T0311793

Principles of Behavioral Economics

This book is unique among modern contributions to behavioral economics in presenting a grand synthesis between the kind of behavioral economics popularized by Richard Thaler, earlier approaches such as those of the 1978 Nobel Laureate Herbert Simon, evolutionary psychology, and evolutionary economics from Veblen and Marshall through to neo-Schumpeterian thinking. The synthesis employs a complex adaptive systems approach to how people think, the lifestyles they build, and how new production technologies and products are gradually adopted and produce changes. Using a huge range of examples, it takes behavioral economics from its recent focus on 'nudging' consumers, to the behavior of firms and other organizations, the challenges of achieving structural change and transitioning to environmentally sustainable lifestyles, and instability of the financial system. This book will be of great interest to academics and graduate students who seek a broader view of what behavioral economics is and what it might become.

Peter Earl is Honorary Associate Professor of Economics at the University of Queensland, Australia.

Principles of Behavioral Economics

Bringing Together Old, New and Evolutionary Approaches

PETER E. EARL
University of Queensland

CAMBRIDGE
UNIVERSITY PRESS

University Printing House, Cambridge CB2 8BS, United Kingdom

One Liberty Plaza, 20th Floor, New York, NY 10006, USA

477 Williamstown Road, Port Melbourne, VIC 3207, Australia

314–321, 3rd Floor, Plot 3, Splendor Forum, Jasola District Centre, New Delhi – 110025, India

103 Penang Road, #05–06/07, Visioncrest Commercial, Singapore 238467

Cambridge University Press is part of the University of Cambridge.

It furthers the University's mission by disseminating knowledge in the pursuit of education, learning, and research at the highest international levels of excellence.

www.cambridge.org
Information on this title: www.cambridge.org/9781316515099
DOI: 10.1017/9781009091053

First published 2022

A catalogue record for this publication is available from the British Library.

ISBN 978-1-316-51509-9 Hardback
ISBN 978-1-009-09589-1 Paperback

Contents

Figures

Tables

Preface

Behavioral economics has not yet arrived at the point at which a standard formula for its textbooks has emerged, let alone its own superstar textbook author. Publishers and authors are at the high-stakes stage of making investments in experiments aimed at producing the winning formula that will be the behavioral equivalent of conventional economics texts such as those by Mankiw or Varian. This means that it is not too late to offer a fresh alternative vision of behavioral economics that instructors and students might find more interesting and of wider practical relevance than what has so far been offered. This book presents such a vision, and it has been written so that it can be used as a textbook. However, although I have also created an archive of online support materials that can be viewed at my personal website (https://shredecon.wordpress .com), this book is a work of scholarship rather than one that follows the pedagogical strategies of today's big textbook publishers. It is much bolder than previous attempts to package a vision of behavioral economics in a single volume. To get a sense of what makes it different and why the differences matter, it is useful to know how it came to be written.

I am not a recent convert to behavioral economics, or even someone who got interested in the field when it began to take off around the turn of the twenty-first century. Rather, I've been viewing myself as a behavioral economist since the late 1970s, having been introduced to the field as an undergraduate a couple of years earlier by Ajit Singh, my director of studies at the University of Cambridge. After completing my BA with first-class honors in 1977, I stayed on at Cambridge to work on my doctorate, which I eventually finished while working in my first academic position, a lectureship at the University of Stirling in Scotland. There, Professor Brian Loasby, the UK's most eminent behavioral economist of the time, had been my mentor and external PhD supervisor. His influence permeates this book, not merely when I refer to his work explicitly but also via the book's emphasis on the processes by which people come to know what they know and change how they view the world. Decades later, it had become very clear to me that where I had got to as a behavioral economist was very different from the perspective arrived at by others who were calling themselves behavioral economists. When I began to write this book, I envisaged the end product as my magnum opus, a legacy volume in which I would bring together everything I had learned about behavioral economics. It would be a means for sharing my vision of behavioral economics, which I felt had much more to offer than the approach that had become popular.

A few years before I started to write this book, I had merely envisaged writing an update to a pair of books that I had written either side of my 1984 Cambridge doctoral dissertation on "A Behavioral Analysis of Choice," namely *The Economic Imagination: Towards a Behavioral Analysis of Choice* (1983c) and *Lifestyle Economics: Consumer Behaviour in a Turbulent World* (1986b). That book would have been called "Consumer Lifestyles and the Economic Imagination." After the release of the copyrights of the old books had been granted, I started trying to figure out how to merge and update them. I soon realized that, even though many of their ideas would be carried forward, I was going to need to write a new book from scratch. This was partly because one of the things that I wanted to achieve was to get modern behavioral economists interested in taking a behavioral view of the firm, via the literature through which I had first been introduced to behavioral ideas. What had been known as the behavioral theory of the firm back in the 1970s had failed to become part of modern behavioral economics and had instead morphed, via Nelson and Winter's seminal 1982 book *An Evolutionary Theory of Economic Change*, into part of modern evolutionary economics. Bringing it in required a much bigger book, and this was what I mapped out and started to write in July 2017.

The book's initial working title was "Beyond Misbehaving: An Evolutionary Approach to Behavioral Economics." I would be offering an "evolutionary approach" not merely by drawing upon modern evolutionary economics but also by exploring links to much earlier strands of evolutionary economics, particularly the late ninetenth-century contributions of Marshall and Veblen, as well as to modern-day evolutionary psychology. The "beyond misbehaving" phrase was there to signal two things. First, I was offering a view of behavioral economics that did not focus mainly on consumers failing to take the decisions that a "fully rational" decision-maker supposedly would take. Second, I was alluding to my intention to show how there is much more to my vision of behavioral economics than is offered in the work of Richard Thaler, the superstar among modern behavioral economists. Thaler is almost ten years older than me, but he, too, began his journey as a behavioral economist in the mid-1970s. However, his starting point was different from mine – he was trying to understand the impact of workplace risks on occupational choices – and it led him to take what I had come to see as a much less radical approach to behavioral economics, one that was based on a much more limited set of influences than mine. In 2015, Thaler had published his intellectual autobiography under the title *Misbehaving* and the subtitles *The Making of Behavioral Economics* (on the cover) and *How Economics Became Behavioral* (on the title page). The initial working title for the present book thus alluded to the title of Thaler's book. It would help to signal my agenda to anyone familiar with the latter, and I also hoped that, by having a title that had some key words in common with it, some potential readers would end up discovering my book while searching for Thaler's one on the Internet.

Thaler had called his book *Misbehaving* because it deals with his persistence in portraying many everyday choices as being at odds with what the theories of the economics establishment predicted. He was able to explain such behavior with the aid of a rather simple set of tools that he had developed after getting to know the work of psychologists Daniel Kahneman and Amos Tversky in the late 1970s. Thaler's knack for using his simple toolkit to explain how "supposedly irrelevant factors" (SIFs) could be driving people to act in ways that mainstream economists viewed as irrational had eventually brought him great career success. However, I felt that his success partly reflected the fact that he had misbehaved in academic terms far less than I had done. What I had been offering and would be reiterating as I went "Beyond Misbehaving" was a more complex view of human action that raised far bigger questions about the usefulness of mainstream economics as a means for understanding real-world behavior. However, although those who had picked up my contributions had mostly been nonmainstream economists, I was not setting out to dismiss Thaler's achievements. As it turned out, I soon had to explain elsewhere why I thought Thaler's contributions had been so significant and offer my critical reflections on his work. This was because, shortly after I began writing this book, I had to take time out from it, for it was announced that Thaler had been awarded the 2017 Nobel Prize in Economics (formally, the Sveriges Riksbank Prize in Economic Sciences in Memory of Alfred Nobel), and I was commissioned to write what has become a frequently downloaded paper (Earl, 2018) about his life and work.

I had greatly enjoyed Thaler's *Misbehaving* and particularly liked how he had managed to write it in a style that would be accessible to the intelligent lay reader rather than merely to an academic audience. Mindful of this, I set out to make this book just as easy to read, though I knew that by writing in this way I would be breaking the norms of professors who expected it to read like a typical research volume. It was a writing strategy that turned out to be crucial for the book's easy transition into a work that could be used as a textbook by students whose professors found its vision compelling.

From 2016, I had set Thaler's *Misbehaving* as the required text for students at the University of Queensland who were taking my course on Behavioral and Evolutionary Economics. Thaler's book was much more engaging than any of the existing behavioral economics textbooks, none of which delivered anything that better suited what I was teaching. Moreover, because I had long taught that course with a lecture sequence based on the history of the field, Thaler's account of how he got his ideas and struggled to win acceptance for them fitted very well. It was a great hit with my class. The trouble was that, in the absence of a textbook that matched what I covered, I had to supplement *Misbehaving* with a long list of primary sources as recommended readings. Such a strategy is risky in an age in which, sad to say, being a "full-time student" typically means "trying to find time to study while holding down a part-time job to pay for my studies." Hence it was natural that, for the 2018 and 2019 iterations of the course, I not only shared a growing number of draft chapters with my students but also restructured the course around the book's sequence of contents. These proved to be my last two opportunities to teach the course, for it was then reallocated to a young colleague who, inevitably, transformed it into a narrower course in modern behavioral economics, built around an existing textbook. But the 2018 and 2019 iterations ensured that I got used to the idea that what I was writing could play the textbook role; they also left me with a new set of lecture slides and other teaching resources that could be useful if anyone else wanted to go "beyond misbehaving."

Ultimately, the original working title had to go, in order to signal more clearly the book's integrative approach and its potential usability as a textbook, at least for more committed or advanced students. In calling it *Principles of Behavioral Economics*, I am not merely trying to signal that it pays much more attention to methodological issues than existing behavioral economics texts do; I am also alluding to its relationship with Alfred Marshall's (1890) *Principles of Economics*. This relationship comes partly via its use of Marshallian ideas, particularly when considering the evolution of firms and industries, and partly because, as with his *Principles*, this book performs a dual role: it presents an integrative account of the field to academic peers in a way not previously offered, and it provides them with a means of teaching that account without having first to write their own textbook or jeopardize their teaching evaluations in the way that one inevitably does if trying to teach via extensive reading lists of primary sources. The costs of tooling up are also reduced by the teaching resources that are available to instructors via my personal website.

The thinking behind the abandoned "Beyond Misbehaving" title and the book's eventual subtitle can be better appreciated – along with what makes this book different and why it may be worth using as a teaching resource – if one is aware of the distinction that Esther-Mirjam Sent (2004) has drawn between "Old Behavioral Economics" (OBE) and "New Behavioral Economics" (NBE). This was in a paper that she wrote to try to make sense of growing interest within the mainstream of economics in employing ideas from psychology, which is one of the things that those who call themselves behavioral economics have long been doing. In Sent's analysis, OBE refers essentially to behavioral economics contributions that were produced prior to 1980 or that have been produced since then by those who have adhered to OBE ways of doing behavioral economics. This is the kind of behavioral economics for which Herbert Simon was awarded the 1978 Alfred Nobel Memorial Prize in Economic Sciences and is the kind that I have practiced. NBE refers to a different kind of behavioral economics that began with an article by Richard Thaler (1980) that was published in the very first issue of the *Journal of Economic Behavior and Organization* and was the first application of prospect theory, a theory of choices under conditions of risk, that psychologists Daniel Kahneman and Amos Tversky had developed and had published in *Econometrica* in 1979. What is currently taught in most behavioral economics courses, and dominates in existing textbooks, is essentially concerned only with NBE. In this book, by contrast, I offer a vision of behavioral economics that blends compatible elements from both OBE and NBE, with a strong evolutionary emphasis. This opens a wider range of research opportunities and areas in which to make novel policy contributions than is possible if one is only focusing on NBE. In doing so, it may help to secure a more sustainable future for behavioral economics.

Those who pioneered NBE or jumped on its bandwagon have done so seemingly without engaging in deep methodological reflection. As a result, they operate in a way that is methodologically quite incoherent (see Dow, 2013). Core to NBE is a focus on the idea that humans are, by nature, fallible as decision-makers because they have evolved to use a set of simplifying heuristics to cope with the challenges of the complicated world in which they find themselves. Those who practice OBE can accept the part of the preceding sentence that follows "because," but they have issues with the part that comes before it. The key issue is the alleged "fallibility" of human decision-makers, which in NBE is seen relative to what a "fully rational" economic agent ought to do if the context of choice is viewed from the standpoint of rational choice theory. From the standpoint of OBE, that theoretical benchmark is inappropriate for most of the decision-making contexts that humans must deal with, for rational choice theory focuses on closed problems with well-defined sets of options, preferences, and constraints, thus making it possible to specify optimal choices. Much of the research from which psychologists such as Kahneman and Tversky inferred that humans use a shared set of "bias-inducing" heuristics when taking decisions was undertaken via laboratory experiments that entailed closed-choice problems, such as choosing between lotteries with payoff matrices that were simple and predefined.

From the OBE standpoint, the world outside the laboratory setting is primarily a world of open-ended problems: we spend our lives trying to figure out what problems we are up against, what the potential solutions might be, what games other people are trying to play as they interact with us, what we really want, and what we can afford to pay. To cap it all, the world keeps changing, often in ways that are hard to anticipate. In the real world, it may be impossible even for rational choice theorists to figure out what a "rational" choice is. Indeed, the very notion of optimal choice turns out to be logically problematic if choices are open-ended, as these choices are mired by a set of problems of "infinite regress" that we have to cut off in an arbitrary manner by employing some kind of rule or heuristic.

The fact that NBE has anchored itself to the rational choice reference point and has not challenged the idea of optimization in open-ended choice settings may look very odd in methodological terms, given that NBE emphasizes so much the role of heuristics in decision-making. But it is precisely this that has helped NBE to thrive within conventional economics departments. If empirical anomalies are raised and can be made sense of by NBE, then outsiders are left with the impression that the economics establishment has all bases covered: where conventional economics fails to fit the facts, its NBE arm comes to its rescue. By having NBE research and teaching taking place in its midst, conventional economics shows how open it is to empirical evidence. Meanwhile, its theorists get on with doing what they do, as if, generally speaking, the conventional approaches to economics offer the go-to toolkit for understanding how the economy works.

Practitioners of NBE seem not to have noticed that they have been allowed to thrive because of the protective role they have been playing for conventional economics, for it was a role they could play while seeming to criticize the latter by exposing the anomalies that they went on to make intelligible. Nor do they seem to have realized that their continuing alliance with conventional economics and acceptance of the "full rationality" reference point put them in a vulnerable position if conventional economics is ultimately recognized as inapplicable to much of real-world economic behavior.

That recognition is long overdue, given that its insistence on building particular kinds of formal models limits it to closed-choice situations and frequently to producing models that cannot be tested. But behavioral economics may now be so well established that it is in a position to break out of this symbiotic relationship and set out to become the dominant way of doing economics. To do this, however, those who have been NBE enthusiasts need to get to see the bigger picture of the limitations of the conventional economist's way of looking at the world and start to realize the wider potential of a stand-alone behavioral approach. This is what the present book is designed to foster by bringing together elements from both OBE and NBE. Their paths have diverged for the past four decades, but the future for behavioral economics lies in bringing them together.

The lack of engagement that contributors to, and students of, NBE have had with those who have gone down the less traveled road of OBE means that the former are largely oblivious of the dysfunctional impact that the relationship between NBE and the established core of economic principles has on how practitioners of NBE see the world and hence on their capacities for identifying where economics might benefit from taking a behavioral approach. For example, take the fact that most consumers will never buy even a single unit of most products. From the established core position, one would see this in terms of mathematical corner solutions and/or transaction costs that impede the division of access to indivisible products via short-term rental arrangements. The transaction cost point may indeed be worth keeping in mind when we are thinking about the functioning of markets for indivisible products, but the corner solution idea points toward a presumption that relative price changes can, in principle, always induce switching between products. In reality, this may not always be the case; instead, it may be that, for much of the time, people are actually choosing in ways that preclude substitution. The presumption in favor of substitution typically is so ingrained that even those who call themselves behavioral economists do not notice how widespread are cases of unwillingness to substitute. Hence, they fail to reflect on what this means for how economic systems function. If behavioral economists were armed with alternative perspectives from OBE, they would see a far wider range of research opportunities and areas where new policy insights could be needed.

In bringing compatible strands of OBE and NBE together in this book, I aim to promote an approach to economics that involves following the rule that economic analysis should be based on what is known about the nature of the human predicament and how people try to deal with the world in which they find themselves. This methodological rule can accommodate the contributions of both OBE and NBE. It is very different from one that says – as has increasingly become the case despite the rise of NBE – that economic analysis must be done in terms of formal mathematical models, even if this entails making assumptions that are clearly at great variance with what is known about reality. Basing analysis on what is known about reality need not preclude formal mathematical modeling, but such modeling may not be necessary in order to derive logically robust insights of real-world relevance. From the perspective that underpins this book, the analytical strategy is to employ behavioral foundations consistently rather than only reaching for them to address anomalies or when designing economic policy. Insofar as we do end up labeling some behavior as dysfunctional, we will not be self-constrained to applying such labels with reference to what an idealized economic agent would be expected to do. However, the synthesis offered in this book generally offers a more positive view of human behavior, consistent with the evolutionary success of humans as a species. It turns out that, even where optima are elusive, it can still be possible to identify reliable ways of achieving reasonable outcomes, as well as ways of choosing and/or choices that it would be wise to avoid.

I think that Sent's NBE/OBE distinction is invaluable for making sense of the history of behavioral economics since 1980. However, despite this, and despite the wording of this book's subtitle, I will proceed, as far as possible, without referring to NBE and OBE in the chapters that follow. I hope this will help readers to end up with the kind of integrated view of behavioral economics that I am trying to foster. For students who are not used to being taught about contending perspectives in economics, the challenge of having to get to grips with behavioral economics alongside conventional economics will be big enough in its own right. For their sake, and for coherent thinking when working toward new policies, it is better to draw a sharp distinction between behavioral and conventional ways of doing economics, rather than allowing matters to become cloudy due to NBE still really being part of what it seems to be challenging. So, let us now proceed to what I hope is a coherent and constructive blend of old, new, and evolutionary approaches to behavioral economics.

Acknowledgments

I owe an immense debt to those who taught me at the University of Cambridge and got me started on the road that led to the writing of this book. After Ajit Singh introduced me to behavioral economics, he encouraged me to read a number of works that provided a bridge from the behavioral approach to the evolutionary ingredients that Alan Hughes introduced during his lectures on industrial organization. The inspiration I got from Ajit and Alan was reinforced by Ken Coutts and Geoff Meeks. Then, at the University of Stirling, my emerging interdisciplinary view of economics and economics method greatly benefited from working with, and support from, Sheila Dow, Brian Loasby, Richard Shaw, and Susan Shaw. Two Stirling alumni, Neil Kay and Clive Spash, have also had big long-term impacts on my thinking and on this book, while a third Stirling alumnus, Stavros Drakopoulos, helped me, via his parallel work over many years, to maintain my conviction that I was right to take hierarchical choices seriously.

The evolutionary aspects of this book have benefited greatly from the many interactions I have had with John Foster, Jason Potts, and Tim Wakeley over the past quarter century and from those with Brendan Markey-Towler more recently. I also wish to thank Lana Friesen for suggesting that choices of mobile phone service contracts would provide fertile territory for a joint research project in which we might apply behavioral insights and experimental methods. The years that Lana and I spent on the project delayed the commencement of this book and progress on it, but, because of what I learned during the project, the final product is much better than it otherwise would have been. The research on that project would not have been possible without an Australian Research Council Discovery Grant (DP1093840). I also wish to acknowledge the extent to which the writing of this book has been aided by the truly superb library resources at the University of Queensland.

Given the scale of this book, it was with some trepidation that I submitted my proposal to Cambridge University Press partway into the fourth year of writing. But Cambridge seemed to be the most appropriate publisher to work with, given where the seeds of my career as a behavioral economist had been sown. It has been a delight to work with my editor Philip Good, his assistant Erika Walsh, and their colleagues at Cambridge.

Last, but by no means least, I thank my partner Annabelle Taylor for all the love and support she has given, which has made this book possible. This includes her enduring, without ever complaining, four years of my "absentminded professor" preoccupation with the book, especially during my frequent wrestling with the sequence of its contents.

1   What Is Behavioral Economics?

1.1   Introduction

A recurring theme in this book is the necessity of recognizing that people differ in how they see things. This applies not merely to, say, how they see a particular product, job opportunity or business strategy but also to how economists characterize behavioral economics. It is possible to get a sense of this by comparing my 1988 characterizations of behavioral economics (in the introduction to Earl, 1988) with those offered later by Tomer (2007) and Thaler (2015) or by contrasting the coverage in textbooks such as Baddeley (2013), Cartwright (2014), Dhami (2016) and Wilkinson (2012). What behavioral economics has been taken to be has changed over the years, with a particularly major change occurring in the last two decades of the twentieth century. But historical accounts of this differ, too: see Sent (2004) and Heukelom (2014). There is not even a consensus about when the first "behavioral" contributions to economics were made.

In this book, the oldest sources referred to are Adam Smith's *Theory of Moral Sentiments*, published in 1756, and his history of astronomy, published posthumously in 1795; otherwise, the earliest sources come from the period 1870–1910. However, it was not until after World War II that the adjective "behavioral" started being applied to some contributions to economics, most notably George Katona's pioneering attempts to apply psychology to understanding macroeconomic phenomena (e.g., Katona, 1951) and Herbert Simon's (1955) work on decision-making. Simon's contributions earned him the 1978 Alfred Nobel Memorial Prize in Economics Sciences, but nowadays it is common to see his work being completely ignored by those who call themselves behavioral economists. Simon's focus was on decision-making in organizations, and it led to the development of a "behavioral theory of the firm" by his colleagues Richard Cyert and James March (1963). Their work was widely known in the mid-1970s when, as a Cambridge undergraduate, I was first introduced to behavioral economics. But today Cyert and March's book receives scant attention from most behavioral economists even though by 2020 Google Scholar listed it as having notched up over 30,000 citations.

Modern behavioral economics has become largely focused on consumer behavior rather than organizations, with much attention given to the work of psychologist Daniel Kahneman, co-recipient (with experimental economist Vernon Smith) of the 2002 Bank of Sweden Prize in Economic Sciences in Memory of Alfred Nobel. It was

Kahneman, together with the late Amos Tversky, who did much of the research on which modern behavioral economics builds. That research became widely known in relation to economics due to Richard Thaler using it as a means for making sense of patterns of behavior that he had noticed and saw as being at odds with conventional economic thinking. Neither Kahneman nor Thaler have sought to promote earlier behavioral economics alongside more recent work. Instead, they give the impression that behavioral economics started around 1979–1980 with the publication of Kahneman and Tversky's (1979) article on prospect theory and that theory's use by Thaler (1980). All in all, this is a very curious state of affairs: a cynic might suggest that it looks rather as if the earlier work has been airbrushed from the history of economic thought by the strategic redefinition of what constitutes behavioral economics. A more charitable and reflexive view would see the situation as resulting from insufficient familiarity with the earlier literature, as a result of the way that scholarly search processes work in the face of information overload (cf. Earl, 1983a, 2017b, 2018).

This book is unusual because it adopts a pluralistic approach, blending elements of both pre- and post-1979/1980 approaches to behavioral economics. Given this, one possible way of introducing behavioral economics would be via a focus on the distinction that Esther-Mirjam Sent (2004) drew between "Old Behavioral Economics" (OBE) and "New Behavioral Economics" (NBE) when she was trying to make sense of the growing interest in behavioral economics that was evident at the turn of the twenty-first century. I have sometimes adopted this strategy, comparing and contrasting the "old" and "new" approaches (as in Earl and Peng, 2012). On this occasion, however, the emphasis will be on things that would characterize the modus operandi of someone who wants to practice a pluralistic way of doing behavioral economics with a view to achieving a powerful grand synthesis of compatible aspects of approaches to behavioral economics that have hitherto not been integrated. So what follows is an introduction to the kinds of things you may find yourself doing if you become the kind of behavioral economist that this book has been designed to produce. Along the way, I highlight past debates about the benefits of, and need for, some of the unusual things that such a behavioral economist may be open to doing.

1.2   As Is, Not "As If"

The theories that economists build are akin to maps: they help us by presenting a simplified picture of reality. The simplifications that theories and maps entail need to be consistent with their purpose. Consider, for example, the iconic London Underground Map. The purpose of the map is to show users of the Underground the routes that are possible and thereby to help users choose how to get to where they want to go. It was a challenge to do this clearly, but the map's designer, Harry Beck, managed to come up with a clear, fit-for-purpose map that works by only using straight lines (whereas the actual routes entail many curves), with all junctions thereby being at 45° or 90°. This abstraction has the effect of distorting the relative distances between stations. But this is not misleading so long as users accept that its role is to enable them to work out routes rather than accurate journey distances.

Similarly, when economists construct their models and analyze aspects of the economy, they do so by applying methodological rules that differ depending on what kind of economics they practice and what they try to achieve. At its core, behavioral economics entails constructing economic analysis on foundations that embody knowledge of the challenges that human decision-makers face and how they *actually* behave in trying to deal with them. This knowledge can come from a variety of sources, as will become evident as this chapter proceeds. The golden rule for behavioral economists is that they do not try to make their own lives easier by making false assumptions about how people make their choices or about what people have to grapple with when choosing. For example, we know that there are limits to human attentive, information-processing, imaginative and short-term-memory capacities. These limits impede attempts to take rational decisions: in Herbert Simon's (1957a, p. 198) phrase, humans suffer from "bounded rationality." Knowing this, behavioral economists try to see what these limitations imply about behavior in the situations they are trying to analyze. In other words, despite the problems that these limitations pose for their own work, they do not assume them out of the way to make it easier to construct economic models. If the use of an analytical tool would require us to make assumptions that we know to be false, it is the tool that has to be set aside, not what we know about the nature of real human decision-makers.

The golden rule means that if we find ourselves unable to use the kinds of mathematics that economists normally use, we will have to find and learn other forms of mathematics that can accommodate what we know about reality (for example, graph theory or fuzzy set theory), or we will have to confine ourselves to doing our analysis in words, not symbols. Although mathematical methods are generally not used in this book, this is not to say that the material cannot be given a mathematical treatment. For example, aspects of the theory of the workings of the mind that underpins the arguments in Chapters 4 and 7 of this book have been represented mathematically with the aid of graph theory by Brendan Markey-Towler (2018), one of my former doctoral students. Readers who are interested in more formal approaches are strongly encouraged to consult the work of Shiozawa et al. (2019), which complements at many points the perspective offered in this book.

To insist on doing economic analysis based on how things are goes against the arguments in a classic paper by Milton Friedman (1953) that conventional economists have used frequently to justify building economic models with patently unrealistic assumptions. Friedman argued that the usefulness of an economic model lies in its ability to predict something about how the economy works. In his view, models are merely instruments for getting predictions; hence what counts is whether our predictions are realistic, not how we arrive at them. It can thus be OK for economists to theorize "as if" something is true even if they know it is patently false, so long as this leads to a realistic prediction.

Behavior economists reject this defense of unrealistic assumptions on several grounds. For one thing, although Friedman's paper is frequently referred to as a means of justifying "as if" theorizing, economic models often yield no testable hypotheses, and the only proof offered for their validity tends to be a mathematical proof. A core part of intermediate economics teaching, namely the analysis of consumer behavior via indifference curves and budget lines, epitomizes this problem: it does not even predict that a rise in a product's price will result in a reduction in its sales. Secondly, a theory that seems to predict correctly despite being based on patently false assumptions is, in essence, getting the right answer for the wrong reasons. If conditions change, it may cease to predict accurately and thereby cause major embarrassment for those who have used it as a basis for policymaking. A theoretical framework based on knowledge of how things really are is less likely to cause such embarrassments. Finally, it has been evident that in the face of evidence that contradicts the predictions of their models, economists have been prone to cling to the models rather than start trying to build models with more plausible assumptions. Rabin and Thaler (2001) once likened this behavior to that of the pet shop proprietor in the famous Monty Python "dead parrot" comedy sketch, who used all manner of arguments to deny that the parrot he had sold was dead. However, they then pointed out that, unlike die-hard conventional economists, the pet shop proprietor did, in the end, agree there was a problem and offered the customer something else. The "as if" justifications continue but, in effect, the inconvenient evidence gets swept under the carpet. Fortunately, such behavior has become less acceptable as knowledge of empirical anomalies has become more widespread: behavioral economics owes much to Richard Thaler for his work (with a number of coauthors) cataloguing behavior that contradicts the prevailing wisdom about what a "rational" economic actor ought to be observed to do. This work appeared as a series of "nomalies" articles in the *Journal of Economic Perspectives* and many of them were conveniently reprinted in Thaler's (1992) book *The Winner's Curse*.

Following Thaler's critiques, economists working on policy design and chasing research funds have increasingly become open to models based on knowledge of how things are. However, old habits have proved hard to shake off: some of the work that is being presented as behavioral economics is still pretty much in the "as if" mold (see Berg and Gigerenzer, 2010). Where predictions are in short supply, much of the core of conventional economics continues to consist of models that are justified via the "as if" argument. From the behavioral perspective, the core needs to be changed, too, in line with the golden rule. A more realistic approach may require junking traditional models, but it may also open new areas for analysis: for example, those who insist on theorizing "as if" people have "given" "complete" preferences that provide a basis for choice in any situation are denying themselves the opportunity to engage in research to understand how people develop the capacity to make choices as they find themselves in new territory.

It needs to be stressed that the behavioral approach does leave room for keeping economic analysis manageable by leaving out some aspects of reality. At any moment, we may opt only to focus on the significance of some of the things we know about the human condition. For example, we may know that people tend to suffer from "seasonal affective disorder" – in other words, they are prone to get somewhat depressed during the winter due to fewer hours of daylight being available – and we may acknowledge that this could affect the kinds of choices they make in the winter. But we may leave this out of our analysis where it seems peripheral to the problem at hand. If we are, say, trying to design long-term policies that might result in more people paying off their mortgages before they retire (an issue raised in Thaler, 2015, ch. 9), we can feel comfortable about leaving out this aspect of human behavior. Even though depressive moods may affect spending in winter months, it may be of no relevance for whether a policy will work as the years run by. But in other contexts – for example, if we were modeling stock prices or the demand for different kinds of TV programs over the course of the year – we might want to include it. (For a study of the impact of hours of daylight on stock prices, see Kamstra et al., 2002.)

Being selective about the behavioral knowledge that we use as ingredients in analysis is a different kind of abstraction from that normally evident when the "as if" approach is being employed in conventional economic analysis. In the behavioral approach, we limit the predictive or explanatory power of our analysis by opting not to include some things we might have included. We do not proceed by bringing in things we know to be false. However, it needs to be acknowledged that behavioral economists are prone simply not to refer to things they potentially might have included in their analysis, rather than explicitly drawing them to the reader's attention in the way that economists conventionally do when making heroic assumptions and adding "other things equal" clauses. With a mass of knowledge on which to base analysis, behavioral economists will try to avoid getting bogged down by always noting the knowledge they are not deploying. It is thus important to be alert to what is possibly being left unsaid, as well as to what has been said, in a piece of behavioral analysis.

As an example of this, consider Richard Thaler's (1980, p. 43) anecdote about Mr. H, who mows his own lawn, declining the offer from a neighbor's son to mow it for $8 but also declining another neighbor's invitation for him to mow the latter's similarly sized lawn for $20. Thaler suggests that Mr. H looks irrational in terms of standard economic theory, since he seems to value the time it takes him to mow one of these lawns as worth less than $8 *and* more than $20. However, Thaler's anecdote presents very little information about the context of Mr. H's decision. Mr. H may actually see mowing his own lawn both as a form of exercise and as a means for catching up with neighbors, which he will have to forego if he accepts the offer from his neighbor's son. On the other hand, to mow the other neighbor's lawn as well as his own may entail both more exercise than he feels he needs and losing time for the other things he wants to do. He may also see this as implying a dent to his social standing: he will become, in effect, his neighbor's servant if he mows the latter's lawn and accepts the money. Thus, if Mr. H behaves as per Thaler's description, he may be operating perfectly logically in terms of how he treats his options. But we will only see this if we get a sense of what his goals are and how he sees the world.

Once we accept the realities of being human, we must rethink how we judge whether human behavior is "irrational" or not. Most modern behavioral economists have chosen to deal with this by using, as a reference point, the orthodox economist's view of how people ought to behave, even though that view attempts to model decision-makers "as if" it is cognitively unconstrained. Such an approach is not taken in this book: as humans, we are what we are, and we live in the world as it is, so the quality of our choices should not be judged in terms of a view of "rational" behavior that assumes out of the way the mismatch between our cognitive capacities and the demands that the world places upon them.

If we are not going to use an idealized way of specifying what constitutes "rational" choice, and hence what is meant by "irrational," what other benchmark(s) can we use? A pluralistic approach seems worth considering. Thus, we might say that behavior should be viewed as irrational if it results in the decision-makers in question doing any of the following:

- Selecting products that are demonstrably dominated by other products as means of meeting their needs, but only in cases where it would have been possible to discover the superior products by using search strategies that are not "exotic," i.e., by using search strategies that other members of the population use in the context in question.
- Making choices that can be shown to contradict their stated goals.
- Failing to meet the basic needs of themselves and their family members despite having similar resources and educational backgrounds to those who are able to meet these needs.

Such criteria need to be viewed as applying to behavior in the longer term. In the short term, poor outcomes may simply reflect bad luck in unpredictable or complicated environments in which it would be unreasonable to expect decision-makers to do well always (cf. Richardson, 1953). Taking a long-term view of behavior helps to ensure that we do not judge people as poor decision-makers with reference to outcomes that others have achieved because they were lucky.

1.3   Decision-Making As a Process

Behavioral economists find it useful to build their analysis of decision-making around the idea of a "decision cycle." John Dewey, an American philosopher, proposed this concept in his 1910 book *How We Think*. For Dewey, the process of making a decision begins with the recognition of a problem, necessitating the discovery of possible solutions, which in turn need to be evaluated for how well they might serve as a means for solving the problem without causing other problems to arise. It is only after the process of search and evaluation has finished that the decision-maker is in a position to choose what to do. Implementing the decision will not always turn out to be possible and sometimes the decision-maker will need to resort to "plan B" or resume the search process. Sometimes, a plan will not be implemented because products turn out to be unavailable, but changes of plan may also be the result of discovering, when talking to suppliers, that a mistaken view has been taken of what the product that was initially preferred has to offer or what needs to be done to solve the problem. Often, though, the extent of success of the choice only becomes apparent after it has been implemented and a hindsight review has been conducted. Such a review may lead to the start of another decision cycle, due to the original problem having not been fully solved, or a new problem having been generated by the chosen solution (for some excellent examples, see Loasby, 1976, ch. 5).

Clearly, the search and evaluation stages of a decision-making process sometimes take virtually no time, whereas in other contexts, the process is drawn out over weeks, months or even years and entails the use of multiple sources of inputs for assessing the options that are discovered. In the latter cases, the decision cycle may involve many sub-cycles on the way to the final choice, such as decisions about how to try to find potential solutions and whose input to use when assessing them, with disappointing options forcing a rethink about how to find some better contenders. So, although Chapters 3 to 8 of this book are organized mindful of Dewey's decision cycle idea, it will be emphasized repeatedly that context matters for how decisions get made. This means that our behavioral analysis contrasts sharply with the view of choice presented traditionally in economics: we do not have a "one size fits all" view of choice, and we emphasize the search and evaluation processes that precede the choice stage; we do not simply assume that the decision-maker already knows what the available options are, along with what they each have to offer. Moreover, we recognize that in cases where decisions are reached rapidly, it may be most unwise to theorize "as if" the decision-maker is able to arrive at a decision quickly due to already knowing about all the available options: choices can also be made rapidly by, say, selecting a default option, or following the recommendation of a trusted friend, without considering alternatives.

The decision-cycle perspective necessarily entails bringing psychology in and appreciating the nature of knowledge. A traditional economist sees an occasion for a choice as a self-evident result of a "shock" to which the decision-maker needs to re-optimize his or her actions. But what we know is that two people in the same situation may view it very differently: one may see many problems, while the other may see no cause for concern and may even see it as an opportunity to improve his or her situation. The nature of things – including problems and potential solutions to problems – is not self-evident; rather, it is something that the individual has to construct in his or her mind. As behavioral economists, we take an interest in how people do this. We thus focus on how they allocate their attention to competing incoming stimuli and decide what to make of the stimuli to which they give their attention. Hence behavioral economists make considerable use of the literature from psychology; indeed, the phrase "psychological economics" has in the past often been used as a synonym for behavioral economics. However, we may also need to follow the lead of Brian Loasby (2000) and call upon what philosophers say about the challenges of knowing what is going on and knowing when to change one's model of an aspect of the world.

Once we start viewing choice as a process that is linked to what the decision-maker knows and how that knowledge changes, it becomes necessary to start viewing the rationality of a choice in terms of the process of deliberation that it entailed rather than in terms of whether the outcome was the best the person could achieve in the circumstances. A behavioral economist thus finds it useful to borrow Herbert Simon's (1976) distinction between "procedural rationality" and "substantive rationality." The former term refers to what constitutes "appropriate deliberation" in a particular context, i.e., *how* the choice ought to be made, whereas the latter captures the traditional economist's concern with whether the strategy or object that was chosen was consistent with the decision-maker's goals and constraints. In the real world, where decisions are taken under time pressure and with limited cognitive capacity, "appropriate deliberation" may entail the use of effective decision-making shortcuts (commonly referred to as "heuristics") rather than trying to gather and take account of all the information that might be available. Decision-making methods of this kind may not be completely reliable but may serve us better than more thorough methods that slow down the process of reaching a choice and thereby cause opportunities to be missed (for example, opportunities to save the lives of those who have arrived at a hospital's emergency admissions department: see Gigerenzer et al., 1999).

Real-world decision-makers face the challenge of finding or creating effective ways of making decisions and then calling them to mind in appropriate contexts. We are not born with all the decision aids that it might be useful to have; worse still, some of those that are hardwired in our brains may actually be highly dysfunctional. This being the case, an obvious role for the economist is as an agent who develops knowledge of effective ways for choosing in challenging situations and shares this knowledge with the wider population of decision-makers. These "ways for choosing" can include quantitative methods such as the operations research techniques that have increasingly been used in organizations since the end of World War II (Simon, 1976, pp. 75–77) but can also consist of simple "do" and "don't" rules for dealing with the challenges of everyday life.

Conventional economics focuses on substantive rationality in relation to the goal of maximizing utility or profits and presumes that it is possible to specify what the substantively rational choice would be in any situation that needs to be analyzed. However, optimal choices may be impossible even for economists to work out in complex and changing choice environments, or where the decision-maker's view of the world evolves during the process of addressing a problem. In this book we recognize that, where optimal choices are problematic to identify, the goals that people strive to achieve may not be reducible to the maximization of utility in terms of a preexisting and well-defined preference system or an unambiguous notion of profit maximization. Rather, people pursue multiple goals that are often arbitrary, open to revision and capable of being met in multiple ways, and/or have a social dimension that focuses on what they achieve relative to the attainments of other people. For example, goals may focus on meeting particular sets of performance standards or achieving better-than-average outcomes. The discovery that others have moved ahead can thus be viewed as a problem, kick-starting a new decision cycle. If choices thereby result in something akin to an arms race, it is hard to view them as substantively rational, but that may not preclude us from assessing the quality of the processes of deliberation that resulted in the choices being made. Yes, it may be futile to engage in a status race, but some ways of trying to enhance our status may be better than others.

1.4   The Role of Introspection

Although behavioral economics is well known for employing inputs from psychology, it is important also to acknowledge potential for using other sources of insights into how people behave in the economic system. This section and the two sections that follow it cover sources that behavioral economists employ from time to time that are seen as out of order in terms of the rules of conventional economics. We begin by considering introspection. This technique entails the behavioral economist exploring the implications of accounts of his or her own behavior in a particular kind of situation and/or in respect of a particular kind of products. These accounts may range from short vignettes (as in Earl, 2001) to something more Proustian that runs to many thousands of words (as in the "much too long" version of Earl, 2012). The comments at the end of Section 1.2 about Mr. H's lawn-mowing choices were informed by my introspection on how I might feel, given my experience as a suburban resident with lawns to mow, if I had been presented with options like those that Mr. H faced. Though I am not Mr. H, my introspection opened the possibility that there might be more to his decision than Thaler had allowed for when presenting it as irrational.

Potential for using introspection in economics was recognized over a century ago by early writers in the deductive, anti-empirical "*a priorist*" tradition that is often associated with the "Austrian" school of economic thought. They called it the "psychological method." As Terence Hutchison (1977b, p. 159) notes, those who worked in this tradition saw economists as having a great advantage compared with natural scientists, since economists can observe the process of economizing from within, whereas natural scientists can only observe natural phenomena from the outside. Despite this, introspection came to be frowned upon as a tool of economic analysis. This had much to do with what Hutchison (1938) wrote shortly before World War II in his inquiry into economic method. As a visitor to Nazi Germany, the young Hutchison had been dismayed to see what could happen if policies were based on misguided subjective beliefs. He was thus keen to make economists focus on ideas that were capable of falsification and then subject these ideas to empirical tests.

In his critique of the early followers of the "psychological method," Hutchison (1938, pp. 131–141) was careful to keep "introspection" separate from "*a priorism*." Despite remarking critically about the dangers of economists generalizing their own perspectives as if these applied to all economic agents, Hutchison argued that introspection does have a place in economics. That place is at the early stages of theory formation; unlike the "*a priorists*," he did not see it as obviating a subsequent stage in which theories are tested. Unfortunately, to judge from what happened subsequently, economists failed to read Hutchison's writings closely. Despite his very clear (1938, p. 163) summary remarks, they ended up conflating introspection and *a priorism*. Thus began the prejudice of economics against using introspection about their own lives as a source of ideas for theories about the economic behavior of people in general.

When a behavioral economist nowadays presents results of extensive introspection (as I did in Earl, 1986b, section 7.2, 2001, 2012), this is not done as an attempt to construct a generally applicable *a priorist* analysis. Rather, and consistent with Hutchison's perspective, it is done in order to suggest empirical research opportunities that might otherwise go unnoticed. Via introspection, behavioral economists may notice areas where the conventional wisdom seems to misrepresent how they take their own decisions. Further reflection on what they view themselves as doing may result in testable hypotheses that counter the conventional wisdom. The presentation of introspective analysis may also be useful if it provokes readers to do some introspection of their own in the same context and thereby add to the list of issues that it may be worth researching systematically in that area. (So, if you were Mr. H, how would you see those lawn-mowing options?) This way of using introspection and the style of papers that employ it are borrowed from researchers such as Gould (1991, 1993, 1995) and Holbrook (1995) in marketing. Their use of introspective methods for analyzing consumer behavior was itself inspired by literature from philosophy and psychology extending back as far as confessional essayist Michel de Montaigne ([1533–1592] 1963).

Source credibility is a major issue in introspective research. Devious researchers might deliberately write partly fictitious accounts of their behavior, while well-intentioned researchers might unwittingly include fictitious content due to memory lapses that result in them creating false connections between elements that they recall with accuracy (Wallendorf and Bruchs, 1993, pp. 343–345). Cognitive dissonance theory (Festinger, 1957) and the "sour grapes" phenomenon (Elster, 1983) – both of which are employed later in this book – suggest that the mind tends to twist perceptions to remove inconsistencies or downplay the attractive aspects of rejected or unavailable options. Even the observable elements of an introspective account may be hard to verify, as witnesses may be impossible to trace and may have had little incentive to remember the events in question or may have incentives to concoct alternative accounts (e.g., when the potential witness is a former partner). Fortunately, there are three things that behavioral economists can do to help their introspective work to be taken seriously.

First, they should apply the technique to an area of high involvement (in the sense of Laaksonen, 1994). In other words, they should choose an area of major significance to them personally. This may be an area about which they can display an abnormal level of knowledge and where they can reveal painful connections between their use of that knowledge and the state of their personal relationships and finances. Involvement reduces the risk of memory decay if it results in frequent reflection about past choices and experiences.

Secondly, behavioral economists should use introspective techniques in areas in which the complexity and richness of the details they provide may be taken to imply fact rather than fiction. This is because it would take far longer to flesh out a largely fictitious account around the skeleton of an actual experience than it would to write an account that flows freely from memory.

Finally, behavioral economists can enhance the credibility of their introspective contributions by choosing their areas of analysis so that they can play the economics equivalent of the "humiliation game" that figures in David Lodge's (1975) novel *Changing Places*. The game described by Lodge is played by English literature academics at a party. To win, a player must confess to having not read a work of English literature that no one else will confess to having not read. In other words, it requires one-upmanship in being poorly read, something that professors of English literature would rationally be reluctant to do in the presence of their peers. By analogy, behavioral economists can win credibility for their introspective reflections by confessing to choices that economists would not view as rational in prospect, or by revealing errors of judgment that were discovered in hindsight and which could have been avoided by operating more like a "rational economic agent" (an "econ" in Thaler's shorthand). Claims that introspective accounts are accurate will be more credible if such accounts publicize potentially embarrassing aspects of researchers' lives (cf. the confessions regarding sexual energy and draft evasion in Gould, 1991).

1.5   The Role of Anecdotes, Screen Data, and Text

Similar issues arise in respect of the use of anecdotes, i.e., stories or vignettes that refer to particular instances of behavior. Self-knowledge derived via introspection can be a source of anecdotes that one behavioral economist shares with others, but anecdotal evidence about behavior can also be sourced from social networks, published historical accounts, blogs and other media. In the past, economists who tried to use anecdotal evidence as a basis for challenging received wisdom would face a hostile reaction from their peers. The latter would typically argue that the source of the evidence might be questionable and that it was "just" an anecdote that did not necessarily say anything about the behavior of the wider population. Such reactions are understandable: an anecdote could be, say, a myth that has spread around a social network and even if the event it describes actually did occur, it might be utterly unrepresentative of what happens in that class of situations, rather like a statistical outlier. However, some anecdotes may be hard for economists to dismiss because they do seem to encapsulate behavior that is common, even if it had not previously been noticed and argued to be problematic for established theoretical perspectives. Moreover, at some point, a growing portfolio of anecdotes that point in the same direction starts to carry evidential weight akin to that of data set gathered systematically using statistical principles.

Richard Thaler's relentless use of anecdotes in his critiques of orthodox economics (described in Thaler, 2015) has probably played a major role in making anecdotes much more acceptable within economic analysis. Nowadays, it is common for introductory anecdotes to be used to "motivate" (the readers of) journal articles. It seems that a well-chosen anecdote can now be deployed as a representative case for a wider class of behavior that needs to be explained.

Some behavioral economists have noticed potential for using other informal sources of evidence about how people behave or view the process of choice. They are open to examining the economic content of product reviews that consumers post online, the ways in which professional product testers reach decisions (as in Earl, 1986b, ch. 10; 1995, ch. 4), or the ways that novelists and writers for the stage and screen portray consumer behavior, career choices and the behavior of firms and other organizations (as in Earl, 2011). Some of us use clips from movie and TV drama to generate discussions in our classes, and behavioral labor economist Arthur H. Goldsmith has even offered an entire course on "Socio-Economic Themes in Literature and Film" in his role as Professor of Economics at Washington and Lee University.

Given the issue of source credibility, it might seem odd for a behavioral economist to be prepared to engage with works of fiction when searching for insights about economic behavior. However, the writers of works that deal with economic issues can be viewed as having reflected on how people would likely behave in the situations about which they are writing, so the drama is potentially a useful guide to what ordinary people may do; it seems hardly likely to have been twisted with a view to supporting or challenging any particular piece of economic theory. In some cases, works of fiction may be based on inside knowledge of the industry at the heart of the drama, or on insights gleaned from people who work there.

For those who are nervous about making use of fiction, an alternative way of employing textual sources in behavioral research is to make use of company archives, as business historians do. Indeed, for those working on a behavioral approach to the firm, works in business history can prove an invaluable source of insights, as I found when writing *The Corporate Imagination: How Big Companies Make Mistakes* (Earl, 1984).

1.6   Questionnaires and Ethnographic Research

It is natural for behavioral economists to be open to using interviews and questionnaires to find out about the choices that people make and how they make them: if we want to find out why people behave as they do, why not ask them? One reason for not doing this is the cost of conducting such research, especially on a large scale. There is also the problem of "respondent fatigue" whereby the reliability of answers starts to become compromised if a survey takes longer than about twenty-five minutes to complete. However, today's behavioral economists would probably be wise to proceed mindful of the reception that awaited pioneering work of this kind in the 1930s and 1940s. This research arrived at findings at odds with conventional economic thinking and it was not well received. In the UK, members of the Oxford Economists' Research Group (OERG) studied issues such as how prices were set, and the responsiveness of investment decisions to changes in interest rates, by interviewing small samples of managers and having them complete questionnaires. They published their findings in a new journal, *Oxford Economic Papers*, which was swiftly reviewed by Cambridge economist Austin Robinson (1939). He acknowledged that their methods gave them flexibility for dealing with the unique situation of each manager that they interviewed, but he was concerned that he could not judge whether leading questions had been asked to steer responses in particular directions. He pleaded that in future articles reporting such studies should include full details of the questionnaires that had been used. In the days before journals allowed authors to upload "supplementary online materials" at the journals' websites, this could be problematic due to its impact on the length of an article. This was especially so if the length of a questionnaire had ballooned out due to attempts to explore particular issues from various directions in order to check for consistency in responses and ensure that the analysis could not be accused of "leading" the participants in particular directions.

The OERG's work, along with subsequent questionnaire-based research conducted in the US by Richard Lester (1946) on how managers took their decisions about how many workers to hire, also became the target of a full-blown critique, this time by Fritz Machlup (1946). He was concerned about small-scale studies being reported and about the risk of semantic differences between researchers and their subjects leading to erroneous inferences being drawn by the former about the validity of conventional economic theory. Interestingly, despite emphasizing the case for large-scale systematic studies, Machlup seemed also to signal the potential benefits of adopting an ethnographic approach to studying economic behavior: as Lavoie (1990) notes, Machlup took the view that if these researchers had spent more time in close contact with their research subjects, they would probably have come to realize that the managers were actually doing something akin to the marginal trade-offs predicted by conventional economic theory, even though their replies in interviews and questionnaires gave the opposite impression. However, the effect of Machlup's critique was to pave the way for Friedman's (1953) "as if" approach to economic method rather than to encourage economists to start operating more like anthropologists and mingle closely with the subjects of their research or operate like a proverbial "fly on the wall."

As with interview-based behavioral research, ethnographic research clearly can be very time-consuming and challenging to write up in the compact format of a journal article. However, it can be especially effective for understanding the thinking of particular groups and how this affects their behavior. So far, behavioral economists have done little research of this kind, but its potential is evident from work by sociologists and marketing scholars in areas as diverse as the New York bond market (Abolafia, 1996, 1998), behavior in shopping malls (Underhill, 2001), the Harley-Davidson Owners' Group (Schouten and McAlexander, 1995), high excitement leisure experiences such as white-water rafting (Arnould and Price, 1993) and skydiving (Celsi et al., 1993), and how the Internet is changing the process of buying a car (Barley, 2015).

1.7   Experimental Studies of Behavior

The use of experiments has become widespread in economics in recent years, largely as a result of the pioneering work of Vernon Smith (1991). Behavioral economists make extensive use of research involving experiments, but their view of the role of experiments and of what constitutes an acceptable experiment is different from that of the conventional experimental economist. There is considerable potential for confusion here, since Smith shared the 2002 Bank of Sweden Prize in Economic Sciences in Memory of Alfred Nobel with psychologist Daniel Kahneman: Smith is not a behavioral economist, whereas Kahneman has had a huge impact on behavioral economics via experiments that did not follow Smith's recipes for how experimental economics should be done. Potential for confusion is increased by Smith's (2008) use of the term "ecological rationality" in a way that differs markedly from its use in behavioral economics via the work of psychologist Gerd Gigerenzer and his colleagues (1999, p. vii). For Gigerenzer, "ecological rationality" pertains to whether the decision-maker is using decision heuristics that "are adapted to the structure of the environment in which they are used." It thus has a similar meaning to Herbert Simon's notion of "procedural rationality" that was outlined in Section 1.3, except that it perhaps does a better job in prompting us to keep in mind the importance of context. But for Smith, "ecological rationality" means a situation in which trial-and-error processes eventually result in a market operating efficiently.

The approach that Vernon Smith pioneered focused on using experiments to find out how markets work. A key feature of his experimental method is the use of significant performance-based financial rewards to motivate research subjects to do the best that they can when acting as players in experimental markets. The setting for such experiments is typically a computer laboratory in which groups of participants can be presented with different "treatments" that enable the impacts of different variables to be assessed, other things equal, in a very strictly controlled manner. In experimental markets, participants can be playing buyer or seller roles, much as in a real-world financial market, but in other experiments the participants are often playing some kind of economic game with some of the other (typically unidentified) participants in their laboratory session.

Behavioral economists often follow Smith's method to test their theories and to test their policy ideas in a laboratory setting. But they are also open to evidence gathered from a much wider range of experimental formats. Most importantly, they take seriously findings of experiments such as those described by Ariely (2008), Kahneman (2011) and Thaler (2015) even where the experiments did not entail the use of performance-based rewards to motivate the participants. Such experiments may involve simple hypothetical choices that entail some kind of gamble, with the focus being on, for example, whether the way the choice is presented to the participants makes a difference to what gets selected. Much of the research that uncovered the "heuristics and biases" to which we will frequently refer later in this book was conducted in this way. In turn, some of the findings became foundations for constructing alternative theories, as in the case of prospect theory (Kahneman and Tversky, 1979).

Behavioral economists are also open to the idea of using experiments that put participants into naturalistic choice environments rather than highly controlled but stripped-down approximations of real choice environments. Different questions may require different kinds of methods. For example, take the case of choices of mobile (cell) phone connection plans, an area that I have studied with my colleagues Lana Friesen and Christopher Shadforth. A highly stylized experiment was fine for exploring the impact of usage uncertainty and different types of plan formats on the extent to which people waste their money by choosing needlessly expensive plans. We were able to isolate the impacts of these issues in a laboratory setting via an experiment in which the participants only faced choices between seven imaginary plans. They were allowed to make a sequence of twenty choices, with no penalties for switching between plans, over the course of an hour as they attempted to minimize their notional spending on a particular pattern of service usage (see Friesen and Earl, 2015). By contrast, when we wanted to study how people search for good-value plans, and the difference it makes to have access to online market aids such as product comparison websites, our experiment had a naturalistic design: in one treatment we used an offline archive of clones of the actual service providers' websites, and in another treatment we simply allowed participants to search freely on the Internet in their attempts to find the cheapest plan for a particular usage pattern (see Earl, Friesen and Shadforth, 2017).

In line with the pluralistic view that behavioral economists have of the nature of rationality, their experiments do not focus purely on finding relationships between variables of interest and the choices that research subjects make; they are also interested in the routes by which participants in experiments arrive at their choices. Some of their experiments therefore come under the umbrella term "process-tracing analysis." As is evident from the handbook edited by Schulte-Mecklenbeck et al. (2011), process-tracing experiments can range from the kind of work that neuro-economists do – in which brain scanners are used to study what happens in the brain when particular kinds of decisions are being made – through to analyzing transcripts of people "thinking aloud" as they make decisions, a technique known as "verbal protocol analysis" (for the classic handbook on this, see Ericsson and Simon, 1993). A logical extension of the latter method, in experiments that involve subjects working on computers, is to record what they say in thinking aloud as the soundtrack of a screen-capture move of what they do on the computer screen while undertaking the experimental task. This method was used in the Earl et al. (2017, 2019) study of mobile phone plan choices. Before Apple gave the world computers that could make such recordings by using its Quicktime app, Payne et al. (1993) pioneered the use of a software package called MOUSELAB that made it possible to record how research subjects searched for information in a stylized screen environment rather than by using a web browser.

As with research involving the use of interviews and large sample questionnaires, process-tracing research is very resource-hungry. This is because of the huge amount of data that each subject may generate and the need to run protocol sessions on a one-to-one basis so that the administrator of the experiment can provide prompts to "keep talking." Unless data collection is automated in the manner of the studies that used MOUSELAB, the data must be transcribed and coded manually prior to any analysis. This can be incredibly time-consuming: in the study reported in Earl et al. (2017), each of our forty-one participants had an hour to complete the task, so nearly forty-one hours of videos and their soundtracks had to be painstakingly analyzed. Because of this, nearly three years passed before we had managed to find enough time to finish writing it up. It should thus be no surprise that, whereas economics experiments in computer laboratories often have 100–200 participants spread across various treatment groups, process-tracing experiments often involve 20–100 participants, with the total number tending to be inversely related to the duration of the task. The good news is that even with small samples, statistical analysis is still possible, with the aid of nonparametric techniques.

In an ideal world, behavioral economists involved in policymaking would test the relative efficacy of their policy proposals via field trials in areas that are representative of the wider population to which it is intended to apply them. This is the behavioral economics equivalent of what a firm does when it engages in "test marketing" rather than risking a nationwide launch. Field experiments can be used to trial multiple policies by assigning different policies to different localities, thereby to get a sense of their relative cost-effectiveness. However, field trials may be impossible to organize in some policy contexts, such as where the policy ideas involve the government imposing regulations of one kind or another about how private sector providers of a particular kind of product must present their offers on their websites. Clearly, in such a case, the alternative strategies could not be trialed simultaneously in different regions owing to the providers' websites being organized to function on a national basis. This problem can be avoided if the policies are simulated in different treatments in a computer laboratory experiment. It was the latter approach that Lana Friesen and I adopted in the context of policies for enhancing mobile phone plan choices. We used a six-treatment experiment to study the relative impacts of three different plan information policies and two training strategies, compared with a baseline, no-intervention treatment (see Friesen and Earl, 2020).

It is important to note that however behavioral economists conduct experiments, they need to use their findings mindful of the replicability crisis that has been going on in scientific research and from which psychology has not been immune (see OSC, 2015; Spellman, 2015; Schimmack, 2018). Given that experimental findings may not be as robust and widely applicable as their proponents have claimed, the wise behavioral economist will look at them cautiously, giving serious thought to whether there are any theoretical bases for taking them seriously in *a priori* terms and to whether and when they seem to "ring true" in terms of everyday experience.

1.8   Behavioral Rules and Routines

The picture of real-world decision-makers that behavioral economists have pieced together from the diverse sources considered in the Sections 1.4–1.7 is very different from the imaginary "homo economicus," who can employ all relevant information to find optimal choices instantaneously. However, it is consistent with Dewey's (1910) decision cycle perspective on choice and Simon's (1976) view that the future for economics lies in studying procedural rationality and helping people to take decisions more efficiently. What behavioral economists have ended up with is a view of humans that is neatly captured by Gigerenzer and Brighton's (2009) notion of "homo heuristicus." People use rules and other simplifying aids to cope with the complex world in which they find themselves. These may be stand-alone aids to choosing, or may be nested together or ordered sequentially, as with decision-making procedures and routines.

A useful analogy here is to think of the mind as being rather like a computer: it comes with some things programmed in from the outset, to which other "apps" can be added. Indeed, we may view the mind as being like a computer that has rules for finding and installing updates to its set of apps by itself, though sometimes it needs external inputs to activate its programs or install additional apps. The heuristics that are hardwired into the human mind can be viewed as constituting human nature insofar as they are shared by the bulk of the population. Other heuristics get installed as a result of the social context in which decision-makers develop, as with the process of nurturing, or are personal creations, tentatively put together by modifying or splicing existing heuristics, and only retained if they seem to work satisfactorily in practice.

Although these heuristic devices are, by definition, supposed to be decision-making aids, not all of them are conducive to good choices. But in acknowledging this, we should not lose sight of the positive role that heuristics play in making life manageable. Indeed, as we will later see (in Section 4.2), if people did not have rules and heuristics at their disposal to call a halt to a variety of "infinite regress" problems that lurk within open-ended choices, they would be prone to suffer from decision paralysis. Unfortunately, the kind of modern behavioral economics that is presented in most textbooks and is typically applied to government and corporate policies by "behavioral insights teams" focuses primarily on seemingly dysfunctional heuristics that are part of human nature. These heuristics are seen as biasing judgments and choices in ways that are contrary to the interests of those who use them. On this line of thinking, humans are, as Ariely (2008) puts it, "predictably irrational." This makes their behavior susceptible to manipulation by firms and governments. However, in principle, people can be taught how to override their inherited fallibility, think more like statisticians and use better heuristics than their less-well-educated counterparts. This latter view underlies self-help behavioral economics books such as Belsky and Gilovich's (1999) *Why Smart People Make Big Money Mistakes and How to Avoid Them* and has become the basis of what is known as the "boost" approach to behavioral public policy (Hertwig, 2017).

In the pluralistic version of behavioral economics that is set out in this book, much attention is of course given to heuristics that compromise the quality of the choices that people make. These dysfunctional heuristics include not merely some that are part of human nature but also others that are not innate and which some members of the population have, by one means or another, come to use. However, we also draw upon the work of behavioral researchers such as Gigerenzer and his colleagues, who see some heuristics very positively, characterizing them as "fast and frugal" tools for making effective choices.

From the latter standpoint, it is natural to focus on differences between people, rather than merely on heuristics that are common to the bulk of the population, in order to find rules that are worth sharing across the entire population. For example, some people possess a set of heuristics that makes them capable of operating in a "streetwise" manner, whereas others lack these heuristics and will consequently be at risk in certain kinds of settings. Those who have especially "fast and frugal" ways of deliberating in a particular context provide benchmarks for procedural or ecological rationality. Their ways of operating may not be the best that humans will ever develop, but they provide exemplars of current best practice. Note here the plural with "exemplars": when members of a population have somewhat different needs and constraints in a particular area of choice, no single set of heuristics may constitute "the" best-practice way of deliberating.

1.9   Computer Simulations

Behavioral economists were very quick to start using computers to model decision-making. Richard Cyert and James March's (1963) book *A Behavioral Theory of the Firm* is a landmark contribution in this respect, as well as for the theory that it sets out, while Herbert Simon was a major contributor to computing sciences and a pioneer in the field of artificial intelligence. For them, the link between organizations and computing was very straightforward. They saw organizations as operating via decision rules that were often embodied in formal policies and procedures about what should be done in particular situations. Decision processes could therefore be mapped in terms of decision trees involving binary "yes/no" nodes with the direction of the answer to a question then leading, in an "if, then" manner, either to an action or to a further question to consider. Once these maps of decision processes had been constructed, it was an obvious next step to turn them into computer programs and see how well they could predict what the organization would do as its environment changed. Trial-and-error processes or statistical analysis could be used to calibrate the extents of a response to a particular problem (for example, how much a department store would lower its prices if it found its inventories getting "too large" and the point at which it would decide to have a "sale") and thereby improve the model's predictive capacity.

Computer simulations play a major role in Gigerenzer et al.'s (1999) research program on "fast and frugal" decision rules, providing a means to test how effectively simple rules work in particular contexts. It has also become common for researchers to develop "multi-agent simulations" to explore what happens in markets populated by a variety of "agents," each of whom is conceived as a set of decision rules. Groups of these "agents" can be assigned different sets of rules, such as rules for when to buy or sell in response to the latest information about prices. Such models enable the analyst to see, for example, how chaotically a market behaves depending on the types of rules used to make decisions and the distribution of such rules among the population of decision-makers.

1.10   Adding the Evolutionary Perspective

This book's approach to behavioral economics is distinctive not merely because it brings together ideas from OBE and NBE but also because it frequently offers an evolutionary perspective on behavior and the functioning of economic systems. The latter has several facets, each of which is underpinned by a Darwinian view of how evolution takes place. This view has three stages. First, some kind of *mutation* occurs in the organism in question. Secondly, there is the *selection* part of the process: if the mutation increases the organism's relative competitive strength, the organism will have a bigger chance of surviving long enough to reproduce, whereas rival organisms will have a reduced chance of doing so. Finally, there is the *retention* part of the process: the mutation is passed on to the next generation if the organism in question breeds. Without the breeding phase, the advantages that the mutation conferred will be lost when the organism that hosted the mutation dies. If the competitive fitness-enhancing mutation is retained down the generations via the breeding process, the population of organisms with the mutation will grow. This will make life harder and harder for other species in the same environment and for members of the same species that lack the fitness-enhancing mutation.

One way this book incorporates this Darwinian perspective is by employing the evolutionary psychology perspective advocated by Cosmides and Tooby (1994) and Cohen and Dickens (2002). This entails trying to understand modern behavior by examining what would have conferred evolutionary advantages on early hunter-gatherers. Central to evolutionary psychology is the idea that modern humans should be viewed as if they have a genetic endowment that is not significantly different from that of their hunter-gatherer ancestors. The basis for this is that, in terms of evolutionary time, modern humans are merely an eyeblink away from early members of the Homo genus who colonized much of the world and from whom Homo sapiens eventually emerged as the dominant species. The hunter-gatherer period is viewed as the only one in human history that is long enough for evolutionary processes to have had enough time to select genes that were especially conducive to survival and reproduction in a particular environment. Hence, if the evolutionary psychology perspective is correct, modern humans must be coping with their choice environment by deploying, or building upon, whatever they have inherited from, and which conferred evolutionary advantages on, ancient hunter-gatherers.

The evolutionary psychology perspective has potential to help us explain why, for example, modern consumers are susceptible to obesity via excessive consumption of food that contains a high proportion of fat and sugar. Our hunter-gatherer ancestors faced an environment in which their access to food was highly variable. This meant that they needed to have calorific reserves to call upon when fresh food was in short supply. Their survival chances would thus have been enhanced if they happened to have a genetic preference for sweet, fatty foods that could replenish their calorific reserves. However, because their access to food varied a lot, their reserves did not accumulate in the long run and hence did not compromise their abilities to reproduce and rear children to adulthood. Those who did not favor such foods would have failed to build up these reserves and would have been more vulnerable and less likely to pass on their genes. A genetic preference for these foods thereby got passed to the present day. However, today's affluent humans can eat regularly and have ready access to the kind of junk food that helps them build up calorific reserves way beyond what they need (see further, Brooks, 2011; Burnham and Phelps, 2019). Evolutionary processes have not yet had enough time to select a population without such dysfunctional preferences.

The evolutionary psychology perspective implies that behavioral economists should perhaps reflect more critically about "heuristics and biases" than they have normally tended to do. If the heuristics that make humans "predictably irrational" are hardwired via the genes that modern humans have inherited, then we may be wise to reflect on how these heuristics might have been retained because they enhanced the competitive fitness of early humans. In some contexts, the ways in which they were of benefit to early humans might still apply today. We will be on the lookout for such contexts as this book proceeds.

In addition to focusing on the selection of genes in competitive environments, the behavioral economist can consider how evolutionary selection takes place with respect to rules and routines. This is what today's evolutionary economists do, much influenced by the seminal work of Nelson and Winter (1982). In contrast to the biological view of evolution, this perspective sees evolutionary change as being initiated by innovative thinking rather than any random mutation of rules or routines. This perspective brings together ideas from the behavioral economics of the 1950s and 1960s and merges them with the "creative destruction" view of capitalism offered by Joseph Schumpeter (1943), a view that focuses on technological competition rather than price competition. In contrast to "as if" theories of the firm that tend to assume firms are identical, the evolutionary approach sees firms as differing in the knowledge, rules and routines that they use when competing.

Firms with operating systems that are better suited to winning customers will enjoy growing market shares. Their ways of doing business will become more and more widespread as they build on their success by growing their existing operations and/or by opening new factories and branches that they operate in the same way. Their success will come at the expense of their rivals. Their ways of doing business may also spread due to rivals copying them. The global spread of franchising as a business model provides a good example of these processes. Franchising is not merely a means by which pioneers of franchise systems were able to grow the geographical presence of their brands and achieve economies in purchasing inputs and promoting their products; it is also a system that other entrepreneurs have copied and applied to a wider and wider range of products and services. However, there is no guarantee that the operating systems that survived and grew in one period will have what it takes to continue to do so if the competitive environment changes.

What applies for rival business organizations is also relevant for understanding cultural evolution. Social groups with ways of thinking and choosing that give them advantages over other groups that think and choose in different ways will prosper and have a bigger chance of passing their operating systems on to successive generations via social nurturing processes, even if these heuristics are not embedded in genes. These considerations help, too, if we are trying to understand the historical path taken by academic disciplines and schools of thought. For a particular view of behavioral economics to flourish, its core ideas need to be passed from generation to generation. This may be impossible if the proponents of these ideas cannot obtain academic posts that enable them to develop their ideas and teach them, and/or if they cannot attract postgraduates with the capacity to pick up their ideas, extend them and pass them on to the next generation. Difficulties that they face in these respects may be ones that they understand and would even be able to correct if they were prepared to operate differently. Yet, "on principle," they may opt not to make the changes necessary to ensure a bigger legacy, for such changes may compromise the form that their legacy takes: they may prefer to accept the costs of being able to say, "I did it my way."

The evolutionary perspective begs the question of what determines the fitness of an organism or way of operating and hence whether it can prosper and grow, or at least have a niche within which it can survive. Over many years, I have sought to address this question by examining what limits substitution and what confers resilience as conditions change in the external environment. My conclusions repeatedly ended up dwelling on matters of structure, i.e., on how things are connected, either in our heads or as elements of our lifestyles and the strategies of the organizations at which we work. However, I did not know that I was thinking about the economy in terms of what is known as a "complex systems" perspective, until I had the pleasure of supervising Jason Potts's doctoral dissertation (published in 2000 in slightly expanded form as *The New Evolutionary Microeconomics*, for which Potts was a corecipient of that year's Schumpeter Prize). Modern evolutionary economists have enthusiastically embraced this perspective, but it deserves also to be an important part of a behavioral approach to economics. On this way of thinking, the structural architecture of a system affects its adaptability. As Potts showed (*ibid.*, especially chapters 2–5), it is a way of thinking that is at odds with conventional economic theorizing but, as we will see, it provides a powerful means of understanding why some ways of thinking and behaving are particularly conducive to survival, happiness and prosperity, whereas others result in life being much more of a struggle than it needs to be.

1.11 Outline of the Rest of this Book

The behavioral approach to economics that is assembled in this book can be summarized in a single paragraph. It is a way of doing economic analysis that takes account of what we can learn from psychology, introspection, informal sources and systematic research, about how people try – sometimes remarkably effectively, sometimes ineptly – to cope with challenges that are an inherent part of life. The choice environment and human cognitive limitations inhibit the discovery of optimal courses of action and prevent decision-makers, and the economy in general, from settling into a state of equilibrium. A behavioral economist is not prepared to theorize "as if" these challenges do not exist by assuming decision-making environments to be simple and static or by assuming decision-makers have all the capabilities they need to handle them effortlessly.

In the chapters that follow, we apply this view both to consumer behavior and the behavior of organizations, as well as considering its macroeconomic implications. In contrast to the conventional economist's strategy of viewing all actions as being motivated by a desire to maximize "utility," Chapter 2 offers a multifaceted examination of what motivates people to do what they do. Instead of assuming some kind of representative "utility function" with a particular simple mathematical form, the chapter ends by emphasizing that individuals differ in their mixes of motivations and it sets out techniques for uncovering how people see means–ends relationships between the things among which they choose and the goals they try to pursue.

In Chapters 3–8, we use Dewey's decision cycle framework to examine how people decide they have a problem to solve and figure out what to do about it. However, these five chapters do not follow what might seem the obvious sequence of (a) problem recognition, (b) search for solutions, (c) evaluation of options, (d) choice and decision implementation and (e) hindsight review. There are good reasons why I opted not to follow this sequence but working out which sequence to adopt instead was far from straightforward, for reasons I will now explain.

Because decision-making may entail a looping process, with hindsight review leading to recognition that there is still a problem, stages (a) and (e) need to be considered together and it may not even be a good strategy to begin by considering problem recognition and hindsight review jointly and proceed from there, via analysis of the search and evaluation stages, to an analysis of choice. Indeed, this structure would have run the risk that, if traditional economists read this book, they would end up viewing the analysis as assuming, as they would normally do, that the result of choice is a state of equilibrium. My intention is to present a view of human action in which problems frequently do not get completely eliminated and intended solutions often beget new problems. Given this, there is a case for putting problem recognition at the end of this block of chapters and to begin instead by analyzing search behavior on the presumption that a problem has already been recognized.

Such a structure might also appear to have advantages when it comes to understanding how problems arise and how they come to be recognized. Problems are personal constructs: problem recognition entails deciding that we have a problem and what its nature is. This is itself a problem that may necessitate a search for possible explanations of what may be going on, followed by their assessment, before we reach a verdict about what the trouble is and hence what kind of a solution we need to find. Problem recognition is thus inherently bound up with the issues that comprise the other stages of a decision cycle, ensuring that a decision cycle in effect consists of a set of interlocking sub-cycles.

Alternative sequences run into the same issue whereby making sense of one stage of the decision cycle is best done with an appreciation of what happens in other stages. Rival search strategies must be evaluated and choices made between them. Evaluation entails a search (including in one's mind) for possible ways of construing what one is looking at, followed, if there are multiple contenders, by a choice of which view to take. The choice stage may require a search for possible ways of choosing, and assessment of them, with the rejection of options that seem problematic begging the question of how their problems are recognized as such. What we have, then, is a tangled web (cf. Hofstadter, 1979); any strategy for analyzing decision cycles in a linear way entails an arbitrary choice about where to begin.

After spending much time experimenting with different sequences of material, I ended up with a structure that minimized the need to flag topics as being discussed further – in particular later sections – because it enabled me earlier to introduce key themes and concepts that crop up repeatedly in later chapters. This structure opens a bigger can of worms at an early stage than some other structures did, but it does so in a way that does not require them all to be dealt with comprehensively on the spot. It proceeds as follows.

Chapter 3 examines in detail, and with the aid of the complex systems perspective, why life tends to be more like a relentless sequence of problem-solving episodes than mainly a steady state or the smooth unfolding of a planned growth strategy. Chapter 4 addresses the process of cognition in respect of both how people come to know they have a problem and how they size up their options for solving it. Chapter 5 examines how they deal with uncertainty when they are trying to form their expectations. Chapters 4 and 5 largely ignore the question of how decision-makers come to have the information they use as a basis for their assessments. However, Chapter 6 focuses on the behavioral economics of searching for solutions to problems whose existence has been acknowledged. Chapter 7 examines the origins of relative valuations that we assign to alternative courses of action, i.e., what determines which ends decision-makers pursue. It revisits some of the issues explored in Chapters 3 and 4, doing so from a complex systems perspective. The ideas from this chapter are then developed further in Chapter 8, where we examine, finally, how choices are made. From Chapters 7 and 8, we will see how emotional factors and the rules around which we build our lives affect the extent to which we become attached to, or are keen to avoid, particular products and activities. Here we see that there is much more than the issue of whether the "price is right" to understanding whether or not people are open to changing their behavior and that it is not the case that "everyone has their price."

By the end of Chapter 8, we will have covered all the stages in a decision cycle. However, before moving on to Chapter 9's examination of how firms and governments can employ insights from behavioral economics to try to influence our behavior, it may be useful to revisit Chapter 4 to get a sense of having completed a full decision cycle loop. Indeed, because of the challenges of presenting a linear account of a decision cycle, the ideal thing to do is to return to Chapter 4 and read (or at least skim through) again from there through to the end of Chapter 8.

Chapters 10 and 11 focus on what used to be the heartland of behavioral economics, namely the behavior of firms and other organizations. In these two chapters, we focus particularly on learning and the determinants of how bold firms are in approving investment decisions, as well as on the challenges of getting a firm to function as a team. Chapter 10 is concerned with factors that affect organizational productivity.

Unlike a conventional profit-maximizing view of the firm, it takes seriously the impact of managerial operating and leadership styles and internal politics rather than presuming that organizations generally adjust swiftly to changes in knowledge about what constitutes "best-practice" methods. It ends with an examination of the challenges of implementing revolutionary change when an organization is struggling to survive. Chapter 11 picks up from there to consider how the competitive process plays out as a never-ending innovation-driven battle between firms. It focuses mainly on choices that firms make in relation to their external environments and how these choices are affected by learning processes within firms and populations of potential customers. What emerges includes a distinctive behavioral/evolutionary view of supply curves and pricing. Although it is only these two chapters that focus on firms and organizations, it should be noted that earlier chapters sometimes use illustrative material regarding choices in the workplace rather than merely giving examples that refer to consumer behavior.

The last two chapters of the book take us into the territory of behavioral macroeconomics. Chapter 12 focuses particularly on the role of confidence as a driver of aggregate demand in affluent economies and on the behavioral foundations of business cycles. Once again, the complex systems perspective proves to be useful – this time in relation to the resilience of the financial system as people experiment with new financial instruments. Finally, Chapter 13 explores the question of whether humanity's consumption of natural resources can be scaled back, to reduce its impact on the environment, without necessarily reducing how happy people are and how fulfilling they find their lives to be. This is a complex issue that takes us into the territory of both "ecological economics" and what has become increasingly known as "happiness economics." However, it turns out that there is a lot we can say about it even if we draw mainly upon material from earlier chapters of this book.

2 What Motivates Us?

2.1 Introduction

The goods and services that people consume, and the things they do in organizational and/or self-employed roles, are merely means to ends. In fact, as Jonathan Gutman (1982) emphasizes, human action typically involves "means–end chains" in which one thing is a means to something that is in turn a means to something else, and so on, though such chains only have a rather limited set of links before terminating at the end that really matters to the person in question. If we are to understand and anticipate behavior without taking a "black box" kind of approach, such as predicting choice via a stimulus–response–reinforcement model, we need to understand the kinds of ends that the decision-makers in question pursue and how they see possible choices in relation to these ends. Gutman developed the "means–end chain analysis" method for doing this, using research methods that are outlined in Section 2.10 of this chapter (for examples of applications of this method, see Olson and Reynolds, 1983; Reynolds and Gutman, 1983, 1984; Gutman and Alden, 1985; Reynolds and Jamieson, 1985; Laaksonen, 1994). Gutman's method has been influential in marketing, but it has so far had little impact in economics.

As far as economists have been concerned, the ultimate end of all behavior is the maximization of "utility." Moreover, they have conducted their analysis in terms of "representative agents" whose consumption patterns were in effect microcosms of the entire economy because they were modeled in a way that normally ensured they would be expected to buy some units of every product. This seemed an acceptable approach to economists because they wanted to analyze market-level behavior and were therefore not particularly interested in the idiosyncrasies of individual preferences. But the theories that economists construct around "utility functions" beg the questions of what is meant by "utility" and how the utility that people derive from a given product might be measured by anything other than their willingness to pay for it.

Economists had originally accepted the thinking of utilitarian philosophers such as Jeremy Bentham, who saw happiness as depending on the extent to which people experience pleasure rather than pain. However, from the 1930s onward, mainstream economists have often sought to avoid thinking about utility and preferences in terms of the extent to which activities bring pain or pleasure. This left them seemingly exposed to Joan Robinson's (1964, p. 58) claim that "[u]tility is a metaphysical concept of impregnable circularity; utility is the quality of commodities that makes individuals want to buy them, and the fact that individuals want to buy them shows that they have utility."

Behavioral economists are wary about reducing all behavior to the pursuit of utility, for they recognize that human behavior may be driven by a variety of forms of motivation, and the significance of these drivers may vary between contexts as well as between individuals in any given context. They have a good reason for getting to know what these drivers of behavior might be: although they are open to asking people why they do what they do or about their attitudes to particular courses of action, and although they could in principle use techniques such as Gutman's "means–end chain analysis" to probe for the deeper drivers of behavior, they are not usually in a position to gather information at a moment's notice about the particular drivers of choices in the situations that they find themselves having to analyze. Knowledge of the key motivating factors that drive human behavior may help them at least to form hypotheses about what is going on in the context they need to analyze. Moreover, even where time and other resources are available for conducting such research, a theoretical framework can be useful for deciding which information to gather and for interpreting it.

This book is written on the premise that, in order to understand how to bring about changes in behavior, it may be useful to understand why some people are already doing what policymakers are aiming to promote, whereas others are not, even if the financial positions of the latter are like those of the former. Hence, we dispense with the "as if" view of utility-maximizing representative agents. In its place, I offer a more complex, multifaceted view of motivation that allows us to have both a general view of the underpinnings of human action and a means of understanding differences in behavior via some factors being more relevant for some people in some contexts. The framework presented in this chapter draws on a variety of perspectives that psychologists, economists and others have offered about what motivates humans in general. After discussing these theoretical perspectives, the chapter ends by outlining techniques designed to find out how individuals see their worlds and to identify their personal means–end chains, without interrogating them within the confines of a questionnaire that reflects the analyst's preconceptions.

2.2   Hierarchically Ordered Needs

The conventional economic wisdom sees overall well-being in terms of the sum of utilities derived from the things that a person chooses. On this view, economizing entails focusing on the different marginal utilities to be obtained by spending a bit more in one area rather than another so that the total utility is maximized. The presumption underlying this view of the process of economizing is that consuming additional units of a product adds to utility, albeit at a progressively decreasing rate. Diminishing marginal utility supposedly provides an incentive to consider consuming other goods, whose marginal utilities are higher per dollar spent, rather than continuing to consume more and more of a good that one has already been consuming.

Though eminently plausible in some contexts, this vision of the consumer may leave us a bit uneasy about its ability to encapsulate the behavior of those who have a seemingly boundless passion for collecting particular kinds of products or those who become compulsive hoarders. However, a more basic issue that should concern us is whether it is a good idea to view all choices as serving the same need with differing degrees of effectiveness. An alternative approach is to see people as having multiple needs that they rank in order of priority. On this view, less important needs will only be attended to if this can be done without compromising the ability to meet higher-ranking needs. Viewing needs in this way does not preclude a person from ranking alternative combinations of goods in order of preference, but it does preclude adding up any kind of total for utility.

This nonadditive, hierarchical way of thinking can be seen in the writing of an Austrian economist, Carl Menger, who came up with his version of utility theory shortly after Jevons devised the one that became the conventional economic wisdom. Menger ([1871] 1950) gave the example of a farmer's choices following a bad harvest. The farmer's first priority would be to feed himself and his family. Any remaining produce would be used for meeting other needs in the order of their importance, beginning with seeds for next year's crop, followed by food for farm animals, and so on. A hierarchical view of wants and needs is also evident in the work of Alfred Marshall (1890), as Endres (1991) has shown.

A similarly hierarchical view of human needs can be found in Ralph Hawtrey's (1926) book *The Economic Problem*, but with an additional insight: he distinguished between "defensive" and "creative" consumption. By the former, Hawtrey meant activities or goods that serve as means to remove or prevent pain, injury and other sources of distress, whereas the latter pertains to consumption undertaken for positive gratification. Some products can serve both functions: for example, parents may purchase a gigantic Toyota Landcruiser 4WD to ensure the safety of their children on the school run (defensive consumption) but it may also be a means by which they can take vacations in which they explore remote areas (creative consumption). As people become richer, they can remove sources of distress such as hunger, being too cold or too hot, being mocked by others because of shabby clothing, and exhaustion from long working hours. They also become more able to reduce the drudgery of domestic chores by purchasing labor-saving appliances. Of course, being rich brings needs for new kinds of defensive expenditure, to ensure that one's possessions are not stolen or trashed by others. Generally, though, as Hawtrey (1926, p. 190) observed, "The rich man can afford to be fastidious in avoiding whatever he finds uncomfortable, fatiguing, unhealthy, disgusting or ugly."

Though largely forgotten in conventional economics, the perspectives offered by Menger and Hawtrey can be seen as precursors to a very well-known psychological view of motivation, namely Abraham Maslow's (1943, [1954] 1970) proposition that human behavior is underpinned by a "hierarchy of needs." (Maslow's analysis provided the basis for two books on "humanistic economics" by Lutz and Lux,

1979, 1988.) In Maslow's theory, the most basic human needs are physiological: we cannot live without adequate access to air, water and food, and we will perish in many climates if we do not also have shelter. Next in the hierarchy come safety and security needs, followed by social belonging, esteem and, finally, self-actualization (by which Maslow meant our desire to live to our full potential, something that, in Hawtrey's terms, may entail being able to engage in a desired form of creative consumption). Much later, Maslow (1971) added an even higher need, namely "self-transcendence," which we can view as the desire to meet our other needs via means that take account of our human obligations to each other and to the rest of nature.

A particular kind of product might serve a variety of these needs: for example, a meal may be a means for meeting basic physiological needs, but it may be consumed socially in a way that brings family members close together or earns praise from guests at a dinner party; for some, being able to cook meals to a very high standard might be a means of self-actualization. Eating a particular kind of food could even be a means toward self-transcendence, as with those who try wherever possible to eat organic, vegan food in order to limit the harm they do to the environment and the suffering they cause for other species, rather than for any health benefits that such a diet might offer.

In Maslow's view, people focus on addressing their most important unmet need and are only willing to consider trying to address lower-priority (but higher-level) needs if they can see ways of doing so without compromising their higher-priority "basic" needs. Consider again the case of food. Our self-transcendence need will have to remain unmet if meeting it would stand in the way of meeting our needs to belong and receive esteem. Such a conflict might arise if we believe that the people around us view those who practice organic, vegan diets as weird and therefore tend to avoid them. But we will also not allow our attempts to win esteem to compromise our abilities to feed ourselves.

Maslow's perspective was dramatically foreshadowed in the opening scene of Puccini's opera *La Bohème*, in which the clash that the lead characters face between their physiological needs and self-actualization is resolved by a decision to try to keep warm by burning the manuscript that one of them has been writing. More recently, the documentary series *Victorian Slum* (directed by Emma Frank, 2016) has illuminated the dilemmas that the poor faced in slums in London a century and a half ago. The immediate obsession of the slum-dwellers was with earning enough money for their weekly rent; they were prepared to go without food in order to avoid being evicted in weeks when their earnings were too low to pay for both rent and food. Although they lacked financial reserves, the reserves of their own bodies were usually enough to enable them to avoid having to switch focus to buying food at the cost of being forced out on to the streets. Their calorific reserves were replenished via a diet that involved buying bread and jam by the slice from local corner stores, and often their accommodation was so basic that cooking was not even a possibility.

Evolutionary processes seem much less likely to have favored humans who were motivationally hardwired to want to maximize total utility rather than to operate in the nonadditive manner envisaged in Maslow's famous theory. A conventional economist would no doubt defend the additive view of preference and utility by saying that, if we are starving, the marginal utility of food becomes extremely high, ensuring that we will divert out expenditure away from other areas. The problem with this view is that if the decision-maker lacks foresight, the need to substitute may be perceived too late, taking the decision-maker by surprise. If so, the decision-maker's past profligacy in other areas may result in an inability to prevent starvation. By contrast, people will be less vulnerable to unforeseen problems if they are programmed to keep asking themselves whether choices that might be means to meeting lower-priority needs put them at unacceptable risk of being unable to meet their basic needs. The latter are more likely to have made provision, "just in case" their worst fears are justified, to ensure they can meet their basic needs: taking the hierarchical view, and always being concerned with basic needs, promotes planning rather than operating in a reactive manner.

People may differ in how strongly they are programmed to keep their basic needs in mind when choosing. Their programming in this respect can be both genetic and the result of social learning and/or inferences from personal experience. Social groups in which keeping basic needs in mind is a norm will tend to thrive in a surprise-prone environment relative to groups in which the norm is to enjoy life today and be confident in one's capacity to deal with whatever tomorrow brings.

Today's debates over the need for action to limit greenhouse gas emissions provide food for thought in relation to this evolutionary perspective. The conventional economist's view of decision-makers seems well suited for characterizing the "climate skeptics" who deny scientific evidence about human-induced global warming and who presume that, if it does turn out to be a problem, relative price adjustments will ensure it is only a temporary one. To the rest of us, who are better characterized by a hierarchical view of motivation, the climate skeptics may seem like the alcoholic who, when told that she is endangering her life by consuming too much alcohol, presumes she will be able to cut back on her intake before the damage to her liver becomes fatal. Our inadequate knowledge of when it would be safe to stop doing something that could threaten our long-run survival matters far less if we have a sense of priorities and a concern with meeting basic needs and we therefore operate on a "safety-first" basis (see also Aldred, 2012).

To end this section, it is also worth reflecting on the evolutionary role of human sexual needs. Maslow included sex on his list of basic physiological needs, whereas he saw the needs for intimacy and to be part of a family as elements of the lower-priority group pertaining to "social belonging." Regardless of whether he was right to make this separation, we should keep the need for sex in mind as a motivating force in the economy. Human sexual needs drive economic activities via expenditure aimed at attracting and keeping sexual partners, such as spending on grooming, clothing and jewelry, dining out, in bars and nightclubs, and so on. Sexual needs are powerful enough to drive risk-taking behavior that often has among the most expensive downsides of any of the choices that humans make. These include the impact of unplanned pregnancies or sexual scandals on career options, and the impact of divorce settlements on financial status. However, these needs seem to have a powerful role to play in the evolutionary fitness of humans as a species.

Most species mate because they are genetically programmed to do so, rather than because they receive the payoff of sexual pleasure. Clearly, to a degree, humans are programmed to want children: most people naturally find babies and infants attractive and yet fail to think ahead about the risk that children will grow to be obnoxious teenagers, while women who do not have children at an early age may find themselves feeling prompted to make up for this via their hormonal "ticking clock." This kind of genetic programming is reinforced by social norms and pressures to produce children. However, with their abilities to think and reason, humans can override such programming if they can see a case against producing (more) children.

Humans might reason, as some indeed do, that sexual activity is ridiculous and/or that it is potentially dangerous due to the risks of sexually transmitted diseases, complications associated with childbirth and the impact of children on resource pressures and their parents' stress levels. With a capacity to think but no motivation to pursue sex for reasons of pleasure, humans would probably have had far lower reproduction rates. Because sex was the route to reproduction, the ability to experience sexual pleasure would naturally get selected in the event of mutations that gave some humans the capacity to experience (more) sexual pleasure, and an associated motivation to pursue it. Evolutionary processes would naturally select a capacity to experience sexual pleasure that was both intense and fleeting so that humans did not lose the urge to pursue it. Were it possible to store such pleasure in one's memory, it would be possible to replay the experience in one's head (rather as we can do to some degree with a movie or piece of music), thus reducing the need actually to keep engaging in sexual activity (see further Earl, 2013).

The development of contraceptive technologies has enabled humans to pursue their sexual motivations even when they have decided that it is not a good time to be producing children. As a result, population growth will depend increasingly on: (a) the presence of people who think little about the negative consequences of producing children or who are not prepared to challenge family and social norms that value the production of grandchildren; (b) adherence to religions that rule out the use of contraception; and/or (c) the existence of patriarchal societies in which women who can see the downsides are denied the right to choose to limit their risks of having children.

2.3   Novelty, Comfort, and Pleasure

Humans have a basic physiological need for novelty in the flows of stimuli that they receive. Our senses have evolved to function on the basis of changes in the stimuli they detect, both in terms of type and intensity. If incoming stimuli do not change, our attention will wander in search of something more interesting or that is a potential threat. Given this, the kinds of products that will sustain our interest rather than motivating us to go shopping for something novel are those that keep enabling us to have pleasurable new experiences and/or keep providing us with what marketing professionals call "surprise and delight" by offering new opportunities that we had not fully anticipated.

Notice here that it is the potential for novel stimuli that is key to something holding our interest: something that has previously given us a flood of novel stimuli but is not expected to continue to do so will lose our attention. George Shackle took this point further during the 1940s when he was developing a novel theory of choice under uncertainty. He noticed, via introspection, that the human imagination enables us to engage in "enjoyment by anticipation" (Shackle, 1943, 1949). In other words, we can give our brains the opportunity to process imagined stimuli by rehearsing in our minds what it might be like if possibilities that we presently imagine eventuate. He saw this as a means of explaining why people stake money on lotteries and bets despite finding it hard to imagine that they will win: once they have made their gambling commitments, they can enjoy the excitement of thinking about what they would be able to do if they did win. Until the results are in, these novel possibilities remain feasible. From Shackle's standpoint, conventional analyses of gambling will be prone to underestimate the demand for lotteries because they focus on the probability-weighted expected utility of the gamble being successful and ignore enjoyment by anticipation that, win or lose, the gambler is able to experience.

Shackle portrays this phenomenon as starting at the point at which the decision-maker commits to the gamble: it is only by purchasing the lottery ticket that we are opening the (very slim) prospect of winning a huge sum of money. If Shackle's analysis is correct, consumers will have a motivation for making commitments for consumption activities such as vacations, dates, weddings, concerts and sporting events well in advance of the time necessary to ensure the event can be organized. There is, however, an exception to the idea that we will get much more out of an event to which we have been looking forward for a long time than if we arranged it just before it happens: we may delight in seeing how good we are at running our lives impulsively, making choices in the thrill of the moment rather than via planning.

Yet perhaps Shackle did not go far enough in considering the motivational significance of the human ability to enjoy things purely by imagining experiencing them. When we are shopping, whether by exploring what is on offer at "bricks and mortar" retail sites, browsing via the Internet or by having tradespersons visit us to discuss our home improvement ideas, we get streams of novel stimuli that can serve as "food for thought" even without making any commitment to spend any money. Like daydreaming, spending time searching and browsing relieves us from boredom by helping us meet our need for novel stimuli. The information we gather from this process is typically incomplete, leaving us needing to create mental stories of how life might be if we purchase particular items (see further Bianchi and Patalano, 2017). On top of this, as emphasized by Tibor Scitovsky (1985), the modern shopping environment provides sensory stimulation in addition to what we get from viewing the products themselves: the modern mall offers us opportunities to eat, socialize and enjoy a climate-controlled environment full of visual and other stimuli (see also Underhill, 2001).

So far, the discussion of the motivational side of the need for novelty has focused on novel stimuli or imagined prospects that are welcome sources of excitement, i.e., things that give us hope. But we should not forget the motivating effects of stimuli and thoughts that we prefer not to have to deal with – in Hawtrey's terms, the things that distress us, the things that we fear. The lives of today's poor or our poorer ancestors are characterized by stress associated with uncertainty about where the next meal is coming from, whether the rent can be paid, and so on. These basic needs, combined with very limited resources, make life for the poor a series of gambles in which hopes are focused on keeping distress at bay, rather than on new experiential opportunities. Because of these preoccupations, this kind of life may not be boring, even where jobs and domestic chores fail to provide stimulation. Being able to put a meal on the table may be enough to give a sense of achievement.

With affluence (and, some might say, with social welfare systems), life may become so devoid of actual and prospective discomfort that it fails to meet the need for novel stimuli. Awareness of Hawtrey's notions of defensive and creative consumption led Scitovsky (1981) to argue that excess comfort in modern affluent societies is the reason for the pursuit of high-excitement activities. These may entail actually putting one's life at risk, as with mountaineering, or merely escapist entertainments in which one gets engrossed in following the fortunes of others as they deal with major challenges. In some cases, as with theme park rides or white-water rafting and jet-boat tours, the consumer is given the sense of living on the edge, but the experience is presumed to be managed so that no one (normally) gets injured or dies.

Although humans have a physiological need for novelty, and insufficient novelty is unpleasant to us, manifesting as boredom, there are limits to the amount of novelty that we find pleasant. As Scitovsky (1976, 1981) emphasized, the relationship between the amount of novelty we face and how comfortable we feel takes the form of an inverted U-shape rather than being monotonic: at some point, a rise in the degree of novelty or intensity in incoming stimuli produces a maximum level of comfort and further increases may eventually reduce our comfort levels so far that we want to be elsewhere, just as when we are bored. However, while our level of comfort is a function of the level of stimulation that we are experiencing, the level of pleasure that we experience appears to be a function of changes in the level of incoming stimuli: highly pleasurable activities thus commonly involve escalating stimuli levels in terms of intensity and novelty, beyond what we would find ideal if they were sustained, up to a point of climax after which stimuli flows fall sharply, enabling us to relax and reflect on what we have just experienced.

While sex would be an obvious example of this, it may be wise for readers to reflect instead on the experience of enjoying movies and live artistic experiences, books that one simply "can't put down," the excitement of sporting events and exhilarating touristic experiences. If well designed, these kinds of activities are utterly attention-arresting "flow" experiences (see further Csikszentmihalyi, 1990) during which consumers at no time are motivated to consider anything else. Where everyone knows that the activity has a particular limited duration, and suppliers have reputations for not going "too far," the prospect of temporary sensory overload can be enticing. However, the problem for the supplier (to which we return in Section 10.12) is to know how far it is safe to go when competing by offering novelty.

2.4   The Need for Achievement and the Instinct of Workmanship

Closely related to Maslow's idea that humans have needs related to esteem and self-actualization is another need that may prevent people from idling their time away in comfortable surroundings, namely, the need for achievement (commonly abbreviated to *n-Ach*). This need is best known via David McClelland's (1961) book *The Achieving Society*, but psychologist Henry Murray had suggested it earlier in a book that also predated Maslow's analysis. It was based upon clinical and experimental research he had conducted with colleagues at Harvard University, using fifty "men of college age" as research subjects. Murray (1938, p. 164) defined the need for achievement as the desire "[t]o accomplish something difficult. To master, manipulate or organize physical objects, human beings, or ideas. To do things as rapidly, and as independently as possible. To overcome obstacles and attain a high standard. To excel one's self. To rival and surpass others. To increase self-regard by the successful exercise of talent." Murray's thinking complements an even earlier contention, by the pioneer of evolutionary and institutional economics, Thorstein Veblen (1914), that humans have an "instinct of workmanship": people are programmed to want to do what they do well and take pride in being able to do this. The higher the standards that we set ourselves, the more we are going to find ourselves engaging in problem-solving activities and learning something as well as coming closer to satisfying our need for achievement. These human traits have obvious benefits in terms of evolutionary fitness.

The need for achievement has attracted most interest in relation to workplace motivation and its impact on productivity, with McClelland advocating the use of measures of *n-Ach* in personnel selection processes. But as well as differences in *n-Ach* possibly accounting for performance differences among individuals within a group, it seems possible that intergroup differences in *n-Ach* might help explain differences in economic performance between nations. This could result from native populations having evolved differently in their genetically inherited achievement needs. However, national differences could also arise due to genetic foundations for *n-Ach* being amplified socially, via cultural norms that favor behavior consistent with pursuing this need (see also Clydesdale, 2021). Having a "mañana mentality" and a casual attitude to quality would not be conducive to survival in global competition against economies in which the need for achievement was higher. If our thoughts turn to cultural stereotypes, it is hard not to think of Germany and Japan as likely exemplars of the latter. Indeed, the Japanese even have the word *karōshi* to denote the phenomenon of death from overwork. We might thus expect, if we had internationally consistent and reliable measures, to find a correlation between *n-Ach* and per-capita levels of national income. This is the proposition for which McClelland remains well known, but its empirical validity remains controversial (for a short survey, see Gilleard, 1999).

It is important not to let the usual focus on *n-Ach* in relation to the workplace divert our attention from its significance in relation to what people do when they are not at work. As Cairncross (1958) pointed out long ago, economists are prone to be blind to the amount of unpaid work that people do at home. Like firms, we can choose to pay others to supply us with goods and services, or we can engage in do-it-yourself. Economists would conventionally emphasize that the incentive to opt for the latter strategy, rather than specialize on the basis of comparative advantage, arises due to relative prices being distorted by taxes. However, do-it-yourself activities may also be more effective than overtime working as a means toward meeting our need for achievement; indeed, those of us with a high need for achievement may feel very restless if we have not got some kind of domestic project under way and/or are not challenging ourselves with new tasks and/or what Hawtrey would class as "creative consumption" activities.

2.5   Identity Management

Identity came into economics mainly via the work of George Akerlof and Rachel Kranton (2000, 2010) and it surfaces at several points in this book as a driver of behavior. In essence, the term refers to a person's sense of self, i.e., how a person answers (at least, in his or her head, if not in public) the question "Who am I?" We might think of this as reflecting the person's assessment of his or her personal qualities such as "I'm politically conservative, kind, reliable and patient, and a bit of a workaholic, but I'm slack when it comes to exercise and I don't dress as well as I should." However, psychologists distinguish between "self-identity" and "social-identity," with the latter term focusing on how people answer the identity question with reference to particular social groups to which they feel attached and whose values they share, often with pride (Tajfel and Turner, 1979). The groups that are part of our social identity may be formal, with regular gatherings (for example, "I'm a freemason" or "I'm Hell's Angel") or comprise merely people with particular socioeconomic status and/or sets of beliefs (for example, "I'm a Western Suburbs matron" or "I'm a Republican"). Being a member of one kind of group often precludes being a member of other groups, and hence people often operate with a strong sense of "us" and "them," as in "I'm a vegan behavioral economist who is passionate about music, whereas my colleagues seem mostly to be omnivorous mainstream economists who are passionate about sport; we hardly ever mix socially."

Identity is thus closely related to Maslow's view that people have a need for social belonging: group membership and a sense of solidarity help us meet that need; we feel less like lone, unreasonable, possibly crazy or misguided outsiders if we join existing groups or succeed in forming new ones. Identity may also relate to the need for esteem, with the esteem that others grant us affecting our sense of self-worth insofar as we choose to take seriously what others think of us. For some, being members of an "out-group" and always being put down by members of the dominant "in-group" can be painful even if they believe that the dominant group has a view of the world that is misguided and/or indefensible. The need that some "out-group" members feel for social esteem may be such that in the end they attempt to meet it by "selling out," i.e., changing sides and thereby losing the approval of the minority group that they leave. Other "out-group" member may be able to tolerate being put down by the "in-group" due to being taken seriously by "out-group" members that they respect.

Joining a group may entail other costs if our existing values do not align well enough with the expectations of the group's members: we may have to adjust our consumption and expectations in order to be accepted and enjoy the benefits of membership. With some groups, membership entails being willing to go through challenging initiation rituals and we may only get to that stage after cultivating the approval of an existing member who is then prepared to recommend us for membership. In some case, no matter how far we are prepared to bend to join a particular group, membership will not be open to us because there is something about us that is at odds with the group's organizing principles (as in the case of, say, all-male clubs that refuse to allow women to join).

Much of economic behavior can be viewed as a means toward the end of identity management. This view underpins a recent attempt by Shrum et al. (2013) to reconceptualize the notion of materialism. In everyday parlance, the term has tended to refer to the notion that the acquisition of goods is the key to happiness. Shrum et al. (*ibid.*, p. 1180) propose that "materialism is the extent to which individuals attempt to engage in the construction and maintenance of the self through the acquisition and use of products, services, experiences, or relationships that are perceived to provide desirable symbolic value." A key aspect of this way of viewing materialism is the phrase "the extent to which": different kinds of identities will entail different levels and forms of spending.

There may be many means to attaining a given identity-related goal. Shrum et al. point out, for example, that if we see our appearance as significant for our self-esteem, we can try to achieve improvements by spending on cosmetic surgery (a materialistic method) or by taking more exercise and dieting (which may not necessarily entail any spending). Those who solicit gifts and/or try to ensure they will receive legacies are being materialistic in Shrum et al.'s sense, whereas those who make charitable donations are not unless they do so in order to acquire or enhance a relationship that has symbolic significance to them. (An example of the latter would be where a person donates money to his or her alma mater, subject to the gift being given extensive publicity and his or her name being attached to the building, scholarship or professorial position that it finances.)

Although personal wealth and social and institutional factors constrain the identities that people can uphold, it needs to be said, foreshadowing Section 2.9, that identities are essentially personal constructs: we try to figure out who we are and then see whether the idea we have is workable and whether we can be comfortable with what it turns out to entail. This is not to say that people always try to establish who they are without recourse to external inputs. For many, it is important to have a sense of their family roots, as is evident with the popularity of genealogical research as a leisure pursuit. We may also look to external stimuli in trying to construct a view of how we fit into the world. Taken together, the messages that marketing campaigns send out promote a highly materialistic perspective on what we should see as important. Depending on how we are brought up and the groups that we join, social norms can operate as "institutional hidden persuaders" (Hodgson, 2003) that oppose or reinforce stimuli coming in from marketing.

In modern economic systems, stable sets of values associated with a sense of self make it much easier for firms to predict demand for their products: imagine how chaotic things would be if, say, people who saw themselves as opera-lovers one day, reimagined themselves as devotees of boxing the next, and so on, and if there were no inherent reason for the switches of identity across the economy normally to offset each other. There are obvious evolutionary foundations for the tendency of identities to morph slowly, for early humans would have benefited if they happened to have a sense of identity and needs for social belonging and esteem. Groups can achieve things that individuals cannot, especially when group members are proud to be members and hence are committed to upholding the group's goals. Coordination failures are less likely when group members agree on particular principles and rival groups know what their rivals' binding principles are. Moreover, without any particular goals or principles to define who they were and to strive to attain or uphold, early humans would have fewer problems that they felt motivated to solve and hence less need to be creative.

A more subtle reason why evolutionary selection processes would have resulted in humans having a sense of identity is that identity reduces cognitive load and facilitates decision-making. Identity does this in cases where we think of ourselves in ways that preclude certain kinds of behavior from being open to us. If we say, for example, "I'm not the kind of person who listens to country and western music or who breaks into cars or houses if the opportunity arises," we are imposing additional constraints on our set of feasible choices and hence on the set of possibilities we need to consider: it is easier to work out what music to listen to on our headphones when we go out jogging and we do not keep getting diverted from jogging and listening due to scanning for opportunities to engage in theft. Operating according to a stable, slowly evolving set of rules in turn reduces the cognitive load of people who know us, for we rarely surprise them (see also Parsons, 2000).

Identity is closely bound up with the ways in which we are motivated to behave in relation to changing fashions and the extent to which we set out to acquire things that will enhance our social standing. It is to these social aspects of motivation that we now turn our attention.

2.6   Fashion and Status

It is hard to deny the existence of behavior that is motivated by concerns about being fashionable or about one's place in the social pecking order. However, acknowledging the significance of such behavior poses a problem for conventional economists. At the core of conventional thinking lies the notion of equilibrium, but equilibrium seems unlikely in a world in which some people see themselves fashion leaders and others view themselves as avid followers of fashion. Concerns about status clash with economic equilibrium, too, since one person's rise in status threatens the status of others, thereby motivating the latter to retaliate.

These challenges to conventional utility theory were recognized in a remarkable, fearlessly subversive paper by Caroline Foley (1893). Fullbrook (1998, p. 711) describes Foley's work as "a manifesto of sorts" for consumer behavior research in societies that have advanced beyond merely living at subsistence levels. In considering the drivers of fashion, Foley does not merely challenge static utility theory and presage research on the desire for excitement by suggestion that humans have a craving for change; she also (1893, p. 461) argues that swings in fashion are driven by "love of distinction," "imitation," "the desire after equalization," and "the expression of social consciousness," the last two of which Fullbrook (1998, p. 713) suggests we should see, respectively, as the desire for conformity and the desire to signal one's membership of a particular social group or that one is embodying the "spirit of the age."

Some of those who follow fashions may view themselves as "late adopters" rather than the sort of person who "rushes to jump on the latest bandwagon." Either way, if fashions change in their social circles, they will at some point have to change accordingly to uphold their views of how fashionable they are. But at any moment it is always more a case of "when" rather than "if" there will be yet another change of fashion: as new fashions become established, would-be fashion leaders will become increasingly motivated to experiment with innovative choices that few, if any, others have made. If we view ourselves as fashion leaders and no one follows us, we must try another experiment and hope that it will be more successful in attracting followers and thereby provide evidence that we are indeed fashion leaders. If our choices are widely followed, there will sooner or later come a point where we will have to try something different in order to stand out from the crowd. If we fail to do this, we risk losing our leadership role to other innovative consumers. The fashion treadmill thus continues to keep turning. Though clearly at odds with orthodox equilibrium analysis, it is amenable to being modeled using simulation methods (see Andreozzi and Bianchi, 2007).

Even those who studiously cultivate a disdain for fashion and feel no need to establish themselves as fashion leaders may sometimes find their identities hard to maintain unless they experiment in new areas. It is not simply that those who are determined to stand out by being different may become motivated to search for a new way of being different due to others emulating their behavior. There may also be the kind of problem revealed in the introspective writing of Holbrook (1995, ch. 10): those who have cultivated a distinctive identity in one environment (for example, being a jazz aficionado at high school in their hometown, while all their classmates listen to pop music) can find it very unsettling to move to a new environment in which their choices seem nothing special (in Holbrook's case, becoming a student at

Harvard after growing up in Milwaukee, Wisconsin). As Holbrook (*ibid.*, p. 330) recalls, "[A]ll at once, I found myself in the midst of hipsters in every domain – music, art, literature, film – claiming interests so esoteric that they tapped into levels of nonconformity whose existence I had scarcely suspected."

Those who seek to elevate their social standing are similarly likely to have to develop relevant knowledge of what is normal in unfamiliar social settings, for failure to conform to the relevant norms could mean failure to be granted membership of the social groups they seek to join. The motivation to spend in ways that signal one's wealth is a consequence of everyone knowing that it is unacceptable to demonstrate one's wealth by walking around with a certified statement of one's total assets pinned to one's shirt. Less widely known is how to engage effectively in spending on "conspicuous consumption" – i.e., on products and services where one's level of spending and/or consumption are visible to a target audience rather than being privately enacted. It is necessary to demonstrate that one understands the entry codes of one's target group by consuming the right kinds of status symbols. Newly rich consumers still see the world from the perspective of the group from which they are trying to elevate themselves, so their early attempts to signal that they have "made it" are likely to be more impressive to that group than to the one they aspire to join. Until they crack the code and start signaling their success in a suitably subtle manner, the "new money" upstarts are likely to be viewed by the "old money" establishment as brash and lacking in taste.

The significance of social norms for how members of different parts of society run their lives is emphasized in the seminal contribution to the economics of conspicuous consumption, Thorstein Veblen's (1899) book *The Theory of the Leisure Class* (for surveys of the history of conspicuous consumption and writing in this area, see Mason, 1981, 1998). The timing of Veblen's work should be noted, along with its title: the book predates the modern world in which working-class incomes are high enough to permit spending aimed at "keeping up with the Joneses" rather than merely spending to meet basic needs. Conspicuous consumption in the suburbs may indeed be a major driver of economic activity today, but, historically, status-seeking behavior was economically most significant at the top end of society.

The rich have never been content simply to be in the upper echelons of society. On the contrary, history reveals them as engaging in vigorous competition to live more lavishly than each other. For some, spending on their country homes and feasts was a means of buying access to policymakers that they hoped to influence, but only a select few would be able to attract monarchs to stay on their estates. Their discretionary spending in such status races trickled down to the lower levels of society, via employment opportunities on their estates and in the production of luxury goods. Veblen's book captured this at the time when traditional landed gentry found themselves facing new competition from successful industrialists, just before their world was further disrupted by World War I. However, he emphasizes that the pursuit of status via displays of trophy products has been going on for as long as human societies have been able to generate surpluses beyond basic needs, or able to capture the fruits of rival groups' surpluses. Given the track record of the rich, and with income inequality on the resurgence in the twenty-first century (see Piketty, 2014), we should expect production increasingly to be skewed toward luxury products for the superrich.

Veblen's view of the leisure class included the idea that the household head gets pleasure not merely from the leisurely lifestyle he enjoys and the prestigious, high-quality goods that he consumes but also by being able to make it possible for other family members to consume similarly and from seeing them enjoy leisure. Veblen called the latter "vicarious" consumption and leisure. Clearly, it is a different kind of vicarious consumption from that which Scitovsky had in mind when discussing scope for people to pursue their needs for excitement via spectator roles. The household head could even take pride in making it possible for members of household staff (who had their own status ladder, from the butler downward) to enjoy their limited consumption and leisure opportunities. In Veblen's time, middle-class household heads had to work, unlike the upper-class household head, but even they could enjoy vicarious consumption and leisure from the knowledge that their wives and children did not have to go out to work in order to support their material lifestyles or meet basic needs.

So strong are fashion- and status-related motivations for spending on consumption that productivity growth since Veblen's time has done much less to increase leisure time than some economists predicted (most notably, Keynes, 1930). Nowadays, however, the motivation to be upwardly mobile or, at least, to keep up the appearance of not going down the social ladder has produced a middle class of dual-income households. Labor-saving appliances have played a vital role in making this possible. Indeed, Ha-Joon Chang (2010) argues on this basis that the invention of the washing machine was more significant than the Internet.

Fashion cycles and status-driven consumption behavior may seem to be dysfunctional beyond their contributions to helping people meet their needs for novelty. However, as argued in Chai et al. (2007), they contribute to evolutionary fitness to the extent that they drive creative thinking and lead to experiments that enhance the stock of knowledge. Societies in which everyone knew their place and did not try to advance or differentiate themselves would provide few incentives to innovate except to deal with external threats or population pressures. New knowledge generated to profit from fashion and conspicuous consumption expenditure may initially only benefit high-status individuals, but it may trickle down eventually to the lowest levels of society: for example, the innovations pioneered in luxury cars tend sooner or later to become standard features in even the cheapest models (as with, fuel injection systems, antilock brakes, airbags, etc.). Moreover, where status symbols and fashion products are durable goods, ownership may trickle down, too: the rich pay hefty premiums for being the first owners before trading up to the next generation of products. They thereby enable less affluent consumers to purchase the trade-ins (or donations to charity shops) secondhand at discounts that are way beyond what physical depreciation would imply. Where we should be concerned, however, is in respect of the possibility of products being designed to last only for the duration of the fashion cycle. As well as being resource-hungry, these "fast-fashion" products cannot trickle down to poorer members of society.

2.7 Building Systems and Keeping Entropy at Bay

Even in an age of fashion cycles, worn-out or nonfunctioning consumer durables still trigger many decision cycles. The physical deterioration of our durable assets can be viewed as a manifestation of an entropic process whereby structures disintegrate unless energy is expended on maintaining them. Such processes impinge on us in many parts of our lives. If we do not put effort into maintaining our social networks, our connections will fade away, much as neural networks in our brains, and the capacities that they give us, will fade if we do not keep activating them. Our homes become filthy and untidy unless we invest time and other resources in keeping things clean and in organizing our possessions, returning them to their places of storage after using them. Our health and appearance will decay without investments in exercise and grooming, and our gardens will start looking unkempt and eventually become like jungles if we leave them untended.

People differ in their willingness to tolerate or allow these entropic processes to work. Some clearly are not distressed by them: they "let themselves go," along with their property, despite not being short of the wherewithal to prevent this from happening. However, for others, building and maintaining structures is a major concern, sometimes to the point of obsession.

The extent of our concern with keeping things in good order may be something that we choose, viewing it as part of our identity. Some of us may want to be viewed as "laid back," whereas others are anxious to avoid the negative social connotations that may be attached to having low standards in this respect: note here that the original meaning of the word "slut" was a slovenly, untidy woman, not one who had many casual sexual partners. As Veblen (1899) saw it, being immaculately presented was a way to show others that one could afford the time and/or other resources needed to keep things spotless. But a degree of motivation to invest in developing and maintaining systems may be the result of evolutionary selection processes favoring those with a genetic disposition toward being organized and building systems, or who live in societies where this is the social norm. To be sure, an obsession with maintaining order can be dysfunctional, crowding out opportunities to acquire other experiences and grow as a person: for example, a life of cleaning, tidying, keeping the garden in order and polishing the car may preclude getting out and getting to grips with the wider world. However, so long as such extremes are avoided, evolutionary processes generally favor people and societies that are prepared to invest in keeping entropy at bay and that look for opportunities to build systems.

This is not just to do with the obvious health benefits that come from good hygiene, or with the impact of grooming on the kind of partner one might attract. Being organized also increases productivity in several ways. First, arranging things in hierarchical systems is a means of reducing the impact of human cognitive limitations. In the absence of any system of organization, we will waste time and miss opportunities while trying to find things: just as supermarkets help us to shop by grouping by categories the items that they stock, so we organize what we buy from them when we get it home and store it in our pantries and refrigerators. Secondly, when we build systems, we often get the benefits of positive externalities between their components: in other words, in some sense "the whole is greater than the sum of the parts," so there is some kind of "synergy" effect to be achieved from grouping them together according to particular rules. For example, when we select clothes to wear, we do not do this randomly but with a view to the overall effect that they will produce in combination; inconsistencies in style and unmatched colors and patterns clash with evolved aesthetic sensibilities (cf. Dutton, 2003), whether these are hardwired or have been passed down the generations socially. The same may be said for interior design and décor and in respect of cooking: random combinations may violate our systems-based sense of what constitutes good taste. Moreover, those with an inclination to build systems can also achieve benefits in terms of physical outputs, as when a vegetable garden is constructed with due attention to relative positions of plants that may affect each other's access to shade and light and the kinds of insects that are likely to be attracted.

2.8　The Diderot Effect

A variant of behavior that is a means to the end of maintaining structures is "the Diderot effect," brought to the attention of modern social scientists by Grant McCracken (1988). It was first described by the eighteenth-century French philosopher Denis Diderot in an account of what happened as a result of him being given the gift of a very fine dressing gown (Diderot, 1775–1777, pp. 5–12). Keeping the gift and disposing of his old dressing gown was the start of a spiral of spending that left him heavily in debt. Diderot's financial disaster was the result of viewing his possessions as complements and striving to maintain consistent quality between them. The new dressing gown upset the order that he had previously achieved: it made his other clothes look tawdry. Replacing the contents of his wardrobe would not solve the problem, for the clothes would look too good for the wardrobe, and if he replaced the wardrobe, it would make the rest of the furniture in his bedroom look substandard, and so on. He would have done better to keep his old dressing gown and dispose of the gift, rather than trying to elevate the general standard of his possessions (and, in the process, his identity) to the standard signified by the new dressing gown.

Nowadays, we may see this human motivation to achieve consistent standards as being a major driver of expenditure on home improvements, often in conjunction with technological or space constraints associated with upgrading a deceased consumer durable. For example, our old refrigerator may expire, and we replace it, not with something of the same size and appearance but with something bigger that is more capable of handling our current needs. This may then cause a cascade of spending if we have to remodel the entire kitchen to get the new refrigerator into the right place and as a result of the new refrigerator making the rest of the kitchen look out of date. After we have renovated the kitchen, our laundry starts looking out of date, so we renovate it too, but then the adjacent downstairs bathroom seems inconsistent with the emerging look of the house and it seems absurd to give this one a makeover without doing likewise, and achieving a better deal from the contractors, for the upstairs bathrooms. The expenditure that began with the new refrigerator thereby escalates fifty-fold or more, all because of our pursuit of consistent standards.

The environmental consequences of the human susceptibility to the Diderot effect ought to be a cause for concern. Diderot's discarded possessions probably were fit to be reused by others, but things work differently with home improvements. The pursuit of consistent standards results in many things that had been serving perfectly adequately in functional terms being torn out of homes, tossed into skips and taken off to landfill sites. Moreover, with attention and funds focused on stainless-steel appliances, granite benchtops, and so forth, the uptake of products such as solar electricity and battery storage systems may be delayed for years.

2.9   People As Scientists

In his two-volume magnum opus *The Psychology of Personal Constructs*, George Kelly (1955), a clinical psychologist at Ohio State University, offered a very different view of human action from what we have so far considered. Kelly's approach to psychology involves an "as if" method that is strikingly different from "as if" economics: he suggests that it may be useful to view people "as if" they are scientists trying to predict and control the world around them. Kelly's book led to the emergence of a new "constructivist" school of thought in psychology, and it has won adherents in marketing, organizational behavior and management. Brian Loasby and I were the first to air its potential for use in economics, at the 1981 meeting of the British Association for the Advancement of Science (in papers later published as Loasby, 1983, and Earl, 1983b; more extensive economic applications followed in Earl, 1983c, 1986a, 1986b).

Kelly (1969) reported that he came up with his "people as scientists" view of human action one afternoon at Ohio State University, where his schedule involved consultations with some of his patients, in his role as a clinical psychologist, and with some of his students, in his role as a teacher. He realized that in both roles he was trying to help people who were having trouble making sense of parts of their lives. They had ways of thinking that could not effectively accommodate the things they needed to handle, with the result that their lives were getting into a mess or their chances of doing well in their studies were being compromised. The underlying problem was that, in some parts of their lives, they were having trouble constructing effective personal views of the events that made up their past, present and future world. Personal construct theory was Kelly's vision of how people construct their views of the world by using rules and building frameworks for organizing their thoughts. However, what he proposed was not merely that human behavior is shaped by *how* people construe themselves and the world around them but also that, for humans, *the essence of living a life is predicting and controlling events.*

In Kelly's view, people go through life trying to develop their abilities to predict and control events, or at least limit the extent to which their ability to do so shrinks as the world changes. Hence, he is inviting us to see choices as means to testing our predictive systems in new areas, refining our appreciation in areas where we already have some effective constructs and ensuring that our predictive systems will not leave us at the mercy of events. Rather than maximizing "utility" in terms of a "given" preference ordering, we develop our distinctive personal views about the areas in which we want to enhance our abilities to predict and control events – in other words, the areas in which we will try to develop our knowledge. We tend also to be concerned with how effective a view we have of ourselves, i.e., our identity, or in Kelly's terms, our "self-construct." The latter concern is not surprising: to find the external world hard to fathom is bad enough, but to lack a view of oneself that seems to fit the facts must be very scary indeed.

Kelly's focus on prediction and control does not entail viewing well-adjusted people as nervous about having any of their hypotheses falsified. If we know that normally we are not confounded by the consequences of our actions, and that normally we can get to grips with new situations or get back under control things that we have temporarily neglected, then we are likely to feel able to venture beyond our comfort zones and see how we fare. To be sure, sometimes we get "more than we bargained for" in a way that results in us finding ourselves out of our depth and struggling to figure out how to cope. However, we are often able, so to speak, merely to "stick a toe into the water" in an unfamiliar area. Knowledge gleaned from such a trial may be useful to us in future, helping us judge more reliably whether we would be able to handle a particular kind of situation.

There are three main ways in which to see choices as serving as means toward predicting and controlling events. First, if we lack constructs in a particular area we may experiment in that area as a means toward forming hypotheses; in other words, our choices may generate information that we hope to use inductively to generate some general hypotheses about this area. For example, if we have never tried a particular kind of cuisine and are open to doing so, a night out in a restaurant that specializes in serving it provides a basis for forming constructs about what to expect on other occasions when this kind of cuisine is being mentioned. We may have started out with no clear expectations, but we form a sense of what it "is like" by comparing and contrasting this kind of food with other kinds for which we already have constructs.

Secondly, what we choose may provide a means by which we can test hypotheses that we have already formed via induction or deduction. For example, we can check whether we were wise to generalize about a particular kind of cuisine based upon our initial experience of it or from what we have inferred it will be like after reading about it or hearing the reports of others. Similarly, if we have had an entrepreneurial idea about a new way of earning a profit, we can put it to the test of the market (cf. the "entrepreneurs and venture capitalists as scientists" analysis offered by Harper, 1996). The choices that we make may provide us with the opportunity to test several hypotheses. Money spent on new clothes and at the hairdresser may be an investment in testing how other people react to an idea we have about ourselves, but it may also be a means toward testing our constructs about other people, as when we get ready for a first date with someone. On such an occasion, having made such investments, we get to test our hypotheses about what the other person is like and we may get to form more elaborate constructs about them and, sooner or later, about other aspects of the world that we end up sharing with them.

Finally, our choices may be of strategies or objects that we construe as means of insulating ourselves from situations that we predict we would find it difficult to predict and control. Clearly, this would be in line with Hawtrey's notion of "defensive consumption."

Some of the things we choose may serve as means to the ends of prediction and control in multiple ways. As an initial example, consider what we can get from watching television. We can get to know more about the world, test our knowledge of the world and test our abilities to anticipate events and cope with situations that we have not so far experienced. Secondly, consider car ownership. It may make life easier to predict and control by enabling us to avoid being at the mercy of unreliable and inconveniently time-tabled public transport, enable us to explore more of the world, open new social experiences by changing how other see us and permit us more readily to test our capabilities and visions of how the world can be changed (for example, by enabling us to transport inputs we need for our do-it-yourself home-improvement projects). Finally, consider activities that entail battling against entropy: from a Kellian perspective, they clearly come into the "control" category, but they can also entail testing hypotheses. For example, building and maintaining a garden as an ordered system requires a capacity to form hypotheses about what will grow success-fully and about how to ensure weeds, insects, fungi, and so on do not prevent the garden that we have imagined from becoming reality. In the process of trying to make the garden happen and keep it under control, we also have an opportunity to test aspects of our theories about ourselves by discovering what we are capable of doing and how much we know.

2.10   Techniques for Uncovering Means–End Chains

George Kelly's (1955) book *The Psychology of Personal Constructs* is significant not merely for its "people as scientists" view of human action but also because it was there that Kelly proposed his "repertory grid technique" (henceforth RGT) as a means for uncovering how people view areas of their lives. The word "technique" is significant here, because what Kelly proposed is a method that does not entail the researcher constructing a questionnaire and asking research subjects to respond to it. Instead, Kelly's technique is designed to coax people into revealing their personal repertoires of constructs – i.e., the dimensions that they use when characterizing phenomena – in whichever aspect of the world is the focus of an investigation.

RGT captures how the person in question sees the world at the time it is being applied; if it is reapplied months or years later, it is quite likely that the set of dimensions that it reveals will have changed somewhat. In this section, we will be exploring the technique in the context of mobile (cell) phone handsets, an area where there has been spectacular evolution over the past three decades. It would not be surprising to discover that many buyers have growing repertoires of constructs and yet lag behind those of more "geek-like" consumers. It needs to be stressed, however, that if applied today, RGT may not capture all the constructs that the person in question might call to mind tomorrow, or even later today. Without a recent cue, we may fail to call to mind things that do matter to us: for example, if RGT is applied to motor vehicles, most people will probably not mention that they would prefer a car to have good brakes, unlike someone who has recently had to do an emergency stop or been driving an unfamiliar car whose brakes perform surprisingly differently from those of their usual vehicle.

In its original form, RGT was used merely for uncovering the basic level of cognition, such as the features in terms of which a consumer construes a set of rival products or the attributes a manager may consider when hiring staff. However, Kelly's doctoral student Dennis Hinkle ([1965] 2010) devised several extensions to RGT when studying why people differed in their tendencies to resist making changes in their lives. These extensions make it possible to probe more deeply into how people see the world and to discover structural relationships between their constructs. One of these extensions, "construct laddering," is central to Gutman's (1982) "means–end chain analysis" approach to understanding consumer behavior. But soon after seeing Gutman's contribution, I realized (Earl 1986a, 1986b) that Hinkle's other extensions had significance for understanding the extent to which people are open to change and their responsiveness to changes in market incentives. Hinkle's work thus has a key role when we explore these issues in Chapters 7 and 8.

The Kelly-Hinkle techniques are nowadays normally implemented with the aid of a computer, using applications that make it easy for research subjects to follow the process and for the researcher to record data. They work as follows.

First, we specify the area of interest, such as how the research subjects see rival mobile phones, holiday destinations, their colleagues, possible careers, and so forth. We then begin the RGT phase by asking our research subjects to list around ten alternatives in this area. These may include not merely options currently available but also ones that were previously available or that the research subject wishes were available – for example, if mobile phones constitute our area of inquiry, "an iPhone 13," "My first mobile phone," "my ideal mobile phone." Some research subjects may be so unfamiliar with the area in question that they have trouble coming up with a ten-item list, even if prodded to include a wider variety of conceptual items (for example, "a mobile phone that would suit an elderly person"). If so, we get them to do the best they can with a shorter list. Kelly calls each item on the list an "element." These elements will comprise one axis of the "repertory grid" that emerges via RGT. The other axis on the grid will comprise the repertoire of constructs that the RGT is designed to uncover.

Constructs are elicited as follows. We ask the research subject – let us call her Susan – to take the first three elements on her list and tell us in what ways they are similar and in what ways they are different. If Susan says, for example, "My first mobile phone didn't have a camera, a touch screen, QWERTY keyboard or Internet access, unlike an iPhone 13 or Samsung Galaxy, both of which offer all of these features," we have elicited four of Susan's constructs for her repertory grid of mobile phone constructs. When she runs out of things to say about the first three elements, we then ask her to focus on elements 1, 2, and 4 and repeat the process, followed by elements 1, 2, and 5, and so on, for all possible three-way combinations until we eventually get to elements 8, 9, and 10. In these rounds, we speed up the process by emphasizing to Susan that what we want to hear from her are similarities and differences that she has not pointed out in the preceding rounds.

It is common for no further constructs to emerge long before all the possible three-way compare-and-contrast attempts have been made. Typically, unless the research subject is very unfamiliar indeed with the area in question, or is an expert in the area, one will end up eliciting around eight to fifteen constructs, some of which will be the same as those elicited from other participants in the study. Some of the constructs may be dichotomous in nature (for example, "color screen versus black-and-white screen"), some may imply a measurement scale (for example, "bigger screen versus smaller screen") and some may have a single point of focus rather than being clearly dichotomous (for example, "smartphone versus not a smartphone"). The last type is particularly common when participants lack much experience in the area in question and have not picked up the terms and concepts that those with more expertise habitually use.

With the repertory grid thereby constructed, we can now apply the first of Hinkle's extensions, namely his "construct laddering technique." We do this by getting Susan to focus on one construct at a time and asking her to tell us which pole of the construct she prefers and why she prefers it. The reasons Susan expresses for her preferences will reveal further constructs: for example, she might say, "I prefer a clamshell phone because when it rings, you just open it and you're able to hear the other person right away; you don't have to touch any buttons or screen icons at all." We can probe further on the basis of these replies and derive yet more constructs: for example, if asked why she prefers not to have to press a button or touch an icon to reply to a call, Susan might say, "I'd be hopeless at hitting the right button, especially if I were not wearing my reading glasses or were out in bright sunlight that made the screen impossible to read. I fear I'd always get flustered when the phone rang and fail to hit the button before the other person rang off, or I'd hit the wrong button and cut them off by mistake, and I'd then have to call them back." We can then repeat the process, laddering to yet another layer of constructs: to continue the example, if we then asked Susan why she prefers to avoid getting flustered and having to return missed calls, the reply might be, "It's so embarrassing, and it means I end up having to pay for the call."

Applying the construct laddering technique is rather like peeling away a layer of an onion only to find another layer below and repeating the process until we get to the core of the onion. However, it turns out that the systems of constructs that people create for coping with the world often have far fewer layers than all but the smallest onions. Typically, in only half a dozen or fewer steps, we will find that our research subjects start giving responses to the effect that "I can't say why I prefer this, I just do, period!" In such cases, the constructs about which we are asking them need to be seen as what Kelly called "core constructs," the things that really drive the person's behavior. In the example we have been using, Susan's core constructs may be only a step or two away: we seem to be heading toward her identity, i.e., to how she sees herself. Taking the laddering process further might well reveal that Susan sees a clamshell phone as a better means for maintaining her self-image and social image as a capable, in-control kind of person, and for avoiding having to wrestle with the possibility that she is a rather mean and penny-pinching kind of person: using a clamshell phone limits the number of times she will have to consider whether she will return the missed call, a call that, by owning a mobile phone, she probably feels she should not have missed in the first place.

Construct laddering processes need to stop when the participant gets to the "I prefer it because I do" stage. It is not ethically acceptable to try to probe any further, for this will cause distress. The means–end chains that are elicited from seemingly unrelated constructs often terminate on shared core constructs. In doing so, they can bring out dilemmas that the research subjects may have trouble resolving with any of the products available to them. For example, if Susan sticks to using an old-fashioned clamshell phone as a means for avoiding identity-related issues associated with missing calls, the trade-off may be that of not having Internet access on the fly, which could cause embarrassment by other means and earn her the label "Luddite" for resisting what has become an affordable and very widely adopted technology. Whether she sticks with a clamshell phone or switches to a touch-screen smartphone, the phone may be both a means of avoiding anxiety and a source of it. She cannot be in complete control. However, she may be able to work out which is the lesser of the two evils – or perhaps she might consider getting an iPad Mini with cellular access, to keep in her handbag as a means of ensuring she has mobile access to the Internet despite sticking with her clamshell phone.

The relationships uncovered by the construct laddering process are typically presented as inverted treelike diagrams, with the constructs that were first elicited listed along the bottom row and the core constructs at the top, with lines showing how they are linked to intermediate constructs and how intermediate constructs are linked to each other. However, relationships between constructs can be explored further and then represented using Hinkle's two other extensions to RGT, namely "resistance to change grids" and "implication grids," which are explored in Chapter 7.

2.11 Conclusion

The wide range of motivational perspectives explored in this chapter offers a much more comprehensive starting point for understanding why people do what they do than is offered by the conventional economist's utility theory framework. It takes time to soak up these diverse perspectives and develop a keen eye for which of them may be especially helpful for making sense of what is going on in any particular context, but they leave us with a dynamic view of decision-makers. Although their sets of underlying motivations may not be changing, people do change in terms of their knowledge, how they see the world and their place in it and in which motivating forces are at the forefront of their decision-making processes at any moment. However, even though particular motivations may come to the fore in particular contexts, it is important to maintain a pluralistic approach rather than to focus merely on what seems to be the key motivating need in the situation being analyzed. This is because dealing with one need may allow other needs to come to the fore or prevent other needs from being met. Moreover, the means by which one person tries to meet a particular need may impinge on the capacities of other people to meet different needs.

For example, if we think about the leisure classes in the second half of the nineteenth century purely with a focus on sources of status being enjoyed by the head of household, it is easy to forget that the women of the house may have had a seriously unmet need for excitement in their lives. If we do note the latter issue, it takes us on to being able to understand the success of department stores as a retail innovation at that time. The success of these stores depended on some women being bold enough to be pioneering customers and, in the process, changing established views about how to construe women who were out on the city streets without chaperones. It also had consequences for the supply of labor to serve the rich and ultimately played a significant role in female emancipation and winning female suffrage. The inclusion of public restrooms was crucial to the success of such stores as places where women could spend extended periods of time shopping, for they enabled women to meet some of their most basic needs. (See further the excellent two-part TV documentary directed by Aitken, 2010.) This was happening around the time utility theory was being worked out, but utility theory is not particularly useful for analyzing what was going on. All that the utility maximization perspective can say is that the innovating department stores enabled women to enjoy more utility. The means–end chain approach that underlies this chapter, coupled with the pluralistic analysis of the ends consumers may be pursuing, provides a fruitful starting point for analysis that does not require us to reduce the behavior of the stores' customers to utility maximization.

One thing we have not done in this chapter is venture into the territory of neuro-economics, typified by experiments in which decision-making is studied by putting research subjects in brain-scanning machines and studying their brain activity while they are making decisions. This omission does not signal that later chapters will proceed without reference to knowledge of how the brain works, for that is not the case. However, we should note here that perhaps the discovery that feelings of pleasure are associated with secretions of neurotransmitters such as dopamine in the brain might come to be seen as providing a basis for removing utility from its "impregnable circularity." If we know, say, that taking the drug commonly known as Ice (Methamphetamine) gives a dopamine hit a thousand times stronger than we get from eating a cheeseburger (see Rawson, 2006), then we can perhaps understand the disastrous addictive attraction of Ice and also see the potential for measuring other marginal utilities in terms of dopamine secretions. However, such an attempt to use research on the electro-chemistry of the brain as a means for modernizing utility theory would be inherently problematic, for two reasons. First, there is the problem of implementing it across the vast range of choices that modern consumers face.

Secondly, it misses the point that choice is a forward-looking activity, and although present choices may be influenced by the outcomes of previous ones, the amount of pleasure derived from a past choice may not be independent of how well the construed outcome matched expectations.

We may thus have to be content with less resource-hungry methods for discovering why people do what they do. The repertory grid and construct laddering techniques that facilitate means–end chain analysis are themselves more resource hungry than clipboard-and-questionnaire methods but are nowhere near as expensive as research involving brain scanners. Where repertory grid and construct laddering methods cannot be used, the perspectives covered in this chapter should serve as useful elements in the design of questionnaires for finding what drives behavior in contexts of interest to researchers and policymakers.

3 Why Is Life So Full of Problems for Us to Try to Solve?

3.1 Introduction

Decision-making starts when we acknowledge that we have a problem. This does not happen merely when we identify an actual or expected shortfall between how things are and where we think they ought to be; we can also present ourselves with problems to solve when we decide that we are bored and fancy trying something new, or when we become aware that we can probably do better than we have been doing but are not sure what our new choice should be. In Chapter 4, we will be considering the processes by which people decide whether they do indeed have a problem to solve. However, it seems worthwhile first to reflect on why so much of life is taken up with problem-solving activities, so this is the focus of the present chapter. Nearly a third of what follows (the multipart Section 3.7) employs ideas from modern evolutionary economics that entail taking a "complex systems" view of the kinds of systems people need to build if they are to limit the extent to which they are at the mercy of events. This will no doubt be unfamiliar territory to many readers, even if they are well versed in modern behavioral economics. However, it has a behavioral economics lineage: some of the seminal thinking about the significance of system architecture for avoiding problems came from the most eminent figure in the earlier behavioral literature, namely Herbert Simon, the 1978 Nobel Laureate. Tuning into the complex systems perspective at this early stage will have payoffs when we consider how the systems that we build inside our heads affect our abilities to adapt as the world around us changes.

In viewing life as a problem-solving activity, it is useful to augment John Dewey's (1910) decision cycle approach to human action with Randall Bausor's (1982, 1984) suggestions for coping with the passage of time when doing economic analysis. If we add a time dimension to the decision cycle, we move to a helical view instead of thinking in terms of loops. The implication of Bausor's analysis is that, taken together, the decision-making processes that we engage in as our lives unfold comprise a complex yarn made up of multiple interwoven helical strands that each start at particular points in time. Sometimes, our choices fail to solve the problems they were intended to solve, so we take the decision helix for that part of our life further via another decision cycle loop. If a decision results in multiple problems becoming apparent, the helix for that area of our life divides into multiple branches as we go forward trying to deal with the various issues. On other occasions, choices do solve the problems they were intended to solve, so the helix in question terminates with a hindsight review, just as the end of a thread may be reached within a textile yarn.

This dynamic view of economizing activities permits a much richer analysis than economists normally offer. For the past century and a half, the modus operandi of the typical economist has been comparative static equilibrium analysis. That way of doing economics proceeds as follows:

(i)   Assume that decision-makers can find the optimal way of behaving in the environment that they are in.

(ii) Demonstrate why decision-makers would not choose anything other than what they have chosen – i.e., show why their choices are optimal – and hence that they are in equilibrium.

(iii) Impose an external shock on the decision-makers, i.e., something surprising in their environment. This is presented in the form of a change in relative prices that results from a shift in market demand (due, for example, to a period of unexpectedly hot weather), a supply-side disruption (e.g., the arrival of migrant workers from war-torn nations, an earthquake, weather that affects crop yields, the entry of new suppliers or the uptake of a new technology) or a change to government policy (e.g., the imposition of a tax or subsidy, or new regulations).

(iv) Assume that the decision-makers remain as they are in terms of their preferences and that they can figure out how best to adapt to their new external environment.

(v)   Demonstrate what their new choice will be and why it is their best choice given the external environment that they now face. They will then be back in equilibrium.

In that way of doing economics, the decision-maker always solves the problem and ends up in a new equilibrium state, staying there until the next shock arrives. The shocks are never the result of choices made by the economic actors whose behavior is being analyzed; they always arise externally. Moreover, the analysis typically proceeds as if the decisions would eventually be reversed if the set of relative prices reverted to the previous configuration: for example, if petrol prices rise, the demand for small, thrifty vehicles will rise, but if petrol prices then fall back in the long run, there will be a switch back to larger, thirstier vehicles when motorists replace their cars, rather than an enduring preference for smaller cars due to motorists having been impressed by how well modern fuel-efficient small cars serve their needs.

In addition to having to address shocks in the external environment that affect everyone to some degree, we each have personal sets of issues that arise via the cards that fate deals to us. For example, a person may be diagnosed as having Coeliac disease and thereafter have to keep solving the problem of finding gluten-free food, a problem that keeps resurfacing as food suppliers change what they offer and as the decision-maker in question moves from one choice environment to another. The symptoms of the disease may, of course, have emerged due to what the person had been choosing to eat, but they only arise because of the underlying problem that, in this case, has genetic roots. Other problems may start for nongenetic reasons that are also completely beyond our control, such the problems that we must deal with due to growing up in a particular set of family circumstances or in a particular part of the world with its associated environmental, economic and/or political issues.

In the real world, unlike the artificial world of a typical economic model, the decision-maker's task is to make life manageable rather than get to an equilibrium state in which no problems are left unsolved that could have been solved. Many of the problems that we identify are to some degree consequences of our own choices. With hindsight, we may regret our choices for reasons that have nothing to do with subsequent changes in relative prices and everything to do with how we went about trying to solve a previous problem. But we may also create problems by trying to defer action. Where resources are limited, it may be impossible to avoid making choices that do not have problematic consequences.

Before the advent of behavioral economics, economists neglected this aspect of everyday life: exploring how people end up with self-inflicted problems or are unable fully to resolve problems that were not of their own making would have been at odds with viewing economizing as the activity of identifying the optimal feasible bundles of goods given the constraints faced by the decision-maker. Here, by contrast, the aim is to highlight what it is about real-world decision-makers and the economy they inhabit that prevents them from settling into equilibrium states after fine-tuning the mixes of products they consume or produce and how they divide their time between work and leisure.

3.2   Bounded Rationality

Many of our self-inflicted problems arise and/or persist because the capacity of the human brain often falls well short of what is needed to solve problems in the best way possible or to address one kind of problem without creating another. This is why, for Nobel Laureate Herbert Simon (1957a, 1982a, 1982b, 1997), the focus of behavioral economics needed to be on "bounded rationality." Three cognitive limitations stand out as especially problematic for decision-makers in the real world, though they do not always result in poor choices even in challenging choice environments.

First, the brain's information-processing speed is a major constraint on filtering out irrelevant stimuli and taking due account of pertinent information: unless we can process information in chunked form, we find it hard to handle more than about ten bits of information per second (Marschak, 1968). This is why, for example, we can have trouble keeping up when taking notes on a lecture or get into difficulties if trying to sight-read a complex piece of music at the intended tempo. If we must make complex choices in a hurry, we may not have enough time to compute all their potential implications even if we are making decisions in an environment that is free of distracting stimuli. The things that we end up failing to consider may then confound our attempts to meet particular ends. If we are cognitively exhausted, the risk that we will make information processing errors increases.

Secondly, although our long-term memory capacities may be prodigious in some areas of our lives, the working memory capacity of the human brain is severely limited: George Miller (1956) famously argued that people can only keep around seven, plus or minus two, things in mind when working on a problem. (This phenomenon is sometimes referred to as Miller's Rule.) Consequently, we are prone to (a) make errors when doing complex mental calculations, (b) forget some of our options if the range of choice is large, (c) fail to keep in mind features of the options that we do manage to keep in mind and (d) forget things we were intending to refer to when considering what to do.

Thirdly, humans have limited capacities to imagine what is possible. This issue tends not to be given the attention that it deserves within the literature on bounded rationality but is a key theme in the writings of George Shackle (1955, 1979). Of course, having a limited imagination often has the benefit of ensuring that we do not worry about things that should not be troubling us – for example, as Shackle (1955) notes, we do not typically concern ourselves with whether there will be a tiger in our bathroom. However, as a result of failures of our imagination, we may fail to check out possibilities that turn out to be relevant to the performance of options that we consider, or we base our expectations on assumptions that lead us to be overoptimistic or unduly pessimistic. Hence, when events surprise us, it is often because we did not even dream that they might be possible, rather than because we viewed them as unlikely (see Section 5.2 for further detail). There is no guarantee that, even in the long run, we will be able to operate with ideal levels of wariness on every occasion.

Bounded though it is, the human imagination clearly has enough creative power to make innovation possible. And because humans crave novelty (see Section 2.3), innovators focus on dreaming up new products rather than merely on competing by finding ways of cutting the costs of making existing products. This is problematic on both sides of the market. As Schumpeter (1943) emphasized, the fruits of innovation tend to be short-lived as the success of a firm's innovations puts its rivals under pressure to engage in retaliatory innovation. This often results in the market lifecycles of innovative products being much shorter than the operating lives of the products themselves. By the time that buyers return to the market to obtain replacements, the competitive landscape may have changed drastically. Even where buyers are more frequently "in the market" for particular products, constantly changing menus of incrementally upgraded options exacerbate the significance of their cognitive limitations by making it harder for them to get better at choosing via experimentation and/or watching the experiences of others.

There are two ways by which we can try to circumvent our cognitive limitations so that we do not end up with avoidable problems. One is to use rules or heuristics to reduce the cognitive demands of making decisions. Some of the heuristics that we use in attempting to solve problems are hardwired products of human evolution. This should mean that they once enhanced the competitive fitness of humans in general. However, as modern behavioral economists emphasize – and as will be shown later in this book (for example, in Sections 4.10, 5.7, 6.5, and 8.3) – they may be counterproductive in some modern-day decision-making contexts. They may also make us susceptible to devious attempts to manipulate our behavior (as discussed in Chapter 9; see also Hanson and Kysar, 1999a, 1999b), leading us to make choices that in some cases will prove problematic. Other heuristics that we use are ones that we have opted to include in our personal repertoires of coping rules after thinking them up for ourselves or seeing them being used by others in particular contexts. Some of these heuristics may be very effective decision aids but others, unbeknown to us at the time we use them, may contribute to generating the problems we later address.

The second way of trying to sidestep cognitive constraints is to outsource tasks that our brains might otherwise have undertaken, as when we write shopping lists rather than relying on our memory, use computers to do calculations, make use of product comparison websites and call upon the heuristics, knowledge and thinking skills of others (see Section 6.8). Precisely how we outsource may be driven by heuristics that end up contributing to problems rather than solving them or preventing them from arising. Our vulnerability here is recognized by the adage "it takes one to know one": we may need some expertise in the area in question to know whom to rely upon as an expert in that area if we outsource aspects of our choice.

The three kinds of cognitive shortcomings so far considered add to a more basic impediment to taking good decisions, namely the limitations of what we know about the world. These knowledge shortcomings – which underpin Kelly's (1955) "people as scientists" view of human action – include gaps and misconceptions in terms of facts ("know-that") and why things happen ("know-why"), in our knowledge of how to undertake particular tasks ("know-how") and our knowledge of other people, including knowledge of what they know and are capable of doing ("know-who") (see further Ryle, 1949). Inadequate know-how may result in tasks being performed poorly, often because poor know-who results in mistaken allocations of tasks relative to expertise. Moreover, one person's knowledge limitations may partly be the consequence not merely of the limited knowledge of those who try to share knowledge with them but also of the latter's limited capacities to put their knowledge into words. Polanyi (1962, 1967) called the latter issue the problem of "tacit knowledge." Following its incorporation in evolutionary economics by Nelson and Winter (1982), tacit knowledge has been widely recognized as a major issue in technology transfer processes.

3.3   Coordination Problems

Many of the problems that we encounter as consumers, workers, managers or entrepreneurs arise because the success of our choices as means to meeting particular ends depends upon the choices that others make or (as when we are trying to solve the problem of what to give someone as a "thank you," birthday or wedding present) how others view the choices that we have made. In a sense, economists in recent years have been acknowledging this via their obsession with trying to model choices from a game-theoretic standpoint. As is evident from some behavioral economics textbooks, behavioral economists have joined in, often using experiments to see how people behave toward others when participating in economic games. However, by allowing their work to be anchored to the well-defined games of mainstream economics, behavioral game theorists have ended up ignoring some important areas where decision-makers need to be mindful of the behavior of others but where the interaction may take place without any well-defined rules or payoff matrix.

One of these areas is how other people can affect our well-being and cause problems for us by behaving in ways that seem crazy to us and seem to require us to respond with particular actions or make it problematic for us to make choices. Here, the key question becomes "What kind of game are they trying to play?" Quite often, the answer turns out to be that they are trying to control other people, as a means of buttressing their own low self-esteem. Eric Berne (1964) opened this area in psychology with his book *Games People Play*. Figuring out what the other party – say, one's partner, a colleague or an elderly parent – "is up to" may be especially challenging if he or she is not actually conscious of playing a game and plays it in a rather inept, inconsistent way.

Of more obvious economic significance is the fact that the success of investment and hiring decisions by managers and entrepreneurs depends on how well the behavior of customers and other firms is anticipated. The original Keynesian approach to macroeconomics (Keynes, 1936) is underpinned by this issue: if entrepreneurs and managers are not sufficiently optimistic about the prospects for selling what their firms produce at a price that covers their opportunity costs, they will cut back on production and employment. In doing so, they will reduce the profitability of their suppliers and the incomes that workers can spend. Collectively, the entrepreneurs and managers might be justified in their pessimism, for those who receive income may choose to delay spending it because they are uncertain about their employment prospects, future needs and the opportunities that technological progress may bring.

If they choose to save some of their income, there is no guarantee that what they save will be lent to fund consumption spending or investment by firms. The money may simply rest in their bank accounts and not constitute an addition to the supply of loanable funds. Moreover, our savings offer no clues about when and how we are ultimately going to spend them and hence about how firms should invest today, if they can access funds to do so, in order to be able to service demand that will feed into the system when we eventually choose to run down our savings. Sad to say, this vision of macroeconomics has largely been lost by academic economists: much of modern macroeconomics is nothing more than scaled-up microeconomics that ignores the "fallacy of composition" problem that arises when incomes depend on spending and spending is not firmly tethered to income.

Even where entrepreneurs and managers are confident about the total volume of demand for a particular kind of product, their investment and hiring decisions remain problematic. Here, the issue is what is sometimes known as "The Richardson Problem" after the work of George Richardson (1959, 1960) on the coordination of investment decisions. Actually, it consists of two problems.

First, there is the "competitive investment problem": the sales revenue that a firm receives on an investment depends on the extent to which other firms invest in creating capacity to produce the same product or a substitute for it. This is so even if each player's contribution to total production is tiny (as is often the case with farmers producing for global markets). If many entrepreneurs and managers can see potential for profits due to growth in demand for a particular product and believe they have the skills required for its production, it is likely that there will be overinvestment, a glut in supply and losses rather than profits. Yet if all hold back from investing for fear of such an outcome, the profit opportunity will remain untapped.

The risks of a coordination disaster will be particularly acute if potential suppliers are scattered across a wide geographical area (and hence are unable easily to see what others are doing) and need to take their investment decisions around the same time (for example, planting for a particular crop). It is this problem that gives rise to boom–bust episodes of wild swings of price and output such as those seen in agriculture (epitomize by the "hog cycle") and the construction of office blocks and apartment complexes. Although seasoned players in such markets may be aware of the problem, such knowledge does not provide a basis for forming "rational expectations," contrary to the claims of Muth (1959). To the extent that such coordination failures are avoided, this seems, paradoxically, to arise from limits to the capacities of market participants to spot profit opportunities, articulate convincingly to suppliers of funds and other resources those opportunities that they do recognize and/or undertake the tasks necessary to bring their visions to fruition.

The second aspect of the Richardson Problem is the problem of coordinating complementary investments. Richardson originally discussed this in relation to the various investments needed to make up the supply chain for a particular product: the viability of an investment at any level of a supply chain would depend on the extent of upstream or downstream investment by suppliers of components and services, as well as on investments that workers make in acquiring the skills relevant to contributing within the supply chain. A firm may run into problems if there is insufficient investment at other stages in the supply chain, leading to limits on how much it can produce or sell or to problems that arise as it attempts to deal with these shortfalls by internalizing the problematic stages despite not having previously developed the relevant capabilities. Nowadays, however, we might also recognize the complementary investment problem in the context of products whose viability depends on investments made in complementary products: for example, electric vehicles depend upon investments in battery-charging stations, while the viability of a computer operating system depends upon investments made in developing apps to run on it. If the investment decisions are taken in a decentralized manner, coordination failures may arise, along with problems for those who adopt the product or technology in question, and the mere prospect of such problems may hinder the diffusion of the product or technology (cf. the problem of "range anxiety" in relation to electric vehicles, a problem exacerbated by the lack of a standard charger interface). We return to this kind of issue in Chapter 11.

3.4   Search Goods, Experience Goods, and Credence Goods

The chances that mere mortals will end up making transactions that prove problematic vary according to the context of choice. It should be noted that some behavioral economists use "context" to refer to how a given choice is presented to a consumer. As we shall see in Chapter 9, that aspect of "context" can indeed affect the choices that people make. Here, however, I am using the term to refer to how occasions for choice differ in terms of the accessibility of relevant information. Economists started considering the significance of information problems seriously in the 1970s, beginning with the work of Nelson (1970), who distinguished between search goods and experience goods, and Darby and Karni (1973), who introduced the concept of credence goods when discussing the economics of defrauding customers. The definitions offered for these three kinds of goods vary somewhat from source to source. My own preferred way of distinguishing between them is as follows:

- *Search goods* are products for which, in principle, it is possible to resolve all issues of knowledge and uncertainty by gathering information *prior to purchasing and using them.*
- *Experience goods* are products for which it is inherently impossible to resolve all issues of knowledge and uncertainty prior to purchasing and using them, but for which it is possible to resolve these issues *once the products have been experienced by the consumer under normal conditions of use.*
- *Credence goods* are products for which it is impossible to resolve all areas of uncertainty *even when a significant time has elapsed after they have been paid for –* in other words, they have inherent problems of uncertainty both before purchase and after they have been supplied and used, whereas experience goods only present buyers with inherent prepurchase uncertainty.

These are "in principle" definitions; in practice, search goods can differ considerably in how easy it is for prospective buyers to obtain information that is potentially available and to be sure that the information with which they have been supplied is correct. Where there are significant costs of finding out about what a particular product has to offer, choices may be made without all the relevant information being gathered. In such cases, proxy rules may be used – just as rules have to be used with experience goods and credence goods – to prevent missing information from preventing a decision on occasions where we have ruled that we do need to make a choice. Where buyers are short of both experience and imagination, they are at risk of making problematic choices unless they are armed with appropriate rules.

The problem that some search goods pose is not simply that information is costly to obtain but that we lack relevant experience or knowledge about that kind of product and thus we do not know what information we should try to find or the significance of some of the information that we happen to discover. If we rule out spending time discovering what we need to know in order to make an informed choice, we can try to generalize from what we know from a seemingly related area of our experience and thereby opt to trust particular brands or people who have previously helped us with choices that seemed to work out well. However, business history is littered with cases in which firms have run into difficulties by trying to extend their brands into territories that require different kinds of capabilities from those on which they had built their reputations. Given this, customers who make such generalizations are likewise sometimes going to experience disappointment. Decision-makers can also try to cope with information and knowledge limitations by building their own mental models of their choice environments by deductive reasoning (see Section 5.3 for further detail). Where these models are naive, they may result in the selection of search goods that were poorly suited to meeting desired ends, or the selection of disappointing experience goods. Where choices entail the unwitting waste of money on credence goods from devious suppliers, the consequence may be problems in other parts of the customer's life that were starved of resources.

The key issues that can cause a good to be an experience good seem to be as follows:

E1 *If the product takes the form of a contingent contract for future delivery, the buyer risks being disappointed due to a dispute over whether a particular state of the world has eventuated or because the supplier has ceased trading by the time a particular delivery clause becomes operative.*

This condition is one of the factors that prevent insurance products from being search goods despite their specifications being stated at length in "product disclosure statements." It is problematic to deal with this by allowing the customer to pay for the contract at the time it expires and decline payment to the extent that promises have not been honored – there could still be dispute about what the state of the world had actually been, or the customer could have been ruined by not receiving the promised service and therefore not be able to fight for redress despite not paying the problematic supplier at the end of the period in question.

E2 *If the product is durable, questions need to be asked about its performance in the long term.*

Durability complicates the choice process because it brings uncertainty into the task of valuing the product: How long may it last? What will it cost to maintain? How long will it be until it is made obsolete by something new, and for how long will the consumer want to use it? These questions may be impossible to answer before choosing because everyday knowledge about the product has not yet become established and market institutions have not yet subjected it to long-term testing or gathered a large sample of data about probabilities of particular problems arising when it is used. In some cases, the product may be so new that its potential durability is greater than the length of time it has so far existed in the market (or even than the time since it was invented). There may also be uncertainty about the longevity of support services (such as how long the manufacturer of a "smart TV" will continue to support the apps that the product in question was able to run at the time it was purchased).

E3 *Some durables have characteristics that hinder the development of a rental market for them. This prevents consumers from avoiding being concerned about long-term performance of these products by renting them instead of buying them outright.*

The feasibility of a rental market for a durable product will depend on the product's nature and mode of use, as these factors will affect the transaction costs of organizing and enforcing rental contracts. The owner needs to guard against potential moral hazard problems whereby renters do not treat the product with the care that they would apply if they owned it. Where the costs of verifying whether the renter has abused the product are high, rental contracts are unlikely to be workable. Rental markets may also be prone to fail in the case of products that are complex to operate and for which no standard operating system has yet evolved. This is because a person who only uses such a product for a short period of time will face high setup costs in getting to grips with using it. (In some cases, it will be viable to rent the product with the services of an operator, as with a taxi that is used as an alternative to a rental car in an unfamiliar city.) By contrast, if there are standard user interfaces, and would-be renters also expect to use the class of product frequently over the long term, then investing in mastering the standard user interface will not lock them into products of the first brand chosen for renting. In the latter case, it is thus far less important to make a good choice of supplier first time around.

E4 *If the long-term price of the product is not finalized at the time the agreement to purchase it is made and yet there are significant switching costs.*

Many of the home mortgages that proved problematic in the USA during the 2007–2008 financial crisis had this characteristic: an initial "teaser" rate was specified, but not the rate that would follow it, and naive homebuyers signed up in ignorance of the kinds of monthly repayments they would eventually be required to meet.

E5 *If the buyer is unable to obtain a demonstration of the product, information gaps may remain.*

Barriers to a demonstration may arise where:

(a) The product is being purchased at arm's length (for example, over the Internet) and at best can only be examined in a "virtual" manner.
(b) The product is subject to quality variability so that examples viewed today are only an approximate guide to what it will actually be like if ordered for future delivery or if the consumer receives an unopened, packaged version of what has been observed in the retail environment.
(c) The product is a unique item being supplied specially for the customer, so at best the supplier can only show examples of somewhat similar products.
(d) The product's performance is a function of its internal condition and this cannot be seen without either making it problematic to use the product at a later date (for example, once peeled, a piece of fruit is less suitable for eating several days later) or without incurring substantial costs of disassembling it and risks of putting it back together incorrectly.

(e) The product essentially consists of information (as with books, magazines and movies), so suppliers will limit demonstrations of it to avoid falling afoul of the "Arrow information paradox" (Arrow, 1962) that once a full demonstration of such a product has been given, the potential customer no longer has any need to buy it.

(f) Although the supplier could, in principle, provide samples of the product, this is uneconomic due to the costs of packaging small lots for sale, measures to prevent customers from taking more than what is necessary for sampling if free samples are provided or the costs of preventing customers from causing damage when testing a nondivisible demonstrator product.

In many contexts, combinations of these factors will apply. For example, a holiday at an unfamiliar destination may involve elements of both (a) and (b), while a used sports car may involve (d) and (f). Note that point (e) depends on the complexity of the information content of the product: complex information flows may be hard to commit to memory, thus limiting the significance of the Arrow paradox.

E6 *If expert knowledge of the product is required from another party in order for the buyers' questions about its characteristics to be answered accurately, the buyers ultimately will have to trust their sources of "expertise," for providers of information cannot be audited without trusting a third party.*

In the absence of bounded rationality on the part of buyers or the possibility of incompetence or opportunism (in the sense of Williamson, 1975, i.e., the guileful exploitation of an information asymmetry) on the part of sales personnel and those called upon to audit their claims, shopping would often be just a matter of asking for information and processing it. Opportunism is potentially a serious issue in contexts where those who are providing advice also stand to benefit from sales achieved because of that advice. However, it may not be possible for customers to ascertain the incentive structure faced by the supplier of the information.

E7 *If a product is complex in the sense of having many features or requiring know-how to operate, buyers may not know what they need to ask about it prior to purchasing it.*

Learning what to ask about such a product or how to get the best out of it takes time, so even if sales personnel try to answer honestly all the questions posed by the buyer, its properties may remain somewhat unclear at the time of purchase. Though a complex product may turn out to have features that cause "surprise and delight," it may also turn out to have irritating quirks. It may be impossible to acquire all the relevant knowledge about its features and mode of operation from in-store demonstrations, websites and market institutions; instead, an extended period of use may be necessary.

E8 *If the product is designed for use with complementary products, its full potential may be impossible to evaluate because some of these complementary products do not yet exist or are not available to be demonstrated with it.*

At the time Nelson introduced the distinction between search goods and experience goods, consumers faced this issue less frequently than we face it today. The usefulness of modern digital products often depends on their ability to be connected to other devices and run programs, which frequently depends, in turn, on their ability to be upgraded. Even if their specifications may be readily available, these kinds of products cannot be search goods in the way the term is being used here, because at the time they are purchased, information regarding some complementary products with which they or their rivals may eventually be used exists nowhere in the system – not even as figments in the imagination of software engineers, film directors or musicians. In situations where rival operating systems have been developed, suppliers of software may also not yet have announced which operating systems they will support (cf. the situation prior to the resolution of the standards battle between Toshiba's HD DVD format and Sony's Blu-Ray DVD). To follow the biggest herd of fellow consumers may be a simple rule for avoiding costly errors when a standards battle is in play between rival new technologies. However, sometimes such battles endure longer than the products in question, as with Apple and Microsoft computer operating systems – in that particular case, following the biggest herd resulted in many users facing problems they would not have had if they had opted for Apple's more user-friendly system, albeit at a premium price.

In the case of credence goods, the factors just considered may also apply at the time of purchase, but the uncertainty about the quality of the deal may persist after the event for reasons such as the following:

C1 *If the product involves a contingent delivery contract and a contingency does not arise during the period covered by the contract, then the consumer receives no evidence about how the supplier would have behaved had the contingency occurred.*

In the case of insurance, for example, rebuy decisions by nonclaimants are inherently based on guesswork unless customers can draw upon experiences of members of their social networks who have had to make claims.

C2 *If the supply of the product is undertaken "backstage" and involves work on the inside of something owned by the customer, the customer may have no evidence that the work has been performed.*

Routine maintenance of a motor vehicle is a classic case of this and was the one on which Darby and Karni (1973) focused: if there was nothing obviously wrong at the time the vehicle was delivered for servicing and nothing is obviously wrong or better when it is picked up, then perhaps nothing listed on the invoice has actually been done.

C3 *If particular know-how is required to confirm that a product has been delivered as claimed, and/or if verifying such claims in effect involve repeating all or most of the work, then the costs of achieving verification may force the customer to trust the supplier's word about what has been done.*

C4 *If the product is one that the customer applies personally as a precautionary device, it is clear when the product has been delivered, but if the event it is supposed to prevent never occurs, there will be no counterfactual to demonstrate it functioned as advertised unless the customer runs a set of controlled experiments or is able to compare experiences with other consumers who made different choices.*

This kind of problem is even more acute when, as with many cosmetics products and dietary supplements, the manufacturers make no precise claims about what the outcome of using it will be or where the outcome claimed is probabilistic in nature.

C5 *If the effects of the quality of what is supplied take a long time to manifest themselves, the consumer may find it hard to disentangle them from other possible causes of what is observed.*

Causal ambiguity reduces incentives for suppliers not to make false claims about the products they have supplied for fear of being exposed as such in the long run.

Lay decision-makers may run into problems due to failing to operate mindful of the issues raised in E1–E8 and C1–C5. However, search goods can also be problematic for those with finite cognitive capacities even where information is readily available: there is a trade-off between avoiding errors that result from failing to gather information versus avoiding errors from information overload (cf. Heiner, 1986). But it needs to be stressed that making good transactions requires not merely information but also knowledge about what information it is worth having in order to make a particular decision and how to interpret that information. It is possible to be armed with information and yet be utterly ignorant about the area to which it pertains (as with students whose examination answers demonstrate the capacity to memorize lecture notes verbatim but no ability whatsoever to do analysis or apply concepts from their courses). This is because the significance of information only becomes apparent if we have a knowledge framework for making sense of it. When armed with such a framework, we can use it to determine which information is relevant to the problem at hand, draw inferences from this information and thereby extend our knowledge. However, our interpretive system – the basis of our "knowledge" – could be misleading us rather than pointing us in the right direction.

3.5   Ambitious Aspirations

The limitations on what decision-makers can know, relative to what they would need to know to make optimal choices, often result in decisions being made with reference to targets or "aspiration level" rather than with any clear idea of what the optimal feasible choices are (see further Sections 4.9 and 6.2–6.4). We use rules or heuristics to set these targets but there is no guarantee that they will be close to the best that would have been feasible. If we set our aspirations needlessly low, we may run into problems that we could have avoided by aiming higher and holding out until we found something that seemed good enough to meet this standard. But if we unwittingly set our sights impossibly high in a particular area, that part of our life will be a chronic source of frustration if we remain convinced that our expectations of what we might achieve are realistic. Even if our aspirations are feasible, being very demanding or searching as if we are going to be able to find the best solution may be dysfunctional because it clashes with the point of what we are doing and prevents us from seizing the moment.

This can be especially problematic in a social context. For example, an impromptu meeting of friends may be wrecked if they decide to go to dinner and one member of the group then insists on deliberating at length over where they should dine. Similarly, if a couple on a touring vacation arrive at an unfamiliar city with no advance booking and one of the pair then insists on checking many motels before deciding where they should stay for the next few days, the search process may consume most of their first evening there. Those in a group who find the fussiness of others exasperating would doubtless agree with psychologist Ellen Langer's (1991, pp. 203–204) contention that the key to well-being is not making the best choice at the outset but being able to feel that we were able eventually to make the choice "come right." So, although avoiding obsessing about which restaurant is the best place for an impromptu meal may (but may not) result in some disappointment when the food is served, what ultimately will matter for the quality of their evening together is whether the group of friends ends up having a memorably convivial evening. If they do, they may soon become oblivious to what they are eating amid their lively conversations.

We may similarly make life needlessly difficult for ourselves and/or others if we set our sights unreasonably high in respect of how much we must know before we are prepared to risk a bad experience or a nagging sense that we may have been "ripped off" by a devious supplier or poorly served by an incompetent one. For one thing, this may mean that we fail to get problems attended to, with the result that they get worse, or we try to fix them ourselves and do the work ineptly. But a lack of trust is also not conducive to acquiring knowledge of who might be trustworthy (for example, among local tradespeople) or to developing capabilities for dealing with those whose products and services disappoint us.

It is not just in relation to the quality of the things we buy or the trustworthiness of suppliers that setting ambitious aspirations can be a source of problems. The goals we set for our own performance standards may likewise be sources of frustration and unnecessary challenges. This may be especially so if we set our sights high in areas that involve social competitions with only a small probability of success. But it can be problematic even when we are not competing with others. For example, setting very high standards about avoiding getting into debt, or the date by which we will be debt-free, may drive us into a "penny-pinching" way of operating that save small sums today but at the cost of necessitating higher overall expenditure in future. High ambition may be particularly dysfunctional where it involves learning a new con-sumption skill: consumers may try, as the expression goes, "to run before they can walk" and consequently may fail to develop any fluency in handling the tasks that they need to master as a foundation for achieving high levels of performance. Always, though, the problem is to know what it is reasonable to expect in any particular area and what the trade-offs are between different areas of our lives.

3.5.1   Utopian Goals

In some cases, life proves frustrating because goals are not just ambitious but utopian. Where people set such goals, they tend to end up feeling depressed and blame their failure to meet them on their personal ineptitude instead of recognizing that the goals were utopian (see further Watzlawick et al., 1974, ch. 5). For example, people who are searching for meaning in life may judge themselves to be failures after questioning all manner of things to no avail – except for the premise that life is meaningless if one cannot answer the question of the meaning of life. "Drop out" behavior is one kind of consequence of disillusionment that follows utopian thinking, even when it might have been perfectly possible for the situation to be reframed in a way that seemed bearable. Some utopian thinkers may repeatedly fail to sustain their interest in anything that they try because each venture fails to live up to their inflated expect-ations. As they drift from one thing to another, they may be failing to realize that there could be a deeper problem: they may have inflated expectations about themselves and dropping out is ensuring that they fail to develop capabilities that could have helped them eventually to get more out of the things they abandoned and thereby could have got them closer to what they had imagined.

A variation on the "utopia syndrome" involves making endless preparations for getting to a distant, demanding goal, without questioning whether the goal is capable of being realized or even whether it will be worth the long journey. Here, we may get escalation of commitment rather than drop-out behavior – i.e., the failure of a particular kind of consumption to meet the end to which it was supposedly aimed may result in an obsession with this kind of consumption rather than withdrawal from it. Such an obsession may detract from moving toward meeting the goal. An example here would be the hobbyist musician who concentrates on assembling a home recording studio of increasingly high technical capacity and studying how to operate the growing amount of equipment, but who uses the limitations of the studio as the reason for not yet concentrating on writing and recording the music that is supposedly its raison d'être. Meanwhile, poorer musicians, who set their standards lower, might get on with the business of making music and record something, of perfectly service-able production quality, with the aid of far less sophisticated equipment.

3.6   The Problem of "Arriving"

Success in meeting goals, or in making significant progress toward meeting them, can itself give rise to problems. Some of these arise where success greatly opens our range of choice by bringing about a quantum leap in what we can spend. In terms of conventional economics, where preference systems are presumed to be complete, consumers will have no trouble adjusting to major expansions of their sets of feasible options. In reality, three kinds of difficulties stand out.

First, there is the problem of adjusting to a loose budget constraint after being used to a tight one that promoted careful monitoring of expenditure. Highly successful sports people and entertainers commonly get into financial difficulties despite their large incomes, as do some major winners of lotteries. Whirlwind success is not conducive to taking care with money, particularly if it involves frantic schedules and international travel, and brings pressures to spend generously and conspicuously, as if one were not constrained. For example, to maintain a high profile in the entertainment business and hence be marketable, it may seem necessary to live extravagantly and be seen moving in the right circles. Those whose earnings suddenly take off will lack experience in choosing financial advisors and managers who have the necessary skills and personal integrity. Consequently, the delegation of personal financial management is prone to result in the discovery that management has siphoned off most of the earnings and/or that there are major problems in meeting income tax obligations.

Secondly, it should be noted that the extent of movement in a budget constraint becomes fuzzy when quantum leaps in earnings and wealth occur, because such leaps dramatically change access to credit. Success often leads managers and entrepreneurs to believe that now "the sky's the limit" for them and to see the world through rose-tinted spectacles. As a result, they embark on unsustainable, debt-financed major expansions of their business activities, with a parallel ballooning of the consumption spending – until reality bites and many of their assets end up having to be sold off at a loss. This is one of the ingredients in the "financial instability hypothesis" of Hyman Minsky that we will be exploring in Section 12.7.

Finally, we should note that for many people, success is problematic because of the utopian standpoint from which they viewed the goals that had been the key focus of their lives. It may be unhelpful to see "arriving" in a new position in life as the end of a journey of struggle, for such a mode of thinking encourages the goal-seeker to believe that the new situation will be nonproblematic (a kind of equilibrium?), when the reality is that life is a process in which "arrival" entails starting a new journey, not a terminal state (Watzlawick et al., 1974, pp. 50–51). Moreover, people can be so preoccupied with meeting particular goals that they devote little attention to developing ways of coping with the success that they so keenly seek.

If attainment of a goal involves a new set of challenges rather than everything at last seeming to be OK, we have a recipe for depression – rather like postnatal depression – after a short-lived period of joy, even though the distance between actual and desired positions has in some senses been eliminated. This issue is amplified where the goal in question pertains to an experience good, as with the goal to become a parent or to get a new job further up the career ladder. A jump up the career ladder that involves switching between organizations can be a source of major dissatisfaction rather than joy if, soon after "arriving," we discover that we have joined an organization that falls vastly short of the operational standards to which we had been accustomed. (Previously, when we were visiting as outsiders and were concentrating on selling ourselves during the process of being interviewed, things there may have looked deceptively normal.) Even in the absence of gross falsification of assumptions concerning the modus operandi of the new workplace, a career move can be a major source of discontent because it unexpectedly seems to require a new set of competencies and/or compromises due to the job itself having been misconstrued.

3.7   System Architecture and Susceptibility to Shocks

When most behavioral economists use the word "architecture," it is in the context that is discussed in Chapter 9 of this book, namely the designs of the environments through which firms and other organizations attempt to shape the behavior of those with whom they interact. In that context, "architecture" means the set of information and options that is presented to the other parties and how it is organized, both at a point in time and as a sequence. Here, and in many other places in this book, we are concerned with the architecture of systems that consumers and members of organizations build as means for coping with the challenges they face.

This section attempts to show how the architecture of these systems is a major determinant of whether their mangers or users will run into problems and what the scale of these problems will be. However, before exploring this issue, it is important to note that these systems are neither static – our lives are very much "works in progress" – nor isolated from each other. The artificial systems that we create for coping with life sometimes complement those that others create. But sometimes system designs are at odds with each other, as when changes at our workplaces disrupt our domestic lives by changing the times at which we must work. It should also be recognized that although human systems are imposed on natural systems, the two types of systems may interact and evolve in a complex manner via intricate feedback loops. For example, human consumption of nonrenewable sources of energy may contribute to global warming, leading more people to install air-conditioning devices powered by nonrenewable sources of energy, further contributing to global warming. In short, the world is a complex system of coevolving complex systems.

3.7.1 Complex Adaptive Systems of Linked Elements

Whether artificial or natural, a complex system consists of a set of elements linked together in a structured way that gives it a distinctive architecture. The evolution of a system entails changing the set of connections between existing elements of that system and/or connecting some new elements to existing ones. Investments of time and energy may be needed to maintain linkages and counteract entropic processes. Social network systems illustrate this neatly: we form new friendships but allow others to lapse by failing to keep in touch, or we fall out with some of those whom we once regarded as friends, and sometimes friends become partners or spouses.

Viewed thus, a complex system is different from what mathematicians and physicists call a "field," for in the latter, every element is connected to some degree with every other element. This distinction is crucial for appreciating the view of economics presented in this book. As Jason Potts (2000) has demonstrated, economists traditionally have followed the "field" perspective and have therefore not focused on how linkage structures affect both the extent of havoc that particular shocks may cause and the capacities of players to survive such difficulties. Moreover, with all possible connections already made, a "field" cannot evolve in the way that a complex system can. In this book, by contrast, our evolutionary perspective on behavioral economics leads us to take a "complex adaptive systems" view and hence to take linkage structures and their evolution very seriously indeed. In effect, traditional economics works with a Newtonian physicist's view of the world, whereas the view taken here is more akin to that taken in chemistry and ecology.

At the level of the household, the complex systems perspective is best appreciated via the notion of a "lifestyle" (introduced to economics in Earl, 1986b). The set of relationships in a modern lifestyle can be very complex, including interlinked subsystems such as:

- The objects within a room and how we arrange them with a view to the fit between them, with some objects being assigned "pride of place" in functional or symbolic terms or are viewed as playing key roles in holding everything together (cf. the rug that gets defiled by home invaders in the Coen brothers' 1998 cult classic movie *The Big Lebowski*).
- The spatial relationships that structure daily lives via their logistical implications (for example, where we choose to live and work and the sets of leisure and "after school" activities that then must be juggled, as epitomized by the modern notion of the "soccer mom" – see Thompson, 1996).
- The families that we create by having partners, children and pets, and the kinds of relationships we choose to maintain with extended family members.
- The nonfamily social networks that we choose to maintain, which are often "bound up" with our work and leisure activities.
- The rules and routines we use to organize and maintain our lives, such as our "ways" of getting to work, how we shop, our exercise regimes, our dietary practices, the sets of clothes we wear, and so on.

As will be shown in Chapters 4 and 7, these structures are underpinned by the cognitive structures that we build as our personal means for making sense of the world and adapting to changes in our circumstances.

Viewed thus, lifestyles are the household equivalent of the distinctive strategies, structures and operating systems that organizations build. As Neil Kay (1982, 1984, 1997) emphasizes from an explicitly system-based perspective, the strategy of a firm involves a commitment to being in a particular set of product markets and supply chains. As firms grow, they typically diversify into lines of business that are to some degree related to what they have previously been doing, build organizational systems to take account of these relationships, and establish complex relationships with members of their supply chains, bankers, customers and – via joint ventures and strategic alliances, interlocking directorships and cross-shareholdings – with other firms, even with their competitors (see also Chandler, 1962, 1977, 1990; Penrose, 1959; Richardson, 1972; Munkirs, 1985).

The capital assets that households and firms use in pursuing their goals are complex systems, too, and should not be viewed, as orthodox economics has tended to view them, "as if" they are made of modeling clay and can readily be transformed to produce any kind of output. Capital assets are often organized into larger systems. They embody connections between system elements that have been built up, layer by layer, over long periods via the successive insights of many people (see Harper and Endres, 2010). Here, we should not merely be thinking of pieces of hardware that comprise many components; we should also acknowledge that they cannot function without specific types of software and human operating systems of rules and routines that are complex systems, too. Moreover, the marketing of output is built around systems, including networks and goodwill relationships and brands (see Harper and Endres, 2017).

In short, from the complex adaptive systems perspective, the world of business is a web of intra- and inter-firm relationships and production, logistical and marketing systems. The only kind of business where such relationships are essentially absent is that of one-off interactions between consumers and fully vertically integrated sole traders, such as when tourists purchase wooden artifacts directly from a craftsperson who works his or her own timber. Moreover, the systems perspective is not one of businesses that operate in the manner of a traditional textbook entrepreneur who is able to switch among all product markets and technologies and is willing to do so depending on where potential profits seem to be the greatest. (Note that the textbook model fails even to capture the economics of the woodturning craftsperson, who has a particular set of skills but lacks many others.) At the macro level, specific obligation-based linkages embodied in balance sheets bind together the financial fortunes of households, firms and financial institutions in ways that regulators of the financial system and players in financial organizations may find bewilderingly complicated (cf. Roe, 1973).

The performance of the systems that people create may change if any of the elements are replaced by nonidentical elements: for example, how effectively a brand functions as a system may be affected by a change in its logo, just as the performance of a team of workers may change if a replacement worker changes the dynamics of the group and/or has different capabilities from the one that has departed. Loss of system elements may be a source of temporary problems, but these may turn out to be chronic in the absence of suitable replacements.

Moreover, systems used in production and consumption typically entail hierarchical relationships between some elements, with some elements being core components without which the system cannot function. The set of core elements, if their specifications are compatible, give the system its ability to do the distinctive thing that it does – its "emergent" capability, in terms of the jargon of systems theory (for a detailed discussion of "emergence," see Harper and Endres, 2012). For example, given a suitable combination of wings, tailfin, moveable control surfaces, power from an engine, instruments, control systems and a pilot, we may have a viable system that we call an aircraft with the emergent property of its capacity for sustained, controlled flight. (A tailplane is not a prerequisite for having an aircraft, as is evident from delta-winged designs such as Concorde, but it appears to be a prerequisite element for an aircraft that can be flown safely if it does not have a delta-winged design.) The loss of one of these key elements may entail the disastrous loss of this capacity.

Other elements have a more peripheral role: losing them may cause some problems but the rest of the system remains viable and broadly retains its identity. In other words, an individual system element, or several system elements taken together, may function, respectively, as prerequisites or corequisites for the functioning of other elements, whereas some elements play no such role. Natural systems such as the human body also have this kind of architecture: for most people, the loss of a finger may be a nuisance, though not so bad as losing a leg, whereas the failure of a major organ may be catastrophic. However, for some people, such as musicians, even the loss of a finger could be a disaster, for their earning power may collapse due to them no longer being able to do their work properly. Likewise, people may not be greatly troubled when some social relationships or products fail, whereas in other cases losses are very significant, since they had built their lives in ways that "revolved around" what they have now lost (see Section 7.7 for further detail).

The challenge for consumers, managers, bureaucrats and government ministers is to build systems whose architectures do not make them susceptible to problems. This is a tall order when people suffer from bounded rationality. The lifestyles that we construct help us to cope with life by giving us a sense of who we are and by removing the need to consider many things that might otherwise have been a drain on our attention. However, despite our best efforts, we may end up constructing lifestyles whose structures ensure that the creation or failure of a particular link may have all manner of unforeseen and unwanted implications. Similarly, the organizational structure of a firm is vital for enabling staff to avoid cognitive overload, but it can result in senior executives being taken by surprise by things that they did not know had been going on elsewhere in the organization (as is possibly the case with the Volkswagen "Dieselgate" emissions-concealment scandal that came to light in 2015). Global financial crises, such as the one that broke out in 2007–2008, may be impossible to anticipate with any precision, but the fact that they do arise periodically should be no surprise if we are aware of the structural complexity of interlocking balance sheet obligations (see also Roe, 1973; Minsky, 1975).

3.7.2   Linkages in the Long Run: Are Systems "Decomposable"?

In trying to cope with structural complexity, people have to approach their situations "as if" the world is decomposable – i.e., as if it consists of a set of independent subsystems. This limits the set of connections they must worry about, along with the potential range of implications of any choice or action. But this "as if" assumption can be dangerous, for in the long run issues that were ignored may multiply into major surprises, such as ecological problems and global economic crises. Nowadays, such long-run interconnectedness underpins chaos theory, wherein it is acknowledged that even something so seemingly minor as the flapping of a butterfly's wings in one part of the world might conceivably set in place a cumulating chain of events that result in drastic disturbances on the other side of the planet. (For an introduction to the economic implications of chaos theory, see Ormerod, 1998.) My own route to this line of thinking came much earlier, via the science fiction writer Ray Bradbury's (1953) short story "A Sound of Thunder." This is a tale about a time-travelling dinosaur-hunting venture that ends up changing the course of history despite the best efforts of the scheme's designers to prevent such a thing from happening. Bradbury's tale coincidentally hinges on one "small" disturbance involving a butterfly: one of the dinosaur hunters steps off a levitation pathway, unknowingly crushes a butterfly and brings it back to the future in mud on his boot.

Human action will stall if decision-makers become petrified that anything they do might have chaotic consequences, so the decomposability assumption plays a vital evolutionary role. Even so, the potential for problems to cumulate is, of course, something that ordinary people do sometimes consider, as is evidenced for several centuries via the enduring popularity of the proverb that sets out the stages by which "for want of a horseshoe nail" an entire kingdom was lost. This proverb offers us a lesson about the importance of allocating resources to the maintenance of subsystems.

Fortunately, the decomposability assumption works much of the time. Many external shocks and many errors and omissions in our behavior do not have disastrous consequences for us. There are three major reasons why this should be so, namely: the presence of buffering to absorb shocks; modular system architecture; and assets that are adaptable rather than fine-tuned for a specific purpose. Let us consider these factors in turn, to show how those who fail – or do not have the resources – to build systems with these features can get into difficulties and suffer what George Richardson (1960) calls "dislocation costs."

3.7.3   Buffering

Three broad categories of buffer can limit the spread of problems in economic systems. First, there is the use of insurance contracts to offset, at some cost, the difficulties that a particular problem might cause. This is not always feasible, due to significant transaction costs and problems of market failure in the face of adverse selection – i.e., the possibility that those at high risk of experiencing the insured-against event will be more likely to buy insurance than are those with low risks of suffering the same event – and/or moral hazard. But insurance may also be problematic for decision-makers who suffer from bounded rationality, due to the complexity of contractual fine print or because there is no amount of compensation that would be enough to offset the loss a person would feel if a particular event occurred. If the latter is the case, limiting the risk may be the preferred strategy.

Secondly, there is the problem-preventing role of strategically created spare time and/or spare physical capacity: at the cost of limiting our ability to do other things, we can make investments in assets that might turn out not to be needed but which we can call upon to rescue us if our activities are disrupted. In engineering terms, this is equivalent to building redundancy into systems and stress-testing them to confirm they meet far higher performance standards than will normally be needed. Thus, for example, jet airliners are typically designed to be capable of being flown even if only one engine remains functioning. Similarly, when buying cars, most of us buy vehicles that we do not intend, wherever possible, to drive "to the limit" in terms of their capacities to accelerate, corner or stop. Instead, we buy much more capable vehicles than we normally need, given how we drive. This is at least in part an act of defensive consumption that gives us the capacity to "put our foot down" to get out of trouble in a way that would not be possible in a vehicle whose maximum capabilities were barely enough for our normal needs.

Thirdly, limiting our financial commitments leaves spare liquidity or borrowing power to deal with income shortfalls or to make emergency purchases of replacements or repairs as the need arises. This financial flexibility comes, of course, at the cost of not being able to do other things that we might have done. If we are prudent, we resist temptation and do not "max out" our credit cards or how much we draw on our mortgage overdraft accounts, or we simply keep funds in reserve "for a rainy day."

Although any individual or organization attempting to operate by "living on the edge" without buffering runs the risk of getting into difficulties, those with meager resources will be particularly prone to having their lives descend into chaos. Those who are well-off and get into difficulties after overextending their commitments may at least have substantial assets that they can sell, or against which they can borrow, to raise funds to stop their problems from multiplying. Where such decision-makers do end up mired with problems, the big driver may be their reluctance to incur trade-in losses and suffer loss of face as the price of removing the problem. By contrast, the poor may be struggling to meet basic needs, with nothing left over for insurance or to maintain assets (such as ageing cars or their own health) that are central to keeping their lives afloat. They will be prone to lack substitute assets to use if other assets fail, get damaged or are stolen. Absent, too, may be complementary goods or services (for example, Internet access) that enable them to solve problems cheaply in terms of both time and money. To the extent that they can raise money via pawning any of their possessions or via "payday loans," the interest charges will be at far higher rates than those that well-heeled consumers have to pay, increasing their longer-term difficulties in keeping problems at bay.

The poverty-stricken consumer's lack of buffering may increase pressure to solve problems quickly, amid other problems, in order to prevent yet others from arising. Bounded rationality is thus much more of a problem for poverty-stricken consumers even if they have sets of decision rules or heuristics that would enable them to get through life just as well as their better-off counterparts if they were similarly endowed with resources. Bounded rationality will be more significant to the poor the less they can call upon social networks to reduce the pressure of trying to solve their problems. Thus, although the poor may not have anywhere near the range of options that others have, being poor can result in cognitive overload and with it the risk of making poor decisions that will generate problems and feed cognitive pressure in subsequent periods (see Bertrand et al., 2004).

In the absence of a significant injection of buffering, it may be impossible for the poor to make their lives less chaotic and escape from such vicious circles. Except in cases where difficulties in meeting basic needs are a matter of poor self-control, the policy implication of this perspective is that governments might be able to save money in the long run by providing poor households with significant lump sums – say, the equivalent of six months of the benefits they would otherwise have received on a weekly basis – subject to their short-term benefits being stopped for a cash-equivalent period. The recipients could then invest part of the lump-sum in chaos-proofing, enabling them to get ahead and reduce or altogether remove their need for support by the time that the period the lump-sum was intended to cover came to an end.

3.7.4   Modularity

Herbert Simon (1962, 1969) used a simple parable concerning two watchmakers to argue that in environments that are prone to being disturbed, evolutionary selection processes will tend to favor modular systems. The watchmakers produced watches that contained similar numbers of parts, were of similar quality and appearance and were offered at similar prices. However, they differed in their designs. One watchmaker produced watches that were not modular, so if there were any interruption while he was assembling them, the components that had so far been assembled would fall apart; it was only when the back of the watch was finally clicked into place that all the parts would hold together as a working system. By contrast, the other watchmaker had designed his watches so that they could be assembled as a set of modules, say, ten modules of ten parts, that would each stay intact on his workbench once they were complete. Final assembly then entailed putting the ten modules together. For the latter watchmaker, the worse that a disruption to the assembly process could cause was the need to have to redo nine steps in the process, either rebuilding a single module or starting the final assembly process afresh. Clearly, if both watchmakers are disrupted at the same rate by phone calls from prospective customers, the maker of the modular watches will experience smaller dislocation costs and will be able to undercut the other watchmaker. The maker of modular watches has a more resilient system and the only cost penalty he suffers is that of the extra stage of putting the various modules together. In an environment that was free of disturbances, that extra cost would be a problem, whereas it is a cost worth incurring when disturbances are possible.

The significance of modularity as a factor that moderates the scale of the problems that we run into in everyday life arises with individual products and with the sets of products or activities to which we make commitments. Regarding the former, note the difference between modular and integrated consumer electronics products. If a component on a modular product fails, it may be possible to repair the product simply by replacing the module in question, unlike in cases where products are not designed to be "taken to pieces." The temptation, though, is to choose integrated products because their initial costs will be cheaper, since they can be made without incorporating interfaces by which components can be connected and disconnected. So long as all components and hardwired connections between them have the same life spans (or at least last as long as it takes for the product to be rendered obsolete by a newer design), we benefit; if not, we may end up with the expensive problem of finding a replacement rather than merely finding someone to undertake repairs.

Of course, that fact that a product has a modular design and can be repaired when a part fails does not mean it should always be repaired when something fails, even if this is cheaper than replacing it altogether in the short run. It makes sense to use the "always repair" heuristic for products whose modules together cost no more than the total cost of the unit and can be installed with negligible effort (as with, say, a Kreepy Krauley swimming pool cleaner). However, where individual modules are disproportionately expensive due to price discrimination and/or transaction cost issues associated with small orders, and/or where labor costs are significant, this heuristic may turn an ageing product into a money sink. Considerable expertise is required to know whether repairs make sense: we need to know the probability that further problems will arise, what the costs of dealing with them will be and the risk of the product becoming obsolete or unsuitable for our needs.

Frankel (1955) raised this issue – which we may call "the sequential wear-out trap" – in the context of businesses wasting money on repairing ageing equipment, but it also arises with household products such as cars, dishwashers and washing machines. Indeed, it can be a significant issue for poor households who lack the capacity to borrow to buy new products that would, over the long run, cost less per month than they end up paying out in their attempts to keep their ageing assets going. There may also be the risk of ending up with a significant write-off if not all parts can be replaced without major cost due to them functioning as core components. An example is where the body of a car suffers from terminal failure due to rust, forcing the consumer to scrap it after having kept everything else in good order by applying the "always repair" heuristic. With full foresight, the rational thing to do with such a vehicle might be not merely to scrap it earlier rather than pay a major repair bill, but also to engage in strategic neglect and not even bother with routine maintenance (cf. the parallel discussion of "defensive investment" by firms in Lamfalussy, 1961, and Earl, 1984, pp. 84–91).

The maxim "Don't put all your eggs in one basket" can be taken as a sign that some people recognize that the risk of running into difficulties is related to the number of modules in which their activities are divided. We might be reminded of this maxim by wise friends if we were to tell them that, say, our retirement plan is to engage, at last, in the self-actualizing activity of making music on a full-time basis. This could all go awry if we become afflicted with arthritis in our hands or lose our hearing: neither eventuality is certain, but both are among the risks entailed in growing old, so we would be wise to cultivate a second interest – as the saying goes, a "second string to one's bow" – that is exposed to a different set of risks or is seemingly risk-free. If we do this, we are in effect dividing our lives into separate blocks in much the same way that the designer of a ship divides it into watertight compartments. The wider the range of risks that we face, the bigger is the set of lifestyle modules we need to create with different risk exposures in order to guard against ending up finding that there is nothing we can do to occupy our time. Such strategic planning is often absent; indeed, on the financial side, we can see this in cases where people end up having miserable retirements due to "losing their life's savings" after having failed to diversify their portfolios of retirement assets.

The household's need to use modular (or failing this, quasi-modular) strategies when exposed to, or taking on, risks has similarities with the analysis that Neil Kay (1982, 1984, 1997) offers about the need for firms to design their business strategies mindful of the risks that their products could become terminally unviable. A firm that is undiversified may have its earnings wiped out by a change of government policy (e.g., if it specializes in making products from asbestos and its business is outlawed on health grounds), by a technological innovation that it does not have the capacity to adopt (e.g., a manufacturer of slide rules in the early 1970s that within a couple of years finds its product completely displaced by scientific pocket calculators), or by changes in fashion (e.g., as with the fate of superstar "prog rock" bands in the second half of the 1970s when they suddenly lost their audiences to punk or new wave acts). Designing a corporate strategy around a diverse set of profit centers that are only partially linked in terms of production technologies and/or the markets they serve is a means of reducing the risk of suffering a devastating blow. However, insofar as there are economies of scale that cannot be offset by economies of scope, smaller firms will be inherently more at risk of potentially fatal shocks, for they will have to accept the risks that go with specialization as they do what they do on the biggest scale they can rather than trying to do many partially related or unrelated things on a small scale.

3.7.5   Adaptable Assets

When the Apollo 13 crew informed ground control in Houston that they had a problem, human ingenuity ensured it did not turn into a disaster. This was despite the crew not having carried with them a spare unit of the oxygen tank that had exploded, depleting their service module's air supply, and there was no way that such a unit could be supplied to them. As Eagleman and Brandt (2017) remind us in their study of human creativity, what happened was that, based on knowledge of what the astronauts did have at their disposal, the support staff were able to work out how to deal with the aftermath of the explosion by improvising an alternative system from a number of items that had been designed for other purposes. This was thus not a simple case of substitution of the kind that traditional economists have in mind when they analyze how people substitute between products as relative prices change, for, in that kind of analysis, the set of technological possibilities is taken as given and known.

The Apollo 13 crew were very lucky to have at their disposal things that could be creatively combined to ensure they continued to have the prerequisites for staying alive in their spacecraft. As Williamson (1985) has emphasized, asset specificity often makes it problematic to deal with surprises inflicted on firms by devious trading partners; it also underpins the risks entailed in investment decisions by households and organizations. Unlike modeling clay, capital equipment is not capable of being refashioned into something else at short notice as the need arises. Moreover, its effective use may require that its operators have specific capabilities, and it may only be viable to employ on a large scale. When these factors are present, entrepreneurs must worry about being wrong in their guesses about the extent of competitive and complementary investment made by other firms (cf. Richardson, 1960). If they find themselves competing against a glut of supply from rivals, or with shortages of inputs, they cannot simply refashion all or some of their assets to produce for another market or to produce inputs for their product at the cost of producing it on a smaller scale. If the world were one of freely malleable physical capital, universal know-how and constant returns to scale, it would not matter if they got their guesses wrong.

In the real world, it is costly to turn unwanted and/or non-repairable durable goods into new goods of other kinds – the more so, the less modular are the goods being scrapped or recycled. Of course, it may be possible to trade in what one has and use the proceeds for something that better fits one's situation. However, this will typically entail a capital loss out of all proportion to the physical depreciation of the asset. With very specific assets, such as dies for making a product that has failed to win customers, the only option may be to sell them for scrap.

In markets where there are strong competitive pressures to invest in highly specific assets to minimize production costs, the human tendency toward overconfidence may be a vital force in the "engine of capitalism" (Kahneman, 2011, ch. 24). Investor exuberance results in expensive problems for some but rich bounties for others, at least for a time, and benefits for the wider population. But committing to a specific product via product-specific assets may put an enterprise into a situation akin to that of a giant panda or other species that have very specific dietary needs and whose food supplies are threatened by habitat destruction.

It was by investing in ever-more specific assets to produce his Model T automobile that Henry Ford made motoring affordable for the masses. But the result for Ford was a production system and marketing orientation that made it very problematic to switch to the Model-T's replacement: as Selznick (1957, p. 110) points out, there was a painful eighteen-month transition that entailed the mass scrapping or costly reengineering of equipment, followed by many years of trying to get away from focusing on cost-cutting and limiting customer choice. Today's automakers are much more aware of the perils of asset specificity. They opt to incur the costs of investing in flexible production systems that limit the costs of switching from one generation of product to another and make it possible to switch the mix of production at any point in time. Unanticipated changes in the pattern of demand are thus much less problematic than they previously would have been. Today's households need to learn similar lessons if they are to keep thriving in a world of rapid changes in the pattern of demand for labor.

Finally, we should note the problem-mitigating role of flexible contracts. Loosely specified contracts may make it possible to decide what to supply or have delivered as contingencies arise. For example, as Coase (1937) realized, and Loasby (1976) reiterated, a firm hires its workers via long-term employment contracts that are vague. This enables it to avoid the costs of hiring staff via highly detailed short-term contracts to cover a known situation, or of hiring staff with highly detailed long-term contracts that contain masses of redundant clauses to cover all imagined contingencies but that might nonetheless fail to cover what eventuates. The price for such flexibility is twofold: (a) having a team of managers to decide what to ask the workers to do once it becomes clear what the situation is, and (b) the potential abuse of contractual vagueness by employees. Consumers can similarly buy flexibility via careful choices of contracts: for example, choosing a flight that can be changed is a means of ensuring that being unable to make a specific flight will be less of a problem than it might have been.

3.8   Getting One's Priorities Wrong: The Nonsubstitution Problem

A key aspect of operating in a procedurally rational manner is to be able to allocate finite attention and other resources at any point in time in a way that deals appropriately with three questions that share the acronym "WIN?": "What's Important Now?"; "What's Important Next?"; and "What's Important Never?" In other words, because we cannot attend to everything that concerns us right now, we need to have effective triaging heuristics that ensure that we neither fail to take advantages of one-off life-enhancing opportunities nor generate significant avoidable challenges in future because of what we try to do right now. Having a sense of what we will be trying to do next is useful insofar as we come across relevant information pertaining to it while dealing with today's focal issues: it may be worth pausing to ensure that we "bank" such information, unlike information pertaining to things that are never going to be significant to us.

Alas, most of us are not as procedurally rational as we might be in this sense. For example, as Herbert Simon (1991) pointed out in his autobiography, most of the time people spend giving attention to the latest news is a waste: it will not help us solve or avoid problems and, so long as someone else in our social networks keeps abreast of the news, we are likely to hear rapidly of anything that really is important. In Simon's view, all we need to do to maintain a broad knowledge of the world around us is spend a bit of time each year browsing in the latest almanac or end-of-year summary.

But time needlessly spent keeping up with the latest news is rather innocuous compared with what may be going on when some people are behaving in ways that cause others to shake their heads and mutter about the former "getting their priorities wrong." What the onlookers might mean when they use this phrase deserves scrutiny.

Conventional economic thinking invites us to view prioritization as entailing the ranking of rival course of action based on their overall benefit–cost ratios, with a discounting technique being used to make it possible to compare costs and benefits that occur at different points in time. Thus, if the relevant cost and revenue data are available (possibly a big "if") for a set of rival investment projects, they can be ranked in order of their internal rates of return. This view rests on the assumption that all costs and benefits can be expressed in the same unit of measurement, thereby making it possible to weigh them together to arrive at overall valuations. Associated with that assumption is the assumption that what matters is the overall net value that a project offers and that there may be alternative mutually exclusive methods by which particular benefits might be pursued. Thus, in order to allocate funds efficiently across different areas, it is necessary first to find the strategy that offers the biggest payoff (for example, investment in buses and busways versus investment in light rail, as means of reducing congestion in a particular area) in each area of interest and then rank the dominant projects from each of these areas.

If the relative prices of the equipment and/or types of workers to be used on the respective projects change, this may affect their relative overall internal rates of return. Indeed, such changes in relative prices may mean that the optimal technique for producing output of a project also changes. If investment funds are currently limited, it may not be possible to go ahead with all the projects under consideration even if they all offer a higher prospective net return than the rate of interest that the funds that are available can earn if they are not spent. This being the case, some of the projects will have to be deferred until additional funds are available. To allocate the investment funds, we simply "prioritize" the projects by ranking them in order of their internal rates of return and work down this ranking, authorizing projects as we do so, until all the currently available funds have been assigned. The remaining projects go on our "wish list" for future implementation.

On this way of thinking, the layperson's notion of problems arising due to people "getting their priorities wrong" has to be interpreted in terms of projects being incorrectly ranked due to mistaken assessments of costs and/or benefits. For example, we might envisage the term being applied to a state government that invests in tourism-related projects while seemingly oblivious of the costs being imposed on the local community by growing traffic congestion. However, if we view this lay expression mindful of Maslow's hierarchical view of needs, a completely different interpretation of it seems possible, an interpretation that goes against the presumptions that decision-makers should always be open to substitution and that relative returns can be reduced to common units for comparison.

From a Maslowian standpoint, priorities arise in hierarchical terms due to the imperatives of, first, physical survival, with social imperatives being attended to only after physical needs have been met, except insofar as achieving a stronger social position is also a means to ensuring basic needs are met. From this standpoint, parents might be said to have their priorities wrong if they are spending the family budget on items that would enhance the perceived status of their children (for example, by buying them high-end smartphones, designer-brand trainers, and so on), at the cost of being unable to meet more basic needs in the long run (for example, leaving their public utility bills unpaid and giving their children "junk" food that is cheaper than more nutritious food, and not having regular dental checks). Such parents seem to be treating conspicuous consumption and the basics of life as substitutes. However, in the eyes of someone who can see what is going on, it may appear that this kind of behavior is foolish. It is likely to create long-term problems such as obesity, rotten teeth or the embarrassment of having to deal with bailiffs and/or the bankruptcy court. Similarly, we would take a dim view of someone who pursued self-actualization goals regardless of the effect this had on his or her ability to obtain food and accommodation.

If we apply a hierarchical perspective to prioritization in firms or government agencies, we may recognize that the ranking of investments may need to be done mindful of the possible presence of prerequisites and corequisites. For example, without adequate standards of literacy and numeracy being achieved first within a region's workforce, measures to attract inward investment may founder due to the local workers being unsuitable for anything but manual laboring tasks. Low wages will not induce substitution if the workers simply cannot perform, or be trained to perform, what firms would want them to do. Likewise, development of export crops from rural hinterlands will not happen in the absence of roads or railways and port facilities. Also, as Schumacher (1973) realized, attempts to raise farm productivity in poor nations by providing gifts of technology designed for advanced economies may soon founder due to the absence of necessary support systems (for example, mechanics to keep farm machinery running).

The importance of getting appropriate combinations of capital assets to avoid squandering the resources available for economic development is central to the complex systems perspective on development offered by Endres and Harper (2020). However, the argument here also warrants consideration in relation to the classic analysis of economic development suggested by Rostow (1960), in which a "take-off" into sustained growth does not occur until a set of "preconditions" are met. Rostow based his analysis on Great Britain's ascendancy and neglected several factors that many development economists would nowadays regard as a basic requirement for promoting investment and economic growth. These are as follows: the absence of corruption; the presence of social stability; well-defined property rights; a stable currency and other institution without which a market system cannot flourish. (For a discussion of these issues in the context of Eastern European economies after the collapse of communism, see Hare, 2010.) Indeed, without many of these most basic requirements in place, it will not even be possible for a government to get basic infrastructure projects successfully implemented.

Those who fail to make investment appraisals with an appropriate sense of the sequence in which things *must* be done and the things that *must* be in place at the same time in order to for something else to be possible or to avoid wasting their potential are likely to create problems by making mistaken prioritizations. To get priorities right in a world of prerequisites, corequisites and complementarities, it is vital to think in terms of production systems and relationships between system elements, rather than focusing on individual projects in the reductionist, substitution-focused way in which economists are conventionally trained to think. (For a behavioral analysis of project appraisal methods in developing economies, see Leff, 1985.)

The same considerations apply within production systems. Those who fail to identify the need to prioritize in a hierarchical sense may find it is impossible to produce output to the desired level of quality while keeping failure rates down to acceptable levels. For example, some products simply *must* be made in a "clean" room or cannot be made by staff who lack particular capabilities. Often, a prerequisite capability for doing a particular job successfully is knowledge that there are prerequisites and corequisites for performing the task successfully. The following example was suggested by my partner, who is a retired primary school teacher. She reported that new teachers who run into difficulties typically do so despite their knowledge of what they are teaching and the latest teaching methods. Difficulties arise because they do not appreciate that the number-one thing they must have in place is adequate classroom behavior management. If the classroom is out of control, the students will learn little, regardless of the quality of what the teacher is saying to them about the subject of that class. Hence "the key" is to be attentive to "spot fires" of particular children starting to behave disruptively and "put these fires out" immediately.

It is indeed bizarre that noneconomists can readily appreciate the priorities ideas in a nonadditive, hierarchical sense and yet most academic economists do not emphasize that some things are "key" to the achievement of other things. Unlike those lay decision-makers who "get" the prerequisite notion, most economists operate on the basis of a "never mind the quality, feel the width" mentality, treating everything as a potential substitute for everything else so long as the price is right. This is particularly bizarre, since they do this in an environment in which hierarchical rules abound. A typical economics degree has prerequisites for entry, followed by a prerequisite structure that determines the sequence in which courses can be taken. When it comes to making decisions about hiring and promotion, those whose track records fail to "tick the right boxes" are typically "ruled out" of contention. In this kind of system, the young academic who is a brilliant teacher and publishes many papers in second-tier journals has very probably "got his or her priorities wrong" if the first priority of the universities whose positions he or she targets is research potential and – regardless of how many there are – second-tier publications cannot offset the absence of anything in the top-tier journals. By contrast, someone who does the bare minimum in teaching and concentrates instead on getting papers accepted in top-tier journals may obtain a probationary position, followed by tenure, even if the acceptance rate of his or her papers in top-tier journals is very low.

Prerequisites and other barriers to substation receive further discussion elsewhere in this book. For now, though, the unwillingness of economists to take on board examples presented as evidence at odds with the general principle of substitution provides a useful reminder to us that problems need to be acknowledged before any remedial action will be initiated.

3.9   Conclusion

Economists are not conventionally trained to view people as problem-solvers whose puzzles and difficulties may often arise due to the creativity of others or be of their own making due to their cognitive shortcomings, restless curiosity and/or incompetence as systems designers. In contrast to the perspective offered in this chapter, the traditional training in economics inculcates a very limited view of problem-solving: problems are only viewed as arising due to external shocks, and people adapt optimally to the changed conditions by making marginal trade-offs – asking themselves "Would it now be better to have a little bit more of this and a bit less of that?" – and thereby arrive at a new equilibrium. The orthodox view emphasizes the role of substitution in arriving at optimal solutions to shocks, whereas the complex systems perspective offered here assigns a key role to complementarities and other linkages between system elements in understanding why problems spread and become challenging to solve.

To be sure, tweaking at the margin may dispose of some problems, as when tuning the engine of a car whose engine is basically in good condition. However, sometimes the entire system, or major components, may be problematic and hence much more drastic changes may need to be made if problems are to be prevented from recurring and/or getting worse. The trouble is, fine-tuning may be precluded in environments characterized by endless streams of innovations, while cognitively constrained decision-makers may be unable to "see the wood for the trees" on occasions where structural changes are needed.

If our biological evolution has equipped us with a tendency to be more confident than we should be, the fact that economic evolution has presented us with much more complex options than were available to our ancient ancestors means that we are likely to be prone to try to deal with today's challenges in a way that falls short of what is necessary to prevent them from resurfacing or ends up causing other problems. However, life may be problematic even if we are wise enough to consider calling upon assistance from experts: we may end up being, as Akerlof and Shiller (2015) put it, "phished for phools" by unscrupulous suppliers of experience goods and credence goods, and of search goods that we lack the time to research intensively or about which we lack the knowledge needed to put us in a position to know the right questions to ask.

4 How Do We Acknowledge Problems and Assess Options?

4.1 Introduction

Problem recognition is a problem in its own right, because problems are not self-evident. The same applies for the potential efficacy of potential means of addressing a problem. To know if we have a problem or potentially effective means of addressing a problem, we must gather information and decide how to interpret it. The systems that we use to do this may to some degree be ones that we have acquired socially or implement because they are among the policies and procedures of the organizations in which we work. But ultimately, these systems are unique to us: they include rules that we have developed for our evolving repertoires of ways for coping with life, including rules that determine whether we will adopt rules used by others and the extent to which we conform with bureaucratic policies and procedures. Because our systems for determining whether we have a problem are personal creations, we will sometimes see a given situation quite differently from how others see it. You may view a glass as half full and hence as an opportunity for refreshment, whereas I might view the same glass as problematic, since it is half empty.

This may seem perfectly obvious and familiar to lay readers, but mainstream economists typically operate "as if" everyone sees things in the same way, with that way assumed to be the best way that economists have so far developed for analyzing the situation at hand. So, for example, in the "efficient markets" theory of how financial markets work, all the players in the market instantly know the significance of each piece of news and do so from the standpoint of the latest economic models, thereby forming "rational expectations." If they differ in their choices of which financial assets to hold, this is the result of differences in their willingness to take risks, not because they draw different inferences from the same information or in some cases have access to "inside information." Here, by contrast, we will be taking the view that differences in behavior often result from people working with different mental models of particular situations. The question of human-induced global warming provides an important instance of such differences. You and I may agree that it is a problem, though perhaps we differ on the question of just how urgent it is, whereas some people operate with a very different view of the world and end up denying there is such a problem. Likewise, we may differ in how we see the pros and cons of alternative technologies for limiting emissions of greenhouse gases. Hence, if economists are to understand why people differ in their behavior, they appear to need to understand how people come to differ in how they think.

In emphasizing the economic significance of differences in how people think, I am taking a "subjectivist" view of human action, a view most associated with economists of the "Austrian school" such as Friedrich Hayek, Ludwig Lachman and Ludwig von Mises. Indeed, Hayek's thinking is assigned a major role in what follows. However, it is a perspective also associated with what is known in psychology as the "constructivist" approach. The pioneering figure here was George Kelly (1955) and his work has a key role in this chapter. In terms of Kelly's approach, problems are "personal constructs," as are the potential efficacies of ways of finding a solution to them and the pros and cons of potential solutions that we dream up in our heads or discover in the external environment.

The subjectivist/constructivist position brings to center stage the significance of the distinction between information and knowledge that was raised in the previous chapter. Incoming stimuli may inform us that, say, we do not exercise enough and that we present ourselves poorly, or that a particular website is the best place to find solutions to particular problems, or that a particular product is the best buy as a means to a particular end, but we do not have to believe these claims. Thus, although we may indeed build information into the mental models that we construct about particular parts of the world, information does not – contrary to common parlance – "lead" us to believe that we have a problem or to the expectations we form about the likely consequences of particular choices. Thus, although this chapter is ostensibly about how we assess whether we have a problem and, if so, what we think of possible ways of solving it, it is more broadly about how we decide what we think we know about the world around us. The analysis that follows explores both subconscious and thinking processes and, along the way, necessitates getting to grips with a trio of philosophical issues of which most economists seem utterly oblivious. The first thing we need to consider is how people allocate their attention, because this will determine which stimuli they attempt to assess.

4.2   Attention and the Infinite Regress Problem

Prior to commencing a decision-making process, we give our attention both to undertaking the acts of production or consumption that we have previously chosen and to scanning the world around us for threats and opportunities. This begs the question of how we allocate our attention between doing and scanning, and between scanning in one way rather than another. Getting the balance wrong could have serious consequences. For example, on the one hand, modern-day users of social networking sites may spend so much time scanning their smartphones for status updates and messages that they end up doing rather little. On the other hand, those who lock themselves away from external stimuli in order to get something done run the risk of discovering too late something personally significant that has been happening outside. We potentially could be making such choices every instant, though sometimes, as when we enter "do not disturb" mode, we make them to cover a particular period of time. We make these choices about how to allocate our attention without realizing that the attention allocation problem cannot be solved optimally: as Berger (1989) has pointed out, it is bedeviled by what philosophers call the problem of "infinite regress." The infinite regress problem will keep arising in this chapter, as well as later in this book, so before we go any further it is important to explore it carefully and understand how the human mind deals with it.

The choice between doing and scanning runs into the infinite regress problem because it is a choice about allocating finite attentive capacity that can only be addressed by allocating finite attentive capacity to it. To consider whether we should be allocating attention to the question of whether we are making the best allocation of attention, we must use some of our finite attention, but is this the best thing to do? The same question keeps arising, seemingly without end. On top of this, there is the need to choose between ways of going about scanning. Attempts to outsource or delegate monitoring to others do not close this part of the problem. Not only is there the question of who should be given the monitoring task but also, as Loasby (1976) points out, there is the possibility that those assigned the monitoring task could have shortcomings and hence they, too, need to be monitored. Constantly checking the performance of a product or person relative to any performance standard does not merely have opportunity costs in terms of time and other resources; the monitoring process may even adversely affect the performance that is being monitored. Moreover, the question of which reference standard should be used also needs to be answered, which begs the question of what possible standards there might be and how these might be evaluated.

These conundrums call to mind one of the problems with the ancient mythological view of Earth as being a flat structure (or, in some versions, the back of a "giant world turtle"). To the question of what supported Earth, the ancient answer was that it was perched on the back of a giant turtle, but those concerned with the ultimate foundations on which Earth rested would then want to know what lay below the giant turtle's feet. If the answer was "another turtle," the mystery remained, as it did if further probing produced the retort "It's turtles all the way down!"

To provide an end point, the infinite regress must be cut off via a rule or hierarchical system of rules. Because the problem otherwise has no end, the layer at which the stopping rule kicks in is arbitrary (Elster, 1984, p. 135) and typically not very deep. In the case of the allocation of attention, one way of sidestepping the infinite regress is by consciously using the rules by which we define who we are and how we go about life, such as "I'm not the sort of person who looks at my smartphone during business meetings, and I keep my social email account turned off when I'm at work." In other words, we have our personal "ways" of operating that will affect when we spot problems and flip into problem-solving mode. These rules are part of our self-control systems, though sometimes they will get overridden by rules from higher-ranking systems. For example, a person who is in the process of trying to find a new partner may find it impossible to resist the urge to check for pertinent social email messages while at work despite normally ruling out this kind of behavior: as Maslow (1943, 1971) argues, it is the most basic unmet need that preoccupies decision-makers.

The allocation of attention is also achieved via unconscious rule-based processes. Evolutionary selection processes have left humans with brains that, like modern computers, can run multiple programs at the same time, with some running in the background rather than being the focus of attention. Our senses have been selected to go into background mode when there is a lack of variation in their respective kinds of incoming stimuli. Departures from reference norms – such as sudden loud sounds (or a situation in which "everything has suddenly gone quiet") or visual punctuations – bring what was in the background back into our conscious attention. For example, one moment we are listening to our car's radio and seemingly driving on autopilot; next, we have switched back into conscious driving mode, oblivious of the radio, in order to deal with something odd that stands out on the road ahead, or to check what caused another driver to sound their vehicle's horn. In short, our brains are, in effect, using "if-then" rules to allocate attention: if a reference norm is breached for a particular activity, then the brain brings that activity to the foreground of our conscious thinking. If nothing is detected that activates these rules, we continue with our existing allocation of attention and remain immersed in scanning or in doing what we were doing – or even just continue daydreaming – rather than getting into problem-solving mode in a different area (see further Koestler, 1979).

4.3   The Process of Cognition

The process of discovering and solving problems begins with incoming stimuli from our scanning and search activities, advertising and our social environments, along with our internally generated ideas about what may be going on and what we may be able to do. It ends with the evaluations and expectations being stored in our brains as networks of neural connections. In this section we explore what goes on during the process and what it means for the kinds of evaluations and expectations that we form.

The analysis presented here draws particularly from three Nobel Laureates – Daniel Kahneman, Friedrich Hayek and Herbert Simon – plus Arthur Koestler's (1975, 1979) analysis of creativity and of the mind as a complex, multilayered system. Of the three Nobel Laureates, Kahneman is the one with the smallest inspirational role, for his (2011, pp. 11–12, chs. 4 and 22) writing about the "associative memory" and intuition mainly reinforces the message drawn from earlier work by Hayek and Simon. From Simon, we take the idea of the mind as a complex system that uses systems of rules, rather like computer programs, to solve problems – in this case, the problem of deciding "What am I looking at here?" Hayek's role here may be a surprise, for he is best known for his writings on how market economies work and why he thinks they work better than socialist systems. Few economists are aware that in his 1952 book *The Sensory Order*, Hayek proposed a theory of how the mind works as a complex system of neural networks. Hayek's book has come to be recognized as a prescient contribution to neuroscience and is a key source for economists who take seriously the distinction between information and knowledge. It has lately begun to attract interest from behavioral economists (see Loasby, 2004; Butos, 2010; Frantz and

Leeson, 2013). Hayek originally worked out his theory of cognition in the early 1920s. It is consistent with – and probably affected – his subjectivist approach to economics in which market signals do not contain self-evident messages but have to be interpreted.

4.3.1   Memory-Based Pattern Detection

To begin, let us consider what happens where we are not actively looking for anything but are nonetheless encountering sensory stimuli, such as when we are idly gazing out of the window of a bus as it passes business premises, billboards, cyclists, parked cars and so on. Our retinal cells receive visual stimuli from these objects and send signals along our optic nerves to our brains, which figure out what we are looking at. If we pass, say, a McDonald's restaurant, we are likely instantly to know what it is, even if we have never previously been along this stretch of road. Moreover, we are also likely instantly to associate it with attributes that are not currently visible (in my case, for example, with alleged copious inclusions of sugar and salt in the burgers and with the lack of vegan or even vegetarian burgers on the menu). We take this for granted as adults, but it is not something that a newborn baby can do, and neither can a digital camera do it even though it can capture the same image as a set of pixels and then store it.

According to Hayek, we can categorize what we are looking at because (a) cognition is based on past experience, stored as memories in the form of sets of neural connections, and (b) we know things in terms of patterns of associations between conceptual elements and objects rather than as unorganized sets of stored sensory inputs. We know what we are looking at if we can find, within incoming sensory stimuli, patterns that match some of the patterns we have formed as means of characterizing things that we have previously experienced. Our instantaneous sense of what we are looking at when we see a particular McDonald's restaurant depends on us having previously encountered and characterized such restaurants as a set of relationships between objects and concepts (for example, "the McDonald's arches logo" and "fast-food restaurant," respectively). These elements in turn are similarly characterized as being constituted by other elements and concepts. For example, "fast" may be viewed as "not taking much time," with "time" in turn being characterized with reference to minutes on a clock-face, and so on. A set of associations that we create to characterize a particular object is essentially a rule for specifying how we construe this object.

Were we gazing out of the bus window as babies, we would have very little idea about what we were seeing despite having the same information coming to our sensory receptors. This is because we would have very few memories to use as templates for finding patterns in the incoming sensory data. Of course, we also would not yet have a language with which we could label and describe anything, but language is not essential for cognitive processes to work: the words that we come to associate with particular phenomena (including brand and model names) are essentially cognitive shorthand symbols that facilitate conscious problem solving, creative thinking, and social interaction.

To start making sense of the world around them, newborn babies need to have some basic hardwired patterns and rules on which to build, and to be programmed to experiment by creating new conceptual combinations and trying to find matches with them, rather than merely to try to find matches with those they already have. Other species inherit some basic survival-enhancing patterns and rules, which we normally call "instincts." For example, Tinbergen (1951) reports an experiment involving young geese and an ambiguous silhouette whose shape was chosen so that it roughly matched the silhouettes of both a hawk (with a short neck and a long tail) and a goose (with a long neck and a short tail). When the silhouette was moved above a pen that contained the young geese, they ran for cover if the direction of its movement were such that the part representing a long tail or long neck was to the rear: it was as if they "knew" by instinct that geese do not fly backward and hence that they were looking at a hawk, which they were programmed to associate with danger.

The dependence of cognition on both stored cognitions and pattern recognition capabilities is evident if we reflect on the capacity of a digital camera as a cognitive device. A basic digital camera can capture as a series of pixels an image that we can see, and it can store it on a memory card that can hold several thousand other images. But what is stored is merely a set of data; it does not signify anything to the camera. However, more sophisticated cameras that embody artificial intelligence can detect particular kinds of patterns, which then trigger them to perform particular kinds of programmed operations. For example, face detection signifies the need to select a particular exposure setting. Similarly, in the case of a camera in a toll road scanning system, recognition of a vehicle registration plate within the photograph triggers search for more refined patterns within the frame of the registration plate, i.e., letters and numbers. The sequence that is found is then checked against a database to determine whether to send an infringement notice to the vehicle's owner or merely to deduct a fee from the owner's prepaid account. Such object recognition systems work in a manner analogous with how our minds work, except that they have a very limited set of things they can recognize.

Because Hayek worked out his ideas long before such technologies existed, he had to use a different analogy to support his argument about the significance of pattern recognition. He pointed out that in a mosaic, it is the pattern of the differently colored tesserae that matters and in that sense a mosaic is more than just the sum of its tesserae. Whether we think in terms of pixels or tesserae, the implication is the same: cognition is an active process even when we are seemingly just gazing passively.

Without memories whose sets of neural connections match those fired up by incoming stimuli, we cannot form cognitions (or perhaps better, we cannot "re-cognize") what we are looking at and identify its potential implications. If we encounter something utterly unlike anything we have experienced, we will have "no idea" what we are looking at, let alone have in our heads scripts to replay that describe what can be associated with it. The situation is rather like having a key that will unlock none of our doors because it does not match any of the patterns of their locks. For example, without having previously memorized the concepts of "bird," "quacking" and "waddling" as being the key aspects of the concept "duck," we cannot characterize a duck as a duck even if it is waddling, quacking and would be seen by others as a bird of some kind. In such a situation, stimuli from the duck may fire up neurons in our brain but the pattern of neurons does not correspond to any stored set that pertains to "duck" because no such set exists. However, if we already have memorized the concepts of "bird," "quacking" and "waddling" and someone nearby utters the word "duck," our brain can form the duck concept and store it for future use by combining the neural connection sets for the existing concepts, plus the one associated with the sound of "duck." Next time we hear someone saying "Look, there's a duck," this will activate a particular set of neural connections and we will know what to expect to see if we look for it.

It may seem, from what has so far been said, that the process of analyzing what is going on, or what a particular option has to offer, entails mentally disassembling it into a set of features. This sounds like the reverse of the process of creative thinking whereby we put together a vision of something by combining concepts we already have stored in our memory (Koestler, 1975; see also Section 6.7). Yet the outcome of analysis is actually like the mental outcome of creative thinking: in both cases, a new set of blended sets of neural connections gets stored in the memory.

In this way, we can usually make at least some kind of sense of new products and new situations, even if our verdict seems inept to more experienced onlookers. For example, on seeing a goat for the very first time, and if the goat in question is rather large and some distance away, a toddler may say, "It's a horse!" Mostly, we do not end up perplexed by novelty to the same degree as the audience at the premiere of Igor Stravinsky's ballet *The Rite of Spring* in Paris in 1913. On that occasion, the complex, dissonant music nearly caused a riot. Stravinsky had broken the norms of musical composition and his audience merely heard a cacophony because they could not find the usual kinds of patterns in the incoming aural stimuli. In general, where incoming stimuli do not fire up sets of neural connections that match those that have been stored as memories of desirable qualities, all we can really do is judge that the object in question is "utter rubbish" (cf. Thompson, 1979).

4.3.2   Finite Attentive Capacity

The more we have stored in our memory system, the greater the number of patterns that our brain potentially could try to find within a set of incoming stimuli. Were the brain to search in an unsystematic, unfocused manner without any pressure to reach a conclusion, it might find many matches that were of rather limited usefulness. The classic "Oscar Wilde Sketch" from *Monty Python's Flying Circus* shows how surreal characterizations can become if the imagination is allowed to range freely: in this piece of comedy, Wilde, Whistler and Shaw show off their wit to the Prince by successively accusing each other of likening him to a "big jam donut with cream on the top," "a stream of bat's piss," and "a dose of clap," all of which they try to justify in ways that turn out to be complimentary (see www.montypython.net/scripts/oscar.php).

The prodigious capacity of the human memory means that evaluation inherently entails a search process within the mind – even when what is being evaluated is itself a possible search strategy. As with any search process, cognition needs to be brought to a halt by a stopping rule that defines when a good enough impression of the object under consideration has been constructed, or by a focusing process that causes the brain to run out of options soon enough for the decision-maker to be able to move on to an adequate decision. In other words, cognition is necessarily what Herbert Simon (1947, 1956, 1959) called a "satisficing" process. It is not like the process of trying to open a door with the aid of a huge, unorganized bunch of keys, with the door only opening if we insert exactly the right key.

Hierarchical decomposition is one means by which the brain can limit the probability of trying stored patterns that do not match up with information contained in incoming stimuli or in information that has been stored previously. This process is akin to the process of sorting mail. These days that task is truncated because an address normally includes a post (zip) code. However, in the absence of such a code, the sorter works up from the bottom of the address, thereby rapidly narrowing down where the letter has to go. Obviously, this will normally be far quicker than indiscriminately asking at one residence after another whether the addressee lives there, until someone answers in the affirmative.

Typically, the starting point for the focusing process entails framing incoming stimuli within a context. For example, in the context of gazing out of the window of a bus, there is no need for our brains to look for, say, fish or books on behavioral economics, for "as a rule" we would not expect to find them in this context, whereas we would, as a rule, expect to see various kinds of vehicles, business premises, roadside trees and so on. If our bus ride ends at a university campus, there will be a different set of phenomena that, as a rule, we will expect to see, and yet another set if the context then becomes that of a lecture theatre or a particular professor's office.

A similar process of focusing comes into play when we are actively engaged in undertaking evaluations. For example, if we were evaluating people for an academic job, we would not need to characterize them in terms of their gardening and housework prowess, whereas if we were sizing up prospective tenants for a rental property, we would not need to consider their potential as researchers and teachers. In either case, we would not need a complete picture of each of the candidates, merely one that our cognitive rules deemed to be good enough for deciding between them. Finding a fit with a particular pattern within the contextual frame may in turn limit how far we need to go down the hierarchy that we associated with that context; for example, if we have in mind some things that would be "deal-breakers" and we check for these at the outset, we avoid having to form evaluations about other aspects of the options that display these features. We will return to this idea in Chapter 8.

How far we can then go will depend on the range of memories we have in relation to that context, as well as on the information we have at hand. For example, if we were gazing through the window of a bus as it passed a used-car yard, we might get only as far as seeing "a car" within a particular set of fleeting visual stimuli. If we have the requisite knowledge, we might conclude it was "a hatchback" and that it was "made by Hyundai," or even get as far as classifying it as "a mid-range 2016 Hyundai i30." If we were able to inspect it closely, we might further conclude that it had "probably covered far more kilometers than its odometer indicates" and hence that "the seller probably should not be trusted." Without having remembered particular patterns, such as how a Hyundai badge differs from a Honda badge, or that a badly worn steering wheel and a huge number of stone chips in a car's paintwork are usually associated with vehicles that have travelled great distances, we will be unable to form a detailed picture of the nature of what we are examining.

The hierarchical process of working down to more detailed levels of analysis is so ingrained that we are rarely aware of it. But it is something that we had to learn. The newborn baby's gaze is not focused but it soon develops rules for looking and hearing that enable it to make cognitive associations and become more skilled in assessing new situations.

In some contexts, we may be able to truncate the evaluation process by consciously applying "fast and frugal" decision rules (Gigerenzer and Goldstein, 1996; Gigerenzer et al., 1999) to the information at our disposal. Indeed, our rules for forming cognitions efficiently may determine the information that we need to gather before we try to form our judgments. For example, suppose we judge whether a particular movie might be worth going to see based on whether the director is one of our favorites and whether it has an average of at least four out of five stars in its review ratings. If so, we do not even need to check what the reviews say or find out which actors appear in it.

The need for the brain to have rules to enable it to move on when it has made good enough characterizations arises not merely because of the finite processing capacity of our memory systems but also because each object that we encounter or imagine is unique in its location in time and/or space if not also in other respects: even a particular McDonald's may be not exactly the same today as it was yesterday, since, for example, different patrons may be there. As Heiner (1983) emphasizes, we cope with the complexity of everyday life by using rules that treat particular things as if they are identical despite their inherent singularity. This in turn makes our own behavior much more predictable than it otherwise would have been. Thus, for example, occasionally a McDonald's may suffer a power outage, get struck by lightning or a runaway vehicle, or be the scene of a shooting or stabbing, and so on, *ad nauseam*, but we form our expectations about going to a McDonald's in terms of what McDonald's is like "as a rule." We form our expectations by expecting it to be pretty much as it usually has been unless we have reason to expect otherwise.

4.3.3 The Likelihood that a Particular Stored Set of Connections Will "Come to Mind"

The foregoing discussion of hierarchical decomposition as a means to rapid cognition entailed a very Koestler- and Simon-inspired perspective on *The Sensory Order*. Hayek himself gives us a different but entirely complementary view of what happens. He suggests that the probability of a stored set of connections being tried as a means of categorizing the meaning of incoming stimuli is a function of (a) the cumulative number of times the set of connections has been activated and (b) how recently it has been activated. Memories we have not called upon frequently or recently are thus unlikely to be used for cognition unless those with a bigger probability of being tried fail to help in figuring out a satisfactory sense of what to make of the stimuli.

If no context has been established to prime the relevant set of stored cognitions, the process that Hayek describes can be quite disconcerting. For example, while I was in my study writing this chapter, my partner was in the lounge watching the 2017–2018 Australia versus England Ashes cricket series on television and, during posture breaks, I would ask her how things were going. Then an email came in from the facilities section at work with the subject line "Bat Policy." It was about what to do if one found an injured or sick fruit bat on campus, but, having not thought about fruit bats for a while, my fleeting first thought was that it might be some kind of health and safety directive to limit injuries on the campus cricket field! But cognitive systems that give priority to finding matches with recently retrieved cognitions have obvious evolutionary merits if we switch environments rather infrequently and/or each switch is only a partial change: our stream of experience thus seems relatively seamless, and we do not have to keep pausing to figure out where we are.

Hayek's analysis implies that what first comes to mind when we are evaluating products can be cued not merely by what we made of advertisements to which we have been exposed but also by the set of experiences we have had, for the latter determine what is salient to us. For example, if the seat in my car has been giving me backache over a long period, I am unlikely to forget to consider carefully the seats on cars that I test as possible replacements for my current vehicle. By contrast, the quality of their brakes probably will not surface as an issue if I have not had to do an emergency stop in ages and if I do not have occasion to do one during a test drive. Things that we would view as important if we have been cued to think about them may thus get ignored if we have not had much occasion to consider them. Instead, we are at risk of focusing our evaluations on things we have repeatedly seen in recent advertisements, even if they might seem rather peripheral were we to be prodded to consider other issues.

Hayek's analysis also seems important for appreciating how people can end up needlessly miserable. Suppose we consider changing jobs because of the political climate in our workplace and how we are being treated there. It may escape our attention that we have a history of feeling like this about our jobs (since we keep thinking about the current job in particular) and we fail to consider how easy our lives are in major respects and how good our jobs are compared with the best jobs that many people can get. If we were to spend less time sharing our complaints with similarly disaffected colleagues and more time at home with our families, this would change the activation histories of work- and home-related memories. This in turn would reduce the probability of us focusing on the downsides of the job or seeing potential benefit from moving to a different one. The solution might thus be to work from home more often rather than at the office.

The process of stereotyping and the significance of brand names can be readily understood in terms of Hayek's analysis. Information received about a particular kind of person or product may be enough to permit a generic categorization to be made, such as "a Muslim" or "an Italian car." However, once the classification has been made, a wider set of associated sets of neural connections will be activated, making it even more likely that the next time we think about this kind of person or object, we will do so in the same way. If the picture created by that set of associations seems good enough for our purposes, the process of characterization stops there without any attempts to see if different patterns can be found in information that is already at hand or is potentially accessible. Thus, for example, suppose we see an advertisement for a new generation of a car offered by a particular brand that we have previously associated with "unreliable" and "rust-prone." Evoking the brand in our memory associates the new model with these undesirable attributes: even if it is much improved over its predecessors, it is "tainted by association." If we do not buy it and experience it for ourselves because of this, and if we do not encounter any reviews to the contrary, we will make the same kind of judgment about the next generation of the firm's products, too, and keep doing so.

There is an obvious role for advertisements here, as a means for challenging this human tendency by countering the set of associations that target customers would otherwise use to characterize the product. Sometimes, though, the process of re-branding a product literally has to entail offering it under a new brand name. A classic instance of this is how, in the late 1980s, Toyota launched its new Lexus brand when it entered the full-size luxury sedan segment of the car market outside Japan. The very idea that a Japanese brand would consider itself a potential player in this market segment also ensured considerable interest from the motoring media. Thereby, the Lexus LS400 was given the chance of coming to mind as a contender in this sector and not being viewed merely as "just a big Toyota."

Though Toyota's strategy was successful, Volkswagen did not copy it a decade later when it introduced its Phaeton model in its first foray into the same market segment. From our Hayekian perspective, it is not surprising that the Phaeton failed despite sharing many components and its underlying platform with the superluxury Bentley Continental. The problem was that if consumers had never previously thought of Volkswagen in this market segment, then it was unlikely to come to mind as a brand to check out if they were looking for a product in that segment. Moreover, even if they had remembered any publicity for the product, there was also the issue of whether members of their social reference groups had any awareness of it: if the prospective luxury car buyers were hoping to end up with a product that would serve well as a status symbol and have a good residual value, it would need to be easily recognized as such by others rather than being open to being mistakenly viewed as a version of the somewhat smaller and much cheaper Volkswagen Passat by the untrained eye. Without extensive and sustained promotion, Volkswagen would not come to mind as a player in the full-size luxury sedan segment. What would come to mind, of course, would be Mercedes-Benz, BMW, Audi, Lexus and (in the USA) Cadillac. But there was no point in Volkswagen copying Toyota's branding strategy. Volkswagen already owned the Audi and Bentley brands, and the point of branding the Phaeton as a Volkswagen probably had a different stereotype-countering mission, namely to use the Phaeton as a "halo" model for enhancing how people viewed lower-tier Volkswagen models.

The powerful stereotyping effect of a dominant way of seeing particular kinds of things is something that you can experience if you type "hollow head or face illusion" into Google and watch one of the many videos that come up in the search results. These videos usually feature a rotating Einstein or Charlie Chaplin mask, and as the mask rotates to reveal its reverse side, you will find it impossible not to see the face pushing out toward you (as well as starting to seem to rotate in the opposite direction), even though the back of the mask has the face curving inward. Try as you may, you will have trouble seeing it any other way. We are not used to seeing faces that curve inward, so if we are presented with something that in all other respects looks like a face, our brain treats it as if it is a normal face that curves outward, even though it does not.

The cognitive rules that our brains develop may initially be rather tentative but over time, as more memories of the same kind accumulate, the sets of neural connections that embody them become increasingly hardwired. In the case of the rules that we use for seeing faces, so firmly ingrained is our way of seeing faces that the hollow head illusion works even when a face is roughly carved into half a pumpkin.

4.3.4   Expert Intuition

The memory- and pattern-based view of cognition provides a way of making sense of what goes on when people with expertise in a particular area are able to make assessments very quickly, especially when sensing that they face a hazard or, in the case of experienced entrepreneurs, a profit opportunity. They may refer to having a "gut feeling," instinct or intuition, but what has happened is more likely to be the result of the fact that an expert is someone who, over the years, has stored a large repertoire of sets of neural connections pertaining to relevant cases and their associated characteristics.

Expert evaluation is just a matter of matching the stimuli from the new situation with a memory and the latter's connotations. As Simon and Chase discovered, chess masters who can play several dozen games at the same time are able to win all or almost all of them not because they have a superhuman capacity to compute the possible decision trees associated with all their feasible moves and their opponents' potential responses; rather, they have extensive memories of what happened in previous games and can use these for assessing each of the games they are now playing (Chase and Simon, 1973; Simon and Chase, 1973). Kahneman (2011) makes a similar argument with respect to the capacity of expert firefighters to size up risks: subconsciously, they can sometimes sense that it is time to withdraw, just before a floor gives way or a beam comes crashing down. They can do this because the patterns of stimuli they absorb set off warning bells in their heads by matching sets of neural connections pertaining to kinds of danger that they have experienced previously. In essence, they know what they are looking at because they have "seen it all before."

4.3.5   Inattention Blindness

The rules we use in cognition normally prevent us from being bemused and unable to choose, but the focus they induce can sometimes have dysfunctional consequences.

If we are attempting to assess something in a particular way, we will not be trying to find matches with other kinds of memories. We may focus on one kind of information in the set of stimuli in question and filter out other kinds of stimuli within which we could have found a pattern that matched a memorized pattern for which we were not looking. This is what commonly happens when students "latch on" to key words they were hoping to see in an exam question and fail to soak up the significance of some other aspects of the question. It is rather like what happens when an organization receives information but acts as if blind to it because it does not get passed on to those who would have seen its significance.

By filtering out much of the information that our sensory receptors receive, we can end up with what has become known, following Mack and Rock (1998), as "inattention blindness." This phenomenon is illustrated by the famous "invisible gorilla" experiment of Chabris and Simons (2010). Participants in this experiment were asked to count the number of passes in a video of a basketball game. At the end of the video, they were asked both how many passes they had counted and if they had noticed anything odd while engaged in the task. About half of them failed to report noticing someone in a gorilla suit moving around among those who were passing the basketball. (A similar result came from a second treatment in which a woman with an umbrella replaced the "gorilla.") The gorilla was not noticed by those whose sensory processes did not lead them to look for anything odd amid the players whose behavior they were observing; they just saw the things for which they were looking. For their expectations to be overridden, something would have needed to put them on the alert: perhaps they would have noticed the "gorilla" had it been bright yellow, three meters tall and shrieking loudly (cf. Section 4.2).

4.3.6   Deconstruction

Cognitive processes sometimes entail the opposite of inattention blindness, namely drawing inferences from missing information rather than failing to process information that was present. We need to be able to do this in cases where information that matters to us is prone not to be volunteered by other parties, such as prospective partners or dates or sellers of used cars and real estate. In such situations, the process of evaluation and expectation formation needs to be based on associations we have previously made between the presence of particular characteristics and what is missing from the stimuli set that we would normally expect to be found in the context at hand. Thus, for example, if an advertisement for a car does not mention its odometer reading, then our rule may be that it has an above-average reading for its age. If our rule is reliable, we may avoid wasting time checking out the vehicle any further. Such a process of inference is akin to decoding the information that the source has chosen to provide, and thereby to discover its subtext. This is like the practice of "deconstruction" that is commonly used in literary criticism and sometimes used by marketing scholars. However, although it is merely a variant on the idea that cognition is achieved by finding patterns in stimuli that match patterns one has previously noticed, deconstruction may be relatively rarely practiced: not everyone is naturally cynical or keen to explain events with the aid of "conspiracy theories."

4.4   Brain Plasticity

Hayek's theory of how the mind works is a precursor to the analysis of brain plasticity (surveyed in Doidge, 2007) offered by modern neuroscientists. If the probability of a neural template being used to classify incoming stimuli is a function of the frequency of its recent and cumulative activation, the way that we will view incoming stimuli is not going to be static. If, on the basis of its probability of activation, a particular stored set of connections happens to get fired up and be found to match incoming stimuli, then its chances of getting used again in that context will increase: the latest activation weighs in its favor, as it is both recent and adds to its cumulative total, whereas sets of connections that were not activated will suffer a reduction in their probabilities of being activated in future (their cumulative activation scores have not changed but there is no recent activation).

Although we might view this process purely as if it is the consequence of the brain using a rule to select stored patterns to test for their fit with incoming stimuli, we should also recognize that the activation of neural pathways, or the lack thereof, has a physical counterpart, namely the process of myelination or demyelination (often known as myelinogenesis). The activation of neural connections leads to the laying down of myelin sheathing around nerve cell axons. The myelin serves as an insulator, enabling the nerve cells to transmit information more rapidly.

These processes can result in our established ways of seeing the world either becoming more entrenched or being displaced by different perspectives. In the latter cases, we move, in effect, from having view A as our normal expectation for the context in question, with view B "barely getting a look in," through "being in two minds" about it, to normally seeing it in terms of view B, with view A coming to mind increasingly rarely as a way of seeing it. Things that once seemed shocking can thereby start to seem normal if we are exposed to them often enough. Stravinsky's *The Rite of Spring* gradually came to be taken seriously as music rather than cacophony – so much so that in 1940, material from it was used in Walt Disney's *Fantasia*. Similarly, people can get used to forms of behavior and products that they once could only view negatively, such as divorce, cohabitation and same-sex marriage; swearing in books, movies and television programs; wind farms, particular styles of cars, hair and dress, political views, dumbed-down higher education, veganism, (non-) smoking, and so on.

The key to opening the mind to new points of view is the frequency with which we are exposed to sets of stimuli that are at odds with our habitual ways of seeing things. But plasticity in thinking is also promoted by encounters with abnormal stimuli that come bundled with stimuli that do not clash with our norms, for then the mind will have to work harder to shunt them aside. For example, it becomes harder to dismiss pro-environment or ethically motivated behavior as "weird" if we are presented with examples of it being undertaken by people that we respect highly for other kinds of behavior that we do not view as weird. Conversely, people will evolve toward more and more entrenched attitudes if – for example, due to geographical isolation – they rarely encounter stimuli that clash with their established way of seeing things and hence are rarely prompted to try putting together new sets of associations or to try templates that they have formed previously but have rarely used. Moreover, if they are armed only with memories of unrepresentative small samples of past cases of a particular phenomenon that displays a lot of statistical variability, they will be at great risk of making poor initial assessments when faced with a fresh challenge of this kind.

4.5   Dealing with Cognitive Dissonance (1)

Unless we confine ourselves to stable, surprise-free environments that we are always able to predict and control, we will keep encountering stimuli that seem potentially at odds with what we think we should be seeing. Such situations could signify that we might have a problem, but this is something we will have to figure out for ourselves. Sometimes, such situations arise because we are receiving stimuli from advertisements that are designed to pose problems for us by presenting us with something better than what we already have: we may see the advertisement as saying that if we do not switch to the product being advertised, we will be underachieving compared with how we could be doing. What once may have seemed perfectly satisfactory has been called into question, but perhaps the message of the advertisement is nothing more than hype that is designed to make us uncomfortable with the status quo. Hence, if we take the bait to prevent ourselves from foolishly underachieving, we may have the uncomfortable feeling that we are possibly fools for believing the message in the advertisement.

Leon Festinger (1957) famously applied the term "cognitive dissonance" to what we experience when we realize there is a clash between contending ways of looking at the world. He argued that the presence of cognitive dissonance makes us feel uncomfortable, motivating us to find a way of achieving cognitive consonance. Evolutionary selection processes would have favored humans who had a tendency to experience such a feeling and motivation to remove it, for inability to resolve how to look at a particular situation could prevent decisions from being made, thereby jeopardizing survival. The picture that Festinger gave of the process of removing cognitive dissonance entails managing the stimuli to which we are exposed or concocting stories by which apparent contradictions can be reconciled. It is rather like a political process that involves censorship and "spin," but it goes on at the level of the individual. However, the strange thing about Festinger's book is the absence of analysis of why we end up managing cognitive dissonance in one way rather than another. Here, by contrast, we will consider several complementary ways of understanding the process. This section views the issue from the standpoint of Hayek's *Sensory Order*. However, first it may be helpful to consider some examples of the process of removing the feeling of cognitive dissonance.

The removal of cognitive dissonance by censoring the information that our brains have to process is memorably illustrated by Akerlof and Dickens (1982) in one of the first papers to appear on the economics of cognitive dissonance. They consider, among several examples, how technicians at nuclear power plants handled the inconsistency between viewing themselves as smart people, since they were doing a job that required unusual expertise, and the idea that they were potentially putting their lives at risk by working where they worked, as indicated by the requirement that they carry radiation monitors with them while at work. These workers dealt with the problem by ensuring that they saw no evidence that they were working in a hazardous place: they only wore their radiation monitors on the days they knew the monitors would be checked; otherwise, they kept the monitoring devices in a drawer – out of sight and, if the drawer is in a steel cabinet, less likely to detect radiation. The "out of sight, out of mind" strategy is also common among those who have got into a mess with debt: they tend to stuff fresh bills into a drawer, often without even opening the envelopes in which the bills arrive, rather than facing up to the reality of their situation and seeking help in dealing with it (see Cameron and Golby, 1990; Lea et al., 1993, 2012). They thereby kid themselves that they can carry on as they have been, such as trying to "keep up appearances" by buying status symbols, while falling behind with their public utility bills.

The "spin" approach to removing cognitive dissonance is rather akin to the processes by which lawyers construct cases for clients that they are defending. It often entails mustering supportive evidence that we might otherwise not have sought and building our scenarios on assumptions that might not turn out to be valid. Questions about the latter, along with any loose ends, may be fended off by applying the "We'll cross that bridge if and when we come to it" rule. Maital (1982) provides an example of this when he considers how consumers who see themselves as "not the sort of person who gets into debt" nonetheless succumb to tempting products that they cannot finance from their current savings. In evaluating these products, they are prone to emphasize the benefit of seizing the opportunity by using their credit cards to make the purchase, at the same time telling themselves that, when they make their next monthly payments on these credit cards, they will be in a position to pay off the balance in full. If it then turns out that they cannot do this, we may expect them to highlight the benefits from having made the purchase and to claim that they will pay off their balance in full soon. But when tempted again to spend, they will have a lower probability of seeing themselves as the sort of person who does not get into debt; if so, they may no longer feel dissonance of that kind when considering doing further spending via their credit cards. It is rather as if, having lost their virginity as debtors, they then lose their inhibitions on that front.

We can begin to understand how the mind may determine how cognitive dissonance is resolved if we recall that in Hayek's *Sensory Order* the probability of a stored notion being called up from the memory and tried for its match with incoming stimuli is a function of both the cumulative activation of the sets of neural connections in which memories have been stored, and how recently these sets have been activated. Stored notions that we have been using for a long time and have been using recently will crowd out those that we have rarely had occasion to call to mind and/or have not ended up using recently to characterize anything. In evolutionary terms we might say that the former sets of connections are stronger and fitter than the latter when it comes to competing for the right to be tried for their match with incoming stimuli. (This is consistent with the process of myelinogenesis that affects the relative speeds at which electrical signals can propagate along nerve fibers.) Weaker sets of stored connections only get activated when the patterns stored via stronger sets do not match incoming stimuli, leading us, as the expression goes, to "rack our brains" for something that will come to our cognitive rescue. A situation of cognitive dissonance would appear from this standpoint to entail two or more well-established sets of connections vying for attention as potentially correct interpretations of incoming stimuli, with the dissonance then being resolved by the strongest one crowding out the other(s).

To get a sense of how this can go on in an entirely subconscious manner it is instructive to consider a famous case from experimental psychology in which the mind is tricked into a seemingly bizarre cognitive error (see Ames, 1952). To experience it yourself, Google "Ames room illusion video" and peruse some of the YouTube items that come up. You will have the disconcerting experience of seeing people appearing to change their height as they walk across a room, something that you know cannot be happening. What is happening in these videos is that the person is walking across a room that has been constructed with no right angles at the corners or anywhere else (for example, in window and door frames). The room is thus utterly at odds with our normal expectations about rooms: prior to being introduced to the Ames illusion, we probably have never seen a room whose alignment is "out of true" to the extent that the Ames room is. But we have seen people change in height as their distance from us varies – nor *actually* changing in height but merely changing in terms of the number of retinal cells that their images activate. With the idea that rooms and right-angled corners go together being so firmly stored in our mind and so frequently activated, our mind is forced to deal with the illusion by allowing the person walking across the room to seem to change height, since *in some contexts* it "knows" that this is what happens. The idea that people cannot change height is cognitively weaker than the idea that rooms consist of walls and floors that meet at right angles; hence the latter wins in the battle for our attention.

4.6   How Do We Know What We Know?

If we ask people why they believe particular things, they will answer either by referring to other things that they believe or by saying, often with evident irritation, "I believe it because I do." As an example of the former, if we ask, "Why do you think product X is better than product Y?" they may reply "Because I read that is so in *Consumer Reports*." If we then ask, "Why do you trust what you read in *Consumer Reports*?" they might reply "Because it's published by a not-for-profit organization and hence has no incentive to present biased reports." This answer, in turn, begs a question, namely "Why does being a not-for-profit magazine rule out the possibility of some of the people who run it being corrupt and receiving benefits from some of the firms whose products they review?" In other words, we are dealing with another example of an infinite regress that will have to be brought to a halt an arbitrary stopping rule. Sure enough, sooner or later, and typically in barely half a dozen rounds, we will get to the "I believe it because I do" stage at which it is wise to stop the inquisition. It appears that human belief systems have no firm foundations and are simply based on rules that people may not have been conscious of using or whose possible limitations they have not even considered. It may seem as though they are fools to construct their beliefs on foundations that seem essentially arbitrary, but logic dictates that is the best that any of us can ever do, no matter how deeply we think.

Related to the infinite regress aspect of the problem of knowledge is an issue known to philosophers of science as the "Duhem–Quine problem." Duhem (1906) and Quine (1951) realized that it is impossible to test one hypothesis without assuming the validity of other hypotheses. For scientists running experiments in laboratories, or astronomers and astrophysicists trying to figure out how the universe works, the Duhem–Quine problem means that there is always the risk of (a) concluding that a particular hypothesis is contradicted by evidence when the problem actually lies with how the evidence was gathered or analyzed or (b) concluding that a particular hypothesis is standing up to empirical scrutiny when actually this only seems to be so because of the way the test data have been gathered and analyzed (see further Loasby, 2000). However, although scientists can never be sure of their findings, they may be able to develop ways of operating that at least seem to yield what Ziman (1978) focuses on in his book *Reliable Knowledge*, namely beliefs that generally ensure that they do not impose disastrous costs on the rest of society. In this sense, reliable knowledge was something lacked by scientists at the German pharmaceutical company Chemie Grünenthal (now Grünenthal GmbH) about the potentially harmful consequences of their drug Thalidomide when it was being taken as an antinausea treatment by pregnant women in the early 1960s. The discovery that it led to thousands of major birth defects came not only as a very nasty surprise to these scientists and the parents of these children but also to the official agencies whose unreliable knowledge had led to the drug being approved for such use.

As with infinite regress problems, the way that the Duhem–Quine problem is disposed of in practice is by applying rules. These rules are typically organized in hierarchically. Taken together, they constitute a standpoint from which to look at the world and thereby become able to pronounce (with, it is hoped, a big enough degree of reliability) whether there is a problem and, if one is deemed to exist, what kind of problem it is and how to go about finding a solution to it.

Lakatos (1970) argues that research scientists make methodological commitments to "research programs" that are built around particular core assumptions and "positive and negative heuristics" (i.e., "do" and "don't" rules) that they take as given. They follow the rules of their research program and thereby pronounce where problems lie, with these problems always being deemed to be peripheral to the core that they are taking as given. (Chapter 1 of this book can be viewed as an outline of a particular behavioral economics research program.) If a scientific research program is having trouble maintaining the range of things it can explain (in Lakatos's terms, if it is "degenerating"), this will be evident in its practitioners having to resort to *ad hoc* arguments in the periphery. The traditional ways of doing economics, based on rational choice theory, seems to be in this situation, with behavioral economists exposing more and more phenomena that seem anomalous from the rational choice perspective. Allowing these anomalies to be explained away via heuristics-based arguments offered by modern behavioral economists deflects criticism that mainstream economists are not open to empirical evidence. Meanwhile, they continue operating as if their view of "rational" choice is a good approximation for what happens in other situations, as well as constituting the right benchmark for how people ought to behave.

In relation to everyday decision-making, the significance of the Duhem–Quine problem is that the rules we end up using to deal with it can result in erroneous inferences. For one thing, we may judge that nothing is wrong when something is amiss and could prove dangerous. The latter can occur where we do not have rules in place to guard against ways that our senses can deceive us, such as the way that we only notice changes if they are big enough to get over response thresholds. Thaler (2015, loc. 568) offers a good example of this: a motorist may fail to notice that one headlight on his or her car has stopped working and hence does not replace the bulb that has failed despite the road ahead being less well illuminated. If the motorist does not have a routine for checking whether lights actually work and is not alerted by someone else (for example, a member of the traffic police) that a light is not working, the presence of a problem with the lights may not be detected until months later when the second headlight fails and the total reduction in illumination becomes bad enough to be noticeable. By that point, it is a different problem.

People are also prone not to notice problems due to the "confirmation bias" that arises because their mode of operating entails looking for evidence that supports their way of looking at the world rather than looking for instances in which their hypotheses are not supported by evidence. Socially sourced rules that are based on misconceptions sometimes cause us to fail to see issues that should be of concern to us or to identify problems that should not really trouble us. As an example of the latter, note that the prospect of missing lunch may seem a problem in terms of the social rule that says we should eat between midday and two o'clock in the afternoon, yet missing lunch normally will not be a problem in physiological terms as the body simply turns to its calorific reserves until the next meal is consumed.

Sometimes, we recognize a problem, but it is not the problem we need to recognize or need to try to solve right now. An important manifestation of this is the kind of "firefighting" behavior commonly displayed by the senior managers studied in a classic piece of behavioral research by Swedish economist Sune Carlson (1951). He found that his research subjects worked long, stressful hours busily searching for, and trying to implement, solutions to problems in their organizations. They were convinced that their situations were just temporary and that they would soon be able to return to a more relaxed pace of work, and work fewer hours, once they had got things under control. The trouble was that their focus on trying to use their existing strategies for dealing with what was going on left them with little time to reflect upon whether they needed a major strategic rethink and to search for a different way of running their businesses or a different line of business in which to operate. Rather than focusing on fighting the "fires" that kept breaking out, they should let some of the "fires" burn unattended and instead give attention to finding a design for a more "fireproof" structure. It was obvious enough to Carlson, but not to them.

In the context of complex business organizations, the problem of knowing what is going on and where problems lie is clearly acute. It will take time for subordinates to pass on information that they judge should be passed up the line, or that their operating procedures require they relay to the next decision point. Managers cannot be always overseeing all their subordinates' actions, but their subordinates may be guilefully concealing things from them. Independent auditors will have to build their analysis on hypotheses whose testing is only possible if they take other things on trust (cf. Wolnizer, 2006, ch. 2). Worse still, the difficulties that a business faces in terms of its key performance indicators (hereafter abbreviated to "KPIs") could have many sources: operational, tactical or, even, strategic. In other words, it could be doing what it does less well than is possible, have poorly chosen products and/or marketing or be in the wrong kind of business given its capabilities and where things are going in its external environment. Moreover, knowing whether a firm has problems and what their nature is also requires knowledge of what rival firms and other firms in its supply chains are doing and what is really driving the behavior of customers. Any data on these issues, if it is available (e.g., via employees poached from other firms or via market research), is not guaranteed to reveal the true picture. But if managers arrive at work each day doubting everything that they and their colleagues are doing, with no idea what problems their organization has or even whether it is operating in areas of business where it has a long-term future, they will have trouble reaching any decisions.

4.7   Personal Construct Systems and Their Blind Spots

Lakatos's (1970) vision of how scientists handle the Duhem–Quine problem is essentially the same as clinical psychologist George Kelly's (1955) view of how ordinary people cope with the problem of knowledge as they go about their lives. However, Kelly's terminology is different. Instead of referring to "scientific research programs," he describes people as using "personal construct systems" to predict and control what happens in their lives. These rule-based systems are hierarchically structured, based on a set of "core" constructs that embody the person's working assumptions about how the world is and who they are. As is explained in detail in Chapter 7, these rules provide the basis for personal value systems and determine whether and where a person is open to change. We can view organizations in a similar way: their operating systems often consist partly of an informal "corporate culture" (see Section 10.11) and partly of a formal mission statement and handbook of policies and procedures. By accepting the vision and modus operandi of the organization for which they work, managers thereby "know" what kind of business they are in and have routines for collecting performance data, with the data normally not being allowed to challenge the organization's raison d'être or core operating principles (see further Earl, 1984, 2002, ch. 1; Harper and Earl, 1996).

As we saw in Section 2.9, Kelly viewed people "as if they are scientists" whose mission in life is to predict and control events, so it is not really surprising that the perspectives that Kelly and Lakatos offered are similar. In constructing *his* theory of how ordinary people theorize about the world, Kelly had in mind a view of the universe akin to that subsequently popularized in chaos theory (cf. Section 3.7): he saw the universe as an integral structure in which seemingly unconnected areas – such as the movement of his fingers at the typewriter and the price of yak milk in Tibet (Kelly, 1955, p. 5) – could turn out to be related via complex chains of causal linkages. People have to abstract from such complexity by theorizing as if they are dealing with a much more modular system in which it is safe only to worry about rather limited sets of connections. The problem is to know where to assume the boundaries of our choices lie: if we make our theoretical modules too small, we may be surprised to find that our choices set in motion unwelcome and unexpected chains of events that we are ill-equipped to handle, but if we try to imagine a huge range of consequences for each choice we consider, we may find it impossible to figure out what our choices would imply and hence we may find it impossible to choose.

Kelly's massive two-volume (1955) book *The Psychology of Personal Constructs* offers an elaborate theory-in-words based around this vision. Although he does not analyze human processes at the neural level, it complements perfectly the perspective that was set out in Section 4.3. As was shown in Section 2.10, Kelly's theory comes complete with a technique for uncovering how people see the world, which was augmented by contributions by one of his doctoral students, Dennis Hinkle ([1965] 2010). Kelly's book led to the emergence of a new "constructivist" school of thought in psychology (see Bannister and Fransella, 1971) and it has won adherents in marketing, organizational behavior and management. When Brian Loasby and I began to explore potential for using Kelly's ideas in economics, we were familiar with Lakatos's view of science and had already been noticing similarities with how nonscientists seemed to operate. From the standpoint of Hayek's *Sensory Order*, Loasby and I were thus going to be open to taking up Kelly's way of thinking as soon as it came to our attention (which was via Charles Suckling, an adjunct professor at the University of Stirling, who had found it useful for thinking about issues in his work as an executive at ICI).

The essence of Kelly's ideas, the first three chapters of his magnum opus, became available in more convenient form in 1963 as *A Theory of Personality*. The latter book's title is very helpful for appreciating his fundamental postulate, namely that "[a] person's processes are psychologically channelized by the ways in which he antici-pates events" (Kelly, 1963, p. 46). Our personalities, as assessed by others, are manifest in things that make our behavior predictable to some degree, and Kelly seems to be arguing that our personalities are shaped by the systems of rules (i.e., "the

Table 4.1. A hypothetical customer's targets and perceptions of a pair of SUVs

Construct dimension	Rating on 0–10 scale										
	0	1	2	3	4	5	6	7	8	9	10
Reliability									T	A	B
Interior space						B	T		A		
Safety								T	B		A
Adequacy of power							T	A	B		
Towing capacity					T	A			B		
Interior quality							A	T		B	
Styling						B	T	A			
Fuel economy					B	T	A				
Off-road capability				T		A			B		
Ride comfort				B	A		T				

T = target for construct; A = rating for product *A*; B = rating for product *B*

ways") that we use to form expectations. For behavioral economists, the significance of his view lies in the implications that his analysis has for the kinds of expectations that people are prone to form and can form and the consequences that their ways of looking at the world have for the choices they make.

Kelly fleshes out his thinking via eleven corollaries to his fundamental postulate, beginning with the construction corollary: "A person anticipates events by construing their replications" (*ibid.*, p. 50). In other words, to form an expectation about something, we ask ourselves what it is like, which is equivalent to trying to find something similar to it in our memory, as per Hayek's analysis. Kelly views this process as akin to seeing how closely we can match the thing we are construing with a template that we have constructed to characterize a particular kind of phenomena. Such a template might refer to, say, "The SUV I'm hoping to find" but this template might itself have been constructed after reflection about the pros and cons of some SUVs with which we are familiar, seen in terms of how they matched up with the view that we have constructed of the ends that we see a car as serving.

Table 4.1 gives a picture of what such a template might look like in relation to findings from market research that asked consumers to rate SUVs from zero to ten on a variety of dimensions. (This kind of information can also be represented in terms of a sawtooth graph, as in Grupp and Maital, 2001; Earl and Wakeley, 2010.) In this hypothetical example, neither product *A* nor product *B* is viewed by the customer as at least matching up to his or her targets. As a spoiler for Chapter 8, it is useful to reflect on what this may imply if thinking in terms of a template means that the consumer does not go on to choose by weighing up the pros and cons of rival products on the dimensions in question. Thinking with reference to a template seems more consistent with the customer ranking these construct dimensions in order of descending hierarchical importance and trying to get as far down the list as possible without failing to meet a target. If so, product *B* falls at the second hurdle as it does not have enough interior space, whereas product *A* falls at the sixth hurdle, as the quality of its interior falls short what the consumer is hoping to find. On this basis, product *A* would thus be preferred to product *B*.

Kelly's individuality corollary emphasizes that people will differ in the templates they use: "People differ from each other in their construction of events" (Kelly, 1963, p. 55). Further reflection on Table 4.1 can give a sense of this and of why Kelly developed his RGT system as an alternative to the use of questionnaires for finding out how people think. Perhaps our hypothetical consumer would have felt uncomfortable with a questionnaire that presented these construct dimensions and required answers in terms of the zero to ten scale. Instead of thinking in terms of "interior space," the consumer might have had in mind, say, "I want an SUV with a third row of seats, and enough luggage space when the third row of seats is folded flat." This might have emerged readily by applying RGT and would have been a clearer lesson for the manufacturer of product *B*, if this product only came as a five-seater.

One reason for people differing in how they construe things is that we each use a distinctive set of rules for constructing associations between constructs. Kelly recognizes the presence of such rules via his organization corollary: "Each person develops, for his convenience in anticipating events, a construction system embracing ordinal relationships between construct" (*ibid.*, p. 56). For example, you might see an SUV as safer than a sedan because you see it as giving a better view of the road ahead than one gets in a sedan, whereas I might see an SUV as less safe than a sedan owing to its higher center of gravity: we can both characterize these different kinds of vehicles in relation to their prospective safety, but we have different "ways" of doing so.

The possibility that we may have our own personal cognitive blind spots is implied by Kelly in his dichotomy corollary: "A person's construction system consists of a finite number of dichotomous constructs" (*ibid.*, p. 59). The operative word here is "finite," and we can illustrate this by reflecting further on the SUV example. Digging deeper into the ordinal relationships of our different ways of thinking about these vehicles may reveal, say, that I do not think about safety in terms of the ease of seeing the road ahead, even when driving a low-slung sports car, unless the windscreen is filthy or on occasions when I am being pushed too close to the vehicle in front of me by an aggressively driven vehicle that is tailgating me. By contrast, you might not think at all about a vehicle's center of gravity; moreover, perhaps neither of us thinks about an SUV in relation to it offering greater convenience in terms of access for senior citizens with poor joints in their legs or in terms of its height making it easier for parents to buckle their children into safety seats. Some of those who end up buying SUVs due to being concerned about problems of entry and egress in lower vehicles might, in turn, not be thinking at all about matters of safety when sizing up their options or, if they are, might simply see it in terms of an official safety rating or the number of airbags that a vehicle has.

The limitations of our sets of constructs also arise via Kelly's range corollary: "A construct is convenient for the anticipation of a finite range of events only" (*ibid.*, p. 68). This means that for any particular context, we will only have a limited repertoire of constructs that we use, with the sets that we use only intersecting to a limited degree between contexts. For example, while we may use the construct "stylish versus ugly" to cars, furniture and houses, we do not assess cars in terms of the construct "bedroom *versus* living room" that we might use when thinking about furniture and houses or assess furniture and houses in terms of the construct "sedan *versus* hatchback."

Because of his constructivist perspective, Kelly avoided the term "learning." He chose instead to see people as sometimes re-construing events after gathering fresh evidence via experience and deciding what to make of it. This is summed up in his experience corollary: "A person's construction system varies as he successively construes the replications of events" (*ibid.*, p. 72). For example, in 2017, after driving a new Hyundai i30 as a rental car, you might have concluded that the i30 pretty much matched a European hatchback, unlike its previous iterations. However, the rules of the way in which we look at the world limit our abilities to change how we see particular kinds of events. As Kelly's modulation corollary puts it, "The variation in a person's construction system is limited by the permeability of the constructs within whose range of convenience the variants lie" (*ibid.*, p. 77). Thus, for example, if you told me about your impression of the 2017 Hyundai i30, I might have found it impossible to believe what you were saying because I took the view that German engineers are always able to stay several steps ahead of those in other parts of the world. If so, I would in effect have been ruling that your evidence-based claim was inadmissible. If I were still thinking like this today, I would anticipate that if I compared a new i30 with the latest Volkswagen Golf, my hypothesis would be confirmed.

Kelly's view that the systems people use to make sense of the world may prevent them from changing how they see some things had an important message for his fellow clinical psychologists: if you want to help your patients toward more enjoyable lives, you will need to understand how their ways of looking at the world are preventing them from doing this by themselves; and, having done this, you will need to work out ways of steering them toward more permeable construct systems in areas in which their rigid ways of thinking are having dysfunctional consequences. But Kelly's view is also profoundly important for economists who want to understand the pace of change in economic systems and the extent to which people will respond to changes in information and relative prices. We will explore this issue at length during Chapter 7.

Although the rules of a person's construct system normally result in them operating in a way that is consistent enough to make them seem to onlookers to have a particular kind of personality, there will be occasions when they surprise others by doing things that seem "out of character." Kelly acknowledges this via his fragmentation corollary: "A person may successively employ a variety of construction subsystems which are inferentially incompatible with each other" (*ibid.*, p. 83). The inconsistency that others see may arise because the person in question has not made a connection between different parts of his or her system for forming constructs, whereas the onlookers have made the connection in question within their respective systems. For example, suppose we have a friend whom we see as a "greenie" and he says he has bought a new Toyota. However, he then surprises us by showing up in an enormous Toyota

Landcruiser rather than the Prius that we had predicted he would be driving. Surely, we think, the vegan tree-hugger ought to know that his choice is going to be bad for the ecosystem!

But there might be method in his apparent madness, and it might turn out that we are the ones who have failed to make some connections. Our greenie friend might have decided to reduce his family's greenhouse gas emission footprint and get closer to nature by ceasing to take his family on vacations that involving flying to far-off lands. Instead, he plans to take them to see the wonders of nature in rugged parts of the country in which they live. The fuel economy of the Landcruiser per passenger will be no worse than that of a jet airliner and they will be covering much shorter distances. Moreover, he may have ruled out using the Landcruiser on the school run, so all in all it might seem a "green" choice in his situation even though he would view with disdain those who use such vehicles as urban runabouts. The lesson here is that we should not jump to conclusions when others behave in surprising ways, and that if we are to understand how people make their choices, we may need quite a deep understanding of the rules they use for organizing their thinking and forming constructs.

In labeling particular people as "greenies," "rednecks," "bogans" (an Australian or New Zealand term that intersects somewhat with "white trash" in its connotations), "ferals," "yuppies" and so on, we are likely simultaneously to be thinking of them in terms of the ways in which they look at the world and the kinds of choices they make. Together, such bundles of associations are what marketers mean when they talk about people with different "lifestyles," which they have long been able to map using a variety of "psychographic techniques" (see Wells, 1975), including those that Kelly and Hinkle devised and which were outlined in Section 2.10. When we assign people to lifestyle categories, we are not denying their individuality: some greenies, for example, may end up choosing to drive a Toyota Prius, others a small diesel car; others may keep an ageing, less economical car going for as long as they can, and others may opt not to own a car at all and instead get around by walking, cycling and/ or public transport. But what we are saying is that they broadly fit a particular kind of template when it comes to the operating systems that they use for running their lives. Kelly captures this via his commonality corollary: "To the extent that one person employs a construction of experience which is similar to that employed by another, his psychological processes are similar to those of the other person" (*ibid.*, p. 90).

People within a particular lifestyle category will find it easy to empathize with each other but may have trouble understanding why other types of people think as they do, even if they can broadly predict how the latter will react to particular stimuli. This leads us on to the final corollary that Kelly attached to the fundamental postulate of his theory, namely the sociality corollary: "To the extent that one person construes the construction processes of another, he can play a role in a social process involving the other person" (*ibid.*, p. 95). Cast in economic terms, Kelly's message is that transactions may fail to take place successfully if buyers and sellers use different rules of thought for forming their evaluations and expectations. For example, consider why the estate agent who tried most diligently to match me up with a house when I first moved to Australia failed to clinch a sale. I told him that I wanted a "low maintenance" house, and he took me to a series of pristinely presented properties, including a couple of former show-homes. However, I ended up buying something slightly cheaper and less well presented. He knew of the house in question and could have arranged a deal with the listing agent to show it to me, but he did not do so because he construed "low maintenance" differently from me. What I had in mind was avoiding anything but brick and tile homes so that I would not need to keep attending to flaking paint on weatherboards or rusting iron-roofing sheets: my concern was with whether the construction materials would best keep the external forces of entropy at bay, not with interior décor.

Success in engaging with prospective customers or suppliers (including people within one's workplace for whom one is undertaking tasks or to whom one is assigning tasks) may thus require taking the trouble to ensure that one understands well enough how the other parties think. Knowledge of how clients think may even go so far as to enable the supplier to anticipate the customer's needs ahead of the customer becoming aware of them, with the customer then swiftly seeing the merits of what the supplier is suggesting. This is the business equivalent of couples who are so attuned to how "their other half" thinks that they not only display a great capacity to finish each other's sentences but appear almost telepathic in anticipating each other's needs.

Kelly's sociality corollary points to another infinite regress problem that could cause decision paralysis in social situations if we did not use rules to prevent it from doing so. For example, if Richard and Jenny are interacting, Richard will be trying to construe how Jenny sees the situation, and Jenny will be trying to predict how Richard sees it. However, Richard could be mindful that Jenny could be planning to adapt her behavior mindful of how she thinks he will be viewing things, which may include a view of how he thinks she will be adjusting what she does based on how she thinks he will be adjusting his expectations, based on his assessment of how she adjusts her expectations of his behavior based on this, and vice versa, and so on, ad infinitum. We get a sense of this at road junctions where no right of way is marked. Opposing motorists commonly hesitate, and, eventually, after waiting for the other to make a move, they may both then get into a frustrating coordination game in which they simultaneously alternate between going and giving way. Road rules enable such games to be avoided, most of the time, as does other people's knowledge of how "as a rule" we tend to view other situations and behave in them (cf. Kelly, *ibid.*, pp. 93, 95).

4.8   Dealing with Cognitive Dissonance (2)

The Kelly-Lakatos analysis of how people use rule-based systems for forming and revising their views of the world can help us to understand further the processes by which cognitive dissonance is managed. In essence, a person's methodological decision to use a particular set of core constructs as the foundations for other constructs means that inconsistencies will be resolved by twisting the peripheral constructs, not those at the core of their system. Their core rules will make it impossible to accept some ways of construing the implications of incoming stimuli. If they say, "I can't believe this," what they mean is that their systems for forming beliefs will not allow them to do so (cf. the organization and modulation corollaries of Kelly's theory). If they do not exclude the stimuli in question, the only way they may be able to accommodate them is by twisting their more peripheral constructs. However, this may not be straightforward to achieve because of the complex webs in terms of which personal constructs tend to be connected. The result can be a very convoluted, even farcical, attempt to hold a set of views together. To an onlooker, it may look as though the person is refusing to admit the real reason for taking a particular stance or making a particular choice, which may indeed be the case. (The scenario of the Landcruiser-driving greenie was constructed mindful of this possibility.)

One way of removing cognitive dissonance in a particular area may indeed be to change some of one's core constructs. However, this could result in the person in question having to experience a period during which he or she does not know what to think in many areas. To get a sense of this, reflect first on the predicament of a woman who discovers, via a friend, something that could be taken as signifying that her husband is cheating on her. If she ceases to trust his marital fidelity, the question of whether she can still trust him in other areas may then arise, leading to major doubts about what she can take for granted about, say, the family's financial situation and hence what kind of life might be sustainable if she sought to patch up the relationship or seek a divorce. By contrast, a story that explains away the possibility of infidelity may have none of these complications, and it might even be true: perhaps, when spotted with another woman by one of her friends, he was indeed "just" having a business lunch despite reportedly having looked sheepishly at her friend when they spotted each other.

In short, some notions must be ruled out in order to allow others to be maintained but ruling out one idea may require us to change many other ideas that depend on it, leaving us with the need to construct alternatives for the latter. If we are going to have to abandon constructs that have previously served us well, we will be vulnerable in those areas until we have developed alternative rules for thinking. In evolutionary terms, our fitness will be enhanced if we have cognitive systems that cope with cognitive dissonance by twisting the construct whose revision has the fewest implications for the rest of our way of looking at the world. We will normally adjust only peripheral constructs, not those that lie at the core of our predictive systems. Where this is not enough (in conjunction with attempts at managing the flow of incoming stimuli) to keep our feeling of cognitive unease down to acceptable levels, we start considering which of our core constructs would be the least disruptive to bend or abandon.

4.8.1   Removing Cognitive Dissonance from Hindsight Evaluations

As well as operating at the stage of expectation formation, the mind's tendency to find ways of removing cognitive dissonance operates at the hindsight phase of a decision cycle. It is worth considering this here, for what the mind does when exercising hindsight often has implications for subsequent expectation-formation and choice. To decide that we still have a problem and/or that our past choice has produced a new problem may cause cognitive dissonance because of other things that we associate with the previous decision or with acknowledging the (continued) existence of a problem.

As we reflect on the outcome of a choice, we will find it difficult to conclude that we should have taken a different option if such an admission conflicts with our self-construct as the kind of person who is a competent decision-maker. There are several common cognitive strategies for arguing that the right choice was made or that letting an opportunity slip away was not a mistake. One is the essence of the Aesop fable that inspired Jon Elster's (1983) book *Sour Grapes*: we argue that an opportunity that seemed better at the time of our choice, but which we could not access, would, in the event, have turned out to be (even more) problematic. Another is to tell ourselves that the areas in which what we selected fell short of our expectations were ones that "didn't matter anyway" even though we had allowed them to influence our choice and we accept that in those respects we could have done better by choosing something else. A third strategy is to attach new emphasis to the aspects of our choice that did perform well. Finally, if we really cannot deny that things have not come out very well, we may try to downplay any notion that we made a bad choice by telling ourselves and/or others that the choice was made in an inherently problematic area that is rather like a lottery in which "You win some, you lose some." Such a way of shrugging off a bad outcome would not be a case of twisted cognition if it pertained to an experience good whose attributes we knew to be notoriously variable – unlike a situation in which the product was really a search good and we had not bothered to do our homework on it very thoroughly.

Such strategies may be hard to get away with where things keep going badly or where we have made a major mistake that other people keep highlighting. In such cases, if people cannot change the ways in which they construe themselves, all they can really do to remove the inconsistency between what happened and their self-construct is to stop their brain from ruminating over what might have been or forcibly try to stop others from interpreting what happened so negatively. Drowning one's sorrows with drink or drugs might serve the former end, while hostile, even violent behavior is a means to the latter. Clearly, it is not uncommon for people to employ both strategies when things go badly awry (see further the discussion of Kelly's view of hostility in Section 7.6).

Reluctance to accept that we have a problem may not merely be associated with the reputational damage that would arise if we admitted that a past choice was a failure. It may also come about because of what we start anticipating will be entailed if we address it. This could include the scope for embarrassment that we will be opening up if we have to move into unfamiliar territory in order to address the problem whose existence we are considering. For example, if we acknowledge that our relationship is a failure, we may be opening the door to the unfamiliar world of litigation and difficult financial circumstances. We can avoid the dread of dealing with this if we conclude that our present relationship is still salvageable. (See Section 5.8 for a discussion of the economics of dread.)

4.8.2   Cognitive Tipping Points

Removing cognitive dissonance by modifying our established viewpoint in an ad hoc way tends to entail a smaller cognitive load than adjusting to a radically different way of thinking. If further stimuli that challenge the same area are addressed by a different ad hoc adjustment, then this marginal change may likewise entail less rethinking than a radical change of view would entail. However, to the extent that each bout of cognitive dissonance does result in some consideration of alternative possibilities, the latter will benefit from the myelination process discussed in Section 4.4, which will increase the chances that ideas involving more radical changes of view will have of grabbing and maintaining attention. Moreover, ad hoc strategies for dealing with successive bouts of cognitive dissonance in the area in question will gradually produce a cognitively unwieldy basis for avoiding change.

If this process continues, the decision-maker may eventually arrive at a tipping point. On the one hand, the decision-maker "gets used to" the idea of thinking or behaving differently. This both promotes myelination of the underlying neural connections and leaves a bigger sense of how downside implications might be addressed. On the other hand, the increasingly cumbersome evolved version of the established way of looking at things may come to look very different from how it used to look and may become difficult to keep in mind in all its complexity. Indeed, its complexity may seriously impede the speed with which it can be fired up and transmitted despite parts of it benefiting from extensive myelination. Once the tipping point is reached, the probability of the new contender grabbing attention will start exceeding that of the old, with demyelination starting to impede the latter's chances of being first to come to mind.

By these processes, the mind can change itself and, in doing so, accept the need to make changes that it had previously resisted. But all this requires cognitive effort, occasioned by repeated exposure to stimuli that generate cognitive dissonance. That effort will be greater the more implications the mind has come to attach to a particular notion (see Sections 7.7 and 8.4 for further details) and the more frequently the neural circuits that underpin them have been activated. Unless a possibility has long been under consideration, the workings of the brain may require it to go through something akin to a farce before a new view can gain traction. The external manifestation of this sort of process is exemplified in Adam Smith's ([1795] 1980) analysis of the history of astronomy: after a long struggle to accommodate improved data in terms of an earth-centered view via increasingly convoluted ad hoc modifications, it eventually became simpler to jettison that view in favor of the Copernican view built around the proposition that the earth orbited the sun.

4.9   The Failure to Meet Aspirations

Problems are both personal constructs and sources of cognitive dissonance. They entail a clash between how the world seems to be and how we think it ought to be, given our way of looking at the world, a clash our operating rules require us to admit that we cannot argue out of the way or deny by censoring incoming stimuli. Rather, to restore cognitive consonance, we must do something. The problem may concern something that looks rather minor, but we acknowledge its existence because denial would imply a major challenge to our system for making sense of the world, since we cannot see a way of telling ourselves that there is no problem without changing one or more of our core rules. For example, if we pride ourselves as being well groomed and discover, after quite a struggle, that there was barely enough shampoo left to wash our hair, we may have trouble denying that we need to get a new bottle of shampoo unless we are prepared to let our standards of personal grooming fall; a new bottle of shampoo may not cost many dollars, but being without one is a big deal in terms of identity management. We might have said to ourselves, as we probably said a few days earlier, that there will probably be enough shampoo left for another shower; this time, however, we accept there probably will not be enough.

The empty shampoo bottle problem is a reminder that, although some problems become apparent without any forewarning, routine scanning of trends in performance data in the external environment may result in other problems being identified as "looming" long before they are deemed to have arrived. But whenever a problem is recognized, a discrete cognitive shift occurs. Sometimes, this is a binary shift on a particular dimension (or, in Kelly's terms, "on a particular construct axis") – for example, from profit to loss or from a functioning system to a system that is "down." However, in cases where performance is measured in scalar terms, the key issue will be where it stands, or is expected to stand, in relation to the target or "aspiration level" that we have in mind. If it falls short and is thereby deemed "not good enough," it is a problem. Where problem recognition is focused on future outcomes, such a target may have two dimensions, specifying both the hoped-for performance level and a target for its likelihood (assessed as, say, its probability) of eventuating. In the latter cases, we have a problem when it does not seem sufficiently likely that we are going to meet the target.

Defining problems in relation to aspiration levels is one of the heuristic strategic we use for dealing with the Duhem–Quine problem. It is central to Herbert Simon's (1947, 1956, 1957a, 1959) "satisficing" view of human problem-solving processes. This is a very different view of human behavior from the conventional economic perspective. In terms of the latter, as relative prices change or as other "shocks" occur, cognitively unconstrained economic agents ("econs," as Richard Thaler calls them) are constantly optimizing on all fronts by fine-tuning the allocation of resources they are using in production or consumption. In Simon's analysis, the presence of finite attentive capacity implies that real-world decision-makers cannot operate "on all fronts" simultaneously. Hence, they need rules for determining what requires their attention and what they can currently ignore. This is the role that aspiration levels play. If these rules present decision-makers with multiple problems, they bring into play further rules to prioritize the problems. They then attend to the problems sequentially, in order of priority. Newly perceived problems will be allowed to jump the queue insofar as they are assigned a higher priority than preexisting problems in the queue for attention.

Simon coined the word "satisficing" as a portmanteau term by combining "satisfy" and "suffice": when we are "satisficing," we are looking for courses of actions that are sufficient to satisfy us in terms of enabling us to meet our goals. In areas where we judge things are going OK, we carry on as we are unless we have discovered credible evidence that we could readily be doing better by behaving differently. In other words, Simon presents decision-makers as using target-based rules to determine whether something is viewed as performing acceptably or not.

On top of being means for sidestepping the infinite regress issue raised in Section 4.2, such rules are necessary where there is uncertainty about the maximum performance that may be expected. In such situations, they are necessarily tentative and open to revision. If performance keeps exceeding aspiration levels, decision-makers will start to aim higher on a regular basis once, in terms of their operating rules, they judge that they have "enough" evidence that their prospects are typically going to be better and that recent performances have not merely been due to luck. Conversely, if they keep failing to meet an aspiration and can see no prospect of finding a means to meet it, they will lower their sights.

Loasby (1976, ch. 6) emphasizes the role of external reference standards in the process of setting aspirations and hence in whether particular levels of performance are viewed as problematic. We may pick up our ideas of what we ought to be able to achieve, or should aim to achieve, via advice from members of our social networks and from observing their attainments. We can also use the attainments of those in related lines of activity as "benchmarks" and study the performance of our rivals – for example, firms in the UK have long been able to get a sense of where they stand relative to their competitors in return for supplying their performance data to the Centre for Interfirm Comparison. If those whom we use as reference points suddenly seem to be doing better, we may infer that we should be able to do so, too, and raise our aspiration levels even though our attainments had not been running ahead of our existing aspiration levels. On this view, being able to observe how others live – via their posts on social networking sites and from international television programs or travel – may be very significant for determining whether people will judge they have a problem of underachievement and need to start searching for ways to do better. No wonder, then, that, prior to the collapse of communism, Soviet Bloc governments limited their citizens' opportunities for visiting capitalist economies and tried to jam incoming television signals.

The aspiration levels that we use to determine whether we have a problem and a consequent need to search for something better may be double-sided, defining an acceptable zone within which we are trying to keep ourselves. In such cases, our problem recognition processes are rather akin to those of a thermostat that is designed to keep the temperature of a room from becoming "too hot" or "too cold." Sometimes, we may be what marketers call "aspirational" in that we operate with both short-term and long-term aspiration levels: if we aspire, say, to be the driver of a new BMW 5-series, today's problem may be that this seems unlikely to be possible if we stay on our current career track, rather than the fact that our current vehicle is merely the closest we can currently get, say, a used BMW 3-series. In the short term, the latter car may seem perfectly satisfactory and may signal where we intend to be going, but we would be dissatisfied if we were still driving such a car in the long term.

Not all the reference points used in judging whether there is a problem for which a solution needs to be found take the form of aspiration levels. Because of the way our sensory systems operate, sometimes the trigger works via the detection of stimuli that are simply different from – in other words, dissonant with – the norm, either in particular ways or as a pattern. If we have made "what has been normal" our preferred situation, we may judge that the arrival of, say, refugee migrants to live in our street poses a threat, even though we may know very little about them. But if we have so far built our lives around being different, we may judge that we have a problem, at least in terms of identity, if we start doing "normal" things such as having a mortgage and commuting to work wearing a business suit – choices that we ended up making in order to solve other problems.

Very simple procedures may be used to determine how well an object or person has been performing. For example, consider the modus operandi of the Deputy Vice Chancellor (Academic) of a large modern-day university that prides itself in achieving high levels of "student engagement." To identify areas of teaching that are problematic in relation to this goal, her operating principles may be that (a) academic staff are required to have their courses and teaching evaluated by students voluntarily and anonymously completing questionnaires prior to the release of final grades, and (b) academics and/or courses are deemed problematic if their respective overall evaluation scores are less than 3.5 on a 0–5 scale. If most staff become able to meet this standard, she may raise the minimum acceptable evaluation score to, say, 3.75 on this scale.

For anyone with some training in research methods and experience in working at the academic coalface, this will seem a very questionable way of operating. For one thing, there is the possibility of relatively small and highly biased samples. It also fails to capture the possibility that some academics are earning high scores by setting simple, easy-to-grade assignments based on multiple-choice questions that students can complete without much work. Meanwhile, other academic staff could be being punished by lazy students because of setting research-based "authentic assignments," that also require some serious thinking, to ensure that the university lived up to its claims that its graduates will be "work-ready."

This senior administrator's seemingly mindless policy does, however, have the virtue that it enables her to monitor what is going on in hundreds of courses across her large domain. It would be impossible for her to sample lecture recording from all these courses, check on the quality of material provided on course websites and examine closely all the course outlines, assessment methods and the distributions of results achieved by the students. If such in-depth analysis were delegated to heads of departments and the latter were issued "please explain" requests when performance standards were not met, then possibly her operating principles might not be a dysfunctional way of trying to find out where performance needed to be improved. However, if all that happens is that she tells departmental heads that particular staff and courses are on her "watch list" and the heads then merely warn the staff in question that this is the case and that they need to do something about their ratings, then the simple principle may prove to be far from procedurally rational as a means of identifying problems.

Where a performance standard is specified, as in the aforementioned example, in terms of an "overall" measure, it is consistent with the traditional economist's focus on substitution: a particular overall score might be arrived at from very different mixes of performances. But "overall" measures of performance in diverse areas may be (viewed as) problematic to aggregate into a global "overall" evaluation. If so, a "tick the boxes" approach to problem recognition may be used. For example, it may be viewed as problematic to grant a permanent position to a probationary academic whose teaching performance is well in excess of the required rating in that area but who has failed to perform adequately in terms of research output. In the latter area, checklists might be used too: does the person "tick the boxes" in terms of publishing in journals with high enough ratings, raising enough research funds, and so on?

Using a nonadditive template to determine whether a problem exists may seem very arbitrary because it entails a specific set of requirements and ignores potential trade-offs. However, as when choosing between potential solutions to problems (see Section 8.3), such templates or checklists greatly simplify the process of defining problems. Moreover, within organizations, they permit consistent, equitable treatment of personnel whose "overall" performance cannot readily be reduced to a monetary figure that indicates their prospective value to the organization.

These processes for defining problems and initiating search are all based upon rules of one kind or another. They may be very effective at preventing disasters in the short term but not be well suited for avoiding long-term difficulties. Insofar as our sense of what is OK adjusts in line with changes in the mean levels of incoming signals, we may fail to notice that the mean has changed. If so, we may be said to be "habituating" to the new norm. This may result in us tolerating things that we would have refused to accept were we approaching the situation for the first time. For example, we may get used to increasingly high rates of unemployment as the crossing of previous politically sensitive thresholds fades into distant memory (see Mosley, 1984). Likewise, we may get used to growing surveillance and censorship rather than taking to the streets to protest or changing our political allegiances. On the other hand, however, becoming accustomed to levels of attainment way in excess of those enjoyed by most people may result in us behaving like unreasonable prima donnas or plunging into despair if our attainments suddenly fall to levels of which most people can only dream.

Given the potential for habituation to have dysfunctional consequences, there will be evolutionary advantages for societies that consist of individuals who are attuned to diverse norms but who are not isolated from each other. By observing how others live and by getting a sense of how they see the world, it is possible to get a better sense of whether and where one really should be recognizing problems and setting out to find solutions. Within organizations, survival may be a function of the mix of standards and aspirations that members set for themselves and expect others to adopt. Those who think in terms of unusually demanding norms (for example, in respect of quality) will be prone to see problems that others do not: the supersensitive types might turn out to be needlessly concerned, but at least they may trigger debates that sometimes turn out to be vital for the continued existence of the organization of which they are part. However, debate has its costs. A largely docile workforce with a leadership that suppresses any dissent will be able to get on with operating in a particular way without consuming resources in debates and inquiries about alternative ways of operating (see Simon, 2005). This might be all well and good for an organization in its current environment, enabling it to outcompete rival groups. However, if the external environment subsequently changed, such an organization might then be very poorly suited to recognizing it has a problem or for finding effective solutions.

4.10   Judgmental Heuristics and Biases

The rules that we use in constructing evaluations and expectations can vary greatly in their effectiveness. Ideally, we would like to have nothing but the kinds of "fast and frugal" decision rules emphasized by Gigerenzer et al. (1999), such as the rules that triage nurses are trained to use. Alas, many of the heuristics that people use in forming judgments and evaluations are dysfunctional and twist the processing of information and forming expectation in ways contrary to the interests of those who use them. The dysfunctional heuristics whose use is easiest to predict are among those that appear to be part of human nature, or that are picked up via processes of acculturation, rather than those that individuals have created for themselves. The good news is that although our inherited rules can have shortcomings, we may be able to override them if we know what they are and have appropriate techniques at our disposal via, say, self-help books such as the one offered by Belsky and Gilovich (1999).

Given that our evaluations draw upon our memories, anything that inherently limits how we remember things can impact upon them. In an Australian television interview (*ABC Lateline*, June 11, 2012), Kahneman emphasized that the mind does not remember entire streams of experience but instead stores impressions based on the most intense level of sensation and the level of sensation at the end of the event. Kahneman's interviewer, Emma Alberici, suggested to him that this would be significant for mothers contemplating having a second child: they will be basing their assessments of the pain they might experience during childbirth on highly edited versions of their first experiences in labor. But this editing process may apply in other, very different contexts: for example, a piece of music that was mostly rather pedestrian might thereby be remembered as having been more engaging, especially if its peak of excitement occurred near the end and there was some kind of climax at the end.

Taken in conjunction with Hayek's view of the mind, Kahneman's point on how memories are formed could help to explain how people who initially were not afraid of flying could develop flight phobia after a flight involving an episode of significant turbulence and a bumpy landing. This may only be a small part of their total flying experience and yet it will loom large when they next consider possibilities that involve flying. Worse still, the more they recall their "bad" flight, the more likely they will be to recall it in future rather than ask themselves whether it is representative of their flight experiences. In the context of buying a car, Kahneman's point implies that we would be wise to confine our test-driving activities to mundane, everyday driving rather than seeing what each vehicle can do if pushed toward its limits: the most exciting part of each test drive will have a disproportionately large weight in our memory, yet a car that is exhilarating to drive fast may perform far less well in typical driving conditions.

But first impressions are also prone to be overweighted during evaluations, as acknowledged in the notion of "anchoring bias." If a house is up for sale with an untidy front yard, prospective buyers will find this looming disproportionately in their minds as something they would need to fix. Worse still, they may take it as signaling more general neglect by its vendor, and, to cap it all, the untidy front yard will also be the last thing that prospective buyers see at the end of a viewing. It is the anchoring process that makes us susceptible to prices whose first digits have been reduced at negligible cost to the supplier: we do not see $9.99 as the same as $10.00 or $29,995 as $30,000 despite the differences being of negligible practical significance. The first digit is what sticks in our mind. As behavioral economists, we know this but still we have to consciously overrule what our minds are programmed to do. Note, however, that from an evolutionary standpoint, anchoring could be fitness-enhancing: given that our attention may get diverted before we can get far into an evaluation, being programmed to take in a first impression means we at least have a chance of remembering something.

Since the use of an existing reference point is necessary when sizing up a new object or event, our evaluations will depend on what that reference point is. For example, consider how behavioral economists with different backgrounds are likely to see the impact of heuristics on the quality of choice. Richard Thaler uses the reference point of the ideal world of conventional economics as his anchor, so he will tend to see heuristics in a negative way; by contrast, after decades of viewing economics from a Simon-inspired standpoint, I will tend to take a much more positive view, like that of Gigerenzer. A pluralistic approach, with multiple reference points, guards against making dysfunctional generalizations, but it is not what we are cognitively predis-posed to use: we are programmed to want to find "the" way to see things; dualistic ("black and white") thinking is cognitively much less demanding than a pluralistic approach that is more conducive to creative and critical thinking. The reference points that we use can also affect our evaluations as a result of our sensory systems working in a stepwise manner rather than registering differences along continuous scales: a difference in the performance of rival products that expert testers can measure may not be big enough to be noticeable to most potential buyers.

If we are presented with several potential reference points, the assessment we make of a given object is prone to change from what it would have been with a single point of comparison. Ariely (2008) discusses this, using examples involving buying a house, a television and deciding which potential mate to approach at a nightclub. A particular house or television might seem expensive in relation to a particular alternative but then suddenly seem to offer really good value for money if compared with something else that offers a bit more for quite a lot more money. Similarly, a moderately attractive person's chances of attracting interest in a nightclub may be enhanced if he or she brings along a friend who is very plain and who will "make them look better" by lowering the average level of attractiveness in their immediate vicinity. In short, we are susceptible to having our evaluations affected by the presence of decoys.

Thaler (2015) emphasizes how his research confirmed his early suspicions that human judgments are often affected by "supposedly irrelevant factors" (SIFs), i.e., things that people would not factor into their decisions if they were thinking like "econs." What he had in mind were not things such as using a person's astrological sign to evaluate their suitability for a job. Rather, he was interested in the impact that factors such as sunk costs and differences between recommended retail prices and actual asking prices have on decisions. We will be exploring these factors in some detail later in this book (see particularly Sections 7.8 and 8.9). However, Ariely (2008, ch. 2) reports an anchoring phenomenon that initially seems a bizarre SIF of a different kind. With Drazen Prelec and George Lowenstein, Ariely conducted an experiment in which they asked MBA students to write down bids for bottles of wine after writing down the last two digits of their social security number and saying whether they would be prepared to pay that number of dollars for the bottle in question. It turned out that the bids and social security numbers were correlated. This finding seems much less bizarre from the standpoint of Hayek's *Sensory Order*, for when asked, in effect, to pluck numbers out of thin air, the mind needs some point of reference, and, as far as numbers go, the social security digits constitute its most recently activated pattern in the context of this experiment.

4.11   Thinking Fast and Slow

In his 2011 book *Thinking, Fast and Slow*, Nobel Laureate Daniel Kahneman provides a detailed account of the research by which he and Amos Tversky identified many of the heuristics and biases that have become core to modern behavioral economics. But he also presents a dual-system view of the workings of the human mind. He argues that, if left unchecked, the mind will use simple heuristics and its associative memory to make judgments swiftly. Kahneman calls this System 1. Underpinning many of the heuristics that System 1 uses is a phenomenon that Kahneman refers to (rather confusingly for economists) as "attribute substitution" or "substitution bias" whereby the mind is prone to deal with conceptually challenging, abstract questions by treating them as if they are different and possibly rather tenuously related questions that they can more readily resolve using simple heuristics (*ibid.*, ch. 9; for a critical examination of Kahneman's thinking in this area, in relation to the wider literature on attributional inference and consistent with the analysis of expectation formation offered here, see Koutsobinas, 2021).

For example, in the UK's so-called Brexit referendum, some voters may have addressed the question of whether they thought the UK should leave the European Union simply by asking themselves how they felt about immigration into the UK. They would thus have largely ignoring economic issues, as well as the fact that by no means all immigrants arriving in the UK are citizens from other EU member nations.

System 1 can be reined in by a slower, more deliberative analytical system that avoids jumping to conclusions and processes information more thoroughly. Kahneman calls this

System 2. Ideally, this dual-system mode of thinking would ensure that decisions are not held up unnecessarily due to unwarranted attention to detail and concerns about ambiguities. However, he argues that System 2 operates in a lazy manner. It is rather like a poorly motivated boss who only occasionally checks what his or her subordinates are doing. We need our System 2 to allow System 1 free rein *some* of the time because there is not enough time to deliberate about everything, but System 2 tends to leave too much to System 1. We thus underutilize our System 2 capacity, wasting time that we might have used profitably to think more before selecting some of our actions.

This can result in poor judgments, as when students quickly interpret examination questions as those for which they have prepared rather than looking at the wording carefully and thereby noticing that something more challenging is entailed. If our System 2 operates in a very slack manner, we may go through life as if driving while asleep at the wheel, rarely reflecting critically on how things are and on judgments and choices that we and others make. Although, as we have seen, the allocation of attention cannot be optimized and *has* to be rule-based, many of us probably need to be more "mindful" (cf. Langer, 1991) about how we allocate our attention. Some things, such as climate change, warrant serious attention but in matters relating to them System 2 often allows System 1 to shape what we do, using rules that worked in the past.

Many economists who read Kahneman's book probably end up thinking that "fast" thinking is the focus of behavioral economics and invariably causes departures from "rational" choices, whereas when people take the trouble to think slowly and reason properly, then they will behave like the "econs" in standard economic models. This is not the message to take from the book, at least not as a general conclusion. To be sure, better choices might come from greater reflection if it results in us deciding to seek advice from those with more experience or expertise than ourselves, or if it results more generally in us asking ourselves whether there might be other ways of looking at our options. Such reflection might also serve to dent our tendencies toward overconfidence – but only if we are prepared to allow this to happen and possibly at the cost of us failing to plunge into ventures that would have greatly enhanced our well-being. However, trying hard to form a clear picture of the potential consequences of making one choice rather than another may simply overwhelm us and leave us "failing to see the wood for the trees" if we lack effective rules for handling information and judging what is important. While we are struggling to figure out "the truth" about our options, opportunities may slip away, either in the context in question or in other parts of our lives to which we have been unable to give attention. Moreover, if we are statistically incompetent and hopeless at calculating compound probabilities when we think fast, we will probably be just as challenged in these respects if we try to slow down and think more carefully about the likely properties of our options.

4.12   Conclusion

When the mind sets about evaluating options and forming expectations about the consequences of making particular choices, it does so based on its systems of associative rules that it has developed via past experience. The process may take place unconsciously or it may entail conscious thought. The depth of analysis that we undertake may vary considerably depending on the context. But regardless of how deep our analysis goes, it is "rules all the way down," including rules that determine how deep we go in undertaking our analysis. This process entails making new connections and can change the probabilities of existing sets of connections being used to evaluate incoming stimuli in future, so the process of making up our minds can also be a process by which we change how we see the world.

As far as possible, I have attempted to keep this chapter focused on what we might call the "positive" aspect of cognition, rather than its "normative" role, for the latter is the focus of Chapter 7. In saying this, I am using the two adjectives in the way that they are used in economic methodology but applying them to everyday decision-making: "positive" refers to building models to make predictions (for example, "If I buy object *X*, I think it will have the following properties or consequences. . ."), whereas "normative" refers to making value judgments about the appropriateness of particular kinds of behavior (for example, "I think it would be a seriously bad move to buy product *X* given what I know about it"). However, keeping the two aspects of cognition separate is problematic, especially when we start considering the processes by which our brains manage cognitive dissonance. When cognitive dissonance is present, we have a clash between what we initially see incoming stimuli as implying, and what we expected to see. The latter is in one sense a prediction, but in another sense it represents our assessment of what we think we *should* see. In a sense, then, our expectations are value laden and that is why they are less likely than the initial interpretation of incoming stimuli to be revised to remove the dissonance. The chances that we will end up seeing what we think we should see are compounded to the extent that the stimuli to which we expose ourselves are filtered because we are looking purposively in areas where we think we should be able to find what we "are looking for."

The personally constructed nature of our experiences and expectations means that although the cognitive processes considered in this chapter yield assessments that are means toward the end of being able to make a choice, they require us to make choices about what to believe and expect. This opens a disconcerting possibility raised by sociologist Harold Garfinkel (1967, pp. 113–114), which we will need eventually to address: our assessments of the potential consequences of choosing one thing rather than another may be shaped to justify choices that have *already* be made by other means, without us realizing that this has happened. The "real reasons" for our choices may be quite different from the surface-level reasons that we give to those who ask us why we chose as we did, even if we are not consciously trying to be deceptive. The "real reasons" may be so deep-seated in our systems for making sense of the world that we are not able to articulate them.

5 How Do We Deal with Uncertainty and Ambiguity?

5.1 Introduction

Decision-makers often experience uncertainty as a result of realizing that the information they have is insufficient to leave them with an unambiguous picture of the problems that they face, or are going to face, if they make no changes, or of the capacities of particular alternatives to serve as means to the ends they are trying to pursue. Despite investing time in search activities, they may still lack information that they would like to have in order to confirm whether they really have a particular kind of problem, and they cannot know the future ahead of its eventuation. They may have been too short of time to undertake comprehensive appraisals of search goods or have doubts because the products in question are experience goods, credence goods, or potentially soon going to be replaced by something better. Sometimes the problem is not one of access to information about what to expect from the available options or from those that could shortly become available; rather, the problem may be a lack of information about the context of use, such as the weather, one's future personal circumstances and tastes, or the tastes and behavior of others.

However, uncertainty should not be seen merely as arising due to information being costly to obtain or intrinsically unavailable. Sometimes it arises due to us having *more* information than we have the cognitive capacity to process: ignorance may be bliss if one suffers from bounded rationality and cannot compute the implications of a mass of conflicting possibilities. We also commonly experience uncertainty because we are aware of gaps in our knowledge or the limits of our imaginative capacities. For example, we may feel uncertain despite having information because we know that we do not know what the information signifies, or we may have a nagging feeling that we have failed to consider, or ask for, information about relevant issues but have no idea what these issues might be. Tacit knowledge can also give rise to uncertainty: we may be left unclear about what to do due to being unable to articulate the nature of our problems or our needs to those who may have been able to provide us with relevant information. The information that could have made things clear may be "out there," but Google may not present it to us unless we frame our question in a particular way.

In these kinds of situations, the constructs that we form regarding problems and prospective solutions will be rather fuzzy. The construct axes that we use can still be either dichotomous or scalar: for example, a woman may not be sure whether or not she will be offered a job for which she has just been interviewed, and she may be uncertain about which point on the salary scale she will be offered if she does get an offer, what her chances are of bargaining successfully for a better deal, or how well she would cope with the job if she ended up receiving an offer and accepted it. However, where we are not sure what we are looking at, we consider the construct axes in question in conjunction with an axis that represents the extent of our uncertainty.

In this chapter we consider how people frame their expectations when they know that they do not know for sure how to construe particular events. The analysis focuses on the constructs that people use to characterize the extent of their knowledge or beliefs in the area in question, and the processes by which they end up assigning ratings that they can factor into their choices (if indeed they are able to do so), or how they otherwise may try to cope despite knowing that they know less than they would like to have known prior to choosing. Toward the end of the chapter, we consider some of the common dysfunctional aspects of these processes and the effects on behavior of feelings of dread about undesired things that could happen as a result of making particular commitments.

5.2   Probable or Possible?

People use a variety of constructs to represent the extent of their uncertainty. For example, economists and psychologists mostly think in terms of probability scales that range from zero to one, in either fractional or percentage terms, because they have been trained to think that way. By contrast, lay decision-makers often seem to distinguish between things that are "probable" versus those that they see as merely "possible," or between events that are "likely" versus those that seem "unlikely." In principle, we might conduct behavioral research using tools such as Repertory Grid Technique (RGT) to discover (a) the ways in which people characterize uncertainty in the situations we are studying and (b) the relative popularity of rival ways that are in use in the population in question. If we did this, the constructs that we initially elicited might include ones that are shorthand proxies for more complex ways of thinking about uncertainty. For example, some of our research subjects might view different brands of cars in terms of the axis "reliable *versus* prone to breaking down," whereas what we may really want to know is what they mean by "reliable" or "prone to breaking down" and hence how they draw the line between the two categories. "Reliable" might mean "never lets you down," but it might instead be a less demanding standard such as "not being expected to let one down more than a couple of times over five years of ownership" or take a statistical form such as "having no more than a one-in-a-thousand risk of breaking down on any day it is being used." To find out what they meant, we would need to probe more deeply.

Rather than undertaking such inquiries, and in the hope of keeping their analysis manageable, most economists, behavioral or otherwise, habitually theorize as if people characterize uncertainty via probability scales that range from zero probability to 100 percent probability. On this view, with a dichotomous construct axis, we might assess an option as having, say, a 70 percent chance of coming out one way and a 30 percent chance of coming out another way. The presumption with the probabilistic view is that, for the axis in question, the set of probabilities that we assign adds up to 100 if we assign each probability as a percentage. Where the axis in question has a scale of potential outcomes, our mental model will often look something like a bell curve, with outcomes near the ends of the scale rated as having zero probabilities of eventuating. However, in some cases, we may envisage heavily skewed or bimodal sets of outcome probabilities. A set of probabilities can incorporate a "residual hypothesis" if we are unsure whether we have considered all the things that might occur. Thus, for example, we might think that, if we choose a particular strategy, it has a 60 percent chance of coming out one specific way, a 30 percent chance of coming out in another specific way, and a 10 percent chance of coming out in a way that we have not anticipated at all. The residual hypothesis means we are open to surprise, such as might occur when we think we have a good chance of getting a particular job but where failure to get it is not the end of the story since, instead, we unexpectedly are offered an internship or a different job within the organization in question. The probability that we assign to the residual hypothesis in a particular context is an indication of the extent to which we acknowledge limits to our knowledge of what could happen there, and the limits to our imagination.

An alternative to the probabilistic approach is the "potential surprise" framework proposed by George Shackle (1949, 1961; see also Earl and Littleboy, 2014). Shackle questioned the wisdom of using probability scores as foundations for decisions other than those about offering differently priced insurance quotations to members of a population of customers, according to the statistical likelihoods that they will experience particular events. Clearly, insurance actuaries can, and do, price insurance policies based on population-level probabilities for customers with different risk profiles. However, at the level of the individual, particular events either occur or they do not. Given this, Shackle suggested that people could form expectations in a nonprobabilistic way by considering how surprised they would be if a particular choice resulted in them experiencing a particular outcome. If an outcome seems perfectly possible, we would not be at all surprised if it took place, whereas if we view an outcome as impossible, we expect to be astonished if it eventuated.

Graphical representations of assessments formed in this way normally look superficially like inverted bell-curve probability distributions, but they are conceptually very different. Clearly, viewing an outcome as impossible is like assigning it a zero probability, but viewing an outcome as perfectly possible is not the same as assigning it a probability of 100 percent, for other outcomes might also be viewed as perfectly or partially possible. Moreover, Shackle's framework is not additive: if we change our view of how surprised we would be if a particular outcome occurred (i.e., if we change our assessment of its possibility), we will only change our assessments for alternative possible outcomes if what we saw as implying a need for us to change our mind for the outcome in question seems also to have implications for how seriously we view any of the alternative outcomes that we have imagined.

Although Shackle's view of how we take account of uncertainty in our mental models is very different from that of an "objective probability" approach based on statistical frequencies, it may be fruitful to try to see how far we can go in creating a synthesis of Shackle's perspective and a subjective probability approach. In the latter, probabilities are not viewed in terms of statistical frequencies of the kinds that insurance actuaries have at their disposal. An attempt to construct such a synthesis seems worthwhile, since, in ordinary parlance, it is commonly said that a particular situation seems "possible, though not probable." Utterances of this kind may often signal that people engage in cognitive simplification by thinking in dichotomous terms rather than in a scalar way. However, sometimes people will be thinking about uncertainty in scalar terms and would not have trouble replying if we were to ask them to rate rival outcomes on a 0–10 "possibility/probability" scale of likelihood. What might they have in mind when they offer their ratings?

In considering this puzzle, it is instructive to recognize that Shackle's approach and the probabilistic/statistical approaches differ in how they see causality. Shackle saw potential surprise ratings as reflecting the extent to which the decision-maker can envisage potential *barriers* to an outcome (for example, our chances of getting a particular job may seem limited because we expect we would score poorly on some of the selection criteria). By contrast, those who think in terms of a probabilistic analysis appear to think of probabilities as shaped by the presence of particular *drivers* (for example, the risk of lung cancer being driven by how much one smokes, whether one lives in an environment where the air is polluted, and so on). It is surely misguided to focus just on either "barriers" or "drivers." Clearly, a "barrier" to something happening may be the absence of a "driver" to kick-start a causal process and maintain its momentum if it runs into obstacles.

Shackle's focus on barriers rather than drivers of outcomes may reflect the fact that his analysis was the product of thinking about active decision-making (such as entrepreneurs considering embarking upon particular creative business ventures) rather than about the possible consequences of acting passively in a particular environment (such as sunbathing on a beach). In the former case, it is the decision-maker who tries to drive the outcome (for example, with respect to a profit/loss construct) by making a particular choice, whereas, in the latter case, what happens will be driven by the external environment (for example, a person on the beach ends up sunburnt or gets stranded as the tide comes in). However, as both Hawtrey (1926) and Kelly (1955) recognized, much of everyday life entails active decision-making aimed at controlling events rather than just letting things happen to us. Certainly, there are times when we operate rather like entrepreneurs in trying to be creative and/or seize opportunities to take our lives in new directions (cf. Bianchi, 1998), but often our actions entail trying to erect barriers against external driving forces – as when we apply sunscreen before relaxing at the beach. Firms, likewise, try to control outcomes by erecting barriers of various kinds against things that their rivals, governments and consumers may do that would limit the returns to their investments. But Shackle largely left it to others to explore risk-taking by consumers and uncertainty associated with operating defensively, and he merely focused his thinking on uncertainty in relation to entrepreneurs making bold investment choices.

Despite the effects that this seems to have had on how he wrote about causality, what Shackle did end up saying about how causal barriers relate to uncertainty and expectation formation is of great importance here. When he revisited his 1949 analysis in his 1961 book *Decision, Order and Time*, he noted that we may reduce our disbelief in a particular prospect if, having recognized some potential barriers to its eventuation, we then imagine second-tier barriers to the potential power of the first set of barriers. For example, at the beach, the sunscreen that we apply to reduce our chances of skin damage may fail to do its job because it lacks water resistance and gets washed away when we perspire or swim. The significance we attach to the potential second-tier barriers to the first-tier barriers will depend, in turn, on the barriers that the second-tier barriers would have to overcome in order to eventuate. If the second-tier barrier prevailed, rather than being blocked by something else, there might be nothing to stop the outcome from eventuating. In the case of avoiding getting sunburnt at the beach, perhaps we can do so even without water-resistant sunscreen if we remember to keep applying the sunscreen that we have with us – but this is possibly a big "if" if we get engrossed in the flow of having fun. Thinking about the determination of outcomes in this way clearly entails another example of the infinite regress problem. In this case, the complexity of the many layers and limits to our imagination constrain how far we can go in considering potential opposing forces, leaving us with an uncertain, foggy view of what is going to happen if we made one choice rather than another.

Expectation formation is further complicated by the possibility that a particular outcome might conceivably be reached in a variety of ways via different combinations of drivers and barriers, with different drivers being needed depending on which barriers eventuate. Hence, where the presence and significance of an imagined barrier are uncertain, an imagined outcome may need to have a powerful and wide-ranging set of potential drivers if it is to seem likely to occur.

Given all this, it might be reasonable, by way of a synthesis, to interpret ratings on a 0–10 likelihood scale as follows:

10 = "I'm sure this is going to happen; I can't see anything that could stop it or anything else that looks at all possible."

6–9 = "It's probable; I'd be more surprised if it didn't happen than if it did, as it has a lot more going for it than it has potentially standing in its way."

5 = "I wouldn't be surprised either way, if it did or didn't happen; I can see just as much reason for believing it won't happen as I can for believing it will."

1–4 = "It's possible, but I'd be more surprised if it happened than if it didn't, since I can see a lot that could stop it from happening and not much to drive it."

0 = "I think it is impossible, and I'd be astonished if it did happen; I'm sure it won't happen, as there's too much stacked against it."

The midpoint rating (5) entails a view akin to what we might have when watching a tug of war between teams that seem equally matched: something will eventually tip the balance one way or another, but we do not have enough knowledge to anticipate which factors might be decisive. However, recognition of the incompleteness of our mental models would also underlie ratings of 6–9 and 1–4.

This interpretation of what people might mean if they were to rate rival potential outcomes on a 0–10 "possibility/probability" scale does not seem to require that the set of total scores for the outcomes they were considering sums to ten except in the case where they assigned one outcome a score of ten, implying that they viewed all other outcomes as impossible. However, neither does it preclude respondents from trying to ensure that their scores for rival outcomes do add up to ten. Some people might be working on the basis that they should think this way and hence take the view that among the barriers they should consider to the eventuation of a particular outcome are the things that they see as potential drivers of other outcomes that seem to some degree possible. Such a view would imply, as per the traditional additive probabilistic way of thinking, that the chances of rival outcomes happening are interdependent.

Clearly, however, there is one serious problem with such an attempt to bring probabilistic and Shacklean perspectives together in a way that does justice to how people speak about uncertainty in everyday life: it seems unable to accommodate the idea that something – or multiple rival possibilities – might seem "perfectly possible" due to having no perceived potential barriers to eventuation. Some people may indeed say that they envisage one or more outcomes as "perfectly possible" in a particular situation, just as Shackle expected, while viewing other outcomes as "less likely." If so, and if they were really thinking about uncertainty in a similar way to Shackle, they ought to resist any attempt we make to get them to rate outcomes using the scale proposed in this section. If they did resist such a request, they ought to be amenable to being asked instead to rate each outcome on a 0–10 scale pertaining to how surprised they think they would be if particular outcomes eventuated. But if they rated more than one outcome as "perfectly possible," it would be instructive also to ask them to tell us under what circumstances they imagine each of those outcomes might eventuate rather than the other(s). If they answered in terms of outcome-specific sets of drivers or barriers that might inhibit one outcome but not the other, this would imply they were not thinking along the lines that Shackle would have expected. Reference to outcome-specific drivers implies that, even though the outcomes are rivals, their prospects are interdependent: something that facilitates outcome A without facilitating outcome B is a potential barrier to the eventuation of B, so they should not be viewing B as perfectly possible.

Where people say they see several rival outcomes as perfectly possible and would not be surprised if any one of them occurred, they may really be implying that, as far as they can see, there is no clear reason why any of these outcomes ought to be ruled out of contention, even though they may be able to imagine factors that might turn out to be decisive for shaping what happens. They may have imagined what these decisive factors might be, but they are unable to predict with confidence what will be decisive. If so, this is different from Shackle's conceptualization of a perfect possibility as something with nothing seemingly standing in its way. It would be a way of thinking more in line with Simon's satisficing perspective. For example, in thinking about the likelihood that a particular person may get a particular job, we might note that this person is one of several candidates who meet all the selection criteria and hence that the members of the selection committee would have to use some kind of tiebreaker procedure to make their choice. We may be able to imagine several different tie-breaking procedures that they might use but be unable to assess any of them as more likely to be used than the others. If so, despite envisaging procedures that could work against particular candidates, we may end up not expecting to be surprised by any outcome and seeing all as having the same chance of success.

Regardless of how we conceptualize uncertainty, we may find it cognitively too demanding to keep a detailed range of possibilities in mind even for a single aspect of one option, let alone multiple ranges of possibilities associated with many options with uncertain performances in multiple dimensions. How will our minds have evolved to deal with this issue?

One strategy that comes naturally to us is to use judgmental rules to collapse ranges of uncertainty into simple dichotomous summary constructs such as "high risk *versus* low risk" or "probably OK *versus* might not be good enough." In some contexts, it may seem safe to ignore things that are statistically very rare and treat as certain the imagined outcomes that have high probabilities or against which we can envisage few credible barriers. Note here how terrorism works in developed economies via engin-eering small changes in the probabilities of events that people would otherwise have ignored, such as getting killed while commuting on public transport or walking on city pavements. Activities that people previously viewed as "safe" are seemingly taken out of that category despite their statistical odds of being unsafe remaining very low.

Shackle's extensive introspections on investment decisions led him to propose a different view of what the human mind does to reduce cognitive complexity. In essence, he concluded that, for each strategy under consideration, entrepreneurs will end up focusing on just two imagined outcomes: the profit outcome that most excites them based on both its size and plausibility (which he called the scheme's "focus gain"), and the loss that most scares them on the basis of both its size and plausibility (the scheme's "focus loss"). He envisaged entrepreneurs as viewing gains and losses of rival strategies relative to what might be obtained via a strategy that minimized risk, such as keeping the funds on deposit. He called this reference point the "neutral outcome." (We might also see it as the aspiration level for the dimension in question in cases where the decision-maker is not sure if some or all of the available options would perform satisfactorily in that area.)

Shackle analyzed the focusing process with a formal "as if" model that was in the style of cutting-edge economic theory in the 1940s. It is rather incongruous for our present analysis, since it involves a continuous "ascendancy function" and presumes that the potential surprise curve of a project's imagined rival possible outcomes is continuous. Figure 5.1 presents an adaptation of Shackle's view of the focusing process, framed in terms of an entrepreneur's view of possible outcomes in terms of their likelihoods, rather than via Shackle's potential surprise notion. The dashed line that runs from A to D represents the entrepreneur's conjectures about the set of possible outcomes that a particular scheme has, with neither a loss greater than A nor a gain greater than D being viewed as possible.

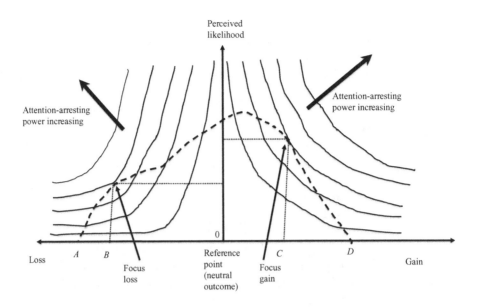

Figure 5.1 Focus outcomes for a scheme of action

The solid curves to the right and left of the vertical axis line at the reference point are what Shackle calls "iso-ascendancy curves." Each point on such a curve has a similar attention-arresting power as any other point on that curve, with iso-ascendancy curves signifying greater attention-arresting power as we move further toward the top right and top left of Figure 5.1. Outcomes that seem highly likely but only slightly different from the neutral outcome will not be of great interest to the entrepreneur, and neither will very large gains or losses that seem highly unlikely. What will excite and be alluring are large gains that seem to have little standing in their way, and what will make the entrepreneur highly fearful are large losses that have little that seems to have potential to prevent them from happening. Shackle's hypothesis is that, for any scheme under consideration, there will typically be just one gain and one loss that have the biggest capacity to attract the entrepreneur's attention, and all the other outcomes that have been deemed possible for each scheme end up getting ignored. The focus gain, C, is the imagined gain outcome that is the most alluring, since it is the value for which the dashed line of conjectures is tangential to the highest achievable iso-ascendancy curve on the gain side of the ascendancy function, while the focus loss, B, is the imagined loss outcome that makes the entrepreneur most fearful, since its likelihood results in it being the outcome whose value on the dashed line of conjectures is tangential to the highest achievable iso-ascendancy curve on the loss or fear side.

Shackle's theory of focusing has a very significant implication: the focusing process will result in us ignoring the extreme outcomes that we had not ruled out as possibilities. In other words, his theory implies a different kind of "inattention blindness" from that considered near the end of Section 4.3 via the "invisible gorilla experiment." It could result in catastrophic decisions if the worst fears we originally entertained turn out to be justified. For example, consider human-induced global warming where, despite the best efforts of climate modelers, there remains uncertainty about how far temperatures will rise if particular policies are pursued. If Shackle is right, the downside focal outcomes that the policymakers keep in mind during their negotiations about alternative mitigation strategies will tend to be rather optimistic compared with the worst-case scenarios that their advisors have identified as possibilities.

5.3   Deductive and Inductive Thinking

Much of what was said in Chapter 4 about how people form expectations presented decision-makers as employing an inductive method for sizing up how things might turn out if they were to make a particular choice. By this I mean that they typically form constructs from new stimuli by categorizing what the stimuli represent in terms of things that they already know. They thereby extend the set of events to which they apply these existing constructs. For example, suppose a tradesman comes to give us a quotation for some renovation work and we notice that his truck is beautifully kept and everything in it seems to be well organized. Based on this evidence, we might infer that if we give him the job, things should proceed as promised: our inductive leap is to extend his way of looking after his truck to how he undertakes his trade. In other words, our rule is that if he seems to display pride in what he does in one context, then we can expect to see him generally displaying pride in his workmanship (cf. Veblen, 1914). Moreover, if this tradesman has been recommended to us by someone who has already used his services and had a drama-free experience, we will feel more confident in our expectation, and still more so if he shows us a folder containing copies of his trade qualifications and testimonials from even more customers. It all adds to what Keynes (1921) called the "weight of evidence" for judging that probably he is someone we can trust to do a good job.

However, forming expectations via inductive reasoning is not a surefire route to successful transactions. The tradesman's truck may be presented in the way that it is purely for show, and his evidence of his successes could be fabricated. Our friend may have been a lucky outlier, and it may turn out that the uniqueness of our renovation task entails things that would result in the tradesman getting into a mess even if he is all he seems to be. The problem of induction is not just an issue in cases such as this; it may also cause major embarrassment for economic modelers, for those who think they have found patterns in the way that financial markets operate that will enable them to predict the future, as well as for business strategists who fail to anticipate game-changing innovations by their rivals or market entry by firms whose track records had given these strategists no reason to believe that those firms would turn out to be competitors.

If we are to avoid nasty surprises or being unprepared for surprises that we could have used to our advantage, we may need to go about forming expectations in a more deductive way. This would entail using our creative and critical skills to consider where the bounds of possibility may lie and what could cause established patterns to break down. If something of relevance to our choice has so far not happened, this does not mean it is impossible. Hence, we should ask ourselves what has been preventing it from happening so far and then consider the kinds of circumstances under which those obstacles could be removed.

This latter, deductive way of forming expectation is the way that Shackle presumed decision-makers to think in his possibility-based alternative to probabilistic thinking. Clearly, in not giving attention to the inductive side of human nature, Shackle limited the contribution of his work as a means of explaining how decisions get made. However, this should not distract us from seeing the significance of his deductive approach to thinking for those who are keen to improve the quality of their decision-making. In his later years, Shackle (1972, 1974) emphasized the possibility of sudden "kaleidic" changes in our environments. (He used the adjective "kaleidic" as an allusion to a once-popular children's toy – the kaleidoscope – that uses mirrors and pieces of colored glass to generate complex patterns: when a kaleidoscope is slowly twisted, the patterns change, often both suddenly and dramatically.) Kaleidic changes might not be wholly without precedents – for example, the 2007–2008 Global Financial Crisis was one in a long succession of somewhat similar episodes – but the unique aspects of each of the episodes that make up a particular class of events may make their timing and fallout inherently hard to predict.

Deductive thinking may provide a means of anticipating what could lie, so to speak, "beyond the horizon." But this style of thinking does not come naturally to most people and it can have the disconcerting effect of making us see a wider range of possible outcomes for an action that we are considering, when what we hoped to achieve was a more narrowly defined view of the range within which the outcome might lie.

Some corporations and organizations have, however, developed a Shackle-like view of the problem of uncertainty and practice something akin to a deductive way of evaluating strategies as part of a process normally known as "scenario planning." The best-known exponent of this technique is the Shell energy company, whose former chief economist Michael Jefferson (1983, 2012, 2014) has provided some very useful accounts of Shell's experience with it and how their thinking linked up with that of Shackle.

In Shell's hands, the scenario planning technique is based on generating rival, internally consistent stories of how the future could unfold and then discussing their possible implications for Shell. These scenarios are not meant to predict the future, but they are useful in helping Shell's strategists to get a sense of where the firm could be vulnerable or of what it would need to do to be able to profit from events unfolding in ways that break with past trends. However, and herein lies a lesson for decision-makers in general, Shell's scenario planners use their deductive skills in conjunction with inductive methods, with the latter being used in assessing how seriously to take the scenarios. In other words, although they are interested in avoiding being surprised by things that overturn current trends, they are not averse to looking at history to find precedents for the key propositions on which they have built their scenarios. For example, in the late 1960s, when they started to consider the possibility of a shift toward highly aggressive behavior by the Organization of Petroleum Exporting Countries (OPEC), they checked to see whether cartels with large numbers of members had historically been able to stand firm. Prevailing economic theory held that the more members a cartel had, the bigger the probability that attempts by it to push up prices would be undermined by members trying to profit by covertly defying the agreed policy. The evidence from previous cartel histories from other industries was not particularly consistent with this prediction, and Shell decided to take seriously the possibility of OPEC engineering a sustained major oil-price hike. The firm chose to invest in a strategy that would leave it well placed if their OPEC vision eventuated, as it did in 1973. On that occasion, the Shell team was lucky and had a scenario that was close to what happened, but the scenario would also have helped them had something else happened to limit supplies of crude oil.

In terms of Kahneman's dual-system view of decision-making, Shell's scenario planning technique seems a powerful means for impeding System 1 thinking and promoting System 2 thinking. However, it should be noted that despite having the resources to work with a wide range of scenarios during any particular planning phase, Shell came to work with just two, designed to embody worst-case and best-case futures for the firm. Originally, they tried working with seven, but this proved too confusing, and attempts to work with three resulted in managers tending to operate as if the middle-case scenario set out how the future would actually unfold. Initially there was also strong resistance to scenario planning on the basis that planning tools should make the future more predictable, not heighten uncertainty.

5.4   Malleable Expectations: Dealing with Cognitive Dissonance (3)

Uncertainty entails a clash of contending cognitive perspectives. It thus adds to our cognitive load, giving us more to keep in mind when we are trying to choose. But it also poses questions about our capabilities when it comes to guessing how things are going to turn out. When we are uncertain, we face the possibility that we will come to regret our choices. Furthermore, worries about having to live with nagging doubts about our choices until uncertainty is resolved may get in the way of thinking clearly about the problem at hand (cf. the discussion of the economics of dread in Section 5.8).

These cognitive consequences of accepting that uncertainty is present are problematic from an evolutionary standpoint, for worries about the prospect of harboring nagging doubts and ending up with regret may result in hesitation that allows opportunities to escape. For humans to make progress as a species, it helps if their unique imaginative capacities go hand in hand with a capacity to take risks with confidence, even though the results may sometimes be disappointing for the particular individuals who made the decisions: failures and embarrassments for some are the price of the wider population benefiting from innovations and experiments that result in the growth of knowledge. We should thus not be surprised that humans have evolved to find ways of denying that they do not know what the future entails or ways of denying that uncertainty matters for their choices. An inherited tendency to try to find ways of eliminating uncertainty or seeing it as nonproblematic would have made our hunter-gatherer ancestors more willing to take the risks that enhanced the prospects of humans as a species. But it is a tendency that may be better attuned to the world of our hunter-gatherer ancestors than today's world in which – as the proponents of scenario planning realize – time spent embracing uncertainty can be time well spent.

We can get a good sense of the malleability of expectations in the context of high-stakes political decisions (such as the 1962 Cuban Missile Crisis) via the theoretical and case study analysis offered by political scientist John Steinbruner in his book *The Cybernetic Theory of Decision*. Steinbruner (1974, p. 123) was inclined to reject outright the notion that people are willing and able to keep in mind ranges of possible outcomes relating to mutually exclusive states of the world. He asserted that it settles on a single course of events and manipulates evidence that something else is happening to maintain the expectation on which the decision-maker's mind has settled.

In making this claim, Steinbruner was implicitly following in the steps of Charles Carter (1953, p. 814) who had argued rather less forcefully that, sometimes, "[w]e may find that, in looking at a fairly close date, a man's calculations are based on a single typical outcome. He has made up his mind about what will, he thinks, happen; he has no side-glances at alternative possibilities." Steinbruner's assertion is probably best seen as a statement of what the human mind generally *tries* to do when faced with uncertainty, rather than as saying that people always manage to whittle down the set of possible outcomes to just one for any choice that they consider. Clearly, we can see such efforts being made, as with Shell's scenario planners when they were presented with three scenarios, but equally clearly, it is evident that people frequently display signs of uneasiness about what is going to happen, even once they have made up their minds about what to do.

To make the case for his perspective, Steinbruner (1974, ch. 4) drew greatly on cognitive psychology, including the Ames room illusion and Festinger's (1957) *Theory of Cognitive Dissonance*. In essence, he argued that the mind is able to construct a workable view in the face of complexity and uncertainty by the following five means:

(a) Deploying images and arguments that involve the use of analogies.
(b) Drawing "inferences of transformation" (wishful thinking).
(c) Making inferences of impossibility.
(d) Highlighting negative images (exaggerating the potential downsides of the schemes they reject, as with "sour grapes" attitudes).
(e) Attempting to obtain social corroboration.

As for what determined the option in whose favor uncertainty is thereby addressed, Steinbruner appeals to a small set of operating principles that the mind applies to limit cognitive load, such as consistency and economy (simplicity and stability) as it tries to accommodate rival contenders as working models of how the future should be seen. His thinking complements the analysis offered in Chapters 7 and 8, where we explore a complex systems perspective on ideas from personal construct psychology (see also Section 4.8).

5.5   What Can We Do If We "Simply Do Not Know"?

In some situations we experience what is known as "fundamental uncertainty": we are unable to rate the probability or possibility of a choice having a particular outcome on any point on one or more of the construct that we are trying to use; we may also feel we have no idea even about whether we are using an appropriate set of constructs and, worse still, we feel that there is no way of obtaining a more bounded picture of how things could turn out in the area in question. The phrase "fundamental uncertainty" is most widely used within the literature of Post Keynesian macroeconomics. The term was not coined by Keynes, but it captures well what he had in mind when he asserted (Keynes, 1936, pp. 161–162, emphasis added) that:

Most, probably, of our decisions to do something positive, the full consequences of which will be drawn out over many days to come, can only be taken as a result of animal spirits – of a spontaneous urge to action rather than inaction, and not as the outcome of a weighted average of quantitative benefits multiplied by quantitative probabilities. Enterprise only pretends to itself to be mainly actuated by the statements in its own prospectus, however candid and sincere. Only a little more than an expedition to the South Pole, is it based on an exact calculation of benefits to come.

And, in replying to critics of his monetary theory of employment, Keynes (1937, pp. 213–214) emphasized that:

[T]he fact that our knowledge of the future is fluctuating, vague and uncertain, renders wealth a peculiarly unsuitable subject for the methods of the classical economic theory... The sense in which I am using the term ["uncertain"] is that in which the prospect of a European war is uncertain, or the price of copper and the rate of interest twenty years hence, or the obsolescence of a new invention, or the position of private wealth-owners in the social system in 1970. About these matters there is no scientific basis on which to form any calculable probability whatever. We simply do not know.

George Shackle was greatly influenced by these oft-quoted words and they probably provided the impetus for his potential surprise approach to uncertainty as an alternative to the (objective) probabilistic approach. However, it should be noticed that, like probabilistic models, Shackle's potential surprise analysis seems questionable where "we simply do not know" in the sense that our uncertainty is so great that any outcome on a construct seems perfectly possible.

So how do people avoid decision paralysis when they face fundamental uncertainty? Keynes offered a heuristics-based answer, suggesting that: (i) we tend to ignore the possibility of unexpected events and use the present as a guide to the future; (ii) we trust the opinions of the wider population, as expressed in current market prices; or (iii) we conform with what the majority of people do, on the basis that they may have more information than ourselves. As Koutsobinas (2014) has pointed out, Keynes's view is a precursor to the attribute substitution perspective on expectation formation that Kahneman employs in his dual systems view of how people assess situations (see Section 4.11).

On close inspection, Keynes's three suggestions point toward two different ways of coping with fundamental uncertainty. The first two entail substituting a simple proxy for the range of uncertain rival outcomes to which it is proving impossible to assign probability or possibility ratings. In other words, we assume it safe to ignore the uncertainty and simply extrapolate, or we assume the current price embodies all the available wisdom, with a low (high) current price relative to some reference point encapsulating prospects that we should assume are viewed, on balance, in a negative (positive) way. The second way of coping with fundamental uncertainty entails giving up trying to find a proxy for how things might turn out if we made one choice rather than another and applying a decision rule, such as "do what most people are doing." This is heresy in terms of a rational choice perspective, as it entails not considering opportunity costs, yet if opportunity costs cannot be computed, it may be a procedurally rational way of operating.

Other decision procedures of the second kind were subsequently suggested by Carter (1953). He argued that we may simply try to reduce the extent to which we expose ourselves to an unpredictable future by deferring commitments (for example, by renting durable goods instead of buying them) until the situation becomes clearer, or by hedging our bets by choosing adaptable assets or a mixed portfolio of assets. If these strategies are not available and it is imperative to make a choice today, then a random choice will be a means for moving forward when we cannot put bounds on the range of possibilities. The mixed portfolio strategy underpins the success of firms that survive for long periods in the entertainment sector. The sales of a movie or album of recorded music may be impossible to predict, and production costs can blow out unexpectedly, but if a firm is big enough to fund many projects at the same time, blockbuster success of a few may, with luck, offset the many that do not take off (cf. De Vany, 2004 and Section 3.7).

The ideas of Keynes and Carter are complemented by two themes in Cyert and March's (1963) seminal contribution, *A Behavioral Theory of the Firm*. One is that firms engage in "uncertainty avoidance." We can get a sense of this by reflecting on how insurance companies behave when faced with a new kind of risk that actuaries cannot price due to the lack of past data. In such situations, these companies are prone either to decline altogether to offer quotations in the areas in question or to offer quotations that are so expensive that they are unlikely to be taken up. The second message from Cyert and March in this area is that firms often seek to achieve a "negotiated environment" by, say, lobbying policymakers for guarantees or to have the source of the uncertainty removed. Clearly, Cyert and March take a very different view of business from what we get from Shackle's (1979, 1988) work, which emphasizes the creative role of bold entrepreneurs who are prepared to test their conjectures by make-or-break experiments that entail plunging into the unknown in pursuit of profit. The latter behavior is vital for economic progress: Kahneman (2011, ch. 24) labels it as the "engine of capitalism" and portrays it as due essentially to overconfidence bias being part of human nature.

However, although Cyert and March's arguments may apply quite often, it is also clear that large organizations are not always able to avoid or eliminate fundamental uncertainty. This is particularly so with innovation decisions, where it may be present in four areas:

1. *Technological and managerial uncertainty* – i.e., whether a concept can be made to work at all, at what cost (including the cost of the diversion of scarce management attention from existing activities: see Penrose, 1959) and by when.

2. *Market uncertainty* – i.e., how potential customers will react to it, which may sometimes be very hard to gauge until a working mock-up can be shown to them. Customer clinics and focus groups may provide limited guidance to the fate of a product if it takes extended periods of actual use before consumers discover what they really want to do with it and develop new habits of use. Because products are used as elements in consumption or production systems, market uncertainty is often bound up with uncertainty about what complementary products other firms may develop. Such products may affect the attractiveness of the product and its rate of uptake. Guessing what such products might be requires the capacity to anticipate the creativity of others as well as their boldness and capacity to execute their visions successfully by particular points in time. Given that people differ in their imaginative capacities, there is enormous potential for surprise here: for example, in the 1970s, when Kodak opted to invest in digital image-capture technology, it would not have been at all clear, if the question were even being asked, how long it would be before photographs came to be stored and viewed on electronic devices rather than as hard-copy prints.

3. *Uncertainty about competitive investment* – i.e., the need to make guesses about the extent of investment in rival products, the prices at which these will be offered and their non-price characteristics (see also Section 3.3).

4. *Uncertainty about complementary supply-side investment* – i.e., the need to guess the extent to which other firms can be relied upon to make upstream or downstream investments (see also Section 3.3). Inadequate complementary investment could increase the costs of making or marketing the new product. This might need to be addressed by vertical integration if it became evident that businesses with the capacity to undertake complementary investments are afraid to do so. Their lack of boldness thus can make it even more risky to go ahead: vertical integration requires even more funds to be committed to produce a given scale of final output and, as writers such as Richardson (1972) and Silver (1984) emphasize, it also usually requires new capabilities to be acquired. In many cases, a product will need to be well advanced in its development before it can be shown to the potential producers of complementary products and/or before the latter become convinced that it is worth investing in something to connect with it.

Firms that are unwilling to innovate in the face of such uncertainty run the risk of being wiped out by those who are prepared to take such risks. But if firms are willing to invest in innovative projects and have staff who are adept at coming up with ideas, they will need a way of ranking rival proposals. The trouble is, textbook techniques of capital budgeting – namely net present value or internal rate of return analysis – require at least probabilistic estimates of costs and returns to reduce each project to a single number. Fundamental uncertainty precludes the use of these techniques, yet it is evident that firms and other organizations (such as bodies that award research grants) do manage to allocate resources to innovate projects. How do they do this?

Neil Kay attempted to answer this question in his (1979) book *The Innovating Firm: A Behavioral Theory of Corporate R&D*. He argued that organizations use a "top-down" process instead of the textbook "bottom-up" method. The "top-down" capital budgeting method is similar to what individuals employ routinely to simplify the process of choice even if they are not bedeviled with fundamental uncertainty (see Section 8.9). Decision rules are used for dealing with trade-offs between different *categories* of spending on new projects (for example, between research and development, then, from the research budget thereby defined, between pure and applied research, and so on, down to increasingly detailed categories and, ultimately, to individual projects).

Use of this sort of technique can begin at an even higher level, such as the trade-off between using resources for marketing existing products (where, it should be noted, payoffs may also be uncertain) versus using them for research and development. It is essentially an inductive method: operating on this basis entails treating the firm's environment as sufficiently stable for reliable decision rules to be developed. For example, managers may have inferred that if they spend 5 percent of the previous year's revenue on research and divide this equally between basic and applied research, then that should be enough to keep them in business. This will then define the budgets that are given to lower-level managers to allocate in a more fine-grained way in their areas of responsibility. Project comparisons are then only made on a within-category basis at a lower level in the process. At that level, competition between those who are arguing the case in favor of their pet projects and seeking to cast doubt on those of their rivals may even result in creative thinking that reduces the extent of perceived uncertainty.

Clearly, it is possible to sidestep perceived uncertainty about creative proposals in a very formulaic manner by making choices based on the track records of those who champion them, along with those of their supporters and/or the teams that will be called upon to implement the projects. This is essentially how bodies that award research grants function in the tertiary education sector. But decision rules that focus on the nature of the projects themselves may be devised to deal consistently with creative proposals, as with checklist systems that classify projects into particular risk categories and set budgetary limits for what the organization is prepared to risk on projects that fall into these categories.

Top-down, rule-based systems of the kind that Kay highlights seem well-suited to, say, a large company in the pharmaceuticals sector that has developed a sense of what the probability distribution looks like for returns to investment in a set of new drugs, many of which will fail and a few of which will become solid earners or spectacular successes, none of whose prospects may be at all clear at the outset. But Kay's analysis seems ill-suited to characterizing decision-making about creative projects that are on a substantial scale relative to the firm's resources and which may "make or break" the firm or at the very least change its fortunes drastically for the short to medium term. In the latter kinds of cases, decisions may have to be based on the "gut feelings" (in the sense of the discussion of expert intuition in Section 4.3) of those in a position to authorize the projects. Where authorization comes from a committee, the internal politics of the organization may have a significant role to play. We will return to this territory in Section 11.12 when considering the behavioral theory of the firm in relation to how competitive processes work.

5.6   The Significance of Brands

Familiar brands can come to our rescue when we are making choices in unfamiliar contexts, such as when buying a particular class of consumer durable for the first time. In such situations, all we may have to work with when forming our expectations are our powers of logic and our past experiences. (Advertisements and sales staff may make cases for particular ways of seeing potential solutions to the problems we are trying to solve but that merely raises the question of what should be made of their claims.) Our knowledge includes our constructs regarding particular brands. If we dare to assume that firms are consistent in what they can do, then we can generalize about the wisdom of buying a product that carries a familiar brand in the unfamiliar context that we now face. It is not always wise to make such an inductive leap, given that when firms diversify into new areas, they normally will need additional capabilities. But it may be a procedurally rational assumption to make if it looks as if the knowhow required for success does not differ greatly between the brand's products that we have experienced and those that we are now considering.

Given that our unfamiliarity with the situation may mean we know little about relevant means–end relationships, the capacities in which we need to trust if we operate in this inductive way go beyond those concerned with the physical quality of the product and its after-sale service environment. We also need to have a sense the brand owner's capacity to know what features people like us will find it useful for the product to have (cf. the combinatorial, complex adaptive systems view of brands set out in Harper and Endres, 2017). If the brand can do this consistently, it may win a string of sales from us in different contexts after initially winning a sale from us for whatever reason and not disappointing us. Each sale reinforces our faith in that brand, adding to the probability that we will apply the same rule in future, if we have the opportunity to do so. Although this would be consistent with Hayek's analysis in *The Sensory Order*, the concept of reinforcement is, of course, a familiar one within the approach to psychology famous for experiments involving rats and pigeons and known as behaviorism. (For a penetrating attempt to view consumer marketing and brand choice from such a perspective, see Foxall, 1990.) It is a way of coping with knowledge gaps without even trying to construct a detailed set of relevant constructs, let alone assign probabilities to them. Where the virgin buyer is purchasing a product that has been around for long enough for competition to have resulted in the emergence of a standard set of features being offered, there will no longer be a role for a familiar brand as a signal that the product will contain an appropriate set of features. However, the brand may still count as a proxy for reliability and after-sales support.

The process just outlined is, of course, a form of satisficing behavior: if we view it favorably, the brand's logo signifies something that is likely be perfectly adequate at doing whatever it is that the product in question needs to do in the context in question. If we make brand-based choices and do not exchange experiences with others, we will fail to discover whether our delight in the unexpected but useful features that the brand owner packages into its products is misplaced due to other manufacturers being able to offer, in the same price band, products that would have impressed us even more.

The absence of familiar brands will not stop consumers from trying to cope in new buying situations by making inferences based on a new product having something in common with familiar products – in Kelly's terms, "by construing their replications." Even if an unfamiliar class of product is technically and functionally very different from things that we have previously consumed, we may still be able to employ some proxies for quality – for example, its country of origin, the length of its warranty or its weight and external finish – that have worked for us as rules in other contexts.

5.7   Heuristics and Biases Associated with Risk and Uncertainty

If George Kelly is right to suggest that human action revolves around attempting to predict and control events, behavior is fundamentally based on the presumption that the world around us does exhibit some kind of coherence. This presumption sits uneasily with the possibility that some areas of life are essentially subject to random events. So it should come as no surprise that, if we are presented with a series of coin tosses, we are prone not to accept the outcomes as random and that we instead try to predict the next outcome based on the succession of recent previous outcomes: if heads has come up several times in a row, we start viewing the probability that the next toss will yield tails as increasing, even though the probability is always fifty-fifty if the coin is unbiased. More generally, we are prone to deploy the heuristic known as "the law of small numbers" (i.e., we are prone to be willing to estimate the nature of a statistical population via sets of data points that are too small to be representative of the population in question). In short, we seem prone to rush to impose patterns and reluctant to live with ambiguity until we have garnered a set of data points big enough for drawing a reliable inference.

Pending the development of our expertise in a particular area, the mind still strives to find patterns to use as bases for action. In the absence of anything better, it is prone to use patterns whose causal connections are questionable. Using astrology or consulting an oracle were prescientific manifestations of this, but modern folk are no less susceptible to basing their choices on assessments that lack causal stories to connect the variables that they treat as being associated. For example, a person may expect to do well in an examination if he or she is armed with a "lucky charm" that they had with them on a previous successful day in the examination hall. This is a very naive form of inductive thinking.

Such behavior is in essence superstitious, but the more unpredictable something is, the more we seem to seek forecasts on which to base our choices rather than accepting its unpredictability and focusing on how well our options are suited to handling the possible range of variation. Gimpl and Dakin (1984) see the commissioning of many business forecasts as a symptom of this and suggest that modern managers and other policymakers are just as prone as primitive tribes to buy into spurious causal notions. They suggest that, for example, upgrading a city's airport to accommodate international flights in the hope it will cause tourists to arrive because this has been observed in other cases is little different from being part of a primitive cargo cult. Overseas tourists may indeed come in larger numbers and arrive via the international terminal, but they might well have come anyway, flying in via an existing hub and taking a domestic connecting flight. The rise in their numbers might also reflect something else, such as rising incomes in source countries.

Many of the dubious causal links that people construct when trying to assess the likelihood of a particular event or outcome of their choices are manifestations of what is known, following the work of Kahneman and Tversky (1972; Tversky and Kahneman, 1971), as the "representativeness heuristic." This entails finding similarities between things and inferring associations between them. For example, if food looks "fatty," we may infer that if we avoid it, we probably will not get "fat," little realizing that excessive intakes of sugars such as fructose may lead us to become obese even if we are on a low-fat diet. These sugars may be concealed in food that does not look "fatty." Poor outcomes also arise because, on top of being prone to base their evaluations on unrepresentative small samples, people often do not understand how to work out compound probabilities. These failings can be exacerbated by a tendency to give undue weight to vivid case examples relative to evidence from large samples summarized in abstract-looking statistics.

An example of the latter sticks in my mind, well over thirty years after seeing it in Nisbett and Ross (1980). It concerns a prospective buyer of a new car who has done his research very thoroughly, including checking consumer satisfaction reports. He is on the verge of buying a new Volvo when he has a conversation at a dinner party with someone who recounts the case of an acquaintance who had a very bad experience with a Volvo that was an utter "lemon." Based on this single horror story, he abandons his plan and buys a different brand. This is an example of what, with their focus on the social side of judgment, Nisbett and Ross call the "man-who syndrome." It is the outlier experiences of others that stick in our minds and loom large when we make decisions, for we can imagine how it would be to end up as they did. Evaluations that are formed socially are also prone to being twisted into conformity with social beliefs (as satirized in the fairy tale of "The Emperor's New Clothes"). We should also note how, in the absence of a well-focused chairperson and strict evaluative guidelines, a panel of decision-makers may compound its own members' tendencies to use inconsistent sets of evaluation criteria across the options. Such tendencies are a good reason for university professors to mark assignments and examination papers with the aid of grading templates.

Human statistical incompetence is not confined to the use of inadequate samples and mistaken probability assessments. Another issue is overconfidence bias that arises due to people not accepting statistics pertaining to their areas of expertise or having failed to seek advice from those with more experience about the odds of particular kinds of outcomes in the kind of territory into which they are planning to go. Kahneman (2011) suggests that lawyers are prone to take more cases to court than they should due to focusing on the singularities of the cases and believing they can exploit them to beat the established odds for success. Regarding the failure to seek advice, Kahneman candidly reports on his unsuccessful experience in a team designing a decision studies curriculum in Israel. After the project had dragged on way beyond its expected completion date, he discovered this was entirely normal with such teams, due to failures to allow for the impacts of factors such as team members' ill health, personal problems and job changes on a team's progress.

It also seems that, in line with Shackle's anti-probabilistic view of the world, people commonly do not even recognize that they face decisions in which it makes sense to think probabilistically. For example, consider how willing people are to buy extended warranties for their consumer durables. These warranties might make sense for, say, those with low incomes and poor access to credit (for example, students buying laptop computers) or for elderly consumers who buy extended warranties for what they believe will be their "last" television and expect to have no need to buy any other consumer electronics products. For most of us, however, the fact that we are continually buying such products and being offered extended product warranties should signal that it might be wise not to treat each purchase as a singular act and instead see it as one instance in a large sample that we will amass through time. If so, our rule should be to decline extended warranties and instead simply repair or replace those items that fail outside of the standard or statutory warranty period. In this way, we would save money in the long term, as we would not be contributing to the profits of the firms that offer the warranties.

The human tendency to treat events in isolation rather than as elements of long-term sets may also help explain the so-called equity premium whereby a diversified portfolio of equities tends over the long term to earn a higher rate of return than risk-free government bonds. Although individual corporations may fail and equity markets in general may go through boom–bust cycles, investors should not require compensation for putting their money into equities rather than risk-free government bonds unless they are getting close to retirement. For the rest of the population, a "kaleidic" collapse in the share market will sooner or later be comfortably offset by a market upswing. The risk of such a collapse thus should not worry us unless we are considering borrowing money to speculate and we fear that whatever causes a temporary collapse could also leave us unable to service the loan.

5.8   The Economics of Dread

Feelings of dread are a further cause of departures of behavior from what would be expected from the standpoint of conventional economic models. Though these feelings are not always associated with uncertainty and ambiguity, they often are and hence seem appropriate for consideration in the present chapter. Dread is the opposite of what Shackle called "enjoyment by anticipation" (see Section 2.3) but which is known by modern behavioral economists as "savoring." Recognition of the significance of anticipation for choices actually goes back before Shackle, at least as far as to Jevons (1905). Indeed, it was Jevons's contribution, along with Scitovsky's (1976) work on excitement, that provided the inspiration for George Lowenstein (1987) to devise a formal model of the effects of the human capacity both to savor and to anticipate feelings of dread (see also Lowenstein and Thaler, 1989; Elster and Lowenstein, 1992).

When we dread something, we get uncomfortable due to thinking about how difficult life could be for us because of what we will have to do if we want to bring about a particular situation (we may call this "prerequisite dread") or due to thinking about the implications for us if, or when, a particular event occurs. The duration of an event should not be forgotten here, for dread may arise in respect of sub-events that seem possible during the process of implementing a choice rather than merely from the act needed to trigger it: for example, I may dread upgrading my computer because of having to wrestle with the options I face and the challenge of figuring out how far I should try to "future-proof" my computing activities, but I may also dread the process of installing the new computer due to the prospect of finding that some peripherals will no longer work or can only be made to work after a lot of hassle.

In formal terms, what has to be done to take account of the impact of dread on choices is rather akin to (and complementary with) what is done in the so-called regret theory analysis of choice under uncertainty, first proposed by Loomes and Sugden (1982) – but with one major difference. The key presumption in regret theory is that how we feel about a possible course of action is affected not merely by what we think could happen as a result of what we choose but also by the extent to which we expect the outcome will cause us to experience regret or rejoicing *after* we know how things have gone, given that we might have done something different. By contrast, in the economics of dread, additional utilities and disutilities are envisaged merely from thinking about what the outcome could be, *before* we know what happens. From the standpoint of Hayek's *Sensory Order*, it is evident that we cannot remove dread by actively trying not to think about the things we are dreading, for that will just make them even more likely to come to mind; rather, if we are to avoid dwelling on a dreadful prospect, we need to be flooded with attention-arresting stimuli of a positive kind or to concentrate on thinking about desired things that may lie ahead.

To the extent that we can anticipate suffering from dread if we make a particular decision, this will make us less willing to make such a choice than we otherwise would have been. However, sometimes we can time our choices to limit the amount of dread we face. If we delay making a commitment for as long as possible (for example, when booking a flight, if we suffer from flight phobia), it may help keep dread at bay, since, until we make a formal commitment to the dreaded event, it is not definitely something that is going to happen. But where a dreaded event is something that we cannot escape, we can eliminate dread insofar as we are able to ensure that the event happens as soon as possible so that we can "get it over with." There is a possible policy implication here for the design of judicial systems that aim to deter criminal behavior: those that are known to operate at a very slow pace before reaching their ultimate verdicts may, other things equal, serve better as deterrents than those noted for meting out swift verdicts.

5.8.1   How Terrorism Works

Reflecting on dread associated with things beyond our control provides a clue for understanding how terrorism works. Normally a theory of risk-taking in dangerous environments would focus just on the disutility of being killed or maimed, measured in terms of lost years of probable life of a particular quality. It would not consider the disutility caused by worrying about the possibility of such a loss – worries that may occur repeatedly. That is to say, the standard model presumes we size up the risks, make our choice *and then put the risks to the back of our mind*. Clearly, this is indeed what we do with some of life's risks: for example, unlike someone who dreads flying, we may judge that flying is safe enough for us and then fly without worrying at all unless something (for example, terrible turbulence) raises the possibility that we are about to become an air-safety statistic. What terrorists seek to do via a steady stream of incidents is ensure that the possibility that we may end up being a victim by being in the wrong place at the wrong time keeps coming to mind with a frequency out of all proportion to its statistical likelihood. Using a variety of weapons and styles of attack enhances this effect. Thus, on each day that we are in any crowded place, we may worry about the possibility of a terrorist attack. Standard theory does not factor in the disutility of not being able to put the possibility of such an attack to the back of our mind after assessing it probabilistically. Vivid news reports keep activating our neural circuits pertaining to terrorism, getting in the way of what we may know about base-rate probabilities of being victims of terrorism. An "econ" would not worry in this way, whereas if we live in environments where terrorists have shown themselves to be active, each day is a fresh day of dread.

Terrorism comes in forms other than those instigated by political and religious extremists. Arguably its most significant form entails domestic violence, in which the perpetrator's partner and children may experience almost chronic dread, even though the actual bashing incidents only occur periodically. The perpetrators of domestic violence may often seem unable to control their behavior but often they do what they do as a means of control. Bullying at school and in the workplace operates in a similar manner. However, not all those who terrorize others will realize what they are doing: dread of terrible situations can come from loved ones via the impact of their poor lifestyle choices on friends and family. Those with addictions to smoking, alcohol and/or drugs might fail to try (or to keep trying) to stop consuming these substances due to their dread of the difficulties they would have if they did so, but to their friends and family, their behavior can be akin to a kind of terrorism. Those close to them may experience ongoing worry that they are going to get bad news about them because of such addictions, even if such news never comes. If that bad news does come, it can bring a sense of relief rather than merely of loss. Policymakers might be wise to advertise the dread that those with addictions cause in others, so that guilt about not being "that kind of selfish person" may have a bigger chance of coming to mind as a counter to the dread about what would be entailed in trying to kick the addiction.

5.9 Post Choice Dread and Loss of Nerve

Before concluding, let us consider the significance of dread that sometimes emerges after we have made commitments. Some of the things that we become concerned about after we have made commitments are issues that do not yet afflict us but which we discover or realize could afflict us at some point in the future. Where these problems have been discovered to have a statistical probability of afflicting those who have made the same choice, they deserve to be called "probabilistic problems." Such problems can arise with consumer durables, though here our probability assessments may be subjective evaluations rather than informed by statistical knowledge. In some cases, we buy goods aware of the risks that they may let us down in particular ways. But on other occasions, probabilistic problems may come as unpleasant surprises, because we engaged in insufficient search before buying the products in question or because no one knew of the issues at the time we bought the products (for example, where we were very early adopters of the product in question).

Where we recognize that, unless we make changes, we now face a particular risk that had not previously troubled us, we need to ask ourselves whether we are prepared to live with it, given that it might take a long time to hit us, if indeed it hits us at all. Conventional economic analysis would view decision-makers "as if" they answer this question by working out the expected (i.e., probability-weighted) utility of the rival probable outcomes for a "no change" strategy versus choosing to bail out and select the best alternative that seems to remove the risk in question. However, this view of the decision ignores the possibility that the decision-maker may factor in anticipated feelings of dread arising if the choice is made to make no change despite the acknowledged downside risks this entails.

Dread that arises from the discovery of a probabilistic problem with something we have already purchased, or from the realization of what could be entailed in a commitment that we have made, will make it more likely that we will "bail out" by disposing of the product sooner than we originally envisaged or that we abandon the commitment altogether. It is worth noting here that in Australian English the word "piker" refers to a person who behaves in this way; as might be expected of a nation famous for its "she'll be right, mate" tendency toward overconfidence, pikers are viewed as wimps. However, in the light of Festinger's (1957) theory of cognitive dissonance, it seems likely that if we bail out of a scheme of action, we will re-construe our options so that bailing out does not seem to imply personal weakness.

Car reliability can be used to illustrate how dread could result in a person bailing out in a situation in which a coolheaded "econ" would probably stick to a plan. Suppose that in 2011, Bruce, an Australian consumer, pays AUD32,000 for a brand-new Volkswagen Golf 118TSI with a 7-speed DSG automatic transmission. At this point, he is blissfully unaware that this type of transmission is prone to occasional catastrophic failure, something he would not have expected from this brand. (Problems of less costly but more frequent natures also surfaced with dual-clutch automatic gearboxes fitted to Ford Focus and Fiesta models around the same time and they later became the subject of a lengthy but successful class action against the manufacturer.) His plan is for this to be his last car powered by an internal combustion engine and that he will keep it until electric cars fall in price to a particular level. Bruce expected that this might occur in 2021. The car generally is most impressive, aside from occasionally faltering when pulling away from a road junction or traffic lights. However, Bruce later reads about the problems with the DSG gearbox and is left unsure whether a recall relating to it has eliminated the risk of failure (and it continues to have its occasional faltering). Now suppose it is 2016: the car is approaching five years of age and has nearly 100,000 km on its odometer. In the past, this is when Bruce would have traded up to a new car, and it is the right time of year for a good seasonal deal. The gearbox has not let him down yet. So should he stick to his plan and keep the car for the expected five further years, or should he trade it in against something else (e.g., a Volkswagen with a later-generation DSG gearbox) and plan to keep that vehicle until electric cars meet his reservation price?

If Bruce were an "econ" (rather than a wimp with European motoring sensibilities), he would try to find out the cost of getting a replacement DSG gearbox and discover that it could be anything from 15 percent to 30 percent of the original price of the car. As an "econ," he would also search for information on the reliability and longevity of the DSG gearbox and discover that so long as servicing is done in accordance with Volkswagen's schedules, the long-term reliability seems much better than implied in the horror stories he has read. If the worst-case cost figures for a replacement gearbox are correct, its failure could entail a bill roughly equal to what the car is currently (2016) worth as a trade-in but probably not much more than the first-year depreciation on a new replacement, quite apart from the interest he would forego on the funds needed to trade up. As an "econ," he would now form subjective probabilities from this kind of information and then factor in the utility he would lose if the gearbox did fail and disrupt his life at some point, taking into account the different kinds of disasters this might entail, along with their different probabilities. The different failure scenarios could include breaking down in the city versus becoming stranded while touring on vacation after breaking down in the outback, hundreds of kilometers from the nearest sizeable town or any mobile phone reception. If Bruce did the research, could do the calculations and was not prone to dread, the answer would likely be a convincing victory for adhering to his plan to keep the car until 2021, risking a disruptive breakdown and, if that occurred, then having to sell the car for scrap. If the DSG gearbox did not give trouble in the ensuring five years, he would probably be around AUD20,000 better off, having stuck to his original plan and not suffered depreciation on a replacement vehicle.

As a real-world consumer, however, Bruce probably would not even have taken the five minutes necessary to gather the relevant information via the Internet. Even if armed with such information, Bruce would be at risk of abandoning the original plan and trading up to a new vehicle to escape enduring nagging fears about being let down by the failure of the gearbox. Each day he used the car, there would be the possibility of gearbox failure. The possibility of the gearbox failing would particularly come to his mind and linger for a while each time the car faltered on pulling away. Instead of merely facing the risk of the inconvenience of a single bad day of gearbox failure, followed by some days spent getting a replacement vehicle, Bruce stands to incur up to five years of nervous motoring that could be avoided by trading up to a new vehicle. The latter could also provide other benefits to help justify abandoning the original plan. Even if enhanced social status is not an issue, bailing out of the Golf and buying a new car offers benefits: he will likely focus on the five years of additional enjoyment that he is going to have from a later-generation vehicle with electronic goodies such as satnav, a touch screen, reversing camera and so on. Some of these new features may also be means of removing other kinds of dread, such as the dread of getting lost or parking. But the price of not sticking to his plan is around AUD20,000 in additional depreciation.

This is a highly specific scenario, but it points to a more general phenomenon, that of people trading up due to dreading unspecified major repair bills as their cars get older. Such bills are unlikely to be anywhere near the additional depreciation they will then suffer on their new or newer vehicles. Though they may be surprised and impressed by the improvements to cars since they were last in the market, it may be dread that is making them head to the car dealers, not the opportunity to get the latest technology. These economically questionable choices can be made to seem more logical by trading to something different rather than merely a newer version of the model that is being traded in, with the differences providing ammunition for constructing a justification that serves as a cover for what is really a choice driven by loss of nerve.

Loss of nerve may also be expected in situations where the decision-maker had not fully thought through the implications of what they were planning or agreeing to do at the time they made the commitment in question. As more information becomes available about what it entails, or as they start imagining further implications of the decision, the events associated with it that lie some way in the future become a source of greater dread than was present at the time the decision was taken. The significance of such an increase in dread for whether or not the decision-maker bails out of the commitment will be greater the longer the period before the dreaded events are expected to eventuate. Indeed, the discovery that the dreaded events are going to be delayed may be enough to produce a loss of nerve.

This line of thinking has significant policy implications: whenever commitments take time to implement, measures that reduce the time it takes to get to whatever it is that is dreaded are likely to reduce the incidence of the commitments being abandoned. For example, consider policies in relation to violence against women. The dread perspective may help us to explain why legal cases concerning sexual assault frequently end up having to be abandoned due to the victims pulling out from facing courtroom inquisitions. Getting justice may literally only require the victim to "have her day in court," but if there is a significant probability that it is going to entail an unpleasant grilling by a defense counsel in the presence of the perpetrator, the victim may experience many days of it in her imagination before the actual day in court (and may also dread reliving it in her imagination many times subsequently). Speeding up such legal processes could thus be expected to have a significant impact on conviction rates for these kinds of cases.

Similar considerations apply for women in relationships with violent partners. Despite having each day to dread what could happen, and despite repeatedly considering leaving, such women may end up staying in these relationships. Each time they start planning to leave, they may have second thoughts due to considering further the struggles they will initially face in reestablishing their lives – struggles that become greater the longer these women are worn down by being in such relationships (see DeRiviere, 2008). In terms of cognitive dissonance theory, we should expect that each time they lose their nerve about implementing a plan to terminate such relationships, they will then (at least temporarily) raise their probability assessments regarding the chances of turning the relationships around. To help to increase the number of women who escape from violent partners, social welfare departments need to introduce policies that reduce these concerns and speed up the process of getting reestablished in a safe environment.

Although most economists have neglected the role that dread may play in making commitments seem problematic and thereby leading decision-makers to abandon things they had resolved to do, lawyers seem to act as though they understand the importance of dread. For example, consider how a lawyer representing a "gold-digging" spouse in a divorce case can seek gradually to grind down the resolve of the other party via a long-drawn-out process of requesting documents. For the other party, the simple act of checking the mailbox on arriving home from work becomes something to dread, along with the consequent hassles of assembling the documents, even though, on most days, no such letter will be there. This is akin to a mild form of terrorism. For some, it may become all too much to bear, leading them to agree to a premature and disadvantageous settlement.

5.10   Conclusion

There is an underlying tension in this chapter between viewing the problem of uncertainty as a problem of forming conjectures in the face of incomplete information and knowledge versus viewing it as a statistical problem in which rules are applied to infer probabilities from what is known about a particular aspect of the world.

In the former view, the focus is often on non-probabilistic situations involving unique events, particularly those that determine the results of what Shackle described as "crucial experiments" that may drastically change, for good or bad, the fortunes of individuals and organizations, with no second chances. In these cases, the decision-maker needs to consider what *could* happen in the situation at hand by deduction, based on creative thinking and logic, and/or induction, based on knowledge of what has happened in the past in somewhat similar situations. With this approach, epitomized by the work of scenario planners at Shell, the focus may be on defining the bounds of possibility in terms of threats and opportunities rather than ending up with probability or likelihood ratings for what seems possible.

The latter view has tended to be the dominant focus of modern behavioral economists, via the work of psychologists such as Kahneman and Tversky. Their work has been "behavioral" in the sense that it presents research subjects with well-defined probability puzzles and tries to infer the use of particular heuristics from the answers that the subjects provide. In such research, the focus is on the extent to which people seem to think like good statisticians, not on the techniques that they use to figure out what could happen and the driving forces behind, and barriers to, the taking place of imagined outcomes. This kind of research is obviously of potential significance for our understanding of how people respond to probabilistic information such as health risks and the costs and benefits of particular treatments or screening procedures. The probabilities may be well known to experts in the field, and knowledge of how lay decision-makers use probabilistic information can be useful for deciding how that information should be presented to them.

Either way, we should keep in mind that how we deal with uncertainties and risks may be driven not merely by the need for our brains to be able to keep cognitive load manageable (which may entail reducing the range of possibilities that are kept in focus) but also by the underlying agenda that our minds are pursuing. Whenever there is uncertainty, it is easy for our conjectures to end up being shaped via the brain's attempts to remove cognitive dissonance.

6 How Do We Search for Solutions to Problems?

6.1 Introduction

The need to gather information can arise when (a) we try to assess whether we have, or are possibly going to have, a problem, (b) we are unsure about the set of potential solutions to a problem that we have acknowledged or about their characteristics or (c) we do not have a problem but are planning to experiment with new means of meeting particular ends. In each situation, we face a challenge akin to that of a senior police officer trying to allocate scarce resources to solving a crime. Despite the efforts of cookie-gathering e-commerce firms such as Amazon to infer what we might be open to purchasing and point us in its direction, the sets of things between which we choose are personal constructs: they result from choices we make about how to find potential solutions to the problems that we identify, how much information to gather about each option and where to try to find it. This means that we must obviate an infinite regress. To choose how to search, we need first to assemble a set of possible ways of searching and evaluate them, which raises the question of how we should go about finding potential ways of searching, and so on, ad infinitum. If, on every occasion for searching, we started by agonizing over whether to use the Internet and, if so, which search engine to use, what will be the best possible set of search words to use, and so on, we would get nowhere. It is thus imperative that we use a rule or routine to stop the infinite regress and get search under way. Other rules and routines may then be applied as the process proceeds and to determine when it stops.

Nowadays, for example, we each may have a default Internet browser and search engine, and as a rule we may never venture beyond, say, the second screen of any set of search results. However, the rules that we employ when searching will differ depending on the context. Often, we will begin with a Google search, but not always. Sometimes, we may head straight to Amazon's website and search there, or we will see what ideas and information a particular friend or colleague can supply. But in other situations, we may search "high and low" by multiple means, and wisely so, for even if we are lucky to have search rules that are, as Gigerenzer and his colleagues (Gigerenzer and Goldstein, 1996; Gigerenzer et al., 1999) would put it, "fast and frugal" in some contexts, they might be woefully inadequate elsewhere.

The issue of what is "procedurally rational" is always present when we are searching (i.e., what constitutes appropriate deliberation for the context at hand or, in lay terms), whether or not we are "going about it in the right way." In practice, search is often undertaken poorly: in a survey paper, Grubb (2015) shows how consumers often suffer from inertia, end up paying more than they need due to doing insufficient search and/or get confused when trying to compare alternatives. Professional buyers, too, may not be particularly good at searching, even though their job is to source inputs efficiently for their employers (see Cunningham and White, 1974).

Though our search rules do not always result in us choosing as well as we might readily have done via other rules, they generally make life manageable by restricting our thoughts and behavior. The moment we start searching for particular kinds of products and/or using particular search criteria, we allow rules to shape the discoveries we make. But this is what we must do to make choice possible, for the number of possible combinations of products that we might buy is mind-bogglingly large in a modern, affluent economy: Amazon.com alone can be used to source millions of different products. The number of possible combinations explodes still further once we take account of scope for adding optional features and the possibility of sourcing a given product from a multitude of suppliers from all over the world.

Operating as if we are "just browsing" is only likely to be procedurally rational if we have no idea what to get to solve the problem at hand. Even in the latter situation, such as when we are at a loss about what might be a suitable present for a relative or friend, we will still impose *some* kind of boundary on where we are prepared to start looking. The search process will typically proceed hierarchically, in the manner echoed and facilitated by website designs: we begin with a broad context (e.g., "a gift for X") and then narrow it down to a particular category (e.g., "something for X's kitchen"), followed by a specific class of objects in that category (e.g., "a platter or dish she can use when having a party"). Hierarchical decomposition of this kind certainly clashes with the standard economics view that all goods are potentially substitutes for each other if the price is right, but it is absolutely vital for decision-making in the face of bounded rationality.

In essence, then, the process of searching is based on the use of rules and hierarchical simplification strategies. This chapter examines some of the challenges entailed in knowing how to undertake search, and how some search heuristics can prove dysfunctional, whereas others can be very effective. However, before we consider the behavioral economics of search in more detail, it is useful to set the scene with an example of a challenging search problem that will be familiar to most readers, namely finding the best-value mobile (cell) phone connection plan to suit one's needs. From the standpoint of traditional economics, we should be approaching this problem mindful of how we might use any given plan differently from another due to differences in unit charges for different kinds of services and differences in the sets of services offered. However, that is far too challenging: it is bad enough to try to find the best plan even if we simply do our appraisals for all the plans we discover in terms of a single, approximate usage pattern based on our knowledge, such as it is, of the number of calls that we normally make, the SMS messages we normally send and the number of gigabytes of data we normally use per month.

Familiar and exasperating though this problem is, few consumers realize just how many plans are available. Many consumers end up paying far more than they need to pay, due to undertaking very little search and selecting a default option (see Section 6.5). Others may make serious attempts to "do their homework" via internet searches, aided by comparison websites, and still end up wasting money due to failing to spot the provider with the cheapest deal or not looking carefully enough at the range of products offered by the provider whose services they use, or not realizing that they did not understand how particular kinds of mobile phone contracts work and hence failing to try to find out. Many end up suffering from "bill shock" after failing to spend enough time studying contractual fine print regarding charges for services such as international roaming. This is, in short, a market very different from the idealized "perfect information" scenarios that economists often find convenient to use when analyzing how markets work. Skill in searching is vital for getting a good deal.

Many other focal examples could be used, such as searching for a marriage partner, a used car or someone to fill a job vacancy. However, as foreshadowed in Section 1.7, there is a very good reason for using this particular example: the writing of this book had to be delayed for several years because I was working with my colleagues Lana Friesen and Christopher Shadforth on a major study, funded by the Australian Research Council, of how Australian consumers coped with this problem in the period 2010–13.

In one of the phases of the project, reported in Earl et al. (2017, 2019), we ran an experiment in which participants were each given an hour to find the cheapest available prepaid plan for serving a particular usage remit. This had to be found from among over 800 plans of all kinds, offered by over 50 providers. These 800+ plans excluded offers with handsets, for the task remit presumed the user already had an unlocked handset. We marooned about half our subjects offline but provided them with an archive that consisted of clones of all the providers' websites; the rest of the participants were able to use the Internet freely but were not given access to the offline plan archive. However, we did not tell any of the participants how many plans there were. The offline participants were given a home page that consisted of links to each of the cloned homepages of the providers' websites, listed alphabetically. A long scroll down the experiment's home page made it possible to see just how many providers there were, but there were no clues to the distribution of plans among providers and no clues (aside from one provider branding itself "Just Prepaid") as to which of them offered prepaid plans. The online participants were not even told which firms offered mobile phone connection services, but they could at least call upon any assistance that Google could help them muster. We asked our subjects to think aloud as they went about the task and what they said formed the soundtracks for individual screen-capture movies of what they did on the way to their verdicts. They were rewarded based on how close they got to finding the cheapest prepaid plan consistent with the usage remit, but it had taken us many, many hours to determine what the best plans were in the two choice environments. If you had been one of our subjects, with just one hour at your disposal, how would you have gone about the task? What would have been "rational" to do in this situation?

6.2   Search as a Satisficing Process

Search becomes a problem in its own right whenever we need to reach a decision without being able to gather all the information that might be relevant to our choice. Such a need may arise because we do not have "all the time in the world" to reach our decisions and/or because of our cognitive constraints on the amount of information that we can store and the speed at which we can process it. For example, if we have just moved to an unfamiliar city to take up a new job, we may have an urgent need to find somewhere to live, possibly somewhere to buy as soon as possible, rather than renting, if it seems that real estate prices are going to rise rapidly. There may be thousands of properties for sale in this city, but if we look at more than about seven in a single afternoon, we will start getting confused and have trouble remembering what we have seen, and there will be much that we are unable to absorb when first viewing a property. Such a search task becomes more manageable if we use (a) simple rules to limit the number of suburbs in which we search (such as those within a particular distance from where we will be working), (b) a short checklist of "must have" features and a price range to limit the set we are prepared to view in those suburbs and (c) rules to reject many of the properties that we see before we stop searching, with the "final" choice being from those that were not eliminated earlier. We thereby may end up only physically inspecting a few tens of properties from the thousands we might have examined.

However, even if we do not have a deadline to meet, and search is not proving cognitively overwhelming, we may opt to reach a decision despite knowing we could have searched further, since searching has opportunity costs because it chews up time. The trouble is, if we stop searching too soon, we may end up selecting something that is inferior to what we might readily have discovered had we continued searching. But then, again, we might be wasting our time if we continue to search. For Herbert Simon (1947, 1956, 1957a, 1959), this implied that search is a satisficing activity rather than a process of optimization: we set aspiration levels as a means of dealing with not knowing how well we might be able to do and we stop searching when we find something that seems sufficiently likely to meet these performance standards.

On this view, search and choice are integrated. Indeed, it may be the case that the decision-maker never puts together a shortlist of acceptable options from which the best is selected; rather, options might be appraised when they are discovered, and further options will continue to be sought so long as nothing satisfactory has yet been discovered. Such sequential searches may be conducted within a frame of expectations about the probable time it may take to find a satisfactory option. If the search process seems to be dragging on without success, the decision-maker may infer that the aspiration level(s) is (are) overambitious and therefore rule out further search, choosing the best option that is still available from those that have already been examined. On the other hand, unexpectedly rapid success in finding an option that matches the aspiration(s) may result in the decision-maker ruling that the aspirations have been set too low and then raising them rather than simply selecting something that meets the original specification.

The aspiration levels used in the process of searching for solutions to problems may be the same as those used during the process of problem recognition. However, sometimes problem recognition may trigger a rethink about what one should really be looking for in the area in question, with the result that new aspirations are set. Some of these may pertain to constructs that the decision-maker had not previously applied in that context. Here, an important issue is how initial aspiration levels are selected. Clearly, it would be unwise to select aspiration levels randomly: if we unwittingly select a wildly ambitious set of aspirations, it may lead us to waste much time in searching for something that is impossible to attain, whereas unduly low aspirations could result in needless underachievement. In the former case, especially if coupled with a reluctance to lower the target, we would be chronically in problem-solving mode and finding life frustrating in that area rather than enjoying what was feasible. In the latter case, life would be much less stressful, but we might develop fewer capabilities due to having less experience in solving problems. Hence, although we may acknowledge our uncertainty about the bounds of possibility, we nonetheless want our aspirations to be in zones that make them serve as useful focal points for our actions.

We noted in Section 4.9 the significance of external reference standards in problem recognition. Outsourcing of aspiration levels is clearly one way of setting them in unfamiliar territory. Another way is via a sampling strategy. Consider what happens on the way to making a commitment to a marriage partner. Via a succession of dates and short-term relationships, people can start to develop their knowledge of the kind of person that they want and can attract. Having figured this out via their sampling process, their problem is how to find and attract someone who matches up to their requirements. Note here that they may be unable to re-attract those whom they have previously rejected; hence, if they come to believe, with regret, that they have little hope of ever finding and attracting someone so appealing as the best person in their sample set, they might end up setting their sights somewhat lower than what that person had to offer (for experimental evidence consistent with this, see Güth and Weiland, 2011). Note, too, that using a sampling method to set one's aspirations entails addressing the question of how big the sample should be if it is to be big enough to be a useful guide.

6.3   A Behavioral Perspective On "Optimal" Search Rules

Simon's satisficing view is very different from that of most economists. For the latter, the essence of the search problem is that it entails basing one's choice on a sample of the information that might have been sought. Hence, it is essentially a problem of statistics and probabilities. If we have appropriate expertise in these areas, or can call upon those who have it, we ought to be able to work out the optimal way of dealing with the search problem to maximize the probability of getting the best result. In practice, however, people simplify search processes rather than acting as experts might act. Though they do not always simplify their search activities in a procedurally rational manner, it should become apparent in this section that viewing search as an optimizing activity has problems of its own.

If we are to search efficiently, it helps to know the size of the pool of potential solutions. This often means knowing the set of potential providers and how many products they have to offer. In the case of a search for the cheapest mobile phone plan to meet our needs, it may be very easy to find out how many providers there are. Participants in the experiment reported in Earl et al. (2017, 2019) could readily ascertain the answer if they thought of trying to find out, though very few actually did show any sign of having such thoughts: the offline subjects merely needed to scroll down the list of links to the archived provider websites, counting as they did so, whereas the online participants would have been readily able to find a list of Australian mobile phone service providers on Wikipedia (if they were willing to trust it as a reliable source) rather than having to check through page after page of Google search results without being sure whether they had gone far enough or might have discovered more via different search terms.

Once one has discovered the number of providers, the next challenge is to estimate how many plans each provider may offer, and how long it will take to find the desired information about each plan. Some plans might not require much attention at all (e.g., because it is immediately evident, just from standard call costs, that they are more costly than the total cost of a plan that has already been considered), whereas unit prices might sometimes take an inordinate amount of time to discover; indeed, it may eventually turn out that some relevant pieces of information are simply not available. Call center staff may be unable to provide answers to infrequently asked questions: in the study of mobile phone connection plan choices, sometimes all that the staff at providers' call centers could do was refer us back to the web pages whose shortcomings had led us to call them.

The first puzzles here are how many providers and their plans need to be sampled to get a good sense of the scale of the search problem. Once this is resolved, the next puzzle is what is the optimal stopping rule to use, given what one discovers via the sampling process. In principle, it is indeed possible to work out optimal sampling strategies and rules for ending search so long as the search problem has been closed (thereby keeping the infinite regress problem at bay) rather than being left open-ended. A classic instance is a scenario known as the "secretary problem." There have been a variety of versions of this problem, but the simplest runs as follows. Suppose that a pile of applications has been received for a vacant secretarial position. The person or committee making the choice looks at the applicants one at a time, in a random sequence, but each time a candidate is considered, a decision is made whether to offer the job to that candidate or send a rejection letter that will preclude the possibility of hiring that person later in the process. The problem is thus rather like that of finding the best marriage partner: in both cases, there is the risk of rejecting the most suitable person from those available. Optimal search thus entails maximizing the probability of finding the best available option. How might this be done?

These days, the decision-maker can turn to Wikipedia for the answer (see https://en.wikipedia.org/wiki/Secretary_problem). First, one should sample some of the applications to get a picture of the distribution of applicant quality. Given the rules of the problem, this entails rejecting all the applicants in this sample set, no matter how good they might be. Hence, there is a risk of rejecting the best applicant. If the sample set is very small, there is the risk of underestimating how good the best candidate might be, whereas the bigger the sample set, the greater is the probability that it includes the best candidate. There is a mathematical solution to the question of how big the sample set should be. In essence, as the size of the pile of applications rises, the size of the optimal sample set rises at a smaller and smaller rate but the probability of selecting the best candidate falls as the number of candidates rises. Eventually, as the number of candidates rises, the size of the sample set, expressed as a percentage of the set of applicants, and the probability of choosing the optimal candidate, expressed as a percentage, converge to the reciprocal of the mathematical constant known as Euler's e – in other words, to about 37 percent. So, if there are 100 applicants, one should see how good the best one is among the first 37 and then keep rejecting the remaining candidates until the random search sequence presents a candidate who looks better than the best in the sample set. This candidate might not be the best one, but the person will at least be close to the best of those outside the sample set unless there is a statistical outlier with outstanding capabilities further down in the pile. Obviously, using this rule might result in the last application considered having to be the one that is accepted, and this person could, in principle, be the best in the pile. However, if the best one is in the sample set, the last applicant considered could be anywhere from the second best to the worst. Whatever the outcome, the process ensures the (rather modest) 37 percent maximum probability of ending up selecting the best applicant.

This search rule is optimal in relation to the given set of applicants, but that set is a consequence of earlier decisions about how and where to advertise the position (or whatever other means was used to ensure there was a given pile of applications to consider). In the case of a real-world "secretary problem," decision-makers might not know the optimal rule for solving it. Indeed, if they did not even know the name given to the problem, it could be problematic to find the solution in Wikipedia, even if they thought of looking there and judged Wikipedia to be a reliable source.

It is the rules of the "secretary problem" that make it problematic to examine all the candidates before choosing. More complicated search problems use limited time and/ or cognitive capacity to force decision-makers to stop searching and arrive at a choice without considering all available options. Time constraints are often present in real-world hiring processes and when people are searching for marriage partners. In the latter cases, those who hope to have children and raise them before retiring cannot keep trying prospective partners indefinitely. Binding cognitive constraints mean that the decision-maker faces the following trade-off: gathering more information reduces the risk of oversight but increases the risk of information overload unless the add-itional information clarifies the problem by making it possible to cease paying attention to information gathered previously (see Heiner, 1986). The trouble is, it is in the nature of an information-processing mistake that we will not be aware we are making it. However, we might be able to assess the probabilities of making mistakes in particular kinds of situations.

The mobile phone plan choice experiment mentioned previously was set up to make it impossible to find out if one had found the optimal plan, even though the investigators had uncovered it (to the best of their knowledge) via many hours of research. One hour was not enough to look carefully at all the plans, and the participants clearly suffered from cognitive fatigue beyond the halfway stage, leading to many errors. In contrast to the secretary problem, it was always possible to revisit options and study them more carefully. The participants had to keep deciding whether they had spent enough time looking at a particular provider's offers, whether to look at another provider's offers or whether they should now call it quits and hope they had found the best plan or a plan good enough to earn them a satisfactory financial payoff for their effort. How would they have decided when to stop?

From Stigler (1961) onward, economists have presumed that decision-makers can form probabilistic assessments of the marginal benefits of search and factor them into their assessments of how far it is worth searching in order to maximize their expected utility: the optimal amount of search could be found by equating the marginal benefits with the marginal costs associated with achieving them.

As a simple example, consider the economics of spending an hour trying to find a cheaper mobile phone plan for our needs than the best we have so far discovered, versus spending an hour doing something else. Obviously, if we earn, say, $50 per hour after tax and we do not think an extra hour spent on searching for a better deal is going to save us at least $50, then we will be wasting our time if we continue to search rather than doing an hour of overtime at work or spending the hour doing something else that we value more than the income we would get from doing overtime. We supposedly will use our probability assessments as weights when making these calculations: for example, if we think there is a 0.2 chance that a particular marginal search will enable us to find a product that is $100 cheaper over the duration of the contract than the cheapest we have so far found, but a 0.5 chance that we will at best only find something $20 cheaper, and a 0.3 chance of not finding anything cheaper than what has already been discovered, then the expected value of the search is (0.2*$100) + (0.5*$20) + (0.3*$0) = $30. If the opportunity cost of our search time is $50, then clearly the odds do not favor continuing to search, and we will choose the best deal from those we have already discovered. (Note that, for simplicity, this example abstracts from the possibility that we experience diminishing marginal utility of money.)

This view of search may seem applicable to the analysis of shopping behavior so long as the cognitive challenges of using probability weights do not seem unduly large. If we are buying a new television, we may indeed be able to consider the relative payoff probabilities of, say, spending an hour on the Internet versus an hour going to the local shopping mall, seeking information from a bricks-and-mortar electrical appliance retailer and coming home. We may also be able to consider the relative payoffs that we might get from using different search terms on the Internet and then assess the relative payoffs from opening one search result rather than another, and whether it may be worth moving on to the next page of search results, and so on. We may likewise be able to form conjectures about the benefits of visiting one retailer at the mall rather than another and from different ways of engaging with the staff in the stores we enter. But Stigler-style models of optimal search beg the question of how the decision-maker arrives at the list of rival search strategies in the first place: just like the options or pieces of other information that they are intended to elicit, rival search strategies are not sitting there in front of the decision-maker and labeled as such. The probability distribution for the results of each search strategy has to be derived from somewhere, too, and this also runs into infinite regress problems. The search problem thus must be closed at some point in an arbitrary manner, by applying some kind of rule.

A conventional economist would doubtless want to argue that we should view the participants in the mobile phone plan choice experiment "as if" this is how they were dealing with questions about when to stop searching, even though the transcripts of them "thinking aloud" as they tried to solve the problem generally did not provide any evidence of them thinking like this. However, to be fair, this could be the result of them becoming so cognitively exhausted that they were finding it harder and harder to "think aloud" as they continued with the task (thereby confirming that it had been a wise move for us also to make screen capture recordings of what they did). To the extent that anything like a probabilistic analysis of the benefits of further search had been going on, it seems likely that it would have been simplified around focal points rather than entailing weighing together rival potential outcomes associated with a distribution of probabilities (see further Sections 5.2–5.4). What the transcripts *did* reveal was a tendency to be so engrossed in the task that most of the research subjects were quite startled to receive the "five minutes remaining" prompt: they had not been monitoring how long they had been spending on the task and tended to rush to a final decision after receiving the prompt, rather than using the remaining minutes to check their calculations and whether the plan they were about to recommend met the "must be a prepaid plan" requirement. In other words, they had been having a "flow" experience, akin to what many of us have experienced when searching or browsing on the Internet, where we suddenly come to our senses after several hours and then comment, "Gosh is *that* the time already?"

We might similarly doubt the plausibility of an optimal search model as a means of characterizing how members of an appointment committee would go about handling the secretary problem if they had significant opportunity costs and had to appoint someone from a pile of 100 applications. It would be possible to compute an optimal size for their sample set if we knew their opportunity costs, but if no one on the committee knew what the optimal sample set was, we might expect them to use a "conventional" number, such as the first ten candidates, as the size of the sample set from which to arrive at their target for the prospective performance that a candidate from the remainder of the pile must offer in order to be acceptable. However, the need for an initial sampling process might be obviated if a set of "essential requirements" had been specified in the job description: the committee could then make the choice simply by selecting the first candidate in the search sequence that did indeed seem to "tick all the boxes." In this connection it is instructive to note an experimental study by Hsiao (2018) of how well people deal with the secretary problem, including variants where there are costs in terms of time and money for considering more candidates. By assuming her student participants would otherwise have been able to work at the local minimum hourly wage, she was able to compute what their optimal search strategies should have been. Typically, Hsiao's subjects did less search than would have been optimal but, despite this, they generally did not end up with woeful outcomes.

Although focusing merely on finding a satisfactory candidate can result in the secretary job not being offered to the best candidate, the outcome may not necessarily be worse than would have been achieved via the optimal search rule after modifying it to include search costs. This is because the latter, likewise, would not guarantee the best applicant will be offered the job; it merely maximizes the probability of the optimal outcome. It could therefore be procedurally rational to do less search than the optimal search rule implied. However, we should recognize that satisficing search rules do sometimes prove dysfunctional even when this is not the result of long-term aspirations being set needlessly low. To judge from Camerer et al.'s (1997) study of the labor supply decisions of New York cabdrivers, the difficulty of getting a taxi at a time of high demand is exacerbated by cabdrivers combining satisficing search strategies with mental accounting based on a daily earnings target. Thus, on days where it was easy to find customers, they reached their target early in their shift and went home, whereas on days where it was hard to find customers, they kept working much longer. Had they set their aspirations on a longer-term basis, they would have reversed their work patterns and earned more or been able to have more leisure time overall. However, this would have been more cognitively challenging than what they did.

In short, from the behavioral perspective, it is misleading to frame the choice of search strategies in terms of constrained optimization. Search must entail the use of rules at some point and optimizing techniques can only be applied once the search problem has been closed. If rules must be used at some point, it may be perfectly reasonable to base the entire search process around them, rather than trying to optimize. Such rule-based approaches to search include using aspirations or targets that call a halt to search when a seemingly satisfactory option is discovered (as in Simon's satisficing analysis), simple routines (possibly ones that Gigerenzer and his colleagues would classify as "fast and frugal") that limits search without specifying any outcome target (such as "get three quotations and choose the cheapest") or some combination thereof. Search that entails satisficing is not necessarily a consequence of the decision-maker being poorly motivated. Rather it may be a consequence of the decision-maker not knowing what the optimal search strategy is once a problem has been closed, either due to a lack of expertise or because no one has yet solved the puzzle for the context in question. Indeed, Herbert Simon proposed his "satisficing" view long before the 1/e rule for dealing with the "secretary problem" was worked out.

6.4 Elusive Optima

The experiment on mobile phone connection plan choices abstracted from an issue that decision-makers must grapple with in the real-world version of the problem: the set of plans offered by the providers keeps changing, as does the set of providers. If we do not have to make a choice today, it may pay to defer choice until after we have seen what is currently, so to speak, "over the horizon." If it is imperative that we come up with a solution today, it may pay to choose a short-term strategy, such as selecting what seems currently to be the cheapest monthly or prepaid plan rather than locking oneself into a long-term contract. But at what point should we cease waiting for something cheaper and try to reap the advantages of a locked-in deal over something that is more flexible but more expensive? This is the mobile phone plan equivalent of the challenge we face in markets where competition focuses on technological innovation – as with cars, electrical appliances and computers – rather than unit prices, as part of what Schumpeter (1943) called the process of "creative destruction." The question of whether to stop searching and make a choice today, or to hope to find something better in the future, also arises with pre-owned goods that are rarely offered for sale: those who hesitate in the hope of finding a better example may run the risk that nothing better comes along and that, in the meantime, someone else will buy the best example that is currently available.

Flux in a market can be so great that the information one has gathered may go out of date before one has had time to do anything with it. Two things brought this home particularly vividly during the research on mobile phone connection plan choices. The first was what happened the day I was finishing a blog piece on the cost of buying an iPhone outright from Apple versus buying one within a plan, using Vodafone's iPhone offers as an example. I had finished the calculations and drafted the blog before stopping for lunch. After lunch, before publishing the piece, I decided to check my calculations and went back to Vodafone's site, only to find that the plans had been changed. My blog had become a piece of economic history even before being released, and I reworked the calculations before hitting "publish." At the level of the market, the kinds of deals Australian consumers were offered changed rapidly, for the better, between the plans in our late 2010 archive and the plans available to our online subjects in 2013 (see the Supplementary Material for Earl et al., 2017). By 2017, when we were still analyzing the rich data from our experiments, life had become even better for consumers, as plans had generally got cheaper and simpler, especially for heavy users of data. Instead of complex call tariffs with two-tier pricing systems, the bigger-capacity plans were increasingly offering unlimited domestic calls and SMS messages, their main differences being between the costs of data inclusions. Once again, I was doing behavioral economic history!

As Sidney Winter (1964) realized, the fact that search and evaluation take time has profound implications for how evolutionary selection processes work in economic systems. Following Milton Friedman (1953), most economists have argued that competition will ensure that those who do not behave in the manner assumed in economic theory will be driven out of markets by competitive selection processes. Although market participants may not be as well informed as hypothetical decision-makers in economic models are presumed to be, the assumption was that it was, in the long run, safe to view them "as if" they operated with full information. This assumption presumed that those who unwittingly happened to stumble upon optimal choices would succeed at the expense of those who did not. In the long run, the latter would be eliminated. However, Winter realized that where information has to be gathered and processed, it is possible that those who happen to have effective decision rules that shortcut the search and evaluation process will perform better than those who gather more information and process it more thoroughly: by the time the latter actually work out what to do, flux in the external environment may have rendered their choices obsolete. Meanwhile, those with what Gigerenzer and Goldstein (1996) came to call "fast and frugal decision rules" would have already been adjusting to the changed conditions. Those with the simple, effective rules could thus outperform those whose choices were more circumspect (see also Hodgson, 1994).

Contrary to the perspective offered by Baumol and Quandt (1964), such decision rules should not be viewed as optimal devices for taking decisions: all that the argument requires is that they are decision rules good enough to force the exit of those who try to take decisions via careful deliberation about marginal costs and benefits. Better fast and frugal decision rules might potentially be devised, but even then, we would not know if they were the best decision-making devices that could be developed.

Flux in markets is also problematic for another defense of the notion of optimization, proposed by Richard Day (1967) who, ironically, later became a significant contributor to evolutionary economics. He suggested that in the long run, via experimentation, decision-makers would stumble upon the best way to do things: satisficing behavior would eventually converge to profit maximization. However, as Winter (1971) retorted, in a world of innovation, many market participants may always be running behind best practice. Failure to find the best options does not necessarily result in these players being forced to exit. Survival does not require them to be "the fittest" but merely "fit enough" to survive in the environment in which they are trying to compete (Alchian, 1950). Indeed, with clever thinking, laggards may even be able to leap ahead for a time, via innovations that change the rules of the game. This would be part of the process that Joseph Schumpeter (1943) labeled "creative destruction." In the long run, optimal ways of doing business do not get discovered via iterative adjustments, for in a world of changing knowledge, there is no convergence to a steady-state equilibrium.

Although flux in markets can make it impossible to identify the best choice in relation to a particular set of means–end chains, traditional economists would still assert (once again via Stigler, 1961) that choices in such settings are acts of constrained optimization, open to analysis using traditional tools. All that is required is that the decision-maker can form a probabilistic assessment of the kinds of better deals that could be "over the horizon" rather than being in the kind of "We simply do not know" situation famously raised by Keynes (1937) where we have no basis, however tenuous, for forming probabilities. Hence, conventional economists presume that despite not knowing when a better product will appear in future and precisely what form it will take, decision-makers can figure out how far to keep searching by factoring such probabilities into assessments of the marginal benefits of searching and comparing these benefits with the marginal costs incurred to achieve them. However, once again, this begs the question of how decision-makers get their probability estimates and whether the computational requirement of such a way of resolving the problem would not be so large as to force cognitively constrained decision-makers to deal with it by applying simple satisficing rules.

Choices that have a social dimension are especially challenging in markets that are prone to constant change. Where the choice problem concerns hi-tech conspicuous consumption products, there is the risk that if one jumps in too soon, one's bragging rights will be short-lived due to the products being superseded by new-generation products that are then purchased by those who held out for slightly longer. More time spent on gathering intelligence about what was beyond the horizon might therefore have been very fruitful. In the case of mobile phone plans, signing up for a needlessly expensive one after a brief search process may limit how much we can spend on other things that have a social impact, such as clothing and grooming products. However, devoting endless hours to the ever-changing problem of finding the cheapest mobile phone plan is likely to keep us from social interaction, limiting the payoffs from being able to be better presented than social rivals. Indeed, if the choice concerns a person's very first mobile phone plan, it is not merely the hours spent trying to figure out the best choice that stand in the way of social interaction; there is also the inability to use the mobile phone to communicate. Moreover, those who use fast and frugal search rules to find a reasonably cheap phone plan will have more time to spend keeping abreast of the latest fashion trends.

6.5   Heuristics, Biases, and Simpleminded Search

How we search for solutions to a recognized problem will depend upon three things: (a) how we construe the problem, (b) our repertoire of rules and routines for solving problems and (c) our habitual styles of thinking when applying these routines. An example of a search rule would be "If I need to find a hotel room, I use hotels.com," and an example of a search routine would be "When finding a tradesperson, I ask for recommendations via my suburb's Facebook page, check their review scores, then work down the list from the top-scoring firms until I have succeeded in getting three to come and give me a quotation." Examples of habitual styles of thinking would be tendencies frequently to think superficially, analytically, dualistically (in a simple "black or white" manner), with an open mind, or creatively. These rules, routines and thinking styles may be revised through time, with the aid of higher-level operating rules, following social interaction, personal reflection on experience, and experimentation. Even if people do choose how, and how far, to keep searching via something approximately like the kind of marginal, probability-weighted trade-off thinking presumed in traditional economic analysis, the strategies between which they choose should be viewed as coming to mind as a result of a cue-dependent process that triggers particular habitual modes of thinking, as discussed in Chapter 4.

6.5.1   Willingness to Search

The effectiveness of our search activities may also be affected by heuristics that are part of human nature, biasing our behavior in predictable directions. Whether we bother searching is affected by the way in which we "frame" the prospective costs and benefits of doing so. For example, we may think about potential savings from searching in terms of the proportion we could save, rather than the absolute amount. If so, we may be willing to incur the costs of checking out a supplier rumored to have what we are looking for at a 20 percent saving on our so-far-best price of $1000 and yet not be willing to incur the same costs to check out a supplier of something else we are searching for, where the supplier is rumored to be able to offer it only 5 percent cheaper than our so-far-best price of $4000. Given that, in both cases, we have a hope of saving $200, our search strategy should be the same in both cases.

This kind of scenario is one of Thaler's (2015, ch. 3) favorites and he illustrates it with reference to differences in willingness to search to save a given sum on a cheap clock radio versus on a television that is much more expensive. A less credible anecdote to illustrate this kind of framing effect would be where the cheap product was a clock radio and a car was the expensive item. For one thing, if the car is not new, its quality may be uncertain relative to the best-value used example that we have so far inspected, so our unwillingness to take the trouble to check it out may be due to us factoring in a risk premium. Moreover, checking out the car also entails the often-loathsome prospect of another interaction with a car salesperson (Barley 2015), whereas a fresh interaction at an appliance retailer does not carry that kind of downside.

Even when we are willing to spend time in a particular search environment to gather information in relation to a particular issue, there is no guarantee that we will focus single-mindedly on our quest. We are susceptible to having our attention diverted – sometime even completely away from our intended search – by the way in which information is presented to us. Consideration of this issue is deferred until Chapter 9, where we explore strategies by which firms may be able to manipulate choices.

6.5.2   Defaults and Other Shortcuts

As Olshavsky and Granbois (1979) emphasize, the process of dealing with problems is often greatly simplified, with far less search being undertaken than would have been readily possible. This may result in decision-makers wasting significant amounts of money that they could have saved had they conducted more thorough research. For example, rather than satisficing as in Simon's basic model by stopping our search as soon as we discover an available option that seems to fit our criteria for acceptability, we might be wise to apply some kind of "oversight avoidance" rule, such as "get another two quotations after getting one that seems satisfactory." But the simplest procedure of all for solving the search problem is the one emphasized by Waterson (2003) and Thaler and Sunstein (2008), namely to select the default option without considering alternatives and even without employing a reference point for defining what is acceptable in that context. For example, when choosing a mobile phone connection service plan, we may head straight to the website of the provider of our landline service and then simply click the one that is listed as "our most popular plan."

Making default choices clearly can prove costly: if we select a default $30 per month mobile phone plan rather than spending a few minutes clicking to and evaluating a $20 per month plan that would be adequate for our needs, we may waste at least $240 over a twenty-four-month contract – and continue to waste money at the same rate if we make the default choice of keeping the plan running after the lock-in contract expires. This is a big price for most people to pay to avoid a few minutes of additional research. On the other hand, accepting the default may in other cases be perfectly reasonable, given the opportunity cost of our time: if it seems likely to take an hour to save no more than we can earn in an hour, we are not necessarily being foolish if we accept the default of allowing our home and contents insurance to be continued via automatic credit card payments at the rate listed in the renewal quotation rather than seeking and purchasing a cheaper product (if we do indeed find one).

A rather more subtle issue underlies the use of social norms as defaults. Going against social norms implicitly challenges the wisdom of the choices that others make even if we do not voice our reasons why we think their choices are flawed. Following the socially normal default strategy thus does not merely economize on our decision-making costs; it also means we are less likely to have to incur the costs of providing justifications for being a deviant. This may prove especially significant if the choice turns out to be problematic, whereas, as they used to say in the computing sector, "No one ever got fired for buying IBM." However, following social norms and failing to engage in careful research before choosing may have severe downsides if the social norms are not well aligned with expert knowledge about the consequences of making such choices.

In the mobile phone plan choice experiment mentioned earlier, no one seemed to choose purely via default settings. In general, though, there was very little sign of any reflection on alternative search strategies. At the outset, virtually none of the offline subjects scrolled down the home page to find out just how many providers there were; rather, many of them just began looking at plans offered by the provider at the top of the alphabetically ordered list and kept working down the list, seemingly acting as if they would have enough time to get to the end of it. Nearly all the familiar providers had names at the other end of the alphabet, but few of our subjects asked themselves whether it would be a good idea to get a reference point by trying to find the cheapest suitable plan offered by a familiar provider. Had they done so, it might have helped them get an idea of whether the unfamiliar providers deserved to be unknown or were being unjustly ignored by most consumers. By contrast, the online participants in the experiment usually began by immediately typing something like "cheap mobile phone plans" into Google. The top results typically took them to mobile phone plan comparison websites, the most prominent of these being Whistleout.com.au, which, fortunately, was probably the least flawed of those available. In most cases, they immediately focused on using these sites, without any critical reflection on the extent to which the sites covered the range of providers (Whistleout.com.au, the most comprehensive site, barely covered a third of the providers, a fact that could have been ascertained in a minute or so via a search for a list of Australian mobile phone service providers), or whether such sites might face conflict of interest problems. In short, the evidence suggested shallow, mindless thinking rather than any depth of reflection on the pros and cons of different ways of approaching the problem.

Doing the first thing that comes into one's head and failing to undertake research on alternatives is not always disastrous. Some who marry the boy or girl next door without exploring alternatives (or who live in cultures where marriages are arranged by their parents) end up blissfully happy, in part due to their (or their parents') prior long-term knowledge of the other party. In markets for goods and services, failure to shop around does not always result in needlessly poor deals: so long as a big enough proportion of customers does search industriously for good deals, competitive pressure may ensure there are no terrible products or products with woeful value for money (cf. Andrews, 1964, p. 102).

In the mobile phone plan choice experiment, disastrous outcomes typically resulted not from plunging into the task in a mindless way but from insufficient vigilance in respect of the task remit's requirement that the chosen plan had to be a "prepaid" product and/or from poor knowledge of differences between types of mobile phone plans and how unit charges are applied. In the face of information overload, it was easy to get sucked into looking at non-prepaid products via their attractive headline prices and then to forget to check whether they were indeed prepaid plans. Some participants evidently ended up recommending non-prepaid plans because they construed "monthly" plans as being the same as "prepaid" ones: certainly, a "monthly" plan, like a "prepaid" one, does not involve contractual lock-in, but if usage levels exceed the amount permitted by any up-front purchase of "included value," a bill for the excess usage would follow rather than the service terminating until a new block of credit had been purchased. Many participants' cost calculations went awry due to failures to understand even the basics of call charges, which commonly involved an initial fixed cost in the form of a connection fee, with calls being timed in sixty-second blocks rather than on a per-second basis. (Our participants commonly operated as though the call blocks were applied to total call minutes over a month, not to each individual call.) However, even with simpleminded search, it was still possible for some participants to find the cheapest plan or one of its close rivals.

6.5.3 Localized Search

Something of a precursor to the modern behavioral economist's emphasis on default-based choices can be found in Herbert Simon's early writings on satisficing behavior. Simon emphasized that humans tend in the first instance to search locally because this is easier to do than casting the net widely and yet may still generate satisfactory results. This heuristic may of course mean that we fail to discover that we could have been setting our sights much higher, and could have been able to meet these elevated aspirations, had we searched within a bigger pool.

The predisposition to search locally can be viewed as an aspect of the availability heuristic. This bias-inducing heuristic calls to mind the joke about the drunk who has dropped his keys in a dark gutter but is looking for them a bit further along the road where a streetlamp provides better illumination. However, even when sober, we are prone to look where it is easy to look, which may not be where the probability of finding a good solution is highest. For example, in statistical terms, there should be a far better chance of finding a suitable potential spouse in a large pool of prospects, yet many people in the market for a mate still resist using online dating sites and rely on opportunities that arise at work or in singles bars, where the pool of prospects is far smaller.

Cohen et al. (1972) have offered what may be viewed as a provocative variation on the idea of localized search, in the form of what they label, possibly somewhat misleadingly, as "a garbage can model of decision-making." Their model is an attempt to capture what is frequently to be observed in administrative systems that operate in a chaotic, incoherent kind of way. Such systems provide easy material for writers of satirical situation comedies about public-service bureaucracies (see, for example, YouTube material from the Australian Broadcasting Corporation's series *Utopia*) that feature staff with very poorly defined objectives, who sometimes have rather little to do but who at other times are to be found frantically throwing together proposals or means of demonstrating that actions of particular kinds are under way. The "garbage can" term captures the unstructured, chaotic nature of what happens, which often entails using ideas that had previously not being taken up or work that had not been completed. The decision-making environment thus brings together: (a) people looking for something to do, (b) advocates of ideas and strategies that have previously not found acceptance as solutions to problems and (c) people looking for opportunities to air issues and find solutions for them. What gets done by such a group of people is portrayed by Cohen et al. (and modeled by them using a computer simulation) as a path-dependent matching process that enables particular tasks to be generated to satisfy the advocates of particular strategies, which satisfy those who have been keen to air particular issues. All the ingredients in the problem-solving process are taken from what happened to be in this "garbage can": the group in question keeps itself looking busy considering problems and finding solutions without searching in its external environment. This is the organizational equivalent of couples forming as a result of who happened to be in a singles bar on a particular night, rather than as a result of careful online search via dating websites. If ideas that previously were not deemed useful are now taken up, their proponents are at last vindicated for the effort they put into them.

The "garbage can" notion is not always ideal for capturing processes in which ideas that some people had rejected as solutions to past problems may get touted and reused as solutions to later problems in roles that had not been anticipated. Garbage cans normally get emptied from time to time, whereas in some cases, the operating rules when something is deemed not currently to be of any use is "Never throw anything away." Hence the situation sometimes is perhaps more like one in which a person with a problem goes to a garden shed or an attic (or a dedicated folder of files of unused ideas on a computer hard drive) in search of something that can be repurposed as the current problem's solution. Reluctance to throw things away may result from unwillingness to accept one has wasted one's efforts (cf. the discussion of sunk cost bias in Section 7.8). However, hoarding on the basis that "it might come in useful one day" is not always dysfunctional: sometimes that day does indeed come along and having the idea, unfinished design, etc., ready at hand can save fresh efforts if it provides a satisfactory solution to that day's problem.

6.5.4   Avoidance of Embarrassment

It needs to be emphasized that limited search can arise for reasons other than time pressure or cognitive shortcuts. A particularly interesting case in psychological terms concerns products whose purchase is seen by consumers as an occasion for embarrassment. Such cases may arise where consumers fear making fools of themselves by revealing their lack of expertise or where the products relate to bodily functions or activities that are not seen as appropriate to raise, even implicitly, with strangers. Waterson (2003) provides a telling case, namely the competitive shake-up that occurred in the UK condom market when these products were moved on to open shelves in pharmacies and hence no longer entailed prospective buyers having to ask at the counter to see alternatives. Before the change of policy, the embarrassment factor favored the dominant brand Durex, which had become practically a synonym for the product, and many buyers would have been hard-pressed to name alternatives. Even today, in the open-shelf environment, we might expect prospective buyers of condoms not to study rival packages at length due to concerns about how they might be construed by onlookers.

6.6   Goodwill and Brand Loyalty

A variant of the strategy of selecting the default option rather than finding and examining alternatives is to not bother searching and instead to give our custom to a supplier we have previously used. We may do this where the problem to be solved is that we are running out of supplies that we have previously purchased, or we need a similar kind of service to one previously purchased from the supplier (as with the services of our regular doctor, dentist, lawyer or car mechanic), or even where we need to deal with the shortcomings or demise of an existing product that we purchased from the supplier (for example, by replacing a deceased Apple laptop with another Apple laptop). In effect, the supplier previously used in that area becomes our default supplier.

Failing to consider any alternatives in these situations may sound like a very sloppy form of satisficing, and sometimes it is. Indeed, in the third kind of case, we fail to punish the supplier whose product has become problematic; thereby we run the risk of giving the supplier an incentive to design products that will go obsolete or are less physically durable than they might have been. To keep us coming back for more, such suppliers merely need to ensure that their products and services meet our criteria for "good enough": for example, if we get at least five years of service out of an Apple laptop before it suffers a catastrophic failure, we may be satisfied with its longevity. However, although repeatedly using the same suppliers can sometimes cost us dearly, it can often be an effective, "fast and frugal" way of operating. Given the uncertainties here, the wise customer may be one whose decision routine includes periodically seeking alternative quotations to check whether the usual suppliers are keeping their offers in line with their rivals, then sticking with them if they are competitive but challenging them, or exiting from dealing with them, if they are not.

In traditional economic analysis there is no basis for preferring one supplier to another if both offer the same price and quality combination. This appears to imply that relative market shares in competitive markets are indeterminate where firms are offering identical deals. On this view, market shares could be transformed by very small differences in relative prices and product quality, which would then invite retaliation. Attachment to a supplier is viewed as a kind of enslavement caused by the presence of "switching costs" or, with experience goods and credence goods, a lack of knowledge about the probabilities of doing better by switching. Switching costs may arise due to the costs of seeking quotations from other suppliers and setting up new contracts, the costs of learning to deal with somewhat different products and/ or their suppliers and the costs entailed in integrating an alternative product into a system of complementary products (for example, changing a computer may also necessitate purchasing new software and/or peripheral equipment). The unknown probabilities problem – formally referred to as the "two-armed bandit problem" but partially captured in the everyday expression "the risk of jumping out of the frying pan into the fire" – will persist if we fail to experiment with alternative suppliers to build up evidence about how reliable they are at satisfying our needs. However, in the absence of such costs or any reluctance to switch that is caused by uncertainty in respect of untried alternatives, the traditional approach portrays buyers as if they are economically promiscuous, ready to switch to wherever they can get the best bang for their bucks.

Things look rather different from an evolutionary perspective: although the enslavement scenario may indeed apply for some contexts, rebuy tendencies often signify mutually beneficial long-term "goodwill" relationships between buyers and suppliers, rather akin to de facto spousal relationships. As with human relationships, things do not always run smoothly in these business relationships: sometimes, the supplier causes disappointment or falls behind relative to competitors; sometimes, the customer seems to be a nuisance (for example, by asking at short notice to change an appointment or the specification of what is to be delivered). But the crucial thing is that over the long term both parties judge they are getting satisfactory returns from doing business together. Having formed a relationship, they will be willing to give the other party credit – in other words, to "cut them some slack" – on the expectation of reciprocal treatment at a later date, should the need arise. The overall evolutionary significance of this arises particularly via business-to-business (B2B) goodwill relationships rather than those between businesses and consumer (B2C). This is because, as Andrews (1964) emphasized, it is the former that dominate in terms of the value of transactions that they affect, through the multiple layers of supply chains involved in the value-adding process before products reach final consumers. Such relationships have been vital in some countries as facilitators of structural adjustments as market conditions change, as with the two-way relationships between giant Japanese firms and their suppliers, discussed by Ronald Dore (2012) in his aptly titled book *Flexible Rigidities*.

This view of the evolutionary significance of goodwill relationships comes from the work of Alfred Marshall (1890) and Philip Andrews (1949, 1964). They drew on their deep knowledge of real-world businesses to argue that the ability to cultivate such relationships is vital for the long-run growth of a firm. There are two main reasons for taking their perspective seriously even in today's globalized world of more aggressive shopping.

First, initial transactions often are not made at random but as a result of network interactions between new customers and those who are willing to share their experiences. This can be compounded by "herding" effects, whereby conjectures about quality and value for money are based on which supplier already has the most customers. Although, once attached, customers are potentially vulnerable to having their inertia exploited, the costs of replacing disaffected customers – who may share their dissatisfaction via their social networks – provides a powerful incentive to keep one's established clientele happy. If an initial transaction or subsequent transaction is a failure, many more transactions may be lost over many years.

Secondly, sticking with satisfactory suppliers can have significant benefits beyond those associated with avoiding the costs of searching. By repeatedly dealing with a supplier, customers enable the supplier to acquire better knowledge of their needs. This will make it quicker to diagnose and solve customers' problems and even to anticipate their needs and know when innovative products will be worth drawing to their attention. Being confident of a regular flow of business from particular customers will make firms more willing to take risks associated with investing in assets specific to supplying those customers. Priority service may also be available when it is required at short notice: a customer known to be a "regular" can be dealt with at less cost than an unknown prospective customer who has not yet established any loyalty and who might merely be "passing through" rather than a definite long-term prospect.

Given these benefits, there is good reason for customers not to sever relationships with suppliers after a disappointing transaction. As Hirschman (1970) emphasized, by "voicing" their dissatisfaction and giving the supplier another chance, rather than simply "exiting" to rival firms, regular customers both let the firm know what it must correct and help ensure it can invest in making the required improvements. In a world of change and human fallibility, firms will suffer from lapses of relative or absolute levels of performance from time to time but satisficing decision processes whereby customers cut them some slack help ensure that the market does not deselect firms that would have been able to perform well enough in the longer term. Being loyal despite a disappointing transaction may thus be rational, though after a run of problems, the evidence may be taken to imply it is indeed time to shop elsewhere.

It should be emphasized that often when clients give suppliers their goodwill, they are not doing this in a one-eyed manner or presuming that the supplier is necessarily going to be the one they will stick with in the longer run. Where there is scope for suppliers sometimes to cause problems, it is wise to diversify when sourcing products and "not put all one's eggs in the same basket": for example, a police service typically will source its vehicles from several manufacturers in order to limit the disruption of having vehicles off the road due to a product recall. In B2B relationships, a major customer may keep giving most of its business of a particular kind to its preferred main supplier (such as its regular advertising agency) while also giving smaller blocks of work to up-and-coming new players. In this way, it signals to the established supplier that it is not to be taken for granted, while also developing knowledge of the capabilities of the aspirant long-term suppliers by seeing how they handle the crumbs of business that it feeds to them. By this kind of limited diversification in its choice of suppliers, the firm limits its vulnerability in the event that things fall apart with the main provider and it needs a trustworthy replacement in a hurry.

Just as B2B goodwill relationships are sometimes polygamous, so brand loyalty of consumers often involve a degree of economic polygamy (Ehrenberg and Scriven, 1999). Over the long term, our needs and wants change, and suppliers' capacities to meet them evolve at different rates. Because of this, we may flip back and forth from time to time between a rather small set of rival suppliers. We are not loyal to just one brand, but we limit our search by not being open to all. Thus, for example, owing to a focus on reliability, we might be loyal to Japanese car brands and at various times buy the products of Toyota, Nissan, and Mazda, without for a moment considering their European or Korean rivals. If so, the only way we may end up rethinking our loyalty is via seeing the experiences of members of our social network with their new Volkswagens and Fords, if anyone we know buys them, or by being forced to drive Kia and Hyundai products when we have to rent cars. After thereby discovering how good the products of the Korean brands have become, we may then try to find out what the facts are regarding their reliability.

6.7   Creative Thinking

A distinction needs to be drawn between external search activities – such as investing time in gathering information via the Internet, visiting retailers or getting prospective tradespeople to come and give quotations – and internal search, where we look for solutions within our minds. The need for external search can be reduced if we take time to trawl through our memories in search of products and suppliers that could help solve the problem we have perceived. But internal search may also entail thinking creatively to form new constructs about the kind of product that entrepreneurs might have thought of supplying (possibly for a different application) that might solve the problem we have recognized. When we use our imaginations in this way, we think like an entrepreneur by constructing new conceptual connections (see Earl, 2003) – new, at least to us, though they might actually be original and even be the basis for us to consider starting a business.

For example, suppose our problem is that of weaning an elderly relative on to using a mobile phone so that we have a backup way of staying in touch now that her traditional landline phone has been replaced by a VoIP service that will not work during an electricity outage. Previous attempts to get her to use a mobile phone have failed because she seems incapable of learning how to keep its battery charged and cannot deal with its user interface due to the keys being too small or her resistance to using a touch screen. We think for a while and then realize what we need to find: a mobile phone that is just like the handset of her cordless landline phone in terms of size and operating interface and which has a dock for charging. This is not like the seniors' phones we have previously seen. However, having used our imagination to envisage the kind of product that might be "out there" due to an entrepreneur envisaging it, we can now conduct a more focused search. Such a search may then lead us to the Olitech Easy Mate Plus, which is exactly what we had imagined might exist (even better, since it also features a programmable emergency button, which we had not thought of hoping to see included). Alas, during the writing of this book, this product ceased to be offered and was replaced with a 4G clamshell model, the Easy Flip, though the latter retained the charging cradle.

Creative thinking is essentially an extension of the process for making sense of stimuli and forming expectations that was set out in detail in Chapter 4. When we engage in creative thinking, we do so by using existing constructs from our repertoires and bending, breaking or blending them (Eagleman and Brandt, 2017). Creative bending entails reimagining a familiar concept in terms of a different scale or shape, whereas creative breaking entails analyzing it in small pieces to understand which elements are necessary for meeting particular goals and what might be done with just some of them. Creative blending typically entails a splicing process that Koestler (1975) labeled "bisociation." From a rather limited initial set of constructs, we can, if we put our minds to it, develop a huge array of more specialized ones, rather in the way that, as Shackle (1979) notes, we can use a couple of dozen letters of the alphabet as elements from which to construct thousands of different words. The ideal seniors' phone that we imagined splices together aspects of a cordless landline phone and something like an iPhone that can be charged on a dock, but not the iPhone's user interface or vast array of capabilities. These elements were themselves created in a similar kind of way: a cordless phone brings together elements of a traditional landline phone, radio technology, a battery charger and rechargeable batteries. These elements, in turn, had emerged from earlier integrative thinking that pulled together elements from yet earlier exercises of the imagination (for example, the traditional landline phone had previously brought together electricity, a system of wiring, a microphone and a loudspeaker), that built on a variety of even earlier connection-making thoughts. In other words, it's constructs all the way down, until one reaches the foundation constructs that enabled us to start using our imaginations as infants.

6.8   Market-Assisted Search and Evaluation

When we use our imagination and memory to find solutions to problems, we are being self-reliant. For this strategy to be effective, we need appropriate experience and a capacity for making mental connections in the area in question. In contexts where we are short of these capabilities, we may often be able to outsource all or part of the decision-making process to those who have superior expertise or operate as hub-like intermediaries. In the terminology introduced to economics in Earl et al. (2017), instead of making "self-reliant choices," we may opt to make "market-assisted choices" as a means of finding better options and identifying them as such. Typically, choices involve a mixture of do-it-yourself and calling upon assistance from the market, but the extent of the mixture and the form that market assistance takes varies with the context of choice.

To appreciate properly the notion of market-assisted choices, it is necessary to think of markets in the way suggested by the leading institutional economist Geoffrey Hodgson (1988), namely as collections of social institutions that facilitate streams of transactions of particular kinds. In turn, a social institution should be seen as any social rule or source to which we habitually head, or are advised to head, "as a rule," for help in finding solutions to a problem. In today's world, such institutions include not merely internet search engines such as Google and online knowledge hubs such as Wikipedia, but also trusted product-specific sources of information and knowledge. The latter consist of for-profit product comparison websites, websites of trade associations, government websites, newspapers, magazines and other media that host advertisements and report on, or review, particular kinds of products. Sources of market assistance can also include people whose inputs we are prepared to consider, such as consultants, sales personnel in retail stores and lay expertise sourced via social networks such as Facebook. In other words, people who are believed to have relevant expertise become go-to institutions in their own right, discoverable with the aid of other institutions but who may sometimes help us by commending yet other institutions as means of solving particular problems.

When search processes are market-assisted, the evaluation stage of the decision cycle is often market-assisted, too. For example, once we start using market institutions to find potential solutions to the problem we are trying to solve, we often move on seamlessly to using them to help us evaluate what we have discovered. An outsourced evaluation may even come before the market institution shows us what is available. For example, we go into a store, explain to the sales staff what kind of product we are looking for and they then show us a restricted set of items that they think will meet the decision criteria we specified or will solve the problem we have explained to them. Internet search engines and product comparison sites can frequently serve us in much the same way.

The distinction between market-assisted and self-reliant choices that was introduced in Earl et al. (2017) grew out of an earlier, more radical notion proposed by Earl and Potts (2004), namely that the idea that there are benefits to be had from the division of labor might usefully be extended from the production side of economic analysis to the preference side. The division of information and knowledge is inevitable in a world in which the set of products keeps changing, where consumer enter markets infrequently and pursue different ends but are all constrained by finite time and cognitive capacity. In its most extreme form, the market for preferences idea extends as far as outsourcing the choices that we make, rather than merely outsourcing inputs that we then use in making our own choices. This extreme is likely where our preferences exist only in a very basic sense and we have very poorly developed means–end chains – for example, when we ask, "What sort of superannuation plan does someone like me need to have?" or "What shall I do when I retire?" or perhaps, the even more basic question, "How can I achieve happiness?" Clearly, there must already be some basic means for choosing, for multiple sources of assistance may be used: if sources differ in the answers they supply, a choice will have to be made about which, if any, of them to use as a basis for choice.

A market for preferences is rather odd in that, unlike a typical market, transactions need not involve any payment to the supplier of information and "if-then" suggestions. For example, someone who provides assistance might merely receive a brief but personal "Thank you" message or socially standardized token reward such as a bottle of wine whose price is well short of what one might have been able to earn in the time it took to provide the assistance. Those who post reviews on online sites such as Amazon.com typically receive nothing beyond, at best, an automated "Thank you." The seemingly one-way nature of the interaction in these cases begs the question of why so many people give their time so freely in posting reviews and helping others to shop in areas where the latter have less experience and/or expertise.

The standard training of economists predisposes them to see the solution to this puzzle in terms of a long-run incentive that is associated with reciprocal behavior. If we fail to make our expertise available today, we might find that others in our social network do not come to our assistance tomorrow when we could benefit from their expertise. In some contexts, the interaction is entirely anonymous but via an intermediary who keeps tabs on who has been contributing. An academic journal operates in this way: those who want to get their work published in a particular journal would probably aim to avoid alienating its editor by repeatedly declining requests to referee the work of others. Some behavioral economists might view those who post online reviews not as operating altruistically but as deriving utility from being able to be seen as owners of the products they review, and from getting good ratings in terms of number of views of their YouTube video reviews or for how useful their review was relative to those posted by others about the same product. Many reviews come from disgruntled consumers and hence simultaneously signal what they could afford and the fact that they acknowledge they made a poor choice. Here, one might presume the utility comes from punishing the supplier by reducing its subsequent sales, as payback for the supplier's failure to compensate them for their bad experience.

Such perspectives may indeed be worth taking seriously, but we may be able to go much deeper by assembling an evolutionary perspective on this behavior (see also Simon, 1992, 1993, 2005). If operating in an altruistic manner benefits a social group, whatever it is that drives the altruistic behavior will have a bigger chance of being retained and passed on to subsequent generations. A relevant trait here is what Csibra and Gergely (2011) have called "natural pedagogy" – in other words, part of being human is a programmed tendency to try to share our knowledge with others. The driving force could be genetic, such as something that hardwires the brain so that a person "cannot bear the thought" of someone else going through what they have been through. For example, if you are gluten intolerant, you may remember what it was like to try to cope with the task of buying groceries and eating out when you were first diagnosed, and it is that memory that makes you volunteer to help someone who has just been diagnosed with the same condition. But altruistic behavior may also be the result of people picking up altruistic norms from the societies in which they grew up, as part of the moral code according to which the society operates (cf. Smith, [1759] 1976). We may thus "do unto others as we would have them do unto ourselves" and contribute to ensuring that this rule gets passed down to future generations. Cultural practices may also be conducive to openness to taking advice, as in societies where there is respect for the wisdom of elders.

6.9   The Source Credibility Issue

Despite the evolutionary basis for people to want to help others make decisions, there is the risk of being led astray whenever one outsources information gathering and/or accepts recommendations. Those who supply information and evaluations may:

- Face a conflict of interest (for example, a real estate agent may seem to be trying to help us but is also acting on behalf of the vendor);
- Be less diligent than they might have been in their examination of the product (for example, in the case of someone undertaking a building or pest inspection on a property that we are thinking of buying);
- Not have the expertise that we think they have or that they profess to have (for example, where a mobile phone comparison site mistakenly lists a particular "prepaid" plan as a "monthly" plan); or
- Express opinions based upon statistically unrepresentative personal experiences (for example, they may have had unreasonable expectations about the hotel room for which they have written a thoroughly negative review on Tripadvisor.com).

This implies that if we opt to outsource our evaluations, we must dispose of another "infinite regress" problem: we need rules for evaluating the likely quality of the information and/or evaluations that we obtain, i.e., rules for judging to whom we should give our trust. Perhaps we should outsource the latter rules, too, but if we do, we run into the same issue. If, on the other hand, we decide to be self-reliant in working out whom to trust, the Duhem–Quine problem kicks in, for we then have to grapple with the question of how we know how to make such assessments. We apply a rule or hierarchy of rules to sidestep this morass, just as we would have had to do when judging whether we faced a problem (see Section 4.6).

The criteria that we use for assessing source credibility take many forms, ranging from relatively unconscious pattern recognition in terms of body language (as with "shifty," "sheepish," "smarmy" demeanors that we have previously encountered and associated with poor outcomes), through to displays of credentials and testimonials. Sometimes, our rules may, in effect, take the form of simple statistical tests, based upon a minimum sample size, average rating and some sense of the distribution of ratings. Online retailers such as Amazon.com often make it easy for us to apply such rules, but they promote the use of a further kind of rule, namely using the reviews that others have "found useful." We can also employ rules that refer to the extent to which suppliers are "market institutions" in Hodgson's (1988, ch. 8) sense. For example, we may trust a firm that has been in business for a very long time, on the basis that it would not have survived so long if it persistently lied to its customers or delivered poor quality and poor value for money. Firms that indicate their membership of relevant trade associations and/or that they have won particular awards invite prospective customers to trust them on the bases of these proxies.

Our stopping rules might be very simple – such as "When judging whether a movie will be worth watching, I always use a review by critic X." Even experts in a field may outsource within their area of interest via very simple rules: for example, in the case of forming expectations about macroeconomic matters, the distinguished monetary economist Charles Goodhart (2008, p. 7) admits to using a very simple rule "Martin Wolfe of the FT is always right." But our rules may sometimes be much more complex, such as "I always rely on the reviews on Amazon when buying books or music, tending to read the first three favorable reviews, look at the distribution of ratings and then look at the worst reviews to see whether those customers seem to have had unreasonable expectations relative to those I'd be using if I had bought the product without reading the reviews."

The risk that suppliers of search and/or evaluation services may present biased results implies that it may be wise to use multiple sources when making market-assisted choices. But here we run into the same question that we run into when getting quotations in a self-reliant way: how many is enough? The experiment on mobile phone connection plan choices that is reported in Earl et al. (2017) added a fresh dimension to this puzzle, for it revealed that the payoffs to using comparison websites varied depending on how competently the participants in the experiment used them. Choices could go awry because the sites themselves were rather complicated: their features (such as calculators and search engines) could be buried on linked pages or not noticed on pages that were examined but which contained too much information. Consequently, there were payoffs to limiting the number of sites visited and focusing instead on learning how to make effective use of those that one did visit.

The rules we use for deciding whom to trust can be based upon the mental models we have constructed in relation to the incentives that our sources have to tell the truth. We may reason that a key issue is whether maintaining a good reputation matters for our source. A supplier with whom we have a goodwill relationship has an incentive not to dupe us since, were we to discover what had happened, we would be likely to take many future transactions elsewhere. By contrast, we might be skeptical about endorsements for credence goods provided by celebrities whose careers are well past their peaks: they are likely to have limited opportunities to supplement their incomes via endorsements, making them possibly more likely to say what they are being paid to say even if they are uncertain about its truth or do not believe it to be accurate.

As economists, we may think these incentive-based lines of thinking are very straightforward and hence are likely to be arrived at by those who lack our training. However, this may be unwise where consumers lack training in critical thinking of a more general kind and have not had enough experience from which to infer reliable or, better still, fast and frugal rules for working out whom to trust. A salutary reminder in this respect is the fact that, in the mobile phone plan choice experiment reported in Earl et al. (2017, 2019), not a single online participant took any notice of providers' claims to be "award-winning," whereas this would have been one of the first things we would have been looking for when assessing which provider's plans were worth considering and how closely we would need to look at their contractual fine print.

Even experts can make mistakes in this area. For an ironic example, consider the fact that, for almost sixty years, researchers on organizational behavior accepted James March and Herbert Simon's (1958) assumption that when undertaking intra-organizational search, it is safe to seek inputs from close colleagues. However, Macaulay et al. (2017) have lately challenged this, reporting non-benign aspects of local search within organizations. With hindsight (and the hindsight bias induced by now knowing that local search environments may not be benign), we may find it surprising that March and Simon took their view and that it was accepted for so long: suitably prompted, we will now start thinking about what could go wrong when people rely on their close colleagues. One issue that may now seem obvious is that close colleagues may be rivals in the process of internal competition for promotion, so they have incentives to be selective in the information they make available to each other, and to proffer plausible-looking lines of inquiry that will ultimately turn out to be fruitless.

6.10   Procedural Rationality When Searching

A recurring theme in this chapter has been how limited is the search that people often do on route to their choices. This can result in them wasting substantial amounts of money that they could have saved at minimal cost – as when people who can only earn a few tens of dollars per hour end up wasting hundreds of dollars on mobile phone plans for which they might have been able to find more cost-effective solutions had they spent an extra hour or so searching on the Internet or sought assistance assistance via their Facebook networks. They may instead have used that time, say, aimlessly watching a couple of cookery shows on TV. But some people are very efficient shoppers, able to arrive at cost-effective choices at little cost. Others, of course, may positively enjoy shopping and spend far more time finding what they want than would be necessary purely to solve the means–end problems that provide the pretext for "going shopping." As Scitovsky (1985) emphasized, even before the interiors of suburban shopping malls came increasingly to resemble marble palaces, modern high-end shopping environments encourage this by offering customers a mass of sensory stimuli and opportunities for social interaction.

The diversity that we can see in how people go about searching begs the question of how we can assess the need for policy interventions to protect consumers from wasting their money. Consider those who continue to shop at malls rather than via the Internet. These shoppers will ultimately pay for enjoying their search experiences rather than searching online and then ordering from a discount retailer. However, given the enjoyment they may get from a shopping expedition, we would be unwise to view them as necessarily irrational if they fail to spend as little as they might have done on means to particular ends. Later in this section, we explore the problems of pinning down ways by which good choices can be made in a particular context. However, it is instructive first to explore some of the evolutionary implications of different approaches to search.

Human tendencies to engage in very limited search become easier to understand if we recognize that what mattered for the success of humans as a species was the mix of decision-making approaches across the population. An obvious basic point is that societies in which people paired up without taking years to find a partner that suited them perfectly were more likely to experience rapid population growth. Secondly, very limited search was sometimes vital for survival, because it ensured quick action. The kind of response systems that enabled our distant ancestors to escape from predators and other pressing sources of danger still come to our rescue today, even though the emergency may be caused by, say, a vehicle rather than a lion. These systems prevent the kind of decision paralysis that may beset a deer that is looking at the headlights of an approaching car. However, the successful evolution of humans has also depended on them not treating all occasions for choice as emergencies. Being able to do this effectively, rather than acting like, say, chronically frightened birds, gave humans the confidence and opportunity sometimes to "think slow," enabling them to search for alternative strategies and to create new ideas rather than just working with familiar possibilities.

Like their ancient ancestors, today's consumers and business decision-makers need operating systems whose rules ensure that they rarely behave impulsively when there is no actual emergency or get obsessed with finding better solutions when there are none to be found or where the payoffs to search are trivial compared with the effort expended. They also need to be able to get an appropriate mix when using their capacities for creative thinking: although creative thinking may be used to find ways to limit our vulnerability to nasty surprises, it consumes attention and can be dysfunctional if it gets in the way of thinking about things that we might be able to do to branch out rather than merely make our existing position more impregnable. Thus, although, from a Schumpeterian standpoint, we might appreciate why Intel boss Andrew Grove entitled his (1996) autobiography *Only the Paranoid Survive*, we would be wise to keep North Korea in mind as an example of how paranoia can result in the allocation of attention going badly awry.

People who lack the capacity to make only a few errors when classifying problems and matching problems with effective mixes of defensive and progressive thinking are prone to end up as clients of clinical psychologists. Among these problem cases will be not merely those suffering from paranoia but also those who get diagnosed as suffering from an "obsessive-compulsive disorder." The latter are chronically over-loaded with problems due to their limited zones of tolerance for departures from their views of how the world ought to be. Other problem cases may include those whose lives have got into a mess due to them repeatedly failing to consider alternatives or due to them procrastinating so much that opportunities repeatedly slip away. In terms of their operating procedures, these unfortunate people seem short on rationality, but most of us exhibit milder versions of these symptoms to some degree in some situations. In some parts of our lives, at home or at work, we can all benefit from better knowledge on how to engage in "appropriate deliberation" and thereby become, in Simon's (1976) terms, more "procedurally rational."

In the case of businesses and other organizations, such knowledge may pertain to the use of computer-based decision support systems and algorithms that save hours of human effort in whittling down zones within which solutions to problems may be found. For example, police investigations may be speeded up via the use of psychological profiling systems to pinpoint potential culprits within a database. But behavioral economists can sometimes help toward better choice simply by making an informed critical assessment of the appropriateness of alternative ways of searching for solutions. Consider, for example, the problem that some participants in the mobile phone connection plan choice experiment ran into regarding getting unit prices for international SMS messages. Often, these figures did not stand out readily among a mass of other information on providers' webpages but sometimes the providers had simply failed to list them. Logically, an appropriate strategy for finding such data, if they are on a webpage, was to use the browser's "find" capability. But if this produced no results, it could have been perfectly reasonable to assume a typical value based on unit charges of other providers, on the basis that the usage remit included only a handful of international SMS messages per month: even a significant percentage error in their unit costs would be unlikely to have a huge impact on the overall cost of the plan in question. With only an hour at their disposal, it would not be appropriate for participants to spend several minutes trying to find such a figure for a single plan by repeatedly scrolling on many of its provider's web pages – yet this is what some participants did.

Unfortunately, it is not always possible to think about the choice problem from first principles in this kind of way. For example, if one faces an alphabetical list of potential suppliers, is it more appropriate to sample from the list at random or to spend the same amount of time working down in sequence from the top of the list or up from the bottom? Should we assume that the top of the list contains a preponderance of poor-value suppliers who choose their brand names (e.g., "AAAA Pest Management") in order to snare those who will, via their normal cognitive rules, begin at the top of the list and work downward? Were this the case, the appropriate decision rule might be to begin with the first firm whose name sounds like it is not deliberately trying to pitch itself at the top of the list (e.g., "Accountable Pest Management," or, perhaps better still, "Adam Friedman Pest Management Services" since the latter is not trying to appeal to fears that customers may have in a sector where service guarantees are inherently problematic). In such cases, the appropriate way to proceed would need to be resolved empirically, not from first principles.

An alternative potentially useful starting point for uncovering what constitutes "appropriate deliberation" in a context of interest is to study the systems of rules that experts in the area use. These systems may never become optimal or be capable of being identified as such if they happened, via iterative adjustments, to do so. Moreover, different experts in a given area may have different operating systems. But they provide benchmarks from which others might be able to learn better ways of choosing. There is, however, a problem with assessing procedural rationality in this way: what an expert might do when checking for a problem and trying to find solutions may not be feasible for the nonexperts to do in the context in which they have to make their choices. Two issues are particularly noteworthy in this respect.

First, there is the "tacit knowledge" problem that Nelson and Winter (1982) introduced to economics via the work of Polanyi (1962, 1967). The experts may be unable fully to articulate how they go about sizing up problems and finding solutions. In common parlance, they cannot explain their "knack," having picked it up over many years by a process of "learning by doing," with aspects of it being unconscious. The expert's way of operating may seem to be "intuitive" or based on "gut feelings," whereas what the policymaker needs – and hopes people will come to use – is a set of specific rules and routines. This dichotomy is often the stuff of TV detective drama series, where the "old school" detective operates "intuitively" in the search for solutions to crimes and thereby keeps running into conflicts with the "new guard" senior management for failing to follow official procedures.

Secondly, there may be differences between experts and nonexperts in the time and resources they have available. An operating system that works brilliantly in the expert's usual environment is not guaranteed to work in a less resource-rich environment of a supposedly similar kind. This is a variation of a problem that is commonly observed, whereby "experts" impose wasteful policy "solutions" on populations without properly understanding the realities of the situations with which the intended beneficiaries have to deal. It may actually be the case that lay decision-makers have much more effective coping systems than external specialists; if so, our focus needs to be on finding what the more successful among the lay decision-makers do in that environment.

If appropriate deliberation is to be inferred by studying what works well in the context in question, we need to proceed in a statistical manner, using a suitably large sample of data from research subjects who differed in the quality of the choices they made; we should not simply publicize what the best performers did and advise everyone else to operate in the same way. The reason for this is that the success of the top performers may be partly due to luck despite making mistakes: if their strategies were applied in slightly different contexts, luck might not be there to offset their strategies' shortcomings. (This is an issue often overlooked by those who write books for business executives about the things that ensured the success of top firms at a particular time.) In the case of the mobile phone connection plan choice experiment, a few subjects succeeded in identifying the cheapest plan for the remit (two of twenty-one offline participants, one of twenty online participants). However, all three did so despite making errors of some kind (in fact, a veritable catalogue of errors in the case of the top-performing online subject). With a different usage remit, there is no guarantee these participants would have been the best performers.

To arrive at a statistical view of appropriate deliberation in a particular context, it is necessary to study behavior in a fine-grained way, tabulating things that some research subjects did but others did not. The next step is to examine how the presence or absence of particular kinds of behavior correlate with a measure of the subjects' success in the task in question. In the experiment on mobile phone connection plan choices, Lana, Chris and I constructed an inventory of over fifty things that it might be appropriate to do. The statistical analysis revealed that the great majority of them made little difference to the quality of the outcome (see Earl et al., 2019). But we discovered that being able and willing to call upon the services of product-comparison websites did improve choices and that there were payoffs to spending major blocks of time using (and thereby getting used to) one or, better, two comparison sites rather than trying to use many different sites. Another predictor of the relative quality of choices was how far participants got into their allocated hour before they calculated a complete total cost reference point, on any plan, for meeting the usage remit. Those who delayed doing this, or never did so, and tried informally to assess whether freshly sighted plans were cheaper or dearer than plans they had been looking at previously were prone to make poor choices. This was so even if their "eyeballing" technique meant that they had a quick look at the offers of a larger number of providers.

It may not be possible always to use such fine-grained research techniques to arrive at a picture of what constitutes "appropriate deliberation" or even, say, the kinds of things decision-makers need to do or avoid doing if they are to end up in the top half of the population in terms of not wasting money or on any other performance measure. But less fine-grained, more cheaply obtained data from surveys can have problems when respondents suffer from bounded rationality. We learned this to our cost in the project on mobile phone connection plans choices, where we had planned to study procedural rationality not merely from the process-tracing experiment but also via data from part of an initial large online survey. We ended up having to abandon our hopes of using data from the survey to shed further light on what was procedurally rational in this context. The problem was that although the survey data included answers to questions about how the respondents had chosen their plans, which might have been worth trusting, we discovered that the respondents' claimed usage patterns were frequently way out of line with their reported monthly spending on the plans that they said they used.

Assessing how procedurally rational people are is also problematic where products serve multiple ends that different consumers value somewhat differently. For example, suppose we were trying to understand what constituted procedurally rational search when buying a car. Here, search strategies could affect both whether people end up choosing a vehicle appropriate to their needs, and whether, given what they buy and what they trade in, they end up finding a good deal. In respect of the former, we might at best be able to classify buyers as having failed or succeeded in searching the market adequately based on whether they ended up purchasing vehicles that were dominated on all relevant dimensions or that expert testers rated as worse than average, overall, for that class of vehicles. The "good deal?" issue centers on a monetary value, as in the mobile phone connection plan experiment, but it could be hard to study due to the enormous set of possible purchase or trade-in combinations and uncertainty about quality differences between vehicles.

Finally, it should be reiterated that we should not presume that the best thing for a population of buyers in a particular market is that they all adopt the search strategies that are used by those who consistently find the best deals. To be sure, a market may need to have enough canny shoppers in order to provide incentives for suppliers to compete keenly. However, if such a situation prevails, the quality of deals that the bulk of the less canny shoppers use may not fall far short of their cannier counterparts. If the less canny shoppers use faster search strategies, they might not judge it was worth the extra time to achieve better deals. Moreover, if everyone started searching in the same way, the supply side of the market might adapt, changing the nature of appropriate deliberation in that context.

6.11   Conclusion

Economists traditionally focus on price as the key factor that determines which transactions take place to balance the forces of supply and demand or to coordinate imbalances between these forces. It should be evident from this chapter that their focus is misleadingly narrow. For a product to get purchased, it must first be discovered by potential buyers and recognized by them, or by those who assist them in the process of choosing, as a potential solution to a problem they are trying to solve. Offering a lower price or better value for money will not win a sale if potential buyers use search strategies that leave them oblivious of products that would have served their needs more efficiently than any of the products that they end up considering. Hence, if we want to understand how, and how well, a market works, it is vital that we understand how buyers construe problems and search for solutions.

This chapter has pinpointed some of the key issues that confront decision-makers when they try to do this and has argued that these issues ultimately have to be dealt with by applying rules. Even though decisions about searching might superficially appear to be acts of constrained optimization, involving the weighing up of prospective costs and benefits in the face of limited time and cognitive power, logic dictates that they are built upon rules that call a halt to inherent infinite regress problems. We logically must operate in a satisficing manner or on the basis of other heuristics and cannot engage in constrained optimization unless we are dealing with simple, closed problems. The evidence suggests that people often could readily be doing much better by using different search rules (see Grubb, 2015). However, search based on simple rules and routines can also be far more efficient, if the rules and routines are appropriate, than time-hungry strategies that involve gathering and attempting to process huge quantities of potentially relevant information.

Implicitly, to use the title of John Hey's (1982) experimental study of search behavior, we have been on a "search for rules of search." But we have not ended up with a definitive list of general-purpose "how to" rules for conducting search. Although the general message is that search is rule-based, the rules that are appropriate for searching for solutions to problems are place-, population-, time-, and product-specific. This point is especially significant in the Google age where our search results and their rankings depend on previous searches by ourselves and untold numbers of other searchers and the links to which we and the latter then clicked.

7 Why Do Some Things Matter More Than Others?

7.1 Introduction

In order to be able to choose, we need to have more than just an awareness of rival products or strategies and an ability to characterize them in terms of what we may expect to get if we select them. We also need the ability to assign values to the prospective performances of our options on the construct axes in terms of which we have characterized them. In other words, for choices to be made, knowledge of options that can serve as means to particular ends has to be combined with a system for ranking rival means to these ends and/or prioritizing the sequence in which we will attend to rival ends or combinations thereof: we need a way of deciding what matters to us, what requires our attention right now.

The paralyzing consequences of being without such a system are evident from neuroscientist Antonio Damasio's (1994) reports of the problems experienced by some of his head-injury patients with prefrontal cortex damage. They could no longer choose, say, a restaurant despite retaining their pre-injury capacities to offer detailed characterizations of a range of familiar restaurants. If we have no system for assigning values, we are indifferent about everything, no matter how much our options differ. Being open to everything closes off nothing. To reason our way toward a choice, we need a system for assigning values; being able to reason without such a system would leave us mentally going round in circles noting the differences between our options.

Now, of course, if we happen to be in a situation for which we have no valuation system, we can ask ourselves what systems we might devise to serve in this role. We may also be able to make use of the market for preferences (Earl and Potts, 2004) and ask others what systems they use, advocate or are aware that others use in this kind of situation. However, both strategies beg the question of how we should value the characteristics of alternative valuation systems; indeed, there is the prior question of whether we should try to figure out our own system of values in the area in question and not even see how outsourced value systems look. This is yet another example of the infinite regress problem, and it will have to be dealt with via a preexisting stopping system or rule that we have inherited or have adopted and incorporated into our personal operating system.

For Damasio, it is the emotional side of the operation of the human brain that provides the necessary foundations for our choices. This chapter offers a similar view, except that it is derived primarily from how emotions are viewed in George Kelly's personal construct psychology rather than by following the neuroscientist's approach of trying to understand where in the brain emotions are generated and the electro-chemical processes they entail. Taking a Kellian view of emotions turns out to offer very useful insights on why some issues leave us untroubled, whereas others lead us to "get hot under the collar" or "go ballistic." The Kellian perspective developed in this chapter also offers a way of making sense of (a) some of the key heuristics and biases that modern behavioral economists emphasize and (b) the extent to which people change their behavior in response to changes in prices, product features and promotion strategies. Responsiveness to changed incentives is, of course, a key concern of economists (e.g., via the notion of "price elasticity of demand") but it is something that they have hitherto been able to measure without being able to predict or explain from their theories of decision-making.

Economists have normally disposed of the question of how things come to matter to decision-makers by simply assuming decision-makers each have a "preference system" that entails a decreasing willingness to make marginal substitutions. From their perspective, it is expected that if we have, say, a great abundance of oranges and no apples, we will be willing to exchange many oranges for an apple, but to obtain a second apple, we would be willing to give up fewer oranges, and so on. The focus is always on substitution, rarely on people as systems builders who may avoid products or activities that they say they "don't like," yet have other things that they "wouldn't give up for the world."

Taking the conventional view of preferences is mathematically convenient: it opens the way to using differential calculus to analyze how it would be possible to maximize utility subject to a budget constraint after carefully considering the costs and benefits of consuming slightly more of some goods and slightly less of others. However, in addition to its shortcomings for making sense of differences in the extent to which people change their behavior in different contexts when there are changes to the terms of the trade-offs that they face, it begs the question of whether evolutionary processes would have selected humans with preference systems akin to those that economists commonly assume. It is instructive to consider this question at the outset.

7.2   The Evolutionary Foundations of Preferences

Most economists follow the lead of Nobel Laureate Gary Becker and his colleagues and prefer to model consumers "as if" they have identical preferences. These preferences are taken as "given" rather than being viewed as things about which there should be any debate. To explain differences in behavior, they focus on differences in constraints and different past experiences that have resulted in differences in capacities to appreciate particular products or make use of them (Stigler and Becker, 1977; Becker and Murphy, 1988).

Becker's way of thinking is an attractive starting point even for behavioral economists. His emphasis on the development of human skills and the need for such skills in consumption aligns well with the complexity of many consumer products. Moreover, if preferences are indeed based on emotions, and if we regard humans as having brains that have evolved to function emotionally in broadly similar ways, then it might be reasonable to proceed as if preferences differ little between people. (Possibly there might be some racial or cultural differences in the norms across population groups, with some being, say, more repressed and/or placid and others being more prone to being passionate and/or excitable in public. However, a climate of political correctness is not conducive to exploring the economic implications of this.) People could have similar preferences in terms of the ultimate ends they pursue, yet might differ in their capacities to use particular products as means to these ends. The main thing lacking from such a perspective is an acknowledgment that differences in choice may also result from different ways of seeing the world.

Now, suppose we accept the proposition that people are basically alike in terms of genetically inherited preference systems and that we also accept the evolutionary psychology position that insufficient time has elapsed for evolutionary selection processes to change inherited preferences significantly since the era of our hunter-gatherer ancestors. If so, we need to view consumers as applying, to today's choices, systems of values that are like those applied by early humans to their hunter-gatherer world. If emotions drove what mattered to early hunter-gatherers, this view implies that today's products and services would ultimately matter to us in terms of these kinds of emotions. For example, if early hunter-gatherers had evolved to experience pride, fear and exhilaration, then these feelings could affect our values, too, making us desire a prestigious car, equipped with all the latest safety aids and advertised as "the ultimate driving machine." However, taking the evolutionary psychology perspective begs the question of what kind of value system would have survived the competitive selection processes that operated in the hunter-gatherer environment. This question raises a set of sub-questions.

7.2.1   Do Humans Need to Be Emotional Creatures?

As any clinical psychologist would attest, and as we will see later in this chapter, emotions can be highly dysfunctional. Given this, there must be a good evolutionary basis for humans to be emotional animals. That basis does not arise because of the need for something to call a halt to the infinite regress problem per se. Choices can be made purely via rules that program responses to stimuli. Decision rules can range from the very simple – as with, say, the rules that program a sunflower's "behavior" as it follows the sun's daily track across the sky – to the very complex, such as those that make autonomous motor vehicles feasible. From this standpoint, we might imagine that systems of rules would have underpinned the choices of Spock, the famously emotionless half-Vulcan character from the *Star Trek* television series. In evolutionary terms, early humans did not need to be endowed with Spock-like decision rules; they merely needed rules good enough to produce outcomes that permitted them to breed and pass their rules on to a new generation. Those whose rules were especially well suited to the environment in which early humans lived thereby would have come to comprise a larger and larger proportion of the population.

To pass on their genes to the next generation of humans, our hunter-gatherer ancestors had to have an adequate propensity to seek, and adequate capacity to attract, mates of the opposite sex, engage in sexual activity with them and then be capable of surviving long enough to rear their children to the point at which they could fend for themselves. The rules that enabled them to do this did not all need to be genetically hardwired. Some rules could be learned socially or personally created and then passed down socially to the next generation. For this social transmission process to occur, the early humans would have needed to be programmed to contribute to – and ensure that, in statistical terms, they live long enough to contribute to – the fitness of the social nurturing system that uploaded these rules into the next generation. So, for example, in relation to the latter, it would have helped the fitness of our species if they were programmed with a tendency toward what Csibra and Gergely (2011) call "natural pedagogy," unable to stop themselves from trying to share their wisdom wherever opportunities arose.

In principle, then, early humans could have functioned as social robots without evolutionary processes having selected them to have any craving for, or determination to avoid, specific sensory consequences of any of their choices. For example, if they were genetically or socially programmed to follow a rule that dictated "avoid all snakes," that could be enough to keep them from being bitten by a snake: so long as they conformed to it, the rule would not need to be supplemented by any fear of being bitten by a snake. If a system of rules were enough to ensure competitive fitness, humans could have evolved to be emotion-free decision-makers who in effect functioned rather like, say, a modern "smart-meter." Such a device can "choose" to turn off power to designated appliances if there is a spike in overall demand and there is money to be made by feeding rooftop solar power into the grid. It has no concerns about what it does and never craves to do things it cannot do. If the behavior of early humans were purely rule-based, studying it might have revealed that they had preferences, in the sense of systems for ranking alternatives, even though they had no emotions or passions shaping their desires to do some things and avoid others.

Such a scenario entails a view of the nature of preferences – if not necessarily of the form they take – that is similar to the one that is implicit in the ordinal approach to preferences pioneered by Hicks and Allen (1934a, 1934b; Hicks, 1939) and augmented by the "revealed preference" analysis of Samuelson (1938, 1948). Prior to their contributions, economists had been working with a view of preferences that had psychological connotations: the utility derived from goods reflected pain or pleasure and was conceived of on a cardinal scale as if it were potentially quantifiable. The view was that, as we consume more and more of a product, successive units produce smaller and smaller amounts of utility. On this view, we choose by finding the point at which the marginal utility of a product is equal to the marginal utility of money (in other words, by considering, "Is it really worth paying the asking price to get another unit of this product, given that I might get more utility by spending the money on something else?"). In trying to rid economics of psychology, Hicks and Allen replaced this cardinal utility framework with an ordinal perspective: to them, there was no need to build preference theory around sensory rewards, since preferences could be specified in terms of whether the decision-maker preferred bundle *A* to bundle *B*, or vice versa, or was indifferent between them, with this set of questions being applied to all possible rival bundles. The idea of a diminishing marginal rate of substitution between different goods thus came into economics. Out went the idea of marginal utility, though economists tended still to speak in terms of utility maximization as the goal of the consumer.

The Hicks–Allen–Samuelson (henceforth, HAS) view of preferences is not normally presented as a complex (and hence potentially cognitively challenging) decision rule. However, a system of preferences that is purely ordinal amounts to a rule: in effect, it says that *if* the budget constraint is such that particular bundles are ruled out, *then* a particular bundle from the feasible set should be selected, whereas *if* the budget constraint changes and rules out the previously optimal bundle, *then* a different specific bundle should be chosen. It makes choice a meaningless, predetermined, automatic process, devoid of any soul-searching or passion (cf. Loasby, 1976, pp. 1–2). Such a rule can be made even more complex if expressed in "state-contingent" terms, whereby the ranking of alternative bundles varies depending on the "state of the world" (for example, whether it is raining or fine and/or hot or cold outside, whether we are sick or well, and so on).

So, if emotion-free systems of rules can provide a basis for ranking alternatives, why have humans evolved to be emotional creatures? From an evolutionary perspective, the answer seems to arise from the capacity humans have for reasoning, a capacity that can result in them questioning the rules that they and others have been using to cope with life's challenges. (In essence, this is precisely what the "heuristics and biases" work of modern behavioral economists does when pointing out how human nature is prone to make us somewhat dysfunctional, and how policies can be put in place to produce better outcomes.) Of course, being able to think and challenge the established ways of operating has been the key to the success of humans as a species. However, the human species could have run into problems if, in the absence of emotions, its capacity to reason resulted in (a) decision paralysis and/or, more importantly, (b) a failure to breed. The former issue is where Damasio's view of emotions (and the limitations of the "I think, therefore I am" position of Descartes) comes in; the latter is one that I raised in an earlier publication (Earl, 2013) and which was outlined at the end of Section 2.2.

Damasio's perspective is relevant for human progress, which is unlikely to happen if people unquestioningly follow existing rules. The capacity to reason and think creatively that has enabled humans to be so successful appears to be at odds with emotion-free decision-making. Where people engage in critical and creative thinking that challenges established rules without anyone having a passionate mission to put in place a particular alternative, the result is unlikely to be progress. Rather, when everyone is willing to listen to everyone else and no one passionately advocates taking a particular line of thinking, the outcome will tend to be paralysis as debates get bogged in the morass of infinite regress. Without emotions, leadership is not going to emerge.

While the prospect of sexual pleasure helped ensure that reason did not get in the way of reproduction, other sensory capacities have been conducive to better risk management as well as making it easier for humans to spread to unfamiliar areas when faced with population pressure. Hunter-gatherers would have been more likely to survive and pass on their genes if they inherited sensory systems that happened to ensure they (a) felt hungry when their calorific reserves were running low; (b) consumed sugar-rich foods, wherever available, to bolster these reserves; (c) were deterred by feelings of nausea from eating rotting food or trying to live in unhygienic surroundings. (d) knew from painful experience that they should avoid getting burnt, tearing their skin; and so on. For example, by nature, most people feel very uncomfortable about even the idea of allowing their flesh to burn. Hence, they prefer to try to ensure that this never happens. In this, they differ from G. Gordon Liddy, one of the characters in the Watergate scandal in the United States in the early 1970s: in *All the President's Men* (Bernstein and Woodward, 1974), he is reported as having held his hand over a candle at a party, keeping it there until his flesh caught fire. When someone asked in disbelief what the trick was, he said, "The trick is not minding."

Human competitive fitness has also been helped by inherited emotions that deter people from trying to operate on their own. These include the pleasurable sense that comes from feeling that one belongs to a particular group, as a counter to negative feelings of loneliness that surface otherwise. These emotions matter due to the significance of both teamwork, for getting things done, and social interaction, for generating knowledge on a larger scale than an individual could achieve. Social support systems also make us more resilient by giving us "the gumption to go on" and bounce back from difficulties in our lives, such as illnesses and physical problems (Jones and Jetten, 2011). Hardwired aesthetic preferences could have been significant for human competitive fitness, too (see Dutton, 2003). For example, with humans having first emerged in the savannah landscape of East Africa, an emotional hankering for such a landscape could have reduced the risk that they would stray into potentially dangerous unfamiliar territory until population pressures forced them to do so. Likewise, it would have helped to have a preference to be near water and trees that humans could readily climb to obtain food, vantage points or safety from non-climbing predators. Such preferences nowadays might manifest themselves in the kind of landscape paintings and parks that humans enjoy.

In short, because humans are thinking beings, their evolutionary success required them also to be emotional beings. But it must be stressed that this conclusion does not take us away from the general idea that behavior is based on rules. Rules control the neurochemical processes that we experience as emotions such as hunger, nausea and fear. However, unlike decision rules that we employ consciously, these rules are hardwired via our genetic makeup: for example, if our taste receptors detect that we are eating something sweet, then a particular set of neurochemical events is triggered in our brain, causing us to feel pleasure. As with the rules that manage our attention (discussed in Section 4.2), these rules work via thresholds: for example, when we start to feel cold as the temperature around us falls, this feeling kicks in at a discrete point. Indeed, the rules that determine the emotional impact of what is going on in our lives are best viewed in evolutionary terms as members of our set of rules for managing our attention to enable us to survive and reproduce.

Some human emotional responses to particularly shocking stimuli are so powerful that they entail involuntary operations such as vomiting or fainting. These responses appear to be associated with the brain sending excessively large signals to the body to prepare for "flight" or "fight" (leading, for example, to excessive production of stomach acid), while itself placing undue demands on the rest of the body (for example, on supplies of glucose) by going into overdrive trying to figure out what needs to be done. Clearly, evolutionary processes have not selected humans with response systems that are ideally calibrated. However, they only need to be calibrated well enough to ensure that, most of the time, responses of these kinds do not occur and prevent us from doing what we are trying to do. Being genetically prone to faint at the slightest difficulty is unhelpful, especially if those who come to assist us are being diverted from more important tasks, whereas being programmed to faint in the event of a major problem may enhance our survival prospects insofar as it results in others rushing to our aid.

7.2.2 Would Early Humans Have Developed Systems of Preference That Were Stable and Comprehensive?

Having a sensory system that results in emotions being experienced when particular stimuli are encountered is not the same thing as having a preference system. The latter is a forward-looking device. It therefore has to embody knowledge about how much of the various kinds of pain or pleasure could follow from a particular choice. Some of our means–end knowledge is confidently held – for example, we may know, from experience or word of mouth, that a durian is a fruit that has a disgusting smell but a fantastic taste – but this kind of knowledge is often very limited and tentative because we and those whom we know lack any experience in the area in question. Problems of knowledge, which lie at the heart of the issues covered in the previous four chapters, call into question the wisdom of following conventional economists in thinking of people "as if" they have comprehensive preference systems, ready to apply on any occasion for choice. This is hard to square with the extent to which modern consumers run into the problem of knowing what to prefer when they travel globally or encounter innovative products. But early humans would have suffered from major knowledge problems, too. As they spread out within Africa and beyond, they ran into uncharted environments in which their initial choices had to entail experimentation and satisficing behavior. If they managed to survive, would they have ended up forming comprehensive, stable preferences of the kind that economists like to assume?

So long as early humans had inherited appropriate hardwiring, being wired to experience particular emotions in particular situations would have made it possible for them to make choices that enhanced their capacities to survive and breed without them possessing relevant knowledge. For example, even with no appreciation of the connection between having sex and having babies, early humans who were aware of the sensory payoffs from sexual activity would have ended up producing children.

Similarly, the pleasures of eating sugary foods would have been conducive to building up calorific reserves without any need to appreciate that this was going on. By contrast, those who had the misfortune to be wired to experience nausea when having sex or eating sugary foods would have been less likely to pass on their genes, leading to this kind of genetic rule vanishing from the population.

As early humans expanded into unfamiliar territory, their emotional response systems – if appropriately wired – would have enabled them to form new preferences for sources of food and materials to use to make tools, hunting implements and means for protecting themselves against the elements. They could tentatively experiment and then, in the light of the resulting sensory experiences, opt to push further or back away. In principle, it might even be possible, via an iterative process of experimentation, for them to build up a complex picture of the trade-offs that were worth making, as in models proposed by Robson (2001a, 2001b, 2002) and Rayo and Becker (2007). In essence, these models end up representing decision-makers rather as Day (1967) represented firms that are operating in an environment in which it is not initially clear how to maximize profits but where the solution is eventually discovered, even if decisions are based on simple satisficing rules, via an iterative adjustment process. The hunter-gatherers are viewed "as if" they use simple satisficing rules to explore their environment. The environment, in turn, provides feedback, which they experience as pain or pleasure insofar as the stimuli take them away from their established reference points, much in the same way that firms receive feedback in the form of profits or losses. They thereby gradually learn what kinds of trade-offs they should make to maximize their utility. To the extent that those with less experience have sensory systems that are calibrated in a similar way, the knowledge of those who have more experience will be worth having as a guide to what matters in life.

The preference systems that emerged from this sort of process would, at best, only become complete for the context in which they emerged. As with Winter's (1971) Schumpeter-inspired critique of Day's (1967) defense of profit maximization (see Section 6.4), innovation and environmental shocks are problematic for the Robson–Becker–Rayo view of hunter-gatherers as eventually developing preference systems that gave them the capacity to make optimal choices. For example, in competing for mates, hunter-gatherers had an incentive to be innovative in how they presented themselves. Existing fashions could thereby have been made obsolete, prompting retaliatory attempts at innovation, just as in the processes of "creative destruction" that Schumpeter emphasized as taking place in competition among firms.

7.2.3   Would Humans Have Evolved to Be Always Open to Making Trade-Offs?

The HAS assumption that there will always be a diminishing marginal rate of substitution between goods entails a view of the shape of preference systems that would have been problematic in the world of the hunter-gatherer. Whenever food was in short supply, a HAS robot-like hunter-gatherer would be at greater risk of not surviving than one whose rules took a hierarchical form based around meeting basic

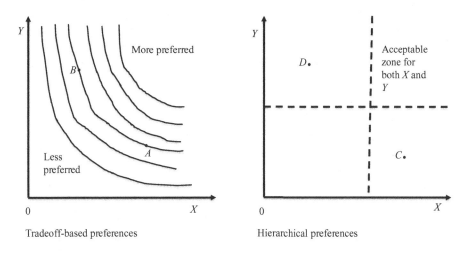

Figure 7.1 Preferences with decreasing marginal rates of substitution versus hierarchical, target-based preferences

needs, as per Maslow's analysis. Unlike a preference system that was always open to substitution, hierarchical preferences would have stopped early humans from jeopardizing their survival prospects by, say, cutting back on finding food if changed conditions meant that it had become more time-consuming (i.e., more expensive) to find food relative to doing other things (cf. Section 3.8). Evolutionary selection mechanisms seem to favor preference systems that are hierarchical, at least insofar as basic requirements for life and reproduction are concerned.

Figure 7.1 contrasts these two different kinds of preference systems. The panel on the left represents preferences as a set of indifference curves whose slopes decrease as we move to the right. In this panel, the consumer is indifferent between rival bundles whose coordinates place them on the same curve (as with bundles A and B in this panel), with preference increasing as one moves to curves toward the top-right corner of the panel. By contrast, on the right-hand panel, the dashed lines represent a pair of targets for basic needs. A bundle in the bottom left quadrant of this panel does not contain enough of either good, whereas bundle C contains enough of good X to meet the target for X but not enough of good Y to meet the target for Y, and vice versa for bundle D. If the most basic need is X but only bundles C and D are available, the consumer will choose bundle C regardless of how much better bundle D is in terms of good Y. If several bundles that have enough of both X and Y are available, then the consumer would choose the one whose combination of goods gets closest to enabling him or her to reach the third goal, and so on if more than one bundle offers enough to meet that third goal. However, if goods are sufficiently abundant in some bundles to meet all basic needs, then perhaps a trade-off may be permitted between any surplus goods that these bundles contain. (If so, the top-right quadrant of the right-hand panel would look similar to the entire left-hand panel.) This is akin to operating via a "safety-first" principle. If applied to risk-taking, it means that the decision-maker is only prepared to gamble with resources beyond those needed to ensure basic needs can be met. On this basis, hunter-gatherers who lacked a surplus of food would have been very resistant to the idea of trying to improve their position by experimenting with agriculture – unless the per-capita supply of food from traditional sources had become so low, due to population growth or depletion of natural resources, that there seemed to be a bigger risk of starving if they did not try to become farmers.

Taking a "safety-first" approach to life in relation to risk-taking is at odds with the view of preferences used in the subjective expected utility (SEU) model of choice (proposed by von Neumann and Morgenstern, 1944) that has dominated conventional economic thinking about risk-taking (and which represented a return to a cardinal utility approach). One of the core assumptions of SEU analysis is the axiom of gross substitution (also known as the "axiom of Archimedes"). This essentially maintains that "everyone has their price," i.e., that we can always be induced to change our behavior in a particular direction via the offer of compensation on a big enough scale to offset the prospective downside of making the change. Where the choice in question involves taking a risk, the SEU model presumes that people compute an overall rating for each available strategy and then choose the one with the highest expected utility. Each strategy's overall rating is derived by summing the utilities they imagine they would get from each of its rival outcomes, weighted by their respective subjective probabilities. From this standpoint, it appears that it is always possible to induce a decision-maker to risk losing everything by reducing the risk of such an outcome to close to zero and/or by raising the size of the tempting outcome's payoff and/or its probability.

From the SEU standpoint, insufficient reward is the only thing that will deter anyone from agreeing to be a mule for a drug syndicate that wants couriers to take drugs into a jurisdiction in which the death penalty applies to anyone caught doing this. Blatt (1979) disputes this: To be sure, some people are prepared to do this sort of thing, but most people regard the behavior of such criminals as foolish, despite being willing to risk their own lives by driving or taking airline flights. The risks of being killed in road or aviation accidents may, of course, be perceived to be lower than those of being executed as a result of agreeing to be a drug mule, but being open to opportunities to earn money in the latter way seems odd if basic needs can be met by other means. Risks aside, most of us would decline such opportunities anyway on the kinds of moral grounds that would have also helped ancient hunter-gatherer societies to thrive.

7.3   Principles-Based Valuations

Behavior that clashes with the axiom of gross substitution is not confined to resistance to taking risks that compromise a "safety-first" principle in respect of the potential for losing one's life or wealth. Everyday experience suggests that people commonly are intolerant of particular kinds of products or situations that entail no such risks; there are things they simply "don't like" for reasons that have nothing to do with price. It is also evident that people sometimes seem to pursue some goals – or have areas in which they pursue ever-higher attainments – seemingly regardless of what they are foregoing in other areas. The key clue to what drives such behavior comes from what people sometimes say when explaining their choices: "It was the principle that mattered" or "I did it on principle." Such behavior reflects the systems of organizing principles that we use to make our lives manageable.

These principles are elements of our personal construct systems and are implicit in the "organization corollary" and "modulation corollary" elements of Kelly's (1955, 1963) theory. They shape our attitudes to our options, playing a role rather like the core assumptions and "do" and "don't" rules (respectively the "positive heuristic" and "negative heuristic" components) in Lakatos's (1970) vision of a scientific research program. The scientist's "hard core" principles may be arbitrary, approximating and sometimes misleading but, as we saw in Section 4.6, without them there is no particular basis for interpreting evidence or trying to push forward the frontiers of knowledge in the scientist's area of interest. A set of principles is a necessary means for avoiding getting bogged down in philosophical debates and infinite regress problems. This applies for us all, not just for academic scientists. In this section we consider how personal systems of operating principles shape our attitudes and the values that we assign to our options. Although we are thereby shifting our focus back to the importance of rules in determining what matters to us, the analysis will later be linked to emotions (Section 7.5).

In Chapter 4, when we introduced Lakatos's analysis of the operating systems of scientists and noted its similarities with Kelly's view of how people in general make sense of the world, our focus was on how decision-makers figure out what has happened or what could be expected to happen if they chose a particular course of action. Here, by contrast, our focus is on how people figure out what they should do, given what they know. In methodological terms, Chapter 4 was concerned with a "positive" question, i.e., how things are, whereas here we follow Loasby (1976, p. 6) and acknowledge that "[c]hoice is a normative activity" – i.e., it is an occasion on which we face the question "Should I do what I'm thinking of doing?" However, just as a hierarchical system of principles provides a way of dealing with the "positive" side of decision-making, so does it provide a means for deriving verdicts about whether the actions we are considering should be seen as appropriate.

The way in which our personal operating systems enable us to do this can be appreciated by likening them to a nation state's legal and constitutional system. Such a system gives the nation's residents freedom to do what they want so long as they conform to the nation's laws. In addition to penalizing those who break the law, the legal system is a means for resolving disputes. If there are disputes about a verdict, the parties may be allowed to appeal to higher courts. Changes to the legal framework are determined by the government of the day and if the residents wish to change the rules under which they are allowed to operate, they may only be allowed to do so legally by following the system's existing rules – for example, by waiting until the next parliamentary election and voting, rather than by bribing parliamentary representatives. If they opt to seek change by staging a rebellion, they will need to get law enforcement personnel to join them, so the ultimate authority (in the absence of a foreign invasion to restore order) rests with the operating principles that members of the police and/or armed forces use. Such a system works on a hierarchical basis: if those in power opt to limit further (or remove restraints on) the behavior of the population, they can do whatever they want so long as they do not lose the support of the police and/or armed forces. As is often seen, nation-states can evolve into systems in which the residents become, in effect, slaves to a dictator and his or her supporting party, whose fundamental operating principle is to maintain power. Life becomes dominated by the ruler's attempts to stay in control. In other societies, there is less of an obsession with staying in control, since principles pertaining to freedom restrain what the governments are prepared to do to remain in power.

From a Kellian standpoint, we are all ultimately slaves to our personal construct systems, and it is the efforts of our systems to continue to be able to predict and control events that drives the values we assign to particular objects and forms of behavior. When we find ourselves facing a situation that we construe as entailing a clash between our principles – which is typically the essence of what is going on when we feel we have a dilemma – we may as a rule look first for a further option that is not beset by this problem. If this fails, we ultimately must resolve it by appealing to a higher-level principle that decides which lower-level principle will be upheld, or whether both lower-level principles may have to be violated in order to avoid compromising the higher-level principle. If the way our systems make us value things is dysfunctional, the only means for recognizing this is from the standpoint of the system we are using. Like a police state, our systems' efforts at self-preservation may prevent us from seeing their limitations.

Our discussions of the management of cognitive dissonance (Sections 4.4 and 4.7) are relevant here. For example, consider how we address the prospect of climate change: if learning how to minimize our carbon emissions and/or implementing that knowledge seems to challenge our core principles, we resist the necessary changes until we are presented either with options that do not violate those principles or with a potentially superior set of principles that we can take up without challenging those at the core of our existing way of seeing the world. In the meantime, we may end up telling ourselves that climate change is not an urgent problem toward whose solution we should be contributing. An ambitious environmental economist might thus do nothing to curb the amount of air travel he undertakes to attend distant conferences, because failing to attend conferences would hinder his promotion opportunities. Hence, if it is pointed out to him that his upcoming conference trip entails carbon emissions on a par with six months' emissions from an average car, he will likely try to argue that if he and other delegates do not go to the conference, this will make it even less likely that emissions will eventually be reduced. By contrast, a colleague who has abandoned any hope of promotion might find it easy to give up travelling to such events and assign more value to spending time reading the latest academic papers and corresponding with some of their authors or engaging with them via Skype or Zoom rather than trying to meet them in person via conference "networking" activities.

The principles that determine our values may be of our own making, but we can also outsource some of them to the "market for preferences" so long as they are not rejected by our principles for what kinds of rules we are prepared to outsource. Thus, for example, some of us choose to be atheists and abide by our own principles for living, whereas others decide to subscribe to a particular set of religious values and allow it to impinge on how they value activities such as drinking alcohol, having sex and children without marrying, operating in a patriarchal manner, and so on. What one person's set of guiding principles allows, or insists upon, another person's principles may exclude. However, similar kinds of behavior are sometimes the result of the application of very different principles: for example, my vegan rejection of pork has a completely different basis from those applied by Jewish and Islamic consumers.

Whether homegrown or outsourced, moral codes or principles may drive many of the valuations that we make, leading us to exclude ourselves from actions that we might have undertaken were we unprincipled wanton agents (see further Etzioni, 1988). However, we can also allow our valuations to be guided by other kinds of principles, such as those that pertain to politics, engineering or aesthetics. Thus, for example, when we choose lounge furniture, we may swiftly rule out chairs and settees that look beautiful but which we judge to be uncomfortable or impractical, as well as those that, according to our aesthetic principles, look ugly. As members of an organization, we may end up using its principles as means of meeting a goal that we use as an organizing principle in our personal lives, as with the conference travel and pursuit of promotion example. Products and potential employers that seem to be at odds with our valuation principles may be ruled out of contention, with clashes between principles being resolved on a hierarchical basis, or by deferring action, rather than by accepting a compromise.

Evidently, a set of principles for organizing our thinking and how we live may rule out many potential options, deeming them to be inappropriate means for getting to the ends that the set of principles leads us to value. It is such principles that underpin comments such as "It's unthinkable that I should do X" (or simply, "I don't do X"), "I wouldn't be seen dead in Y," "I'm not doing that: I'm not that kind of person," and so on. However, our principles may still leave us with room to choose, either because more than one option conforms to them or because they "rule in" more than one possible course of action that we *must* consider.

Sometimes, of course, the principles that we use do indeed leave us with no choice, especially if we have multiple principles that we apply to particular contexts and if these principles set very exacting standards. It may appear that a single principle can be enough to make life frustrating by seemingly removing our freedom to choose. For example, if one is a vegan and all except for one item on the menu are nonvegan, then there is no choice as the vegan principle rules out all the other items. However, note that the frustration is likely to be underpinned by another normative principle, such as the idea that everyone should have a choice if one is presented with a menu of options. Indeed, the frustration may raise a further normative question, namely "Should I patronize a restaurant that denies me any choice?" From a Kellian standpoint, the frustration we experience in these kinds of situations can be appreciated in an even more basic way: when we are in a situation in which we cannot choose, the only way to regain control in that area of life is to exit to a different location. Repeated frustration from applying a principle may result in us questioning whether the principle that denies us choice or ensures we are unable to meet some of our goals is an appropriate one to use as a means for getting through life. If so, a higher-level principle may be needed to find an answer: the principle in question may be a source of problems, but can it be replaced by something else without violating a principle or principles even closer to the core of the system we use for coping with life?

It is easy enough to see how substitution may be problematic in relation to simple dichotomous constructs if our guiding principles label one pole as good and the other as bad (for example, a "party animal" may view someone who is teetotal negatively and immediately rule them out as a potential date). However, systems of principles can inhibit substitution on scalar constructs, too, by specifying a particular dividing point without allowing trade-offs to be made and breaches to redeemed or compensated for by offering especially good performance or taking a punishment or other penalty in another area. For example, the principles that academics apply when grading students will specify a minimum mark for reaching a "pass" standard and not permit a student with a mark that falls short of this to be awarded a pass because the student has, say, a cheery disposition, pleasant nature and tried hard, or was prepared to bribe the examiner.

If we allow such principles to be corrupted via ad hoc variations, they cease to serve the simplifying role that they otherwise play for us. There may also be implications for our identity/self-construct: if we allow ourselves to breach a principle by crossing a particular line either once (with a very firm principle) or "too often" (with a weaker principle), we no longer know where we stand unless we look at our behavior in terms of higher-level principles that redefine the kind of person we are. For example, consider the case of a vegan who is bored with having to eat the same meal every time he or she visits a particular restaurant. If the vegan ends up occasionally losing control and eating a vegetarian meal, there may come a point at which it seems necessary to redefine the working principle for assigning value to different types of food. This could entail, say, relaxing the vegan principle and redefining his or her self-construct to being a "vegetarian" in general, or somewhat less so, to "vegan at home, but at least vegetarian when eating out." But higher-level principles may result in this consumer opting not to abandon a vegan self-construct and deciding to try harder to stick to this ideal without backsliding.

Relaxing our valuation principles or rules may make life more relaxing to some degree, as fewer choices will seem to raise questions about the kind of person we are. However, widening the range of options will make choice more cognitively taxing in other ways. We will be exploring the implications of this in Chapter 8.

7.4   Unconsciously Outsourced Values: The Hidden Persuaders

When introducing the ideas of the "market for preferences" (Earl and Potts, 2004) and "market-assisted choices" (Earl et al., 2017), my colleagues and I were thinking in terms of people consciously and strategically opting to outsource their expectations, valuations or valuation systems. For example, a person struggling to find meaning in life may check out several alternative religious systems and then "convert" to a particular faith. Similarly, a person who has been putting on weight may study various dieting systems and then select one as a basis for choosing what food to eat or may simply adopt one that a dietitian or social network member recommends. However, we should not ignore the role that unconscious cognitive processes can play in the acquisition of social principles for coping with life. The environments in which we are brought up and in which we operate later in life provide us with stimuli that are being generated by the people around us and within which our brains identify patterns. These stimuli include examples of what people do in particular kinds of situations and information about what they experienced as consequences of their choices. Of course, we still must decide for ourselves what to make of this information, but the frequency with which we end up finding the same patterns in it shapes how our minds work because it affects the likelihood that we will try to find such patterns when sizing up stimuli sets that we receive subsequently.

By this process, social institutions can become our rules for cognition and the basis for our lifestyles. These social "hidden persuaders" (Hodgson, 2003) may be every bit as powerful as, or even more powerful than, those from advertising that Vance Packard (1957) famously emphasized. Even if we are not consciously inferring rules from what people in our social circle say or do, our unconscious cognitive processes may be developing sets of associations between particular social phenomena. Seeing particular kinds of choices being made repeatedly in particular kinds of contexts provides a basis for inferring rules that we may then follow until we have occasion to question them. If the pattern seems to be that adults form couple relationships and then have a mortgage, two or three children and a dog and a cat, we will probably come to expect that our lives will be like this unless we see ourselves as being like those who fail to follow the norm. Insofar as we follow such norms, we add weight to them, giving others further instances on which to base their views of normality.

At the very least, the patterns that we infer from what goes on around us provide reference points for what people normally seem to look for in potential means to particular ends and the ends that people normally find worth pursuing. We can use these norms as default settings if we wish and thereby save ourselves the effort entailed in discovering and evaluating alternatives. However, not everyone who grows up in a particular social setting ends up accepting its norms. We will only admit externally developed ways of thinking to our systems of personal constructs and retain them there so long as they remain consistent with high-level rules in our systems that we use for judging when to change our rules. If, by whatever train of events, we create higher-level personal rules that prevent us from absorbing our local social norms, we may end up evaluating our options differently from those around us.

If our lives take place within rather homogeneous surroundings and non-pluralistic cultures (such as rural backwaters, parts of the Middle East, North Korea, and mainstream economics departments in many universities), we may never be exposed to stimuli that challenge the norms that we have previously inferred: we will instead habituate to these norms and fail to build up mental models of alternative lifestyles to which people like ourselves might aspire. For example, if everyone around us says that wind farms are ugly blots on the landscape and potential health hazards, we are likely to end up with a similar view. In effect, we become "social dopes" who follow social norms rather than seeking alternative ways of seeing things and thinking critically about them before making choices (see Garfinkel, 1967; Koppl and Whitman, 2004). For people living like this, the capacity of advertising messages to serve as hidden persuaders will be much more limited than Packard (1957) famously argued.

In open societies, where variation is tolerated among members of social groups, the relative incidence of messages about what is acceptable or constitutes normal behavior may gradually evolve through time. In turn, some members of the group may change the rules they use for anticipating events. If this results in them changing their behavior, they will contribute to further changes in the relative incidence of alternative messages that others receive. Unlike normal behavior that we have seen so frequently that we do not give it a second thought, deviant behavior garners a disproportionate amount of attention because it clashes with normal expectations. But deviants may do much to promote new norms (including pluralistic norms) by providing exemplars of different ways of living. In responding to requests that they justify their behavior, deviants may also provide a basis for their kind of behavior being seen as acceptable by those around them.

7.5   The Trade-Off between Experimentation and Being in Control

Whatever the origins of our sets of operating principles, the fact that we can use these principles to deal with the normative side of choice takes us back to the question of the role that emotions play in decision-making. We have seen that there is an evolutionary role for emotions that relate to whether we are meeting the kinds of needs identified by Maslow, but should we now expect also to find emotions that relate to our capacities to predict and control events, given that the latter could function purely via systems of rules? We will consider this question in the present section, before moving on to examine what Kelly (1955) had to say about emotions – a topic he did not raise until he was nearly 500 pages into setting out personal construct theory.

The evolutionary fitness of our hunter-gatherer ancestors would have been enhanced if they inherited a motivation to predict and control events rather than merely bumble through life in a purely reactive manner. But the balance between the drive to learn (and hence be able to predict better or across a wider domain) and the drive to control is significant for how our lives will unfold. To be sure, being in control is better than being completely at the mercy of events, but an obsession with being in control may cause problems in our interactions with others as well as limiting the extent to which we acquire knowledge of situations beyond our usual range. Since we can only create partial models of aspects of the world, even seemingly familiar territory will be prone to generate surprises. Widening our range of experience may limit the impact of shocks in much the same way that the pursuit of a strategy of diversification enhances the resilience of firms (see Kay, 1982, 1984, 1997). On the other hand, disasters may befall those who are uninhibited in their zest for experimentation and prone to plunge into unfamiliar environments on the expectation of being able to figure out on the spot how to cope with the situations in which they find themselves. Being *somewhat* open to experimentation and thereby to disappointment and loss of control normally allows us gradually to find the limits to our constructs and our capacities for creating new and better ones "on the run." Moreover, in surprise-prone and/or entropic environments, a prerequisite for being able to devote our attention and other resources to experimentation is a willingness to allow some of the things that one might have controlled to get temporarily out of control and out of line with our templates for how they ought to be.

Herein lies a role for emotions that are conducive to growth in our capacity to predict and control events. On the one hand, feeling bored motivates us to try new things and make discoveries. So, too, do emotional rewards associated with the experience of being playful – characterized by James March (1988, pp. 260–265) as entailing suspending our normal operating rules – and "going with the flow," as we do when partying. On the other hand, fear of unexpected consequences and loss of control – of "being caught with our constructs down," as Kelly sometimes put it – makes us hold back from new experiences or at least limit our exposure to risks by merely "putting a toe in the water." The key thing for our long-term success is how these opposing forces are calibrated.

The finite speed at which we can discern associations and form constructs implies that our chances of surviving and reproducing will also be enhanced if we are programmed to have some tolerance for ambiguity and cognitive dissonance. If we do not feel threatened and hence do not back away from something the moment that we realize we cannot figure out what it entails, we have a bigger chance of discovering how it may serve us as a means of predicting and controlling events or how we can prevent it from compromising our efforts to achieve control.

Given this, we should not be surprised by the human capacity for marveling and the emotional "Wow!" buzz that goes with it when we are surprised by something that exceeds our expectations. As Adam Smith ([1795] 1980) realized (in trying to understand the behavior of astronomers by reflecting on similarities between science and everyday life), when people "marvel" at something, it is because they cannot figure out how it can be possible or how it works so effectively. So long as we feel that way about something that has this "Wow!" factor and so long as we are not diverted by the "next big thing," it commands our attention, increasing the likelihood that we will learn something. Likewise, we sometimes experience "surprise and delight" because we have failed fully to anticipate how cleverly a product has been designed to help us to make some things easier to predict or control. Brands that we construe as likely to offer us such an experience will therefore be attractive to us; indeed, one of the attractions of purchasing them will be the challenge of testing how well we anticipate the ingenuity of the designers. These kinds of experience goods clearly have very different emotional connotations from those that we dread buying because the shopping experience clashes with our view of how things ought to be and we construe it as designed to limit our ability to control the outcome (as with buying a car: see Barley, 2015) or because we expect to struggle with vague assembly instructions, complex operating manuals or service suppliers who turn out to be incompetent and/or devious.

These emotions can pull in opposing directions and thereby may have the potential to drive our choices: we may anticipate that a new product will be "marvelous" but dread the beyond-our-control process that we have to go through when buying it, while having repair and renovation work done at home may offer the prospect of restoring control, at least for now, against forces of entropy but come at the price of having to deal with tradespeople who might not be competent or trustworthy.

7.6   The Relationship between Personal Constructs and Emotions

The personal constructs approach to emotions adds a subjectivist aspect to our understanding of this area of the mind. It centers on the relationship between how people see the world and the emotions they experience. We may all experience particular emotions in much the same way in our minds via similar, though possibly somewhat differently calibrated, neurochemical processes. However, the products and situations that we *allow* to trigger these emotions may differ from person to person and, for any individual, may change through time. For example, consider attitudes toward flying. You and I might both have taken our first flights with a sense of excitement rather than trepidation, but now, perhaps, you happily take one flight after another, whereas, after some flights marred by bad turbulence, I may have come to dread flying and therefore now avoid it as far as possible. Even though we both travel economy class, you might not view the seating as claustrophobia-inducing, whereas I perhaps do, and this may be another thing that makes me avoid flying. You might also fly without any concern about the implications of doing so for climate change, whereas, on the rare occasions that I do fly somewhere, I may feel guilty about what it is doing for my environmental footprint.

In other words, just as incoming stimuli do not determine what we perceive, as was emphasized in Chapter 4, so they also do not determine what we feel. Rather, what we feel when thinking about a particular problem, choice or outcome depends on how we form our constructs, i.e., on the rules of our personal construct system and the associations that we thereby make between the things we construe. However, the fact that we all have our own ways of seeing the world does not make it impossible to get a general sense of the kinds of situations in which emotions may kick in and shape our choices.

A simple statement can be used to foreshadow where the analysis below is heading. When we "don't care" about something, it is because we have not created expectations that are contingent on its presence or absence, whereas things matter greatly to us because their presence or absence is something we see as a prerequisite for many of the expectations that we have constructed. It should be emphasized here that the expectations in question can include expectations to the effect that, if we employ particular operating principles, then our lives will be easier to predict and control. Simple though it is, this idea turns out to be very powerful. For me, tuning into the personal construct theory perspective on emotions via Kelly (1955) and the survey volume by Bannister and Fransella (1971) was a key "aha" experience, a "lightbulb moment": suddenly I understood so much more about my own behavior and that of close friends, relatives and colleagues; it also opened my eyes to how some kinds of marketing derive their power to affect behavior.

7.6.1 Kelly's View of Emotions

To tune into Kelly's view of emotions, it is necessary to take his "let us view people as if they are scientists" proposal as entailing more than simply the idea that "people cope with the problem of knowledge in everyday life in ways similar to those used by scientists" (which is how we used it in Section 4.7). What we also need to do is view the essence of living a life as if it is the widening of one's capacity to understand the nature of things and not being at the mercy of events. On this view, as explained in Section 2.9, the things we choose to do are means to the ultimate ends of prediction and control.

From this standpoint, how we feel about how our lives are going, or about the idea of making a particular choice, will depend on what has been happening or seems implied for the systems of personal constructs that we use to predict and control events. The rules of our systems determine what we think we know and how we go about forming our expectations. If they cease helping us to do this successfully in some parts of our lives, we no longer have a basis for action in those areas, which then become a mystery and potentially a source of danger. Given this, we should expect that at least some of the emotions that we experience are those triggered when our brains infer that we face changes in our capacities to predict and control events.

For example, suppose we are at a nightclub and have taken recreational drugs that mess with our brain chemistry – and thereby with the workings of our construct systems – in a way that results in us inferring there is nothing we cannot do. Our brains mark this situation in a neurochemical way that we experience as a feeling of euphoria, which impedes the operations of systems that normally ensure we behave in a guarded manner. A rather different neurochemical process will mark things that seem to entail damage to our capacity to predict and/or control events. For example, we may start feeling depressed if we are finding that nothing that we do seems to make a difference to anything: we might be able to predict events with a gloomy sense of their inevitability, but we see them as opening up no new opportunities for us and we have no expectation of being able to control them. In this sort of situation, our emotional experience is being driven by our way of looking at the world, but we may "feel" very similar to those whose brains are malfunctioning, making them feel depressed despite their lives offering them excellent opportunities. However, the latter may need medication, rather than cognitive therapy aimed at promoting a more positive view of the world.

In writing about emotions, Kelly opted simply to focus on the current or prospective state of a person's predictive system rather than trying to link that state to what the brain is programmed to do (for example, in its endocrine systems) when particular states arise. He defined some emotions in terms of the fit between our construct system and the situation we are in but defined others with respect to the kinds of actions in which people engage.

Kelly (1955, p. 495) defined anxiety as "the recognition that the events with which one is confronted lie mostly outside the range of convenience of one's construct system." For someone who has an anxiety disorder, the problem is that of being convinced that they will not be able to make sense of, and act appropriately in, many of the situations that are part of everyday life. As a result, they may keep avoiding such situations and thereby fail to synthesize new constructs or acquire relevant constructs from other people, and they will not get to see how well they can cope even by using their existing constructs. (Note how this idea complements the Becker–Stigler–Murphy view, mentioned at the start of Section 7.2, of the significance of consumption skills as drivers of the choices we make.) To illustrate what can happen if such consumers are taken out of their narrow comfort zones, I offer the scenario that follows. It is based on an event that occurred in a restaurant in Hobart, Tasmania, in the mid-1980s when my parents were visiting me from the UK. One night, my (then) partner and I took them out to dinner, something that I had never previously done. This was a big mistake, still vivid in my memory over three decades later.

Suppose a person has for years avoided dining out at anywhere but a fish and chip shop and otherwise has lived on plain English cuisine. If this person is then pushed into having a meal at an Italian restaurant, she may experience something akin to a panic attack when faced with food that is utterly unfamiliar, in an environment with similarly mysterious norms of behavior. Attempts by her fellow diners to come to her assistance by supplying relevant constructs potentially could defuse the situation. However, such good intentions could founder if part of the problem is that she sees herself as a person who is able to get by in life without any need for help from others, a self-construct that she normally manages to uphold by confining herself to situations in which it appears to be valid.

This means that she now feels threatened, too: Kelly (*ibid.*, pp. 509–510) sees threat as the emotion that people experience when they see "a major change coming up in their core role structures," though the way he introduces the idea is in relation to social competition rather than a scenario such as our present one. If taking advice is problematic because she sees herself as self-sufficient, she urgently needs a way of regaining control of the flow of events. One strategy is for her to reject assistance, choose something from the menu at random or by copying one of her fellow diners and then sulk for the rest of the evening. In terms of a typical person's construct system, a meal out in an Italian restaurant is a cheerful occasion, where the normal rule is that no one seeks to take control, and everyone tries to keep the conversation flowing freely. If she sulks, throws a tantrum or insists on leaving, she pushes her fellow diners out of *their* comfort zones unless they have experienced all this before and have an effective technique for getting her to lighten up.

Her control-regaining behavior is consistent with Kelly's (*ibid.*, p. 510) view of hostility, which he defines as "the continued effort to extort validational evidence in favor of a type of social prediction which has already proved itself a failure." He likened this to the behavior of Procrustes in Greek mythology, who ensured that any overnight visitors always fitted his guest bed exactly by stretching them or lopping off parts of their limbs. Here, we have an emotion characterized as a form of behavior rather than how the person in question feels, but what drives the behavior seems to be a sense that one's predictive system is being challenged.

This view of hostility may be helpful for understanding many acts of domestic violence: a man whose expectations of life are being dashed by his daily workplace experiences (or the lack of any job at all) may restore some illusion of control (even though to others it seems to display precisely the opposite) by beating his wife, probably after also attempting to "drown his sorrows" via alcohol. Hostility is also a common response to those who defy social norms. Sometimes this takes the form of ostracism, which means that conformists do not have their view of the world blighted by the sight of deviants; a gentler form consists of demands for justification, which can be very trying for those on the receiving end. Another manifestation of attempts to keep a set of predictions intact is where, say, teenagers refuse to listen to critical comments from their parents and make this evident by putting their fingers in their ears – usually then leaving the room after a derisory "whatever. . ."

In everyday parlance, hostility is often construed in the same way as aggression. However, Kelly begged to differ, defining aggression as "the active elaboration of one's perceptual field" (*ibid.*, p. 508). What he had in mind here may be easier to envisage if we see it as applicable to people who (a) act in a "bossy" manner, (b) do not "hold back" from making known their position on a contentious issue, (c) "push their luck" with others to get what they want or (d) take the risk of inviting retaliation from those whom they threaten via an act (of, for example, conspicuous consumption) that is aimed at elevating their social standing. It is also consistent with what goes on when a person behaves in a "passive-aggressive" way, as when a person risks having his or her bluff called by his or her partner, as in, "Well, feel free to book that cruise, but if you do, you'll have to find someone else to share the cabin." Kelly's conceptualization of aggression may also be viewed more generally as connoting behavior that results from confidence that the situation that a particular choice will open will be one that does not result in them experiencing a loss of control. As with Kelly's conceptualization of hostility, his view of aggression pertains to behavior rather than how the person feels, but here the underlying feeling driving the behavior seems to be the absence of anxiety about what may happen as a consequence of the behavior and the allure of verifying that one's ability to predict and/or control is growing.

Finally, let us consider guilt, which Kelly (*ibid.*, p. 502) defines as "the awareness of dislodgement of the self from one's core role structures." It is something we experience when we reflect on something we have done or something that we are currently contemplating, that is at odds with how we normally see ourselves. In other words, such an act casts doubt on our identity. Guilt is thus both a cause of cognitive dissonance and closely related to anxiety: if we are no longer confident of the sort of person we are, predicting our own behavior or figuring out what we should do may become problematic. Once we have experienced the cognitive unease that comes from acting "out of character" in a way that potentially diminishes our view of ourselves, we will be more likely to try to avoid that kind of behavior in future – unless we can keep our identity intact by coming up with a way of justifying the choice as being consistent with it, thereby removing the cognitive dissonance.

Emotional responses have a particularly vital role to play where people have not come to see their lives in terms of developing or at least maintaining their capacities to predict and control events. If we are familiar with Kelly's theory, we can use it to analyze why we feel anxious or guilty in particular situations by considering what these situations imply in relation to our predictive systems. If we can do this, we have no need to "feel" anxious or guilty in order to want to act in a way that will not expose us to things that we lack the capacity to understand or that could damage our capacity to predict and control events. If we have such self-understanding, we can be honest with ourselves and coolly choose what to do based on differences in our accumulated human capital in different areas, in line with the Stigler–Becker–Murphy view of consumer behavior. By contrast, those who are not aware of Kelly's analysis, or who have not reached a similar perspective independently, cannot engage in such analysis. Their prospects for survival are enhanced if their subconscious processes kick in and make them feel anxious or guilty when they consider actions that could take them out of their depth or call their predictive systems into question.

7.6.2   Construct Laddering and the Meaning of Life

We need to be mindful of these emotions when undertaking construct laddering (as introduced in Section 2.10), and interpreting the constructs that we elicit, on route to uncovering means–end chains. Our research subjects may not be comfortable about sharing their emotional hang-ups via this process, and if we try to dig deep with multiple layers of laddering, we are likely to elicit a hostile response if we try to push them beyond the stage of "I believe (or prefer) this because I do, period": their inability to articulate a basis for their beliefs or preferences will probably come to them as an unpleasant surprise.

If Kelly is right about the importance to humans of being able to predict and control events, we should not expect the laddering process to continue beyond a construct that pertains to prediction and control unless it takes us into a loop that keeps coming back to this kind of construct. However, we also should not expect that if we undertake a construct laddering process, our research subjects will necessarily end up explaining that they prefer to meet a particular goal rather than not meet it or prefer to be on one end of a particular construct than the other, on the basis that "it enables me better to predict and/or control events" or words to that effect. On the contrary, construct laddering may arrive at the "I prefer it because I do, period" stage without any mention of this. Many people may go through life without reflecting on what living entails. In some cases, this may be the result of being so busy with the excitement of trying to see what they can make of new experiences, or struggling to avoid being overwhelmed by events, that they do not give much attention to construing "the meaning of life"; in other cases, people may not expect to arrive at an answer and, faced with the disturbing thought that they will never know "what the point of it all is," they simply do not "go there" in terms of trying to find out.

7.7   Implications of Choices and Changed Circumstances

In this section we will be using the term "implication" in the way it was used by Dennis Hinkle ([1965] 2010) in his pioneering work with construct laddering. His theoretical and empirical focus was on how relationships between constructs affect resistance to changes between the poles of constructs. These relationships result from the operating rules of our construct systems, so changing how we see something may, if we abide by the rules of our system, require or allow us to change how we see other things, thereby affecting which parts of the world we seem able to predict and control and to what degree. The changes to constructs that our rules for seeing the world require or allow because of changing a particular construct by switching from one pole to another are, in Hinkle's terms, the "implications" of that initial change.

When we switch from one pole to another on a construct, or from a particular pole to being uncertain about our position on a construct, or vice versa, the implications that we see for our capacity to predict and control events will depend on the implications that we see the change as having for other constructs. Regarding the latter, the range of possible implications appears to be as follows if we prefer pole A to pole B on construct X:

(i)   Switching from pole A to pole B on construct X implies a switch from pole A to pole B on construct Y (i.e., a negative implication of a negative change), or vice versa for a (positive) switch from pole B to pole A on construct X. For example, we might see switching from a large car to a small car as detracting from our social status.

(ii) Switching from pole A to pole B on construct X implies a switch from pole B to pole A on construct Y, or vice versa for a switch from pole B to pole A on construct X. For example, although we prefer a large car rather than a small car, we may see a small car as having advantages in ease of parking or lower running costs.

(iii) Switching from pole A to pole B, or from pole B to pole A, on construct X implies no switch of pole on construct Y. For example, switching from a large car to a small car may not seem to us to have any impact on the reliability of the car that we drive or our view about whether the current president of the United States is fit to be in that role or whether it will be wet or fine this afternoon, and so on.

(iv) Switching from pole A to pole B on construct X implies uncertainty on construct Y, whereas previously we were on pole A of construct Y. This reduces our perceived ability to predict and control events. For example, if we switch from a large car to a small car, we may no longer be confident that we will be able to drive home from IKEA with the kinds of products that we tend to buy there.

(v)   Switching from pole A to pole B on construct X implies uncertainty on construct Y, whereas previously we were on pole B of construct Y. Here, although we view the switch negatively overall, it possibly may improve our position in some areas. For example, although we prefer to have a high-status job rather than a low-status job, we may suspect that having to move to a low-status job might take away the stress we associate with high-status jobs.

(vi)   Switching from pole B to pole A on construct X implies uncertainty on construct Y, whereas previously we were on pole A of construct Y. Although overall we view the switch positively, aspects of it may make us nervous. For example, being promoted to a job with higher status may seem to bring the possibility of longer working hours.

(vii)   Switching from pole B to pole A on construct X implies uncertainty on construct Y where previously we were on pole B of construct Y. For example, switching from a casual job to an established position might seem to increase one's chances of getting a more predictable working week, something that had been impossible in the casual role.

(viii) Switching from being uncertain in respect of our position on construct X to being on pole A (B) on construct X implies that we move from being uncertain about our position on construct Y to being on pole A (B) of construct Y. For example, the news that we have (not) got the job we had been hoping to get means we will (not) be able to move to join our partner rather than continue having a long-distance relationship.

(ix)   Switching from being uncertain in respect of our position on construct X to being on pole A (B) on construct X implies that we move from being uncertain about our position on construct Y to being on pole B (A) of construct Y. For example, when we get news that we have (not) got a job we had been hoping to get, we now know we will (not) have all the disruption associated with moving interstate.

(x)   Switching from being uncertain in respect of our position on construct X to being on either pole A or pole B on construct X has no implications for our position on construct Y.

This set of possibilities can in principle be explored, and the results coded by category, for all possible pairs of constructs that we are able to elicit from research subjects by applying Kelly's repertory grid technique and Hinkle's construct laddering technique in the manner outlined in Section 2.10. In essence, what we would need to do is ask our research subjects to provide the information needed to fill out an N-by-N matrix in which all the N constructs that we had elicited were listed on both axes. The main diagonal of cells would end up blank, since change on a construct cannot have any implications for that construct. To fill out the others, we would successively take constructs on the X axis and ask our research subjects how the way they construed the situation in question on each construct on the Y axis would change if they had to switch poles on the X axis construct. The result would be what Hinkle called an "implication grid." He provided examples of such grids for twenty-eight research subjects, from each of whom he had first elicited ten constructs by applying Kelly's RGT, followed by another ten that he obtained via laddering. However, he did not examine cases where a polar shift on one construct had uncertain implications on another. Instead, he simplified matters by asking his research subjects to say whether, if they had to switch poles on one construct, they felt they would "probably" have to do so on another. (Note: if you read Hinkle's original analysis, be aware that when talking about relationships between constructs in terms of "subordinate" and "superordinate" constructs, his terminology is the opposite of what may seem natural; other personal construct psychologists sometimes use the terms in reverse. In what follows, I have opted to avoid using these terms altogether in order to avoid confusion. It becomes easier to understand the coexistence of these opposing ways of construing hierarchically related constructs when we reflect on expositions of Maslow's hierarchy of needs that involve a diagram in which "basic needs" are often shown at the bottom of a pyramid of needs despite being the needs that are most important to meet.)

Following Hinkle's initial demonstration of the construction of implication grids, personal construct psychologists have used them to study how their patients or research subjects see changes in their circumstances, rather than the implications of choosing to buy one product instead of another. The latter is a more time-consuming task but still possible in principle. For example, we might say, "You have told me that you prefer an SUV to a sedan, but that you prefer a vehicle with a smooth ride to one with a bumpy ride. If you had to switch from driving an SUV to driving a sedan, what would that imply for the ride quality you experienced? Would it be smoother, bumpier or something about which you don't have any particular expectation?" Of course, if we get the reply "no particular expectation," this could actually reflect knowledge of the area in question rather than ignorance: the research subject might see SUVs and sedans as exhibiting great variety (for example, he or she might believe that an Audi Q5 would have a smooth ride, unlike a Hyundai Santa Fe, and this might already be evident from the first round of construct elicitation if those vehicles had been used as "elements" when RGT was applied).

If we are ultimately trying to anticipate choices, we should run the process for the research subject's present situation versus a particular option (for example, "You say that you currently drive a Toyota RAV4. How do you see the implications of switching to a Volkswagen Tiguan for where you would be on the constructs you've provided?") and then repeat the process for the research subject's present situation versus a different option, and so on. Alternatively, we could work with a shifting reference point: i.e., whichever option the research subject preferred from the first pair would then be pitched against a third to explore the implications of choosing between them, with the preferred one from that round then being pitched against a fourth possibility, and so on. This would leave us with a set of implication grids for each research subject, showing how they saw the implications of choosing between rival courses of action in the context in question.

To understand choices, it is important to recognize that relationships between some constructs can flow in both directions. For example, consider a traditional young male who does not yet own a car but aspires to own a large, powerful sedan. If he had such a car and then were forced to switch to driving a small hatchback with a tiny engine, he would see this as implying a shift from a "real man's car" to a "girlie car." Hence, if he went from having no car to being given his late grandmother's small hatchback, he might see it as at odds with his core view of himself as a macho male. To avoid changing his self-construct, he would have to trade the hatchback for something bigger and more powerful. The latter might come with various downsides in terms of its age, economy and ease of parking. Clearly, this kind of example points us back to our discussions in Chapter 4 about the management of cognitive dissonance. Owning the hatchback implies a view of himself at odds with his preferred self-construct. He can remove the cognitive dissonance by changing the car or by changing how he sees himself, or some combination thereof. Strategies for "changing the car" could include (a) keeping the car he has inherited but "hotting it up" with some smart wheels and a personalized paint job or (b) trading it against a somewhat larger and older "hot hatch" that carries a GTi badge, to avoid the negative implications of switching to an even bigger, thirstier car in terms of running costs. So what makes him resist changing one way rather than the other or limits how far he will change on the constructs where he does change?

7.7.1   Implications and the Significance of Losses and Disappointments

Hinkle measured the resistance of his research subjects to switching between poles on their constructs by constructing triangular N-by-N "resistance to change grids" and asking his subjects to identify the constructs on which they were willing to switch from one pole to the other in order to avoid making such a switch on the construct in question. The more of the other constructs they were prepared to switch to avoid change on a particular construct, the higher he ranked that construct in terms of resistance to change. He then hypothesized that the construct rankings he derived from his subjects' resistance to change grids would be strongly positively correlated with the scores he derived from their respective implication grids regarding the number of implications that were associated with flipping between poles on each construct axis. In other words, he expected that a person's resistance to switching poles on a construct would be a function of the number of other constructs on which the person would switch poles if he or she had to make a switch on the construct in question.

This hypothesis was supported by Hinkle's results. To appreciate what he had in mind, it is instructive to start by considering Shakespeare's Richard III: When he cried, "A horse, my kingdom for a horse!" the point was that without a horse from which to lead his soldiers, everything associated with his position as king, and his life, was in grave danger. Getting back on to a horse was, in other words, something that he saw as a prerequisite – necessary, but not sufficient – for preserving everything that mattered to him. For most horse owners, having their horse die or bolt would be far less drastic, merely a cause of sadness or inconvenience.

For a more everyday kind of example, consider the implications of failing a compulsory unit in a degree program and not being able to graduate. Some students may have built up complex mental models of their future that hinge on passing the final examination for this unit. If they find it unexpectedly challenging, much of their vision of the future will appear to be falling apart; they have a big motivation for trying to keep cool and do the best they can. By contrast, other students may not yet have constructed a mental model of the future that hinges on passing that examination. The latter students can be quite nonchalant if they find themselves struggling with it: failure does not have drastic implications for them; they might simply give up and leave the examination room early, telling themselves they will have another shot at it in a future semester.

Notice how multiple levels of implications may follow if a prerequisite outcome fails to materialize, with the number of levels depending upon how detailed a view of the future the decision-maker has constructed. Furthermore, there may be multiple chains of implications fanning out to other constructs from any construct that has a determining role. Constructs can thus differ greatly in the number of constructs that they affect. Consider the plight of Zak, an imaginary would-be graduate. He sees failure to graduate at the expected time as something that will cause terrible disappointment to his parents, which would make him feel very guilty about "letting them down." He also views such an outcome as having negative implications for his self-image, reputation and ability to take up a particular job. Let us for the moment focus on the last of these. Zak may view having to wave the job good-bye as having a variety of implications, such as a reduction in his income in the coming year, not being able to move to the city where the job would be based, not getting the kind of work experiences the job was expected to offer, and so on. The pattern of implications that fans out from the result of the examination seems to be rather like a tree.

However, as we explore further the set of implications, it may turn out that they map into a network that is more complex than a treelike structure. This is possible because the implications of a forced change on a construct may arise not only for constructs that depend on this construct but also for constructs that depend on constructs other than the one in question, possibly even at a level closer to the one that is, so to speak, the root cause of the changes. For example, having less income than expected is a tier 4 construct (failing the examination is tier 1, not graduating is tier 2, not being able to take up the job is tier 3). In turn, Zak may expect that because of having less income, he would have to abandon hopes of buying a decent car to replace his old clunker (tier 5). Zak may view this as implying that he will still have to worry about breaking down and put up with creaks, rattles, a poor sound system, and so on (these are all tier 6 constructs). But he may also see being stuck with his old clunker as implying that he will have to forego some esteem from his peers. Esteem may be a tier 2 construct on a different branch that is likewise affected by the exam result construct, and Zak may also see his social esteem as being dented by not being able to graduate (also tier 2 but on a different branch) and not being able to take up the job (tier 3).

Each chain of implications that flows from a change on a particular construct will have a terminal construct at the other end. To illustrate this, let us continue with the implications for Zak of not passing the exam: if Zak sees one of the implications of failing the exam as that he will have to continue driving a car that lacks a state-of-the-art sound system, this would not be an implication on a terminal construct if he saw it as implying, say, something about his self-image or social standing, or for his ability to use Apple CarPlay. However, suppose that we find out that he views not being able to use Apple CarPlay (a tier 7 construct) as implying changes in the pole on which he would be on some other construct axes (tier 8). These tier 8 constructs may not be terminal ones either, but they might be. Suppose that Zak explains that having to switch from "will be able to use Apple CarPlay" to "won't be able to use Apple CarPlay" will give him a better chance to use his iPhone's capabilities while on the road, with a smaller risk of being fined or crashing and getting injured, killed or harming someone else. If he can give a reason for not wanting to be fined, then "lower risk of getting fined *versus* higher risk of getting fined" is not a terminal construct; indeed, it may have implications in relation to financial, self-image and social esteem constructs to which he has already referred. However, if he cannot articulate why he prefers not to get killed or harm others while using his iPhone when driving, then we have found a terminal implication of whether he has access to Apple CarPlay. By contrast, being able or unable to use Apple CarPlay might carry no implications for you and me because we are not, and do not expect to become, iPhone users; if so, it will be a terminal construct for us, but is one where we can articulate a reason for why it does not matter to us. However, it will cease to be a terminal construct if we start to think that buying a car without Apple CarPlay might prove to be problematic when we eventually came to sell the car.

Where the decision-maker sees constructs as affected by the event in question, the changes on these constructs may be construed as positive, negative or not significant either way. If the decision-maker views an implied change on a construct as mattering in a positive or negative sense but cannot articulate why, this construct must be a terminal one. Such an inability to explain why the change matters has a significant analytical implication. If we have a preferred pole on a terminal construct but are only able to say that it matters "because it does, period," our concern about being on that pole is essentially an emotional one: we feel it matters and have an urge to attain or preserve that position, but we cannot say why. By contrast, if we "simply don't care" about where we are on a terminal construct, we will experience no emotional attraction or repulsion in respect of any position on that construct. In the latter situation, unlike the former, our brain must be making no subconscious connection between the construct and our ability to predict and control events.

7.7.2   Are Terminal Implications the Only Ones That Determine What Matters?

Terminal constructs seem the natural place to focus if we wish to understand how people resolve dilemmas and make trade-offs. These constructs are as deep as people can go in articulating the "ends" that they are pursuing. Given the rules of their personal construct systems, changes on intermediate constructs are what drive the changes on the terminal constructs, but intermediate-level constructs do not matter for any other reason. From a "means–end chain" standpoint, it thus appears that the extent to which a change on a construct matters is a function of (a) the number of terminal implications on constructs for which the construct in question is viewed as having a determining role and (b) the mix of types of terminal implications, i.e., the number of terminal constructs on which the implied move from one pole to the other is a move to a preferred pole rather than in the reverse direction or a move of the "don't care" variety. If, say, a change on a construct implied a net total of eight negative implications via eleven negative terminal implications partly offset by three positive ones, then having to make that change would seem to a bigger cause for concern than a change that only entailed a net total of, say, five negative terminal implications.

If we have no limitations on our ability to articulate and sum the net terminal implications of a change on a construct, then logically we should be able to make an overall assessment of this change without attaching weights to any of the positive or negative terminal implications: if we can explain why an implied change on one construct is more significant than a change on a different construct, we will do so with reference to what the implied change on the former construct implies for other constructs; hence, that construct cannot be a terminal construct. In cases where we "feel" or "sense" that changes on terminal constructs differ in their significance but are unable to articulate reasons, then the relative strengths of the emotional impacts of the prospective changes will kick in as weights.

This "net terminal implications" view is an appealing way to bring together personal construct theory and conventional economic thinking that centers on weighing up costs and benefits. However, I think that there is an alternative implications-based perspective that deserves even more serious consideration in relation to the question that this chapter's title poses. This alternative view is that, when the possibility of change on a construct is being considered, the extent to which that change is welcomed or resisted depends on the entire set of changes implied on the affected constructs, i.e., on the implications for intermediate constructs as well as the terminal ones. This is the view that Hinkle seems to be taking in his work with "resistance to change grids." I followed his approach when first applying his thinking to responsiveness to changed market conditions (Earl, 1986a). However, I soon realized that it begged a big question: Why would having to make changes on intermediate constructs in a particular chain have any significance beyond the implications that ultimately followed for terminal constructs? An answer started to come together when I began to think about what the brain must do to dispose of cognitive dissonance (Earl, 1992; Earl and Wicklund, 1999). (While writing this part of the book, I discovered that my thinking appears to overlap with the "free energy minimization" view of brain functioning proposed since then by the eminent neuropsychologist Karl Friston. Friston's theory is based on thermodynamic principles. For entry points to his thinking, see Friston, 2010, and Raviv, 2018.)

The idea is very simple: To understand why intermediate implications also matter when people consider potential changes in their constructs, we just need to recognize that there are cognitive costs to changing how we think and that these costs increase with the total number of implications of the change, not just the number of terminal implications. This is because, as Kelly emphasizes, the process of seeing things in a new way is a process of construction that takes place from the standpoint of how we already see things in that area rather than out of nowhere. In other words, we begin with our existing model of the area in question and modify it to construct a new one. (If we do get as far as constructing a new model and adopting it, the way we used to think is not dismantled; rather, it gradually fades in our memory, with the neural network that embodies it suffering demyelination as it falls out of use.) If the new model is to be worth having, it must offer a better capacity to predict and control events than the existing one offers. But this will only be evident after we have incurred the effort required to construct it. Where mental models entail simple networks of constructs – i.e., where causal chains are short and the range of terminal constructs is small – it is easy to work out the terminal implications of change, so choices are unlikely to be affected by the prospective costs of constructing a new mental model. In more complex cases, however, the prospect of the mental effort required to build a new model may result in such a model not being constructed, with the decision-maker instead finding a way to avoid having to change on the construct in question.

Consider the rewiring of neural networks that is entailed in building new mental models. In the case of existing construct relationships, registering each implication of a change on an existing subordinate construct is akin to throwing a switch. This must be done for intermediate constructs as well as terminal constructs. Forming a new construct relationship is akin to plugging in a cable to connect previously unconnected system elements. Severing a relationship between construct is like unplugging a cable between them. All this takes energy and may get in the way of doing things that need to be done. To reduce the risk of being eliminated by evolutionary selection processes, human brains therefore need to limit the extent of unnecessary rewiring that they undergo each time they change their views of the world. But they need to be able to do this without it resulting in dysfunctional behavior that jeopardizes their chances of surviving and passing on their genes. When faced with cognitive dissonance, our brains seek to remove it by making the smallest modification to our constructs that is consistent with preserving our capacity to predict and control events.

Consider the prospective cognitive effort entailed in changes on two different constructs that both entail the same number of net positive or negative terminal implications but have implication networks that differ in their architectures, one involving many more changes on intermediate constructs. If forced to choose between changing on one construct and changing on the other, the "easy way out" for the brain is to choose the structurally simpler change that can be made with less energy, since there is less rewiring to do. But we should also notice here a lesson from Adam Smith's history of astronomy (noted at the end of Section 4.8): A succession of small cognitive changes that are alternatives to making a major change in how we think may result in the creation of an increasingly complex structure that becomes unwieldy. When this happens, increases in the amount of energy required to use it and continue making ad hoc modifications will eventually favor making a revolutionary rethink that entails adopting the idea that had previously been rejected. We then go about the task of constructing the more economical mental model that this idea implies.

Resistance to change can, in short, be seen as a means whereby the brain is able to avoid the prospective costs of rewiring itself to accommodate change. These costs increase with the complexity of the mental model in respect of which the possibility of change is considered. But there is a bigger picture that needs to be appreciated here. First, so long as our existing model is not dangerously dysfunctional, sticking with it reduces the risk that we will be unable to act when action is necessary: rethinking complex parts of our lives takes time and in the interim choice may be problematic if we are not sure what our partly constructed new model implies and hence whether we ultimately will be adopting it. Secondly, resistance to change is also a means whereby we avoid the costs of researching things that may be relevant for the construction of a new way of looking at the area in question. The latter has the benefit of reducing the risk that we will make fools of ourselves by asking "dumb questions" or struggling to understand the answers that we are given; hence, avoiding change in one area can be a means for avoiding the risk of collateral damage in other areas of our predictive system. The implications of changes that seem rather minor to some people may seem potentially drastic to others because the latter fear that the process of change could call their core constructs into question. If pushed to consider such changes, their responses are likely to display hostility, in Kelly's sense of the word. The change would have mattered less if they had constructed more modular personal construct systems, with greater tolerance for risking losing control in the interest of developing a system that would serve them better in future.

7.7.3   Loss Aversion

Taken together, the arguments set out in this section can help us make sense of the phenomenon of loss aversion, which Thaler (2015, loc. 637) describes as "the single most powerful tool in the behavioral economist's arsenal." For Thaler, loss aversion simply means that "a loss hurts more than an equivalent gain gives pleasure" (*ibid.*). If humans were not beset by cognitive and knowledge limitations, they would always be able instantly to identify the full implications of changes that seemed to offer enhanced potential for their abilities to predict and control events. However, we are not "econs" and are thus prone initially to underestimate the significance of gains. Moreover, even though we are often able eventually to recover from losses, we are not able instantly to build new mental models as means of plugging holes that losses cause in our views of the world. When we lose something, we do not merely lose access to it; we also need to construct a new set of expectations to replace the set of expectations we had constructed premised on access to it. We are used to this entailing cognitive effort and that it may also require us to incur research costs. We also are used to the fact that our original expectations will keep coming to mind as we think about the situation in question, interfering with the process of adjusting to (or "getting over") the loss (cf. Hayek's analysis of the mind and the significance of neural myelination).

7.8   Sunk Costs, Persistence and Escalation of Commitment

A "rational" decision-maker is supposed to choose with reference to relative prospective net returns to rival ways of using yet-to-be committed resources, not with a focus on recovering sunk costs incurred via past decisions whose outcomes have proved to be problematic. Everyday maxims agree with this, asserting that we should not "pour good money after bad" when we make losses and that we should not "cry over spilt milk." Where milk, so to speak, has been spilt, we should coolly focus on selecting the most efficient way of cleaning up the mess and then simply pour ourselves a fresh glass, with no attempt to recover and drink the spilt milk. In reality, and despite familiarity with such maxims, people often act as though sunk costs matter, treating them not as "sunk" but as needing to be "justified" (Wolf, 1970) and as not having been incurred "in vain." When things do not go as well as anticipated and questions arise about whether they might be wasting time and money, many people display a reluctance to concede that they should abandon what they have been trying to do. They find it difficult to be so coolheaded, and in their attempts to avoid ending up with losses, they are prone to act in ways that end up increasing their losses. In situations where the economical act would be to scrap or throw away an object, personal relationship or plan that has gone wrong, they instead try to make it come right.

The impact of sunk costs on behavior is evident in many areas. Thaler (2015, ch. 8) offers telling examples from a large set that he collected over many years, such as how a decision to drive through a blizzard to a sporting event depended on whether one had bought tickets for it or had merely been given them. He also notes (via DellaVigna and Malmedier, 2006) cases in which those who sign up with a gym discover that they absolutely hate having workouts there but say they are continuing to go "in order to avoid wasting their money." More tragic are cases involving those who start realizing that they probably should not be marrying the person they are about to marry but who nonetheless go ahead with the wedding because so much has already been invested in arranging it. At the corporate and governmental level, we find cases of persistence with major projects (including wars) despite warnings, later proved to be correct, that they will never cover their costs and that further expenditure will merely increase the total loss (for some examples, see Smith, 1963, and Staw, 1976). However, it should be recognized that, in some cases, a succession of decisions to persist with a troubled project may eventually take the project to a stage at which *further expenditure* will have a positive return even though sunk costs are never recovered. The *Concorde* supersonic airliner may be an example of this: unexpectedly high development costs ensured that, overall, the project incurred a huge loss, but for a time, with those costs written off, *Concorde* flew at a profit in terms of its operating costs. The problem was that the latter period was not – and could never have been – long enough to generate a big enough surplus to recoup *Concorde*'s development costs, especially when the calculations were done in terms of present values.

The *Concorde* case has a lesson for modern behavioral economists about the need to be careful when labeling behavior as evidence of "sunk cost bias" or the "sunk cost fallacy." We should distinguish between two classes of behavior associated with the presence of unrecovered sunk cost. One arises due to failure to understand the basic economics of decisions to continue with or abandon an activity. The gym example may imply this. But now consider a case in which someone has an ageing car that is turning into a financial black hole due to frequent spending on repairs. It has broken down yet again, but the person says, "I can't just have it towed to a wrecking yard, for it is only a few weeks since the last lot of repairs." Such a motorist should certainly be focusing on future streams of costs and benefits rather than trying to get value from the costs he or she has recently incurred. However, the motorist's predicament should call to mind the discussion in Section 3.7 regarding "the sequential wear-out trap." What the motorist says now may sound like evidence of a failure to understand opportunity costs properly, but the tragic history of the repair bills may also be understood as a case of what Barry Staw (1976) calls "escalation of commitment." The latter can arise even in situations where decision-makers know that they should disregard sunk costs when choosing.

Escalation of commitment entails repeatedly pouring more resources into a project because of overoptimistic assessments of potential future payoffs and/or underestimates of the costs that will need to be incurred to bring about the outcome that is being used to justify what is being done. Motorists with ageing vehicles may argue that, given how much they have spent already on repairs, "one more" repair bill should be enough to give them a good run of repair-free motoring that will be cheaper than scrapping their car and trading up to something newer: with so much having already been replaced, there may now seem little more that could go wrong. In some cases – for example, when a gambler who has had a bad run of losses at a casino places a very risky bet in a bid to try to recoup these losses – loss aversion and dwindling resources combine to produce "all-or-nothing" risk-taking as the culmination of a process of escalation of commitment. When played out in a social setting, escalation of commitment may be associated with desperate attempts at extorting support of the kind to which Kelly alluded in his Procrustean-style view of the nature of hostility.

It is easy to see how escalation of commitment can occur where there is uncertainty and/or ignorance about the additional costs that will need to be incurred to make a project work. Initially, it may be impossible for those who must consider whether to pull the plug to know whether the project could ever be viable in terms of its net revenue if past sunk costs are written off, so even those who do not want to "pour good money after bad" may end up doing so. In the case of the *Concorde* project, successive decisions to keep spending on it meant that, as time passed, the aircraft became closer to being ready for production. Hence it became easier to argue in favor of pouring yet more money into it even though, with perfect foresight, the project would never have been given the initial go-ahead. Justifying continuation on this basis became especially attractive once the social costs of thousands of unemployed aircraft workers were considered.

With projects such as *Concorde*, accountants may formally (and sometimes "creatively") record the losses as they mount. However, similar but less formal processes may go on in the minds of ordinary consumers. Thaler (1985) suggests that people use "mental accounting" systems to manage their lives, with these accounting systems contributing to people ending up needlessly reducing their well-being by persisting with plans that are not going as well as expected. Each time we buy something we mentally open an account for it – it now "owes us" what we have spent on it – and we hope that by the time we close the account, due to the product ceasing to function or being disposed of, we will not have to record a loss on it. If things do not go well, creative mental accounting is something we can use to keep at bay the uncomfortable prospect of the account ending up in the red. For example, suppose that I buy a pair of shoes. They seem to fit perfectly well at the shoe store, but the first few times that I wear them, I am left with blisters on my feet. This might be inferred as signifying that I should have bought them in a bigger size. Rather than writing them off and consigning them to a local charity's collection bin, I recall that in the past, when I have run into this kind of problem, persistence has paid off because I eventually managed to "break in" shoes that had initially been recalcitrant. I therefore persist in trying to get comfortable in the new shoes by wearing them – actually, wearing them more often than I might otherwise have done – but I am unable to tame them. The mental account for this pair of shoes thus stays in the red. If I stop wearing them, I stop getting the blisters, but I still want a way of getting their account out of the red. So, rather than write them off and put them in the charity bin, I reassign them as a reserve pair to be kept in my wardrobe for emergency use, which gives me a stream of benefits even if an occasion for wearing them rarely arises. Months or years later, when I need more space in my wardrobe, I have a pretext for closing the account for that pair of shoes: taking them to the charity bin in their little-worn condition is something my mind can "spin" to be a benefit: I end up with both extra space and the warm glow of thinking that I'm helping someone else.

The creative accounting that we engage in when returns to our investments are falling short of our expectations is in essence a means of managing cognitive dissonance between our views of ourselves, as competent decision-makers who do not waste resources, and incoming stimuli that might be taken as signifying that we have chosen unwisely and wasted our money and/or time. The ability to see ourselves as competent decision-makers is a prerequisite for actions aimed at predicting and controlling events, so it is something to which we will cling so long as we can see evidence that we still possess it. By committing further resources to the project in question, we can give ourselves a basis for denying that the choice is a failure: the additional resources open the possibility of making the project "come right" by changing the flow of returns that it generates. Given the centrality of a self-construct as a competent decision-maker in our construct systems, this kind of cognitive dissonance management is likely to result in "rose-tinted" perceptions about the prospective payoffs to spending more on an activity that so far has produced poor results. Being viewed by others as a competent decision-maker will also matter if we are to be granted control over events, and this need to "save face" will favor persistence wherever it can be denied that the case for abandoning a project is conclusive.

Although it is easy to see how people may end up engaging in dysfunctional behavior in the presence of sunk costs, especially in a social setting, we should recognize that this human tendency toward persistence has an upside. Those who are too willing to bail out of commitments when the going gets unexpectedly tough may develop fewer problem-solving skills and less knowledge than those who are more prone to sunk cost bias. Bailing out early may result in the former achieving very little but, like those who suffer from sunk cost bias, they may end up wasting large sums of money on things they could have made to "come right." (Recall our discussion of the economics of dread in Section 5.8, where we considered how loss of nerve can result in people replacing their cars more often than they really need to replace them.) In evolutionary terms, tenacity can be a good thing, so long as we do not make our self-images unduly contingent on the success of each project that we embark upon and do not then operate with the stubbornness of a mule.

7.9   Linkages between Things and/or Activities

A key theme underpinning this chapter is the idea that structural complexity in our mental models of the world inhibits our willingness to give up what we have. This complexity can be purely the result of our way of thinking: our operating mode may make particular assumptions and use them to develop rich narratives about how our lives *will* unfold, rather than developing rival scenarios about how events might unfold; other people, by contrast, may not think far ahead and may operate in a more nonchalant or lackadaisical manner, such that nothing seems to matter much to them because they have few expectations whose falsification could raise questions about their abilities to predict and control events. However, the structural complexity of our mental models may also be a consequence of the external structures that we have opted to build in our lives (see also Section 3.7). What we see as the implications of having to give up elements of these structures will be related to whether the elements in question play a core or peripheral role. The loss of a core element can make the system impossible to sustain, yet while it is present, it may be taken for granted due to the frequency with which it figures as a means to prediction and control, with little thought given to what life would be like without it.

The significance of structural centrality can be readily appreciated in relation to the grief that we experience if we lose a loved one around whom we have built many of our expectations, or in relation to the consequences of losing a job that is a prerequisite not merely for an expected lifestyle but also for self-esteem and social standing. But some products and services can also play core roles in our lives. Consider, for example, the extent to which the lifestyles of many affluent families depend on access to a motorcar and how disruptive it would be for a parent to become unable to drive for medical reasons or after being banned for driving while intoxicated. Getting by without a car was easy back in the days when families lived in geographically close-knit communities in which children could walk to school and did not have a mass of after-school activities, and where shopping could be done at local stores on a day-to-day basis. Now, with sprawling suburbs, mall- and supermarket-based shopping, households in which both parents work, and heavy investments in children via after-school activities, a car becomes a core element in family life. Without access to a car, such a lifestyle becomes chaotic and full of anxiety: economies of large-scale shopping are compromised, while after-school activities and even getting to school can become logistically challenging and/or a source of anxiety regarding the safety of children.

In the twenty-first century, Internet access and smartphones have become core components in many people's lives, facilitating enhanced prediction and control in many areas. Because they enable us to have integrated access to a wide range of capabilities, the loss of Internet access or one's smartphone can be a distressing, highly disruptive experience. In this sense, the modern consumer is far more vulnerable than consumers were only a few decades earlier in the dark ages of function-specific devices and media that were stored on individual disks or in hard-copy form.

The economics of smartphones also illustrates related structural issues, namely that what matters depends on the extent to which the systems we build are highly integrated or modular (again, see also Section 3.7): reliability matters much more if we spend $1000 on a multifunction device such as a high-end smartphone than if we spend the same sum on a set of function-specific devices, since, in the latter case, the failure of one has no implications for the others and the cost of replacing one failed element is much less than the cost of replacing the integrated device. On the other hand, being able to have an integrated device also matters because technological synergies (for example, a microphone services telephone, dictation and voice-recording roles in a smartphone) will enable us to get more "bang per buck" in terms of capabilities than if we built a modular system. Moreover, the integrated system allows us to perform linked activities much more seamlessly (for example, taking a photograph and sending it to a friend).

7.10   Social Embeddedness

Social linkages are an additional source of resistance to change. People generally are not socially isolated; rather, they are, as Mark Granovetter (1985) puts it, "socially embedded," taking their decisions mindful of the implications of their choices for their relationships with members of their family and other social groups. Social embeddedness is a phenomenon that is especially important as a determinant of labor mobility. From a behavioral perspective, one should not presume that enticing people to work in remote areas (for example, medical professionals in outback Australia) or to take up overseas jobs is simply a matter of offering a lucrative premium on normal remuneration packages. This is because the prospect of having to sever social ties (or imposing this on their children) or of being unable to be with elderly family members on a regular basis or at short notice may be a "deal breaker."

Given that parents only get the one chance to watch their children grow up or help their parents through the latter's twilight years, what may matter when such positions are being offered are the opportunities to take leave and return home frequently during the period of remote service, not the amount of money that the worker might be able to accumulate by the time that period comes to an end. From this standpoint, mining companies have been wise to switch to having "fly in–fly out" (FIFO) workforces rather than continue building "company towns" adjacent to their remote mines. Their FIFO workers may indeed command a premium for not being able to be with their families all the time, but remoteness ceases to be a deal breaker because social ties are not disrupted over the longer term.

Social embeddedness and sets of linkages within personal construct systems may work in tandem to generate resistance to change when people are presented with market incentives to move on. For example, a father with children of high school age may tell himself, "I'm not the sort of person who disrupts the lives of the rest of my family in order to pursue career advancement." He, therefore, declines promotion opportunities that would involve moving to a different city. Once he has seen his children through to university, his career may still be socially constrained, unless opportunities come up locally, if his elderly parents and/or those of his partner live nearby and he feels guilty at the prospect of moving interstate or overseas, or of making things difficult for his partner. There is a lesson here for would-be high achievers who do not see themselves as self-centered: Concentrate on winning advancement before your children are in their teens, and make sure you live and work in a large city to increase your chances of being able to continue to rise up the career ladder without having to move elsewhere and for your partner to do likewise.

In addition to affecting geographical mobility, social embeddedness is also worth keeping in mind as a driver of norm- and reciprocity-based behavior, which in some cases can lead to corruption. The cognitive mechanisms that Hayek set out in *The Sensory Order* will mean that social relationships will produce a form of availability bias by enhancing the chances that those with whom we have developed relationships will come to mind when we need someone to help us out or are considering who might be suitable for a particular role. In turn, we will come to mind more readily when those who came to our assistance or who benefited from our choices are in need or are seeking to fill the kinds of roles that we might suit. So long as interactions continue working out successfully, the availability bias that comes from social connections may lock out those who are not in the same social network. Moreover, one's sense of obligation increases where ties are shared within social networks, for any failure to reciprocate when a favor is called for may have wider long-term repercussions within one's network.

7.11   Attachment and the Endowment Effect

Our Kelly- and Hinkle-inspired view of why some things matter more than others provides a way of understanding situations in which people say they would not give up something they have "for the world." An example would be where a person resists the purchase of his or her house to make way for a new road or property development. From the standpoint of conventional economics, such behavior is a manifestation of a devious "holdout" strategy aimed at extracting the maximum that the other party is prepared to pay. That sum may be vastly in excess of the normal value of the property in question if failure to take ownership threatens the entire project because there is no way to build around the property. In this sort of case, the implications of not buying out the property owner are drastic for the developer. However, the "holdout" perspective may be mistaken, for reasons that are captured in *The Castle*, a classic 1997 Australian movie. This movie focuses on resistance to compulsory purchase orders for homes adjacent to an airport whose facilities are being expanded. Darryl Kerrigan, the lead character, resists increasingly generous offers before ending up in court and telling the judge that he does not want to move, since "money can't buy what I've got." In other words, in these kinds of situations, the implications of having to move may seem so drastic to the owner of the property that no amount of money will compensate for losing the life to which he or she has become accustomed – even if it is a life (such as living next to a noisy airport) that most people would be glad to avoid.

Those who will not "move for the world" clearly pose major challenges to the social cost–benefit analysis techniques used in appraising social projects that provoke such resistance. From the wider subjectivist position taken in this book, the root cause of such resistance to change is not per se the sets of expectations that the affected parties have built up about how their lives are going to be and their impending loss of control over their lives. Rather, the problem lies with their limited capacities to imagine how they might live better lives if they accepted somewhat above-market valuations and set about reconstructing their lives somewhere nearby: they can see the threatened wreckage of their existing view of the world but cannot yet imagine that things could be better if they accepted the offer. The obvious policy implication is that steps should be taken to assist such people in constructing a positive new view of how their lives might be – for example, by letting them experience living in, say, the more modern accommodation that they will be able to purchase nearby if they accept the offer that they have been given. Those who seek to impose settlements in these kinds of situations need, in other words, to get out of the trap of viewing ordinary people "as if" they are fully informed "econs": If the affected parties have little experience of life in any environment other than where they currently live, the prospect of moving may be a major source of anxiety because they lack constructs for anticipating events in the new environment. They need a head start in forming these constructs, not an infinite amount of cash to compensate for what they are being required to give up.

A related kind of outright resistance to change is commonly evident when the children of increasingly frail elders seek to persuade the latter to move out of the now needlessly large "family home" in which they have lived for decades and into a retirement complex or aged-care facility. In these situations, the key to the elders becoming comfortable about moving can likewise be a trial experience of the new life. An obvious means to this end is for their children to persuade them to take a respite vacation in such a facility while they are taking a break elsewhere.

These cases of resistance to change may also be viewed as large-scale versions of what we may call "attachment," an aspect of emotional involvement that in principle can arise with any consumer durable. What I have in mind here is a view of attachment that goes beyond the term's normal use in marketing theory to connote the relationships that consumers have with brands or particular service providers (cf. the discussion of the notion of "goodwill" in Section 6.6, and Thomson et al., 2005). Here, my contention is that physically identical items can differ in how they matter to us because they differ in the associations that they have with us.

The extent of our attachment to objects that we own is not merely a function of the extent to which we have incorporated them into our expectations, which means we will need to form new constructs if we let these assets go; attachment also arises where durable assets have symbolic value to us because they have been elements in significant parts of our life experience. Continued ownership of the product in question ensures that we have a tangible reminder of the experience with which we associate it; it may also be a trophy that provides evidence of a period in which we seemed to be in control, "going places" and/or "on top of the world." The act of disposing of a product that has served us well "through thick and thin" might seem akin to being disloyal to an old friend. Hence, even if we no longer use such a product very often, we may not attempt to sell it despite being able to say with confidence that we would not replace it if it were stolen and we received an insurance payout equal to its market value. A replacement might be physically identical, but it would not have the same symbolic value.

Attachment can culminate in dysfunctional compulsive hoarding problems whereby homes become so cluttered with goods as to make them dangerous places to live due to the risk of tripping or being hit by falling objects, enhanced fire risks or the risk of picking up diseases via the vermin that move in (for more analysis of the psychology of hoarding, see Frost and Steketee, 2010). The scale of the clutter also tends to result in home maintenance being neglected, as so much needs to be moved in order to get any work done and with no space into which to move anything (see McDermott et al., 2009). George Kelly's view of anxiety seems to offer a fruitful way of making sense of how people end up in such a mess. The items that get hoarded are not merely those that mark significant times in their owners' lives; they may also include potential means of increasing prediction and control, so disposing of them could result in a loss of perceived control. The latter basis for attachment is readily evident where people end up with cluttered sheds or workshops that are full of pieces of things that "may come in useful one day," or where academics' offices end up resembling a waste tip because their occupants tell themselves that any of the journal articles and press clippings could be of use in their research or teaching – even though they seem to have trouble locating anything in the midst of the chaos. In some of the cases I have seen, dysfunctional hoarding appears to result from poor self-control and/ or a "rescuer" mindset that leads to compulsive shopping and an inability to walk past a bargain or to allow things that others are throwing out to end up at the refuse tip.

Attachment provides a way of making sense of the "endowment effect" identified by Kahneman, Knetsch, and Thaler (1990, 1991) and for identifying situations in which this effect is likely to be significant. Under this effect, people who own a particular kind of asset will tend to assign it a bigger value than they would have assigned had they not owned it. The effect would be seen as evidenced by, for example, the tendency of vendors of houses and apartments initially to ignore the advice of their real estate agents and insist on asking prices in excess of market prices for properties like the ones they are trying to sell. However, the endowment effect has been puzzling, for the experiments that demonstrated it merely involved Cornell University coffee mugs and pens, i.e., low-value objects where there might seem little basis for an attachment to be formed. Participants in these experiments who were given either of these items and were asked what they would accept in compensation for giving them back required about twice what other participants were typically prepared to pay to get them. In other words, being given a mug made that mug seem special to the recipient. What could be the basis for this?

The explanation may lie in the fact that a mug received in the experiment was no longer just a mug with a Cornell University insignia but a mug that the recipient had been one of the lucky ones to receive, and, in the years to come, it would be a mug with a backstory more interesting to tell than if the recipient had simply bought it, as Thaler had originally done, in a store on the Cornell campus. A mug that was part of an experiment is no ordinary mug; it is more like a trophy – all the more so with hindsight knowledge of how famous the experiment has become.

It is sometimes possible to buy products that come with readymade backstories that make them worth having. The obvious area for examples is the market for relics from the world of sport and entertainment. In such situations, we may expect a smaller proportionate endowment effect because the personal significance of owning the relic is not the only thing that adds to the owner's reluctance to part with it: ownership of a notable relic also confers bragging rights that may make it worth paying a premium relative to the price of a new example of the same product or a used example with no such provenance. Fernandez and Lastovicka (2011) have studied the demand for relics in the context of the market for guitars. This market includes an expensive equivalent of the prefaded jeans phenomenon whereby some guitar manufacturers charge premium prices for finely copied versions of unique badly worn examples of their products owned and played by notable performers. (The most extreme case is Fender's Rory Gallagher Stratocaster, whose extensively pre-wrecked paintwork accurately reflects the drastic perspiration-induced damage that the original suffered between first being sold in 1961 and Gallagher's death in 1995. It retails for nearly three times the price of Fender's standard replica of the firm's 1960s Stratocaster.) Such instruments do not merely serve as status symbols and conversation starters; they also test whether their owner can tease the same sounds from them that the owner of the original was able to achieve.

7.12   Conclusion

The question that this chapter posed is rarely addressed deeply by economists, but we have dug deeply to address it rather than merely assuming the existence of preference systems that take an analytically convenient form (as conventional economists do) or focusing on the significance of behavior that is at odds with such preference systems (as most modern behavioral economists have hitherto done). In addressing the question, we have explored the evolutionary foundations for having preferences, and the emotional and structural determinant of differences in the keenness of people to meet particular ends or avoid particular kinds of situations. Along the way, we largely avoided reference to "utility" by taking up George Kelly's view that a person's behavior is driven by the attempts of his or her system of personal constructs to enhance, or at least mitigate damage to, its capacity to predict and control events. These systems often function via rules that serve as means for reflective analysis or fast and frugal choices, but emotions kick in to defend them when our rules fail to generate decisions and/or things seem to be getting unpredictable or out of control.

Understanding patterns of implications that people see as following from changing their behavior in particular ways enables us to anticipate who will shrug off particular losses or be desperate to avoid them, or who will see particular gains as life-changing and who would barely be excited by them. For some consumers, being without, say, a functioning mobile phone, or not having the very latest iPhone, may be of no concern. For others, it is a difficult prospect to imagine, because being connected, or being at the leading edge in that area of technology is something that they have chosen to see as central to how they run their lives or to the kind of person they see themselves to be. They are prisoners of their personal construct systems, systems that they built for themselves as means for getting through life. If people wish to change, they are not prevented from doing so by inherited sets of "given" preferences. However, changing the mindsets that drive what we do is inherently impeded by the construct systems that we may need, and want, to change, along with the effort it takes to develop new mental models.

Change will be easier for those who create for themselves a diversified life and a way of looking at the world with many compartments, each based on different core themes: this way of operating means that any disruption is localized. Otherwise, seeing oneself as "open to change" (rather than as "a conservative by nature") or following the rule "try anything once, except folk dancing and incest" (which is attributed to, among others, Sir Thomas Beecham and Oscar Wilde) may help to produce flexibility as economic conditions change. However, if our systems are completely open to change, because they lack any organizing principles, we are unlikely to develop much of an ability to predict and control events. Such an ability is a product of persisting in an area long enough to discover reliable patterns and rules, a process that is defeated if we simply move on and try a different area the moment the going gets tough.

8   How Do We Choose?

8.1   Introduction

With the analysis of the processes of problem recognition, search, expectation formation and the assignment of values behind us, we can now move on to consider how
choices are made. But as we do so, we should not forget that in the preceding chapters
we have at times already had to consider how choices are made, as with choices about
how to define when a problem exists, how to gather information, what to believe and
what matters. In this chapter, we will consider alternative behavioral perspectives on
choice. Some of them are very well known and widely used by those who call
themselves behavioral economists, whereas others are much less well known. As we
proceed, four major areas of contrast will emerge in addition to the tension that
loomed large in Chapter 7 between rules and emotions as drivers of action.

One contrast is that some approaches follow the conventional economist's strategy
of viewing the decision-maker at the moment that the choice is made, whereas others
view choice as a subprocess within a decision cycle, a process that may take a
significant amount of time after the previous stages of the decision cycle have
been undertaken.

Secondly, some approaches focus on the particular "characteristics" or "attributes"
of the rival options, whereas others focus on values assigned to overall gains and
losses of alternatives relative to a reference point.

Thirdly, both "compensatory" and "non-compensatory" views of choice will be
considered. In the former, the weak aspects of a choice potentially could be offset by
strong performances in other areas, whereas, in the latter view, a missing feature or
substandard performance in a particular area may be viewed as a "fatal flaw" and
hence be a "deal breaker."

Finally, some behavioral analyses of choice are presented, like the model of choice
in mainstream economics, as "one-size-fits-all" models, whereas others view choices
as being made in different ways in different contexts. The latter view aligns with
Chapter 2's pluralistic discussion of motivation, for different perspectives on motivation might be more relevant in some contexts than in others. However, it needs to be
understood that in this chapter, the "context" of a decision is viewed in relation to the
type of choice and how the challenges that it entails may impinge on the way that the
decision gets made. This is a broader view than has been common in behavioral
economics: "context" is often used merely in relation to different ways in which a

particular choice could be presented to consumers in order to try to shape their behavior, an issue that we will be addressing in Chapter 9. The present chapter's key concern in relation to context is with how people may be expected to take decisions in different ways in different contexts.

8.2   The Fishbein–Ajzen Model of Behavioral Intentions

The title of this chapter echoes that of a short book by Mary Tuck (1976) that I first read in 1980, around the time I was starting to explore the potential for applying Kelly's personal construct psychology to economics and was immersing myself in what researchers in marketing were writing about consumer behavior. Tuck's book was significant to me because she mounted a vigorous critique of the complex "boxes and arrows" kinds of models that the marketing scholars used (as in Nicosia, 1966, and Engel et al., 1968). She argued that the complexity of these models made them impossible to apply empirically. Instead, she advocated the use of a very simple framework that had just been proposed by psychologists Martin Fishbein and Icek Ajzen (1975). Their model of behavioral intentions predicts behavior via a single equation that relates attitudes and beliefs to behavioral intentions:

$$B \approx BI = (AB)W_1 + (SN)W_2$$

In this equation, B = overt behavior, assumed approximately equal to BI; BI = behavioral intentions ("How probable I think it is that I will undertake the activity in question"); W_1 and W_2 are weights that we could estimate using regression techniques; AB = is the chooser's attitude toward the activity, and SN is the chooser's "subjective norm" regarding performing the activity. Fishbein and Ajzen viewed AB as depending on the chooser's assessment of how likely it is that undertaking the activity will result in each of a number of salient consequences (usually assumed via Miller's Rule to be 7 ± 2 due to short-term memory limitations). For each of these salient consequences, the chooser's rating of its likelihood is multiplied by the chooser's assessment of its goodness or badness, with the resulting scores then being summed together to get the AB value. The chooser's subjective norm regarding the activity is arrived at by summing together scores arrived at in relation to the beliefs of a number (again, usually 7 ± 2) of salient members of his or her reference group. These scores come from multiplying the chooser's belief about the extent to which each particular social referent would approve of the chooser undertaking the activity (that referent's "subjective norm"), by his or her motivation to comply with that referent.

Put simply, the central proposition of the Fishbein–Ajzen model is that two things determine the choices we make: first, our personal assessment of the consequences of taking a particular course of action; and second, the opinions that we believe other people of significance to us have about whether we should undertake the action and the extent to which we are prepared to follow these opinions. The two components are weighed together; so, depending on the relative sizes of the weights, the model can accommodate not merely situations in which personal assessments and social influence both play roles in the choice but also polar cases in which, at one extreme, decision-makers essentially ignore social pressures or, at the other extreme, base their choices very largely on what they believe others think they should do.

Tuck was a very early adopter of this model, but many researchers in psychology and marketing have since shared her enthusiasm for it. By the end of 2020, Google Scholar listed Fishbein and Ajzen's (1975) book as having over 60,000 citations, with some of their other works in the same vein also notching up thousands of citations. This is an extraordinary impact, and it begs the question of why this chapter is not about to offer the same answer as Tuck offered in her book. After all, it may appear that what was said about expectation-formation in Chapters 4 and 5 could readily feed into the Fishbein–Ajzen model by explaining how the respective consequence and likelihood values are arrived at and how people assess what others might feel about whether they should select the option in question in cases where the latter have not expressed their views. It also seems compatible with Chapter 7's Kellian view of why things differ in how much they matter to us, for the goodness or badness ratings in the *AB* component can be viewed as proxies for the net (good minus bad) implications of each of the outcomes, and the respective ratings for motivation to comply with particular social referents can be viewed as proxies for the net implications of complying with the perceived views of each of the social referents. (This Kellian perspective is taken further later in the present chapter, beginning in Section 8.4.)

It is not hard to see the appeal of the Fishbein–Ajzen model. It attempts to acknowledge human cognitive constraints by limiting the number of aspects of the schemes of action being considered and the number of social referents it presumes people keep in mind when choosing. It also brings in uncertainty in a very simple way. It is easy to use empirically at the level of an individual who is considering a range of options, and it accommodates the fact that, when we choose, we are often aware that people we know may have contrasting opinions about what we should do, some of which we are inclined to take seriously and others that we prefer to ignore. Yet, in contrast to its impact in psychology and marketing, the Fishbein–Ajzen model has attracted little interest from economists, even from those in the modern behavioral camp.

This has happened despite the Fishbein–Ajzen model sharing with conventional economic models the idea that a low score in one area can be offset by high scores elsewhere: it is an additive, "compensatory" model of choice both within and between its two major blocks. What ultimately matters, it suggests, is the overall rating accorded to an action. However, in addition to the recognitions of cognitive limitations (which ought to appeal to behavioral economists), there are three aspects of the model that differ sharply from the conventional economic approach to modeling choice.

One issue is that the social component is at odds with the standard reductionist way of viewing human action. To me, this is an appealing feature. However, if one looks at the world from a general equilibrium perspective, social interaction between economic agents opens up the possibility of crowd behavior and thus stands potentially as a threat to the attainment of equilibrium. Given the choice, a typical economist will cling to an existing equilibrium-focused way of doing things rather than jettison it to try to incorporate crowd behavior.

Secondly, the Fishbein–Ajzen model is not specified in a way that entails optimization subject to a constraint and with a diminishing marginal willingness to substitute between the things between which the choice is being made. What it may be viewed as focusing on are options that the decision-maker views as feasible, but the prior stage of determining whether a potential course of action does not breach any relevant constraints is taken for granted. The Fishbein–Ajzen model is typically applied in relation to "discrete choices" (i.e., choices between specific indivisible products or actions), rather than in relation to trading off different amounts of, say, apples and oranges when shopping with a limited budget.

Thirdly, the Fishbein–Ajzen model also differs crucially from preferred practice in economics by focusing on a range of imagined *consequences* of choosing rather than on overall expected "utility." The consequences we get from choosing are akin to, or closely related to, what marketing researchers call "product attributes" and what Kelvin Lancaster (1966a, 1966b), an Australian-born Columbia University economist, called "product characteristics." It was never likely that conventional economics would have embraced the Fishbein–Ajzen view of choice, for they still find themselves unable even to follow Lancaster's approach of viewing consumers as choosing between the bundles of characteristics that rival bundles of goods or discrete items seem to offer as means toward deriving utility. Over half a century on from Lancaster's demonstration of how this could be done (in essence, by blending elements of standard consumer theory and production theory), most economic theorists persist in modeling behavior in terms of choices between goods considered as wholes, i.e., as if the key question decision-makers each have to resolve is which bundle of *products* – for example, the contents of one hypothetical shopping trolley rather than any of the different mixes of products that other trolleys might contain – maximizes their utility. Textbook accounts of Lancaster's approach remain rare (I provided one in Earl, 1995, ch. 3) and it is largely ignored in modern behavioral economics. The behavior of economists in this respect is especially lamentable, since, as Loasby (1978, p. 3) has pointed out, viewing consumers as choosing with reference to product characteristics was not new: Three quarters of a century before Lancaster worked out his formal analysis, Alfred Marshall (1890) had been working with precisely this perspective.

As will already be evident, there is much that I find appealing about the Fishbein–Ajzen model. But I am not about to argue that behavioral economists should see it as a panacea for answering the question that this chapter poses. Two key issues need to be noted. First, like Lancaster's (1966a, 1966b) model, it presumes all choices are made in a compensatory way. This is at odds with our everyday encounters with people who think in terms of "must-have" or "must-not-have" features in the products for which they are shopping or who say that they "don't like" particular products, regardless of the prices at which these products are being offered. Here, we will be taking non-compensatory choices very seriously despite them clashing with the core presumption in conventional economics that substitution can always be induced in favor of something that has disadvantages by offering additional benefits (such as a lower price) on a scale big enough to offset those disadvantages.

My second reservation about the Fishbein–Ajzen approach is that, like conventional economic models of choice, it is a "one-size-fits-all" kind of model. It encourages us to think "as if" making a choice about, say, whether to stay in the armed services (one of the examples discussed in Tuck, 1976) is essentially the same as choosing, say, a holiday or what to put in one's shopping trolley on a weekly trip to the supermarket. Introspection led me to question this, the more so the more experience I had of choosing in diverse contexts. However, my doubts about a "one-size-fits–all" approach to modeling choice also came via reflection on the possibility that people might find that some contexts pose cognitive challenges that others do not, forcing them to adapt in a contingent manner as they moved between decision contexts.

8.3   Prospect Theory

Around the time that I was considering the merits and limitations of the Fishbein–Ajzen model, Richard Thaler (1980) offered economists a different behavioral view of choice, namely Kahneman and Tversky's (1979) prospect theory. Kahneman and Tversky developed their theory as a modified version of subjective expected utility (SEU) theory to take account of inferences they had arrived at by studying the choices that people made when presented with rival hypothetical lotteries involving simple payoff matrices. (The research program that culminated in the publication of prospect theory is set out in detail in Kahneman, 2011.) These choices seemed to differ systematically from what SEU theory predicted and they attributed this to the bias-inducing effects of a number of heuristics. In its intended role, prospect theory has been a remarkable success: according to a survey article by Barberis, it has become "widely regarded as the best available description of how people evaluate risk in experimental settings" (Barberis, 2013, p. 173). But when Thaler commended it to economists, he offered a bigger vision of the theory's potential, having rapidly recognized that it could also be applied to making sense of riskless behavior in everyday life. Beginning with his seminal 1980 paper, much of his work has entailed applying the theory in the latter context. After a leisurely takeoff, his way of using the theory has become commonplace and a key part of modern behavioral economics.

Despite emerging as a modified version of SEU theory, prospect theory overlaps somewhat with Shackle's (1949) non-probabilistic "potential surprise" model of choice under uncertainty (for a detailed discussion of this, see Earl and Littleboy, 2014, ch. 8). However, Kahneman and Tversky seem to have been utterly unaware of Shackle's work when they put their theory together. The feature it most obviously has in common with Shackle's analysis is the idea that potential outcomes are viewed as gains or losses relative to a reference point. Like Shackle, Kahneman, and Tversky seem to have arrived at this idea by introspection. SEU theory assumes that decisions to participate in lottery-style choices are based on the probabilities of ending up with particular levels of wealth and the utilities associated with each of these rival levels of total wealth. However, in order to know what these terminal values will be, decision-makers need to have not merely an idea of the payoffs to rival choices and their respective probabilities; they also need to know how much wealth they have at the time they make their choice, for their subsequent total wealth will be this sum plus any extra that they win or minus any loss.

Kahneman and Tversky questioned whether people normally have such knowledge of their wealth and instead posited that what actually happens is that people frame their choices in terms of gains or losses relative to a reference point. If decision-makers do indeed focus on gains and losses, they do not need to know how much wealth they currently have. However, once we accept the general idea of choices being framed in relation to reference points, it becomes apparent that what gets chosen may depend upon the reference point that the decision-maker chooses to use. Thus, for example, we may make different choices if we use our current situation as a reference point for assessing prospective gains and losses instead of using an aspiration level as our reference point.

Their reference-dependent view of how people think when choosing aligns with Kelly's view that we form constructs by considering what things "are like": we construe everything relative to other things, for there are no absolute measures. Moreover, because choice entails the question of whether to continue as before or do something different, implications-based rankings seem inherently likely to be framed in terms of reference points. For example, if the context is the possible trading-in of a car against a newer vehicle, then one change of construct would be "keep my existing car versus trade my existing car against car X," whose overall implications would be compared with a change on the construct "keep my existing car versus trade my existing car against car Y," and so on. Here, the "do nothing" option is used as a reference point and the alternatives are, in effect, viewed in terms of the gains and losses that are implied relative to that reference point. Of course, in the case where we consider getting rid of our current car, one option that we may consider is to give up owning a car altogether. The latter would have different implications depending on which kind of car-free lifestyle we imagine having. But computing the implications of any of these possible courses of action does not leave us with a measure of the *total* utility we would get; all we end up with is a *change-related* measure.

Having come to view the utilities of prospective outcomes as a function of the distance of the outcomes from the chosen reference point, Kahneman and Tversky then factored into their view of the utility function the idea of loss aversion, i.e., that we feel much greater disutility from a loss than the utility we would get from a gain of the same amount (for further details, see the end of Section 7.7). Thus, although they accepted the assumption from SEU theory that when we become better off the utility we get from our wealth rises at a slower and slower rate for marginal increases in our wealth, they posited that people make decisions with respect to utility functions that have the kind of S-shaped form shown in Figure 8.1. Note how there is a point of

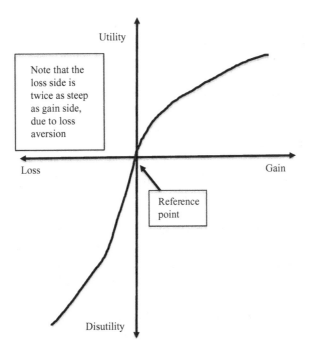

Figure 8.1 An *S*-shaped value function

inflection at the reference point and that the loss arm has a steeper slope than the gain arm. Losses hurt more the bigger they are, but at a decreasing marginal rate. Note, too, that the *S*-shaped utility function is smooth: it does not imply any points at which there is a sudden jump in how the decision-maker feels due to, say, having "made it" by crossing a particular threshold, or due to going bankrupt when losses reach a particular level. In the latter case, where a change of legal status is entailed, probably along with a collapse of social standing, this seems especially questionable.

This *S*-shaped value function is what Thaler seized upon in his early work as a behavioral economist, without even needing to call upon what prospect theory predicts about how people take account of risks when facing lottery-like decisions such as those concerning insurance products. Thaler realized that an *S*-shaped value function could in principle apply to *any* situation in which decision-makers will have to give up something they already have if they switch from their current situation to get something that they do not currently have. In effect, Thaler used the *S*-shaped value function as the basis for a compensatory view of choices that involves two stages: first, work out the utility of gains associated with each option and the disutility of losses associated with each option and then rank the options on the basis of their respective net gains or losses of utility. The *S*-shape led Thaler to the idea of the endowment effect, for which we provided theoretical support in Section 7.11. But it did not require the choice problem to be reframed explicitly in terms of a choice between alternative combinations of specific product characteristics or consequences:

the total gain or loss associated with a particular option would obviously arise from that option's characteristics or consequences, but in contrast to the Fishbein–Ajzen and Lancaster models, this was left implicit. This minor modification to utility theory obviously resonates brilliantly with the pleasure–pain or cost–benefit way of thinking that is central to economics. However, it also aligns well with the "net implications" way of ranking alternatives; indeed, where "gain" and "loss" do not refer to money, they might be viewed in terms of changes in the decision-maker's capacity to predict and control events, with the vertical scale then seen better in terms of excitement and anxiety rather than utility and disutility.

The combination of the reference point and loss aversion implies status quo bias and path-dependent preferences: behavior will not revert to how it used to be if the conditions that led it to change are no longer present. For example, suppose that some years ago fuel became cheaper, and people switched from small cars to large 4WDs. Now suppose fuel prices are back up to where they were previously. If those who previously switched to 4WDs now consider switching back to regular cars, the things they gained when they switched to 4WDs (e.g., "go anywhere" capabilities and perceived better passive safety) are the things they will lose if they switch back to small cars. On the other hand, the things that they previously had to be prepared to give up in switching from small cars to large 4WDs (such as better fuel economy, ease of parking and superior active safety) are now what they will gain if they switch back. The reference point-dependent *S*-shaped value function implies that the things they like about 4WDs will now matter more to them, relative to the things they like about smaller vehicles, than was the case at the time they switched to large 4WDs. Hence, unless manufacturers of thriftier vehicles can dispel the 4WD owners' concerns about losing the things they like about 4WDs, fuel prices will need to rise *beyond* their previous high levels if the 4WD owners are to be induced to go back to driving more fuel-efficient vehicles (see further Kahneman, 2011, ch. 27).

Focusing on gains and losses relative to a single reference point may be procedurally rational for decision-makers and behavioral economists in cases concerning monetary payoffs. However, it needs to be recognized that in other situations decision-makers may find it cognitively easier to use a floating reference point and employ a form of what is known as an "additive-differences" procedure. By focusing merely on differences between one option and an initial reference point, we may easily work out which of the two we prefer. We can then use that one as the reference point and consider the net utility gain or loss of choosing a third option instead, with the preferred option from this pair then being used as the reference point for considering the net utility gain or loss from choosing a fourth option instead, and so on, until we have considered all our options. The preferred option from the last comparison is the one that we select via this process.

This may sound perfectly reasonable as a procedure, but suppose we decide to check our verdict by seeing what happens if the option preferred in the final pairwise comparison is pitted against the preferred option from the first pairwise comparison. If the first-round victor beats the final-round preference, then it appears that we should not select the latter, but if we repeat the process, we will just end up going round in circles. This would be a case of what rational choice theorists call an "intransitive" ranking system, similar to what we sometimes may see in sporting tournaments where, say, Team A beats Team B and Team B then beats Team C but Team C then beats Team A. Such a situation may seem unlikely if we can handle the task of computing the net utility gain or loss for each pairwise comparison across *all* the constructs we have in mind. However, things may go awry if we try to simplify the process by, say, selecting the victor of each pairwise comparison based on which one has the best set of implications on *the most* constructs (for a numerical example of this, see Anand, 1982, p. 161; see also Tversky, 1969). Even if we can compute the net utility gain or loss for selecting one option rather than the other in each pairwise comparison, the scope for intransitivity seems considerable if the reference point for each comparison has its own *S*-shaped utility function.

8.3.1   Dealing with Risk and Uncertainty in the Psychology Laboratory and in Everyday Life

In situations that resemble lotteries, prospect theory predicts that people will not weigh their prospective gains and losses by the actual probabilities. Rather, they will tend to use decision weights that differ systematically from probability values. They will tend to overweight outcomes with low probabilities but underweight outcomes with medium to high probabilities. This perspective, drawn from experimental studies of lottery choices, provides a means of explaining why people are prone to waste money by acting as if they will need to make insurance claims far more frequently than they do: if we only make a claim, say, one year in five, it is not a good idea to spend an extra $100 a year to reduce our insurance excess by $400. Similarly, the transformation of probabilities into tail-heavy decision weights might help explain why some parents opt to ignore official immunization policies, fearing that their children might suffer from very rare side effects.

The experiments conducted by Kahneman and his colleagues that paved the way to prospect theory typically focused on simple lottery puzzles. They often involved substantial imagined payoffs, with the researchers specifying the probabilities of the rival outcome. The puzzles tended to involve merely two-by-two or three-by-two payoff matrices (i.e., they only presented two or three options, each with only a pair of possible outcomes) and much of the excitement for the researchers came from showing that participants may: (a) behave differently depending on how a given gamble is framed; (b) exhibit inconsistent preferences that are at odds with normative theories of rational risk-taking; or (c) seem (as eventually summarized in the decision weight part of prospect theory) to give disproportionately low weight to large probabilities and vice versa.

Outside the psychology laboratory, the prospect theory view of choice may characterize well what happens in some contexts but not others. Clearly, where there are many options and/or each option has a wide range of rival probable consequences, decision-makers may need means of cognitively simplifying their choices. If Shackle's theory of attention focusing is correct (see the discussion of Figure 5.1 in

Section 5.2), then the decision-maker will only have to weigh together, for each prospective course of action, the hope he or she feels in respect of its focus gain, versus the feeling of fear that its focus loss generates. However, a satisficing rule offers another possible way of achieving cognitive simplicity: for example, we might rule that, in order to be an acceptable risk, a scheme must seem (a) to have a sufficiently good chance of delivering a big enough gain relative to a risk-free reference point and (b) to be sufficiently unlikely to result in a loss beyond that deemed acceptable relative to the risk-free reference point. In this latter scenario, we end up only having to look at a pair of outcomes for each option rather than the entire range of its possible outcomes; we also escape the need to weigh them together. (It was this kind of simplified thinking that Shackle presumed in early versions of his model, before he devised his theory of focusing, and he seemed to switch back to it toward the end of his life: see Earl and Littleboy, 2014, chs. 5 and 8.)

Even where cognitive complexity is not an issue, the weighing together of all relevant rival probable outcomes may be ruled out by "safety-first" principles. For example, consider the following real-life choice that my partner once had to make. In 1992, she was a contestant on the Australian television quiz *Sale of the Century*, and, after winning on five shows in succession, she had to choose whether to exit at that point and take all the prizes she had won (whose total value was around AUD90,000) or appear in a sixth show where she would have the chance of either winning an AUD500,000 cash jackpot and keeping her other prizes or losing all that she had won. This choice clearly had a simple payoff matrix, but she tells me that she used a "safety-first" approach to reach her decision to quit rather than go on to the sixth show: by bailing out, she knew that if she sold her major prizes, she would be able to put together a deposit to buy her first house, something that had previously seemed, on her teacher's salary, a distant dream. No way was she going to jeopardize the life-changing benefits that her prizes made possible. She might have been willing to risk losing all her prizes if she had so far won much less and therefore was still way short of her deposit target (and in that situation, had she won, she could have bought a very good house outright).

The "safety-first" view of decision-making operates in a non-compensatory manner, whereas the thinking behind loss aversion runs in conventional compensatory terms. Even so, these two perspectives on why people limit the risks they are prepared to take can be viewed as complementary. This is effectively what Shackle did in the middle period of his thinking on his potential surprise model of choice under uncertainty when he was not implicitly thinking in satisficing terms. He suggested that, after focusing on a single gain and a single loss outcome for each option, the decision-maker would finally rank their options by trading off the focus gains against their respective focus losses. This trade-off would be done in terms of the decision-maker's "gambler preferences" between (to put it rather more simply than Shackle himself did) the allure of focus gains and the fear associated with focus losses. With the former shown graphically on the vertical axis and the latter shown via the horizontal axis, indifference curves for the gambler preference function slope down to the left due to the negative preference toward losses. Each option reduces to a single point on such a map, with the most-preferred option being the one located on the indifference curve that is furthest to the top-left due to the preference for avoiding losses. Shackle normally drew the slopes of these indifference curves in a way that we would now see as implying loss aversion, but also with a perpendicular line some way along the horizontal axis that showed, in effect, the maximum extent to which the decision-maker was willing to expose himself or herself to fear associated with the possibility of making a loss.

Anyone seeking to build "safety-first" heuristics into prospect theory, or into the analysis of choice more generally, would be wise to recognize that safety-first rules may differ in how tolerant they are: even if we have a fear of flying, we might not altogether rule out flying (after all, we may take the view that there are significant ways in which we will fail to "live" if we completely refuse to fly), yet we may rule out particular kinds of air travel, such as on a Russian airline or in a hot-air balloon, as "too dangerous."

8.4   Personal Constructs and Choice

Although I came across both the Fishbein–Ajzen model (via Tuck, 1976) and prospect theory (via Thaler, 1980) in 1980 at a very early stage in my journey as a behavioral economist, I decided not to adopt either of them as the focus for my research on choice. I was already hooked on Kelly's psychology of personal constructs and was in the process of attempting to get a sense of how it might be integrated with Simon's theory of satisficing behavior and Shackle's potential surprise theory of choice under uncertainty. The road that I took would be one less travelled than the other two, but I was far from alone in following Kelly's work: by late 2019, Google Scholar listed over 20,000 citations for Kelly's (1955) magnum opus. But as with the fate of the Fishbein–Ajzen model, very few of these would be in behavioral economics.

One of the subversive things that I found appealing about Kelly's thinking was that it provides a way of making sense of choice without viewing people as "utility-seekers." The essence of Kelly's view is to be found in a component of Kelly's theory of personality that was deliberately omitted when the theory's elements were set out in Section 4.7, namely the Choice Corollary. Kelly (1963. p. 64) expressed this as follows: "A person chooses for himself that alternative in a dichotomous construct through which he anticipates the greatest possibility for extension and definition of his system." Kelly is thus not talking about choices being made in order to avoid pain or get pleasure but as means for improving the functionality of the systems we create as means for predicting and controlling events. The implication of this is that wherever it appears, from the standpoint of our personal construct system, that potential choices would reduce our system's functionality in this sense, we will not "go there." If all available options are problematic, our system will select the one that seems to pose the least damage to its functionality.

From Kelly's standpoint, and as foreshadowed in Section 7.5, the key trade-off that we each face is between gathering a wider range of experience that we can call upon when making subsequent choices (i.e., "extension") versus adding to the detail or precision with which we can construe things about which we already have something of "an idea" (i.e., "definition"). This trade-off is rather like that faced by the board of a firm that has to make a strategic choice between diversifying to a greater or lesser degree versus concentrating on securing its position in its existing product markets. Both kinds of improvements are worth having, so in deliberating about alternative courses of action we will need to construe their implications and somehow decide which are the most significant for our system.

For example, suppose the dichotomous construct in question is "staying single versus getting into a long-term relationship." We may view staying single as having implications of both kinds: on the one hand, it may leave us with freedom to explore adventurous new things – such as owning a motorcycle or taking up tourism opportunities in more challenging parts of the world – (i.e., "extension") without having to worry about dealing with objections that a partner might raise or feeling guilty about imposing anxiety on a partner; on the other hand, not having a partner might leave us with freedom to continue "playing the field" and allow us to get deeper into things that we already do (i.e., "definition"). By contrast, we might view a long-term relationship as opening the door to all manner of new experiences that would be very problematic if we were single, such as those associated with becoming a parent (i.e., "extension"), but it might also seem to be a means of getting more out of the kinds of things we already do, if we have these interests in common with our partner (i.e., "definition").

8.4.1 From Terminal Implications to Rankings?

To understand how people end up resolving the trade-off between definition and extension and thereby select the areas of life in which to develop the capacities of their predictive systems, we need to recall the arguments set out in Section 7.7. We explored there the kinds of patterns of implications that may follow from change on a single construct axis. From a "means–end chain" perspective, it appears that what ought to matter for the decision-maker are the terminal implications of a change on a construct. From that standpoint, the intermediate implications of that change are of interest merely because of the causal role they are construed as playing in determining what happens on the terminal constructs. With this in mind, we now need to consider how people choose between options that differ in terms of multiple construct axes, with corresponding differences in the options' overall sets of terminal implications. If we try to take an economist's view of this, the natural thing to expect a decision-maker to do is weigh up the positive terminal implications of a choice against the negative ones and to rank options according to their net terminal implication relative to one another. Because options are construed relative to one another, the process naturally entails the cognitive ease of using an additive-differences information processing strategy. With any pair of strategies that are being compared, the decision-maker could attempt to a running tally of which one is leading as their net implications are considered across a sequence of constructs until the winner of this pair emerges. Thus, on the first construct option *A* might, say, beat option *B* in terms of its net positive implications, but on the second construct perhaps option B wins, thereby narrowing the overall gap or moving into the lead, and so on.

At first sight, it may appear that there should be no need to attach any weights to any terminal implications to take account of their relative significance. As noted in Section 7.7, if implications differ in their significance, there must be reasons for this – i.e., some or all the constructs on which the choice implies a switch must have implications on other constructs – so some or all these implications cannot be terminal ones. However, there are two situations in which weights may need to be attached. One is straightforward, namely where we have doubts about whether the choice would indeed turn out in a particular way: here, each weight would reflect our assessment of how likely its respective outcome is, or (to the extent that Shackle is right) how unsurprised we think we would be if the outcome eventuated.

The other situation in which terminal implications would seems likely to be weighted is where, in effect, we have an internal tacit knowledge problem and are unable to articulate to ourselves (let alone anyone else) deeper implications of some or all the terminal implications that we are able to articulate. Despite this, we may have a sense that some of these positive or negative implications are more important than others, such that we could rate them in this respect for a researcher. These would be emotion-related weights associated with the mind's sense of what is implied for the functionality of its predictive system. From the standpoint of Section 7.7, these weights would incorporate loss aversion and be proxies for the cognitive costs of having to change expectations on intermediate constructs if one option is selected rather than the other that is being considered as its rival. Hence, the choice could be viewed instead in terms of which action dominates in terms of net *overall* unweighted implications.

Either way, there is the question of whether we have the computational capacity to rank rival courses of action in terms of the net implications (weighted or not, and terminal or overall) of selecting a particular option rather than an alternative, even if we use an additive-differences procedure to simplify the process of dealing with multiple options. Our chances of being able to do this are greatest when the axes in which we construe our options take a binary form and we are not unsure about which pole we will end up on if we select one option rather than the other. Things are much more challenging where the construct axes for the options take a scalar form and multiple outcomes along these scales seem to some degree possible. Shackle's theory of focus outcomes is thought-provoking in relation to how our minds may achieve cognitive simplicity in respect of a single outcome scale. But perhaps we may need to think more as is suggested in the Fishbein–Ajzen model – i.e., in terms of how likely a particular hoped-for or feared outcome is, even if the construct in question has a scalar form – if we try to compute net implications in the face of uncertainty. From Simon's satisficing perspective, such a focal outcome would be our aspiration level on the scale in question. If there are many options and they differ significantly on many axes, ranking via an additive-differences method may prove cognitively exhausting, leading us to lose track of the net implications of a choice even when only making sets of pairwise comparisons.

Finally, and significantly, it should be recognized that occasions for choice are themselves events that need to be construed. Hence, even if a choice problem is in principle simple enough to be addressed in terms of the net implications of pairwise choices, we may construe the decision-making task as simply not worth approaching in this way – if, indeed, we even consider it as something that could be approached in this way. Instead, we may construe the task in a nonadditive way. In other words, if we see choices as occasions for applying hierarchical principles, discriminating tests and other fast and frugal procedures, we may proceed on that basis rather than by trying to figure out what, "on balance," the implications of choosing one way rather than another might be. Although this may entail choosing on the basis of a rather limited view of the implications of our actions, the way we choose may be perfectly adequate for avoiding being at the mercy of events, especially if there are many choices we need to make within short periods of time.

8.5 Choice Overload

For products to be ranked via any procedure that refers to the implications of choosing them, the decision-maker needs to have figured out what these implications are or, at least, what they might be. However, both intermediate and terminal implications of a course of action may only become known after the decision-maker has incurred search costs and the cognitive costs of figuring out what to make of the information that has been gathered. Although prospective gaps in the availability of potentially relevant information may be a cause of anxiety, so, too, may be the prospect of having access to far more information than we have the time or cognitive capacity to process. In both cases, our response may be to delay making a choice. In the former situation, choice deferral is a means of avoiding the possibility that we will change course in a way that we will come to regret; it also gives time for additional relevant information to become available. If we face choice due to awareness that we have a plethora of options that differ in many ways, we may abandon our shopping expedition and head home to do research on the Internet to find a way of simplifying our choice problem. Such a response means that, contrary to conventional economic wisdom, the retailers might have clinched a sale there and then if they had stocked a smaller variety of products and the products stocked had fewer features (Iyengar and Lepper, 2000; Schwartz, 2005; Fasolo et al., 2007). However, given the complex situation that we faced, our action may have been procedurally rational.

But delay is not the only strategy that may be preferred and/or procedurally rational when choices are challenging. An alternative to deferring choice in the hope of building better constructs is to choose by other means well before the terminal implications of many or all our options are clear. This may entail rejections or selections based essentially on first impressions, via "fast and frugal" heuristics (emphasized by Gigerenzer et al., 1999) and/or with reference to simple proxies and brands (emphasized by Olshavsky and Granbois, 1979); selecting the default option, if there is one (emphasized by Thaler and Sunstein, 2008); following social norms or rules for the context in question (emphasized by Hodgson, 1997, 2003); and applying satisficing rules whereby search stops with the discovery of an option that seems, on the basis of other evaluation rules, sufficiently likely to meet a particular (set of) performance standard(s) (as emphasized by Simon, 1955, 1957a) or outsourcing choice to the "market for preferences" (as suggested by Earl and Potts, 2004).

To the extent that we do engage in more extensive and time-consuming decision-making, it may still require us to use heuristics to prevent cognitive overload. Thus, we may search extensively, until we judge that we have got "enough" information but then rank products using an information processing strategy that simplifies our task, such as by applying non-compensatory rules rather than seeking to compute overall values for each of the rival products. Or we may make a compensatory approach cognitively manageable by first deriving a shortlist of acceptable brands or a few intolerant criteria (i.e., by initially using a non-compensatory approach) and then evaluate trade-offs among characteristics of the options on that shortlist.

Choosing via incomplete models of what we may be getting into saves us the effort of figuring out the full implications of the options that we reject. If we make such a choice, our "sense" of what lies in store for us will have to be arrived at by applying heuristics where options that are unfamiliar to us. These heuristics are likely to work in a highly discriminating, non-compensatory manner that combines choice with the formation of constructs and likelihood assessments. So, for example, those who came across this book but decided not to read it might have been "put off" by, say, its scale, contents page and a quick look at the list of references. Via those criteria, they may have inferred that a lot of mental effort would be necessary to absorb its contents and go beyond typical modern approaches to behavioral economics. Unlike readers who have persisted to this point, they do not know what they could now have known, but in the meantime, they may have improved the functionality of their predictive systems in other areas.

Clearly, choices based on first impressions will tend to favor the status quo whenever continuing as before seems to offer a satisfactory prospect and thus does not seem to have drastic negative implications for our predictive system: we know where we stand with our previously favored strategy, whereas we still need to build a mental model of how things will look if we try something different. So, for example, as a rule, we may trade in our Toyota every four years for the current version of the same model, not because we have any passionate commitment to the Toyota brand but because we anticipate no problems if we do so, whereas if, say, we switch to Volkswagen, we do not know whether the ownership experience is going to drive us crazy and we may not even trouble to examine reviews of rival products, let alone reviews of after-sales service experiences. As is commonly said, "If it works, don't mess with it."

Anything new or unfamiliar will have trouble holding our attention unless we somehow already have a sense that the benefits it offers are going to make it worthwhile to incur the effort of figuring out what it implies for our means–end chains. If we have very little idea at all about what a switch will entail, an immediate choice has to rely upon our associative memory, i.e., on what happened when we were previously in this kind of situation and chose to stay with the status quo, switched or decided to explore our options further. If the implications of departing from the status quo are so unclear, all that the associative memory can really focus on are the characteristics of the decision-making context, not the features of the product in question: for example, how have things worked out when we rushed to make changes or refused even to listen to what our friends were suggesting we needed to do, or when we did not say "No, I'm not ready to decide" when a salesperson was trying to rush us to a decision?

If we do delay action and instead engage in search and reflection, we incur costs not merely in terms of time and/or financial outlays but also the cognitive cost of building new mental models of how things are going to be if we make particular choices. In emotional terms, we can go from being anxious (because of our uncertainty about what is implied by the change and our capacity to deal with it) to being much more confident about what to expect and our capacity to deal with it. Such deliberation entails incurring the cognitive costs of building new mental models, so except in cases where, the more we explore our options the more uncertainty we recognize, it seems likely that the more that we have researched and thought about our options, the bigger the weight that terminal implications will have in our choices and the less we will be susceptible to biases that are driven by the cognitive costs of adjusting to change.

8.6   Impulsive Behavior, Procrastination and Weakness of Will

Coolheaded responses to the question of when and how to reach a decision are, unfortunately, by no means guaranteed. The less tolerant we are of living with uncertainty, the more we are at risk of failing to get to the stage of being able to focus on the terminal implications of an appropriate set of potential courses of action. Instead, to limit the cognitive load that our perceived need to dispose of the problem generates, we may seek to restore a sense of control by applying heuristics that produce either of two kinds of behavior. On the one hand, we may rapidly remove the looming uncertainty by selecting a course of action without appropriate deliberation (i.e., we behave impulsively). Alternatively, we can remove ourselves from the choice environment and come up with a basis for arguing the problem out of the way for the moment rather than working on addressing it and finding a timely solution (i.e., we procrastinate).

Taking the view that impulsivity and procrastination are driven by problems of knowledge and the cognitive costs of changing complex systems of constructs is complementary to, but different from, how a typical behavioral economist would see these two kinds of behavior. The later, exemplified by O'Donoghue and Rabin (1999), assign a key role to "quasi-hyperbolic discounting" as a driver of both procrastination and what they view as behavior aimed at immediate gratification. The notion of quasi-hyperbolic discounting is particularly associated with the work of George Ainslie (1992), a researcher at a Florida rehabilitation hospital, and the nature of his patients' difficulties may help to account for the pursuit of immediate gratification being taken as the opposite of procrastination: a drug addict's apparent inability to exercise self-control despite awareness of the severely adverse long-term consequences of continuing to take drugs can be framed as the consequence of grossly overweighting immediate benefits relative to long-term costs. In contrast to our Kellian picture of impulsivity as a rather desperate attempt to clear away a lot of uncertainty, the addict's lack of restraint is seen as entailing calculating as in a rational choice model, except that "present bias" is evident due to the tendency to discount in a roughly hyperbolic manner rather than exponentially.

In conventional economics, people are presumed to have "time preference": to give up a dollar today, they will require it to be repaid with interest that accrues exponentially, at a constant percentage rate per period. This is viewed as perfectly rational and is not what behavioral economists mean by "present bias." If we engage instead in quasi-hyperbolic discounting, we apply a smaller and smaller discount factor to assess the present worth of costs and benefits that arise further and further into the future. In mathematical terms, a hyperbola is a functional relationship between two variables whose values always have the same product. Thus, for example, a graph of a hyperbolic demand curve that shows the relationship between the offer price and the number of units purchased implies the same total revenue (i.e., price times quantity) for any price. Similarly, if we engage in hyperbolic discounting, the discount factor that we apply in any period is always given by $1/n$, where n is the number of the period. As can be seen in Table 8.1, if we engage in hyperbolic discounting, we greatly overweight upfront costs and benefits relative to those in the future, compared with how we treat them if we engage in exponential discounting.

The economics of car ownership may make it easier to appreciate how human tendencies to act roughly as if engaging in hyperbolic discounting can result in behavior that may be unduly driven by present benefits. The decay profile for the value of a hyperbolically discounted dollar is rather like that of the value of a car as it gets older: a new car's value plunges the moment we drive it from the showroom, but as time goes by, it depreciates at a slower and slower rate. Viewed in relation to savings in maintenance costs, the initial fall in the value of a car seems crazy, and, in basic functional terms, a new car may not offer that much more than the previous year's model, yet we act as though it does. When we buy a new car, we seem implicitly to be willing to pay huge sums for whatever new features it offers, for that "new car smell" and for the temporary bragging rights it offers, even though we might have saved thousands by waiting another year or two and buying a nearly new car rather than one that is brand new. But we should not forget the role of dread and anxiety here (recall Sections 5.8 and 5.9): Being able to get a car fixed for free during its warranty period does not compensate for the out-of-control feeling we (expect to) experience if things go wrong. This, and overweighting of the other benefits of a new car, seems likely to limit the impact that the competitive drift of vehicle manufacturers from three- to five- or seven-year warranties will have on vehicle depreciation.

Our willingness to overweight immediate benefits against longer-term costs may seem a tragic aspect of human nature, but perhaps even bigger tragedies arise where present bias drives us to procrastinate. Here, the problem is that we allow upfront costs to loom unduly large, leading us to defer action that would produce a long stream of

Table 8.1. Exponential versus hyperbolic discounting

	Eponential discounting		Hyperbolic discounting	
Period in which cost is incurred or benefit is received	Discount relative to previous period	Present value of $1.00	Discount relative to previous period	Present value of $1.00
1		$1.00		$1.00
2	10%	$0.90	50%	$0.50
3	10%	$0.81	33.3%	$0.33
4	10%	$0.73	25%	$0.25
5	10%	$0.66	20%	$0.20
6	10%	$0.59	16.7%	$0.167
7	10%	$0.53	14.3%	$0.143
8	10%	$0.48	12.5%	$0.125
9	10%	$0.43	11.1%	$0.11
10	10%	$0.39	10%	$0.10

future benefits. If a new course of action has an upfront cost and the decision-maker discounts quasi-hyperbolically, it will seem that delaying action until tomorrow makes it look far less costly in prospect, whereas benefits in later periods only seem slightly reduced in present value if they are delayed. For example, if we are discounting hyperbolically as per Table 8.1, it will seem to us that if we defer incurring the cost of making a change until next period, the cost is only half as bad, whereas delay reduces the present value of benefits by rather little (for example, delaying a $1 benefit from period 9 to period 10 only reduces its present value from $0.11 to $0.10). Hence, it may seem better to delay until another day – but tomorrow it may then seem better to delay until the day after, and so on. For such procrastination to end, the upfront costs of acting will need to fall, or there will need to be a major improvement in long-term benefits (or an escalation in the costs of not changing).

A particularly tragic situation that this analysis leads us to expect is the failure of people to break off dysfunctional personal relationships. Any dread they have about what they have to do to end the relationship will be magnified greatly if they succumb to present bias. To be sure, they might have to incur the costs of a very unpleasant evening in which they announce their intention, and some weeks or months of anxiety and chaos as they set about finding somewhere else to live and getting established there, but the benefits may be great and last for many years, or even decades.

8.7   The Resolution of Dilemmas

Not all cases of delays and/or agonizing before reaching a decision and taking action result from information overload, incomplete knowledge or quasi-hyperbolic discounting. Sometimes, the problem is that we have a very good idea of the implications of selecting any of our options, but they all seem unsatisfactory in ways that matter to us. In such situations, we thus face a dilemma. These occasions are potentially challenging to make sense of in terms of a compensatory view of choice such as the Fishbein–Ajzen model, prospect theory and our "net implications" view of how options come to be ranked. In normative terms, compensatory choice models exhort us to compute overall scores for our options, choose the one with the best score and accept that we can't have everything that we want in life. In this section we consider, via a couple of examples, whether dilemmas can and should be viewed as ultimately being resolved by a compensatory process.

First, take the case of Steve, a semiprofessional heavy-metal guitarist. When playing with his band, he needs to be able to produce wild vibrato effects without his guitar going out of tune. Steve views a guitar with a Floyd Rose locking vibrato system as the only means for meeting this conjunction of requirements. Given this, we should expect Steve to reject instruments that have other vibrato systems, or no vibrato system at all, *regardless of their prices*, as means for playing this kind of music. Here, his decision rule appears to be a non-compensatory one. However, Steve also considers that it is essential that he can easily replace a broken string under the pressures of playing at a gig. He therefore has a dilemma: any guitar equipped with a Floyd Rose vibrato system entails a nightmare if a string breaks, owing to the tiny clamps that hold the string ends in their bridge saddles. These are incredibly fiddly to use, as they are hard to see unless well illuminated. If this is how Steve sees the situation, the only way that he can meet the conflicting goals is to take multiple guitars with Floyd Rose vibrato systems to each gig so that he can switch guitars if a string breaks and then replace the broken string later. But Steve may rule this out due to the cost, quite apart from the extra hassle in transporting equipment to and from gigs and when trying to avoid damaging his gear at his typically small venues with cramped stages. There would also be the risk of having the spare guitar stolen if he had to leave it out of his sight. If the spare guitar strategy is precluded, he will have to sacrifice one of his goals.

From a compensatory perspective, it would appear that, if everything can be reduced to the same unit of measurement, the resolution of a dilemma simply comes down to finding the least bad option in terms of that unit of measurement. This should apply even in in cases where there are technological or engineering barriers to substitution and, more broadly, where people are trying to run their lives on the basis of moral principles or health-related rules (as in the case of those with food allergy or intolerance issues) that preclude some kinds of substitution.

If we take a Kellian view of Steve's dilemma, the solution seems likely to come down to what his choice of guitar implies for his self-construct, which he may see as depending to some degree on how others are likely to see him. If so, the key question for him is whether his image will be compromised most by not being able to play in the way that his heavy-metal guitar heroes do, or by having his guitar frequently go badly out of tune during a song, or to have occasionally to stop a performance for as long as it takes, with shaking hands and dim illumination, to grapple with a fiddly string replacement process. Most nights, he will not break a string, so a guitar with a Floyd Rose system will be fine, but there will always be the dread of what will happen if a string breaks. If he does not compromise on his music but tries to use a guitar with a different vibrato system, he will have the dread and quite often the actuality of having to deal with it going out of tune during a song.

Steve's dilemma thus seems to reduce to a probability-weighted trade-off: whatever guitar he selects, he has something to dread if he insists on playing in that particular style. However, note that although the dilemma reduces to a common unit of measurement, its resolution results in a non-compensatory rule: depending on which way it is resolved, Steve's guitar must or must not have a Floyd Rose vibrato system. If Steve is agonizing about which guitar to use, the compensatory perspective seems to invite us to see his problem as one of adjusting cognitively to the idea that his ideal instrument simply is not available and getting a clear picture of the risks his various options pose.

Let us now consider the rather more complicated dilemma faced by Emma, a "green" Australian consumer. She feels guilty about continuing to drive a car that emits greenhouse gases, but when she thinks about becoming an early adopter of an all-electric vehicle, she experiences "range anxiety," since she frequently has to make a 280km round trip to visit her elderly mother. It is 2019, and there are only three fully electric vehicles within her budget. The most expensive of these is the second-generation Nissan Leaf, which will be just about able to do the journey on a single charge if she drives with restraint. It also looks like it will be the best to drive. The second is the smaller, less powerful Renault Zoe, which also has just about enough range on a single charge. However, it is being marketed only to fleet customers through a mere four dealers across Australia and the nearest one is 1000km away. The third is a Hyundai Ioniq, whose highway range is about 200–225km. It therefore cannot complete the round trip to her mother and back without being recharged. This would need to be done either at her mother's home or at the one commercial charging station currently available on route. The latter's location, about halfway between her home and her mother's, is inconvenient, since if she only recharged there once on each trip, she would barely be able to get home given the Ioniq's range. But charging the car at her mother's would take far too long. In any case, neither her mother nor the charging station has solar power, whereas at home she has a large rooftop solar photovoltaic system and would pay to have a fast charger installed.

Emma initially rules out the Zoe as too small and more an urban runabout than a car for country use. She is also concerned about the hassle involved in buying a Zoe and getting it serviced (will her local Renault dealer's mechanics be able to do the job properly?). So, she initially rules out the Zoe. Having done this, her choice may seem a no-brainer: buy the Nissan Leaf. But then she looks at the specifications of the cars in detail and runs into a dilemma. As a vegan, she wants a car with seats covered in cloth, not leather. She can get this with the Ioniq if she sticks to the base model, but the Leaf comes to Australia with compulsory "leather-accented seat trim." The key issue for Emma is whether she is prepared to jeopardize her vegan self-construct by breaking the "no leather" rule in order to avoid range anxiety and guilt about recharging it from nonrenewable sources each time she visits her mother.

In simple terms, Emma's dilemma reduces to which option will, overall, make her feel as free of guilt and anxiety as possible. This may require her to bring the Zoe back into the picture: it entails no leather if she buys the base model (the premium model has a leather-covered steering wheel and transmission shift) and she realizes that if she purchases a Leaf in preference to a Zoe, she will also feel guilty about putting the Leaf's driver appeal and space ahead of being as leather-free as possible. By contrast, if she buys a Zoe, she can tell herself that she has made the personal sacrifice of going electric via a car that involves a step down in terms of space and performance.

Of course, one way of removing the range anxiety problem of the Ioniq would be by giving up going to see her mother, but this may be unthinkable, as she cannot see herself as "that kind of daughter." Another strategy would be to buy a plug-in hybrid version of the Ioniq, which would remove the range anxiety problem but leave her feeling guilty about not making as big a contribution to reducing emissions as she might have done. If she delays adopting an electric car, she will continue to feel guilty about not doing as much as she might have done to reduce her carbon footprint, but we might expect, via cognitive dissonance theory, that she will end up telling herself that, by waiting, she will soon be able to purchase an electric vehicle with enough range to ensure she can avoid charging it via nonsolar sources and without any need to compromise her aspirations in terms of her car's space and performance. With all these options, everything reduces to prediction and control, centered on whether she is really the kind of person she has viewed herself to be, foreboding about out-of-control climate change and nightmarish thoughts about the consequences of running out of battery power.

Suppose that, in the end, Emma ends up selecting the Renault Zoe despite expecting it to fall short of her aspirations in areas such as space and despite her concerns about the dealership issue. From a "net implications" perspective, we would see her as making this choice because the other options would entail having a much bigger rethink about the kind of person she really is and in other areas of her personal construct system. However, another way of looking at her choice is in terms of her system being something that she has constructed to function in a principles-based manner, with hierarchical rules about the sequence in which she is prepared to sacrifice particular expectations. In the latter scenario, she is prepared to do whatever it takes in order not to compromise her most important operating principle and then only consider her second most important operating principle in terms of the options that enable her to meet the first principle, and so on, as far as she can get down her list. This way of thinking may at times result in her seeming like a martyr to her causes, whereas others, who have constructed different operating systems, may be prepared to "sell out" by selecting "compromise" options in such situations.

Insofar as decision-makers resolve dilemmas via hierarchically ordered principles rather than by exploring net implications in terms of an additive-differences procedure, they will be inherently ill at ease: the remaining unmet aspirations are a problem. By contrast, those whose rules permit them to resolve dilemmas via an additive choice process may arrive at comfortable equilibrium positions after figuring out which compromise solutions achieve the highest scores.

8.8   Non-Compensatory Decision Heuristics

When decision theorists and marketing scholars began studying non-compensatory decision rules, their focus was typically not upon key principles around which people choose to build their lives, such as those in the scenarios considered in Section 8.7. Instead, it tended to be on how these kinds of rules get selected because they simplify choice in information-processing terms. This information processing perspective is certainly worth taking seriously, as is evident from experiments that show how increasing the complexity of the choice environment increases the probability that research subjects will use non-compensatory decision rules (see Payne, 1976; Payne et al., 1993; Norman et al., 2004; Fasolo et al., 2007; Lenton and Stewart, 2008). However, from a Kellian standpoint, and as some of the leading researchers from the information processing school went on to acknowledge (see Luce et al., 2001), it seems unwise to view the use of non-compensatory rules merely as convenient heuristics and neglect their links to emotion-related issues of the kind that go with identity and/or having "no-go" areas in one's life.

Non-compensatory ranking heuristics can take a variety of forms, the simplest of which is commonly known in the marketing literature as a "disjunctive" procedure. It entails focusing on one characteristic and ranking the options based on how well they perform in that area, regardless of how well they perform in any other area. This way of choosing could underpin various kinds of fanatical consumer behavior, such as that of the "hi-fi freak" who is only concerned with sound quality or the "petrol-head" who is obsessed with acceleration and ranks cars on their 0–100km per hour or standing quarter-mile times. It begs the question of how a final choice is to be made if there is a tie between the best performers on that dimension. A "lexicographic" procedure can break ties by successively bringing in other dimensions that are ranked in order of priority. For example, the petrol-head's second priority might be outright top speed, with road-holding ability the third priority, and so on. The adjective "lexicographic" alludes to the similarity between how the rule works and how we operate in order to find a word we want to look up in a dictionary. In the latter case, if we begin at the start of the alphabet, we keep turning the pages until we find the word that has the letters we are looking for in the right sequence; anagrams with the right set of letters are not acceptable. Similarly, a lexicographic decision procedure only entails going as far along the specific sequence of choice dimensions as is necessary to eliminate all but one option. In contexts where the options differ considerably, decision-makers who used lexicographic procedures might reach a verdict without having to go very far down their priority rankings.

Tiebreak procedures may also be required where decision-makers choose by applying what are known in marketing as "conjunctive" heuristics, i.e., heuristics that specify a set of attributes, and their associated performance levels, that a product must have in order to be deemed satisfactory. This is essentially a "tick the boxes" procedure, and a tiebreaker heuristic such as "choose the cheapest" will be needed if two or more options seem to offer enough of all the desired attributes. Conjunctive decision heuristics align well with Kelly's view of personal constructs even though they do not entail adding up the net implications of choosing one option rather than another. From some of the examples that Kelly offered – such as his (1963, p. 121) discussion of why some people marry after rather limited search for a partner, whereas some may end up as an "old maid" – it is evident that he did not view choice as necessarily entailing the weighing up of desired and undesired implications. Instead, he sometimes saw choice simply in terms of an extension of his idea that people make sense of the world by constructing templates and seeing if these templates match up with incoming stimuli. We can readily end up doing conjunctive decision-making by constructing reference points that take the form of templates that then function as decision rules rather than merely as devices for construing things. For example, among our car constructs may be "my dream car" or "the car that would be just right for me" or "a car that would be perfectly OK for me." Such abstractions provide templates against which we can assess actual cars, as illustrated previously in Figure 4.1 in Section 4.7. If our aspirations are sufficiently modest for the constructs that make up these templates, we may find that one or more of the options open to us "ticks all the boxes" and thus seems perfectly acceptable if not actually our vision of what would be perfect for our needs or our dream vehicle.

As with other non-compensatory decision procedures, template-based choices can be achieved with far less cognitive load than would be entailed if we attempted to weigh up all the implications that we can see for each of the options we are considering: we do not need to compute an overall score for each option and store it in our working memory. We also reduce the number of bits of information we will need to gather and process: we stop considering any option the moment it turns out to have a "deal breaker" aspect due to failing to tick one of our boxes. However, depending on the aspiration levels embodied in the template in question, attempts at conjunctive decision-making may founder due to none of the available options seeming to "tick all the boxes" or due to the discovery that more than one option does so. To resolve such problems, we will need to have in repertoires of decision-making rules that enable us to adjust some of our aspiration levels (i.e., modifying the shape of the template) or prioritizing them, as well as for breaking ties (such as "In the event of a tie, choose the cheapest of the tied products").

There are two other major lines of thinking within the literature on non-compensatory choice methods. Both entail a process of sequential elimination that differs from the lexicographic heuristic and provide a means for avoiding ending up being unable to act if nothing "ticks all the boxes." One approach is rather like Maslow's view of needs: it views the sequence of the tests that the decision-maker applies as reflecting a hierarchically ordered set of preferences or principles for choosing. This choice process then works like a hurdle race in which anyone who knocks over a hurdle is disqualified: at each hurdle, any option that does not meet a performance standard is eliminated from further consideration. Consider this in the context of car choices: a hurdle may refer to a particular pole on a simple dichotomous construct (for example, having a full-size spare wheel rather than merely a tire repair kit, or [not] being an SUV) or may entail an aspiration level being met on a scale (for example, one might insist on a car having a 0–100km per hour acceleration time of eight seconds or less, overall fuel economy no worse than 6l/100km, at least six airbags, and so on). The option that survives the most tests wins even if it does not pass all the tests that the decision-maker was ready to apply. More sophisticated variants of such a procedure could bring in subsidiary rules in particular situations, such as a rule decreeing that further search must be undertaken if the option that survives the most tests has not "ticked enough boxes" (in which case the procedure is a hybrid of sequential elimination and conjunctive methods). If two or more options tie for the number of tests that they pass, a simple tiebreak rule is to choose the one that performs best on the next test, where none of them performed well enough to pass.

I first encountered the sequential elimination perspective (along with the non-compensatory heuristics considered previously in this section) via the work of James Bettman (1979, pp. 181–182) in marketing. However, I later discovered that a hierarchical characteristics-based view of choice had been published in economics a few years previously. This was in a contribution that deserves to be recognized alongside Lancaster's characteristics-based model of choice by another Australian economist, Duncan Ironmonger (1972, ch. 2). (Ironmonger worked out his analysis several years prior to Lancaster's model but published it later.) After being inspired by Bettman's work (which itself was influenced by Simon's work on bounded rationality), I went on to explore the economic significance of hierarchically organized preferences in publications such as Earl (1983c, 1986b, 1995, ch. 4) and Earl and Wakeley (2010). (Stavros Drakopoulos has likewise written extensively on the economics of hierarchical preferences, and his work includes some very useful survey articles in this area: see Drakopoulos, 1994; Drakopoulos and Karayianis, 2004.) Rather than using Bettman's terminology, I called this way of choosing "characteristic filtering" to try to ensure it is not mistaken for the lexicographic heuristic outlined earlier in this section, which does not include targets or aspiration levels. By using the "filtering" idea, I also hoped to distinguish this perspective from another that was proposed by Amos Tversky (1972). The latter, which Bettman (1979. p. 182) had also mentioned, recognized that people may use a sequential elimination approach to taking decisions that does not entail a priority order for features that their options must have.

Tversky called his alternative view – which is at odds with the view of choice he and Kahneman later offered in their prospect theory – "elimination by aspects." He suggested that people may attach weights to the various aspects or characteristics of interest to them in the context at hand, but they do not use them to compute overall scores for the rival options. Rather, the importance assigned to an aspect determines the *probability* that it will come to mind and be used initially or subsequently as a filter. Tversky's thinking implicitly complements Hayek's *Sensory Order* view of how the mind works, especially insofar as the probability of an aspect coming to mind as a decision criterion is affected both by how often the person in question has thought about that aspect and by how recently it has been salient to them because of something that they have experienced or an advertisement that they noticed. The weights that Tversky proposed might also be viewed as proxies for the net implications the decision-maker associates with not being able to meet the requirement in question: although it may be cognitively too demanding to compute the overall net implications of a choice in terms of all the relevant constructs, we may at least have an idea of which constructs are ones for which the choice really matters. But in casting these weights in merely a probabilistic role, Tversky is allowing for the possibility that we will get diverted from ensuring that we run the elimination process in a sequence consistent with these weights. With finite attention, we run the risk that the elimination sequence will get distorted by things in our choice environment and/or by guileful ruses of those with whom we interact. Sales personnel or political players may be able to steer others toward particular choices by shaping the sequence of aspects used to whittle down the set of options.

Our brains may find it convenient or necessary in some contexts to reach decisions via procedures that entail a hybrid of compensatory and non-compensatory rules. For example, like conjunctive heuristics, hierarchical filtering and elimination by aspects procedures will founder in situations where two or more of our options "tick all the boxes." At that point, we might reflect on whether any of the aspiration levels we were using should have been more demanding and, if any seem like they should have been, we could rerun the filtering process on the options that have tied. Otherwise, however, switching to an additive-differences approach may be a workable way of breaking the tie between them. Sometimes, we will be trying to make up our minds in situations where products have lots of features and we lack any clear sense of the desirability of some of them. Here, we can try to choose between products that tie in terms of their performance in respect of "key" features by simply counting the number of "miscellaneous" features each option seems to offer and choosing the one that has the most. Via experience, we may later incorporate some of the latter features into our set of core requirements for when we next buy such a product. We may call a decision rule that bundles potential decision criteria together without any weighting or prioritizing a "polymorphous" rule: there are many forms a product could take in achieving a particular total score in terms of the bundled features.

8.8.1   The Procedural Rationality of Non-Compensatory Heuristics

Clearly, these kinds of procedures are cognitively very simple. However, insofar as they entail ignoring many implications of the options under consideration and limiting the set of options that get considered, they could prove far from procedurally rational. In the case of disjunctive or lexicographic heuristics, the products that they favor may achieve their performance on the decisive characteristics at the cost of having many downsides that may cause their gloss to rub off very rapidly. For example, a "super-car" such as a Lamborghini may delight the petrol-head on paper and on an occasional "track day" but mostly may turn out to be an expensive nightmare to own compared with a capable all-rounder high-performance car (such as a Volkswagen Golf R) that is not as fast on an autobahn but is narrow enough to enjoy on minor roads, has more seats and luggage space and can negotiate shopping mall car parks and safely be left there unattended. By contrast, other non-compensatory rules often function in effect as heuristic alternatives to choosing via net implications because they entail the use of target values rather than the best performance on constructs of interest. (This does not imply that firms should view customers who use target-based non-compensatory decision rules "as if" they are doing compensatory trade-offs: when some of our options "tick all the boxes," being offered more than we require in some areas may not make us willing to rethink and compromise by accepting a product that is inadequate in other areas. See further Earl and Wakeley, 2010.)

But aspiration-based heuristics can also be dysfunctional, sometimes tragically so, if the aspirations are needlessly undemanding or unrealistically ambitious. In the former situation, we may fail to learn how much better we might have done. This may have consequences not just now but also in the future: undemanding consumers fail to push suppliers hard to work out ways of doing better. Insofar as people pick up their ideas of what it is reasonable to expect by observing the attainments of those around them, it is easy to see potential for social groups to lock themselves into poor-quality lifestyles and relationships due to "setting the bar(s) too low" in key areas. The risk of this seems especially high where people are anxious about the social conse-quences of unsuccessful attempts to aim higher and about not being in control while searching for solutions that are both feasible and offer much more.

Unrealistic aspirations can result in frustration due to a chronic inability to find something (or, in the case of Kelly's proverbial "old maid," someone) that matches our expectations. Templates that entail overoptimistic ambitions and expectations on some constructs can drive us to hold out for opportunities that are never going to materialize; in the process, they may deny us experiences that we would have found fulfilling and which, with hindsight, we would have deemed perfectly satisfactory. Worse still, disastrous choices may follow due to processes of cognitive dissonance reduction interfering with how options are seen, in order to remove the frustration. Organizations can fall into such traps when trying to hire staff for important positions that they have left unfilled for long periods. Instead of lowering their sights and filling the position, they impose avoidable costs on other stakeholders. Then, in desperation, they may end up kidding themselves into hiring someone who claims to be what they are looking for but then delivers less than they would have got from less disingenuous applicants that they might long since have been able to hire had the job descriptions been less demanding.

Clearly, non-compensatory ways of choosing may make us seem intolerant and inflexible compared with how we will appear if we try to rank our options in terms of their net implications and have the information processing capacity to succeed in such endeavors. Choosing in a non-compensatory way may also seem "irrational" and arbitrary insofar as it entails not using all the information we have at our disposal, for once we have eliminated an option due to its failure to meet a particular test of adequacy, we may consider it no further, regardless of what we know or suspect we might have been able to discover about its performance in other areas. For us to return to an option rejected in this way, we may need to be under pressure from others who challenge the decision we have reached. But having a method of choosing that limits the amount of information we must process may be vital if we are dealing with a huge range of options in a context where many different characteristics are relevant and where the options differ considerably in what they seem to offer. In such situations, it may be impossible to choose with reference to net implications and hence we *have* to use *some* form of heuristic in order to avoid decision paralysis and exert some control over what happens to us.

8.9   When Are Prices Significant?

Aside from reference to a "choose the cheapest" tiebreak heuristic, the significance of prices for decision-makers has received very little attention so far in this chapter. In relation to compensatory decision-making, the price of a product is simply another characteristic to be traded off against other characteristics. Hence, consumers may be willing to purchase products of poor quality if their prices are low enough to offset their non-price shortcomings. Such substitutions may also arise because a lower price enables more units of the product to be purchased, thereby enabling buyers to get more of its non-price outputs for a given amount of spending. Clearly, substitution could be inhibited if, in the face of uncertainty, buyers judge the prospective quality of a product mainly via its price: consumers may be suspicious of products that look a lot cheaper than those to which these products are offered as rivals (see further Scitovsky, 1944; Gabor and Granger, 1966). Lower prices may also reduce the snob appeal of product and their functionality as status symbols (see Leibenstein, 1950).

The role of price is rather different when people choose by applying non-compensatory tests. Except when price is used to assess whether quality is likely to be "good enough" on a particular dimension or is brought into a non-compensatory choice at the end as a contingent tiebreak device, it normally operates early in the choice process by affecting a product's ability to survive a high (top?) priority budget test. Such a filter may be single-sided ("Is it cheap enough?") or double-sided ("Does it fit into my budget range?"). To keep these tests cognitively simple, we will usually set them up in terms of conventional, rounded numbers, such as a $500,000 limit rather than $513,089 when buying a house. Firms that allow their prices to drift slightly beyond popularly employed budget limits may therefore experience major losses of sales; they would be wise instead to reducing their costs, and thereby avoid such price increases, by scaling back the specifications of their products in ways that did not cause them to be no longer able to meet popular non-price aspirations. Where a budget range is used, products priced below the amount that the buyer expects to spend will fail to be examined, even if they might have been great value for money and ticked the non-price boxes the buyer has in mind. A higher price would help their chances of being discovered by such a buyer, but possibly take them over the upper limits of other buyers. It is thus important for suppliers to know the mix of budgetary rules across the population of prospective buyers.

The fact that we use budgetary limits when choosing is a necessary consequence of our cognitive limitations: we are unable to choose by trading off complex bundles of diverse products against each other in the manner assumed in conventional economics. Instead, as recognized by Strotz (1957), we compartmentalize our choices into expenditure categories, attaching budgets to them in a top-down manner. Thaler recognized this, too, when he developed his analysis of mental accounting (Thaler, 1985, 1992, ch. 9, 1999), but he also argued that people set budgets for projects and categories of expenditure to guard against self-perceived weakness of will. Like corporations, they assign budgets to their personally constructed mental compartments and create policies about the kinds of spending that are allowed within them. For example, a couple might choose to limit themselves to spending $100 per week on alcohol and prohibit themselves from consuming more than one bottle per night or spending more than $20 on a single bottle. On this basis, they will refrain from buying a $30 bottle of champagne even if, at the week's end, there is $30 unspent in their alcohol budget. Such rules inhibit the development of more expensive tastes or bad habits. However, their use may cause opportunities to be missed if sticking to them prevents money from being transferred from an account that is in surplus to one for which a temporary deficit is required if a bargain is not to be missed.

Thaler's analysis seems very relevant for manufacturers of electric cars, for if our mental budgeting practices are rather slow to adjust, they may inhibit our adoption of these vehicles. For example, suppose that when I buy a new car, my rule is to keep my spending under AUD35,000. If so, I may rule out an electric car such as a Nissan Leaf, even if I have no range anxiety issues, because it has a drive-away price of around AUD55,000. To my entrenched way of thinking, the Leaf is ridiculously expensive for a car of its size from a non-premium brand. (Note how the inclusion of compulsory leather in the interior in the Australian version may be an attempt to give the Leaf more of a "premium" image.) I may reject it in this way even though it would save me AUD3,000 per year in running costs. Things might be very different if Nissan Australia took note of how some electric cars are priced in Europe and offered the car on a "batteries not included" basis for AUD35,000 but offered to lease me a battery pack for not more than $3,000 a year and suggested the latter could be paid for from my vehicle fuel budget. (Making leather merely optional would be wise, too!)

Finally, whether compensatory or non-compensatory decision heuristics are employed, the asking price of a product may affect choice insofar as it has an impact on whether we see it as a "rip-off," a "bargain" or simply as being offered at a "fair price." This is an issue that I raised in passing (see Earl 1986b, pp. 260–261) around the time that Thaler, too, was thinking that this was an area worth researching, as part of his mental accounting project. In terms of conventional economics, how we categorize the price we are being asked to pay for a product should be irrelevant to our choice; all that should matter is the product's relative price and the utility we expect to get from it if we buy it. Yet it seems obvious that our willingness to pay a particular asking price is affected by how we view that price relative to a reference price: the difference between the two affects what we think of "the deal" we are being offered.

My thinking on this issue assumed that prospective buyers have the capacity to look at what they are being offered and assess the size of the profit margin the supplier hopes to extract from them. We may have no formal expertise as cost engineers and accountants, but we can often hazard reasonable a guess with the aid of proxies for what has gone into making the product and by comparing it with what other suppliers are offering. Then, if we feel the profit margin is excessive, the prospect of giving in to the supplier's "rip-off" strategy clashes with our desire to predict and control events: we feel we should not "have" to pay *that* much. On the other hand, the presence of something that surprises us because it seems a bargain bolsters our sense that we are good shoppers and not at the mercy of suppliers.

Thaler attempted to make sense of the significance bargains and rip-offs somewhat differently, by offering a modified version of utility theory. He drew a distinction between "acquisition utility" and "transaction utility." The former is what the consumer expects to derive from consuming the product – implicitly, it is a compensatory view of the net benefits the consumer expects to get from how well the product serves as a means to meeting various ends. However, "transaction utility" is something else that the buyer gets (with a bargain) or loses (with a "rip-off") depending on the difference between the price paid and the reference price. Thaler's analysis is thus a further application of the idea that utility is reference-dependent, that is central to the S-shaped value function in prospect theory.

One of Thaler's favorite illustrations of this is the "beer at the beach" scenario that he used in his empirical study of the existence of transaction utility. He posed to his subjects the question of how much they would authorize a friend to pay to get them a beer while they stayed on the beach. Even though the beer brought back by the friend would be the same regardless of where it was purchased, subjects who were told the only nearby supplier was a run-down convenience store were, on average, prepared to pay significantly less than those who were told the only nearby supplier was an upmarket beachfront hotel (Thaler 1985, p. 206). This finding is clearly problematic for the conventional analysis, as it entails willingness to pay being affected by factors other than the characteristics of the beer itself.

Thaler interpreted this as arising because subjects do not see paying a higher price to the hotel as a "rip-off," since the hotel offers more value for money (for example, a better atmosphere), even though they are not going to be accessing any of this when they consume the beer on the beach. This finding has a sinister implication: by offering additional features, even if these are not actually desired by customers, a supplier may be able to raise the reference price that potential customers use when appraising the prospective deal. An asking price that would have seemed a "rip-off" if those features had not been included may thereby be deemed acceptable.

Thaler's analysis of the psychology of pricing offers a plausible way of making sense of why supermarkets that offer "weekly specials" tend to thrive at the expense of those that offer "everyday low prices" despite there being no difference in the overall costs of a typical week's shopping or in the range of products that are being stocked. As he notes (Thaler, 2015, loc. 1005), "Getting a great deal is more fun than saving a small and largely invisible amount on each item." This is not inconsistent with the success of discount chains such as Aldi in wresting market share from traditional supermarkets by offering a much more limited range of grocery products with conspicuously low everyday prices, as well as spectacular "weekly specials" on fleetingly stocked non-grocery items that conventional supermarkets do not stock at all.

The analysis of choice so far offered in this chapter implies that, in the real world, the relationship between prices and quantities may not take the simple inverse linear form that economists typically assume. If many consumers use similar rules to decide what to buy, then a "demand curve" may have discontinuities at the prices at which such rules have an impact. Moreover, insofar as buyers commonly use rules that specify a "minimum price" to limit search costs or use price as a proxy for quality or status impacts, there may even be segments in which raising a product's price will increase its sales. If buyers choose in a compensatory manner by weighing up implications of selecting one option rather than another, the extent to which a price will need to change to induce changes in behavior will be a function of how its implications are viewed. In some cases, where buyers see few, or zero, non-price implications of choosing one product rather than another, a small rise in a product's price may result in mass defections to its rivals: in essence, the buyers see that they would be crazy not to save money by switching. In other cases, only a very substantial proportionate change in price will result in switches of behavior, owing to the change entailing the need for buyers to reconstrue their lives across a wide range of areas. Not changing will have its own implications – the more so, the greater the change in relative prices. Hence, if buyers think in a compensatory manner, there will eventually be a point at which a price increase is big enough for it to "pay" to switch.

8.10   A Multilevel Rules-Based Perspective

As this chapter has progressed, we have increasingly seen choices as being driven by decision-makers' repertoires of operating principles and heuristics. Such a view of choice is an extension of the rule-based views of cognition, search and valuation that were offered in the previous four chapters. What we appear to have is, in essence, a rule-based view of choice. This section is an attempt to pull together some core themes that underpin such a perspective (see also Hodgson, 1997, 2010).

The first thing to notice is that we can have rules operating at a variety of levels and taking many different forms. Lower-level rules can be those external to us, that are deemed admissible by the higher-level rules that we use for running our lives, but they can also be internal ones that we have developed personally.

Secondly, habits should normally be seen as rules that have probabilities of being employed in particular situations rather than as rules that we will always apply in particular situations. Just as consumers seem to be polygamous in terms of brand loyalty and switch within their particular sets of acceptable brands as time goes by, so they will tend to evolve multiple ways of acting in a particular kind of situation in order to deal with variation within it. Moreover, although search activity is rule-based, the list of possibilities that ends up being considered can be affected by chance and contingent factors, as well as by what we have previously considered and experienced. From the standpoint of Hayek's (1952) *The Sensory Order*, it is to be expected that which rule initially comes to mind as a possible means for reaching a decision will depend on which rules have been used recently and/or frequently in the kind of context in which we believe ourselves to be. So, for example, if last time I changed my car I sold my existing vehicle privately, the idea of doing this is more likely to come to mind first than it would have been if I had traded my previous car in to a dealer – even if the way it comes to mind is in "never again" terms because I experienced a lot of hassle on that occasion. However, so long as whatever decision rule comes to mind is not at odds with our higher-level rules in the context in question, it may be allowed to determine the outcome. If multiple decision rules come to mind, higher-level rules will be brought into play to determine which one will be used.

External rules include those of legal and social institutions regarding what people should do in particular contexts, the extent and means of information gathering about options and/or how to choose between the options on one's agendum of possibilities. For example, a person whose removal expenses are going to be paid by their new employer might be required to get three quotations from removal companies and to choose the cheapest one. If the person had, via another rule, already got a preferred supplier in mind, such an external rule might be circumvented by using other rules to get more than three quotations, of which at least two were more costly than that of the desired carrier. Such a guileful strategy – which would be a case of "opportunism" in Williamson's (1975, 1985) sense – might be ruled out on moral grounds as, in effect, "not the sort of thing that someone like I see myself as being would do." If so, this would be an example of a higher-level rule dominating. Some social conventions for how to behave in particular contexts may, of course, have economic underpinnings. For example, they may be low-cost means of efficiently coordinating social behavior. However, more generally the contention here (see also Choi, 1993) is that rules get selected by other rules: people will break with conventions if these are at odds with their higher-level rules; if not, and if their established rules seem sufficiently likely to result in satisfactory outcomes, they will continue to follow them. If rules are to continue to be used in a particular context in the face of rival contenders, they must be deemed good enough for that purpose. Otherwise, they will be "ruled out."

The higher-level rules are what stop the seemingly infinite regress of "choices about choices," in the same way as the "core axioms" of a scientist's research program provide an anchor not merely for devising models but also for interpreting empirical results (see Sections 4.6 and 4.7). Overall, the set of rules that comprises a person's cognitive and decision-making system is rather like an onion, with many layers, but if one keeps going up to a higher level, the core is eventually reached. A person's cognitive core can be thought of as the individual-level equivalent of a nation's constitutional rules and supreme court: they are there to determine which lower-level rules are permitted to operate (i.e., which ones are not "ruled out of court") and to arbitrate when several lower-level rules are admissible but produce contradict-ory results (Earl, 1986b, pp. 145–147). But we should not forget that these systems are not quite at the core: if they pose enough of a challenge to the needs and aspirations of the population, revolutionary change may occur. Another way of thinking about higher-level rules is as analogous to the operating systems of computers, with the lower-level rules being akin to application programs that are capable of running with a particular operating system.

In the context of this chapter, an important role of higher-level rules is for determining in what kind of context agents define themselves as being. Thus, for example, if we have a lower-level rule that says, "When in Rome, do as the Romans do," it will not be brought into play unless we have identified that we are indeed "in Rome." Note also that if we are "in Rome" and observe a variety of forms of behavior in particular contexts there, then we need another high-level rule to pronounce whose behavior should be copied, such as "follow the action of the most respectable-looking person you can see." That, in turn, would require a rule for judging who might be more respectable than someone else.

Lower-level rules for search, evaluation and choice within a particular context can take many forms, some of which may result in consumers seeming to choose as if they have preferences of the kind assumed in standard analysis. Some rules might thus provide a means for judging the likely payoff to further search, while some rules might spell out trade-offs whose terms are acceptable, sometimes in ways that imply diminishing marginal rates of substitution. However, other rules might be very different from those entailed in the conventional economist's view – such as ones that say simply "buy the product that is recommended as the 'best buy' in a particular consumer magazine," or ones that are non-compensatory, like those considered in Section 8.8.

The set of rules that a person uses will evolve through time, with new rules (discovered from external sources or created internally) being added to their repertoire so long as they are deemed admissible by the person's core constructs. Sometimes, acceptance of new rules will require that particular existing rules are abandoned (for example, "Don't judge a vehicle's safety by its size, but by its ANCAP or ENCAP rating").

While the notion that choices are based on the application of an evolving framework of hierarchically related rules is a general one, the key point is that it allows for the possibility that consumers may evolve very different forms of rules for dealing with different contexts. In some contexts, the consumer may use rules that deem it is worthwhile to search extensively in particular ways, while in other contexts search processes may be truncated by using decision rules suggested by particular individuals or agencies, with different rule suppliers being used in different contexts. Sometimes, consumers might be expected to approach problems in a pluralistic manner, using different rules to form perspectives on what to do, and then move from being "in several minds" about the choice to "making up their mind" via a higher-level rule for judging, which is the best rule to apply in that context.

8.11   Predicting Choices

Because rules limit the sets of things that people consider and find acceptable, a rules- or heuristics-based view of decision-making is inherently more useful as a means toward making predictions about behavior than is the standard economic approach that collapses simply to a vision of everything being traded off against everything else. Indeed Ronald Heiner (1983) has gone so far as to argue that the prediction of human behavior is possible *only* because human cognitive limitations force people to base their decisions on simplifying rules. Rules for reducing the cognitive load of taking decisions make life simpler by ensuring that we do not consider all the potential trade-offs that an "econ" would consider. In other words, we do not address each occasion for choice in all its rich singularity; instead, we select rules from our repertoire of decision aids. Hence, it should be possible to predict a person's behavior – at least in probabilistic terms – if we know which rules this person has in his or her repertoire, and the person's propensity for employing them to identify contexts and address problems in particular contexts.

Heiner's insight does not apply merely to the capacity of economists to predict behavior; it can readily be appreciated in relation to everyday social interaction. The people we know have their personal ways of operating and habits of thought that are the essence of what we view as their personalities. Normally, people we know well do not surprise us by acting "out of character" relative to what we know about how they tend to think. Firms, likewise, have particular styles of operation (their corporate cultures as well as formalized policies and procedures) that facilitate internal coordination, while inter-firm coordination is facilitated by firms having gradually evolving strategies that keep them to a limited range of markets and particular kinds of supply chain structures (see further Section 10.11; Selznick, 1957; Earl, 1984; 2002, ch. 1; Schoenberger, 1997). Because there are significant cognitive costs to changing how we think (as explained in Chapter 7), these systems of rules normally evolve gradually rather than frequently being given revolutionary makeovers. This means that we will have a good chance of anticipating the behavior of those whose histories we know well.

However, when we are trying to anticipate the behavior of those whom we do not know, we have a problem: which rules will they apply in the context that we need to analyze? If presented with a problem context, the typical behavioral economist will look for ways in which heuristics that people *in general* use could affect the choices that get made. For example, given that people are unduly prone to select default options, one obvious question to address is what the default is in the context at hand. By contrast, this book mostly follows Kelly's (1955) "personal constructs" approach: the emphasis is on the *personal* repertoires of rules that make us the individuals that we are. These rule repertoires are the everyday person's equivalent of the methodological rules that determine how a particular kind of economist addresses contexts of interest. Clearly, emphasizing that people use different operating systems makes analysis more complicated because, in any particular context, it admits the possibility that people may make their choices in different ways, even if they end up doing the same thing.

For example, consider decisions about getting cars serviced. The decision may be initiated by a rule supplied by the manufacturer, such as, "This vehicle must be serviced every 15,000km or twelve months, whichever comes first," but the vehicle owner may work with a different, personally constructed rule. Once the decision has been initiated, several strategies are possible: choose one of the manufacturer's dealerships, choose an independent "no-name" service agent or take a "do-it-yourself" approach. If so, the vehicle owners need ways of assessing the likely differences in quality of work that would result from each strategy, as well as the likely financial cost and time that will be involved. Different decision-makers may base their assessments on different models of the situation.

Some consumers, for example, might trust manufacturer-authorized service agents on the following basis: "The brand owner has a very big incentive to ensure its service agents do the job properly: if tales emerge of bad practice from even a few of these service agents, trust in the rest could be undermined. Loss of revenue from servicing the brand's vehicles could cause major issues for the economics of the dealerships insofar as they would normally expect to make more from servicing each vehicle than from the initial sale. To keep its dealership network intact, and the prices of its cars affordable, the manufacturer has a major incentive to ensure there are no horror stories about how the authorized agents service its products" (cf. Klein and Leffler, 1981). Other consumes might not believe there is any greater basis for trusting a manufacturer-authorized service agent: they might reason that "an independent, local business has a very strong incentive to avoid lapses of quality since the proprietor may have used the family home as collateral when taking a loan to finance the business, and thus risks losing the house if bad local publicity causes customers to stay away, whereas an employee of a manufacturer-authorized dealership only stands to lose his or her job by letting quality slip." However, some who take the latter view might still choose a manufacturer-approved servicing agent rather than their independent local service station, on the following basis: "The main dealer will be able to get the job done more efficiently because they can draw upon a bigger sample of cases to help them diagnose problems and have factory-trained personnel and access to the latest computerized diagnostic tests. Hence, although I may be contributing toward covering bigger overheads, it should work out cheaper for me, one way or the other, in the long run."

Ideally, then, if we want to understand behavior in a particular context, we need to gather data on the rules and mental models that people commonly use, and their respective usage rates (cf. Boland, 1986). If, due to a lack of time or other resources, we do not gather such data, then how can we offer anything beyond the comment that "in this context people will use rules or models from their personal operating systems to arrive at their choices"? If that were the best we could offer as analysts, it would be worth no more to our clients than if we had tried to view the situation from a conventional economic standpoint and concluded that choices depend on how people weighted up marginal trade-offs.

What we need to be able to do is identify when members of the target population will be likely to use particular kinds of rules that will "rule out" particular types of action, thereby making their behavior somewhat predictable instead of it being the case that "anything goes, depending on relative prices." Where the data that we would like to have are unavailable, we must adopt a deductive strategy and engage in what we may call "meta-cognitive situational analysis." This form of analysis can also be a means for deciding which data we should try to gather if we are able to seek data from a sample of the target population. The "situational analysis" aspect entails dissecting the context of interest into its distinctive features, while the "meta-cognitive" aspect entails thinking about potentially plausible ways in which the decision-makers in question would think about it. In other words, in contrast to the "rational expectations" approach of conventional economics – in which it is assumed decision-makers operate "as if" they are using the best available economic model – we try to put ourselves in the minds of the types of people whose behavior we are trying to understand. Introspection may give us some leads as we do this (so doing it on a team basis may be wise as a means of getting a wider range of perspectives), but we can also apply what we know about how the human mind works, in ways that go beyond knowledge of "heuristics and biases."

The "situational analysis" aspect of what follows does not mean we are adopting the method of situational determinism that Latsis (1972) accuses orthodox economists of employing to build what he calls "single exit" (i.e., deterministic) models. Situations do not determine which rules people apply to make their decisions. Rather, people use the rules of their personal operating systems to decide what situation they are in, and it is only once they have done this that they decide which rules from their operating systems should be employed to deal with it. Implied here, and central to situational analysis, is the fact that the context in which a decision is made comprises a variety of characteristics, just as does the product or the output derived from a product that is the focus of the decision. This brings the possibility that contexts of choice could themselves be subjects of preference and choice. For example, some consumers may be nervous about contexts involving the challenges of new technologies, whereas others may revel in contexts with masses of facts for them to acquire before they choose, and so on. Sometimes it may appear that consumers have decision-making contexts imposed upon them, but even here there is usually a "fight or flight" choice to be made.

We have already considered the significance of information and knowledge for how challenging a decision context is, and hence for how decision-makers try to cope (see, for example, Sections 3.4, 5.6 and 8.5). In the rest of this section, the contexts that we consider are ones that entail more psychological and social aspects of context that tend to be overlooked if context is merely viewed from the standpoint of the "heuristics and biases" approach to decision-making.

8.11.1   Personally Significant Choices

In the light of our implications-based view of the determinants of why some things matter more than others, the obvious focus for situational analysis is on the potential implications of choices in the context in question for the decision-maker's ability to predict and control events. In terms of Laaksonen's (1994) contribution to the literature on means–end chain analysis, what we need to consider is the extent of the decision-maker's "involvement." Here, one obvious issue is whether we are dealing with "routine" purchases or what Shackle (1949, 1972) called "crucial experiments" that entail one-off choices that may have major implications, for good or bad, depending upon their outcomes.

It is at first sight tempting to see single-use products that are purchased to meet needs that arise repeatedly as fitting into the "routine" or "low-involvement" category: a lackluster performance by whichever product is chosen today does not lock the consumer into buying it on future occasions. The choice of such a product can be seen as a replicable event that adds data to the consumer's sample pool. By contrast, a durable could involve a substantial capital loss if a mistake is made and the consumer attempts to reverse the decision by trading it in against something else.

On closer examination, however, the potential downsides of experimentation are not necessarily a simple function of the life span of the product or its price relative to the consumer's total budget. Even rather minor outlays may have significant implications, in relation to the consumer's personal constructs, if they are undertaken or cannot be implemented. These implications can arise for quite subtle situational reasons. For example, consider the significance of the fact that a regretted purchase of a relatively cheap durable is less easy to disregard than a disappointing consumable of similar price. This is because the durable remains as a nagging physical symbol of poor judgment unless the buyer disposes of it. In cognitive terms, neither storage nor disposal is likely to be costless, though a giveaway via social media or for a "white elephant" stall at a school fete provides a way out that avoids the guilt of disposal via the rubbish bin.

Note also that the risk associated with a particular product may be affected by its context of consumption. For example, a bottle of wine for an evening meal at home has fewer potential implications than a bottle of wine being chosen to take to a dinner party where one needs to make a good impression. Likewise, the reliability of a rental car matters less if one is renting for a long period with no itinerary, rather than briefly to get to and from a particular event. In the latter case, fear of having our plans unravel is likely to result in us favoring big-name rental car firms whose vehicles are typically only a few months old, whereas in the former cases we may be far less anxious about using cheaper rental firms whose cars may be as old as the ones we own. This emotion-based perspective is different from an information economics liquidity premium perspective that would see big-brand car rental firms dominating in short-rental contracts because they are well known and save us the cost of searching for a cheaper deal in an unfamiliar location. (If the rental is only for a short period, the likely price premium of sticking with a big brand hurts less.)

A choice may thus be akin to a "crucial" one, even if it does not involve a major *initial* financial outlay, if its context involves risks of nontrivial *subsequent* costs in terms of a need to buy yet more products for damage-control purposes, or in terms of psychological costs of embarrassment. If the consumer knows that a set of costly implications would not arise, or at least has a low probability of arising, with particular brands, then "safety-first" considerations are likely to rule out trying other brands with unknown probabilities of performance or with known higher variances in performance than familiar brands.

8.11.2 Contexts in Which the Consumer's Requirements Are Uncertain

Uncertainty about what to purchase can arise in contexts involving durable goods if buyers are unsure about their future circumstances. This is a different kind of context from that where consumers know what their circumstances are but are uncertain about means–end relationships and product performances. In the latter case, they can choose with the aid of the market for preferences, unless the set of possible choices includes products that are too new for it to be able to handle them in a reliable manner.

Consumers can deal with some contexts of these kinds by postponing action, or may at least be able to limit their risks of costly errors by:

(a) renting products initially rather than buying them outright (for example, in a situation in which it is unclear whether a child is going to make a long-term commitment to learning a particular musical instrument);

(b) hedging their bets via the selection of a "happy medium" between two different views of what might turn out to be the best kind of product to go for (which seems likely if contrasting scenarios are imagined and neither seems more likely than the other); or

(c) selecting products with an eye to their option values – in other words, their versatility, amenability to upgrading, and so on. (For example, if consumers are looking for a sporty car but are uncertain about whether they will be starting a family or need frequently to carry bulky items, a "hot hatchback" has considerable option value compared with a roadster or high-performance sedan.)

Strategic thinking would not be necessary if perfect secondhand markets existed: if they did exist, consumers would not face risks of capital loss beyond those reflecting physical depreciation if they wished to undo their choices. Because of this, the importance of making the right choice is far greater when buying a durable than when buying a consumable with a similar expected cost per occasion of use.

8.11.3 Contests with Social and/or Institutional Dimensions

The social side of consumption, emphasized in Section 2.6, is central not merely to the work of Veblen (1899) and others on conspicuous consumption but also to the literature on positional goods spawned by the work of Fred Hirsch (1976). Positional goods are those whose value to us is a function of how much of them we have relative to other consumers, rather than our absolute level of consumption of them. For example, housing is a positional good if most people would prefer to be in a situation in which they lived in a 3,000-square-foot house and the average size was 2,000 square feet, rather than one in which they lived in a 4,000-square-foot house and the average size was 6,000 square feet (see Frank, 2007, who also examines many other examples of positional goods).

Some of the key contextual features that determine whether a good is positional or potentially usable as a status symbol are as follows:

- The product's consumption must be *conspicuous* or must be something that those who own or consume it can credibly boast about owning or consuming, in a way that those to whom the boast is directed will understand as signifying their relative inferiority in that area.
- If the likely cost of the product cannot readily be inferred from its features, or its consumption is being boasted about rather than being undertaken conspicuously, the product must be *cognizable* from its brand and/or model name so that its price can readily be assessed as an indicator of the owner's wealth (for a more detailed discussion of this issue, see Earl, 2002, pp. 160–162).
- There are *physical externalities* with products in the same category owned by other consumers (for example, if the passive safety capabilities of a motor vehicle are a function of its mass relative to the mass of a vehicle that collides with it, one needs a heavier vehicle than other road users to achieve the goal of being less at risk than those with whose vehicles one collides).
- The product is *exclusive* because there are barriers to reproducing it, so one person's access to it prevents another from consuming it once spare stocks run out due to growing demand.

If we use these dimensions to identify contexts involving positional goods, then we will not be surprised to observe behavior akin to an arms race there, with expenditure on them crowding out expenditure on non-positional goods despite it being difficult for the typical consumer to make headway relative to the rest of the population.

Whether or not the consumer is purchasing a positional good, the task of working out what might be a smart purchase is much simplified by the extent to which the context of choice is a market characterized by a well-developed set of social institutions (in the sense used in Hodgson's 1988 analysis of markets). This is not just because it permits market-assisted choices; established standards simplify choices by leaving buyers free to focus more on other characteristics. In contexts where buyers rely heavily on the verdicts of particular reviewers, market share may end up depending on how closely firms manage to tailor their products to fit the decision rules that these reviewers use. If it is socially well established what is "cool" versus what signifies that the buyer lacks taste (in British slang, what is "naff"), then the context is one in which consumers who deviate from socially favored choices need to be well armed with arguments to justify their choices publicly – unless, of course, the context is one of private rather than social consumption.

Market turbulence associated with changes of fashion is a source of risk, not merely financial via its effect on resale values, but also in terms of one's social reputation if one places the wrong bets on what will be "in" and what will be "out." For those who seek to avoid such risks rather than reveling in the possibility of developing and maintaining a reputation as being ahead of the pack, following the biggest herd of fellow consumers may seem the most obvious strategy.

Outsourcing of choices is something that consumers in a social world can do quite consciously as a means of avoiding poor outcomes (i.e., in an attempt to be procedurally rational). But in some cases, it is hard not to conclude that choice is essentially institutionalized by social convention: we do what is done in that kind of situation and operate as "social dopes" rather than rational economic actors carefully considering alternatives (cf. Garfinkel, 1967; Koppl and Whitman, 2004). For example, it is not intrinsic to a funeral that the mourners should wear formal black clothing, but we would not think for a moment of showing up in beachwear even if we anticipate a blazing hot day and know that our grief and respect for the deceased will be conspicuous via other aspects of our behavior. Our decision set is much reduced by these social norms (see also Spread, 2011).

8.11.4   Contexts Involving Goods Whose Value Is Intrinsically Uncertain and/or That the Buyer Expects Eventually to Dispose of in a Secondhand Market

An excellent exemplar of this kind of context is the challenge of buying a work of art (see Beckert, 2020). This kind of product entails a different kind of uncertainty from that associated with an experience good such as a used car that might turn out to be a "lemon" (as per the analysis in Akerlof, 1970) or a new car whose drawbacks (such as seat comfort on a long journey) cannot be discerned via a test drive. Here, the problem is that we may find a particular artwork aesthetically appealing but are wary of buying it because we are nervous about whether the asking price is reasonable or because we are fearful of paying "too much" for it if it is being auctioned. Paying an appropriate price or getting a bargain is important not merely in relation to our potential embarrassment or to the kudos we will gain from members of our social network who, on viewing the artwork, ask what we paid for it; the price we pay will also determine the kind of return we can enjoy from it as an investment. In this context, the provenance of the object and the standing of the supplier are key to its market value, and we can obtain opinions on these factors via a variety of market institutions. (We may allow our appreciation of such objects to be shaped via inputs from the market for preferences, too, such as adult education art classes.)

Much the same concerns are inherent in contexts such as buying real estate or financial assets or investing in wine. But the question of potential resale value arises with any durable good. The more expensive a durable good is, the more likely it is that transaction costs will not prevent it from being traded on a secondhand basis rather than being consumed by its original owners until completely worn out or rendered obsolete. This brings an intersubjective, speculative dimension to durables choices, which can be characterized via Keynes's (1936, ch. 17) "liquidity premium"-based analysis of portfolio choice (see also Townshend, 1937; Earl, 2002, ch. 11). We may anticipate that unless there is no other way of reaching a particular end, consumers will keep well clear of brands and model specifications for which they have reasons to suspect rapidly crumbling residual values and a lack of interest at trade-in time. Thin markets entail a high probability of a long wait before someone comes along looking for the product in question, so a wise dealer will have a risk premium in mind when deciding on the trade-in value and may even refuse to make a trade-in offer, mindful of the opportunity costs of thinly traded products in terms of space for stocking things that are more frequently in demand. (Both of the imaginary consumers in Section 8.7's discussion of dilemmas – Steve, the wild-vibrato guitarist, and Emma, the early adopter of an electric vehicle – would suffer much more, at resale time, than those who have mainstream buying rules.) In short, choices of durable goods may be shaped by conjectures about what others will be looking for in used-goods markets, rather than determined by what they personally would ideally prefer.

8.12   A Pair of Contrasting Cases

The view of choice that we have been considering presents new challenges for the economics classroom that need to be appreciated by instructors and students alike. Because it works in words, without the usual technical challenges of mastering graphs and mathematical formulations, weaker students are likely to slip unwittingly into relying on introspection when asked to analyze decision-making in a particular context; instead of dissecting the situation at hand and drawing inferences with the aid of theoretical tools, they will be prone to the misapprehension that "it's all common sense, really." However, strategically chosen problem contexts can counteract such tendencies to engage merely in "person in the street" introspection based only on personal experience. The obvious way to nudge students into reflecting via behavioral perspectives is to ensure that some of the chosen analytical contexts are ones of which the class members are likely to have very limited or zero experience. It is also important to ensure a mix of search, experience and credence goods – ideally with some ambiguity about which category is the appropriate one for purposes of classification.

This section gives two examples to show how the approach works in practice. Rather than being designed to lead to a focus on bias-inducing heuristics, both cases were chosen primarily to test an appreciation of the informational and institutional drivers of choice.

8.12.1   Context 1: Arranging the Funeral of a Relative Who Has Died Suddenly

Funeral services are likely to be experience goods: each funeral is to some degree a unique event, so reviews of suppliers can at best only be an approximate guide. To some extent, funeral service companies can provide information via illustrations on their websites and in their catalogues, and they can show potential customers their facilities. But some elements will have to be experienced to be appreciated properly, such as the attitude of the staff, the pace of the event, the quality of the food at the reception afterward, and so on. The choice of provider thus is made with some uncertainty. Inexperienced choosers may find it more like a credence good: even though they will be able to see what was delivered, they may not know how much was *really* necessary. Hence, they need trustworthy advice about what they should authorize.

In any case, the word "suddenly" implies limited scope for doing in-depth search about the relative merits of possible rival suppliers of funeral services, since it is common (i.e., social institutions dictate) that, unless there is a major delay due to an autopsy, a funeral should be held within a matter of days after a person has died. Given the difficulties that many people have in facing up to their mortality, we may expect it to be common for friends or relatives to find themselves in this situation, rather than for the deceased to have researched the market and set out detailed specifications about which firm to use and the form the service should take. That being the case, we should expect the market to have adapted to simplify the search process and here we can indeed note that while it is in principle possible to shop around for specialist suppliers of caskets, flowers, a venue, catering, and so on, the typical funeral services firm is a one-stop shop that reduces transaction costs considerably. Even so, those making the arrangements will typically find, if the geographical context is a large urban area, that there are multiple one-stop providers vying for business.

There are other factors here that add to the information problems faced by the person who chooses the service provider: they may live far away and have no local knowledge, or they may have no experience of funerals and thus have little idea what they should sign up to have provided or what constitutes a reasonable price. The nature of the product may also be one that seems at odds with extensive shopping around and haggling over the price or what is to be included in the deal. In terms of social norms, this is not a time for doing that sort of thing.

The potential vulnerability of the person choosing the funeral service provider is enhanced by the shock that they have suffered. But the need to get the best deal may be somewhat limited if they are not themselves paying for it (unless they can see that it will reduce the sum that they inherit from the deceased's estate). There is thus a problem of agency here, though the person to whom it falls to arrange the funeral may be trying to keep in mind what the deceased would have wanted, along with what other attendees might be expecting (cf. the Fishbein–Ajzen model).

If shopping around is unlikely in this context (beyond perhaps a few initial phone calls to get a rough idea of charges and to confirm availability – the latter a crucial checklist requirement – then we would predict that market institutions may play a major role. These could include how long a company has been established, its membership of the relevant trade association (as signaled in its advertisements and website) or perhaps online reviews, recommendations from members of the decision-maker's social network, neighbors of the deceased or the solicitor with whom the will was made.

It may also be the case that some brands of funeral service providers stand out more readily when the person makes initial investigations. Here there is potential for the Klein and Leffler (1981) analysis to apply: customers are likely to expect that quality is more likely to be assured if it appears that investments have been made in establishing the brand and applying it across many providers: a bad experience could have severe repercussions the return on this investment. Multibranch funeral services may also be vaguely more familiar to potential customers if they have been taking advantage of their ability to spread the fixed costs of advertising to generate a higher profile, with a wider geographical reach than single-branch businesses. We should thus not be surprised to find that in recent years the funeral services sector has been characterized by mergers and takeovers and the emergence of suppliers with a considerable presence, in contrast to the industry's traditional old-fashioned family firm image.

As a way of simplifying the choice process and reducing transaction costs, suppliers may be predicted to offer standard bundles of funeral service products (basic, deluxe, etc.). The social aspect of funerals may affect the level of product that gets chosen: there may be issues of respect for the deceased that make it hard for those arranging the funeral to choose only the most basic service. Such a choice might also cast them in a bad light with friends and family, so again the Fishbein–Ajzen analysis may be relevant.

8.12.2 Context 2: Choosing Which Movie to See for an Evening Out

This is typically a socially consumed experience good whose choice may involve a joint decision in which several people's decision rules need to intersect. The experience good aspect arises because a movie is a complex flow of information that is too much for reviews to capture fully and which cinemas only partly preview for free in order to motivate customers to pay to see what has not been previewed (cf. Arrow, 1962).

Checklists seem likely to be used in this context. Although there is uncertainty about detailed aspects of the rival movies, it is common for movies to be classified by genre and censor's rating (adults-only, parental guidance recommended, etc.). If a movie is a sequel, uncertainty is much reduced and likewise, to some degree, if the movie is based on a well-known novel or television series. Such movies may also present less of a challenge to prospective viewers in the sense that, when watching them, they will have to make less of an effort to get to know the characters and plotlines. Very broad kinds of categorization may also provide clues about the kinds of challenges different movies will present: "art-house" films may not offer "Hollywood endings" (cf. Scitovsky, 1976, 1981, on differences in the desire for comfort, pleasure and excitement among consumers in modern societies). The sheer range of movies, venues and viewing times on offer in a large city implies that, to avoid information overload, would-be moviegoers are likely to include in their checklists requirements such as time, venue, length, genre, star rating by trusted reviewers, acceptability of the stars and/or the director, how friends have rated it, whether it is coming to the end of its run and the probability of it being available later on DVD or Netflix if missed now. In a small town, with only one cinema, matters could be different: Miller's Rule would be less obviously relevant.

The context of choice here may differ quite significantly between moviegoers for reasons other than their location. Some may have overriding reasons for suspending their usual decision rules because of the particular social nature of the evening, such as a male being open to a "chick-flick" rather than an action movie because he is on a date. Features of potential venues further complicate the choice, again pushing consumers toward using intolerant checklist rules to whittle down the choice, such as whether parking is too difficult, the sound system too loud, the décor too tatty, and so on. This may result in the venue being chosen first by one rule and the movie then being chosen, via a different rule, from what is available at the selected venue – or vice versa.

The switch from single screen to multiplex cinemas in recent decades has changed the context of choice in several ways. It has increased the total range of films between which to choose (adding to information overload) but also the range of venues at which a given film might be viewed. The latter may have simplified the choice problem insofar as it has enabled more consumers to have a regular venue rather than needing to visit a wide range of venues in order to see the variety of films they wish to view. The ability to run trailers of movies being run both concurrently and in the near future at a particular venue may also help mitigate bounded rationality problems to some degree by concentrating the regular clientele's attention on a particular set of films. Multiplex cinemas also simplify choices by enabling parents and children to see different films that are running at the same time rather than the parents having to deal with child-minding logistics; they also make it easier for customers simply to make a sudden decision to go to the movies at a particular venue and work out what to see once they arrive, as the probability of there being *something* acceptable that is starting shortly is increased.

From the standpoint of information economics, we might expect the presence of stars and their current standing to be seen as a good signal of movie quality. Stars need to be careful when choosing the movies in which they appear, for box-office disasters can be bad for their reputations. Thus, their willingness to appear in a film is a kind of celebrity endorsement of it. However, as De Vany (2004, ch. 4) has demonstrated in his book *Hollywood Economics*, there is much less empirical support for this than we (and the movie production companies) might expect: in statistical terms, no star is a "sure thing." His book instead emphasizes the importance of network effects, such as word of mouth, as the means by which consumers deal with the inherent uncertainty regarding movie quality. It is also possible that some people may use production companies' brands (Sony Pictures, Touchstone, Disney, etc.) as a means of simplifying their choices: different production houses specialize to some degree in different genres.

8.13   Conclusion

The pluralistic approach taken in this chapter reflects the presence of alternative views within the scholarly literature on decision-making. It also seems appropriate given that individuals may call upon different ways of taking decisions on different occasions and those who end up opting to do similar things may arrive at their conclusions in different ways. However, I have been offering this pluralistic approach to decision-making within a single general view, acknowledging that decision-makers have repertoires of ways for reaching decisions and treat life as a series of experiments aimed at prediction and control. This is a dynamic, evolutionary view of how people go about choosing, in which, as they accumulate experience, they will change their propensities for using particular decision rules in particular contexts.

All this is likely to be perplexing to economists who would like to use a single type of heuristic as a general "as if" basis for analysis. Such economists would probably feel that an additive differences procedure might be the best single one to select, but it is by no means obvious that it would be worse to select a non-compensatory procedure such as characteristic filtering or elimination by aspects. If consumers do not set highly demanding tests when using non-compensatory procedures, they may end up with choices that do not seem grossly intolerant, even though their procedures reject some products because of single failings. However, a compensatory heuristic is absolutely at a loss to explain situations in which consumers are conspicuously intolerant, refer to rejected possibilities as "having a fatal flaw" or "an Achilles' heel" or where they "single out" a particular characteristic to say why "in the final analysis" they chose a particular option. With a compensatory heuristic, there is no basis for identifying particular characteristics as determinants of choice.

It has not always been possible to keep the analysis in this chapter separate from the issues we explored in the previous four chapters. In large part, this is because our focus has typically been on open-ended decision problems that are bedeviled by infinite regress problems whose closure necessitates the use of rules of some kind: economizing has to be done in terms of the mode of choosing as well as in relation to the alternatives under consideration. In the earlier chapters we emphasized the choices that must be made about how far to search for information about potential problems and solutions, and about what to believe about the consequences of particular courses of action. Here, we have particularly emphasized the challenges of processing all the information that earlier phases of a decision cycle may generate. However, although it has been shown in this chapter that some information processing strategies may be more procedurally rational than others for handling such information, we have also acknowledged that it may sometimes be better to keep things simple by gathering less information in the first place. But this chapter has also recognized that choices may be affected by the willingness of decision-makers to "go there" in terms of buying into a particular kind of decision-making context as a means for being able to choose a particular kind of product. The probability of a problem being left unsolved will be increased if its solution requires us to enter a decision-making context that we loathe and/or dread because it appears to entail scope for not being in control, making fools of ourselves, having to demean ourselves by haggling to avoid a sense of being "ripped off," and so on (cf. the discussion of car buying in Barley, 2015). This will be particularly so if our dread is compounded by present bias. There is thus room for suppliers to win market share purely by improving customer expectations about the buying experience.

9 How Can Firms and Governments Influence Our Choices?

9.1 Introduction

The question that this chapter's title poses has a very simple answer if it is viewed merely from the standpoint of conventional economics, where every choice is an act of well-informed constrained optimization with respect to a given set of preferences and a given set of options. All that firms can do to attract customers is offer lower prices. Public sector policymakers can only attempt to shape behavior by: (a) changing the relative rates of tax applied to different product categories; (b) changing income taxes and thereby changing the consumer's disposable income; or (c) imposing regulations that affect the set of products that can be supplied.

Evolutionary economics points to three further policy instruments for inducing behavioral change: (d) offer people new, more efficient means of meeting their goals; (e) introduce new systems for facilitating the uptake of products and services; and (f) supply members of the target audience with new routines whose adoption will contribute to the end that the policy designers are promoting. In each case, the policymaker should be mindful of the bounded rationality of the those whose behavior the change is intended to influence. As an example of (d) and (e), consider how, in the third quarter of the nineteenth century, the Singer Corporation drove a revolution in how people made clothes: As part of its mission to commercialize the sewing machine, Singer pioneered the use of a franchise-based distribution system that made it easy for people to learn about its products and finance the purchase of them. As an example of (f), consider a government agency that is trying to promote healthier ways of living by suggesting routines that help toward this and which are very simple, unambiguous and specific, as with "Improve your health by switching to low-fat milk" rather than "Eat healthy food" (this example is from Heath and Heath, 2010, pp. 15–17). This way, the target audience is not presented with a problem to analyze, with scope for being diverted from it before they find a solution. If the supplied routine entails a sequence of actions, the policy may aim to counter memory limitations via the use of an acronym, as with "PASS" when using a fire extinguisher (Pull the pin, Aim, Squirt, Sweep). Clearly, there may be scope for combining incentive-based, innovation-based and routine-supplying strategies as complementary means by which firms and governments can seek to meet the interests of their stakeholders.

In this chapter we will take the foregoing for granted as we explore what are commonly called "behavioral insights" on how firms and governments can seek to influence behavior or may even have scope for manipulating choices without those who are being manipulated realizing what is happening. The use of these insights commonly entails designing the decision-maker's information environment (for example, the layout of a shopping mall or the design of a website) and the ways in which information about products and services is presented, with a view to triggering the use of particular heuristics that will be conducive to the selection of the (kind of) option whose selection the policymaker is trying to engineer. In many ways, these modern behavioral insights simply reinforce intuitions that businesses have long since been applying to try to shape buyer behavior (see Hanson and Kysar, 1999a, 1999b).

The analysis offered in this chapter takes us into the zone where behavioral economics overlaps with marketing, a zone that can be rather uncomfortable to enter in ethical terms. Those who offer behavioral insights might hope that their suggestions will only be used for designing policies aimed either at enhancing the well-being of those whose behavior the policies are designed to shape or at protecting people who are at risks of having their behavior manipulated in ways that conflict with their personal interests by firms and governments. However, there is the risk that these behavioral insights might end up being deployed against the interests of customers and political constituents by those whom they have taught, who apply them without being constrained by moral principles. I therefore hope that readers of this chapter operate via an ethical perspective based on a sense of justice, fairness and sympathy of the kind central to Adam Smith's ([1759] 1976) theory of moral sentiments.

9.2   Confusopolies

Markets that were once dominated by state-owned monopolies or a limited set of local suppliers protected by import controls have in many countries been opened to competitive entry in the belief that more choice is always a good thing for consumers. However, the new entry that resulted from such policies has sometimes been accompanied by the emergence of the market form that has been dubbed as a "confusopoly": Buyers face a proliferation in both the number of suppliers and in the range of products that suppliers offer, on such a scale as to generate information overload. In such a market, finding the most appropriate option to select becomes a major task, even for those who have a good sense of their requirements and ready access to the specifications of each product that is being offered. This was the central challenge for research subjects in the study of mobile phone connection plan choices that I undertook with my colleagues Lana Friesen and Christopher Shadforth, to which I have referred in earlier chapters. The subjects in our experiment struggled despite facing a much easier task than their real-world counterparts: The research subjects were given a specific usage profile, whereas, at the time of that study (the early 2010s), real-world mobile phone users in many cases would have had little idea of their prospective usage, for this was the period of the transition to smartphones and the unfamiliar world of mobile data usage.

Of course, offering a confusingly large array of differentiated products can some-times be counterproductive. It can result in some consumers deciding not to buy anything from the array, rather than trying to figure out which product suits them best (see Iyengar and Lepper, 2000; for a wider analysis of the effects of choice overload, including its emotional impacts, see Schwartz, 2005). Alternatively, it may drive buyers to shop with firms such as Aldi that, in effect, shop on the behalf of customers by offering, within each product category, a single product that will satisfy most buyers and which is offered at a price that benefits from economies of large-scale production and promotion.

But there is a good reason for creating confusion, especially in markets for must-have products (such as mobile phone connection service plans) and where the costs of offering each addition to the range of products are trivial (as, again, with mobile phone connection service plans). The reason is that, if it is too cognitively challenging or time-consuming to assess the array of products in terms of their characteristics, decision-makers will resort to using heuristics in order to choose. The supplier therefore has scope to influence choices by providing cues to use particular heuristics. In the case of mobile phone service offers, this can entail suggesting which plan is designed for a particular kind of customer (even if the design was based on what the specified class of customer might be prepared to pay rather than their likely usage pattern), listing a particular offer as "our most popular plan" (whether true or not), or saying that it has a particular unique feature.

If consumers are using heuristics to reach their decisions, firms that offer far simpler product ranges than their rivals will only increase their chances of success if they can trigger the use of heuristics congruent with what they are offering, for a small range of objectively better-value products will not dominate via its actual value for money if no one is bothering to do the calculations necessary to rank products on this basis. We might expect that such a supplier could have a chance if an expert third party invests time in finding out which firms really are offering the best value for money and the supplier in question is then able to promote its products by referring to such findings. However, as previously noted, Lana, Chris and I found that our research subjects gave no special attention to plans that had won awards from credible third-party sources.

In some cases, product proliferation can be a key aspect of a price discrimination strategy aimed at ensuring that buyers pay what they are willing to pay rather than what they need to pay to meet their objectives. The market for electric guitars is consistent with this, with the major firms offering huge ranges of products that embody their iconic standard designs but carry different model designations. Here, entry-level products (sourced from China) may be as little as 10 to 20 percent of the price of "prestige" or "professional" versions made in Japan or the United States, with mid-range versions coming from Indonesia, Korea, and Mexico. Multiple products and variants of them are offered at each level without economies of large-scale production being lost, since the variation is achieved largely by assembling different combinations of a limits set of parts. To try all the products at the different levels would take an inordinate amount of time and likely incur "frown costs" from staff in music stores (cf. Section 9.9). However, if the products are promoted so as to invoke the heuristic of judging quality by price, buyers can avoid confusion by concentrating in the price band that suits their budget. If all goes well for the manufacturers, buyers who can afford to pay more than entry-level prices will never try lower-tier instruments and hence will not discover how good they now are (compared with how entry-level products were when they started playing), and those who are willing to pay for top-tier products will not even test mid-tier offerings. There may indeed be quality differences that correlate with price, but the product proliferation strategy reduces the probability that buyers will discover how small these are and start asking themselves whether the marginal gains are worth the time it would take to earn the money to pay for them, or what else they could buy with the extra money. To the extent that the instruments in question are going to be used publicly and their model tier can be discerned readily from their headstock brand logo despite it otherwise being difficult to know the model tier, conspicuous consumption motives will also contribute to the success of such strategies.

9.3   The Gruen Transfer

The design of retail environments is a more pervasive area in which stimulus overload is used as a means of influencing consumer behavior. The key design technique is rather like that employed by Wikipedia and YouTube, whereby large numbers of explorable links are presented to users. In the case of Wikipedia, these links are offered with helpful rather than guileful intent. Even so, they can act as diversion that keep the user browsing rather than staying on the site for only as long as it takes to get the information that was being sought. Let us consider first the architecture of shopping malls, whose economics Jason Potts and I examined critically (Earl and Potts, 2000) long before we knew of the pioneering role that Victor Gruen played in establishing this way of shopping.

In the early 1950s, when Gruen designed the world's first region-serving, fully enclosed, climate-controlled shopping mall – Southdale Center, at Edina, Minnesota – he did not set it out as he should have done if he were trying to make it as easy as possible for shoppers to locate and buy everything they had come to purchase on a "one-stop shop." Had he done so, the mall would have had a hub-based configuration, with car parking below and/or on its roof. Shoppers would have entered by coming into a central circular hall whose edge was ringed by the entrances of all the mall's shops. The floors of the shops would have been shaped rather like slices of a pie. Such a configuration would have been akin to a mathematical "field," for it would have enabled shoppers to go in a direct line between any pair of shops. The distances that shoppers would need to walk, per transaction, could have been very short if they spent most of their time at the mall in the mall's stores, for the hub-hall's diameter would then only need to be big enough to enable it to accommodate those shoppers who were going between stores. Even so, walking times could probably be minimized, for consumers who wanted to do comparison shopping, if similar stores were located as a group of neighbors on the hub-hall's circumference. This would ensure that shoppers never needed to walk a distance equal or close to the diameter of the hub-hall to reach a similar store.

Instead, Gruen designed the mall as a means of keeping shoppers shopping. Rather than having a field-like configuration, his approach to a mall has the architecture of a complex system that makes it necessary for shoppers to walk long distances as they shop, with stores that sell similar products typically being located as far from each other as possible – except for the "food court" of eateries that provide the sustenance for those undertaking their longer-than-necessary shopping expeditions. This is the means to what has become known to marketers as the "Gruen transfer," whereby shoppers are exposed to a mass of stimuli designed to divert their attention from the purpose of their mall visits, ideally (from the standpoints of the mall management company and its tenant stores) with the result that shoppers start to consider buying – and, in some cases, actually go on to buy – things that were not on their minds when they came out to shop there. In some cases, the mass of stimuli helps shoppers to remember things that they will soon be running out of, so the mall captures their latent demand that day when otherwise there might have been the chance that it would have been satisfied later at a rival mall. But in other cases, the stimuli serve, in effect, as seeds for demand that otherwise would not have existed.

Stores are designed to generate the Gruen transfer, too, with the product lines that customers most commonly intend to buy being located as far as possible from the store entrance and reached only after navigating around aisles and/or racks of other potential claims on their attention and spending capacity. And, just in case customers are not coming in for items at the back of the shop, it makes sense to locate the checkout area there, too, unless there is a good reason (such as to deter shoplifting in a store that has few staff) for it to be near the entrance. Indeed, IKEA stores are designed to try to ensure that customers take a particular walk, with no shortcuts, that takes them past every type of product on the way to the checkout. Similar principles are employed in the design of online retail environments, where, for example, even after one has eventually got to the page for the product of interest, it will often be impossible to examine its specification or reviews without scrolling through suggestions of complementary products and/or other products purchased by those who previously purchased the item in question. By providing lists of "recently browsed items," some website designers acknowledge the risk that we may get diverted and lose track of things that we have viewed as we browse in an online store.

The analysis of retailing offered by the neo-Marshallian economist Philip Andrews (1964, 1993, ch. 6 and 7) emphasizes the demand-generating role of retailers and their choices of what to stock. However, he envisages Gruen-like effects taking place in different ways in stores that offer different, but intersecting, sets of products. His analysis provided a means of understanding why manufacturers might wish to control the retail prices of their products and prevent discounting. It is readily illustrated with reference to the retailing of books and, indeed, Andrews was a supporter of attempts by publishers in the UK to continue to be allowed to engage in resale price maintenance.

Consider books that are sold both by specialist bookstores and by general merchandizers. The latter typically sell only a narrow range of books, mainly current and perennial best sellers, and their book-buying customers can be divided into three groups: (a) those who entered the store on a mission to buy something else and, via the in-store Gruen transfer, ended up making an unplanned book purchase; (b) those who were planning to buy a best seller from a bookstore but did not get to it, as they went initially to the general merchandizer for another type of product, noticed the book there that they were intending to purchase and bought it there as they did not expect it would be cheaper at a nearby specialist bookstore; and (c) those who went to the general mechanizer expressly with the intention of getting the best seller there, rather than from a nearby specialist bookstore, because they expected the book to be offered at a discount at the general merchandizer.

Group (a) customers are the only ones that publishers would prefer general merchandizers to serve. This is because publishers are likely to benefit from bigger Gruen effects if would-be book purchasers go into stores that carry a wider range of books than merely the best sellers. Moreover, if specialist bookstores lose profits that they would otherwise have made from selling both best sellers and other books to groups (b) and (c), they will be less able to finance holding stocks of slow sellers (or incur the costs of handling customer orders for such books). They will also be less able to experiment with carrying stocks of books that are not yet on best-seller lists. Matters will be exacerbated if the bookstores match the discounts offered by the general merchandizers: The bookstore may lose more profit from those who would not have purchased best sellers in general merchandizers, anyway, than they gain from keeping group (c) customers away from the general merchandizers. If publishers are not allowed to engage in resale price maintenance, the long-run result may be that there are fewer specialist bookstores and fewer books being published. This may not represent a welfare gain to book lovers, even if it means that prices of best sellers are lower than they otherwise would have been.

9.4 Contractual Complexity

Suppliers can also induce buyer confusion by presenting offers that are computationally challenging (for example, multipart and/or multitier pricing structures used by energy and telecommunication utilities) and/or which entail many restrictive clauses that are hard to understand or keep in mind when choosing (as with contracts offered by insurance and car rental companies). Choosing good-value products and/or avoiding nasty surprises in markets where such offers are commonplace requires the buyer to have relevant expertise (or "literacy") regarding the meaning of the terms of the offers and to take the time to apply it diligently – rather than being snared by a particular aspect, or a few aspects, designed to induce heuristic-based choice and the abandonment of attempts at careful analysis. The project that I conducted with Lana Frisen and Christopher Shadforth on mobile phone contract choices provided a great opportunity to study this type of confusion, both in its own right and when it is combined with confusion caused by the sheer numbers of plans and providers.

The first phase of the project entailed a large online survey with a representative sample of 1,018 respondents. One of the concerning things it revealed was how many of them could not calculate the cost of a call correctly and did not understand how a bill is worked out if the plan involves – as many Australian plans did at the time (2010) – the purchase of an amount of "included value" (also referred to simply as "value" or "credit") that is greater than the number of dollars that have to be spent to get it (as with a plan that offers "$450 included value for $29"). We used the following three questions to test these two essential skills.

Suppose you have a mobile phone contract with the following conditions:

• Voice-call connection fee: 35 cents per call
• Standard voice call: 40 cents per thirty seconds or part thereof

You make one phone call for two minutes and thirty-four seconds. How much will the call cost you? (Respondents were invited to tick one of the following.)

(a) $1.95 (b) $2.00 (c) $2.35 (d) $2.40 (e) $2.75 (f) not sure

Now suppose you are on a "cap" plan that offers you "$150 included value for a minimum monthly spend of $20." An individual voice call costs $0.50 per minute (or part thereof) with a $0.40 connection fee, and a standard text message (SMS) costs $0.25.

(i)   What will you have to pay for using this plan in a month in which you send sixty standard text messages and make seventy voice calls, with each call lasting exactly one minute?
(a) $20 (b) $50 (c) $78 (d) $98 (e) $150 (f) not sure
(ii) What will you have to pay for using this plan in a month in which you send eighty standard text messages and make 100 voice calls, with each call lasting exactly two minutes?
(a) $20 (b) $30 (c) $150 (d) $160 (e) $170 (f) not sure

It turned out that only 11 percent of our survey respondents provided three correct answers. The correct answer to the call cost question is $2.75. (Only 42 percent of our sample provided the correct answer.) A call of two minutes and thirty-four seconds uses up six thirty-second call blocks. The end of the call is disproportionately costly, as the final four seconds require payment for a complete thirty-second block. The call blocks cost six times $0.40 = $2.40, and to this the $0.35 connection fee must be added.

In relation to the two monthly cost questions, it should be noted that the "cap" term has since been prohibited for use with mobile phone plans in Australia, due to the industry regulator having judged it to be misleading. At the time we were gathering out data, it was used by providers to denote the then dominant form of non-pay-as-you-go plan in which the customer received a monthly bill with two key components: a block of "included value" in the form of credit to be used during the next billing period, plus charges in the month leading up to the current bill for use in excess of the amount covered by the "included value" paid for via the previous month's bill. This form of plan would now be listed as being "postpaid" to distinguish it from a pay-as-you-go plan (also known as a "prepaid" plan), and the modern terminology will be used here.

The way that a postpaid plan with "included value" works is rather like having to buy a block of foreign currency to pay for phone services denominated in that foreign currency, except that once the block of foreign currency is used up, the prices that are then charged use the same numbers but in terms of domestic currency. In effect, this means that if $20 buys $150 of "included value," the cost of using the phone once the "included value" has all been used up jumps to 7.5 times what it had previously been. It is like coming home from a country whose cost of living is much less, where prices look the same in terms of the local currency but where it would take 7.5 units of that currency to buy a dollar back home. When the bill is sent to the customer, these charges for usage beyond the "included value" are added to the upfront charge for the next block of "included value" to be used in the next billing period. If the block of "included value" has not been fully used up by the end of the billing period, the customer forfeits the unused part, and the bill merely consists of the charge for a new block of "included value." Such forfeiting was common, as customers who were fearful of "bill shock" tended, as a kind of insurance strategy, to buy much more "included value" than they would normally need.

With postpaid plans working like this, the correct answer to the first monthly cost question is $20. (Only 35 percent of our large sample provided the correct answer to this question.) The answer is $20 because the usage charges are less than "included value." The one-minute calls are $0.90 each (one call block plus the connection fee), which means seventy calls will use up $63 of the "included value." At $0.25 each, the sixty standard text messages use $15 of the "included value." Calls and text messages thus use up only $78 of the $150 included value (so one could nearly double the rates of usage and the monthly cost would still be only $20).

The correct answer to the second monthly cost question is $30. (Only 19 percent of our large sample provided the correct answer to this.) This time, the usage exceeds the $150 "included value" that has been purchased by spending $20 upfront. The two-minute calls each use up two call blocks and each one costs $1.40 (i.e., twice $0.50 for the call blocks, plus $0.40 for the connection fee), so 100 of these calls uses up $140 of the "included value." The eighty standard text messages, at $0.25 each, cost $20. Total costs are thus $140 + $20 = $160, but $150 of this is covered by the "included value," leaving an extra $10 of charges to be added to the upfront charge of $20 that has to be paid each month, making a total of $30 for this month.

It is worth noting that, at the time of our study, some providers were offering what they called "prepaid cap" plans that involved charges specified in relation to "included value" but with customer simply buying a new block of "included value" when the existing block was used up or the expiry date was reached. In other words, two-tier pricing was not entailed with these plans; rather it was as if all the services were being charged in a different currency. The providers that offered these plans tended to make them look like their postpaid counterparts, but they would not always involve the same outlay. If the figures in the final question had referred to a prepaid plan involving the same "included value," it would have been necessary to buy a new block of credit (i.e., "recharge") before the end of the month and if usage continued at the same rate, this block would run out before the end of the next month. If usage ran at this rate for a year, it would be necessary during the year to buy enough blocks of credit to get twelve times $160 of included value, a total of $1920. Thirteen $20 purchases of credit would be enough for this, with a little to spare, since thirteen times $150 = $1950. The total annual cost of the prepaid "included value" plan would be thirteen times $20 = $260, whereas the postpaid version would cost, at this rate of usage, twelve times $30 = $360. The expiry period could be an issue if one were computing the annual cost of such a plan, as some offered prepaid "included value" that lasted for only twenty-eight days rather than a calendar month. If one's usage never exhausted the included value each month (as with the first monthly cost question), then a postpaid plan billed per calendar month would be cheaper than a "twenty-eight-day expiry" prepaid plan with identical unit charges, included value and upfront credit purchase. Clearly, it could be worthwhile to think very carefully when choosing plans based around buying "included value," especially if a provider offers sets of postpaid and prepaid plans that seem to have the same unit charges for each service.

When Lana and I studied the impact of mobile phone plan designs on the quality of plan choices, we used a computer lab experiment in which our research subjects only had to choose between seven plans. The subjects who struggled the most were those in the treatments with "included value" styles of plans that entailed two-tier pricing with higher marginal costs once the "included value" has been used up. These subjects performed better than those in the large representative sample of our online survey when presented with the same three mobile phone plan literacy question, but not spectacularly better: only 18 percent offered correct answers to all three questions. As we noted in a paper about this experiment (Friesen and Earl, 2015, p. 246), a quarter of the subjects got all the answers wrong, 37 percent got only one right, and 22 percent only got two right. There was a significant positive relationship between the efficiency of subjects' plan choices in the experiment and both how well subjects performed on these questions and their experience as users of these complex types of plans.

Lana and I had designed the "mobile phone plans" in the experiment with a view to seeing whether comparing a small set of complicated plans led the subjects to choose by employing simple decision rules. To set bait for our subjects, we designed the treatments so that the best two plans were never the ones that dominated on a particular feature, such as "lowest call cost" and "biggest included value." The experiment required subjects to have twenty shots at choosing, in both "certain" and "uncertain" treatments, so we were able to infer whether subjects were initially caught by our bait by seeing how the pattern of choices changed during the experiment. Sure enough, the bait plans were more popular at the start than later, though learning was very slow in the treatments where subjects only knew what their usage would be in a probabilistic sense.

The price of failing correctly to understand and/or compute the implications of complex mobile phone contracts sometimes results in "bill shock" on such a scale as to entail personal bankruptcy. Normally, however, the sums involved are tiny compared with those that can arise from taking out complex loans with an incomplete picture of what the loan contract entails. Those who take out secured loans would be unwise to apply the heuristic, "It must be safe for me to borrow this much, since they wouldn't lend it to me if they didn't think I could repay it," without reading and making sure they understood the fine print of the loan's "product disclosure statement." This is because, if the value of the collateral (for example, the family home) has been rising, the lender may profit even if the borrower defaults. If would-be borrowers merely ask what the monthly repayments are going to be, an opportunistic supplier may give them a figure for what the initial payments will be without advising them that these could rise due to the loan having an initial fixed-rate period after which it switches to a variable rate that the supplier intends to make much higher. This appears to have been an issue with many of the "subprime mortgages" in the United States that went in to default in the 2007–2008 Global Financial Crisis.

9.5 Teasers and Shrouded Attributes

The mortgages with initially low interest charges that were commonly issued to subprime borrowers in the early 2000s combined the challenge of financial "fine print" with another manipulative device, namely the teaser. A teaser product offers what initially seems to be an excellent deal as bait for signing the customer up to something much more expensive. Teaser-based strategies can take a variety of forms, such as:

- Low, or even zero, initial prices for addictive products or products with high switching costs, with the price then being increased significantly once the customer has become hooked. Examples here go well beyond drugs, and mortgages for the financially illiterate, to many online services and apps, and even to lawyers that offer free initial consultations.
- Attractively cheap "base model" products to lure, say, car buyers into showrooms that turn out never to have them in stock or available for delivery any time soon, but where finance is readily available for customers to purchase higher-grade models. The showroom's demonstrator vehicles, of course, will never be models from the bottom of the range.
- "Drip pricing" whereby the initial attention-grabbing price entails many exclusions that can be addressed by add-ons on the way to the checkout, as with budget airlines whose advertised prices fail to mention, say, departure taxes, baggage charges, additional charges for in-flight refreshment and entertainment service, and so forth. Having arrived at the destination, the airline traveler may face further add-ons with car rental services (e.g., more comprehensive insurance, satnav, safety seats for children, unlimited daily mileage) and with hotels (e.g., to park the rental car and use telecommunication services).

- Supplying durable products at prices that may not even cover their manufacturing costs, with a view to making an overall profit by charging prices way in excess of production costs on complementary consumables that will need to be purchased repeatedly over the life of the durable product. The supplier may use proprietary interface designs to prevent buyers from using generic consumables. Obvious examples here include computer printers and electric toothbrushes, but we should also note scope for carmakers to design their dealership franchise contracts in ways that reduce the initial price of the car and impose very high servicing costs on the buyer. The servicing may be expensive due to inflated charges for the work that is done, or because the original cost of the vehicle was kept down by using components that were cheap but needlessly short-lived.
- Not including in a quotation everything that will be necessary to get to the result the client needs (for example, when a devious builder quotes on renovation work) and then presenting the additional work as something which was only "discovered to be necessary" after the contract had been awarded and the work commenced. If the customer lacks relevant expertise and only seeks a small number (possibly only one) quotation, there may be a good probability that the supplier will be able to get away with this if it is a common practice in the industry.

In some cases, combinations of these strategies may be used to conceal from customers the potential overall costs of what they could be getting into.

The computer printer and hotel room examples are used by Gabaix and Laibson (2006) in a paper where they explore why such strategies persist rather than being revealed for what they are by competitors who simply offer upfront the big picture of what the product is going to cost. Gabaix and Laibson see these strategies as means of exploiting buyers who are naive and/or fail to think ahead and who hence fail to seek details of the full bundle of products before purchasing any part of it. They thus see the suppliers as able initially to "shroud" some of the components of a typical consumption bundle in order to make a sale on the unshrouded part, after which they gradually reveal the other things that go with what has already been agreed will be purchased. (They call the add-ons "attributes" but those in their examples are actually products, since they are ordered separately.)

A supplier who ceases using teasers and shrouding might instead price each of the components based on their marginal costs plus a markup, or offer an all-inclusive bundle (sometimes called a "banquet-style" product). Either way, such a supplier needs to be mindful of the extent to which there are "sophisticated" customers as well as those naive enough to take the bait of a cheap initial transaction. The sophisticated buyers may currently use their knowledge to avoid paying for add-ons: for example, as regular visitors to a hotel, they may know where they can find free on-street parking nearby and know to bring a mobile Wi-Fi dongle for their laptops. Hence, Gabaix and Laibson argue that if the hotel switches to include "free parking and Wi-Fi" within a room price that is higher than that previously charged for the room without these attributes, the sophisticated customers may switch to a rival that continues to cross-subsidize room prices by charging for add-ons at prices well above their marginal costs. The loss of these customers will not necessarily be offset by bookings from less sophisticated customers as a result of the latter seeing the add-ons-included price and realizing that the full cost of rooms advertised with teaser prices may be higher if the add-ons are included. Indeed, if the add-ons-included price is higher than naive customers have budgeted to pay, they may not even bother to look at a hotel that does not pursue an attribute-shrouding strategy and hence they will fail to be nudged by its offer to think more carefully about what they will really end up having to pay. Given this, it may be more profitable to continue with teaser pricing for rooms and initial shrouding for add-ons.

If we bring in other theoretical ingredients from behavioral economics, it is easy to see how people can end up succumbing to these strategies, much as an online dater may succumb to someone whose dating profile happened not to mention things that would have been a complete turn-off had they been revealed at the outset. Sunk cost bias may kick in as one proceeds further into a transaction and starts discovering hidden additional costs. We might also expect that quasi-hyperbolic discounting will result in the benefits of completing the deal today being exaggerated compared with those that could come from bailing out of an unfinished transaction today and beginning afresh, with more diligence, on another occasion.

DellaVigna and Malmedier (2004) have explored how firms can take advantage of consumers who are prone both to engage in quasi-hyperbolic discounting and to be myopic about how much self-control they have. Such consumers will underestimate their probabilities of consuming later, even if there are no "shrouded attributes," and they are aware of potential future costs. For example, people may sign up for credit cards, tell themselves that they will only use them as convenient means of payment (which may be a free service if they spend enough via their cards to escape the annual card fees) and that they will not use the extended credit facilities that come at with onerous interest charges. But many still go on to use the extended credit facilities (cf. the discussion in Section 4.5 of the analysis of credit card use offered by Maital, 1982). Likewise, people may tell themselves, "I know that this printer is so cheap because the manufacturer is selling it at a loss with a view to me having to pay their rip-off prices for the ink cartridges. But I'm confident that I'm only going to use it sparingly, as I intend to keep documents in electronic form wherever possible." Despite this, they may find themselves printing hard copies much more often than they imagined.

But there are also markets in which the teaser is a future price for something that the weak-willed consumer never gets as far as consuming after taking the bait and paying a hefty *upfront* fee to gain access to the teaser offer. DellaVigna and Malmedier suggest that this is to be expected where the buyers are intending to invest in improving themselves by doing something that otherwise they do not enjoy, such working out at gym. Gym owners may make losses on the small minority of gym members who become exercise junkies, but they expect to profit handsomely from the upfront fees of those who fail to make much use of the facilities in the long run, even if sunk cost bias initially keeps them coming in despite them hating the experience. (The impact of sunk cost bias will decay as time passes – see Wolf, 1970.)

Of course, bailing out is always a possibility for would-be customers who have not yet formally signed up to a deal that is starting to look much more expensive than it first appeared. In some cases, a mandatory "cooling-off period" may even offer scope for bailing out afterward. However, in face-to-face transactions, bailing out may be impeded by concern about losing face. Such concerns are to be expected among those who lack confidence about how to behave assertively and do not want to end up seeming to be someone who had been too stupid to realize that they could not really afford what they had come out to buy. Amid this, the processes of resolving cognitive dissonance would doubtless kick in. If the consumer opts not to bail out, becoming resigned to having to spend much more than expected may entail becoming open to the thought that "probably, no matter where I try to buy this sort of thing, I'm going to run into these kinds of practices."

However, from an evolutionary perspective, we should recognize three reasons for doubting whether these bait-based strategies will be successful in the long run. First, naive consumers may become more sophisticated as they get more experience in the area in question or in life generally. For example, after having been caught out with, say, the running cost of the first printers they buy for their home computers, they may switch to more expensive, more durable office-style printers after researching the prices and capacities of printer cartridges. When choosing in unfamiliar areas, consumers may increasingly start applying the heuristics that "if a deal looks too good to be true, there's probably something fishy about it." Secondly, the market for preferences is likely to become more efficient, not merely due to new market institutions being created (as with the advent of TripAdvisor in hotel choices) but also because of more consumers sharing their experiences through existing institutions and more people in the consumer's social network having acquired relevant experience. Finally, entrepreneurs may eventually figure out ways to offer substitute complementary products at lower prices than those asked by those who supply the teaser products. Examples here include the emergence of suppliers of refilled printer cartridges and non-franchised car servicing firms that specialize in servicing brands that have developed reputations for "rip-off" service pricing.

9.6   Principle of Persuasion

Suppliers need ideally to be able to present their offers as trade-off-free options that offer desirable benefits. If there are any obvious downsides to what they offer, they run the risk that people will reject them due to loss aversion or because the prospective benefits come at the cost of omissions or shortfalls that are classed as "deal breakers" by those who employ non-compensatory decision rules. If products have aspects that are likely to be viewed as downsides, then the supplier needs a means for getting prospective customers to accept the offer before they start thinking about these issues – i.e., they need a means to keep the downsides "shrouded" and increase the probability that potential customers will make their decisions via simple heuristics that favor the product being offered ("System 1 thinking," as Kahneman would put it) rather than switching into a more analytical ("System 2") way of choosing. Failing this, they need a convincing means of defusing objections. Conversely, those who try to prevent past adherents to their products from taking up alternatives need a defensive strategy that cuts short any consideration of the latter by focusing on their downsides and points to what could be viewed as "fatal flaws" in terms of non-compensatory decision rules.

Marketing and political strategies that are designed to function like this work, in effect, by mustering skills akin to those of magicians and rhetoricians to divert attention along pathways that conceal problems with what is being advocated, highlight problems with rivals while concealing their strengths and seek to provoke visceral reactions or cut to the core of the audience's systems for making sense of the world. Strategists can systematize how attention and emotions are to be managed in particular situations into routines that include contingent clauses for where to take the interaction next if a ploy has failed to elicit the intended response and has produced a particular kind of objection. For brevity, and in line with the terminology of marketing practitioners, we may call such a routine a "sales script." In this section we explore some of the sales script ingredients that are known to increase the probability that a person will behave as the persuader wishes.

9.6.1   Cialdini's Six Principles of Persuasion

The most influential contributions to the literature on persuasion are arguably those of psychologist Robert Cialdini, particularly his classic (1984, 2009) books that have achieved millions of sales. Cialdini sees persuasion as a science rather than an art, but his experimental research has been inspired by his knowledge of the practice of persuasion, derived via undercover ethnographic research that he undertook in sectors such as telemarketing and used-car retailing. Reduced to its essence, Cialdini's research points to the following six principles for inducing people to behave in the way that the would-be persuader desires.

(1)   Reciprocation
The evolutionary success of humans has been aided by our willingness to be docile and cooperate with, or support, those to whom we feel obligated because of what they have done previously for us. Given this, the persuader (let us call him Josh) needs to provide a basis for the other party (let us call him Ethan) to construe that Josh has chosen to give him something that he was not obliged to give. Ethan is thus more likely to agree to buy what Josh is trying to sell him if Josh seems to have been unusually focused on helping him, investing a surprising amount of time in doing so. This principle implies an extension to Thaler's idea that when a manufacturer publishes "recommended retail prices" for its products, it provides a reference point for customers to use in deciding whether a retailer's discounted price represents a "bargain." Even if discounting is widespread, Josh's store may also seem to be giving a gift by offering a better-than-normal discount upfront rather than promising to match any better price that the customer can find elsewhere, and by offering to "throw in, for

free" some complementary items (floor mats for a new car are a classic example) if Ethan agrees to the deal at the price Josh is offering.

(2)   **Scarcity**

Cialdini's research revealed that people are suckers for scarcity. So, if Josh can credibly argue that what he is offering is hard to find elsewhere, he will increase the probability of getting Ethan to agree to the offer – especially if Josh seems to be using information that itself is not widely available. Cialdini (2014) goes further than noting the advantages of being able to offer a product with a unique feature, for he shows how loss aversion can be exploited by emphasizing to customers not what they will gain from the unique feature (or unique combination of features) but what they will lose if they opt to buy an alternative.

(3)   **Credibility and Authority**

The probability of getting to yes is an increasing function of the credibility accorded to the persuader. For Cialdini, even if it is not possible to point to a portfolio of credentials, it is possible to set bait for believing that the persuader can be trusted. Ethan is more likely to succumb to Josh's sales pitch if Josh volunteers that he regards at least one particular feature as a shortcoming relative to rival products, rather than shrouding all the weak points of what is being offered. (Of course, he should choose what to reveal after getting a sense of what might not be a deal breaker.) This could be done in a way that results in it being seen as a gift, as in "My boss wouldn't be pleased to hear me say this, but I think you should know that . . ."

(4)   **Likeability**

From a conventional economic standpoint, Ethan's view of Josh in any areas other than credibility and trustworthiness should be irrelevant to whether Ethan accepts the deal that he offers. Cialdini's research suggests otherwise. Ethan will be far more likely to accept the offer if he views Josh as a pleasant person, rather like himself, who makes him laugh and gives him compliments rather than seeming an aloof know-it-all during their encounter. Physical attractiveness counts, too.

(5)   **Social Evidence**

People are more willing to agree to do things that it is evident others have commonly agreed to do. Hence, if Josh can make a credible claim like, "This is our top seller for this kind of product," or, "This is one of the world's top-three sellers," or, even, "This is actually the same as the one my wife and I have, which we bought before I started working here – here's a picture on my phone of her with our one," he will increase the probability that Ethan will agree to buy it, especially if Ethan feels uncertain about its characteristics or whether he should buy such a product.

(6)   **Commitment and Consistency**

It is not surprising, in evolutionary terms, that people seem to operate as if genetically or culturally programmed to try to honor commitments that they have made and attempt to act in ways that are consistent through time: operating like this facilitates progress by enhancing trust and reducing coordination failures. This implies that it may be possible to get people to agree to do a succession of things if one can "get a foot in the door" by getting them initially to agree just to do one thing and, when they have done it, complimenting them on how well they have done it and asking them to agree to do something rather more demanding, and so on. Cialdini's experiments confirmed the power of combining this principle with the reciprocity principle (and often a sense of what would commonly be viewed as a reasonable request), via a strategy that begins by asking much more of the other party than they seem likely to find acceptable. When they reject the request, the persuader indicates that the request was a long shot that he or she would likely have declined, too, and then asks whether the person might be able to assist with a rather smaller task. By not trying to pressurize the person into accepting the onerous request, the persuader has in effect made a gift to the other person, giving that person something easy while seeming likely then to be chasing someone else who might accept the onerous task.

This strategy may be adapted to a retail setting: for example, suppose that Josh has been talking with Ethan about a range of products that are available at various levels. If he then asks Ethan if he would be interested in the top-tier model, he has scope for employing teaser and decoy strategies if Ethan says that the top-tier model is much more expensive than what he wants to spend and/or is better equipped than he needs it to be. Josh then concurs, "The manufacturer certainly does charge quite a premium for the extra 'bells and whistles.'" He follows this by jumping to the bottom level of the range. If he gets Ethan to commit to buying the entry-level product, he may then see if he can talk Ethan up to the next tier. A strategy for doing this would be to say he will have to go off and check availability, even though he knows perfectly well what the stock levels are. While away supposedly doing this, he primes a colleague that he may need to bring him in to the act: he will say that the entry-level product is out of stock, with no supplies imminent (thereby playing to Ethan's present bias) but that they do have a single mid-tier model available (playing to the scarcity principle). If Ethan is unwilling to budge, Josh will float the idea of in-store finance to facilitate spending more than the entry-level price. If that fails, he catches the eye of his colleague and asks whether the entry-level model that he had noticed in stock but listed as "sold" is actually a confirmed sale, whereupon the colleague, who supposedly handled that sale reports, "No, that one fell through this morning; they couldn't get the finance approved." So, Ethan at least ends up honoring his claim that he would be prepared to buy the entry-level product, and there may yet be scope for selling him some add-ons before the transaction is finalized.

9.6.2 Emotional and Visceral Ploys

Around the time that Cialdini was uncovering his six principles of persuasion, it occurred to me (Earl, 1983b, 1983c) that the analysis of emotions in Kelly's (1955) *Psychology of Personal Constructs* could be employed to influence consumer behavior. My initial focus was on how firms could attempt to bring customers to them via marketing their products in ways that reduced consumer anxiety and concerns about seeming foolish or impecunious in interactions with sales personnel. This seemed to be part of what some of the UK's building societies were trying to do at the time as they set about competing more forcefully with the main high-street banks by presenting themselves as friendly club-like institutions in contrast to stuffy, aloof banks. But soon I realized that there was scope for more devious emotional ploys that involved strategies aimed at generating an uncomfortable emotion to trigger a perceived need and then presenting the product in question as a means to satisfying that need. In other words, show consumers an area of their lives in which they may not be as in control as they imagined; then show how the product that is being advertised enables them to restore their control in that area.

It came as no surprise to me to discover that others had drawn similar inferences from other approaches to psychology, even prior to Kelly's work (for example, see Irving and Feschback, 1954) and that a substantial literature has emerged on what are commonly called "fear appeals" and how they can be used in marketing (for a short survey, see Block, 1999) and in areas such as the promotion of public health (see Witte and Allen, 2000; Peters et al., 2014). Fear-inducing verbal scripts may cut more readily to the core of the worldviews of members of the target audience and trigger the desired response if they are supplemented by vivid images that produce a visceral reaction of the "Oh, that's so gross!" kind. For example, in the campaign to promote switching to low-fat milk that is analyzed by Heath and Heath (2010), the ploys included not merely the information that a glass of regular milk contains as much saturated fat as in five bacon strips, but also showing journalists that the fat from a gallon of full-fat milk would fill a small tub. (Likewise, if one is trying to make products less intimidating, designing them to have baby-like cuteness may increase their allure.)

Guilt is another emotion that a persuader can seek to exploit. An example here is the "guilty mother" ploy evident in, for example, how some pharmacies advertise dietary supplements that are being claimed to increase height growth in children, boost their immune systems, and so on. If a mother views herself as the sort of person who always does the best she can for her children, she may feel guilty if she sees these advertisements and finds them credible but thinks she will not buy the product that is being promoted: failure to purchase it clashes with her self-image. Of course, these strategies are not guaranteed to succeed, as consumers who are being emotionally targeted by multiple campaigns may simply not have the wherewithal to buy all the products and hence may be left feeling needlessly anxious, threatened and/or guilt-ridden.

9.6.3   Script Duration and Pace: Using Ambushes and "Ego-Depletion"

Sales scripts get their power from the finite information processing and connection-making capabilities of the human brain, augmented in some cases by norms of appropriate social conduct. If the window for the persuader's audience is presented as or taken to be only open very briefly, there is considerable scope for success in persuasion because the audience simply does not have enough attentive capacity to adopt a reflective, analytical "System 2" way of processing the persuader's message. By contrast, where the persuader has scope for controlling the duration of the interaction, the challenge is to design a script that is paced and sequenced in a way that enables the persuader to align the audience's thinking mode with different aspects of the package that is being promoted.

Consider first an example – from Australian politics – of how an effective "brief window" strategy can work where voters only hear what politicians say via soundbites broadcast in news reports that attempt to cover many stories. Men in Australia's Liberal–National Coalition use a very simple, soundbite-friendly script for resisting the imposition of gender-based quotas for their parties' parliamentary representation. It entails referring to core party values: if journalists raise the issue, they are simply reminded – and duly report – that the two Coalition parties stand for a meritocracy, and hence it is vital to select candidates based on their merits rather than by using quotas such as those that refer to gender. Because of the script's effectiveness as a means for shutting down discussion, this remains an area where the Coalition lags woefully behind the Labor Party opposition, which has long been using gender quotas in preselecting candidates for potentially winnable seats.

If one pauses to reflect upon it, this script may seem hypocritically at odds with the use of faction-based quotes in the allocation of ministerial roles. Worse still, it begs the question of whether appropriate criteria are being used for assessing the merits of would-be electoral candidates. However, it has repeatedly been enough for soundbites in the news broadcasts that are seen as providing enough news by the mass of the population that does not bother with news sources that offer deeper analysis. This script would fail to do its job if the typical voter were lightning quick as a critical thinker, for the weakness of the argument could be inferred, and remembered for future use, before the news report moved on to the next story.

Secondly, note how the stereotype of a high-pressure salesperson as "fast talking" implicitly acknowledges that such a person's capacity to bamboozle prospective customers into a particular choice comes from not leaving them enough time to discern potential weaknesses in what is being said and assemble a riposte that will force the seller off-script, into a zone for which no answers that will enable a return to the script have been (or, worse still, could be) prepared. The sales script is designed to keep the prospective customer focused on what is being said, rather on what is not being said, and it leaves no space to engage in deconstruction.

Ambushes of customers work in the same way. For example, consider customers in electrical appliance stores who are suddenly invited to purchase an extended product warranty by the salesperson who is walking them over to the checkout desk. Readers of this book will be in a position (from the end of Section 5.7) to offer an instant, crushing rejection of such a proposition, that will (as I have seen from using it) completely derail the salesperson from the script. But the lay consumer is unlikely to be able to work out the relevant economic argument on the spot. Even the well-trained economist is likely to feel forced to give in if ambushed by a hone renovation contractor who suddenly announces his "discovery" that additional work is needed and asks for assent to do it right away as otherwise it will bring all the scheduled work to a halt. Getting anyone else in to give a quotation on the additional work will seem problematic, especially during major domestic upheaval without a functioning kitchen or bathroom because of the work that is under way, and the consequence of such a display of distrust in the contractor may be difficult to assess. If we were in such a situation, we would probably just give the go-ahead, with a quiet sigh of resignation, even if we had reminded ourselves about present bias and quasi-hyperbolic discounting.

The fact that human cognitive processes require time to arrive at their best constructions of a situation is of significance in relation to our capacity to be "composed" when dealing with someone who is trying to persuade us to do something that clashes with our interests or our views about how the institution for which we work should be operating. We may have enough time to figure out what we think is wrong with the position that the would-be persuader is taking but not enough time, within the window we have for commenting upon it (e.g., a particular agenda slot at a meeting), to organize it into a script that we can deliver coherently and without seeming to be arguing in a way that is "emotional" (as opposed to lucidly and coolly passionate) rather than "rational." Those who can shape the flow of a meeting to ensure their opponents cannot object in a composed manner will thereby increase their chances of persuading other meeting participants to accept their case. Their opponents will find it easier to be composed and garner support from others if they can spot an easy-to-articulate "fatal flaw" in the proposal rather than having to demonstrate that it has a multitude of small shortcomings that add up to a poor overall deal.

Let us now turn to situations in which those who seek to influence others attempt to do this by setting up the choice environment to ensure that the decision-making process cannot be concluded rapidly. An example of this is the retailing of luxury cars, in which the choice process is protracted due to buyers being presented with a huge range of choices and options (e.g., regarding powertrain, color, wheel type, steering wheel design, interior trim combinations, entertainment systems, safety features, etc.). Clearly, this will be expensive in terms of the salesperson's time and giving such choice will inflate production costs by making production logistics more complicated and limiting the extent to which potential economies of scale are achieved. However, the payoffs may be substantial, for a reason that go beyond potential to charge more by giving customers a sense that they are in control and producing a personalized vehicle that is exactly what they want. The key reason why this strategy may be profitable seems, via the work of psychologist Roy Baumeister and his colleagues, likely to be that the purchasing experience results in "ego-depletion" because it runs for hours and involves so many choices.

The work of Baumeister and his colleagues is related to the dual-system view of thinking popularized by Kahneman (2011) and involves extensive use of experiments, both in the lab (see, for example, Baumeister et al., 1998) and the field (using fatigued IKEA customers in mixed methods research reported in Sjåstad and Baumeister, 2018). Baumeister suggests that people have finite cognitive resources that they can apply to supervising their own behavior to ensure they do not act impulsively, and to exercising free will by making choices. The problem is that this volitional resource is rather like a battery: it runs down as we use it, and we then need to take a break from exercising self-control and taking an analytical approach to problem-solving in order to allow our self-control capacity to recover. When we are in an ego-depleted state, our capacities for effective analytical thinking tend to be set aside: we become less inhibited about what we are doing (Baumeister, 2014) and resort to taking decisions in a simplistic, System 1 manner (Baumeister et al., 2008).

To extract as much as possible from their customers, luxury car brands need to be more sophisticated than simply prolonging the process whereby customers specify precisely which combination of features they are going to have. Dragging the process out may indeed, as everyday parlance would put it, "grind down" the customer's resistance to spending. But ideally, the big-ticket options need to be scripted for discussion at the end of the transaction, where the customer's strength of will is at its most depleted. If sales personnel get customers to agonize over body color and trim combinations early on, they will have a much bigger chance of getting them to sign up for expensive safety packs and suspension options later in the proceedings. Wise customers will plan their shopping strategies carefully to limit their vulnerability to these kinds of ploys if they have a sense of the limits of their self-control and know that they will become more vulnerable to impulsive choices if they have been going through a long session of choices and self-restraint. This could entail them doing a lot of preliminary research online and drawing up their preferred specification and a list of questions they want to have answered at the showroom so that they limit the extent to which the salesperson's script controls the process. Unfortunately, however, the research reported by Sjåstad and Baumeister (2018) shows that people in an ego-depleted state become less willing to invest effort in planning. We might thus expect that customers at luxury car showrooms will be less likely to enter them with such a plan on a Saturday morning than on a Monday morning, since by the time they finish work on Friday, they are likely to feel too exhausted to spend the evening planning their strategy for the following morning.

9.7   Nudges

Given what has been said so far in this chapter, we may doubt that consumers will generally be operating in a procedurally rational manner. Instead, we may be concerned that they are at risk of being, as Akerlof and Shiller (2015) put it, "phished for phools" by guileful businesses unless they can, and do, call upon assistance from market institutions that supply them with fast and frugal heuristics that they can remember to apply instead of resorting to using inherited heuristics that were selected by evolutionary processes in the hunter-gatherer era. This risk seems especially acute if we factor in the possibility that they will be presented with false claims about products and will fail to discover this due to having unwarranted confidence in their decision-making capabilities and hence failing to employ the wisdom available via market institutions. There may thus be a role for the state to try to influence behavior so that consumers operate in a more procedurally rational manner.

One way of doing this is to apply paternalistic regulations that are informed by what we know about human decision-making. For example, mandating a "cooling-off" period in which significant decisions can be cancelled gives consumers time to do further research and reflect more carefully than they were able to do under time pressure or in the face of "ego-depletion" (see further Camerer et al., 2003). However, although this kind of paternalism can be helpful without imposing costs on sophisticated consumers, widespread use of regulations is likely to be politically problematic due to the business sector being able to find ways of arguing that it interferes with consumers' freedom of choice and will deter business investment, thereby reducing employment opportunities. Something less heavy-handed than regulations could thus be necessary if behavioral insights are to be applied to help consumers in economies where there is powerful opposition to anything that threatens the freedom of firms to choose how to try to influence buyer behavior.

Richard Thaler and Cass Sunstein's (2008) influential book *Nudge* fills this gap by fleshing out the notion of "libertarian paternalism" that they had floated in an article five years earlier (Sunstein and Thaler, 2003). It offers a seemingly trade-off-free route for political conservatives to get involved in trying to shape behavior without limiting freedom to choose. Thaler and Sunstein's key idea is that policymakers can try to steer consumers into welfare-enhancing choices by designing the way that choices are presented (in their terms, the "choice architecture") mindful of the heuristic and biases that are known to be part of human nature and to affect choices by driving people to take account of "supposedly irrelevant factors" that would not be part of an "econ's" way of choosing. A "nudge" does not change the set of options or the set of relative prices or entail the imposition of a regulation; rather, it simply involved a change in the way that options are presented, or the provision of additional information. So, for example, Thaler and Sunstein suggest that to nudge college students into healthier eating at college cafeterias, it might simply be necessary to place the healthy choices at the front and at eye level in display cabinets, where they would more readily grab attention, and place the unhealthy products in places where they could only be seen and selected if the students took the trouble to look for them. The influence of the food companies might thereby be countered without, say, banning sugary foods from the menu or pushing their prices up by imposing a "sugar tax."

After first being picked up by the UK government and applied, with assistance from Thaler, by its newly created Behavioural Insights Team (BIT), the ideas from *Nudge* have been applied widely around the world (for a comprehensive survey of "lessons from around the world," see OECD, 2017). Australia, for example, has its BIT equivalent, the Behavioural Economics Team Australia (BETA) and private sector consulting firms that specialize in offering policy insights based on behavioral principles; like several other countries, it also has a well-established annual "Nudgathon" competition in which teams from universities and public and private sector "nudge units" try to showcase their abilities to apply behavioral economics to a real-world policy problem, such as getting more people to engage in volunteer activities or to improve the uptake of restorative justice programs. (Perhaps not surprisingly, some of the winning Nudgathon teams have concentrated their efforts on influencing the judges via the "architecture" of their presentation pitches, rather than on trying to demonstrate, within the brief presentation window, that their proposals were firmly grounded in behavioral economics.)

The libertarian paternalism idea grew out of a paper that Thaler and Sunstein had written with Christine Jolls (Jolls et al., 1998) in which they sought to establish that behavioral foundations would be better for law and economics than those from rational choice theory that had previously dominated. A behavioral approach admits the possibility that, for example, perceptions of fairness can drive behavior, with real-world consumers sometimes being prepared to impose costs upon themselves to punish those whose behavior they judge to be unfair. They saw scope for behavioral manipulation instead of consumer sovereignty insofar as people are predictably irrational. However, instead of suggesting that it might be possible to train lay consumers to transcend their natural shortcomings as decision makers (as per the "boost" approach outlined in Section 9.8), Thaler and Sunstein opted to "pathologize" (Mehta, 2013) the lay population and show how knowledge of human shortcomings could be used to steer people into personally or socially beneficial choices. Thus, if we know that people are prone to adhere to defaults, we can nudge them into becoming organ donors and participate in retirement savings programs by making these the default actions from which people have to opt out if they do not wish to participate: fewer will participate if nonparticipation is the default and those who are willing to join have to incur the costs of opting in – even if those "costs" merely entail ticking a box on a form and submitting it. The nudge approach to policy is thus very soft compared with heavy-handed regulation and can be very cheap indeed to implement.

Probably the most significant nudge-style policy to be implemented is the "Save More Tomorrow" retirement plan in the United States that was designed by Thaler and Benartzi (2004; see also Benartzi and Thaler, 2007). This plan can be viewed as a counterweight to the attempts of the US corporate sector to get consumers to spend today money that they might be wiser to save to spend after they have retired. By agreeing to lock away, until they retire, fund that they might have used for discretionary spending, consumers can guard against their lack of self-control (one of Thaler's long-standing interests: see Thaler and Shefrin, 1981; Shefrin and Thaler, 1988; Thaler, 1992, ch. 9) and not fall prey to tempting bait from suppliers inciting them to spend right now. Given that consumers might be afflicted with loss aversion, too, the architecture of Save More Tomorrow entailed not merely making entry to the scheme the default choice; it also sought to counter loss aversion by advising potential adopters that the initial contribution rate would be very low and that when the rate rose as the wages of the scheme's members rose, they would not experience reductions in take-home pay.

Although nudge-based strategies may not restrict choices and may only be partially successful in steering behavior in the direction that their designers intend, they nonetheless ultimately deserve to be viewed as manipulative devices. As such, they raise an ethical question: how would those who are "nudged" view the impact of this on their well-being? This is especially significant in two kinds of situations. One is where people are being nudged to sign up for medical screening procedures that entail risks and the possibility of stress and pain due to them being initially given a false positive diagnosis; the other is where the nudge is for the benefit of the wider community or the government. (An example of the latter was an early BIT-designed nudge to reduce the number of people who were late in submitting their income tax returns. The nudge worked via the norm of social conformity with a reminder letter that noted that the addressee was in a small minority of those who had not yet submitted their tax returns: see Thaler, 2015, loc. 4978–4990.) Thaler and Sunstein advocate using randomized control trials to assess the impacts of nudge strategies before they are unleashed on the wider population. Where such trials are undertaken, the trial population might then be surveyed to find out how they felt about being nudged. This *ex post* way of applying what Thaler and Sunstein call the "as judged by themselves" (AJBT) criterion for deciding whether to proceed beyond the initial trial makes good sense from a behavioral standpoint, since many things that we resist doing due to fears of change turn out to be things we are glad to have done if we end up choosing to do them. However, it would not be surprising to discover that nudge-based policies are often put in place without the trial phase to see how effective they are and how well they seem to stand up in terms of the AJBT criterion, while the criterion itself begs the question of what to do if some people are glad to have been nudged but others regret the choice they made as a result of the nudge. (For further critical analysis of the philosophy of nudging, see Sugden 2009, 2018.)

9.8   Boosts

Because of its pathologizing emphasis on bias-inducing heuristics, the literature on the nudge approach to policymaking has tended to give inadequate attention to the deficiencies in personal knowledge that result in people behaving in ways that are contrary to their best interests. As should be evident from the approach to behavioral economics presented so far in this book, these knowledge gaps have three main forms:

(a) "Know-that" deficiencies: i.e., decision-makers have inaccurate, incorrect or (where no consensus exists about the facts) insufficiently qualified information of relevance for the choice in question (for example, about causal factors for health outcomes, about consumer rights or about characteristics of particular products).

(b) "Know-how" deficiencies: i.e., people lack the capabilities needed to understand the significance of particular kinds of information and apply it without making mistakes (for example, in relation to how the risks or returns of a particular medical screening activity or procedure apply to them personally, or what the information in a product disclosure statement for, say, insurance, a mobile phone connection plan or a mortgage implies about the charges that they might face); and/or

(c) "Know-who" deficiencies: i.e., decision-makers do not know the right people to trust, and seek assistance from, so that they can deal with deficiencies (a) and (b), or to act on their behalf (for example, which politicians they should take seriously, which financial advisors they should hire or avoid, and so on).

If such knowledge deficiencies are the cause of people acting because of, say, "fake news," "urban myths," conspiracy theories, mistaken calculations and risk assessments, and bad advice, an alternative to using nudges to steer them in better directions may be to design policies that "boost" their knowledge and supply them with "fast and frugal" heuristics to use to enhance their decision-making in complex situations.

This philosophy has been propounded by European behavioral scholars such as Gigerenzer (2015), Grüne-Yanoff and Hertwig (2016) (see also Hertwig, 2017), who see great scope for education and training to enable humans to take high-quality decisions and override the "heuristics and biases" that have been accorded so much attention in modern behavioral economics. For these writers, dysfunctional inherited heuristics for making probabilistic judgments can be countered by, for example, education in statistics early in school curricula, with the effects of such training tending to be retained rather than decaying through time (see Gigerenzer, 2015, pp. 373–376). Indeed, Gigerenzer has even gone so far as to argue, via his research, that the view that humans do not naturally operate in a Bayesian way if they are dealing with probabilities may actually be the result of researchers presenting subjects with risks expressed as percentages (for example, "a 75 percent probability of") rather than what he calls "natural frequencies"(for example, "the chance that three out of four") that are cognitively simpler to use. There is an obvious irony here, for this also supports the idea that the frame used for presenting information may affect behavior rather than being a "supposedly irrelevant factor."

The dividing line between a boost and a nudge can be fuzzy, as is implied in the notion of an "educative nudge," whereby people are provided with some information that is intended to trigger a form of action. An example of such a nudge is the use of automated reminders to students who have missed a deadline for an assignment and are in danger of suffering penalties for late submission (see Motz et al., 2021). Indeed, we might even regard cigarette pack warnings that "Smoking can damage your health" and online retail prompts that "Customers who bought this item also bought . . ." as both boosts and educative nudges: perhaps some people would otherwise not have known about the hazards of smoking or been aware of the items that may complement the item whose webpage they are examining.

Although boosts may seem preferable to nudges on libertarian grounds, boosts may require public policymakers to make major upfront investments to enable people to make procedurally rational decisions in a particular area. Such investments could include designing new modules in statistical thinking and home economics for school curricula, designing adult financial literacy classes and running them in public libraries, running information campaigns in mass media, and so on. To ensure that those at whom the boost programs are aimed pay attention to them, it may be necessary to implement them in conjunction with nudges that are aimed at prodding people to ask themselves whether they should acquire additional knowledge of a particular kind before making the choice they are currently considering. In some cases, boosts might even be made compulsory with requirements that particular levels of attainment be met after one has undertaken the boost program. This is, in effect, what happens when we learn to drive or when an employer attempts to influence workplace behavior via requiring employees to undertake online training module on fire safety, workplace health and safety, ethical conduct, sexual harassment, and so forth, as part of each employee's induction and, in some cases, with refresher boosts every few years. But we might irk the libertarians by taking this approach into other areas, such as requiring consumers to undertake, and pass satisfactorily, a short course in financial literacy before they can apply for a credit card, or complete and pass satisfactorily a basic module on how mobile phone connection service plans work before they can sign up for such a plan. In relation to the latter, it is noteworthy that when Lana Friesen and I ran a computer lab experiment to examine the impact of five kinds of regulatory intervention, including information provision and mobile phone contract training, on the quality of mobile phone plan choices, we found it was the training that had the most significant beneficial impact on subjects' choices (see Friesen and Earl, 2020).

These kinds of policies would be consistent with the notion of "asymmetric paternalism" proposed by Camerer et al. (2003), where the idea is to design regulations that benefit naive consumers without imposing significant costs on those who do not benefit from the regulation because they already have the relevant forms of knowledge. Thus, the opportunity cost of the time spent working through the training module and completing the assessment task might be nontrivial for naive consumers. However, they might still end up with a net benefit by then being able to avoid wasting money. For example, imagine that online purchasers of mobile phone plans were prevented from lodging their orders by a government-imposed system that first required them to pass an online mobile phone contract literacy test. Consumers with the relevant knowledge would be able to jump straight to the test and enter the correct answers in only a couple of minutes, whereas naive consumers might need to spend, say, half an hour working through the module before taking the test. Yet the latter could still benefit. For example, if someone earns $20 per hour and has to spend half an hour taking a mobile phone contract literacy module instead of half an hour of work but ends up saving $10 per month on the phone plan, they will reap a nontrivial net benefit that may extend over many years.

9.9   Discouraging Unwanted Customers

Before concluding, let us consider what Kotler and Levy (1971) introduced to academic marketers as "demarketing." Such an activity will initially seem most peculiar to economists, but it is practiced for reasons that make good economic sense from a behavioral standpoint and which apply across areas as diverse as online dating, retailing and the management of public welfare agencies.

First, we need to note the finite service capacity of the supplier, both in terms of physical space and human cognitive resources for responding to queries, monitoring what the prospective customers are doing with items carried in stock by the supplier and for finalizing transactions. Like a manufacturing business, a service supplier needs normally to be operating with spare capacity in order to be able to serve new clients who may turn into long-term members of its clientele and provide recommendations to others. If a store is too crowded for comfortable browsing and staff are rushed off their feet trying to deal with customers, service standards will suffer, and some prospective customers may exit to shop elsewhere, or even decide not to enter in the first place.

Clearly, one way of dealing with crowding in a retail setting is to post higher prices for the products that are being stocked. However, this carries the risk of attracting more competitors in the long run rather than solving the problem of maintaining and growing the supplier's pool of goodwill (cf. Section 11.2). There is also the question of whether higher prices would result in the exit of those that the business in question would prefer were not present even if crowding were not a problem. The retailer's problem is that not everyone who enters a store is intent on making a purchase: some may simply be "shopping" as a leisure activity that enables them to explore an area that they find interesting, try things they know they cannot afford to buy, "hang out" with their friends, or even test their skills in playing social games with the sales personnel. These faux shoppers may limit the attention that can be given to genuine shoppers and exit after damaging stock or leaving it in disarray. Unless retail staff have effective heuristics for identifying them, the faux shoppers will waste their time and prevent them from earning their sales bonuses or commissions.

The faux shoppers are not the only problematic group to which demarketing ploys may profitably be aimed. There are also actual customers who are undesirable because either they are overdemanding of service relative to the amount they spend or, because, by later being seen to have purchased a product, they deter a more profitable group of customers from buying it. For brevity, we may call the latter the "wrong kind of customer."

A classic example of the former is the hypochondriac customer at a medical practice if the practice is paid (as per the UK's free public health system in the days when I was one of its customers) according to the number of patients it has registered rather than on a per-consultation basis. Such a system provides strong incentives for medical practitioners to solve their patients' problems rather than overservice them, but the practitioners' ability to do the former is reduced if their time is chewed up by hypochondriacs. A rather similar problem arises within universities, where a disproportionate amount of academic staff time is chewed up on inquiries from a small number of students. In a market context, overdemanding customers, like many overdemanding students, may seek personal service as their first port of call, rather than after attempting to "do their homework" about what is available and how it might suit their needs; they may also operate in a prima donna style, as if there is nothing wrong with attempting to change the details of what is to be supplied even after a deal has been struck.

Where products are publicly consumed, it is possible that a very small proportion of the wrong kind of customer, or even a single individual of significance, may spoil a market in this way. This applies especially if their public consumption receives wide media coverage and becomes common knowledge. One notable example is that, in the UK, the Burberry clothing firm had to battle to keep its traditional market of affluent buyers after its distinctive checked caps and scarves became part of the uniform of choice of many of the UK's "chavs" (young consumers from "council houses and violent" by background) (*Economist*, 2011). Another example is the slump in sales of denim jeans in the UK from 1997 to 2001 that was credited to the so-called Jeremy Clarkson effect (Borg, 2001) whereby their association with a high-profile middle-aged TV presenter resulted in them being no longer seen as hip. Carmakers have also discovered the downsides of having their products find favor with footballers, popstars and drug dealers, to the alarm of their previous customer bases. Not merely may such customers "lower the tone" of the brand in the way that John Lennon was famously viewed as doing when he customized his Rolls-Royce with a psychedelic paint job; there can be damage to resale values, due to the high-profile customers tending to treat these normally durable assets as disposable and being less careful about maintenance, with potential buyers of used examples not necessarily being able to discover their provenance.

The driving away of customer that firms would like to have by those that they are unable to exclude can happen without media headlines to fuel the process. Consider the following three examples. First, note the difficulties that carmakers Saab (a now-defunct Swedish firm) and Jaguar (a British firm that was eventually taken over by the Indian firm Tata) faced in widening the markets for their cars. While German premium brands prospered, Saab and Jaguar floundered, their main buyers being seen, respectively, to be liberal intellectuals and managers close to retirement rather than pushy high-flying professionals in their thirties and forties. Secondly, note that with products such as restaurant meals that are consumed in public, suppliers may find their long-run plans compromised if they are unable to exclude overly boisterous nouveaux-riches or "riff-raff" who fail to follow the norms of their traditional customers. Thirdly, online dating services might be able to command higher fees and generate far better network externalities via satisfied users if they could find ways of keeping timewasters, liars, weirdos, "gold-diggers" and sleazy subscribers away from their membership lists. Barriers to doing so leave other prospective customers with a classic "lemon" problem of the kind identified by Akerlof (1970): the probability of finding the right kind of subscriber is reduced, and search costs are increased, by the presence of those of the wrong kind, and this may deter customers of the right kind from using such services.

The faux customer, overdemanding customer and wrong kind of customer problems arise in large part because, unlike members of clubs, people who enter business premises as prospective buyers do not have to pay a membership fee or meet membership or entry standards that are set and enforced by an individual or committee. Thus, while, say, a nightclub may specify a particular dress code and hire bouncers to keep out or evict clientele who are deemed undesirable, suppliers in a market typically operate with their doors unlocked when they are open for trade: anyone can make inquiries about what is being offered and anyone with the where-withal to make their desired transaction can be a buyer. From this perspective, the obvious way to address these problems is to devise a means of turning access to the products or services in question into a club-like arrangement. But this requires those with gatekeeper roles to have appropriate heuristics for sizing up would-be members.

Such heuristics are not always easy to find. Consider the higher education sector, in which elite universities can operate like clubs and yet exhibit chronic failure to determine which applicants will turn out to be students who fail to meet the providers' expectations for the effort they put in or how they behave on campus and/or who demand to be "spoon-fed" or "play the system" by using a highly litigious approach to getting the grades to which they feel entitled. (Of course, a limited ability to be fussy about whom to admit will ensure that such issues will also afflict universities that are lowly, poorly funded institutions; unlike the elite institutions that are swamped with applicants that seem from their credentials to be admissible, the lower-tier ones do not even have the luxury of trying to operate like a club.)

Admission heuristics employed in elite universities may entail pattern recognition capabilities of a tacit kind that provide the basis for "intuitive" judgments by staff who have years of experience in the area in question. To ensure that such capabilities are maintained, admissions panels will need to combine those who have relevant experience (in conjunction with ultimate veto capacities) and those who are likely to be capable of developing it in the long run by making cognitive connections between what they observe when interviewing and how those whom they admitted went on to perform. To the extent that the knowledge required for making effective admissions decisions is of the tacit variety, it will be problematic to program them into websites that ask and process a set of questions for determining who will be allowed access. This is not merely a challenge for long-established elite providers of education services. Another significant area where the admission issue arises is in the financial services sector when loan applications are being considered (see also Section 12.6).

When firms are unable to create effective club-like arrangements but are aware of the possibility that costly customers could undermine what they are trying to achieve, they can use demarketing strategies such as the following – some of which reverse the design principles that were prerequisites for the success of nineteenth-century department stores (cf. Section 2.11 and Aitken, 2010):

- To the extent that frontline staff *do* have reliable heuristics for identifying potentially desirable customers, employ a policy of not initiating interactions with anyone identified as "doubtful" and frowning distantly at anyone who is viewed as a "timewaster" to indicate that they were nonetheless being watched. Those who are not genuine prospective buyers may tire of waiting for service and/or the chance to try a product and will then exit, whereas those who have initially been misclassified and want to purchase something that is in stock may start getting assertive about their need for service.

- Display high-value items in locked cabinets and display an "ask before you try anything" rule.
- Attempt to deter long-stay shopping by all except for genuine would-be buyers by providing very limited seating and no restroom facilities.
- Bundle products together so that the entry price of being a customer is raised without increasing the overall cost of being a committed customer: the "chavs" would not have been so readily able to encroach on Burberry's market if they had been asked to buy complete Burberry outfits rather than merely the more peripheral Burberry items.
- Make the supply of the product subject to a set of restrictions about what can be done with it and/or devise other means of limiting the areas over which buyers have discretion. For example, a property developer can use covenants at the time of sale or lease to ensure that a townhouse complex operates with, in effect, its own system of byelaws, enforced by an on-site custodian, while the scope for neglecting gardens and general upkeep can be limited by a design that minimizes private garden space and by having external maintenance work undertaken via a body corporate, funded by a levy.

In the public sector, there are two main kinds of reasons why customers need to be deterred: (i) there are insufficient resources to service clients, some of whom might be serviced instead by private sector providers at the clients' (or their insurance companies') expense, and (ii) there are clients who seek forms of support (for example, by claiming welfare benefits) despite having potential to be self-supporting. Clients can be deterred from seeking public sector support via measures that impose costs upon them in ways that seem needlessly to chew up their time, make them physically uncomfortable and give such an impression of bureaucratic incompetence as to cause exasperation when clients are waiting to receive service, and to cause dread of going through the same experience the next time they are called in. For this, it is useful to require extensive form-filling that may only be possible to complete after having found details in one's records. Call centers should have long waiting times, and if clients are required to present themselves for face-to-face assessments, there should be long periods of waiting in areas with too few, poorly upholstered chairs that it is probably wise to screw to the floor so that frustrated clients are unable to use them as weapons if they decide to "go ballistic." From the standpoint of, say, public sector hospital managers, it would be ideal if the clients that they succeed in driving to experiment with private sector hospitals will be so captivated by the vivid contrast between public sector austerity and the luxury hotel-like private sector ambiance that returning to the public sector is unthinkable. Once patients have tried the private hospital system, their reference point regarding health care will shift, with loss aversion then inhibiting a return to the public system. Dread of having to make such a return can be kept at bay by paying for health insurance.

9.10   Conclusion

The analysis in this chapter leaves us in a position to offer some reflections on an important question that the chapter's title did not pose, namely "Do people need to be protected from attempts by firms and governments to influence their behavior?" Addressing it at this point provides a way of pulling together threads from what was covered as we explored means by which firms and governments can seek to influence behavior.

Real-world decision-makers potentially seem to be very vulnerable to having their behavior manipulated by those who stand to gain by exposing them to cunningly designed marketing ploys that deliberately or intuitively employ behavioral insights. Such ploys can:

- Divert the attention of consumers toward products that they will find tempting.
- Wear down the resolve of consumers who are trying to limit their spending.
- Exploit the most basic emotions of consumers, leading them down scripted pathways that may not be in their best interests.
- Manage the flow of information to extract every extractible dollar from them, such by deliberate creating confusion and even by using outright lies.

Although, as Akerlof and Shiller (2015) have emphasized, today's consumers enjoy far more protection than, say, their counterparts a century and a half ago, they are much more at risk of being manipulated on the basis of sophisticated modern knowledge about how humans are genetically programmed to behave, in conjunction with capacities to process masses of information about individuals obtained by spying on what they do online. We live in a world of much greater complexity, under time pressure. As a result, even search goods often have to be chosen on the basis of incomplete information and knowledge, so we may sometimes inadvertently give our trust to suppliers that do not deserve it. In a world of globalized competition, where market deregulation and rapid technological progress has intensified the struggles of businesses to survive, firms may find it hard to hold back from competitive practices that an impartial spectator would view as morally questionable and devoid of sympathy regarding their impacts on customers (cf. Smith [1759] 1976; Etzioni, 1988). Even in markets where existential competitive pressures are absent, pressure from bonus-hungry managers and top-tier executives seems to result in practices that show scant regard for the notion of corporate social responsibility (Szmigin and Rutherford, 2013).

However, when we recognize that real-world consumers are vulnerable because they lack the omniscience of an "econ" and are genetically prone to employ heuristics that can sometimes be dysfunctional, we should also acknowledge that they are not born with fully formed preference systems and that they usually operate within social networks. Given this, there is potential for some marketing ploys to provide food for thought as people attempt to construct a sense of how they might wish to spend their time and money. Moreover, real-world consumers can learn how to improve their decisions, by drawing on their analytical skills and with the aid of their social networks and other market institutions. Their skills in avoiding being manipulated can also be enhanced if governments and public sector broadcasting services that are not slaves to corporate interests set out to educate them about how marketing processes work. (For example, the Australian Broadcasting Corporation has offered prime-time television programs that do precisely this, in the form of many seasons of "*The Checkout*," a consumer affairs program that sometimes has included guest slots from Dan Ariely, and *The Gruen Transfer*, more recently simply called *Gruen*, in which marketing professionals critically and wittily analyze marketing campaigns.) Unfortunately, it may prove difficult to nudge consumers to boost their decision-making skills rather than watching reality television and cookery shows, so investments in creating populations of sophisticated consumers may need to occur in school curricula.

Populations of consumers can thus become more sophisticated, though perhaps not fast enough to keep up with the growing expertise of those who seek to influence them. However, within such populations there will inevitably remain those who are especially naive and vulnerable. To the extent that choosing in procedurally irrational ways results in consumers being "ripped off" (for some examples of "rip-off" ploys, see Akerlof and Shiller, 2015), consumer protection frameworks and means of obtaining redress need to be in place. It is to be hoped that such systems will be simple to use and well funded, rather than run in unsympathetic ways that align with the principles of demarketing.

10 What Determines the Productivity of an Organization?

10.1 Introduction

In addressing the question that the title of this chapter poses, we will be focusing on the human element in production rather than on matters of engineering such as the extent to which a production system employs the latest machinery or is automated. Although humans are collectively capable of designing extraordinarily complex systems of technologies, and although decision-makers in organizations often bring considerable expertise to their jobs, they remain mere mortals when they are at work, beset with problems of information and knowledge that they have to handle by using rules, heuristics and routines, just as they do when operating as consumers. This should already be evident from organization-related examples used in previous chapters, but it is important to recognize that the very existence of organizations in which people have specialized tasks and specific reporting relationships is a consequence of bounded rationality and the divisions of knowledge. To appreciate the difference that it makes to organizational performance to have organizations populated by real people rather than "econs," we need to understand the nature of organizations from the inside; it will not be enough to view organizations "as if" they are "black boxes" in which employees simply do exactly what an entrepreneur requires them to do in order to maximize profits.

This chapter therefore takes us into territory opened in the first two decade after World War II by two research programs that both have so far had their main impacts in business schools rather than in economics. They are rarely brought together in an integrated perspective, despite being based on complementary ways of thinking (Pitelis, 2007). One was fired up by the work of Edith Penrose at The Johns Hopkins University in Baltimore. Penrose's (1959) book *The Theory of the Growth of the Firm* focuses on the role of distinctive sets of human resources in shaping the evolution of firms and on managerial constraints on the pace at which firms can accumulate and effectively mobilize human resources. It led to the development of what has become known as the "resource-based" or "competence-based" approach to the firm (see Foss and Knudsen, eds, 1996). The other research program emerged in Pittsburgh at what is now Carnegie-Mellon University and was the product of collaboration between Herbert Simon, James March and Richard Cyert. The output of their multidisciplinary research culminated in Cyert and March's (1963) seminal book

A Behavioral Theory of the Firm, which sought to integrate economics and organization theory and made extensive use of computer simulation methods.

Penrose's work is best viewed as an extension of Marshall's (1890) evolutionary approach to the firm. Marshall's vision had seemed best suited for understanding dynastic family-controlled firms, yet even at the time his *Principles* appeared, such firms were increasingly having to compete with, or were being turned into, joint-stock companies that were reaching unprecedented sizes and were run by salaried managers. During the first half of the twentieth century, such firms grew larger still, often diversifying as they did so. At the end of his life, Marshall (1923) was increasingly recognizing this, but it was Penrose who first provided a framework for understanding how large, diversified corporations evolve.

Central to Marshall's analysis was the idea that the fortunes of businesses depend crucially on the people who run them and on the capacities of entrepreneurs and employees to learn how to do their jobs better as they accumulated more experience. He saw firms as being prone to cease growing and prone eventually to go out of business due to their failure to ensure that those who ran them had the vision, skills and motivation to keep them thriving. No matter how gifted its founding entrepreneur had been, the fortunes of a firm would always depend in the long run on how it handled succession issues and whether the staff that it recruited had skills that conferred advantages in its changing external environment. A well-established firm could eventually die as a result of failing to keep developing the requisite knowledge for survival as technologies, tastes and ways of doing business changed. Sheer size did not guarantee survival, for large firms could turn into sluggish bureaucracies and lose their markets to more adaptable newcomers.

Penrose took a more optimistic view and portrayed firms as having great potential for long-run growth so long as they were able gradually to build and maintain teams of staff with desirable sets of capabilities that other firms could not readily replicate. As we shall see (particularly in Section 10.7), her theory, like Marshall's, has learning at its core and thus does not take a static view of productivity and efficiency. It is a theory that is "behavioral" via its focus on human capabilities, and it was informed by her studies of business history. Its core messages were gradually reinforced empirically by three acclaimed books on the evolution of firms produced by the great business historian Alfred Chandler (1962, 1977, 1990).

By contrast, the Carnegie trio's research program began with Simon's 1942 doctoral dissertation in political science at the University of Chicago. In 1947, two years before Simon moved to Pittsburgh to join the Carnegie faculty, his dissertation was published in revised form as *Administrative Behavior: A Study of Decision-Making Processes in Administrative Organization* (4th ed., 1997). Though still mostly read by management and public administration scholars, this book was viewed as being of "epoch-making" significance for economics by the committee that awarded Simon the 1978 Alfred Nobel Memorial Prize in Economic Sciences. It was in *Administrative Behavior* that Simon began setting out his satisficing view of decision-making under bounded rationality. However, much of the book is about the challenges that organizations face in trying to ensure that their members will work together effectively to enable the achievement of organization-level goals. There is a key role for leadership in such processes, and Simon had been greatly influenced in this area by Chester Barnard's (1938) book, *The Functions of the Executive*, a work based on Barnard's many years of senior management experience in the telecommunications sector. In collaboration with March, Simon went on to write another classic, *Organizations* (March and Simon, 1958), around the time that March was working on articles with Cyert (Cyert and March, 1955; 1956; Cyert, Feigenbaum and March, 1959) on how organizational factors affect the behavior of large firms. Cyert was the economist of the Carnegie trio, but he was also very much an enthusiast for working across disciplinary boundaries.

As should be evident from this sketch of its origins, the behavioral theory of the firm is focused on the internal organizational operations of firms. It is very much a theory about how people behave in organizations, in which organizations are viewed as social systems that interact with an external environment consisting not merely of rival firms but also customers, firms involved at other stages in their supply chains and public policymakers. As such, it is profoundly different from how economists typically find it convenient to depict firms. Moreover, although firms may have a fiduciary duty to maximize earnings for their shareholder, the behavioral approach to the firm acknowledges the impossibility of pinning down precisely what this entails in a world of complexity and uncertainty. Thus, instead of portraying firms "as if" they are profit-maximizing entities, the behavioral approach acknowledges that managers in the real world focus on a variety of KPIs, in respect of which they set short-run and long-run targets as proxies for what they need to do to keep generating satisfactory earnings for their shareholders.

The challenges of reaching decisions and the organizational processes by which they are in practice resolved are glossed over in conventional analysis, as are the challenges of achieving outcomes that the decisions are intended to produce. This is done by treating each firm "as if" a lone entrepreneur decides which factors of production to hire, the quantities of products to produce and the prices at which they will be sold, and how to respond to changes in external conditions.

Ignoring the organizational aspects of production systems may sometimes be OK for analyzing very small firms where the "boss" is also the owner. However, even this might be unwise in some cases. For example, suppose we are studying the music industry and wish to understand the rise and fall of rival bands. It is perfectly reasonable to think of bands as very small firms, but they are notoriously prone to disagreements about the way forward and the musicians in them frequently have problematic relationships with their managers.

With larger organizations, it seems unwise to assume that everyone is interested in making profits for the shareholders and that information about problems and potential solutions is simultaneously available to, and seen in the same way by, everyone in the organization who needs to know what is going on. Moreover, when managers cannot be watching all their subordinates all the time, they run the risk of unpleasant surprises due to the latter misconstruing what they were expected to be doing or choosing not to perform as their managers had hoped they would.

To open up this territory, it is useful to give some attention to the meaning of efficiency and productivity (Section 10.2) and to the nature of organizations and employment relationships (Section 10.3), rather than heading straight to an examination of the Marshall/Penrose and Barnard/"Carnegie" perspectives.

10.2   Alternative Perspectives on Efficiency and Productivity

Empirical studies of efficiency and productivity have proliferated in recent decades, with econometricians developing more and more sophisticated techniques to facilitate such research (see Coelli et al., 2005; O'Donnell, 2018; Sickles and Zelenyuk, 2019). These studies normally show that some organizations in the sector in question are operating inside the best-practice "efficiency frontier" that the researcher team has estimated. To an econometrician, such organizations are "inefficient" in the sense that they are using needlessly large amounts of inputs to generate their output.

The discovery of evidence of significant inefficiency should be a cue to look for policies that might result in improvements in efficiency, but this requires an appreciation of the underlying causes of the observations. For a behavioral/evolutionary economist (and probably many managers and intelligent lay people), the obvious places to look to explain efficiency differences and thereby assist policy designers would be:

- the competence and motivation of the workers,
- how well inventories of parts and the scheduling of production of different types of output are being managed,
- the organization's structure and operating system and
- the age and type of the equipment that the workers use

We will be considering all these issues in due course, though the last, particularly associated with the work of Salter (1960), is deferred until Chapter 11. However, obvious though they might appear as areas central to efficiency, they are not where the dominant economic approach leads its disciples to focus if inefficiency surfaces as a topic.

Economists typically view production-related choices "as if" those who make them have access to a "book of blueprints" that specifies all the different ways in which factors of production can be combined and how much output can be achieved from any of these combinations. An entrepreneur supposedly can get the technological knowledge from engineers and then work out simultaneously the cost-minimizing, profit-maximizing technology to use, the rate of output to produce per period and the price to charge. Insofar as fixed costs may be shared between multiple products to achieve "economies of scope," the entrepreneur must do these computations in respect of alternative product combinations. This optimization exercise entails combining the engineering knowledge with knowledge of factor markets and demand conditions for the product(s) in question. The entrepreneur is then presumed to hire the set of factors of production consistent with all this and to end up using the profit-maximizing technology in a best-practice way. On the typical economist's view, productivity thus tends to be as good as it can possibly be in terms of measures such as the ratios of inputs to outputs or number of units of output produced per worker per month. In other words, firms are viewed "as if" they are always "technically efficient."

Given this, the only things that will make average total costs of production higher than they need to be are distortion in markets. Here, there are two usual suspects. One is the possible abuse of monopoly power by firms, as holding back output to drive up prices will drive up average total costs due to fixed costs being spread across fewer units of output. The other is that there could be distortions in factor markets, such as wages being pushed up by the actions of labor unions. These external sources of inefficiency entail deadweight losses to society, but what is produced is presumed to be produced at the lowest cost possible given the distorted set of input and output prices.

Harvey Leibenstein (1966, 1976, 1978, 1989) challenged this view and sought to replace it with a perspective more in tune with management and lay views of the meaning of efficiency and inefficiency. He suggested that the kind of (in)efficiency that economists seem to have in mind should be labeled "allocative (in)efficiency" and that it was typically of much less significance than what he chose to label as "X-(in) efficiency." If a firm is suffering from X-inefficiency, its costs per unit of output are higher than they need to be. As a behavioral economist, Leibenstein argued that this is a consequence of people in organizations failing to search as far as they could have done for ways of enhancing productivity and/or failing to work as hard as they could have done. He suggested that X-inefficiency can persist for four reasons:

(a) *The Production Function Is Imperfectly Known and Incompletely Specified.*

This encompasses two issues. First, a firm may be operating inside the production possibility frontier because its managers are unaware of the existence of more productive technologies. Secondly, whatever technology they are using, workers do not know how it needs to be used to extract maximum productivity (as when, say, they are using a computer oblivious of the things it can do and the shortcut keystrokes that they might be using). This in some cases is due to the tacit knowledge problem, whereby they can only get the "knack" for performing a particular task via a process of "learning by doing" rather than from instructions. Although they may accidentally discover better ways of doing their jobs when working under pressure, loss aversion is a deterrent to active experimentation in the midst of trying to get things done when they are confident that familiar recipes will be good enough to enable them to meet production targets. The full potential of production systems thus sometimes gets discovered belatedly, but sometimes never. This issue applies not merely in respect of equipment but also in relation to knowing what particular colleagues can do.

(b) *The Market for Factors of Production Is Not Perfect.*

People typically are not "in the market" for a better job every day and hence can be unaware of jobs that would have suited them better than their current positions. Instead, we should expect them to search for a better job only when they are failing to meet their aspirations, unless they employ a periodic search routine to get a sense of what is "out there" and hence of whether they might reasonably aspire for something better. Whether or not they then discover the currently available job that would most suit them will depend upon the search rules that they use. When such considerations are coupled with the uncertainty and ignorance that prospective employers face when choosing between job applicants, it seems unlikely that the labor market will work efficiently as a matching device. Because of this, managers who might have been able and willing to shake up performance in organizations that were trailing badly in productivity and efficiency relative to their rivals might thus end up having a rather easy time, working in organizations that already have excellent operating systems and would function well even with less capable managers. Meanwhile, lower-caliber managers could be struggling in the midst of working for under-performing organizations, where there was much scope for a managerial shake-up.

Similar issues apply in relation to the use of management consulting services. Indeed, as was evident in a classic UK study (PEP, 1965) produced just before Leibenstein published his first paper on X-inefficiency, ambitious "thruster" firms may be more likely than low-achieving "sleepers" to hire management consultants. If a firm suffers from what is known as the "not invented here syndrome" whereby managers have the arrogance of presuming they know best, any suggestion that fresh perspectives from consultants might be worth obtaining are going to be swiftly dismissed.

The shortcomings of factor markets may be connected to issue (a) in respect of physical assets as well as human resources. Research by Loasby (1967 [reprinted in Earl, 1988, vol. 2]) on the impact of UK regional policies on the location decisions of firms can be read as providing examples of this. The policies in question could make it impossible for firms to obtain the Industrial Development Certificates that were prerequisites for expanding or building new premises outside designated "development areas" (a euphemism for "relatively depressed areas"). They thus got in the way of the normal tendency of entrepreneurs and managers to look for local sites and then stop searching if they found somewhere that they deemed satisfactory near their present location. In some cases, being forced to look further afield led to the discovery that not only were cheaper sites available but also that the transportation logistics were better, confounding long-held presumptions (as with bookstore chain W. H. Smith, which ended up moving its main warehouse from London to Swindon, about eighty miles away: see the book-length case study in Loasby, 1973).

(c) *Employment Contracts Are Specified Incompletely.*

As Coase (1937) realized, in a world of uncertainty and surprises, there are transaction costs to be saved, and flexibility advantages to be gained, by not spelling out precisely what a worker is expected to be doing at a particular moment. However, this leaves workers with some discretion about the effort and care they put into their work, especially since their bosses have only limited capacities to monitor what they do in response to instructions that were intended to flesh out what they have formally signed up to do. Clearly, what workers achieve could be limited if they exploit vagueness by acting in a self-serving way, but they might also not be completely clear what their bosses want and may even be reluctant to seek more clarification for fear of making a bad impression.

(d) *Competitive Pressure Is Weak.*

Where members of an organization are not constantly having to worry about its survival, there is less of an incentive for managers to seek to extract higher levels of productivity from their subordinates, or for anyone to be innovative. Nobel Laureate Sir John Hicks (1935) captured the essence of this when he wrote that "the best of all monopoly profits is a quiet life." In a similar vein, proponents of free trade commonly speak of the adverse effects of tariffs and quotas in terms of "featherbedding," i.e., overstaffing and underutilization of workers in firms protected from international competition.

Leibenstein (1966, p. 407) emphasized that in the face of uncertainty about how rivals might respond, oligopolies will tend to engage in conservative policies of tacit collusion. For example, as a rule, they may not change their prices unless the acknowledged "price leader" makes a move. But just as firms may not wish to risk inadvertently starting a price war, so promotion-hungry workers who would like to impress their bosses may be wary of starting a destructive "effort war" with their similarly minded peers. They may also be aware of the risk of having to deal with the social pressures and punishments – such as ostracism and vindictive damage to one's car – that can be applied to those who step out of line by working so hard that it makes others look bad. (It is interesting here to note that, in Singaporean English, there is an economically apt word for someone who behaves in this way, namely a "spoilmarket.")

The "quiet life" perspective makes it easy to see why Leibenstein thought it was so important for economists to widen their view of efficiency: if we know what a firm's costs are, but not what they could be or could have been, we are likely to underestimate the deadweight losses being caused by barriers to competition. If we acknowledge the possibility of X-inefficiency, our reference point should be the price and output combination that would have emerged if the barriers to competition had not been there and if, in their absence, unit costs had been driven lower due to the need to match rivals in order to survive. If we merely try to estimate the price and output combination that would have emerged in the absence of barriers to competition by referring to actual costs, we will likely be inferring too small a difference between actual and potential prices and actual and potential outputs.

Leibenstein's X-efficiency concept overlaps somewhat with what Philip Andrews (1949), a Marshall-inspired member of the Oxford Economists' Research Group, had earlier labeled simply as "managerial efficiency." Like Marshall (1890, 1923), Andrews was well aware from his engagement with the business community that firms in an industry typically differ in how well they are managed. However, he saw this primarily as a result of differences in knowledge and sought to emphasize that competition is often so powerful as to limit opportunities for a "quiet life." His view was a precursor to the "contestable markets" view of competition proposed by

Baumol, Panzar, and Willig (1982) in which it is argued that firms are concerned about losing their markets not merely to existing rivals but also to firms that they view as having the potential to cross into their territory and challenge them. In other words, the Andrews/Marshall view implicitly downplays factors (c) and (d) but emphasizes factors (a) and (b) from the preceding paragraphs. From a pluralistic standpoint, it seems wise to keep both perspectives in mind as we proceed. Although we should be on the lookout for potential competition's mind-concentrating and motivational capacities, we should also recognize that, in some contexts, managers and workers in incumbent firms may indeed be untroubled by fears that other firms will enter.

The X-efficiency perspective points to ways in which organizational productivity can be increased that have profoundly different distributional consequences. However, the distributional dimension of productivity growth makes overall efficiency gains from policies problematic to identify except in situations where there is a Pareto improvement, i.e., where some people end up better off but no one is left worse off.

Clearly, if we focus on factors (c) and (d), the implication is that the output per head might be greater if policies were implemented to induce people to work harder. Such policies could include more tightly specified job contracts or the removal of regulations and trade barriers that limited scope for potential competitors to enter markets. However, it is less clear that such policies improve "efficiency" in the sense of enhancing overall well-being. Some people may benefit from better service or from cheaper products, but they do so at the cost of others working harder (see further Stigler, 1976; Martin, 1978). Moreover, putting more detail into employment contracts can be counterproductive if it limits flexibility. This is clear from what happens when labor unions use a "work to rule" policy to try to win concessions from employers. Normally, their members would employ common sense to deal with unexpected contingencies, but when they insist on doing everything "by the book," the disruptive effects can be not far short of what they could have achieved by going on strike.

By contrast, if we focus on factor (a) and potential for improvements in knowledge, it is evident that productivity growth can come from working smarter rather than harder. However, this, too, can entail a mixed blessing in terms of social well-being if the productivity benefits come at the cost of some workers losing their jobs. Much may depend on who works in a smarter way – innovative thinking, in terms of leadership, job design and the assignment of roles, may result in people ending up feeling happier despite working harder without being paid more for doing so. Depending on how the changes were managed, employees might end up feeling happier about their work via, say, a better sense of sharing a common purpose with their colleagues and of "all pulling together." Indeed, as Peter Hanson (2013) argues in *The Joy of Stress*, there can be great benefits to not having a quiet life: thus, in some cases, workers may throw themselves into their work with gusto after at last being put in a position where they feel they are being taken seriously and given more responsibility, even if they are not yet being offered any more pay. Without such recognition and new challenges, and especially if their geographical mobility is limited due to social embeddedness, they might otherwise have quietly "rusted out" in a rather depressed state, feeling increasingly disengaged from the organization in question.

Hanson's emphasis on the long-term downsides of an unduly quiet life can be taken as a cue for us to make sure that we do not lose sight of the dynamic dimension that adds to the difficulties of judging the efficiency with which an organization operates. Here, as with the great environmental questions of our time, the key question is whether performance is sustainable or is merely being achieved today at the cost of running down assets and failing to invest in technologies that are prerequisites for future survival.

To be sure, it is sometimes true that immediate existential threats may concentrate minds so wonderfully that innovations are swiftly achieved, and long-resisted changes are implemented virtually overnight. In 2020, the Covid-19 pandemic triggered many examples of this, such as the widespread move to working from home and the switch that universities made to online teaching. However, such examples of frantic adaptation in emergency conditions should not lead us to view organizations as being any more capable of extracting peak-load levels of efforts from their employees, day after day, than students are of sustaining the kind of performance that they sometimes demonstrate via a couple of "all-nighters" in which they dispose of backlogs of assignments. For one thing, there is the eventual "burnout" effect on the health of workers from being constantly under extreme pressure to meet current output targets. But such organizational environments are also not conducive to innovation and productivity growth: for that to occur, workers need to have time to think and research new possibilities. The perils of viewing efficiency improvements themselves in a static way are evident if we recall (from the end of Section 3.7) the difficulties that the Ford Motor Company ran into after years of being obsessed with finding ways of making its Model T cars more cheaply. That obsession was served at the cost of failing to build up capabilities for designing and putting into production successive new models with much shorter life cycles than the Model T had enjoyed.

10.3 The Nature of Organizations and Employment Relationships

Production processes usually involve complex systems that bring together and add value to components produced in other complex systems. These systems may, at different times, involve the use of workers and equipment that at other times are used to make other things. Orders and deliveries can fail to materialize at their expected times, and absent workers or breakdowns of equipment may cause production to be disrupted. The complexity of such systems in terms of interrelationships and feedback loops can mean that even staff with years of experience can have great trouble figuring out why, for example, they are unable to meet delivery deadlines due to production bottlenecks despite having plenty of inventory in terms of components. Such a situation and how a manager gradually gets to grips with it are brilliantly explored by Eliyahu Goldratt (2004), an Israeli management consultant, in his novel *The Goal*. We get a great sense there of how running a production system does not entail iterative adjustments akin to tuning a car engine until it is running smoothly; rather, it is more like trying to deal with a pandemic without complete knowledge of network interactions, where the task is to keep chaos sufficiently at bay to meet performance targets. If the mix of orders keeps changing, scheduling and/or prioritization strategies may need to keep being rethought if bottlenecks are to be kept at bay and inventories are to be kept under control.

Organizations are complex systems, too. They consist of contractual and role relationships, along with operating rules and routines. They get created as means for running complex production systems in the presence of uncertainty and limits to human information processing and imaginative capacities. Hierarchically structured role relationships reduce the chances that members of an organization will suffer from cognitive overload due to being expected to deal directly with inquiries and requests from too many other members or due to having to figure out what too many other people should do, communicate it to them and verify that requests have been actioned properly.

The need for inquiries and requests to be initiated and addressed arises because organizations are by nature "problem-solving institutions" (Loasby, 1990). They are not the only way of getting complex production processes to occur in the presence of problems of information and knowledge but, in many situations, they are more efficient and reliable than alternative means for doing so. In principle, a complex set of tasks can be undertaken by a set of independent contractors each of whom has struck a deal to deliver a particular product or service at a particular time, subject to particular conditions prevailing. For example, individual A could rent premises from individual B, along with access to capital equipment owned by individual C, and work there adding value to semifinished goods supplied by individual D before selling the output to individual E, and so on. In such an arrangement, everyone is his or her own boss and has to operate like an entrepreneur in deciding which deals to do to earn an income by spending less on inputs than is received from selling his or her output. Some people do operate like this, as sole traders, but they forego benefits that others achieve by working for an organization. The latter have a much simpler life as far as contracts are concerned: if they work for just one organization, they only need one contract; they do not have to hire other factors of production, as everything is laid on for them.

Organizational membership does not come about via a series of momentary contracts that each specify what one must do at a particular moment. Rather, it entails formal or implicit relational contracts that last for nontrivial periods of time (months, years or even decades) during which members get known by some (if the organization is large) or all other members as having particular capabilities, missions and modes of operating, and a particular role in the organization. Because the contracts that define each member's relationship with the organization run for significant periods of time, they need to be designed to deal with both the impossibility of predicting future events with complete accuracy and the possibility that the pool of knowledge available to deal with things that happen will keep changing. Since human imaginative capacities are not infinite, the problem of uncertainty does not merely entail not knowing what will happen but also entails not even being able to be sure if what is going to happen is on the list of imagined possibilities. Hence, these contracts need to be able to accommodate surprises that are not mentioned in them. Leaving vagueness or "wriggle room" in contracts is a means for achieving this, but is also necessary because they need to be kept simple enough to be workable and capable of being put together soon enough for them to apply to issues from a desired starting point. Usable contracts are unlikely to be arrived at if negotiations continue until there is nothing left to discuss since, despite their bounded imaginative capacities, people may be able, given time, to imagine a huge range of possibilities, leading to an overwhelming amount of contractual "fine print," much or all of which could turn out to be redundant. Keeping contracts simple and flexible also limits legal bills when contracts are being devised.

10.3.1   Contracts of Employment

Simon (1951) pointed out in one of his early contributions that there are two basic contractual formats by which people establish their membership of an organization. Simon called one type an "employment contract," seemingly unaware that Coase (1937) had already made a similar characterization and drawn similar inferences when analyzing the nature of the firm. (In turn, Leibenstein, 1966, seems to have been unaware of both contributions when he gave these contracts a role in his X-inefficiency analysis.) Such a contract promises the worker a specific income, but the task is only partly specified. This means that the worker's boss can decide what to ask the worker to do as events unfold. It is thus an excellent means for dealing with surprises, but the boss's request may come as a surprise to the worker even though they fall within the loose terms of the contract. When the worker is given a task, the boss will not be specifying exactly how to perform the task or what the exact outcome must be – as with, say, "I'd like you to teach the final-year undergrade course in behavioral economics next semester." Indeed, the boss may not even have the expertise to perform the task effectively. But the missing details are also not completely addressed by the organization's manuals of policies and procedures. Hence, what then happens is partly up to the worker. This means that the outcome may range anywhere from being a great disappointment to the boss, to something that is an unexpectedly impressive display of industriousness, knowledge and creative thinking. Whatever it is, with an "employment contract," the worker gets paid the same amount.

The other type of arrangements is what Simon called a "sales contract" but which we might prefer to call a "payment-by-results contract." Here, the worker has discretion about how to use his or her time but knows that payment depends on what he or she achieves, with the reward being structured in relation to a specific set of possible outcomes. So, for example, the commission that a sales assistant in an appliance store receives might simply be a fixed proportion of the sales revenue that this person achieves, or there could be different percentages for different kinds of products. The incomes of workers employed via such contracts may be affected not merely by their effort and competence but also by what is currently in stock to sell and which prospective customers come into the store. Their income is uncertain, as are the organization's sales. For the boss, there will be the risk that they will focus on achieving a particular target income (like the cab drivers in the study by Camerer et al., 1997) and will lower their efforts once they have reached their target, with the result that sales that could have been achieved will be lost.

With both kinds of contracts, there is scope for the performance of the workers to have consequences for what other members of the organization are asked to do or end up doing altruistically, or for the incomes that can be achieved by those who are on sales contracts. The two types of contracts are often combined to some degree, as when a salesperson is hired by a deal that entails both a "retainer" and performance-based pay, or where an executive receives a performance-based bonus as well as a salary.

The difference between the two types of contracts is significant for the boss who must pay the worker. If a worker is hired via a "sales contract" and is not very productive, the worker's remuneration will suffer accordingly. In future, the boss may be able get the desired volume of the output in question by hiring more workers, but in the meantime, the worker's poor performance may impose costs on the organization (e.g., costs of financing unsold inventory). But with an "employment contract," the situation is rather like signing a blank check: the details of what is to be done are only partly spelt out, giving the boss flexibility regarding what the worker can be asked to do in return for a given wage. However, because of the vagueness of the contract, the boss may be unable to refuse to pay the wage if the worker's performance is disappointing. The challenge for the boss is thus to "get" the worker to deliver a fair day's work for a fair day's pay so that both sides to the contract are satisfied.

10.3.2   Rates of Remuneration

The distinction between "employment contracts" and "sales contracts" should lead us to start wondering how pay is determined in the case of employment contracts, given the uncertainty that firms are trying to deal with when hiring workers via such contracts. The standard economic wisdom is that firms should be viewed "as if" they pay their factors of production their respective marginal revenue products, with the number of hours of labor time hired for a particular task being determined by the point at which the marginal revenue products of the worker equals the marginal cost of hiring an extra hour of the labor type in question. That view can seem reasonable where jobs involve repeatedly performing the same task on one's own. For example, if the owner of an orchard expects to earn $1 per kilo of its fruit net of the costs of getting it sold, fruit pickers will be worth hiring at $20 per hour (if that much is necessary to attract them to do the work) for as long as it takes to complete the harvest if they can pick more than twenty kilos of fruit per hour; if they can only pick nineteen kilos per hour but require $20 in order to be willing to do the job, then it is not worth hiring them, as it would be better to let the fruit rot rather than lose $1 per hour per worker hired.

How should the employer deal with the risk of the workers not working at least at the necessary rate? With such a simple job, it should be possible to obviate this risk by devising a "sales contract" arrangement whereby the worker is paid a per-kilo amount rather than an hourly rate: so long as workers can be found who are prepared to pick fruit for less than $1 per kilo, a profit can be made from having the fruit picked. "Employment contract" arrangements come into their own when such clarity is absent. However, their simplicity severs any clear link between pay and the employee's performance.

Workers hired on fixed salaries typically undertake a range of tasks whose mix depends on what their line managers ask them to do as events unfold. Many play their roles as members of teams, where their productivity is affected by the quantity and quality of their coworkers' contributions. This all makes it problematic to assess the revenue that would be lost in the absence of a particular worker over the duration of an employment contract. Such issues were already evident from the 1946 study by Richard Lester mentioned in Section 1.6, but Simon's work implies that productivity can also be a function of the quality of the relationship between managers and workers. Managers who alienate their workers may get less from them than they might have done with a given employment contract, whereas, in difficult times, inspirational management styles may prove decisive in giving workers hope, quelling their anxieties and ensuring their attention is focused on performing in an altruistic, collegial manner (see further Wallis et al., 2009).

As we think about the difficulties that traditional wage theory has in accommodating the vagueness of Simon- /Coase-style employment contracts, we also need to recognize the "efficiency wage hypothesis" (see Akerlof et al., 1986), whereby paying better wages can actually increase a firm's profits due, for example, to employees working harder and being less prone to absenteeism. Here, the problem is that the relationship between pay and performance may be hard to predict reliably, especially since the performance of the worker may depend on how fair he or she feels the deal is (which may change as new colleagues are discovered to have been hired on different terms or with different levels of experience) and on how the worker feels about how he or she is treated by the organization in ways that are not seen as due to the worker's line manager's actions. And, if a worker is threatening to quit unless offered a better deal, the true cost of employing a replacement may be hard to assess, both ahead of advertising the position and after the closing date for applications: those who apply will differ in their capabilities, attitudes and how long they take to acquire organization-specific know-how.

In some cases, uncertainty about these areas is compounded by the need to consider the impact on other areas of the organization's performance if a particular job slot remains unfilled. Sometimes, there will be other workers (and there might be many to consider) who could be required to put some of their normal duties on hold (or have them assigned to others) and serve as substitutes. In other cases, it may be perfectly clear that if a position is left unfilled, some production will be impossible because other members of the production team lack the specific capabilities required to perform the task in question: for example, if an airline is short of pilots, its ground staff or flight attendants will not be capable of filling the gap, and safety regulations will limit the number of extra flight shifts that the available pilots can be asked to do. Substitution and assessments of returns to spending marginally more or less on human resources rather than capital equipment are also frequently precluded by basic engineering and ergonomic considerations that limit the set of available technologies that so far have been invented: for example, when it comes to digging a ditch by a particular deadline, the choice is more likely to be between a gang of workers, each equipped with a shovel, or one worker and a small excavator rather than about the worker–shovel or driver–excavator ratios.

All this means that the relationship between productivity and pay is rather tenuous. As a result, decisions about the hiring and retention of workers normally must be made by applying decision rules regarding the types of workers sought, which applicants are to be regarded potentially as at least satisfactory, how those deemed appointable are to be ranked, which kinds of remuneration packages can be offered, and the terms under which workers can be promoted or have their employment contracts extended or terminated. For example, as Simon (1957b) and Lydall (1959) argued, one way of designing an organization's remuneration structure when marginal revenue products are unknown is with reference to the positions that workers hold in the organizational hierarchy and the number of subordinates they have or the aggregate pay of those who report directly to them. A more basic version of this is to employ the rule that subordinates must be paid less than their bosses. A different rule-based approach is set out by Wood (1978), who suggests that relative pay should be understood in terms of social norms about what it is fair for particular kinds of workers to receive.

Where the number of workers in a production system is determined by technological or engineering considerations and/or health and safety rules, it may in any case be possible to rank alternative production technologies without reference to marginal revenue products. Depending on what the decision-makers in question decide to assume about what the respective systems' labor costs might need to be to attract enough workers of appropriate caliber, it may be possible to rank the systems via their relative *total* costs and revenues. In cases where workers are being hired for positions that do not entail the production of marketed outputs, the authorization of the positions will need to be rule based, with proxy rules being used to rank the applicants. For example, managers of a university can use budgeting rules and student–staff ratio targets to decide which faculties are to be allowed to hire new staff, with rules regarding acceptable mixes of staff at various levels then being applied to determine the levels at which hiring will be done. In turn, the prospective performances of entry-level academics may be proxied by the rankings of the institution from which they obtained their PhD and the journals in which they published their first papers. Similarly, simple formulae based on what has seemed adequate in the past may be used to work out how many sales representatives to employ to cover a particular geographical region, or police officers of various grade to allocate to particular kinds of cases, and so on.

10.4   The Marshallian View of How Unit Costs Evolve

The Marshallian view of organizational productivity centers on the knowledge held by the organization's members, the sum and internal distribution of which will be unique to each firm and hence hard, if not impossible, for rivals to replicate. This is not to say that the quality of an organization's capital equipment is not significant; rather, the point is that, except in fully automated systems, the quantity and quality of output achieved with the aid of physical assets depends on human inputs.

A simple, music-related example may help convey this point. Staff in musical instrument retailers sometimes privately use the phrase "dentists with Alembics" (DeVoe, 2019) as a disparaging code to denote rich customers who make their money via professions other than music and spend it on ultra-high-end gear that they use as hobbyist musicians. The latter still end up sounding very ordinary, because they lack the kind of musical talent that enabled electric bass virtuoso Stanley Clarke to achieve fame in the 1970s from his playing on a very expensive Alembic bass guitar. By contrast, as can be seen via many YouTube demonstration videos, in the hands of a skilled musician who can set up a guitar properly, knows how to get a good sound and can play well, an absolute bottom-end instrument can be very hard for even an experienced listener to distinguish from a premium product.

Being able to match the best performers may thus depend, literally, on knowing the "secrets of their success." However, following Nelson and Winter (1982), we should also note that the tacit knowledge problem may stand in the way of picking up those secrets, even if it is possible to hire someone who knows them, is prepared to do his or her best to share them and is able to engage the full attention of those who need or wish to acquire them.

Thinking about productivity with a focus on access to particular kinds of equipment is also unwise insofar as it diverts attention from the human element in the design of methods of production. The production systems that organizations use are not selected from a "book of blueprints" that covers all possible combinations of spending on physical and human capital in the manner of the Cobb-Douglas production function that is so frequently used in economic models. Rather, as Marshall (1890) acknowledged, production functions are incomplete and the set of available technologies (not all of which may be available to be purchased by organizations that would like to use them) is a result of past problem-solving activities and the knowledge and creative insights applied at the time the problems in question were being addressed (see further Loasby, 1982). Indeed, the incompleteness of the "book of blueprints" often results in firms not buying, from outside suppliers, technologies that already exist. Instead, they develop their own technologies for making the things they intend to make. Either way, some of the things that could have enhanced productivity, such as better ergonomics, may not have been among the problems that were being attended to at the time particular pieces of capital equipment came to be designed or selected. If a firm routinely involves workers who will have to use a particular piece of equipment in the process of choosing it, productivity may be higher than if the choice is left to production engineers who are less able to spot some kinds of potential issues when assessing contending technologies.

In fact, the production technology and the design of the product itself may jointly affect the productivity of a firm. For example, consider what happened in the late 1970s when Honda first began its partnership with the now-defunct UK carmaker

British Leyland (later the Austin Rover Group and, finally, MG–Rover). Honda allowed British Leyland to assemble the Honda Ballade sedan and market it in slightly modified form as the Triumph Acclaim. The assembly quality of the latter turned out to be far better than British Leyland had been achieving with its own products. This seemed to be because Honda's designers habitually set out to ensure that there was only one way that components could be fitted together and that they would readily fit together that way (Edwardes, 1983). In other words, quality was designed into the product. Without that approach to design, it was possible for assembly line workers to force-fit some components, leading not merely to a low-quality look along joining seams but also eventually to issues that sapped customer goodwill and imposed warranty costs on the firm. Having a superior design and engineering philosophy and staff capable of implementing it may thus be a way to achieve excellent results without necessarily having line workers who are as capable and/or committed to quality as those of rival organizations.

Marshall viewed the unit costs of a firm as tending to fall if it survived long enough to get well established and grow. One way these cost reductions could come was from switching to larger plant. This could entail not merely various forms of "economies of increased dimensions" and spreading the fixed costs of indivisible inputs across a bigger volume of output (i.e., the kinds of advantages that supertankers enjoy in construction and crewing) but also from greater "division of labor," with workers being given more specialized tasks on which to concentrate their attention. In some cases, specialized workers could capture higher earnings as their in-depth training enabled them to apply more knowledge and solve problems more rapidly and to a higher standard than generalists had been able to do (much as occurs when regional health service provision is consolidated by switching from using small local hospitals that lack specialist staff in most fields to sending patients to a few massive hospitals that are often further away but have many different specialists).

In other cases, larger-scale production is a means by which tasks can be simplified, enabling cheaper, less skilled workers to be used (a strategy pioneered by Henry Ford and nowadays known as "Fordism"). These larger production systems could be, and indeed might have to be, freshly designed rather than chosen from an existing "book of blueprints"; in other words, in Marshall's way of thinking, economies of large-scale production often come about by filling in knowledge gaps in the production function rather than choosing a cost-minimizing means of expanding output from an existing production function that already exhibited economies of scale in the manner depicted in conventional textbook versions of production theory.

However, for Marshall, unit cost reductions could also come within existing production systems as a result of managers and workers learning on the job how to save time and/or reduce wastage of materials. Such growth in their competence as individuals or teams could have a statistical dimension, with the variance in input use or output quality decreasing through time and the associated probability distributions becoming narrower and their peaks moving in the direction of reduced unit costs and/ or reduced defect rates as the process of production became less "hit and miss" and good performances less a matter of luck rather than expertise.

It is instructive to reflect on these learning processes in relation to the ideas of Hayek and Kelly that we used in Chapter 4 to understand cognition. It seems likely that the process of neural myelinogenesis will be involved insofar as learning entails improved dexterity and/or the speeding up of capacities to identify patterns or spot that one is drifting away from a target. When we get the knack for doing something well, our initial successes may come purely by chance, but they will increase the probability that we will employ the same sets of neural connections when we are trying to do the same thing again. The speed with which the more efficient sets of neural combinations crowd out the less efficient ones looks likely to depend partly on how we think about doing the task and partly on the extent to which we are prepared to allow our unconscious processes to take over. If we mentally rehearse what we have discovered we need to do, we enhance our chances of success, whereas if we are anxious to avoid mishandling the task in a particular way, we may increase the probability of our neural system doing it in precisely that way because our negative thoughts reinforced the associated set of neural connections. (This is a variation on the phenomenon popularized by "The Germans" episode in the famous comedy series *Fawlty Towers*, whereby saying "Don't mention the War" to someone prior to a meeting will increase the chances that the person will do precisely this during the meeting. It is also why addictive behavior is so hard to stop if the addict keeps thinking about stopping it.)

From the standpoint of personal construct psychology, the ability of staff in an organization to improve its or their productivity depends on them being motivated or jogged by a surprise to experiment with a different way of construing the kind of situation in question. Without this, the accumulation of experience will not produce consciously figured-out improvements. Kelly (1963, p. 171) rams home this point by referring to a college administrator with thirteen years of service, whose dean had spoken of as having had only one year of experience, repeated thirteen times. Whether learning takes place will thus be affected by how workers construe their job roles. If bosses and workers know that they are expected to be constantly on the lookout for ways of cutting costs, and that they will be rewarded for meeting cost-reduction targets, they are much more likely to learn how to deliver such results than are workers who have received no such instructions and who see cost reductions as likely to reduce their employer's demand for labor and increase the probability that they will lose their jobs. One of the keys to the ability of Japanese firms to improve productivity during the 1960s and 1970s was being able to cultivate the former view. They did this partly by institutionalizing systems for suggesting improvements, empowering workers to stop assembly lines if they spotted defective products and paying employees significant annual bonuses that were based on the firm's overall performance. But they also ensured that workers were willing to engage with the pursuit of productivity improvements by demonstrating that when ways of saving labor were identified, surplus workers would then be redeployed within the growing organization rather than being retrenched (see Adams and Kobayashi, 1969; Dore, 1973, 2012).

Finally, we should note the role that Marshall gave to "external economies of scale" in his analysis of how unit costs fall as firms and industries develop. Here, his focus was on networks of interacting firms, particularly those clustered together physically in related lines of business, as with firms today in Hollywood, Silicon Valley and many other districts that are well known as homes to concentrations of particular kinds of businesses. Firms in a "Marshallian business district" have to contend with strong competition that local monopolies avoid but they also enjoy benefits that go beyond cost reductions that come from collectively operating on a big enough scale to make it viable for specialist ancillary service providers to set up (for example, firms that specialize in repairing Hollywood studios' movie cameras). Their marketing and hiring costs are reduced when the districts in which they are located acquire brand-like institutional status as go-to areas for particular kinds of products and jobs. However, as Neil Hart (2013) reminds us, Marshall's view of external economies of scale is particularly focused on the knowledge advantages that firms can glean about the mysteries of their area of business – the "tricks of the trade" and the "secrets of success" – that may give others a competitive advantage. Not only may knowledge seep out via social mingling but also being located amid firms in a similar line of business may make it easier to recruit personnel who are willing to switch between firms and bring their knowledge with them.

10.5   Learning Curves

It is abundantly evident that Marshall was right to emphasize organizational learning and to take a dynamic view of costs and productivity. In everyday discourse, we commonly hear people talking about having to struggle up a "steep learning curve" after taking up new workplace roles. Their lack of experience results in them facing many surprises at first and not knowing where to turn to for help or having initially to struggle to solve unfamiliar kinds of problems by themselves. Gradually, however, their pace of work speeds up as they build up an effective knowledge base and repertoire of routines that involve "shortcut" methods compared with the routes they initially took to completing their tasks. In graphical terms, the laypersons "steep learning curve" seems to be best depicted by putting the "hours so far spent in the job" on the vertical axis and "accumulated output" on the horizontal axis. The curve would initially rise steeply from the graph's origin, toward the graph's right-hand top, with its slope becoming less and less steep as the recorded total of hours spent on the job increased.

The formal literature on the impact that learning has on costs is usually seen as having begun with Theodore Wright's (1936) paper on how the unit costs of assembling a particular design of aircraft fall over its production run. This was a different phenomenon from what had earlier been observed with Ford's Model T. The unit cost reductions achieved for the Model T over its almost two-decade production run (1908–1927) involved changes in the technology and scale of production, and the development of more refined Model T–specific tooling, under pressure from Henry Ford to find cheaper ways of making the Model T. With aircraft assembly, the process of building aircraft more and more cheaply seems more spontaneous and attributable to learning within a given context. It could simply entail operations taking place in a

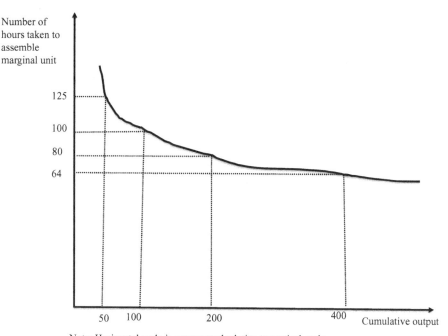

Note: Horizontal scale is compressed relative to vertical scale

Figure 10.1 An "80 percent" learning curve

particular hanger, with a particular number of workers, but the finished aircraft would be rolled out with increasing rapidity as the workers got more adept with their individual tasks and in working as members of teams.

Figure 10.1 presents a graphical example of a learning curve, which is typically drawn with the axes arranged – in contrast to the layperson's view – to show unit costs falling as experience increases. Note that the horizontal axis indicates *cumulative* output, not the amount produced in a particular period. The costs can be recorded in terms of average unit costs on production so far undertaken or, as in Figure 10.1, in terms of the labor hours for assembling the marginal unit of output. The example in Figure 10.1 shows an "80 percent" learning curve in which the marginal costs of production falls by 20 percent over each successive doubling of accumulated output. Hence, the time it takes to assemble the second unit of output would be 80 percent of the time it took to assemble the first unit, with assembly times falling thereafter at a slower and slower rate. In Figure 10.1, the 100th unit takes 100 hours to assemble, and if we had space on the graph to show how long it would take to assemble the 800th unit, its prediction would be 51.2 hours, i.e., 80 percent of the time that the 400th unit took to assemble. Such a level of output takes us beyond the scale on Figure 10.1: for large range of cumulative output, it is common to use logarithmic scales on learning curve graphs, and, if depicted thus, the learning curve is a downward-sloping straight line.

Knowledge of the learning curve phenomenon can be self-reinforcing insofar as it is built into targets that are set within firms. Moreover, to the extent that a particular production system in "on" a particular learning curve and that learning curve can be mapped in terms of a marginal cost function with respect to accumulated output, it is possible, with the aid of integral calculus, to predict how long it will take to reach production targets by using the current production system and workforce. In effect, the capacity of the production system for the product in question keeps expanding, but by a progressively slower rate, with each extra unit of output that is made. Knowledge of the learning curve phenomenon means that, if we have got data on how costs have declined with output so far and are confident that we can stay on the curve that the data imply, it is possible to bid for contracts to deliver specific quantities of the product based on the average costs we expect to achieve over the duration of the production run. If we are confident that we will indeed be able to stay on the learning curve that we have estimated, we can offer a price that will give us a profit over the production run even though it may entail taking a loss at first. For aircraft companies building bombers, and for shipyards that were rushing to assemble standardized "Liberty Ships" during World War II, the discovery of the learning curve phenomenon was thus very timely.

Although the learning curve phenomenon is often discussed in relation to the labor time it takes to produce a complete product, we should not lose sight of it when thinking about learning at the level of a particular operation in a production system that produces a variety of products. For example, one of the things that enabled Japanese carmarkers to enhance their competitive advantage was that their workers learned faster and faster ways to change dies in presses that stamped body panels (see Grimsdale, 1990). This enabled them more readily to achieve economies of scope by offering variations on their key models to suit diverse customer preferences: the presses could spend more and more time stamping panels rather than being idle for long periods while the dies were being changed.

10.6   Effects of Experience, Pride and Anxiety

The accumulation of experience often makes it possible for workers not merely to perform a given task more rapidly but also to perform tasks to a higher standard than they were previously able to attain or, at least, to increase their probabilities of being able to achieve particular types of outcomes. It is the expectation that this will be the case that enables, for example, partners in law firms to command much higher fees than their juniors. (Evidence that experienced lawyers do indeed think differently from newly qualified ones can be found in the 2015 doctoral dissertation produced by Peter Macmillan [one of my past students], using the technique of verbal protocol analysis. His study entailed analyzing transcripts of recordings that he collected via Skype from practicing competition lawyers with different experience levels. After being given briefing notes on a set of competition law cases that at the time were being considered by the Australian Competition and Consumer Commission, these research subjects had then been asked to "think aloud," as they perused these notes, about which of the cases would end up going to court.)

However, employees who are committed to doing a good job and have considerable experience in what they do are not necessarily going to be more productive than those who are less industrious and have accumulated less experience. This is because the quality of work only needs to be good enough to satisfy the requirements of those for whom it is being carried out. Offering excessive quality chews up time, so it may be possible to save time by replacing experience workers who "can't stop themselves" from overservicing their customers, with less experienced workers who nonetheless have enough experience and motivation to get a good enough job done more rapidly than the former take to perform the task to their needlessly exacting standards.

This has an important implication for a firm that has made a name for itself in producing premium products and now decides to expand by diversifying into sub-premium market segments. If this firm is operating in a Marshallian business district that specializes in the kind of premium products it has been making, then it may be unwise to try to expand its operations there by hiring local workers experienced in making premium-grade products. Such workers will be prone to be overdiligent in what they do, thereby slowing the pace of production and raising unit costs. To keep costs down, it may be necessary to build the sub-premium products somewhere else, where workers do not have such backgrounds and are less obsessed with the quality of what they do. (This point was inspired by the discussion of the Gar Wood boat-building company in Selznick, 1957, and is a spoiler for the discussion of corporate culture in Section 10.11.)

It should be noted here that overzealous commitment to quality may be the fault of those who decide on product specifications rather than the line workers who build the products. A telling example of this, that I recall from an article in the UK motoring journal, *Car Magazine*, in the early 1990s, concerns the attitudes of different vehicle manufacturers toward providing "under the skin" quality: Toyota did not get its workers to paint the steel seat frames of its luxury Lexus LS400, since owners would not observe whether or not the seat frames had been painted, and there was no need, in that context, to paint the steel to limit corrosion; by contrast, Citroen wasted money by painting the seat frames on its lowly AX hatchback.

In some cases, such as when fielding queries from colleagues or external clients, the problem of experience-driven overservicing is a consequence of workers not knowing what their clients need from them and lacking skills in extracting details of the latter's goals and knowledge of the area in question before trying to serve them. The human tendency toward "natural pedagogy" (Csibra and Gergely, 2011) may thus kick in, with a far wider range of advice being offered than is necessary because the expert has seen the diverse challenges that can befall people in this area and is keen to help the other party avoid them.

But there is potential for other underlying psychological drivers to be at work here. The expert could simply get a buzz from "showing off" his or her expertise or may spend too long reiterating and reinforcing key messages to a particular client due to having trouble discerning whether the client has absorbed what he or she has been saying. Overinvestment of time on tasks can also be a form of obsessive–compulsive behavior that is driven by anxiety and ignorance of how rival workers perform in similar roles. Consider, for example, professors who end up with very poor productivity as researchers due to chewing up much of their time in accumulating and managing teaching resources that "might come in handy one day" and freshening up their lecture presentations every year in ways that do nothing for their teaching evaluations or the attainments of their students. Though such professors may complain about how time-consuming teaching preparation is, it may also be a means of keeping them away from thinking about what research they might do if they had more time, and all the challenges and potential blows to their self-esteem that such research could entail.

10.7   The Receding Managerial Limit

In her *Theory of the Growth of the Firm*, Edith Penrose (1959) gives center stage to learning by managers as the key determinant of the sustainable pace at which firms can grow and enjoy economies that come from being bigger. At any time, a team of managers has finite attentive capacity. Hence, if attention is given to new projects at the expense of existing activities, productivity levels of the latter could fall due to shocks not being adequately addressed or entropic organizational processes being left unchecked. New projects may require attention to be given to the process of hiring new staff, inducting them and ensuring that they work effectively in teams. Rushing this process can hold down productivity due to managers not yet having the "know-who" needed to allocate roles effectively or appreciate which staff member needs which kind of mentoring. Indeed, if many new staff are taken on simultaneously, managers may initially have trouble even putting names to faces. Moreover, managerial attention is also likely to be consumed by "teething troubles" with new projects that involve innovative methods and/or products or diversification into unfamiliar territory. To "debug" these unanticipated problems, managers often need to oversee or coordinate attempts at problem diagnosis, followed by experiments with new operating routines until a set of routines is arrived at that seems satisfactory as a means for meeting performance targets.

We should also be mindful of the demands placed on the attention of managers by the challenges of having to close or sell off parts of their business whose profitability they have not been able to sustain, and by the need to address succession problems when staff retire or when key, hard-to-replace staff resign. As Chandler (1977) emphasizes, one of the things that facilitated the emergence of giant firms from the last few decades of the nineteenth century onward was the creation of career development systems to ensure that succession problems could be avoided via a steady stream of promotions up the various layers of their organizational hierarchies. Using internal labor markets and a "grow your own" policy that begins with the organization's management training program for new recruits is a way for managers to sidestep the attention-related costs and risks that go with recruiting staff from other organizations and integrating them into existing teams. However, this comes at the cost of limiting the inflow of potentially useful fresh perspectives that managers could get by hiring staff from other organizations (cf. Loasby, 1983).

In the long run, however, the capacity of a management team normally grows as problems with new projects and personnel get addressed and business can then be left much more to run "normally" via tried-and-tested routines, with more being left to subordinate layers. Penrose therefore writes of a "receding managerial limit" to the growth of the firm: today, managers may be flat out overseeing long-established activities and trying to get recently established ones to run smoothly, but before long they will have spare attention to give to bringing more resources and activities into their realms.

There is scope for management teams to grow their organizations at a faster pace by taking over other organizations that are already well established in the area of interest, rather than through hiring new staff and acquiring new premises and equipment. However, corporate mergers and acquisitions have a long history of turning out to be, as Meeks (1977) put it, "disappointing marriages," in contrast to the rosy promises issued by their proponents. This should not be a surprise, for integration may entail merging incompatible operating systems and mindsets, with turf-guarding activities by those who fear they will lose territory and influence as a result of attempts to achieve economies of scope by sharing product inputs in a way that involves "rationalization" at their division's expense.

The complexity and uncertainty that entrepreneurs and managerial teams face when trying to grow their businesses make it hard for them to know how rapidly they can attempt to grow without getting into difficulties. This can result in them generating jerky or cyclical growth trajectories for their organizations even in the absence of macroeconomic instability (see Earl, 1984, pp. 12–16, 69–72). Some growth proves unexpectedly easy, sometimes leading to euphoric expansion that turns out to be unsustainable. Some projects prove unexpectedly difficult to implement, in some cases leading to unwarranted loss of confidence and overly hesitant subsequent expansion. In some case, attention and other resources then get diverted from more profitable uses due to senior executives and other managers falling prey to sunk cost bias on finding bewildering problems with a major investment in new territory that they had mistakenly construed as similar to their firm's usual areas of business. Learning about what growth can be handled successfully will be difficult where corporate growth involves a succession of novel experiences rather than merely "rolling out" clones of what has been implemented previously. But even where lessons might be learned, the way that managers view their firm may prevent them from properly understanding how previous setbacks arose. As Loasby (1983) reminds us, calling in consultants can counteract this, if they construct the world differently.

10.8 Managerial Authority and Worker Docility

As we move from Penrose's neo-Marshallian view of the firm to the "Carnegie" perspective, it is important to be mindful of the significance of Barnard's (1938) book

The Functions of the Executive for how Herbert Simon viewed the functioning of organizations. A key issue in Barnard's book is the nature of managerial authority, which, like the ability of a teacher to control his or her classroom, is a prerequisite for being able to lead others to do what one wants them to do. The problem is that authority does not come automatically with the role of manager or teacher; rather, it is granted by the manager's subordinates and the teacher's pupils. If subordinates do not respect their boss, they can choose to act in ways that are contrary to what their boss needs them to do. When subordinates fail to do what is being asked of them, the manager is often the one who will need to change his or her operating system first if productivity is to increase. There are limits to the punishment that a manager can apply for insubordination: obviously, making an example of recalcitrant workers by flogging them is ruled out these days, but even three centuries ago, when a ship's captain could order such a punishment, it could backfire completely and result in a mutiny if applied too frequently. Modern-day managers who are battling against game-playing, disrespectful workers are prone to discover that the latter have studied the rules and have ensured that the extent of their insubordination is not so bad as to provide enough of a basis for their dismissal. Even where workers have crossed that line, their dismissal will not be without costs to the boss who dares to dismiss them.

It is this issue that underpinned Simon's (1951) interest in the nature of the contracts by which workers are hired (see Section 10.3). Contractual flexibility is desirable in a world of bounded rationality and surprises, but workers may abuse it and may also give their bosses problems by failing to comply with what they are formally required to do. Hence, for Simon, following Barnard, a key challenge for a manager is to figure out how to earn authority and, with it, a docile workforce whose members will identify with the espoused goals of the organization and will operate altruistically and/or collegially rather than always operating with a self-serving mentality. Insofar as Veblen (1914) was right to ascribe an "instinct of workmanship" as part of human nature, and insofar as jobs are of a kind that are intrinsically interesting to do and serve as means of meeting a need for achievement, docility may not be hard to achieve. But it will be an uphill battle where workers have a lazier disposition, jobs are boring and/ or unpleasant and where some workers decide they can meet their need for achievement by playing games and succeeding in thwarting the manager's best efforts.

An excellent illustration of how managers can struggle to win authority is provided by Alvin Gouldner's (1954) classic ethnographic study of what happened in a gypsum mine when a new manager was appointed. Prior to the new manager's arrival, the operating system at this workplace was quite informal: there was a culture of working hard but a very casual approach to issues of health and safety. The new manager was horrified to observe the latter and he sought to replace the norms that the workers had evolved with a formal set of policies and procedures. This was viewed by the workers as a heavy-handed imposition and their compliance was poor. But bringing in additional supervisors to try for force compliance was not the way to get the desired result. It made the new regime seem even more heavy-handed and distrustful of the workers. A more gradualist, consultative approach, that better engaged the workers via examples of win-win improvements that had been achieved elsewhere in rather similar contexts, would probably have helped the manager win authority rapidly and saved him a lot of time: getting high productivity entails developing and maintaining relationships, and it cannot be achieved simply by drafting rules and hiring more supervisors (cf. Huising and Silbey, 2018). Moreover, if workers feel their bosses do not trust them, their natural response is not necessarily going to be to act in a way that will earn trust; rather, if they believe their way of operating has been reasonable, their response to the boss's challenge to it may be to act in ways that signal they are not willing to legitimize the boss's authority role.

Workers will be more likely to be docile, altruistic and collegial if they fear the demise of the organization that employs them and are unable to see easy ways of finding alternative employment. However, such fears can often seem absent in the Carnegie trio's behavioral view of the firm. To understand why this is so, two things need to be appreciated.

One is the extent to which March and Simon were not merely interested in firms that had to survive the test of market viability; they were also trying to understand organizations such as police departments, public service entities and public-sector universities that were funded wholly or in large part by governments granting them budgets to spend rather than by revenues from selling products and providing services.

The other is that March and Simon's classic contributions on organizations were made prior to the rise of strategy-focused management research and education, that was followed by increasing efforts to run budget-based organizations in more "businesslike" ways. Much of this was a result of management consulting firms (most notably McKinsey) and business school academics realizing that organizations could generate stronger internal competition, along with a clearer idea of production costs for each of their outputs, by adopting an organizational structure of the kind that Williamson (1970) labeled as an "M-form," i.e., by creating divisions (rather like miniature firms within a firm) on the basis of product categories or according to where production occurred. This view rejected the ideas that organizational efficiency would be best pursued via a structure based on specialized departmental functions such as human resources, finance, research and development, production and marketing (which Williamson labeled as a "U-form" structure to reflect the consolidation of particular functions into departmental units). The idea was that if a firm has a function-based structure, departments will blame each other for poor overall performance, for if decisions are taken to axe some areas of business, there will still be a need for their particular function to serve those areas that remain and any that are added. By contrast, staff in each division of a firm with an M-form structure have a stronger incentive to cooperate as they could all lose their jobs if their division is closed. (Restructuring into an M-form is not as straightforward to implement as it might first seem, particularly due to the presence of complex synergy links or economies of scope between products or between operations at different locations: see Earl, 1984, ch. 9; Kay, 1984, ch. 6 and 1997, ch. 12.) The next step, to which Williamsons (1975, 1985) also provided theoretical impetus, was to ramp up the pressure of competition via the threat that activities could be outsourced to specialized external suppliers if costs of having them supplied internally could not be reduced to comparable levels.

After being applied in firms, particularly from the mid-1960s onward, these ideas were applied from the early 1980s to organizations such as universities and public health systems. Organizational restructuring along such lines essentially entailed a "divide and rule" strategy based around creating a "funder–provider split" in which the organization's head office (the "funder") decided which product divisions (the service "providers") would receive funds or be sold off or closed down on the basis of their KPIs. This business-school view that organizations could be run in a more "rational" manner proved attractive to those who adopted the neoliberal/neoconservative way of thinking that came to dominate politically in many countries from the late 1970s or early 1980s. What followed were widespread attempts to increase the pressure of market competition by deregulating markets and privatizing public sector providers of goods and services (see Earl, 2002, pp. 84–87, for a list of the core assumptions and operating rules of this policy philosophy; for critical analysis of it, see Saul, 1993).

With all this lying in the future, it is not surprising that March and Simon (1958) presented a view of organizations as places in which life did not have to center on ever-present existential threats, and where there could be a tendency (which we would nowadays call "sunk cost bias") toward "persistence" with problematic projects long after it should have been clear that they needed to be abandoned. This rather cozy view of organizational life carries through into Cyert and March's (1963) *Behavioral Theory of the Firm*. Instead of having to be future-focused and constantly under pressures to achieve cost reductions, there was considerable scope for members of organizations to "muddle through" by operating in a passive, reactive manner. Indeed, it can be argued that the Carnegie trio's work provided the impetus for business school to concentrate on developing many of the tools of strategic management that were applied in subsequent decades to counter the antirational picture of how firms and other organizations could function. (A key early contribution of this kind, where the departure from Cyert and March is emphasized, is the work of Ansoff, 1965, who had recently joined the Carnegie faculty after working at the Lockheed Aircraft Corporation.)

It can be tempting to conclude that much higher levels of X-inefficiency (relative to contemporary best practice) would have been widespread in firms in the decades before Leibenstein coined the term, than in firms today. But we need to be mindful of the changes in the distribution of effort and reward between then and now. The former era may indeed have been one in which lower-tier bureaucrats lived the kind of internally focused, not client-focused, life aptly satirized by the New Zealand playwright and TV screenwriter Roger Hall as one of "gliding on." (The first episode of the TV series that Hall wrote under this title is available at nzonscreen.com/title/gliding-on-1981/overview.) In busier moments, their actions could be generated by the kind of "garbage can" process set out by Cohen et al. (1972) (see Section 6.5). In budget-based organizations, much work was being done without well-defined objectives and KPIs to meet, with, for example, detectives and professors being left to get on with their jobs as they saw them. Back then, organizational employees frequently got by without any mission statements, team-building "retreats," corporate plans or handbooks of policies and procedures. But they may have had more time to get on doing what they thought they were employed to do, due to having to spend less time in meeting aimed at developing formal plans and policies, or in compiling reports on what they had achieved, to satisfy demands from higher officials whose salaries were paid on the expectation that they would extract more efficiency and thereby save money. (Roger Hall went on to satirize the latter world, too, in the 1990s TV series *Market Forces*, latterly available on Amazon Prime.)

10.9 Stakeholder Rivalry and Cooperation

Having accepted that uncertainty and complexity make it impossible to know how to maximize returns for shareholders, Cyert and March modeled firms in terms of Simon's satisficing perspective. They portray top-tier managers as setting multiple aspirations as means to try to ensure that their firms stay in business in the long run and offer returns good enough to prevent a shareholder revolt or a hostile takeover raid. These aspirations can take a variety of forms, both generic – such as targets for the rate of return on capital, rate of growth of assets, market share, acceptable debt–equity ratios and acceptable ratios of inventory to daily sales and/or production – through to those that relate to, say, the rate of rollout of new products by a particular division or the opening of new retail outlets. These goals provide a means for assessing performance and serve as foci for action. Where firms are divided (as per the "M-form" model) into "profit centers" akin to mini-firms, head office can function as an internal capital market by examining divisional performance in relation to such targets.

This satisficing, multiple objectives view of what the firm is striving to achieve was enough to make Cyert and March's (1963) *Behavioral Theory of the Firm* by far the most radical among several "new theories of the firm" that appeared in the late 1950s or early 1960s and became standard fare for undergraduate students in industrial economics until the early 1980s. Unlike Cyert and March, other authors kept the idea that something was being maximized but used the presence of imperfect capital and product markets as a source of opportunities for managers to maximize something other than profits, such as the firm's sales revenue (Baumol, 1959), rate of growth (Marris, 1964) or the utility that managers could get from spending on "pet projects" and making the most of their expense accounts and other perquisites such as opportunities to spend on lavish corporate offices, luxury cars, corporate jets, etc. (Williamson, 1964).

These contributions were belated theoretical sequels to empirical work from the 1930s where it had been argued that the rise of large joint-stock companies meant that, in contrast to family-owned, family-operated firms, owners delegated control of operations to salaried managers (Berle and Means, 1932). Dispersed shareholdings limited the risk to managers that they would have to face takeover raiders if they failed to maximize profits, while imperfect product markets were assumed to mean that supernormal profits were potentially available for shareholders but instead could be sacrificed by managers in pursuit of other objectives. However, except for Cyert and March's *Behavioral Theory*, the "new" theories all portrayed the managers as being able to run their firms in a cost-minimizing manner: ordinary workers were not seen as beneficiaries of the discretion that the market imperfections afforded to managers. It was "as if" the managers had complete authority over the workers. (For a more detailed exploration of the methodological aspects of these contributions, see Loasby, 1989, ch. 7.)

There was an obvious policy lesson in such models: if managerial remuneration packages were designed so as to align managerial and shareholder interest by giving managers carefully design stock options and profit-related bonuses, then managers would try to maximize profits. With that lesson learned and applied, these models no longer seemed to have a role in explaining corporate behavior and they faded from the industrial economics curriculum. With the behavioral theory of the firm viewed as just one of this set of theories, it shared their fate. This was despite the view of decision-making on which it was based remaining relevant whatever the incentive structure under which managers operated.

10.9.1   Subgoals

Except for Cyert and March's contribution, the theories just referred to are best described as "managerial" rather than "behavioral" theories of the firm though their proponents were all trying to come up with models that presented a more realistic view of managerial behavior. The original 1963 edition of *A Behavioral Theory of the Firm* included a chapter by Williamson (a doctoral student of Cyert and Simon) that was essentially a cut-down version of his (1964) PhD-based book on utility-maximizing managerial behavior. However, it sat uneasily with the rest of the book and was removed in the second edition (Cyert and March, 1992). But Cyert and March did not merely replace *any* kind of optimization with a rule-based, satisficing model of decision-making in respect of multiple firm-level goals; they also broke new ground in economics by offering a vision of the firm centered on the pursuit of "subgoals" by all of what are nowadays referred to as the organization's "stakeholders." In other words, the behavioral theory of the firm is not just about managers versus shareholders: *anyone* with a stake in how the firm performs is to be viewed as part of the firm and as a rival claimant to other parties involved with it. Moreover, members of any class of stakeholders, including managers, are not presumed to share the same subgoals.

Cyert and March's focus on subgoal pursuit is a logical extension of Simon's earlier focus on the significance of vaguely specified employment contracts and the implications of Barnard's view that, to get things done, managers would need to win their authority from their subordinates: if managers fail to cultivate their authority effectively, they increase the risk that those whom they supervise will pursue personal subgoals rather than doing their best to help the managers deliver acceptable outcomes in terms of their organizational unit's KPIs and hence assist with the attainment of the organization's overall targets. But it is not just employment contracts – including those of managers at various levels and in rival departments or divisions – that entail fuzzy relationships and thereby permit the pursuit of subgoals. Relationships with external stakeholders, such as customers, supplier of inputs, bankers, shareholders and the wider community, are also fuzzy.

Each stakeholder seeks to get benefits by contributing to the pool of resources that makes the organization's output possible. Workers and managers contribute their time and effort. Depending on their roles, they may also incur psychic costs of work, such as stress, burnout and feelings of anxiety and frustration associated with not being in control. In return, they receive remuneration, along with satisfaction from any sense of achievement, belonging and control that they get from their work and being part of the organization in question. Shareholders and other providers of finance receive dividends or interest payments in return for incurring financial risks. Strategic alliance partners and other entities that have relationships with the firm or organization in question commit resources to activities whose returns depend to some degree on the effort and other resources provided by other stakeholders. Customers provide revenue and, perhaps, feedback and goodwill or loyalty in return for receiving output. The wider community may provide infrastructure and incur the costs of negative externalities such as environmental pollution but may benefit from the multiplier effects that the firm or organization has on the external economy via its local spending on inputs, the spending of its employees and its impact on the attractiveness of the area as a location for other businesses.

10.9.2   Organizations as Common-Pool Resources

It is easy to see scope for disaster if we view an organization's stakeholders with a focus on them each trying to capture as much of the organization's output for themselves while minimizing their inputs. Viewed thus, the pool of resources that the stakeholder provide may appear to be at risk of suffering a fate akin to that of a common-pool resource such as a fishery that falls prey to overfishing because there are no property rights to restrict how much anyone takes from it. Wherever a stakeholder's relationship with an organization is not spelled out in full detail in a readily enforceable manner, there is scope for self-serving behavior that has negative impacts on other stakeholders. Where employment contracts specify remuneration in a way that is not tightly related to output, workers can try to take a leisurely and inattentive approach to their tasks, leading to poor productivity and to quality levels that customers may find annoyingly low. But organizational rot can arise at higher levels, too: as Williamson (1964) recognized, managers have scope for abusing their expense accounts for personal benefit and for diverting investment resources into "pet projects" rather than supporting proposals that would be more consistent with the firm's stated objectives. They may also find it convenient to turn a blind eye to environmental issues and pile demands on their workforces while holding down pay and dividends in order to pay themselves more. In the case of government bureaucracies, the plundering of public resources could entail tendencies of officials to treat their jobs as sinecure. Getting them to do anything may require bribery, and when allocating resources, they may act in a nepotistic manner. These kinds of behavior are not desirable ingredients in a recipe for long-term prosperity or personal and environmental well-being.

Although the operations and long-run fates of some organizations are indeed redolent of a "tragedy of the commons," what is normally going on is something more subtle than simpleminded self-serving behavior. Cyert and March invite us to view the firm as an incompletely specified coalition of interest groups in which the various players recognize that although their interests differ, they run the risk of becoming unable to meet their personal goals if they fail to moderate their claims and extend their cooperation enough to help others to meet their respective goals. Being greedy and uncooperative is risky as a member of an organizational coalition, for other stakeholders may respond by reducing their inputs or by exiting the coalition altogether, with their replacements coming at greater cost or with fewer skills. To a degree, stakeholders in an organization thus stand or fall together. The trouble is, they cannot be sure how far they can push their luck when bargaining over returns to becoming or continuing to be a member of that coalition.

Negotiations over returns to membership of an organizational coalition inevitably entail opportunity costs for those involved. At the very least, such negotiations divert attention from undertaking other activities. In some cases, continuing to engage in negotiations precludes being able to enjoy returns to membership of the organization: for example, if workers go on strike in the pursuit of better pay, they lose pay at the current rate and output is lost. Such costs provide a good reason to accept a deal if it seems to offer a sufficiently good chance of meeting one's aspirations, so long as one lacks good reasons to believe that a better deal can be struck. However, before reaching that point, it may seem worthwhile to incur the costs of negotiating, after setting a much more demanding "gambit price" rather than simply offering a "take it or leave it" deal that is consistent with one's aspirations: not only is there the possibility that the other party may accept a deal that offers more than the minimum that one would accept (the latter is often referred to as one's "transfer earnings"), but also, as Shackle (1949) emphasized in his analysis of bargaining, there is the chance to signal, via one's rate of "climb down," how determinedly one will be willing to bargain on future occasions.

10.9.3   Treaties and Alliances

This coalition-based view of the nature of an organization can be seen as working at several levels and it can be instructive to think of a firm in terms of a "nexus of treaties" perspective (cf. Aoki et al., 1990) rather than as a single coalition of agents who are willing to participate despite their differences. Such a nexus can include relationships both inside the legal boundaries of the firm and between the firm in question and other firms, such as those involved in its supply chain or those with which it has a strategic alliance, interlocking shareholdings or overlapping directorships (see Blois, 1972; Richardson, 1972). However, the "treaties" concept tends to make one think of formal contracts, whereas we also need to keep in mind informal relationships between individuals, teams and/or organizations that often have an obligational aspect akin to an implicit contract about the kind of behavior that parties expect from each other. In other words, as with goodwill relationships between customers and suppliers, relationships within and between firms may be of an unwritten but sometimes spoken form that amounts to promising that "I'll keep supporting you if you keep supporting me and, in the long term, do so at least as effectively as a competent alternative source would."

Within a large organization, policies are often worked out and/or agreed upon by departmental or interdepartmental committees whose members' interests clash. Committee decisions may entail a voting process in which outcomes are shaped by the relative sizes of sub-coalitions. Sometimes, being a member of a coalition requires one to vote in favor of something that goes against some of one's own interests in order to ensure that fellow coalition members can meet their interests and thereby ensure that the coalition does not fall apart. This is an investment for future meetings when the latter will reciprocate. As in war and diplomacy between nations, what matters is not winning every battle but winning a set of battles that, taken together, leave one satisfied that one's aspirations have been met. The same applies at the level of treaties between companies – i.e., for the successions of deals that a firm does with its strategic alliance partners (see Kay, 1997, ch. 10).

Viewing organizations with a focus on coalitions, negotiations and treaties brings out the political dimension of their operations. With resource allocation based on decision rules and bargaining rather than well-informed estimates of marginal costs and returns, organizational politics can have a profound impact on organizational productivity growth. Those who advocate particular choices today may have an incentive to pursue short-term benefits rather than focusing on the more distant future: for example, they may expect to have retired or moved on by the time problems become evident. Such problems in principle could damage the reputations of those who are known to have advocated the projects in question, but in practice they may end up being blamed on those who were assigned the task of administering them. In the long run, bargaining processes can determine the extent to which profits are available to invest in productivity-enhancing technologies or (as will be explored further in Section 11.12 in the next chapter) whether bold new experiments will be embarked upon instead of incremental extensions to, and/or upgrades of, existing activities.

With everyone associated with an organization potentially focusing on pursuing their personal goals, any sense that the decision rules according to which the organization runs lack firm foundations or are being applied in ways that unfairly benefit others is likely to lead to reflection on whether an alternative set might be used that better favored one's own interests. Such concerns also have considerable potential to affect the productivity of an organization. For one thing, there is the potential for everyday "office politics" to harm productivity by diverting attention from the tasks at hand, to workplace relativities. There is also scope for perceptions about the distribution of payoffs between rival stakeholder groups to have an impact on attitudes and behavior. For example, whether workers respond to management requests by offering (to use terms from Williamson, 1975, 1985) "consummate cooperation" or merely complying in a "perfunctory" manner may depend on the extent to which they view the distribution of returns between bosses and workers as fair. In other words, competitive success may require more than just the capacity to understand what will appeal to customers, develop procedurally or ecologically rational operating routines and assemble an appropriate set of capabilities. If the political climate in an organization is toxic, great products may fail to be offered, routines may be flouted and capabilities may be wasted (see further Lazonick, 1990, 1991).

10.9.4   *Voltaire's Bastards*

Given all this, it is not hard to see why the U-form corporate structure fell out of favor and why the M-form has been enthusiastically advocated and adopted. In a U-form structure, there are obvious dangers that strategic decision-making will be highly politicized if it is left to, or based purely on advice from, a committee that consists of representatives from each of the function-centered divisions. A way of trying to avoid this is to allow functional representations merely to be made to a chief executive officer (CEO) who then makes significant decisions single-handedly or as part of a governing board that otherwise consists of nonexecutive directors elected to represent shareholder interests. However, the CEO's bounded rationality and finite attentive capacity can then prove a constraint on figuring out what to make of the claims being made by functional representatives as they lobby for resources and react to proposals with an eye to the implications for their functional areas. It could prove very difficult for a CEO to get to the bottom of what has been going on if the rival functional representatives make conflicting claims. Moreover, the CEO's assessment of these claims is unlikely to be independent of his or her past area of expertise.

By contrast, the M-form structure reduces cognitive load on the CEO. Dividing the firm into a set of, in effect, subsidiary firms that each report to head office in terms of identical sets of KPIs makes it possible to make comparisons between different activity areas in a much simpler way. The CEO can also take advice from a team of strategic planners who can be ruthlessly dispassionate, since they do not have operational empires that they are trying to grow or need to defend. The emotional detachment of strategists in large corporations is further facilitated by having them work in a corporate head office building located well away from the operating divisions that their choices affect.

Tendencies for the backgrounds of strategists and CEOs to bias decisions in particular directions are potentially attenuated in organizations with M-form structures by appointing them from other sectors so that they will apply more generic business skills. So, for example, we may see corporate hi-fliers who begin their careers in major accounting firms, take an MBA and eventually move from running a car company to running a ministry of defense (cf. the career of Robert McNamara, discussed in Saul, 1993) or have a career that, after tertiary education at a military academy and in law, entails running, successively, a mining company, a brewery, a national airline and retail chains (cf. the career of the late Australian businessman James Strong). This, of course, has the downside that those who are parachuted into areas in which they lack specific experience of the kind that is emphasized in the Penrose's neo-Marshallian view of the firm may make dysfunctional choices due to ignorance despite their emotional detachment and repertoires of rules that were supposed to enable them to be rational decision-makers. The title of John Ralston Saul's (1993) book *Voltaire's Bastards* implicitly acknowledges this issue and invites us to consider whether the authority granted to such leaders is legitimate.

10.10   Organizational Slack and Its Uptake

The inherent uncertainty about what rival stakeholders will be willing to accept may mean that some or all the stakeholders involved in an organizational bargaining process end up with a deal that offers a prospective return in excess of the minimum that they require in order not to reduce their contributions or exit the organization altogether. In such situations, Cyert and March see "organizational slack" as an unintended by-product of the conclusion of negotiations: it is the difference between the sum of returns that coalition members are receiving and the sum of the minimum returns they are prepared to accept in order to be willing to remain part of the coalition. Like strategically chosen buffers and reserves, organizational slack makes a coalition more resilient than it otherwise would be in the face of shocks. But organizational slack exists purely because of uncertainty: the fact that it existed can only be confirmed in a later negotiation phase when it becomes apparent that some coalition members are prepared to make sacrifices in order to continue to enjoy benefits from membership of the coalition.

To appreciate the nature and significance of organizational slack, consider a situation in which an organization suffers an external shock that results in some stakeholders being unable to meet their aspirations. For example, a rise in input prices may eat into a firm's profit margins, thereby limiting what will be available for managers to spend on "pet projects" and bonuses for themselves if they leave output, prices and dividend payments unchanged. Suppose the managers now opt to risk annoying the firm's customers, by raising prices, and/or shareholders, by pruning dividends. To the extent that customers continue to buy despite the increased prices, they are enjoying less consumer surplus than before, and the managers may regret not previously having taken the risk of increasing prices. Likewise, they may discover that cutting dividends does not result in their jobs being jeopardized due to shareholders selling the firm's shares to takeover raiders: had the managers known that this would be the case, they would have reduced dividends previously. Alternatively, the managers might opt to cut wages of production line workers, something they would not have done while they were meeting their aspirations. It may turn out that they can get away with this, but there is the risk of workers defecting to other organizations or going on strike.

If such strategies leave the membership of the coalition unchanged, there was enough organizational slack to absorb completely the shock of the input price increase: the size of the "pie" of net returns to coalition membership has been reduced and the relative slices received by the various stakeholder groups have changed, but all stakeholders are continuing to meet their aspirations. Some stakeholder groups may still be enjoying "slack payments" in excess of their transfer earnings.

Such outcomes are more likely in situations where an external shock comes after a period in which things have been going well for the organization and aspirations have lagged way behind attainments, the "slack payments" having not yet been factored into what their recipients normally expect they ought to receive. It may also be easier to get a particular group of stakeholders to accept less in situations where what is available to them if they try to switch to other organizations has also fallen.

In other situations, however, there may not be enough organizational slack to absorb an external shock completely – either in absolute terms or in relation to the strategy that the managers experimented with to address the problem. Unfortunately, managers may not be able to reverse their experiments if they discover that slack did not exist to a sufficient degree in areas where they thought it might exist. For example, if managers try to deal with competitive pressures by refusing to grant pay increases, some workers may leave, and the same may happen if the managers then try to extract more output from the remainder. It may not be possible to rehire those who quit or to find equivalent replacements by reversing these policies. After forming relationships with other organizations, former employees may discover just how much better they could have been doing if they had bailed out much earlier; they may now resent having been taken for granted by the organizations to which they had given their loyalty. (The same may be true where disgruntled customers take their business elsewhere.) Perhaps the managers would have been able to capture the resources they sought if, say, they had instead cut shareholder dividends, but that, too, could have misfired. Even where many organizations face similar problems, external reference standards may fail to change because others seem not to have the same afflictions.

Viewing organizations and the uptake of organizational slack in this way seems to point to a less dynamic view of productivity than that which emerges when we see problem-solving activities as a driver of the growth of knowledge. If managers suspect that organizational slack may exist, they may view experiments in trying to renegotiate the distribution of returns among stakeholders as an alternative to experimentation with new ways of operating as a means of trying to address shocks. If the managers' hunches are correct, docile workforces, apathetic shareholders and undemanding customers may bear the costs of an external shock by accepting, respectively, stagnant wages, stagnant dividends and/or share values, and products that are falling behind those offered by competitors in terms of quality and/or innovation – at least, until their patience is exhausted.

An organization whose managers deal with an increasingly tough competitive environment by taking up slack that had accumulated when times were easier is likely to have trouble catching up with more dynamic rivals when the supply of slack is exhausted: unlike its rival, it is probably failing to develop routines (for example, regular performance reviews) for identifying areas where it could be improving its performance and developing routings for doing the latter. Note also that the exhaustion of organizational slack can occur via a cascading process. For example, if managers continue to push their luck without appreciating that their workers have had enough of putting up with slow wage growth or falling real wages, the result may be a prolonged strike. The disruption of supplies that this causes may, in turn, be so severe that it leads to the exit of long-established customers, who otherwise might have continued buying in ignorance of better deals they could have obtained elsewhere.

10.11   Corporate Culture and Openness to Criticism

The probability of needlessly poor productivity is increased if there is no shared sense of purpose or of how things are normally done in the organization of which one is a member, for everyone then has to work out their own ways of dealing with colleagues. Colleagues who know each other well may use that knowledge (as per Heiner, 1983) to predict each other's behavior as they try to pursue conflicting subgoals, whereas there will be major scope for coordination failures during interactions with unfamiliar colleagues.

Subgoal pursuit, blunders and confusion may be attenuated, and the chances of adhering to the strategy that an organization's leaders are trying to pursue will be increased, if members of the organization employ a shared system of go-to assumptions, values and operating rules that happen – or have been designed – to ensure they respond to decision cues in ways that align with the intended strategy. A shared system of this kind constitutes a "corporate culture," and it nudges behavior in the preferred direction by limiting the need for members of the organization to figure out their own rules for how to operate when working there. Employees may pick up the operating culture of their organization via lessons in "How we operate here" or more subconsciously via the kinds of inferential process envisaged in Hayek's *Sensory Order*. To the extent that individuals build similar operating models and then respond to decision cues in ways consistent with the rest of the corporate culture, the chances of everyone ending up roughly "on the same page" and, thereby, of successful coordination can be increased (cf. Kelly's commonality and sociality corollaries). Some of the implicit values that members of an organization have picked up as part of its corporate culture may only kick in as restraints, rather like moral norms, when people realize that they or their colleagues are considering possible courses of action that conflict with their unwritten views of themselves as members of the organization and/or their firm's strategy; indeed, for much of the time, they may not even be conscious of some of the means they use to reach particular goals and a lot of the time could be thought of as being on "autopilot."

The management training programs that many major corporations invest in can be viewed in this context as akin to installing their corporate operating systems at an accelerated pace in the minds of their graduate recruits. (A more cynical characterization would be that these programs brainwash the recruits into "company men or women.") Investments in grand buildings and facilities (such as those of "elite" universities) are also a way of trying to ensure that staff identify with high organizational expectations and operate accordingly. But attempts to change employee mindsets in ways aimed at improving productivity can also be made on a much smaller scale.

As an example of the latter, consider some simple changes introduced at what is now one of the largest UK musical instrument retailers, Anderton's Music Co., when it dramatically upscaled its operations and moved away from its roots as a rather informal high-street store. A goal of this upscaling was to win more business by appealing to affluent hobbyist musicians who expected professional standards of service. From that point, staff wore uniforms and took their lunch and coffee breaks in a dedicated back room rather than at service counters (Anderton, 2020). Such changes were means of ensuring that staff would identify with the store's mission (rather than merely being readily identifiable as staff) and be focused on the needs of customers; they would be less likely to be confused with, and waste time chatting to, those who merely saw the store as somewhere to hang out. Without thinking ahead and making these changes, Anderton's could have failed to engage those who had a lot more money to spend than their previous local customer base.

The idea that shared systems of rules, values and assumptions can affect efficiency can be traced back at least as far as the work of March and Simon (1958) and Selznick (1957), with the latter making it a key part of his analysis of the role of leaders in shaping the ways in which firms operate and the enduring impact that a particular leader can have. However, corporate culture did not blossom explicitly as a concept until the 1980s (influential sources include Smircich, 1983; Schein, 1984; Kilmann et al., 1985; Lorsch, 1986; Camerer and Vepsalainen, 1988; Green, 1988; Kreps, 1990), around the time that managers in the West were waking up to the different operating systems that Japanese firms used and wondering about whether and how they might be taken up in the West. Japanese firms wondered about this, too, and, in 1984, Toyota and GM commenced a collaboration called NUMMI at an existing GM plant in Fremont, California, that badly needed turning around. The partnership lasted for a quarter of a century, as a means for both firms to find answers, with Toyota going through a "learning by doing" process as it introduced its system, while a few GM managers watched what happened (see Gomes-Casseres, 2009). (After the venture ended, the plant was acquired by Tesla.) However, Japanese vehicle manufacturers (like their Korean counterparts in more recent decades) deliberately did not set up their US "transplant" factories anywhere near Detroit or other established car-making cities in the United States: by building on greenfield sites further south and recruiting and training workers locally, they had a bigger chance of ensuring that their recruits would absorb *their* operating systems, untainted by those of the US firms, and hence be able to achieve better quality standards, a faster pace of production and good labor relations.

Despite the involvement of Colin Camerer, one of the key figures in modern behavioral economics, in the takeoff of the corporate culture idea, it remains rather underused within behavioral economics except through the "identity economics" work of Akerlof and Kranton (2000, 2010). However, potential for using behavioral policy tools such as nudges to reshape organizational cultures and thereby enhance workplace performance has been recognized outside economics by management consultants and in the human resource management literature (see Miller et al., 2018). Nudges have also been recognized to have a complementary role alongside bureaucratic rules and corporate culture as means for enabling managers to ensure that frontline workers comply with regulatory policies (see Huising and Silbey, 2018).

10.11.1 Cultural Change in Organizations as a Coevolutionary Process

Organizational cultures change through time, even without conscious efforts by leaders to shape them in particular ways. They get built up, elaborated and eroded by social interaction among the changing population of individuals that comprise the organization, which affect those involved via the processes set out by Hayek in his *Sensory Order*. Cultural change in organizations is a "coevolutionary" process: individuals who join an organization may contribute to its productivity via the behavioral examples they set and by the policies that they design, but the mood and mode of operation of the organization may also "rub off" on them unless they have developed strong core constructs that rule out such changes.

For example, those who join ethically challenged organizations may previously never have had to ask themselves about the ethics of what they were doing. They may gradually absorb the prevailing ethos and then help transmit it to the next generation of recruits. This process may entail a slippery slope whereby naive employees who might elsewhere have picked up, and adhered to, a nonsubstitutable ethical norm instead absorbs the idea that "sometimes you have to make a bit of a trade-off to get things done," with the extent of ethical compromises gradually growing thereafter. Such a perspective has been employed by Augier and March (2008) to understand how mainstream economists, trained to assume that values are always open to being traded off, have ended up increasingly seeing nothing wrong with chasing the rewards that came from being able to display technical prowess via models that became increasingly divorced from reality and incomprehensible to nonspecialists. Augier and March observe *(ibid.*, p. 103) that, via this process, "[l]oss of realism becomes an affordable cost rather than a personal failure."

Of course, effective leaders within a firm should be able to influence their organization's culture rather more than they let it influence them. Productivity potential is likely to be squandered if entrepreneurs and managers focus unduly on installing technologies and the formal aspects of their organizations; they need also to be able to make strategic use of informal tools such as stories, myths, legends, symbols, the language they use, ideologies, rituals and ceremonies to motivate their subordinates to operate in ways consistent with where they want to take their organizations (see further the sources surveyed in Smircich, 1983).

10.11.2 Corporate Cultures in the Context of Industrial and National Cultures

The operating systems of firms are unlikely to be independent of the "ways" in which the industries in which they participate routinely operate. This is not just because the mobility of personnel within an industry is conducive to blending knowledge and what is seen as normal practice but also because organizations will attempt to emulate corporate cultures that appear to confer competitive fitness, and those whose cultures prove dysfunctional will tend to wither. Thus, for example, if a "student-centered" culture works as a means for meeting KPIs, universities that operate as if students are only tolerated as a means of paying for research do so at their peril; likewise, if operating with scant regard for ethics seems to pay off in sectors such as financial services, then financial institutions that have been operating in a more ethical manner may be driven to learn the dirty tricks of their rivals. Corporate leaders who wish to steer their organizations away from industry norms may thus face an uphill battle.

The attempts of corporate leader to enhance productivity by steering the culture of their organization in a particular direction may also be impeded by deeply ingrained aspects of the culture of the country in question. We can get a sense of the problem via remarks made by Graham Spurling, the head of Mitsubishi Australia at a time when concerns were being expressed that Australia could end up squandering its potential and end up like a Latin American "banana republic" due to growing foreign debt and poor productivity growth. Spurling (1985, p. 74) commented that Australia faced "a major attitudinal and motivational problem." Echoing the irony intended in the title of Horne's (1964) book *The Lucky Country*, he then argued that

[t]he concept of Australia as the lucky country is real to the extent that most Australians believe that our economic development is automatically assured by our rich endowment of natural resources and our ability to somehow manage. It is an expectation, or faith, that has little to do with the realities of a post-industrial society. The reality of Australia becoming the poor nation of the Pacific is directly related to the common assumption that it could never happen.

Over three decades later, the lucky country mentality may still be an issue for Australia, with its manufacturing sector having largely been wiped out, as import controls were gradually relaxed, leading to increased dependence on resource exports.

10.11.3 Effects of Corporate Culture on Creative and Critical Thinking

The culture of an organization can play a key role in facilitating productivity growth and guarding against sunk cost bias if it makes frank and fearless constructive criticism something that members of the organization expect to receive and address, and which they are expected to offer in relation to work that colleagues have done or ideas that colleagues are proposing. However, it is not easy to engineer such a culture if it is widely believed that those whom one criticizes are likely to resent being criticized rather than welcome criticism as something that provides an opportunity to do better. This is especially so in relation to upward feedback where the recipient is able to fire or deny promotion to the critic.

We can get a sense of how things can go badly awry in this respect if we reflect on reactions to feedback within universities that market themselves as "student centered" but where teaching staff do not normally provide extensive written feedback that emphasizes the students' mistakes and missed opportunities. Let us consider what is likely to happen if a newly recruited professor provides precisely this sort of feedback.

If the students come to the university from school environments in which they have not experienced criticism, they are likely to be shocked, especially if they have track records as high achievers, if the new professor provides critical feedback on their work. This feedback will clash with their core self-constructs, and its apparent brutality will appear out of order if, as modern fee-paying students, they view education services products like any other product that they buy, where suppliers set out to be nice to them. The professor may construe such students as "millennial snowflakes" who lack resilience and have an unwarranted sense of entitlement. But the professor may also find it difficult to take on board feedback meted out by students who claim that he or she is "unapproachable" and who react poorly to the feedback the professor has slaved long and hard to provide. The students' reactions may seem very strange to the professor, who does not have a self-image as "unapproachable" and who makes available generous consultation opportunities and sees the few students who take up these opportunities as usually being very pleased with the attention they get. To the professor, having to deal with criticism is central to his or her work as a researcher, and it is core to the university experience, something that the students are going to have to get used to. Ideally, the professor would also give more positive comments, where these were warranted, but there is not enough time to do so. Given this, it may seem that, in order to generate acceptable teaching scores, the professor will have to operate as he or she sees most colleagues as operating: dumb down what he or she tries to teach so that there is less of a need to be critical, which will also leave more time to write positive comments. The professor's teaching scores improve as a result of adapting to the institution's teaching and learning culture, but the students are likely to learn less.

So what kinds of systems of rules can be used to promote critical thinking about existing ways of doing things, and about current and proposed projects, without incurring hostility from those on the receiving end? One approach is to put the question of whether a project continues in the hands of those who have not been involved in championing the project, giving its initial go-ahead or working on it. The absence of such involvement should make coolheaded decision-making possible, for it is not the reputations and self-images of the reviewers that suffer if the project is abandoned and the work put into it deemed to have been in vain. This is what the "M-form" organizational structure is supposed to achieve, as are anonymous refereeing processes that are used in academic publishing and in the allocation of scientific research funds.

In smaller organizations, where everyone must work with everyone else, there is the risk that what needs to be said about the shortcomings of a particular project may not be said, for fear of upsetting colleagues and then suffering payback. The provision of anonymous suggestions boxes is one obvious step in the right direction. Change will be easier if review processes focus on lessons that the organization would not have learned if the failed projects had not been started. Keeping minutes of who said what in meetings provides both a means for quelling hindsight bias, thereby encouraging staff to make proposals without fear that, if things go awry, they will be subject to criticism on the basis of issues that no one had raised at the time the go-ahead was given. Such minutes also provide evidence by which effective critics can build their reputations and be taken seriously, due to being able to say, "I told you so!" But more important may be a climate in which the norm is to think in a pluralistic manner, where everyone accepts that no one's decision-making is guaranteed to come out right every time and that there may always be scope for learning from colleagues. For extensions of such thinking, there is much to learn from Pixar Animation cofounder Ed Catmull's (2014) memoir *Creativity, Inc.*, which charts the processes by which Pixar succeeded in ensuring that individual egos and insecurities did not hold sway and prevent Pixar from making changes that were necessary if it were to avoid squandering its creative potential.

Where one group within an organization has come to dominate, it is often the case that any major kind of change is difficult to achieve without the use of external agents of change, such as consultants or managers hired from other organizations. But even these agents may end up finding that their ideas are rejected or strongly resisted, on the grounds that they do not properly understand the organization's situation. Sometimes, the "new blood" may even end up absorbing the organization's existing way of thinking.

10.12   Pathological Organizations

Before concluding this chapter, it is worth extending the discussion of corporate culture to take account of the work of Manfred Kets de Vries, Danny Miller and Peter Friesen on dysfunctional corporate cultures (see Miller and Freisen, 1984; Kets de Vries and Miller, 1984, 1988). They reasoned that if we view a firm's culture as the organizational equivalent of an individual's personality, then it may be instructive to consider how we might expect firms to operate if they were afflicted with personality pathologies – i.e., tendencies toward excessive use of a particular neurotic style or way of thinking – akin to those that prove dysfunctional for individuals. Kets de Vries et al. therefore reflected on organizations with the aid of the (then) current psychiatrist's bible, the *DSM–III* diagnostic manual produced by the American Psychiatric Association (1980).

An organization whose way of operating has a particular systemic disorder may have grown to have the disorder because it has been led by an individual or team that suffers from the individual-level equivalent of the disorder. However, this is not the only route to such a pathology: the organization's way of operating may reflect the combined path-dependent effects of many events and individuals' ways of operating, rather in the way that a particular scientific research program's core assumptions and operating rules may emerge from many contributions over a considerable period of time. Kets de Vries et al. see each organizational pathology that they identify as being underpinned by a particular need or preoccupation, such as the following, some of which are particularly at odds with what is conducive to generating productivity and growth via constructive criticism and experimentation:

(a) *The Need for Grandiosity* ➜ *Impulsive Organizations*

The operating style of an impulsive organization resembles that of an individual with a histrionic–narcissistic personality disorder, which may indeed be the pathology of the firm's leader. Someone with such a personality uses dramatic behavior as a means of demonstrating their prowess and to impress and dominate others. In the corporate context, this entails running the organization in a very centralized, top-down manner that can prove chaotic for subordinates. Leaders of such organizations use their charisma and their latest grand acts as means of diverting attention from problems arising from past choices. This kind of leader focuses on giant projects and on growing the organization very rapidly. In the case of a firm that is in this situation, that growth typically is via mergers and acquisitions that demonstrate its leader's prowess as a dealmaker but also symptomize a lack of caution or interest in potential for problems. Because leadership in this kind of organization is focused on drama rather than detail, and on the initiation rather than the execution of grand designs, outcomes are likely to be poor, eventually leaving creditors disappointed.

(b) *Helplessness and Hopelessness* ➜ *Stagnant Organizations*

This kind of organization operates rather like a person who has a depressive personality that is possibly the result of having suffered a major setback that wiped out their confidence in relation to being able to predict and control events. In many respects, it is the opposite of the impulsive organization. A focus on past problems that crowds out acknowledgment of past achievements is likely to lead to capabilities being underestimated, with the result that the organization's imaginative or creative capacities are not exercised to address current problems. The problems thus persist, as evidence of the organization's lack of capacity to solve them. Anything novel or bold thus seems too dangerous to be worth trying, as it may generate new problems (for example, retaliation by competitors). Instead, the focus is on getting by on the basis of routines that seem to work, pending the arrival of a rescuer, though given the lack of self-esteem, it is viewed as unlikely that a white knight will appear. Anything that is nonroutine tends to result in decision paralysis rather than experimentation, so change tends to be very sluggish. Like a person with a depressive personality, an organization pervaded by a feeling of hopelessness badly needs to create more ambitious goals and operate in a less risk-averse manner.

(c) *The Need for Control* ➜ *Compulsive Organizations*

This kind of culture is the corporate equivalent of being afflicted with an obsessive–compulsive disorder. It can result in organizations failing to make necessary changes despite having very industrious managers who are not merely "going through the motions" of doing their jobs in the manner of those in stagnant, routine-based organizations. Obsession with "running a tight ship" can mean that a firm with this affliction heads to the rocks due to being overly focused on its internal processes and reporting requirements rather than on what is going on in its external environment, such as the changing requirements of customers. Being obsessed with keeping everything under control tends to result in chronic firefighting behavior of the kind that Carlson (1951) observed in his study of executive behavior.

Managers of this kind of organization would have more time to devise effective strategies if they engaged less in "micromanaging" their subordinates and instead trusted them more and gave them more discretion over budget use and for taking on-the-spot decisions. Moreover, insofar as the obsession is with short-term performance targets, those who are being managed may be less able to engage in creative thinking that could have major long-term payoffs. Highly formalized management styles such as this are inherently problematic in surprise-prone environments where quick action may be needed but is prevented due to failure to delegate responsibility. Much of modern Western managerialism has tendencies in this direction, in contrast to the Japanese style of business in which, for example, a production line worker can halt the line if he or she spots a problem with quality, rather than the quality problem being left for an inspector to identify at the end of the line.

(d) *The Persecutory Preoccupation* ➜ *Paranoid Organizations*

Paranoid individuals operate in an excessively vigilant manner, treating others with distrust and suspicion, and tending always to be on the lookout for new enemies. Their inability to trust others makes them prone to go into "denial" mode and act in a hostile manner (in Kelly's sense of the term) when their ways of thinking and acting are challenged. Clearly, at the level of a firm operating in a Schumpeterian environment of "creative destruction," some degree of paranoia is an asset, unlike hubris (see Grove, 1996). But operating with a siege mentality may result in a futile focus on keeping competitors at bay in cases where technological progress or changes in taste mean that the firm's existing products are doomed. In such a situation, the firm should be looking for ways of redeploying its resources and augmenting its capabilities. Unfortunately, a paranoid firm is unlikely to be open to forming strategic alliances as a means to the latter end. Paranoia in relation to external threats may be accompanied by, or preceded by, an internal operating style that results in paranoia among employees. Paranoia at the top is likely to lead to highly centralized systems, with considerable effort going into gathering information to ensure compliance with directives and minimize the risk of anyone doing anything that could cause reputational damage for the organization. An especially watchful eye will be kept on the activities of labor unions, though short-term contracts or extensive probationary periods will be favored to make it easier to remove anyone who "rocks the boat." Managers will categorize their subordinates based on whether they are "with" or "against" the organization; those construed as "disloyal" (who may simply be raising important questions) will tend to be fired or denied promotion.

(e) *The Need for Detachment* ➜ *Politicized Cultures or Schizoid Organizations*

This kind of organization operates in a highly politicized manner from the second level downward due to the leader being someone who operates in a cold, aloof manner, seemingly being unwilling to trust others, having no concern about operating in isolation and feeling no need to communicate in ways that go beyond just sending decisions down to lower levels to be actioned. The leader's detachment results in lower tiers lacking a coordinated sense of how the organization should run. This opens the way to the emergence of rival cultures within the organization as rival second-tier staff step in to fill the vacuum in a self-serving way by trying to win resources from the leader and cultivating support from lower levels. These executives will be prone to managing information in ways that suit their personal agenda and to try to stifle each other's plans, focusing on internal power plays rather than the need to keep adapting the organization to changes in the external environment. Sadly, it is hard not to think of some "ivory tower" universities as commonly operating like this, with top-tier staff being viewed by those engaged in teaching and research as out of touch with realities of life at the "frontline" or "coalface," and acute interdepartmental rivalry ensuring that, instead of interdisciplinary cooperation, there tends to be needless waste of resources through activities being duplicated.

As with individuals (for example, paranoid schizophrenics), combinations of such corporate personality types may exist, and they may evolve through time depending on who is in power and how events unfold. Some shocks may trigger major "never again" transformations, but even if such resolve comes abruptly at the top of the organization, changing any aspects of its culture in ways that seem necessary may entail a far longer process across the entire organization.

10.13   Conclusion

Three areas of tension underlie much of this chapter: between the roles of bosses and their subordinates, between formal and informal aspects of how organizations are allowed to operate and between maintaining productivity today by not squandering current capabilities and increasing productivity by generating new knowledge. A conventional training in economics is conducive to presuming that it should be possible to discover optimal trade-offs in these areas: between the costs and benefits of having closer supervision and the costs, in terms of subgoal pursuit and coordination problems, as well as benefits of allowing more discretion; between the costs and benefits of devising and negotiating more detailed job contracts and more prescriptive organizational policies versus those of having vague contracts and allowing informal rules to evolve freely as contingencies arise; and between concentrating on generating profits by established methods of producing an existing product range versus giving attention to designing new products and production systems and speeding up the process of earning revenue from them. Furthermore, it would be natural to want to design the structure of an organization mindful of the costs and benefits of achieving economies of scope via a U-form function-based structure versus achieving better motivation via an M-form structure that pitches product or geographical divisions into internal competition, or via an efficient combination thereof.

Viewing the problem of organizing production systems in terms of such trade-offs can be productive, but it has two shortcomings. One is that it diverts attention from the emphasis that Marshall and Penrose gave to the importance of on-the-job learning in the context of production system that are already operating. The other is that it begs the questions that Simon, March and Cyert pose about how managers might ever find the optimal system for getting their organizations to be as productive and efficient as possible in the long run.

There are certainly some broad principles for them to apply. In relatively surprise-free environments, formal systems in which much activity is prescribed by existing rules may be effective. But organizational chaos is likely to arise where attempts are made to run things in a highly formalized way that does not take sufficient account of bounded rationality and potential for surprise: complex formal structures and operational rules are prone to ensure that attempts to change anything generate complex webs of disruptions and that the organization experiences difficulty in taking advantages of opportunities that were impossible to anticipate in great detail. Hence, where the environment is less stable and quick adaptation is needed, or where the focus of the organization (or a particular part of it) is on generating creative disruptions, the manager's role needs to be much more as a coordinator or facilitator than as a supervisor, with workers being trusted to apply their knowledge in appropriate ways.

These kinds of principles are central to what is known as the "contingency approach" to organization (see Burns and Stalker, 1961; Woodward, 1965) but they do not close the problem. To go beyond these basic principles, managers can at best merely experiment with specific ways of dividing up their areas of responsibility and assigning tasks, and with the styles of operation they use to try to get their subordinates to do what has been requested rather than pursue subgoals.

The question that this chapter posed is of vital significance if we are trying to understand changing relative standing of firms within an industry and changes in international rankings of income per head. However, such an understanding also requires us to appreciate how structural change occurs in economic systems as a result of competitive interactions between firms and the evolving behavior of their customers as new technologies are introduced. This is the focus of the next chapter.

11 How Does the Competitive Process Work?

11.1 Introduction

In this chapter we attempt to understand how economic systems change through time. This entails appreciating how evolutionary selection processes determine the rise and fall of: (a) types or genres of products, production methods and operating systems; (b) variants within these types or genres; and (c) economic entities such as households, firms and nations. Three knowledge-related changes drive these processes, namely: (i) changes in what is known and believed; (ii) changes in who has access to what is known; and (iii) changes in the capacity of those with knowledge to apply it after recognizing its potential implications. These changes drive what Schumpeter (1943) called "gales of creative destruction," whereby innovations render some technologies and ways of operating and earning a living obsolete and provoke critical and creative thinking that results in further changes. This means that the economic system does not tend toward equilibrium, even though there may be periods of normality in some industries: incumbent players are usually under pressure to come up with better ways of doing things, for even if they see the benefits of having a competitive truce among themselves, there may remain the risk of challenges from new entrants with innovative ways of doing things. Hence it pays to devote resources to innovation and to finding ways of improving quality and cutting costs.

To aid the understanding of how competition produces structural change in the economy, I present in this chapter a synthesis of behavioral and neo-Schumpeterian ideas. This is pretty much what Richard Nelson and Sidney Winter (1982) sought to do in their seminal book *An Evolutionary Theory of Economic Change*. However, the present synthesis benefits from being able to draw upon contributions that Nelson and Winter seem to have been unaware of or which were made after their book appeared. Nelson and Winter's synthesis of behavioral and Schumpeterian thinking results in a "population ecology" perspective that goes well beyond Marshall's (1890) attempt to liken the rise and fall of firms within industries to the life cycles of tress and other plants within a forest. However, in the body of this chapter, we make rather little explicit use of their work, important though it has been in helping to maintain interest in pre-1980 behavioral economics. The approach that will be taken reflects the fact that, as Nightingale (1997) has argued at length, their population ecology perspective had a precursor that deserves to be acknowledged and much more widely known, namely Jack Downie's (1958) book, *The Competitive Process*, a work not cited by Nelson and Winter.

The question that this chapter poses is thus an allusion to Downie's book. I first read *The Competitive Process* as an undergraduate, five years before Nelson and Winter's book appeared. It had been mentioned in class and it made an enormous impression on me when I considered it in relation to the behavioral theory of the firm. Sections 11.2–11.4 of this chapter take us from a neo-Marshallian view of competition to what we get if we blend Downie's approach with ideas from the previous chapter. When Nelson and Winter's book appeared, it largely served to confirm the picture I had already formed, though it enhanced it in two ways. One was by adding tacit knowledge as an impediment to the ability of firms to emulate the performance of their more successful rivals by poaching personnel from them or making technology transfer arrangements with them. The other, considered here in Section 11.5, was how it modified the Darwinian approach to evolutionary economics via its focus on the replication of rules and routines as economic growth and structural changes occur. The latter eventually provided the basis for the "micro–meso–macro" framework developed by Kurt Dopfer, John Foster and Jason Potts to aid the understanding of how economic systems evolve. Their widely cited framework is employed extensively in Sections 11.6–11.13 of this chapter.

11.2   Competitive Rivalry In Mature Industries

We begin with the neo-Marshallian perspective on competition that emerged from empirical studies of manufacturing firms conducted in the United Kingdom by the Oxford Economists' Research Group (OERG) in the 1930s and 1940s. Involvement in this work eventually led the OERG's Philip Andrews to a radical reconsideration of the economics of the firm (see Andrews, 1949, 1964, 1993; Andrews and Brunner, 1975; see also Irving, 1978, and Jacobsen, 2017; for further discussion of Andrews and of related lines of thinking in institutional and post-Keynesian economics, see Lee, 1999). This research was conducted in the context of firms that were working with well-established technologies that could be used to make a wide variety of outputs and whose customers often were other firms. Competition was intense but normally it did not result in destabilizing price wars, for firms sought to win customers from rival suppliers on a face-to-face basis or submitted tenders to get contracts without knowing the details of their rivals' offers.

The intensity of competition that Andrews observed resulted in him being hostile to the behavioral theory of the firm despite the research methods that he used and his insights regarding the simplifying rules and routines that people use for coping with real-world economic complexity. He rejected elements of the behavioral theory of the firm that allowed for behavior at odds with the pursuit of long-run profits. Indeed, in a lecture he delivered at Harvard University in 1966 (posthumously reprinted as the first chapter of Andrews and Brunner, 1975), he characterized the behavioral approach to the firm, the idea of satisficing and managerial theories of the firm as "ways of evading economic analysis" (*ibid.*, p. 1) due to their failure to take proper account of the power of competition. In addition to his emphasis on the power of competition in product

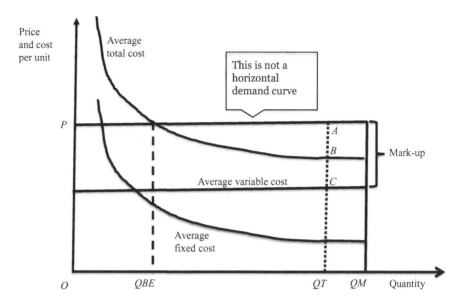

Figure 11.1 The "normal cost" view of pricing

markets, he saw divisional rivalries inside multiproduct and multiplant firms and "internal competition" between promotion-hungry staff as providing impetus for cost reductions and product improvements (Andrews, 1964, p. 80; 1993, ch. 9).

The picture of competitive behavior that Andrews put together in the context of the OERG's research was at odds with the theories of perfect, imperfect and monopolistic competition that displaced Marshallian thinking after Marshall's death in 1924. The industries that the OERG studied contained firms with nontrivial market shares (which meant they were far from "perfectly competitive") but they did not seem to enjoy significant discretion over their prices or hold prices to the level they wanted by restricting output. They did not work out their price and output choices by practices that seemed akin to equating their marginal costs and marginal revenues, and they did not seem to change their prices in response to short-term fluctuations in demand or costs. The alternative view of price and output that Andrews assembled from the OERG's research findings is shown in Figure 11.1. It entails a simple, rule-based way of coping with the complexities of the business world, but its underlying logic is richer and more complex than the theories it was intended to displace. For clarity, Figure 11.1 does not show how Andrews sometimes took account of overtime work undertaken at higher hourly rates of pay, as this does not change the essence of his analysis.

In Andrews's model, the firm sets its prices by applying a markup to its average variable costs at its target rate of output and sales. This markup is shown in Figure 11.1 by the distance between A and C, which would leave the net margin shown by the distance between A and B if sales are at the target rate, shown in Figure 11.1 as QT. This target (which we might also call the firm's "sales aspiration") is somewhat less than the maximum rate of output the firm can achieve, which is indicated by the vertical line at QM. (Early in the firm's time in the market, QT may seem to lie some way in the future, with the initial aspiration being to get to QBE, the break-even level of output and sales.) The firm will aim to grow its capacity ahead of growth in its sales, keeping $QM > QT$. This leaves the firm able to service more customers if it is lucky enough to get them. The firm produces as much as it is able to sell at the cost-based price that it works out and quotes to its prospective customers. If sales are less than the target level, it will review its competitive position and marketing strategy to figure out why sales have been disappointing and how it might be able to do better. If sales are greater than the target level, it will review its capacity expansion strategy, for if the new customers can be retained in future, it will wish to ensure it still has capacity to serve even more in future periods. Since its long-run average total cost curve is not U-shaped, the volume of business that the firm can do is not constrained on the cost side in the long run. The constraint on the growth of the firm's size and sales aspirations is its ability to grow its clientele of customers. This will be easier to do if demand for the kinds of products that it makes is growing and if its rivals start to disappoint their customers in terms of price, quality and delivery dates, causing them to start looking elsewhere.

What we have here is a view of pricing that does not refer to a demand curve. The firm is not viewed as "having" a demand curve for its products. One reason for this is that its demand position is not static. Customers come and go from markets as their needs and locations change through their life spans, and customers who were once loyal may be lost by firms that let their standards of service and value slip, either in absolute terms or relative to what is thought to be available from their rivals. Amid this evolving population of buyers, the firm is trying to grow its goodwill base of regular customers and enhance the probability of winning one-off customers even if they cannot be turned into "regulars." This is why it needs to have spare capacity: it does not want to have to decline to serve its repeat customers in order to seize opportunities to serve unfamiliar customers, and it does not want to turn new customers away, particularly when a successful initial transaction may be the start of a long-term relationship. But pricing is also done without reference to a demand curve, because the industrial context is that of a competitive oligopoly in which it is impossible to know how rivals will respond to changes in its prices and where it could be costly to recover customers if it experiments with a price that is viewed as "too high" and results in its customers experimenting with seeing how its rivals serve them. The markup on costs that yields the asking price for the product is set with a view to keeping the firm in business and growing it in the long run.

These long-run considerations rule out short-term price changes in response to changing market conditions. In the event of a spike in demand, a firm will normally respond not by raising prices but by increasing output via the spare capacity buffer or, if that buffer is inadequate, by adjusting waiting list times. This ensures that the firm is seen to be engaging in fair play rather than trying to take advantage of customers in times of temporarily high demand. It thus helps generate customer goodwill rather than triggering customers to wonder what other devious practices it might seek to get away with (cf. the investigation into buyers' views on the pricing of snow shovels undertaken by Kahneman et al., 1986). If this means that waiting lists build up when there is a spike in demand, these will need to be seen to be handled fairly, for example, via "first come, first served" rules rather than on the basis of side payments by those who have more money and are not willing to spend time queuing. However, deviating from normal prices could be hazardous in other contexts, too, in other ways. In a business-to-business context, heavy discounting to win a contract may be viewed with suspicion regarding the quality of what is going to be delivered or about the firm's ability to stay in business and become a regular supplier. In consumer goods markets, unpredictable price variability may damage goodwill by making shopping more difficult or making it harder to be confident of being served at a particular price in the absence of a forward contract (as would be the case if restaurants varied their prices each night depending on how many customers seemed to be around) (cf. Alchian, 1969, pp. 113–116).

Hence, even in the absence of any costs of changing price list (on menus, in catalogues and, nowadays, on webpages), prices are normally adjusted not because of changes in demand but because "normal" costs – i.e., long-term costs – are viewed as having changed. Short-term fluctuations in production costs will not normally result in price changes. (It should also be noted that in large organizations, where sales information could have to pass across many desks before reaching the person who is responsible for setting prices, price changes would be at risk of being based on out-of-date information by the time they were actioned: see further Cyert and March, 1955.) Where retailers run seasonal "sales" or discount items "for clearance," such price reductions usually reflect rule-based write-offs of mistaken over-ordering of particular lines of stock, to make way for more saleable stock (see the simulation model of department store pricing in Cyert and March, 1963). Otherwise, periods in which prices are reduced to address weaker demand are based on industry-wide rules of an institutional kind, such as discounted movies and pizzas every Tuesday or "Black Friday" sales that "everyone knows" to expect.

In setting its markup, the firm's managers are acutely aware of the costs of winning back customers if they pitch it too high. Here, the issue is not merely one of customers shifting their goodwill to established rivals. Even if it were achieved via collusion among the existing suppliers, greedy pricing could backfire due to triggering entry, both by new players (even from the firm's own staff setting up in business based on their experience and their connections with the firm's existing customers) and by established firms from industries that have rather similar resource requirements. It is therefore in the long-run interest of the firm to set its prices slightly below the level that would-be entrants need the market price to be for them to find it attractive to enter the market. By moderating their demands on customers and giving no impression to potential rivals that fat profits lie ready for the taking, incumbent producers in an industry will enjoy larger sales in the future. They also reduce the risk that the market will be spoilt by the entry of "fly-by-night" suppliers whose presence would make it harder for anyone to buy with confidence regarding quality.

This conclusion about the role and appropriate level of prices may seem similar to that of the "contestable markets" view of competition proposed by Baumol et al. (1982), but the latter is based on an orthodox view of demand rather than one that is evolutionary and relationship-based, as is especially evident by Baumol et al.'s focus on what it will take to deter "hit-and-run raiders," i.e., firms that can enter without worrying about any sunk costs if they later have to exit. Zero sunk costs might be plausible in relation to entry based on using existing equipment and skills but not in relation to investments in marketing and building relationships with customers (see further Davies and Lee, 1988).

Of course, managers will face uncertainty when trying to assess how low their prices will have to be to serve this entry-deterring role, and they will not always arrive at appropriate conclusions. But since the pricing rule entails a markup only on variable costs, they will at least have a good chance of assessing their own costs reasonably accurately, without having to address complications associated with shared overheads with their other products. They may also have been able to gather intelligence about how efficient their firms are relative to the industry average (for example, by subscribing to bodies such as, in the UK context, the Centre for Interfirm Comparison, that serve as market institutions by providing subscribers with benchmarking information, or via consultants with expertise in the industry and from hiring former employees of rival firms). If they are aware of an industry norm for the typical percentage gross markup that has evolved and seems to be effective in limiting entry, then they may set their prices by adjusting this markup norm to take account of what they know about how their efficiency stands relative to the industry norm and adding it to their variable costs. This rule is their way of proxying the unknown opportunity costs of their potential competitors.

11.2.1   Retail Pricing

When Andrews (1964, 1993, chs. 6 and 7) extended his thinking to the context of the prices that consumers faced when shopping, his emphasis on the power of competition meant that he viewed differences in relative prices of rival products essentially as reflecting differences in the quality of what is supplied. His work views "rip-offs" as uncommon and only allows for bargains that rivals do not match (such as "weekly specials" at supermarkets) on the basis that it is at the level of the typical shopping basket or trolley load of goods, not the individual item, that long-term competitive pressure exerts its disciplinary force. From the perspective of Andrews's work, we should not see competitive pressure as being compromised due to the laziness and ineptitude of many shoppers or due to them being too busy to experiment rather than sticking to their established shopping habits and routines. The argument that he offers us here draws on a point made by one of his students, Neville Ward-Perkins (see Andrews, 1964, p. 102), namely that the presence of even a small minority of canny shoppers (say, 10 percent) may be enough to ensure market discipline and a focus on finding ways of offering better value for money. This is because the latter group could be enough to make entry attractive if incumbent suppliers adopt a slack attitude and/or try to "rip-off" the rest of the population of buyers. Nowadays, this argument is made even more powerful by the more sophisticated market for preferences that the Internet and social media have made possible.

Despite this, Andrews's analysis can appear somewhat overoptimistic in some markets in the short run. There is evidence of persistent dispersions in the value for money that firms offer, with consumers wasting money at greedy suppliers (cf. Grubb, 2015), while the limited restraining power of potential competition is shown by the actual entry of new players who are prepared to spend many years building market shares by applying new rules to offer better value. (The experience of the Aldi supermarket chain comes to mind as an example here.) Incumbent suppliers can thus seem to be focused on competing with each other and giving insufficient thought to new entry, with some enjoying years of profits on the basis of having become a default choice (as with, say, former state monopolies that have been privatized) despite charging higher prices than their rivals. But in the long run, under the pressure of *social* competition, people generally do seem to learn how to improve their living standards, thereby keeping up pressure on suppliers to improve their offers. The consumers who get "ripped-off" and/or fail to adopt innovations that would have enhanced their well-being will tend to be those who are socially isolated. Consumer-protection policies may indeed be needed to prevent them from being, as Akerlof and Shiller (2015) put it, "phished for phools." However, a strategy of trying to earn profits by exploiting the ignorance and dysfunctional heuristics of such buyers is ill suited for growing a business in the long run. Indeed, we should probably view it as the last resort of those who lack the imagination required to compete in an honorable way.

11.2.2   A "Price-Minus" View of Costs Instead of a Cost-Plus View of Pricing?

We end this section by considering a question that Smyth (1967) posed after reflecting critically on studies that purported to demonstrate the existence of cost-based prices. Smyth invites us to consider whether products may be "built to a price" rather than sold at prices that are based on existing cost levels (see also Earl, 2002, ch. 10). If managers and entrepreneurs plan to introduce new products or consider trying to enter an existing market, the prices currently being charged for similar products will provide a reference point for their decision-making. Prices that have been set with a view to deterring new competition will fail to do so if potential competitors believe they can come up with a better product at the same price (or, at a slightly higher prices that is still within the same "price range") or that they can offer a similar product and succeed in selling it at a lower price that will yield an acceptable return on their investment. If their target rate of return and reference prices are already given, the question then becomes whether they can find a way of producing a suitable product at a low enough price.

Smyth discusses such explorations in relation to cost accountants being able to arrive at acceptable recorded costs without breaking their established rules. Cost aspirations might also be met by:

(a) opting not to include some product features at all or offering them to a lower standard,

(b) outsourcing or offshoring to lower-wage businesses the production of components that they could not produce so cheaply in their usual production facilities,

(c) working out innovate ways of making the product, either in its manufacturing process or by redesigning it so that is has fewer parts or can use more parts from other products in the firm's product range and

(d) attempting to take up organizational slack or X-inefficiency by changing work practices and remuneration arrangements.

Clearly, given loss aversion and the possibility that potential customers will use non-compensatory decision rules pertaining to spending budgets and product features, firms that hope to compete by offering products that are in some areas superior to existing alternatives have to be careful about cutting back on other features and/or letting their products get too expensive.

11.3   Productivity Growth and Structural Change

Let us now extend the neo-Marshallian approach to examine how industrial structures change and prices fall in the long run as a result of the discovery of cheaper production methods. Cost-reducing methods typically take time to be adopted, and industries are normally populated by firms whose productivity levels differ because of differences in how they are run, where they are located and which generation (or "vintage") of technology they are using. To grapple with the heterogeneity of firms that populate an industry, it is useful to employ a simple framework from Wilfred Salter's (1960) book *Productivity and Technical Change*. This book is based on the PhD dissertation that Salter wrote in the mid-1950s as an Australian graduate student at the University of Cambridge.

Central to Salter's study of how productivity grows through time is the idea that whether an existing production plant is worth operating depends only on whether it can cover the non-sunk costs of operating, i.e., the costs that can be avoided if production does not occur. These costs consist not merely of variable (or "direct") costs of line workers, materials, components and energy but also payments for managers, salaried workers, overhead staff, lighting and heating, local authority property taxes and loan-servicing charges that must be paid if the operation is to remain solvent. Like Andrews and Brunner (1975), I prefer to call these costs "paying-out" costs. The plant should only be taken out of operation if the minimum average paying-out cost that can be achieved is greater than the market price (i.e., the average revenue) that the firm can get from the output that it can be used to produce. If the price per unit that the firm can achieve from selling output from the plant is greater than the average paying-out cost per unit, then the plant should be kept in operation. The earnings that result from the difference between price and average paying cost can contribute to paying off any remaining debts that were incurred in building and

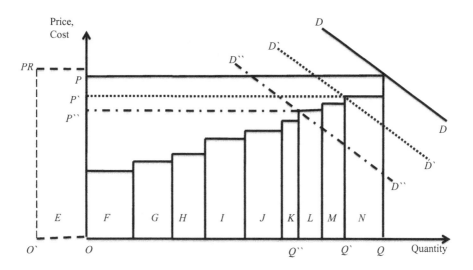

Figure 11.2 A mature industry suffering from declining demand

equipping the plant or, if no such debts remain, it can be paid out as dividends to shareholders or ploughed back into new investment. By contrast, firms will only invest in new production facilities if they expect that, over their planning horizon, they can achieve a satisfactory return in terms of the net profit margin between their average revenues and their average total costs.

To illustrate theoretically what he was analyzing empirically, Salter devised a simple but powerful diagrammatic framework, which is employed here via Figures 11.2 and 11.3 to explore the process of structural change in an industry. Figure 11.2 extends what evolutionary economists call a "Salter diagram" mindful of the discussion in Section 11.2 of Andrews's "normal cost" approach to pricing. It depicts an industry of suppliers whose production systems differ in their productivity. Each rectangular block labeled from *F* to *N* represents a particular production system, and it should be kept in mind that a single firm may produce a particular product using several production systems at different locations or even within a particular factory. The width of each block represents the normal or target rate of output for the production system in question. The height of each block represents, per unit of output, the costs that must be paid out to produce the normal or target rate of output. In a "Salter diagram," we rank these blocks in order of height, rising from left (most efficient) to right (least efficient).

Initially, the demand curve for the industry's output is *DD*, with output *Q* being sold at price *P*, with all the existing production systems able to reach their sales targets. The firms in this industry have set their prices just below *PR*, the price required by a prospective entrant, whose prospective output is shown by the width of the dash-edged block labeled as *E*. So long as the incumbent firms keep their prices below *PR*, entry will not occur. The industry seems to be in a steady state despite the very different margins that are being earned on average paying-out costs by the owners of the various production systems, with plant N barely earning a return on its non-sunk costs. However, although each production system on average achieves its target rate of output without piling up any new losses, their different operating margins means that some might be earning satisfactory profits on their investments, whereas some of the others might even be running "under administration" due to having failed in servicing debts incurred to pay for their fixed capital in previous periods. Note also that even if demand for the industry's output did not change, the steady state might be disturbed by changes in its cost structure, such as the invention of a more productive technology (which we will shortly consider) or if the wearing out of any of the existing plant results in its replacement by a more modern production system that has a different normal capacity level, as in a scenario where, say, N is scrapped and replaced by a plant similar to F and such a plant's average total costs are less than P.

Now consider what happens if demand for the industry's output starts to decline, shifting from DD to $D`D`$, then to $D``D``$, and so on. If we were viewing the stepped set of blocks as akin to a supply curve for the industry, we would expect that competition for orders would result in price $P`$ and industry output $Q`$ when demand shrinks to $D`D`$, forcing the closure of plant N and that the market price would fall to $P``$ and output to $Q``$ when demand shrinks to $D``D``$, with plants L (which no longer earns a net return if the price is $P``$) and M being shut down. However, from the standpoint of Andrews's normal cost analysis, what we might expect is that the firms will stick to price P initially and try to figure out why they are no longer meeting their sales targets. As demand for the industry's output shrank, average costs would rise for each producer. Eventually, the realization that the industry is not suffering merely a temporary fall in sales within "normal" bounds will lead to a breakdown of restraint, with more aggressive pricing as, led by the most desperate player, the firms scramble to win orders. It would be at this point that the less efficient operations are shut down.

Now consider Figure 11.3, which shows an industry with a similar starting point but this time the disruption is that firm E has invented a new vintage of production technology with lower production costs. Here, E's required price for entry (PR) is less than the prevailing price, P, even though E is building a brand-new production system and PR thus must cover the average *total* cost per unit of output as well as leaving a profit margin. If E's target level of output and sales is equal to the distance from O to $O`$, $E$'s entry means that we must move the origin on Figure 11.3 to $O`$ and shift the industry's demand curve to the left by the same amount as E's addition to the industry's capacity, i.e., to Figure 11.3's $D`D`$ demand curve. The industry's price would fall to $P`$, with production systems $M$ and $N$ being shut down, and total output now being the amount from $O`$ to $Q`$, leaving the owners of production system E with a healthy margin beyond their required price. Average costs in the industry have fallen, with buyers benefiting from lower prices. However, this may not be the end of the story, for given E's high profit margin on the full costs of production, the owners of E might consider building a duplicate plant and/or other incumbents, or new players, may be tempted to try to replicate E's technology. There is clearly potential for excessive capacity creation to occur, as per Richardson's (1960 competitive

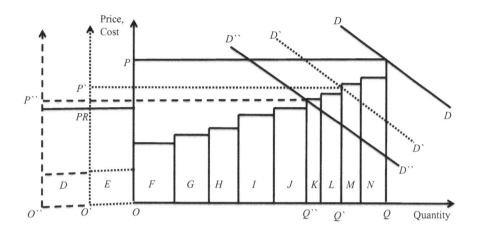

Figure 11.3 Structural change induced by the uptake of a new production technology

investment coordination problem. Figure 11.3 implies that a single clone of $E's$ production system, shown as block D, would prove viable: it would bring the industry price down close to PR, as it would add somewhat more capacity than would be lost due to K and L being forced to close. By applying the previous argument, we should expect the price to fall to $P``$, with the industry's output being the distance between $O``$ and $Q``$, the move of the origin to $O``$ implying that the demand curve is moved to $D``D``$.

If we consider Figures 11.2 and 11.3 mindful of Chapter 10's discussions of X-inefficiency, learning curves and organizational slack, a more complex view of the process of structural adjustment emerges. Instead of the exit of marginal production systems being purely the result of falling demand in the industry or capacity creation by firms that can achieve lower average unit costs by investing in the latest technology, we may also expect to see changes in market share that result from changes in the productivity of existing plant. If any existing operation moves further down its learning curve, its respective block on a Salter diagram will become wider and its height will decrease since, within a given period, it can now produce more output with its workforce, with average costs per unit of labor inputs and non-sunk overhead costs also falling.

Heightened competitive pressure resulting from capacity expansion via both new investments and learning may result in search for ways of reducing costs in plant represented by blocks toward the right of the diagram. This may result in the discovery of ways of reducing X-inefficiency by changing operating practices, and/or successful experiments to see if there is any organizational slack by, say, seeing if workers will tolerate working at a faster pace after some staff have been retrenched. The blocks representing plant where this happens may either become wider and lower, as with learning curve effects, or they may simply be reduced in height due to the normal rate of possible output not being changed but it now being achieved with fewer workers, with some of the workforce having been retrenched.

These changes will change the relative viability of the rival production systems, possibly even by enough for their positions in order of efficiency to need to be rearranged. If there is a major productivity-enhancing shake-up at a plant that was on the verge of being shut down, another plant might be forced to close instead. Another scenario might be that a high-cost plant is taken out of operation but is then shipped off to a low-wage economy instead of being sold for scrap and is then brought back into operation. In this latter scenario, the height of its block might be reduced enough for it to be re-ranked much further to the left on the diagram, even if its width initially is smaller than before due to its new workforce lacking experience in using it and there being tacit knowledge barriers to transferring expertise even if the original managers are sent to oversee its recommissioning at the lower-wage location.

If technology is expected to advance very rapidly, firms may run into difficulties if they follow pricing strategies aimed at deterring existing and potential rivals from adding to capacity by investing in the latest technology. Prices set at the entry-deterring level may be impossible to sustain due to capacity in the industry currently being less than the demand that there would be at these prices. Moreover, if new technologies appear shortly after firms have invested in the then current technology, entry-deterring pricing may prevent them from earning a normal return on the investment they have recently made. Given this, it would make more sense to accept the inevitability of investment in technologies that will sooner or later push prices down. Having accepted this, one might then make investment decisions based on whether customers will accept prices that are compatible with a very short payback period for one's investment before such prices are rendered unsustainable by the arrival of output from the next generation of production technology.

11.4   The Transfer Mechanism versus the Innovation Mechanism

The structural adjustment processes that we have just considered via the Salter diagram framework are consistent with the key ideas in Jack Downie's (1958) remarkable book, *The Competitive Process*. It was written around the same time (1954–1956) that Salter was working on the Cambridge PhD that became his (1960) book. Downie, who was born in 1919, was ten years older than Salter and wrote his book while working at the Oxford Institute of Statistics on a two-year secondment from the Economic Section of the UK Treasury. The timing of their writing and the shared interest of Salter and Downie in how productivity growth takes place was not all they had in common. After returning to Australia, Salter, too, became a public service economist and, tragically, both he and Downie died prematurely in 1963 on overseas appointments – Salter in Lahore from heart failure and Downie in Paris from a seizure. (For excellent studies of their respective careers and contributions, see Weber, 2009, and Nightingale, 1997, 1998.)

Like Salter, Downie was interested in how overall productivity changes in industries that consist of firms that differ in their efficiency. However, Downie offered an even more dynamic picture by recognizing the feedback relationship between the profitability of a firm and its capacity to invest in productivity-enhancing equipment. (By extension, this relationship applies to investment in improved products, but Downie did not take his analysis there despite evidently being familiar with Schumpeter's [1943] thinking on creative destruction in relation to both process and product innovations.) This feedback relationship will work to the cumulating advantage of firms that, for whatever reason, have above-normal profitability, whereas firms that are struggling with below-normal rates of return will find themselves in a vicious circle in which their relatively limited ability to invest makes it harder for them to reduce their unit costs, forcing them to exit.

This idea became a major ingredient in Robin Marris's (1964) *Economic Theory of "Managerial" Capitalism*. There, it was integrated with ideas from Edith Penrose's (1959) *Theory of the Growth of the Firm*: a firm that had abundant profits and the associated ability to raise external finance would need to be mindful that it could run into managerial problems if it attempted to grow very rapidly. Marris succumbed to the temptation to model managers as if they could work out an optimal rate of investment that would enable their firm to grow at the fastest steady rate that was sustainable in the sense that the managers would be able to generate enough profit to fund the investment rate that they could safely handle without getting into a mess and inviting attention from takeover raiders. However, behavioral economists would recognize that managers might in some cases make the mistake of "biting off far more than they can chew," with adverse impacts on their firm's profitability and hence on its ability to invest during subsequent periods. These adverse impacts might even be so bad that the managers were unable to engineer a recovery – especially if the projects in question were ill conceived rather than causes of what we might call "corporate indigestion" and they then succumbed to sunk cost bias. (I have shown elsewhere that Marris's framework can be adapted to explore such possibilities: see Earl, 1984, pp. 12–16.)

Unlike Marris, Downie did not build a deterministic model of the competitive process. Instead, he offered pathways to alternative scenarios of how industries could evolve via the interplay of two key processes that he then investigated in relation to what had happened in the UK during the Interwar and early post-World War II periods.

Downie's book appeared just too soon to incorporate, as Marris did, Penrose's analysis of short-term managerial limits on the growth of firms. But like Penrose, he took seriously the possibility that firms might be able to grow very large and keep growing as time passed. He did not accept Marshall's (1890) view that the size of firms would be constrained due to them going out of business after losing the drive and vision of their founding entrepreneurs within a few decades or family generations. Downie was concerned with what the implications for competition policy would be if growth in firm size did not go hand in hand with increasing inflexibility and compromised productivity. Consumers might ultimately suffer if output increasingly came to be dominated by the lowest-cost producers via the feedback relationship between profitability and investment: industries might thereby become monopolized, with prices being jacked up after the competitors had been driven out. However, the well-being of the population might also be compromised if the most efficient firms were prevented from driving out their less efficient rivals.

A conventional training would lead most economists to assign a key role to economies of scale in such a process. However, Downie was enough of a Marshallian to realize that productivity advantages could also come from having better knowledge than rivals and applying it effectively. But regardless of how they were achieved, lower costs per unit would enable a firm to grow its market share by investing its capacity at a faster rate than its rivals. Unless demand were growing at an even faster rate, the firm with the lowest unit costs would eventually force the exit of all the less productive firms. Customers would get progressively better value for money as this process played out, but if it resulted in monopoly, would the threat of potential entry be enough to ensure the remaining player did not abuse its position or "rest on its laurels"?

Downie applied the term "transfer mechanism" to the cumulating feedback systems that enable the most productive firms to capture market share. But he did not presume this "mechanism" would necessarily operate unchecked. Rather, he recognized that it might be counteracted by what he called the "innovation mechanism." By this he meant that the firms that currently enjoy the lowest unit cost levels may face challenges from, and lose market share to, innovative start-up enterprises or existing rivals that come up with significant productivity-enhancing ideas as a result of recognizing the long-term existential threat that they face and trying to find a way of getting round it. Downie's thinking in this respect is clearly very similar to what was emerging around the same time within the Carnegie research program; it is also complemented by Leibenstein's X-inefficiency analysis. However, we should notice that the innovations that established lower-productivity firms come up with need not be step-up responses after managers have examined performance data and issued a wake-up call to their colleagues; they could also result from creative thinking or discoveries made during routine work in which these firms engage because they realize that, in the long run, they will continually have to find ways of doing better even if their current profits are enough for them not to arouse interest from takeover raiders.

What we might end up seeing, if the innovation mechanism is powerful, is that product markets do not end up turning into monopolies; instead, they may tend to operate rather like sporting leagues in which the rankings of teams move around through time, with some teams being relegated to lower-tier competitive arenas, or being disbanded, and new teams sometimes eventually learning how to perform well enough to become credible competitors in the league in question. However, the ability of the innovation mechanism to counteract the transfer mechanism depends on how rapidly firms wake up to the threats they face and their capacities to change. Firms are not guaranteed to see their falling cost competitiveness in terms of learning curves and increasing returns to scale; they might instead see the problem in terms of worker attitudes, incentive systems and how factories are being managed. If so, their response may focus on cost cutting within the existing technology system – i.e., reducing X-inefficiency and taking up organizational slack – without actually engaging in the innovation that will be needed for longer-term survival.

The periods for which Downie investigated empirically the interaction between the transfer mechanism and the innovation mechanism were times where trade was far less free than in the world of globalized markets that gradually took shape from the 1970s onward. However, his empirical analysis has never been updated, because those who have wished to undertake the task (myself included, in my first idea for my PhD) have not had the luxury of having access to the raw (i.e., firm-level) UK Census of Production data that Downie had been able to use due to his position as a public servant.

If Downie had been writing in the late twentieth and early twenty-first centuries, he would doubtless have paid more attention to the processes by which firms in newly industrializing economies can disrupt existing competitive leagues and gradually work their way up toward the premier technology battlegrounds. If he had done this, he might well have seen the need to introduce an "imitation mechanism" into his analysis. This starts in economies with much lower wages and/or with protection against imports. Because of their limited initial knowledge, firms in such economies concentrate initially on serving local customers or those in export markets who are less affluent and hence less demanding in non-price terms than those that the experienced, dominant producers serve. Their progression to more advanced products (for example, from making mopeds, to increasingly powerful motorcycles, light cars and eventually on to luxury vehicles) has often entailed outright copying or reverse engineering of established products or learning via licensing product designs and production methods from dominant players. The latter have been prone to be oblivious of, or to discount heavily, the possibility that their licensees may one day become their rivals (for an excellent video documentary of this in the context of the rise of the Japanese motor industry, see Grimsdale, 1990).

The present-day significance of Downie's transfer mechanism is easy to appreciate if one reflects on the dominance of modern tech giants such as Google, Amazon, Facebook and Microsoft. Here, we should keep in mind potential for improving products, too. The economics of modern tech giants often entail near-zero marginal operating costs (because their products are based on programming) and increasing network externalities. Once they have bigger market shares than their rivals, they can invest far more in programming, to offer more sophisticated services than their rivals and yet enjoy smaller average fixed costs than their rivals. So, for example, Microsoft Office apps will tend, other things equal, to have a richer range of features than Apple's equivalents because more people use Microsoft software. However, Apple's ability to survive reflects another aspect of modern business that reinforces Downie's concerns about the potential for the competitive process to tend toward extreme industrial concentration: large modern firms tend also to grow by pursuing economies of scope, i.e., they diversify their ranges of products by exploiting further their existing investments in technology, manufacturing and marketing. This sharing of investments reduces average fixed costs compared with those incurred by a rival firm that has a smaller product range. Apple's desktop and laptop computers, its iPad tablets, iPhones and Apple watches take product complementarity to a higher level: these products are not merely based around different combinations of technology modules but are also designed to be synchronized with each other and have similarities in their user interfaces.

11.5   Nelson and Winter's Neo-Schumpeterian Evolutionary Analysis

As Marshall (1890) had realized, there are obvious parallels between the struggles that individual living organisms and entire species face as an inherent part of being alive and the struggles that firms and industries faces as an inherent aspect of capitalism. There are also parallels between the symbiotic relationships that we can observe in biological ecosystems and the relationships between businesses that Blois (1972), Richardson (1972) and scholars of Japanese business (e.g., Dore, 1973, 2012) have played key roles in bringing to the attention of economists. However, we obviously also need something equivalent to the idea of a gene if we are to take further this parallel between biological and economic evolution. For Nelson and Winter (1982), the notion of a rule or routine is the economic equivalent to a gene in the process of natural selection: just as species are carriers of genes that shape their competitive fitness in biological ecosystems, so technologies, organizations and products are carriers of rules that shape their competitive fitness in commercial ecosystems. This way of thinking integrates readily with the rules-based view of cognition and decision-making set out in earlier chapters of this book.

On this modified biology-inspired view, changes in the rules that economic entities carry will change their relative competitive fitness and hence their probabilities of prospering and growing or struggling and going extinct. In evolutionary biology, genetic mutations can be viewed as occurring randomly: over millions of years, successive tiny random changes in genes can be passed down countless generations to produce new organs, reproductive and mobility systems, and new species, with diverse species continuing to survive so long as their genes confer enough competitive fitness upon them relative to others that may try to occupy their environmental niches. But changes in relative competitive fitness of rule-carrying elements of economic systems do not typically arise via random mutations of rules. Rather, they result via people exercising their capacities for critical thinking and making creative connections.

The Post-It Notes produced by 3M provide a good illustration of Nelson and Winter's view that problem-driven creative changes drive the innovations that propel much of the structural change that takes place as economic systems evolve. Post-It Notes are often seen as the epitome of an accidental innovation, but they came about partly because of a connection being recognized. Indeed, Post-it Notes emerged via something akin to the "garbage can" decision process proposed by Cohen et al. (1972) that we considered in Section 6.5: a failed attempt to create a new superstrong adhesive left 3M scientist Spencer Silver with a "solution without a problem," with six years elapsing before his colleague Art Fry realized that Silver's unexpectedly weak adhesive could be used as a temporary means for attaching bookmarking notes. Note, too, that 3M was routinely funding scientists such as Silver to search for new technologies and new ways of applying technologies rather than only switching into search mode due to the failure of its managers to meet their aspirations or KPIs or after perceiving an existential threat to the organization. The competitive fitness of firms thus continually changes as a result of purposive action rather than having to await random mutations in their ways of operating.

Nelson and Winter's analysis integrates this innovation-focused Schumpeterian view of the nature of economic evolution with some of the behavioral ingredients that we employed in the previous chapter: they drew on the Carnegie group's work on decision rules, satisficing and problem-solving behavior and on Penrose's view of the firm as a pool of resources with distinctive capabilities. Like those in business schools who have extended Penrose's perspective, they recognized that these capabilities could be augmented via learning within the firm, but that other organizations could find it difficult to replicate them completely whether via reverse engineering the final product or via technology licensing. (For a collection of key papers on the "resource-based" view of firms, see Foss, 1997.)

In Nelson and Winter's analysis, a firm's ability to survive and grow depends on whether its operating rules and routines lead it to offer products whose features and prices are congruent with what potential buyers are seeking. Some of these rules and routines will embody knowledge that is common to all players in the industry or embody policies imposed by government agencies, trade associations and so on (as with health and safety procedures, product standards and design rules); some will have been outsourced via technology licensing deals, but others will embody the specific know-how of its human resources. If the firm's operating rules and routines lead it to offer products whose designs do not appeal to prospective customers or are poorly executed and/or not offered at competitive prices, then it will be pushed out of the market. Meanwhile, the market shares of firms that have been better able to contain their costs and satisfy and/or cultivate market preferences will grow.

We can get a sense of what evolutionary success looks like if we reflect on the growth of a franchise-based business system such as McDonald's, as more and more McDonald's restaurants are set up around the world as clones of existing ones and are operated via the same formula. Nevertheless, although such business systems may seem to spread like a plague, their futures are not guaranteed: if they fail to adapt to changes in how their rivals compete and in what customers want, they will not survive in the long run. Moreover, when a franchise formula is broadly congruent with market selection processes across a wide geographical area, it can be jeopardized by attempts of franchisees to try to improve their performance by applying their local knowledge and breaking the rules by changing the products somewhat (see the empirical study by Winter et al., 2012).

11.6   The Micro–Meso–Macro View of Structural Change

From the complex adaptive systems standpoint that was introduced in Section 3.7, the process of growth and structural change in the economy entails change in the set of elements that constitute the economic system and changes in the architecture of connections between these elements. The population of consumers changes, as does the pattern of goodwill relationships that consumers have with firms, the popularity of different purchasing rules and the ways of behaving that underpin consumer lifestyles. As a result, the popularity of individual products changes, with implications for the population of firms that supply them. The set of capital goods and consumables being offered to firms and households changes, too, as new products are created by constructing new combinations of elements as people have new ideas about what might be possible and as knowledge grows about the set of feasible combinations (see further Endres and Harper, 2012). As knowledge grows, the complexity of the economic system increases in terms of the production systems that create outputs, the range of outputs and the connection-making capabilities required to make them. Some products, such as computer printers, may seem to be lighter and made of less physical "stuff" than they used to be, but they are only possible as a result of more advanced knowledge being employed to design and manufacture them.

Progress in economic science works in this way, too, as should be evident from reflecting on what has been happening in this chapter as we have moved to a progressively richer view of economic evolution. The next stage is to combine the complex systems view with the rules-/routines-based view of economic evolution that Nelson and Winter offered. This is essentially what has been done by Kurt Dopfer, John Foster, and Jason Potts in their attempt (Dopfer et al., 2004) to provide a means for understanding what happens, and why, as innovators seek to interest others in new products, production methods and/or ways of running business and social systems. They call it the "micro–meso–macro framework." It entails a much more radical, more general use of the notion of a "rule" as the unit of selection than evolutionary economists had previously used. This section introduces their framework, and Sections 11.7–11.13 employ it to illustrate the dynamics of structural change. As the framework's name indicates, it entails three levels of analysis.

11.6.1   Micro

This is the level at which individuals and organizational entities use rules as means for meeting the ends that they are pursuing. It is the same level as conventional microeconomic analysis, except that Dopfer et al. are viewing production, consumption and other activities as entailing the selection and use of rules rather than objects. This does not mean they ignore the things on which orthodox microeconomists focus their analysis of choice. Rather, they view objects and human agents as carriers of rules, just as evolutionary biologists view living organisms as carriers of genes. Thus, when we decide to start producing, consuming or doing anything else (for example, interacting with others in social settings) in a different "way," we adopt particular rules and rule-carrying objects in place of others that we had previously been employing. Our change of behavior thereby changes the relative populations (i.e., the relative popularity) of particular rules in the economic system. If everyone has stopped using a particular rule, it has, in effect, become extinct, though obviously it is much easier to revive extinct rules (as with "retro" and "reissue" products) than it is to recreate an extinct species, even if we can map the latter's genome. If a defunct rule is to be revived without using a reverse engineering process, the key thing is that the rule is stored somewhere in the system, along with the set of rules for building and operating objects that carry it. Sometimes, of course, rules that go extinct end up being forgotten, as with many languages, crafts and knowledge from ancient times about how to build particular structures.

To tune into this perspective, let us first think about production systems. At the micro level, there may be many different "ways" that are being used to make a product, with different levels of productivity (cf. Section 11.3). Each "way" comprises a particular set of physical, institutional and human elements and embodies a set of rules specific to that system. The system's technology embodies a particular set of design and operating rules. The system's institutional rules specify the context in which it is operated, such as the formal structure of the organization in question and its policies and procedures, plus the more informal rules that constitute the organizational culture. Finally, the personnel involved in the production system each have their own operating systems of cognitive rules that determine how they will view issues that arise as they do their jobs. Their personal operating rules will determine, for example, the extent of their compliance with instructions issued by their bosses and the extent of their altruistic contributions to making the system function effectively. It is via these systems of rules that the evolutionary selection process functions at the micro level, with some systems thriving and others being taken out of operation and broken up. Their fates depend on how congruent are the outcomes that they make possible with the decision rules of their funders and intended customers.

On the consumption side, households will differ in how they operate "as a rule," and members of a multi-person household may likewise go about doing things in different ways and with the aid of different consumable inputs and durable assets. In the case of food, some may have adopted particular dietary practices but differ in the specific kinds of meals they consume within the rules of any given diet, in how they get their meals, in the technologies they use to cook their meals if they do not outsource them and in which household member(s) shop(s) for ingredients and cook(s) the meals. Through time, the rules that constitute these household practices will change but at different times and in different ways across the population of households. (For a practice-based view of household behavior, see Shove et al., 2012.)

11.6.2 Meso

Dopfer et al. (2004) argue that it is instructive to take this rule-based view further by acknowledging that, in addition to the micro-level systems that make up an evolving economy, there is also a more generic level, which they call the "meso" level. In their terms, a meso is a rule that defines a generic category of production method (e.g., the basic oxygen method of making steel, the electric arc furnace method of making steel, cooking with a wok, cooking with a microwave oven, etc.), product (e.g., a hatchback car, a smartphone, a bicycle), mode of organization (e.g., an M-form corporate structure, a franchise system) or a social or political rule or philosophy (e.g., democracy, family planning, gender equality, sustainable living, "living together" instead of marrying). Micro-level aspects of the economy are the specific manifestations of generic, meso-level rules, with different micro-level carriers of the generic rules applying them in their own ways.

Thus, when analyzing an industry, we might classify production systems into several meso categories, each pertaining to a particular generic "way" of producing the output in question. The systems categorized in a particular way may differ in their productivity because they comprise different vintages of that particular technology and workers with different levels of experience and motivation, and so on. Likewise, a particular generic product category may comprise many manufacturers' own visions of what to offer as a product that has the essential features that make it a member of that category. For example, some vehicles classed as SUVs may not have a third row of seats or offer four-wheel drive, but they all entail raised ground clearance and an elevated driving position relative to conventional sedans and wagons. The specific SUV models that manufacturers try to sell are the micro-level carriers of the SUV meso.

Meso rules can be conceptualized at multiple levels. For example, consider what, "as a rule," we mean by "a bicycle." In its most generic sense, a bicycle is a self-propelled personal transport aid whose user is required to sit astride a frame connected to two wheels and to be able to maintain balance when in motion. However, as the bicycle has evolved, it has gone from the crude "hobby horse" (with no pedals) to the "penny farthing" (with pedals, very different diameter wheels and no cog and chain system) to the "safety bicycle" (with a triangle-based tubular frame, pedals and a cog and chain system that includes a free-wheel device), which in turn has morphed into more specific categories such as "mountain bike," "road bike" and "BMX bike."

The "meso" level of analysis lines up well with the analysis of cognition that was presented in Chapter 4 and the idea that cognitively constrained decision-makers typically consider substitution within a category when choosing (e.g., Apple versus Android smartphones, or LG versus Samsung Android smartphones), or substitute at the category levels (e.g., monthly phone budget versus monthly leisure budget) rather than between specific options that are in different generic categories. But the meso idea also enables us to analyze economic evolution more readily, for during the period in which members of the population of economic entities use a particular meso, the specific micro-level things that come into its generic category may come and go. This is central to the process of "creative destruction" that Joseph Schumpeter saw as driving the evolution of economic systems, and Dopfer (2012) credits Schumpeter as being the pioneer of meso-level thinking in economics.

11.6.3   Macro

Because Dopfer et al. see economies as complex systems in the sense set out in Potts (2000), they offer a very different view of the "macro" level of the economy from the conventional usage of "macro" as applying to aggregates and economic indicators at the level of the economy as a whole. By integrating Schumpeterian thinking with the complex systems approach, they end up with a view of the "macro" level of economic analysis that focuses on how structural change takes place as growth processes play out in economic systems. The process of structural change entails changes in the connective structure of the economic system, so in the Dopfer et al. view, the macro level of an economy evolving through time is rather like a roll of cloth whose pattern evolves as it comes out of a loom. These changes of system architecture entail not merely changed rates of connections between economic entities, operating rules and assets that embody particular rules; they can also include changes in the extent to which particular kinds of complementary relationships are employed in processes of production and consumption. This rewiring of the overall connective structure of the economy is both a result and a driver of changes in the elements (technologies) that are brought together to create new micro-level carriers of existing and new meso rules or rule-based concepts.

Hence, for Dopfer et al., "macro" evolution pertains to how the structure and operation of the economic system as a whole change due to the interaction between different meso rules, i.e., how the uptake trajectory of a particular meso (mapped in terms of how the size of its population of users changes through time) impacts upon other meso trajectories and is in turn affected by the latter. This "macro" evolution emerges out of micro-level changes in: (a) how production is organized as a result of particular meso rules being adopted (e.g., interactions between the uptake of computer-aided manufacturing and the uptake of global offshoring as a business model); (b) what is made (e.g., in the use of touch screens and digital storage media in car audio systems); and (c) the lifestyle systems that people build (e.g., the interconnected uptake of dual-income suburban living, commuting by railway, car ownership, supermarkets, fridge and freezers, frozen food and time- and labor-saving appliances such as washing machines and microwave ovens).

Macroevolution of this kind is inherently challenging to predict. This is partly because of complex feedback links between the often path-dependent uptakes trajectories of different meso elements in the economic system and partly because of the role of entrepreneurial or innovative thinking in spotting ways of creating new systems. This unpredictability is not merely a problem for economists, town planners and other policy analysts; it also afflicts firms and consumers. For example, when smartphones first appeared, conventional taxi companies may not have imagined the possibility of a ride-sharing app such as Uber; likewise, those who bought early smartphones had little idea of the range of apps, e-commerce, and streaming opportunities that would soon start making these phones more valuable to them and how their lives might consequently change.

11.7 Meso Trajectories

A key aspect of the micro–meso–macro view of structural change is that it is a process that takes place through time: even the most brilliant innovations are rarely taken up instantly by all those who adopt them. Evolutionary economists think of meso adoption trajectories as typically having the kind of S-shaped uptake trajectory shown in Figure 11.4 and comprising three phases: origination, adoption and retention or decline.

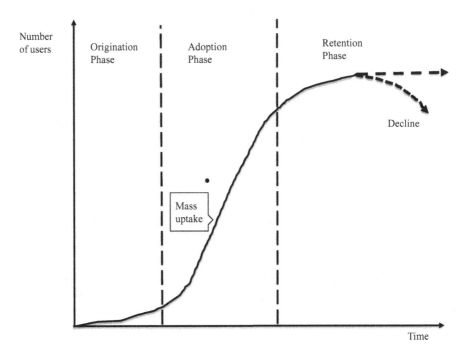

Figure 11.4 A stylized meso trajectory

The *S*-shaped curve of a meso trajectory resembles the kind of trajectory seen with the spread of a contagious disease. This should not surprise us here, for social network structures will have significant roles to play in spreading information about new products and ways of doing things. Diffusion trajectories that take a broadly *S*-shaped form have been identified for many products and production processes: early studies included those by Griliches (1957) on hybrid corn and Bain (1964) on television ownership in the UK after World War II.

In stylized form, the shape of a meso trajectory is like that of a stylized product life-cycle trajectory for a micro-level carrier of a meso rule. However, it should be noted that individual products may be launched at any stage during the trajectory of the meso that they carry. Some products launched during the original phase may be withdrawn even before the meso is widely adopted, whereas others that carry the same meso rule may even be launched during the meso's period of decline and be specially designed to cater for the remaining users. Also note that, during the period in which particular individuals are users of a particular meso rule, they may use successive carriers of that rule (for example, successive generations of Apple iPhones that carry the smartphone meso). As with actual product life cycles, actual meso trajectories may differ significantly from the smooth *S*-shaped curve shown in Figure 11.4. For example, some adoption and retention phases may last for decades, other for much shorter periods and sometimes (as with the resurgence of enthusiasm for vinyl LPs that had previously been displaced by CDs) meso rule enjoy a "new lease of life" after long periods when they were out of favor.

Sections 11.8–11.13 consider the drivers of the three meso trajectory phases shown in Figure 11.4 in relation to what happens at the micro and macro levels. These sections include extensive case material, much of which is not cluttered with references. However, in each instance, the relevant Wikipedia entry provides further details and opens the door to relevant sources. If you visit Wikipedia for such material, you might pause and reflect that you are engaging with an innovation that was catastrophically disruptive for sales of traditional printed encyclopedias but was just one of many innovations made possible by the uptake of the Internet and personal computers.

11.8   Meso 1: Origination

Schumpeter was careful to distinguish between inventors (those who first have an idea about a new product or production process) and innovators (those who take risks pioneering the commercialization of new products or processes). He was wise to do this, for the process of creative destruction that an invention could generate will not get under way until someone steps forward to take a commercial gamble with it, which in some cases is not until decades after the inventor first had the idea. Although some innovations originate with rival research teams that are simultaneously trying to make roughly the same idea work, it is rare that the race to be first to market is a tie. As a result, the origination phase of a meso trajectory normally coincides initially with the accumulating sales path of the first product to be marketed that follows what becomes how the product will be thought of "as a rule." Here, in contrast to the analysis presented in Section 11.2, pricing is highly discretionary, for either there is patent protection for the first-to-market monopolist or the potential for rivals soon to come up with better versions will be so evident that, as the saying goes, "it pays to make hay while the sun is shining."

There is often scope for debate about which is the micro-level product with whose introduction a meso trajectory commences. Should we view a meso trajectory as beginning with the first design to "write the rules" of the meso, or should we see it as beginning with a design that is merely a partial harbinger of what will become the rule in the area in question? This is not a mere semantic issue, for the evolution from harbinger products to rule-setting or game-changing designs often entails what we might call "meso-splicing."

For example, consider the "hatchback car" as a meso. If we think of this simply as a small car that does not have the rear overhang of a sedan or wagon but has a wagon-like rear door and fold-flat rear seats, we might see the meso as beginning with the 1959 Austin A40 Countryman produced by the British Motor Corporation (BMC). But the A40 packed much less interior space into its dimensions than a modern hatchback does, since it was powered by a longitudinally mounted engine that drove the rear wheels. This format was hardly ever adopted aside from the 1975 Vauxhall Chevette in the UK, the first hatchbacks made in Japan from the early 1970s to the early 1980s and the BMW 1-series from 2004 to 2019. The generic "hatchback" design that was widely adopted by manufacturers (even, in the end, by BMW) and customers is one that achieves space efficiency, reliability, and ease of maintenance by having a transverse-mounted front engine, with the gearbox end-on to the engine and the power transmitted to the front wheels by unequal-length driveshafts, with an electrically driven cooling fan and front-facing radiator.

On this spliced-meso view, the hatchback that wrote the rules for its genre was the three-door version of the little-known Autobianchi Primula that was manufactured from 1964 through 1970. Autobianchi was a niche producer of small cars, and its co-owner Fiat used the Primula as the test bed for this drivetrain meso. Designed by Dante Giacosa, the Primula's drivetrain format became the small-car norm. It was also gradually applied in much larger vehicles as engineers became better at taming the torque-steer problem (associated with the unequal-length driveshafts) that was encountered when it was first used with powerful engines. It eliminated problems inherent in an earlier water-cooled, transverse engine, front-wheel-drive system devised by Alec Issigonis for BMC. In the Issigonis design, the engine and gearbox shared the same oil sump, and an engine-driven fan cooled a sideways-mounted radiator. BMC brought this design to the market in 1959 in the original Mini (marked as an Austin Seven and a Morris Mini Minor). In its own creative splicing, Austin used the Mini's system in its 1969 Maxi hatchback, but other carmakers did not emulate it, and eventually Austin came to use the system pioneered in the Primula.

Meso-splicing will happen more readily where commercial innovation environments function rather in the way that academia functions as a system for generating knowledge. Jason Potts (2019) calls this kind of environment an "innovation commons," the core principle being that those who come up with new ideas are duly credited for their creative insights, but others are then freely able to draw upon them to make further creative advances. (This is essentially what has happened in the writing of this book: with the aid of an excellent library, I have been freely able to use hundreds of sources and integrate them into a novel synthesis, while giving credit to the originators of the ideas.) Potts's thinking echoes our earlier Koestler-inspired discussion of creativity in which it was emphasized that new ideas do not spring from nowhere and instead emerge as a result of people making new sets of connections between existing elements. Once we recognize the genealogy of innovations, the case for innovators being able to confine access to their ideas to those who are prepared to pay a license fee seems questionable: each contribution is only possible because of what has gone before, so putting a series of licensing hurdles in place to enable each creative connection-maker to capture rents is likely to have adverse effects on the growth of knowledge. (On this view, patents and copyright protection should be brought to an end and academic publishing should all be done on an open-access basis, with publishers deriving their earnings by being able to charge authors fees for getting their contributions quality-checked and valued by peer-reviewing processes.)

Once an innovator kick-starts a new meso, the origination phase in some cases takes many years, with a sequence of faltering attempts to make it work well enough and cheaply enough to take it on to mass adoption. For example, smartphones grew out of attempts to merge mobile phones and personal digital assistants, beginning with the IBM Simon Personal Communicator in 1994. The Simon had a touch screen, but its usefulness was limited by a very short battery life and a tiny memory. It was only on the market for about six months and was discontinued before the term "smartphone" was coined. Its successors were more capable but generally came with a built-in miniature QWERTY keyboards rather than a touch screen. It was not until 2007, via the first Apple iPhone, that the smartphone meso was clearly established, with a focus on Internet connectivity and a touch screen large enough to make this practicable.

Given its feeble performance compared with even the first iPhone, the fact that the IBM Simon was withdrawn so soon is far less remarkable than the fact that in its brief life it achieved sales of 50,000 units despite being priced (in 1994 US dollars) at $1099 without a contract or $899 (later $599) if purchased with a two-year operating contract. The combination of premium price and restricted capability relative to later products of the same meso is very commonly observed with innovations. Initially, their customer base will typically be confined to those who have a lexicographic kind of preference for whatever it is that the pioneering product offers that gives its users some kind of competitive edge. These initial adopters want it as a means to get (or stay) ahead, regardless of its cost and/or technical limitations. The competitive edge may be in terms of social competition, i.e., the bragging rights that its user will (briefly) enjoy but may also come in relation to business use (as with the IBM Simon's mobile ability to send and receive faxes and emails), sport (as with early carbon-fiber bicycle frames), the creative industries (as with the pioneering Fairlight CMI sampling keyboard instruments purchased by superstar musicians and leading recording studios in the late 1970s), press photographers (with the first digital SLR cameras) or in the defense sector.

It is in such competitive contexts that dramatic differences between the prices of the first iterations of a meso product and those for earlier ways of serving the same end may not matter. As far as the pioneering adopters are concerned, the innovation pays for itself in terms of the time it saves, the deals that it makes possible, and so on. Otherwise, it is normally procedurally rational with high-tech innovations to delay adoption on the basis that the value for money that they offer will soon increase as knowledge advances in the area in question and spreads more widely via the innovation commons. The growth of (access to) knowledge typically leads to more suppliers contesting the market and offering a wider range of choice, along with general performance improvements. Prices of new products typically fall, consistent with Marshall's long-run analysis, as the scale of production increases, learning curve effects are achieved and the pressure of competition increases, driving producers away from monopolistic behavior and into cost-based pricing.

At the macro level, the origination phase of a meso brings discoordination and disruption to existing order – though not always with abruptness akin to the effect of a cat joining a gathering of foraging birds. Purveyors of older ways of servicing the same ends will not merely find it challenging to win any further adopters; they will also find that rebuys from past adopters tail off as the latter switch to the new meso at replacement time (or earlier, if the innovation is so attractive as to lead them to depart from their usual replacement cycle routines). Investment in producing and carrying stocks of complementary products for those of the challenged meso will begin to dry up, thereby limiting further that meso's appeal. For example, when CD players were launched, record companies and record stores faced the risk of ending up with vinyl LPs that they would not be able to sell even if they waited in the way that they would normally expect to do with slow-selling albums. The record companies thus had an increased incentive to issue new recordings only in CD format and the record shops had a bigger incentive to make space for CDs. The greater difficulty that this posed for customers when it came to finding particular vinyl LPs was a signal that sooner or later it would be time to give up buying new LPs altogether. Similarly, vehicle manufacturers would have begun considering the implications of CD technology for the design of in-car entertainment system: would they need to replace audio cassette players with CD players or offer both? Three and a half decades later, the music-streaming meso gave vehicle dashboard designers a similar dilemma, but this time the question was whether to continue to provide in-car CD players and storage space for CDs.

11.9   Impediments to the Adoption of a New Meso

Given that real-world consumers typically have considerable experience of new types of products getting cheaper and better, we should not be surprised that mass adoption of a new meso takes time. Prospective adopters do not have to be "econs" to see the benefits of waiting and in the meantime continuing to operate in their usual way. For example, consider Sarah, a consumer in the early 2000s who typically has been spending $1000 a year on photographic film and photo processing, and who does not have the professional photographer's need for instant access to her photographs. Sarah may be readily able to see that she would be throwing money away if she buys a digital SLR camera whose price she expects to fall by more than $1000 in the next twelve months, even though the marginal cost of a photograph taken with the latter is close to zero if she just keeps reusing the same memory card and stores photos on her computer's hard-drive rather than getting hard-copy prints. Hence, even if Sarah had purchased a non-digital SLR just before the digital ones came out and then delayed switching for several years, we should view her behavior as procedurally rational rather than a sign of sunk-cost bias and dysfunctional mental accounting. On the other hand, if she *did* become an early adopter of a digital SLR camera in order to keep getting SLR capabilities with the benefit of instant access to her photographs, then we might reasonably view her behavior as implying quasi-hyperbolic discounting.

Where new and old applications of meso rules entail investments in durable assess, delays in adopting the new means to the end(s) in question can be perfectly rational precisely because of the presence of sunk costs in respect of the older meso, even if there are no expectations of falling prices and improved capabilities for the new meso. The key point here, as in the Salter diagram analysis in Section 11.3, is that, in order to be preferable, the newer way of doing things must offer the prospect of average *total* costs that are less than the older way's average cost in terms of new outlays on operating overheads and variable inputs. If the latter average cost is smaller than the average total cost for the new technology, it pays to keep on using the old technology until it wears out even if, at that point, it would make no sense to replace it.

Rapid adoption of a new meso, or the failure of an innovation to take off at all, is not merely a matter of procedurally rational resistance by potential adopters based on the kinds of logic raised in the previous two paragraphs. Ahead of such concerns as potential barriers to the adoption of a new way of doing things lie other kinds of barriers that are easily recognized if one views choice from a behavioral perspective.

11.9.1   Where Initial Micro-Level Applications of the Meso Have One or More "Deal-Breaker" Flaws

Loss aversion and non-compensatory decision rules may stand in the way of adopting new types of products whose new capability requires the sacrifice of something hitherto taken for granted. Electric vehicles exemplify this: they may offer spectacular acceleration, smoothness and silence and provide a means of reducing one's carbon footprint, but all this comes at the cost of questions about their usability on long journeys where charging stations are few and far between. Even if not viewed as "too expensive," these vehicles may thus be commonly ruled out except as urban runabouts and delivery workhorses. In other cases of initial resistance, the new concept requires no sacrifice aside from the asking price but has a design shortcoming that renders it inadequate in terms of what the user might reasonably expect it to be able to do. For example, in 1975, when Sony became the first supplier of videocassette recorders on the domestic market, its original NTSC-format Betamax machines could only record for one hour, thereby failing to be able to do a time-shift recording of an entire movie. Any significant uptake of the VCR required cheaper machines that could record for several hours, even if this came at some cost in picture quality, and this was what other brands' machines were soon able to offer via the VHS technology standard.

11.9.2   Conflicting Micro-Level Standards

Given the technical challenges of making some meso concepts work, we should not be surprised to see, at the micro level, firms differing in the philosophies that they apply in trying to implement a particular meso concept. Sometimes this is no impediment to the meso rule achieving widespread adoption, with the alternative philosophies even persisting as meso rules in their own right because their differences make them attractive to different customer groups (as, for example, with the solid body electric guitar meso, divided between the single-coil pickups and bolt-on neck philosophy pioneered by Fender, versus the twin-coil pickups and glued-in neck philosophy pioneered by Gibson: see Port, 2019). But in some cases where manufacturers differ in their design philosophies and offer incompatible applications of a given meso concept, it is procedurally rational for prospective customers to wait to see which standard dominates. This applies particularly in two kinds of situation where a failure to choose the dominant meso will entail having to write off a significant investment.

One of these cases is where the adopter must invest time in learning how to use the product in question and different user interfaces are where the different design philosophies manifest themselves to prospective users. If one backs the philosophy that fails to become the dominant standard, upgrading to subsequent generations of the product will involve investing time in learning how to use the dominant system. It thus pays to wait and see what the dominant interface will be. Of course, once a meso standard has been established, such learning costs will be a barrier to the uptake of a rival new meso. This will be especially the case if they are inflated by quasi-hyperbolic discounting and/or dread of being temporarily less than fully competent during the transition period and if the existing way of operating seems perfectly adequate (as with the continued dominance of the QWERTY typewriter keyboard and the failure of the ergonomically superior Dvorak keyboard layout to take off as an alternative meso).

The other situation is where the adopter must invest in an asset whose value depends upon it being used in conjunction with complementary products whose supply will be curtailed if it fails to become the dominant standard. Suppliers of such products will hold back, too, if the production equipment is also standard-specific. Consider again the case of videocassette recorders in the late 1970s or early 1980s. The initial significance of three rival standards (Sony Betamax, Philips V-2000 and VHS) was limited if buyers only expected to use a VCR for making their own recordings, for in that case these machines would continue to be useful so long as blank videocassettes of the right kind were available. But as soon as opportunities to rent prerecorded content appeared, the logistics of supplying content favored having just one format. Hence, it became procedurally rational to wait to see which standard dominated if one were planning to buy a VCR as a means for playing prerecorded content.

11.9.3   Limited Availability of Complementary Products

Disappointing supplies of complementary products will delay adoption of a meso even in the absence of a standards battle and even in cases where the technology has no shortcomings when first launched. Obvious examples here are the limited ranges of CDs and DVDs that pioneering buyers of, respectively, CD players and DVD players had to contend with, just as pioneering buyers of phonographs and televisions decades before had faced, respectively, a limited range of recordings and few programs to watch. Given such issues, other areas of spending may be favored pending acceptable growth in the supplies of complementary products.

Related to the complementary products issue as a barrier to the initial uptake of an innovation is the possibility that its appeal is a function of how many others have adopted it. This is known as a situation of increasing network externalities. Internet dating services provide an excellent example: the probability of being able to find a very good match via such a service depends on how many subscribers it has. If such a service has very few subscribers, it will only be likely to serve the needs of those who do not have firm checklists about the kind of person they are trying to find and/or who are attracted by the idea of being able to identify readily who is "in the market" and approach them without having to have the social skills required for doing this in traditional settings.

11.9.4 Ignorance and Incomprehension

An innovation will not even be considered by potential adopters if they do not become aware of its existence because:

(a) they are not exposed to stimuli about it due to shortcomings of the innovator's marketing strategy, or
(b) they do not discover it by themselves or with the aid of market institutions because of limitations of the search strategies that they use to solve problems to which it would be relevant, or
(c) they do not search in the area in question due to setting their aspirations needlessly low in that area.

The willingness and ability of retail suppliers to obtain and display stocks of new products may thus be a vital driver of demand for them. This point is overlooked in a conventional economic perspective that view supply and demand as independent of each other, but it is, as Andrews (1964) recognized, something we need to take seriously if we accept that real-world decision-makers are not omniscient. (See further the discussion of Andrews's thinking in Section 9.3, in relation to the "Gruen transfer.")

Even if those whom we might view as potential adopters do discover a particular innovation, there is no guarantee that they will perceive it in a way that results in them wanting to invest time in learning more about it. To appreciate why, it may be useful to revisit Chapter 4's analysis of cognition and Section 7.7's analysis of resistance to change: people with long-established ways of thinking may have trouble viewing new offerings as their suppliers or proponents want them to be viewed. The cognitive processes of the target market or audience will tend, out of cognitive habit, to try to make sense of them in terms of their established mental models.

An example of this, from the history of economic thought, is relevant here, because it pertains to the cognitive challenge that many readers probably faced when on reaching the discussion of the behavioral approach to pricing in Section 11.2. The "normal cost" theory of pricing differs fundamentally from the standard theories of price and output that involve equalizing marginal costs with marginal revenues. However, when Philip Andrews (1949) set it out in his book *Manufacturing Business,* his reviewers simply did not "get" the difference and tried to view it as a wordy restatement of either the theory of perfect competition or the theory of imperfect or monopolistic competition (see Irving, 1978). Moreover, a decade earlier, Andrews's colleagues Robert Hall and Charles Hitch (1939) had themselves failed properly to grasp the nature of the departure they were making in their "full cost" version of the new approach: at some points, they needlessly flipped their analysis into marginalist terms (see Lee, 1984). In other words, their minds had taken them through the kind of process that happens when we watch one of the videos of a rotating "hollow head." I, too, went through the same kind of process before I "got" what was different about the Oxford approach to pricing.

Similarly, even if the need to switch to a new way of doing things is recognized, or where it is imposed from outside, cognitive habits can make the change difficult for those who try to achieve it. It is not just those who are addicted to, say, drugs or alcohol who are prone to "backsliding" in the face of temptation. For example, it has been evident since the 2007–2008 Global Financial Crisis that, despite pressures for firms in the financial services sector to adopt the meso of "corporate social responsibility," major banks have continued to engage in ethically questionable behavior, as in the case of Westpac, one of Australia's largest banks, that was fined AUD1.3 billion (US$923 million) in 2020 for twenty-three million breaches of anti-money-laundering rules. (For analysis of organizational struggles with ethics in the face of ongoing temptation, see Kaptein, 2017.)

11.9.5   Bounded Imagination

Bounded imaginative capabilities can inhibit interest in a new meso despite target customers having no trouble understanding what they are being shown. This issue seems to underpin the cautionary tales that are central to Clayton Christensen's (1997) famous book *The Innovator's Dilemma*. Christensen was attempting, with the aid of a set of case studies, to understand how major producers of an existing technology could fail to survive transitions to new alternative technologies that they had initially resisted. At the heart of this tended to be the fact that the new technology, in effect, solved problems that target customers did not *yet* see as problems and that it did so in a way that imposed a cost that users of the existing technology would indeed see as a problem.

Christensen's initial case focused on computer hard drives, where the issue is especially easy to understand. The first small hard drives for computers could not be produced with storage capacities that matched existing larger hard drives, which computers had already been designed to accommodate. The established makers of large hard drives failed to think ahead to a world in which the small hard drives had been developed further to offer more capacity and would be sought after by computer makers who were increasingly competing with a focus on laptops and/or reducing the amount of office or desk space that their products occupied. Since the established hard drive manufacturers and their customers were not initially interested in buying the new technology, the firms that pioneered it initially had to focus on developing relationships with customers for whom compactness did matter but who did not view smaller memory capacity as a problem (such as in medical electronics devices for hospitals). That provided enough of a foundation for them gradually to develop high-capacity miniature hard drives and go on to capture the customers of the established hard drive manufacturers, with the latter manufacturers then not having the capabilities needed to make the smaller drives and thereby stop customers from switching.

The significance of bounded imaginative capacity as a barrier to the takeoff of a meso may depend on the extent to which those with less bounded visions have begun to supply complementary products. For example, back in the early 1980s when personal computers were first offered as appliance-like objects, a common reaction was, "Why would I need a computer for my home?" At that time, the range of software packages was very limited, so knowledge and imagination were prerequisites for being interested in the idea of getting a personal computer. If one could imagine using a personal computer only to do word processing, an electric typewriter with a small memory to enable typos to be removed and text to be rethought on the run might seem perfectly adequate.

11.9.6 Limited Supplies of Complementary Learning Resources

In an academic context, the supply of complementary learning resources (e.g., tutors, courses and textbooks) that would-be adopters can use has obvious significance as a meso adoption barrier; indeed, it was one that the behavioral economic meso has had to overcome. But it can arise in many other areas, such as in relation to the uptake of music genres and complex, hi-tech products. For example, prior to the advent of YouTube, it would also have been significant in the spread of technically challenging ways of playing music that could not readily be inferred simply by listening to the recordings of those who pioneered them. This was especially so where the recordings were only available via vinyl LPs that made it difficult to play small samples repeatedly or at slower speeds. More generally, in an age of increasing technological complexity, those who pioneer the adoption of innovations need to be bold enough to presume they will be able to make what they adopt work ahead of others uploading "how-to" Internet resources that make it easy to solve operating problems without having to find answers (if they are there to be found) in the manuals supplied by manufacturers. For others to follow, it can be vital for them to have confidence that bold pioneers will have shared their discoveries and have not overridden human tendencies toward "natural pedagogy."

The pool of freely shared "how-to" knowledge may be called the "user assistance commons" for the product or meso in question. This type of commons complements the market for preferences and market-assisted choices. It also augments Potts's (2019) origination-facilitating "innovation commons" with similar implications in relation to the social benefits of altruistic behavior: if, as a rule, pioneer adopters keep their new "how-to" knowledge to themselves (as is more likely if they see the product as a means for getting themselves a competitive advantage), society will accrue benefits from innovation more slowly, since slower adoption rates and/or the need to invest more heavily in customer support systems will reduce returns to investing in offering such technologies.

11.9.7 Innovator Overload

The problem of potential adopters failing to "get" an invention or other creative product is especially significant where the person in question is a gatekeeper (as with journal referees and editors) or a potential provider of resources needed to make the invention available to, and/or noticed by, the wider pool of potential adopters. If those in such positions are unable to construe it in a supportive manner, the only way for it to go from a mere invention to the stage of being offered to the wider world is for the inventor personally to make the necessary resource commitments to produce and/or market it. In some cases, this may require formally starting a business (see further Hodgson, 2004).

The pressure that an innovator faces can be compounded due to skepticism on the part of potential suppliers of components who would need to invest in product-specific dies and tooling in order to deliver the components that the innovator wants to order from them. In such a situation, the innovator will need more financial resources due to having either to pay for the product-specific investments (as, for example, vacuum cleaner innovator James Dysons did when initially outsourcing the manufacture of plastic moldings for his game-changing product) or to make components in-house because no external suppliers are prepared to take the risk that the product will fail and leave the innovator unable to pay its bills. Where external skepticism forces innovators to engage in vertical integration – an issue emphasized in Langlois and Robertson (1995) – the meso's takeoff will be held back insofar as the innovator has to produce on a smaller scale due to having to invest in more stages of production, with greater scope for problems to arise due to a wider range of capabilities needing to be acquired in order to make and (if potential distributors are skeptical, too) market and distribute the new product.

In some cases, internalization of activities may arise because innovators can see potential for the tacit knowledge problem to get in the way of external supply chain participants being able to deliver what is needed. For example, they may worry that they will be unable to ensure that external distributors really "get" how it will be necessary to change the mindsets of their staff in order to ensure that customers receive the correct messages. In relation to this, it is worth reflecting on how Tesla's early managerial challenges were increased by a determination to have its electric cars distributed via Tesla-run showrooms rather than franchised dealerships – a strategy that ran into legal diversions in some US state due to being deemed anticompetitive under state laws. The managerial challenges of building an in-house distribution system added to those that Tesla faced by having a highly vertically integrated production system (that conferred the benefit of enabling easier within-model hardware updates). Given all the demands on the scarce attention of Tesla's management team, it is not surprising, from the standpoint of Penrose's theory of the growth of the firm, that Tesla ran into quality control and supply bottleneck problems as it increased its scale of operations.

11.9.8   System Non-Decomposability

Finally, and mindful of Section 3.7, let us consider the significance of Herbert Simon's (1962, 1969) notion of system decomposability for the process of structural change. An innovation will have a far bigger chance of being rapidly adopted if it is in essence a module that can be installed in place of a functionally inferior module within an existing system (see Langlois and Robertson, 1995; and Pil and Cohey, 2006).

If a modular innovation comes without any patent restrictions on its use, adoption may be very rapid via other suppliers imitating the originator. An example of this is the sudden spread of multivalve cylinder heads in vehicle engines in the early 1980s. The concept had originally been devised for a Peugeot racing car in 1912 but had not been commercialized at the time. The performance-enhancing multivalve head could be introduced essentially as a bolt-on module without having to reengineer the rest of a car's engine, let alone the bulk of the car itself. Indeed, in its first application to a mass-market sedan, in the 1973 Triumph Dolomite Sprint, the engineers managed to design a four-valves-per-cylinder arrangement without even moving from a single camshaft to a twin-cam cylinder head. However, the substantial increase in power did necessitate wider modifications to the previous Dolomite model in its "Sprint" form, notably to ensure the drivetrain could handle the extra power.

Much incremental innovation is facilitated by the modularity of products, whereas radical changes in one area may require radical changes elsewhere in order to be effective. For example, building enough battery capacity into an electric car to give it both a long cruising range and low center of gravity precludes simply fitting an electric drivetrain and battery system to an existing car platform; instead, it is necessary to invest in an entirely new vehicle architecture with the weight of the batteries spread out beneath the passenger compartment.

The multivalve vehicle engine meso also provides an interesting illustration of another issues, namely how technological constraints can sometimes force engineers to choose between meso rules that ideally would be complementary. In the 1990s, Audi and Toyota achieved further performance improvements by switching some of their engines to five valves per cylinder. However, other manufacturers did not follow their lead and Audi and Toyota did not persist with the idea, as this configuration did not leave enough space in the cylinder head area to incorporate an electronic gasoline direct injection system. The latter, first introduced by Mitsubishi in 1996, offered major benefits for economy and emissions.

Clearly, if innovations take a modular form, their uptake may fail to become widespread if their originators offer them without taking account of standard interfaces (such as the USB standard in computing, and MIDI in digital music) that potential customers use to connect modules together. This matters also in contexts where performance-focused buyers wish to be able to customize their purchases by *replacing* some of a product's components with those from aftermarket suppliers. Adoption will be hindered if such buyers discover that this is not possible if they buy an innovative design, even if the product follows the "interchangeable parts, bolted together" manufacturing meso that originated with the mass production of guns during the American Civil War. It is also procedurally rational even for prospective customers who are unlikely to want to customize an innovative product with after-market modules to check the extent to which the product's components are interchangeable with those designed for earlier products. Any inability to replace modules with such aftermarket components provides a procedurally rational basis for delaying adoption: if the innovation flops, long-term maintenance could prove problematic due to spare parts not being available and the impossibility of substituting them with "standard" modules.

The issues raised in this section can occur in many combinations. For an example that also serves as a bridge to the next section, consider resistance to the uptake of dietary philosophies such as vegetarianism or veganism. Their first adoption hurdle is a cultural norm: the mindless consumption of meat. For those who wake up to ethical, environmental and/or health consequences of their existing diets, the challenge is then to imagine what vegetarian or vegan diets would entail. This is now much less of an issue in Western countries than it was several decades ago, for modern consumers can readily find in mainstream supermarkets what are, in effect, meat-free modules to slot into traditional "meat-and-two-veg" recipes; there is no need to imagine how one might learn to come up with, say, Asian-style meat-free meals that are completely different from what one is used to having. The emergence of meat, dairy and fish substitute products enables a complete transition to vegetarian or vegan diets to be made without cognitive overload from trying new recipes supplied via the user support commons of social network contacts, cookery books and "how-to" programs on TV food channels. Moreover, nowadays the switcher's imagination is less taxed due to more cosmopolitan restaurant dining having become the norm, with menus that display the kinds of diets to which dishes conform. Finally, as deviant diets have become more widely adopted, those who adopt them have had less reason to fear that unimaginative members of their social circles will subject them to tiresome demands for justification of their dietary practices. By contrast, if we scroll back half a century, there were so many impediments that adoption would have been unlikely unless driven by an overriding ethical principle.

11.10   Meso 2: Adoption

From a conventional economic standpoint, it would be natural to view the widespread uptake of a meso as being driven by: (a) falling prices of the products that carry the meso rule in question, (b) improvements in the overall value for money the products offer (as in the optimizing, compensatory model of choice among characteristics proposed by Lancaster, 1966a, 1966b) and (c) rising incomes. If people in similar financial situations adopt particular meso rules at different points in time, this should not seem particularly surprising, for their circumstances may differ in other ways and they may differ in their tastes; moreover, without getting deeper into debt than they are willing to go or financial institutions are willing to allow, people will need to prioritize how they spend their money.

Clearly, in some cases, the sequence in which people adopt a particular set of rules could indeed be driven by compensatory value systems in the manner envisaged by Lancaster. However, in others, adoption sequences may be driven by hierarchical principles being applied in path-dependent ways that are triggered by problems and which are related to macro-level changes.

Consider, for example, the uptake of domestic air-conditioning systems by those who live in tropical and subtropical climates. One household may have been planning to install such a system but then defer doing so for a couple of years after bringing forward bathroom renovations to solve an unexpected and urgent plumbing issue and then succumbing to the Diderot effect. Another household may be getting fed up with rising summer temperatures but opt, on green principles, to delay fitting any air-conditioning until after they have installed a large rooftop solar photovoltaic system. Eventually, both households do get air-conditioning but, in the meantime, they help to drive other meso trajectories. If we aggregate up from households to lifestyle groups, it may be possible to anticipate, at least probabilistically, the order in which members of particular groups will adopt particular meso rules (cf. Pyatt, 1964; Paroush, 1965; for a study of structural change in patterns of household expenditure, based on the *S*-shaped curve idea, see Woollett, 2007).

Explaining why meso adoption times differ is easier than explaining why *S*-shaped meso trajectories in particular are observed. From the standpoint of conventional economics, one might try to do this via a combination of (a) a roughly normal distribution of income whose mean income gradually increases and (b) decreasing marginal utility from improvements in the quality of the products in question. If the distribution of income is highly skewed in favor of the rich, there will be a more rapid initial takeoff than is commonly observed, followed by a long period in which the long tail of the less well off in the distribution gradually becomes able to afford the product. The ability of less affluent groups to adopt the product will be increased by the willingness of past adopters to upgrade to later generations of the products and thereby allow their heavily depreciated initial purchases to trickle down to poorer buyers via markets for secondhand goods. This trickle-down process will be attenuated if past adopters experience decreasing marginal utility from product improvements and opt to go for longer periods between upgrades.

However, a mass-market bunching of adoptions might plausibly be interpreted instead as being due to a major part of the population of adopters choosing via rather similar non-compensatory decision rules that specify price and non-price targets that must be met if they will be willing to adopt the meso in question (cf. Earl and Wakeley, 2010). Non-price targets could have a technological basis: for example, in the uptake of digital photography in the early 2000s, tech-savvy photographers may have realized that the emergence of two-megapixel cameras marked the point at which one's photographs would have similar resolution to the high-definition computer and television screens that were being adopted around the same time, even though they would still fall short of traditional film-based photographs for printing off as hard copies. Meanwhile, more serious photographers might have been holding out until, say, they could get "a digital SLR camera for less than $1000" despite knowing that a few years after that point had been reached, such cameras were likely significantly cheaper than their target price.

Rather similar effects seem likely to play a major role in the electric vehicle meso, where the key issue, aside from an "acceptable" price, is conquering "range anxiety." Given the need for comfort or rest or dining stops, affordable electric vehicles with a highway range of 350–400km are likely to be needed, along with a sufficiently dense network of fast-charging stations (with adjacent dining facilities, etc.) if electric vehicles are to be deemed acceptable for general-purpose use. This is obviously well short of what can be achieved by most petrol- and diesel-powered cars, but three to four hours at the wheel is at much as many motorists would drive without taking a break.

As behavioral economists, we would expect such targets to be set in terms of popular and rounded numbers (e.g., 10, 50, 100, not 9, 43, 92, etc.). We would also be mindful of the significance of social demonstration effects and the market for preferences as means by which the behavior and knowledge of earlier adopters begins to snowball. The bunching of targets may be amplified by institutional factors such as the provision of safety ratings for new cars, requirements that electrical appliance and vehicle retailers display energy consumption figures or star ratings on products in a standardized form, or requirements that energy efficiency ratings must be specified by real estate agents when residential properties are listed. If scores on such systems come to determine the marketability of the goods to which they are attached, these rating systems may become major drivers of the meso trajectories of box-ticking technologies. Thus, we may end up with a bunching of decision rules and of what is being supplied. Moreover, even if buyers themselves do not yet personally desire some new features, they may be wise to ensure that the durable products they buy are equipped with them if the features in question seem likely to become normally expected by the time that they come to try to resell what they are now buying.

11.11   Meso 3: From Retention to Decline

In the absence of radical creative thinking and innovations, we might expect that meso trajectories would continue for long periods once they reached their peak level of adoption, with production then settling down at the level necessary merely to satisfy replacement demand. During such periods, micro-level change might still be going on, with product life cycles terminating as better products were introduced. This is pretty much what we can observe with kitchen appliances such as refrigerators, dishwashers and microwave ovens, which have become viewed as standard and essential features of kitchens in homes in advanced economies – though, of course, such meso rules are still in their adoption phase in less affluent economies. At the macro level, coordination will return in the retention phase, with the ripple and backwash effects to and from other meso trajectories gradually drying up. For example, agribusiness firms and supermarkets will have adjusted to the changes in eating and shopping habits that refrigeration appliances made possible, the market for cool boxes for transporting chilled and frozen food around will head toward the retention phase, and so on. But meso trajectories often turn downward, sometimes sharply, and meso rules in some cases may even go extinct in almost all their applications (as with the vacuum tube thermionic valves that were once key components of radios, televisions and many other electronic devices but which were driven out of all their applications, except from microwave ovens and high-power guitar amplifiers, by the adoption of transistors). Indeed, some adopters of a rule may already have abandoned it before its usage rate peaks.

The eventual abandonment of a meso by its users can be a consequence of users switching to products that embody new technology rules and/or switches in their decision rules. For example, consider the process of structural change in the automotive sector. Imagine that some motorists use the decisions rule "must have a 0–100 km per hour acceleration time of around eight seconds" as a proxy for whether a car will have "enough get up and go" and be "safe enough for overtaking." These motorists might apply this rule when purchasing cars with very different types of engines across the decade as they grapple with rising fuel costs. In the 1980s and 1990s, they may have driven V8-powered cars but in the early 2000s they adopt cars powered by the latest, more economical V6 engines whose power matches that of their previous V8s. In the 2010s, they switch to cars with turbocharged four-cylinder engines that offer even better economy, and by 2020 they find themselves choosing between Honda Accord and Toyota Camry hybrids that offer a spectacular further increase in fuel economy yet can dash from 0–100 km per hour in around eight seconds. These motorists end up adopting cars with hybrid power trains not because of any green principles but by looking for cheaper running costs without compromising on performance. Others who end up buying Accord or Camry hybrids may never have required their cars to have that much acceleration, with their adoption of the hybrid meso entailing a switch from conventional four-cylinder Accords and Camrys after becoming nervous about climate change and deciding it is time to adopt greener principles. Other motorists, meanwhile, are abandoning the sedan or wagon motoring mesos and switching to SUVs that they view as superior in other ways and which they can adopt without breaching their running cost rules if they buy variants with turbo-diesel engines. The rules that make these motorists want SUVs may be ones that they have long used (e.g., they may look for the safest vehicles in their price range and view SUVs as safer than lower vehicles), or they may be employing rules that they have not previously used (as with ageing motorists with worn limb joints who find it difficult to get into and out of lower vehicles).

Where the origination and adoption phases of a new meso drive the decline and/or extinction of an existing meso, the extent of disruption for established producer will depend upon the differences between the meso rules in terms of the capabilities and equipment required to embody them in products and how swiftly producers wake up to the impending change of rules. For vehicle manufacturers with flexible production systems, a rapid shift in demand from sedans or wagons to SUVs may pose few challenges beyond, say, designing suspension systems that can maintain sedan-like ride quality without compromising cornering stability. By contrast, for firms that specialized in making mass-market record turntables, the switch to CD players was a disaster, since two technologies were utterly different.

11.12 Boldness versus Conservatism

The pace at which the economy changes and the shapes of meso trajectories associated with economic evolution depends on the boldness of investment in innovations as well as the total amount invested in developing and adopting innovative products and processes. In this section we will examine how the innovative boldness of firms is affected by how far existing meso trajectories have progressed, via the impact this has on competitive conditions and via the shifting internal politics of corporate coalitions.

11.12.1 Alternative Approaches to Improving Products

Firms face a three-way choice when considering how to invest to improve their product offerings in order to try to avoid being swept away by processes of creative destruction. They can:

(a) continue to invest in ways of improving their products without adopting any new meso rules;
(b) improve their products and/or diversify their product ranges by adopting meso rules that they have previously left for others to adopt; or
(c) seek to improve their products and/or diversify their product ranges by investing in the origination of a new meso.

Each of these options potentially could apply to the same area of performance improvement. For example, a vehicle manufacturer could continue trying to improve the fuel economy of its cars by, say, (a) finding further ways to improve their aerodynamics, (b) fitting a hybrid petrol-electric drivetrain modeled on the "synergy drive" system that Toyota originated with its 1997 Prius or (c) investing in, say, a radical new composite material and 3D printer system to produce car body shells that rewrite the rules of the game via dramatic economy-enhancing weight savings.

Firms differ greatly in their boldness, both in terms of where and how they seek to "push the envelope" and in how far they are prepared to "put all their eggs in one basket" rather than hedging their bets. It is rare for a firm only to follow strategy (c); it would entail coming up with succession of original products that it commercializes and then simply abandons or whose production rights it then sells to other firms rather than developing new generations of them. The ups and downs of the British electronics entrepreneur Sir Clive Sinclair's career roughly epitomize this approach and the risks that it entails. Some firms may go through periods when they pursue all three of these strategies simultaneously, but other firms are consistently conservative or unimaginative and only attempt to use strategy (a) or strategies (a) and (b), always operating as imitators and never attempting to be innovators. However, sometimes a firm will opt to not follow its rivals in adopting a new meso, because it imagines a much more radical future technology that it tries to originate while still making incremental improvements by continuing to follow older rules (i.e., it pursues a mixture of strategy (a) and (c)). Such a strategy of not adopting an intermediate meso generation might make sense even where the incremental costs of getting to a particular performance level are higher with the old meso due to it running into diminishing returns. The logic here is like that which underpins the Salter diagram: by skipping the intermediate meso, the firm may avoid significant fixed cost associated with that technology, which may more than offset the higher incremental costs of raising performance via the old technology until the radical new meso is viable to bring into use.

Clearly, these strategies differ in the amount of uncertainty that they entail and hence in the risks of costs blowing out on the way to achieving the performance goal or making a concept work. With option (a), the firm is engaging merely in incremental improvements and may be hoping to continue along an existing learning curve with a reasonably confident estimate of how costs will run into diminishing marginal returns. With option (b), the new meso may amount to little more than a modular change that the firm can outsource to a more experienced supplier if it is nervous about its internal capacity to imitate the concept: so, for example, in the early 1980s, Toyota outsourced the cylinder head design of its high-revving 4A-GE engine, its first sixteen-valve four-cylinder offering, to motorcycle maker Yamaha before then working out in-house how to simplify the camshaft system for its wider range of more economy-focused engines. But with a brand-new meso, the firm may lack precedents and trusted partners, making the venture very much a "leap into the unknown," a case of the "We simply do not know" variety discussed in Section 5.5.

If the new meso entails technical challenges, rushing it into production may lead to reliability problems and catastrophic consequences for the firm's goodwill. Here, once again, the history of the front-wheel-drive hatchback car is instructive. A key new challenge with front-wheel-drive systems was to design a reliable and easy-to-use clutch and gear-change system. This was something that those who designed the 1969 Austin Maxi failed to achieve in time for the car's launch. This was particularly problematic, since the car was fitted with a five-speed gearbox, a decade before this feature was widely adopted. The difficulties that drivers of the Maxi experienced in finding the desired gear had a disastrous impact on that car's reception and they got progressively worse as the cable in the linkage system stretched with use. By contrast, Fiat had earlier displayed wise caution when it only used the customers of its minor co-owned subsidiary Autobianchi as the guinea pigs for Dante Giacosa's radical front-wheel-drive system (and Fiat's new rack-and-pinion steering system). We might similarly view Japanese automakers as operating wisely when they lagged half a decade behind those in Europe in abandoning rear-wheel-drive in their small cars. In waiting until they got their designs right before launching them, they ended up with vehicles that not only caused no new problems for their customers but also had designed systems so slick to use that their cars then became vehicles of choice for driving instructors and thereby played a formative role in setting the standards that new drivers came to expect.

Even if bold ventures do not run into problems of execution, they can still run into difficulties due to being too bold for prospective customers to handle. Back in Chapter 4, we had an example of this: the initial reception of Igor Stravinsky's *The Rite of Spring*, a very radical creative work that did not match the cognitive templates of concertgoers. Such resistance can be encountered even where the boldness of a product's design is conducted largely within the rules of an existing meso and yet the product proves cognitively too challenging to accept because of the leap forward that has been made from established reference points. Eventually, customers will probably get used to a radical design, especially if rival firms offer products that go some way in the same direction. Indeed, a radical design may age much better and eventually enjoy a longer product life cycle than its more conservative contemporary rivals. But in its early years, those who championed and authorized it will be blamed for any negative impacts that its excessive boldness has on its manufacturer's performance.

However, firms that seek to limit these technical and market risks by operating in a conservative manner risk losing their customers to rivals that offer more innovative products and yet manage to avoid technical difficulties and customer resistance by not going *too* far in one step. Herein lies a more basic kind of innovator's dilemma than that set out by Christensen (1997): how bold should a firm be? On the one hand, there is the risk that boldness may fail in the market even if it does not run into cost blowouts associated with capability shortfalls and unforeseen problems. On the other hand, conservatism may cost more in lost revenue that it saves in avoiding the costs of innovation if rivals adopt more radical strategies and customers eagerly adopt their products. There is no easy way to answer this basic question, especially in the absence of industrial espionage to find out what rivals are planning to offer. It is a question that is further complicated by uncertainty about how rapidly any headway that an innovating firm gains might be dissipated due to rivals imitating and extending things that it did successfully.

11.12.2   Boldness as a Function of Market Structure and Meso Trajectory Stage

In setting out his "creative destruction" view of the dynamics of capitalism, Schumpeter challenged the prevailing view that consumers will suffer if industries come to be dominated by a limited number of firms and that strong competition is conducive to technical progress. He suggested that it only makes sense for a firm to invest in a bold innovation if it has enough market power to keep rivals at bay long enough to capture a satisfactory return on its investment. Where a large player is also diversified and the innovation is in just one area of its business portfolio, failure will not be a disaster for the firm as a whole; indeed, as with giant pharmaceutical and entertainment companies, it will normally be expected that many bold ventures will not get as far as being offered in the market due to technical issues or will be commercially unsuccessful. These failures are the price of achieving blockbuster successes when it is impossible to be sure which bold ventures will succeed. By contrast, the owners of a small, undiversified firm could stand to lose everything by being adventurous on a very limited budget that they have scraped together in part by mortgaging their homes. Even if their firm has a winning formula, supernormal profits will be short-lived if many copy its ideas and are correct in believing that it will be unable to enforce its property rights over them. For the small firm, competitive logic favored waiting for others to find better ways of doing things and then copying them.

But Schumpeter's perspective is open to challenge on several grounds. First, consider how things look if we combined Leibenstein's (1966) X-inefficiency analysis with the ideas of loss aversion and satisficing. These ideas seem to point in the direction of dominant firms not being prone to be bold in what they do: if a quiet life is a good enough life and it is hard to see how others might upset it, why do anything bold? If it works, don't mess with it. This leads to an "inverted-U" view of the relationship between market share and the propensity to innovate, in which the propensity to innovate is absent if market concentration is very limited or extremely high; it rises as one moves from either end of the concentration scale (see further Peneder and Woerter, 2014). This view may seem perfectly reasonable if one is used to thinking of innovation in relation to established products being produced in industries that differ in their degrees of concentration. However, a different kind of competitive logic seems to make sense if we try to anticipate patterns of innovation through time as a meso trajectory unfolds. It is to be found in the Downie-like analysis of dynamic competition offered by Burton Klein (1977), who supports his thesis with case study material from the automotive, aviation and electronics sectors.

Klein argues that, in the early years of an industry, there is much instability in market share rankings as firms experiment with rapid revisions to their designs, trying to find a winning formula. Technological progress is thus extremely rapid in this period, but once a standard kind of design becomes accepted as the way forward, cumulating processes set in and, from Downie's perspective, it could be said that the innovation mechanism is then largely swamped by the transfer mechanism. Not only are many firms driven out of the sector but also the pace of progress slows, with innovations being mainly of an incremental rather than radical kind. Klein's view is thus that of innovation been most rapid when an industry is least concentrated, with innovation falling as concentration increases.

Central to Klein's analysis is the uncertainty that the pioneering entrepreneurs face about what the dominant design is going to be. For example, in the early days of the automobile, gasoline, steam, electricity and diesel were all contenders as means of propulsion. There was also no standard interface between the driver and vehicle in terms of pedal and levers, with initial views even differing on whether a steering wheel or tiller bar was the way to steer. But this uncertainty about the winning formula comes with confidence that the product in question does have a bright future. This means that where proponents of different approaches to the product can all convince themselves that they have a plausible case for why their vision might be developed into the one that dominates, the situation is rather like a lottery in which any ticket could win, with fortunes to be made by those who hold the winning tickets. This means that the risk-taking situation is quite different from that of an *established* industry of many small firms, none of which is going to have a chance of making a spectacular leap forward by innovating.

Klein does not explain the willingness of the pioneering entrepreneurs with reference to the ideas that we employed in Chapter 5 of this book when discussing risk-taking. But those ideas support his analysis. Loss aversion will be trumped where those experimenting with different formulae feel they are in with a chance that their particular variant will hit the commercial jackpot. Moreover, by taking risks that may be of great personal significance, they are also able to avoid the prospect of regret that they would suffer if they did not invest in their vision and it turned out to be successful in someone else's hands (cf. Loomes and Sugden, 1982). If their gamble fails, they can say "At least I tried," and they may have learned some lessons that will enable them to get backing from venture capitalists who appreciate that entrepreneurs typically need three or four ventures before they hit on a winning formula (cf. Richardson, 1953). In the meantime, they gain "enjoyment by anticipation" (Shackle, 1943, 1949) from being part of the lottery.

Many of them will fail, but the rewards may indeed be enormous for those whose formulae take off, with the latter growing into the giants of the industry. The transfer mechanism will favor the latter, whereas those whose formulae the market rejects will be hard-pressed to invest in imitating them because it is those whose gambles paid off who have the profits to reinvest and the biggest ability to raise external funds to take their vision to much larger-scale production. This process leads to increasing concentration of market shares in the hands of fewer firms as the industry matures. However, Klein argues that as concentration increases, the remaining firms will have the resources to imitate any bold innovations by their rivals. Because the returns to bold innovations are thus likely to dry up rapidly, increasingly oligopolistic players follow the now-established rules of the game and merely experiment with incremental improvements that may gain them a temporary increase in market share for a relatively small investment. If the industry is to be disrupted by a new meso, it will tend, as in Christensen's studies, to come, Tesla-style, from outside.

The behavioral theory of the firm seems very much in line with Klein's view of oligopolistic organizations in mature industries. The theory's focus is not on bold, heroic and flexible entrepreneurs engaging in crucial experiments but on managers who operate on the basis of routines, including routines for allocating funds to research and development (Kay, 1979). These managers engage in "uncertainty avoidance" and are reluctant to embark on major projects until they have lobbied public officials to achieve a "negotiated environment" (Cyert and March, 1963).

When we factor in potential for an entrenched corporate culture to affect how a firm sees the world, we can readily see how, in line with the cases presented by Klein and Christensen, new players who are implementing new meso rules may become dominant. The incumbents may fail to wake up to the impending demise of the meso within whose rules they have been working. The incumbents thereby fail to undertake in good time the kinds of changes that will be necessary for their survival. As Schoenberger (1997) recognizes, these change-impeding aspects of routines and corporate culture are especially pertinent in relation to the firm's operating system: for example, a car firm that has for years had a supply-driven view of its business will tend to keep viewing its distribution system as a means to "move the metal" via pushy sales methods, even if its crumbling market share ought to be taken as a signal that it needs to use its distribution system much more as an intelligence gathering resource for finding out what customers want and then ensure the designs and production systems are changed accordingly. But insofar as a new meso requires fundamental changes in capabilities in order to introduce and operate new technologies, fears of change may be justified even though procrastination may be fatal as it allows early adopters to gain learning advantages.

11.12.3   The Creative Instability Hypothesis

Although the behavioral approach to the firm augments our understanding of Downie's innovation mechanism and helps us to make sense of the patterns that Klein and Christensen identified, it is not at odds with the fact that some firms appear to focus consistently on using innovation as a means to maintain their competitive advantage. An innovation-based strategy is in essence a rule for how the firm is going to operate and it may be applied for many years and give rise to a supporting corporate culture. Thus, for example, Selznick (1957) argued that the Mercedes-Benz had long been pursuing the strategy of pioneering innovations in automotive design. Around the time he wrote, the firm was pioneering fuel injection systems. In the ensuing decades, it has continued with the same strategy, with technologies such as antilock braking systems and electronic stability controls, and during the writing of this book the firm began offering electric vehicles; it was not about to allow Tesla to leave it behind in that area.

However, as Jason Potts and I realized, Cyert and March's vision of the firm as a coalition of agents with different subgoals could be a starting point for understanding cases in which firms do not pursue consistently bold or conservative strategies but instead oscillate between such strategies as the years go by. We called our analysis the "creative instability hypothesis" (Earl and Potts, 2013, 2016), doing so partly because it is related to the "financial instability hypothesis" proposed about the banking system by Hyman Minsky (1975, 1982b). (Minsky's hypothesis is explored later, in Section 12.7.)

At the heart of the Earl and Potts analysis lies the tension that is inevitable between a firm's "creatives" (i.e., design engineers and stylists in a manufacturing company, artists signed to firms in the cultural and entertainment sector, and so on) and its "suits" (i.e., those who are responsible for its financial performance). By nature, the creatives will be much bolder than the suits; indeed, creatives may have "pet projects" that they want to carry out essentially because of their curiosity about whether they can succeed in turning their visions into reality and about how the intended audience will react, rather than because they are confident that the projects will be highly profitable. The task of the suits is to ensure that the "grand designs" of the creatives are held in check so that they can deliver acceptable results to shareholders. The trouble is, the suits do not know how hard they need to rein in the creatives, given that being conservative could result in the firm being left behind by rivals that allow their creatives more freedom. Sometimes, the suits fail to rein in the creatives enough, leading to projects that are bedeviled with technical troubles, cost blowouts and deadline overruns and/or which run too far ahead of what customers can understand or are prepared to tolerate. When faced with financial difficulties, the suits do call a halt to boldness, taking the firm into a period of conservatism in which the focus is "bean counting," watching every cent of spending. In turn, the financial recovery that "bean counting" achieves eventually makes it hard to justify continued conservatism if customers start to crave something more exciting and rivals seem to be moving ahead by being more adventurous.

Sometimes, the suits are unable to stop creatives from going ahead with bold visions simply because the creatives have more votes than the suits in committees and at board level when projects are being authorized and budgets approved. This is essentially what underlay the bankruptcy of Rolls-Royce in 1971 after it ran into trouble developing the pioneering RB2–11 jet engines that it had agreed to supply for the Lockheed Tri-Star airliner. The Rolls-Royce engineers were determined to rewrite the rules of jet engine design by making extensive use of carbon fiber (which they eventually succeeded in doing after the firm was rescued by the UK government) and their votes outnumbered those on the financial side (Grant, 1977, p. 96). Often, however, project champions will need to win support from finance-focused colleagues. Wherever there is acute uncertainty about a creative project's potential costs and revenues, the latter must follow their instincts, and these may be affected by the rhetoric of those who act as champions for the project. The less expertise the finance staff have in common with their creative colleagues, the less they are able to know how skeptical they should be about the claims that are being made.

Of course, experienced financial staff are likely to be wary of the "grand designs" of their creative staff and know that, where projects do run into difficulties after gaining approval, they will have a battle on their hands to limit budgetary escalation. In such situations, it is unlikely that creative staff will suggest that the project was a mistake that should be abandoned. Indeed, anyone involved in approving the project (including any financial officers who agreed to it) will be prone to succumb to sunk cost bias because their credibility is in question and remaining uncertainty provides opportunities for claiming that, with more resources, a floundering project can be made to come right (see Section 7.8).

Given the scope for creatives to be promoting "pet projects" and all the uncertainties associated with assessing their proposals, the creative instability hypothesis is that decision-making about the extent of creative boldness that the firm should embrace is open to tidal shifts between boldness and conservatism, driven by changes in beliefs among the decision-makers in question. As with tidal shifts in a nation's politics, it may take only a small proportion of voters to switch their preferences for a major change to be brought about.

The idea that there could be such tidal shifts complements the suggestion of Cyert and March (1963) that managers give "sequential attention to goals" and thereby cause their organizations to "go round in circles." However, the underlying thinking is somewhat different. Cyert and March see the tendency to give sequential attention to goals as resulting from bounded rationality: because managers are beset with finite attentive, information processing and memory capacities, they fail to perform value-integrating trade-offs of the kind envisaged in conventional microeconomics. Instead, they focus on whether targets for particular hierarchically ranked values are being met and then concentrate resources on addressing the highest-priority unmet goal. However, due to their inability to think through all the implications of a change of policy, success in respect of that target eventually comes at the cost of failure to meet another goal, with attention then shifting to designing a policy to meet that goal, and so on.

By contrast, the creative instability hypothesis takes account of the significance of fundamental (non-probabilistic) uncertainty rather than focusing on bounded rationality. As Dunn (2000) has emphasized, these two concepts do not reduce to the same thing: fundamental uncertainty does not arise from problems in processing information; rather, it a problem of knowledge that arise from desired information not yet being available. In the case of creative boldness, fundamental uncertainty results from not knowing how far it is necessary and safe to push the boundaries when strategies of rivals and acceptability to customers are not yet known. This is often because these other parties have not yet even made up their minds or imagined what they would do if presented with a particular bold new product rather than because insufficient intelligence gathering has been done by the firm in question. Similarly, the capacity of the organization to bring a vision to fruition at a particular cost is uncertain because the bounded imaginations of its staff leave them open to potential for surprises that they may not know how to handle, rather than because of being overwhelmed by thoughts of all the things that could happen in trying to make a concept work (see also Section 5.5).

In the presence of such uncertainty, news about the outcomes of past decisions and the boldness of rival organizations may affect the credibility of claims made by different players involved in collective choices about significant projects. When boldness has recently paid off, or rival organizations simultaneously seem more confident and to be posing bigger threats by acting more boldly, it will be harder for the financial "bean counters" to dismiss the "grand designs" that their creative colleagues propose. Organizational slack will tend to develop, too, for in such an environment, the creative staff may seem to be in a stronger position to move elsewhere if they are not granted the resources, from growing profits, to try to realize their "grand designs." If the financial "bean counters" could be certain that the authorization of "grand designs" would prevent the firm from meeting its KPIs, they would refuse to support such projects. In the face of uncertainty, they may err by supporting overly bold projects but then get more assertive as the consequences of that support become apparent. If, in the latter event, creative staff put up with being reined in and do not defect to other organizations, this would be a case of organizational slack being taken up.

Overshooting will cause credibility problems for those who advocated the projects in question, but if conservative strategies result in a firm falling behind its bolder rivers, we should expect defections from conservative to radical camps. Those who "went too far" (or whose conservatism was discredited) may even quit or be fired and be replaced by executives with less radical (more radical) agenda and/or reputations. While a focus on cost cutting and offering products that offend no one may restore profits after an episode of overshooting, sooner or later there will be signs that being more radical does pay, as some rivals succeed with experiments aimed at satisfying what Scitovsky (1981) called "the desire for excitement in modern society": there are limits to the amount of novelty a consumer can tolerate at any moment, but once consumers have got used to past novelties, they will be prepared to step once again some way out of their comfort zones to relieve boredom.

It needs to be understood that the creative instability hypothesis is not a general theory of the determinants of creative boldness in organizations. Though it is based on the idea that rival organizations take their cues from each other about how bold they should be, it does not entail a claim that *all* organizations fail to achieve broadly stable creative trajectories. Rather, it is a way of making sense of why some firms oscillate between "grand designs" and "bean counting." When there is no obvious way of remaining profitable in a world of Schumpeterian competition, we should not expect all firms to succumb to the processes just outlined. In other words, some firms may suffer from something akin to a manic–depressive disorder, but many firms may opt for more consistently effective kinds of strategies that reflect the kinds of deep-seated corporate cultures emphasized in the work of Selznick (1957). So, for example, a carmaker might consistently employ a "middle of the road" blend of conservatism and imitation if, unlike Mercedes-Benz, it does not have a premium market segment from which it can extract margins to pay for pioneering new technology modules that eventually trickle down to less well-heeled buyers. Another might opt to be broadly similar but seek to keep its adaptive innovative capabilities alive by maintaining a division in which more experimental things can be done for niche markets, with potential halo effects for its more conservative mainstream products, and so on.

11.13   The Changing Division of Knowledge and Division of Labor

As technologies evolve, the combination of increasing complexity and bounded rationality favors the development of increasingly specialized capabilities. This happens naturally due to individuals having different experiences as they go about their work and leisure activities. Their experiences depend on their experiments with the aspiration levels they set and how they try to meet them. Making their expectations come true may only be possible if they can solve problems that they encounter. It is through such problem-solving activities that they increase their know-how, their knowledge of how to make particular things happen, sometimes with new pieces of equipment that they have invented and which embody some of their new knowledge. But the new capabilities that emerge from problem-solving activities can also pertain to know-how regarding the formation and management of relationships inside organizations, with other organizations (such as those involved in their supply chain) and with customers (see further Loasby, 1998). Such processes of generating experience-based know-how also occur within households, with the division of knowledge not merely providing a basis for differences in lifestyles but also for the existence of the market for preferences.

Those who are highly ambitious and set out to make bold concepts work will run into problems that they might have avoided had they opted to cruise along and simply imitate systems that others have pioneered. However, in the long run, those who have managed to survive in the latter way will be making themselves more vulnerable, since they fail to put themselves under pressure to develop their problem-solving capabilities. By extension, we should expect firms that have for many years followed the rules of a particular meso, and have finely tuned their corporate cultures to it, to find it much harder to adjust to the rules of a disruptive new meso than those who have had to contend with a succession of short-lived meso rules. The latter will have been under much greater pressure to develop capabilities in change management and cultures that are open to change. It thus becomes easy to understand how established "old school" competitors can suffer from inertia and get wiped out by entrants to their markets who lack experience in the market in question. The latter may bring in a new meso and be open to learning how to handle unfamiliar territory because they have already had to do this repeatedly elsewhere (see further Robertson and Langlois, 1994).

This chapter has so far focused on how the growth of knowledge affects the market shares of firms and the uptake of technologies through time. But the experience-based growth of specialized know-how will also affect the division of activities between firms in respect of vertical integration and horizontal diversification. Indeed, some of the experiments that a firm conducts in these areas will be means of addressing particular problems, with know-how then being generated that leads to further changes in the firm's internalization and product-mix strategies.

For example, a firm may experiment with internalizing a stage in its supply chain after being let down by a devious or incompetent supplier or no longer being able to find anyone willing to supply at a viable price. Bringing some component production in-house or diversifying the firm's product range may also be a way of using up surplus capacity that has arisen due to learning within the firm running ahead of growth in its ability to find new customers (see Penrose, 1959, ch. VII; Moss, 1981).

On the other hand, firms may conclude that the capabilities required for growth and survival in their area of business are such that they should switch to outsourcing things they have previously done in-house. Two contrasting examples should be noted here. One is where the firm's managers conclude that some of the knowledge that the firm has developed in a particular area can be codified into an instruction manual that could provide the basis for expansion via a franchising system that would be attractive to those who lack the imagination and skills necessary to start up original business ventures. The firm thus ceases trying to grow by opening more branches of its own and instead specializes in developing products and processes for the franchise system, maintaining the system's integrity and engaging in bulk purchases of inputs for the franchisees to use.

The other noteworthy example of increasing specialization is characterized by Richard Langlois (2003) as the "vanishing hand of capitalism." Here, rising techno-logical complexity results in firms accepting that they cannot keep at the leading edge in areas where they used to produce inputs in-house. They therefore seek to retain competitive advantage by sourcing these inputs from specialists. Carried to the extreme, this consequence of bounded learning capacities could eventually result in, say, a car firm that does little more than control its brand and sign off designs to be produced for sale under that brand, while outsourcing all the styling, engineering, components and final assembly. It might even outsource the contracting with these input suppliers – in much the same way as the building of a one-off skyscraper is outsourced by the property developer to a construction management company that hires and oversees a diverse set of contractors (see Earl, 1996). This way of operating also enables the firm to limit its exposure to unpredictable changes of technology and patterns of demand.

The "vanishing hand" view of modern capitalism that Langlois offers is an extension of work he conducted with Paul Robertson (Langlois and Robertson, 1995), which examined, with evidence from several case studies, how the extent of vertical integration changes as meso trajectories unfold. As noted earlier, although a do-it-yourself strategy is often forced on entrepreneurs by skeptical suppliers of finance and component at the origination stage, it also enables the pioneers of a meso to gather feedback more readily from customers, make frequent improvements to products and ensure that potential customers are provided with a vision of the product's potential that does not get distorted by a marketing intermediary. However, as the nature of the meso becomes established and adoption takes off, the original reasons for vertical integration start fading away and competition becomes increasingly focused on both price and the addition of features as opposed to getting the meso to work effectively and getting it understood by potential adopters.

The growing sophistication of the product and moves to larger-scale production require a growing range of capabilities, not all of which there will be time to develop in-house while trying to keep up with or drive the evolution of the meso. With pressure to contain costs and improve the product, the constraints on capability development are likely to push managers to examine where their emerging compara-tive advantage lies relative to other players. Some will conclude it lies in producing particular modules and then concentrate on becoming key players in those areas, whereas others will see their distinctive edge in terms of being able to anticipate the sets of modules to bundle together for particular types of customers. The growing expertise of more fussy customers may also mean that the market for modules in the area in question develops not merely to supply manufacturers who integrate them into appliances (for example, loudspeakers or turntables for makers of "radiograms" in the early years of hi-fi home entertainment systems) but also to supply modules (for example, loudspeakers housed in their own enclosures) to connoisseur consumers who take pride in using their knowledge to design their own systems.

However, when a new meso emerges, suppliers of products that carry the old meso rule will face a dilemma over what their internalization strategy should be if they are uncertain about the extent and duration of any residual market: to the extent that they are still vertically integrated, should they start to outsource those activities to reduce the risk of having to exit? Or should they internalize the production of more compon-ents (for example, by buying up suppliers from whom they have been sourcing components that are unique to the meso in question) to try to make the residual market more secure? (See further Harrigan, 1980; Silver, 1984.) The latter strategy may provide ways to (a) eliminate the risk that the exit of a key module supplier will wreck the residual market by preventing the systems in question from being put together or kept going, (b) ensure that customer confidence is maintained and (c) make it easier to gather intelligence from, and adapt designs for, the changing needs of residual customers.

11.14 Conclusion

The emphasis on the relentless pressure of competition and processes of creative destruction in modern capitalism that permeates this chapter may seem somewhat at odds with the previous chapter's behavioral analysis of the firm. There, we explored potential for managers and workers in firms to be pursuing their own subgoals rather than doing as much as they can to enhance long-term profits. Here, we began with Andrews's view of the power of potential competition as a driver of search for ways of retaining existing customers and attracting new ones, and it was not until the creative instability hypothesis was being outlined that we returned to the idea of subgoal pursuit.

However, what we should conclude is that although Andrews was right about the tendency of the behavioral literature on the firm to concentrate on internal operations and downplay pressure from the external environment, the behavioral approach to the firm is compatible with a world of strong competition. This is because, as was stressed earlier in this book, decision-making via satisficing rules and other heuristics is necessary in order to deal with the infinite regress issue that attempts to maximize profits or personal well-being run into in the presence of open-ended choice problems. However, the use of such decision-closing devices in these contexts does not mean that we should view all managers and workers as setting their aspirations so low that they grossly waste the potential of the organizations in which they work.

The pace of innovation will be set by those who find it easy to think creatively and/ or by those who set ambitious standards for themselves and their subordinates to meet. Limits to imaginative capacities, along with knowledge gaps about what rivals (including potential entrants) are planning or are capable of achieving, make it impossible to know how exposed one's organization is to external threats. It is thus inevitable that mistakes will be made in judging what standards to aim for in terms of cost reductions and product improvements or in which new technologies to invest. Depending on the bets they and their rivals place, business leaders may find themselves in virtuous or vicious circles that link profitability and investment. However, these feedback loops will not operate deterministically, as there may be potential for innovative breakthroughs, for organizational slack to be taken up, for X-inefficiency reduced in organizations that come under pressure and for exhaustion or hubris to set in at organizations that have enjoyed sustained success. Even if firms fail in the long run due to their inability to envisage and/or finance cheaper production methods and better product to the extent that their rivals do, the logic of the Salter diagram should remind us that their deaths may take many years to eventuate.

12 Are There Any Behavioral Insights for Macroeconomists?

12.1 Introduction

We now turn our attention from the "macro" of the micro–meso–macro framework, with its focus on intersectoral connections between meso trajectories and how the structure of the economy changes through time, to the "macro" of conventional macroeconomics that focuses on the performance of the economy as a whole in relation to economic indicators such as rates of unemployment and inflation and changes in the balance of international trade and payments through time. It is remarkable that capitalist economies perform as well as they do in terms of these indicators, given that the price signals on which market coordination is supposed to depend are often absent in relation to goods and services to be delivered in future. As Keynes (1936, p. 210) emphasized, when people opt to save, they do not signal when they will spend their savings or what they will use their savings to purchase (see also Section 3.3). Investing in creating capacity to serve future demand therefore entails a leap of faith, but such faith does not guarantee successful coordination at the level of the macroeconomy, even when supplemented by routines and heuristics as means of avoiding economic paralysis when the future cannot be known (see also Section 5.5). The essence of Keynes's view thus appears to be neatly captured by Loasby (1976, p. 167) in a single sentence: "Unemployment in a market economy is the result of ignorance too great to be borne."

Keynes's analysis understates the potential for real-world market economies to get into difficulties, for there are other issues to be kept in mind. First, the Schumpeterian innovation processes that underpin the micro–meso macro framework generate uncertainty on both sides of the market about what will be available at what point in the future and about when products will enter their decline phase or when their life cycles will suffer more sudden truncations. Herein will inevitably lie the competitive and complementary investment coordination problems emphasized by Richardson (1960). Finally, the disconnect between income today and spending today is increased by the availability of credit, the provision of which adds further areas of risk, especially as modern financial innovations such as the securitization of loans are viewed as providing ways by which those who set up loans can pass the risks of default on to others.

Yet despite all this, conventional macroeconomic thinking in recent decades has largely focused on building "rigorous" macroeconomic models on microeconomic foundation that center on "econs" who make optimal decisions about consumption, saving, investment and production. These models failed not merely to predict that the 2008 Global Financial Crisis (GFC) would happen when it did; they seem to have left their proponents, who tend not to be well versed in macroeconomic history, not even thinking that something like the Great Depression of the 1930s might ever happen. In other words, the models were technically rigorous but lacked enough "feel" for how economies work at the macro level. By contrast, armed as I was with the key perspectives set out in this chapter, I had been anticipating something akin to the GFC sometime before it erupted. Indeed, I had been introducing many of these perspectives to my students since the early 1980s, and in the six years leading up the GFC I had been giving particular attention to both how a highly leveraged property portfolio can be built in a rising market and why it could be dangerous to pursue such a strategy (see Earl and Wakeley, 2005, ch. 13). With the complex adaptive systems perspective coming explicitly into my teaching during that period, my students should have been well equipped to appreciate the problems of systemic risk in modern financial systems, unlike those taught in the mainstream reductionist way.

The GFC provided Nobel Laureate George Akerlof and soon-to-be (2013) Nobel Laureate Robert Shiller with a golden opportunity to try to generate interest in the benefits of taking a behavioral approach to understanding why the macroeconomy is prone to experience business cycles and financial crises that economic forecasters frequently fail to anticipate. They seized this opportunity by writing their 2009 best seller *Animal Spirits*, which can be thought of as their manifesto for behavioral macroeconomics. Their book's title is a phrase that Keynes (1936) had used in his *General Theory of Employment, Interest and Money* during the Great Depression of the 1930s as he sought to understand much the same set of issues as Akerlof and Shiller.

The analytical approach that Akerlof and Shiller take in *Animal Spirits* has much in common with the strategy that Richard Thaler used so successfully to cultivate interest in behavioral economics more generally. Like Thaler, they use the dominant full rationality view as their reference point and set out to expose its shortcomings, this time in relation to its failure to ensure that economists anticipated the GFC. Again, like Thaler, they see the shortcomings of orthodox thinking as resulting from economists erroneously viewing a particular set of factors as irrelevant. However, they do not simply borrow Thaler's set of supposedly irrelevant factors (SIFs). Instead, they offer their own set of SIFs and it is this set that they call "animal spirits." It consists of the following five elements:

- *Confidence*, which Akerlof and Shiller see as a key but fickle driver of expenditure in the real world of uncertainty. They particularly emphasize the word's origins in relation to its middle syllable, which refers to trust, because firms and consumers will only hand over any of their wealth, undertake work or make commitments to others if they feel they can trust the latter's prospectuses and promises to deliver particular products, services or payments to them. If confidence collapses, so will economic activity, but if confidence is buoyant, the economy will boom, making it easier for people to honor their economic promises, thereby encouraging others to have confidence to spend even more. The Keynesian income multiplier will thus tend to be amplified by feedback loops that determine the level of confidence and, in turn, expenditure.

- *Fairness*, which means that the deals that people are prepared to do, such as when bargaining about wages or setting prices, can depend on what the parties in question stand to get or would have to give up *relative* to others, rather than on the absolute amounts that they would receive or have to give up. In contrast to the orthodox view of the economy, Akerlof and Shiller see the real-world economy as a place in which concerns about fairness can cause macroeconomic performance to suffer if they prevent market-clearing prices from being generated or give rise to inflationary processes that reduce the effectiveness of price signals.

- *Corruption*, which Akerlof and Shiller see as contributing to macroeconomic instability by leading people into financially dubious contracts from which others benefit at their expense. In turn, the shortcomings of such contracts trigger or amplify financial failures, as with the issuing of "subprime mortgages" and the inappropriate ratings that were given to the securities into which these mortgages were bundled in the run-up to the GFC. As corruption becomes evident in the financial system, it shatters trust, thereby reducing confidence. Given that Akerlof and Shiller often portray those who operate in a "corrupt" way as being akin to sellers of "snake-oil remedies," they might have been wise instead to tag the behavior they had in mind via the term "opportunism" that Oliver Williamson (1975, 1985) used as a shorthand for behavior that entails the guileful pursuit of self-interest. However, their use of "corruption" also pertains to behavior of the kind that the term is used to characterize in evolutionary and institutional economics, namely behavior that involves people pursing self-interest by failing to follow rules to which they are supposed to adhere (see Neild, 2002).

- *Money illusion*, i.e., the difficulty that real-world decision-makers have in keeping track of or anticipating changes in the real value of their wealth and money incomes in terms of what it can or will be able to be used to purchase. People may thus misjudge, for example, the value of wage offers or how much they need to save for retirement if they use simple heuristics to make such assessments because they lack good mental models of how the economy works and are unable to calculate correctly the implications of compounding inflation versus how their incomes and savings capacities could grow in the long term. (For a study of how people try to anticipate the compounding effects of GDP growth and how accurately they do so, see Christandl and Fetchenhauer, 2009.) Many simply do not even bother to attempt such calculations.

- *Stories*, i.e., the narrative accounts that people construct for themselves or come to know of from other people and which serve as means for making sense of life and figuring out what to do. These stories may play key roles in helping people form their identities and get a sense of focus in their lives, while stories of choices and their consequences may be used as substitutes for formal knowledge of how things work and of the probabilities of particular outcomes. But the heuristics used in constructing and remembering such stories may make them unrepresentative and misleading. This can prove unfortunate if people use them as a basis for decisions about key issues such as their career direction, their housing choices and their investment strategies. This can be particularly tragic if pertinent facts, based on large samples of data, are not actually that hard to find and would reveal the shortcomings of such stories, perhaps even exposing them as myths – as Akerlof and Shiller use a significant chunk of their book to demonstrate. Shiller's (2020) book *Narrative Economics* takes this theme much further, emphasizing the significance of narratives that capture the imagination so readily that they go viral.

All five of these elements surface from time to time in this chapter. However, although this book has only a chapter-length consideration of lessons from behavioral economics for macroeconomists, what follows covers a wide range of behavioral perspectives and manages to go more deeply into some of the precursors to the vision that Akerlof and Shiller set out and frequently refer to as "their" theory.

12.2   Alternative Views of Speculative Markets

To begin, we need to reflect on how prices are determined in markets for financial and physical asset (including real estate and major works of art), foreign currencies and commodities such tin, oil and pork bellies. These markets are not venues in which prices are, as Gardner Means (1935, 1972) put it, "administered" in the way that manufacturing and retail prices are by being posted either on a take-it-or-leave-it basis or with the expectation that there may be some margin for negotiation. (The "administered-price" analysis of pricing that Means offered is the US equivalent of the "normal cost" approach, discussed in Section 11.2, that Andrews developed at Oxford: see further Lee, 1999.) Instead, prices in these markets emerge via auctions or spontaneously amid numerous bids to buy or sell being cried out on a trading floor.

Values arrived at in these markets dominate in primetime TV new coverage of business affairs, as well as in the specialist business media, for they are of great macroeconomic significance. Raw materials prices feed into manufacturing costs, and the prices of existing assets affect the attractiveness of investments in producing new substitutes for such assets. However, current prices in such markets have inherently speculative foundations since they reflect the expectations of market participants regarding what the assets' respective future prices are going to be. As Hugh Townshend (1937) realized, this means that the stability of both relative prices and the general level of prices ultimately hinges on the stability of expectations: the whole edifice of prices is, as it were, held up by its own bootstraps, and if conventional notions about prices break down, economic order may not be maintained by the kinds of underlying objective sets of preferences and supply conditions that economists so often assume to underpin our daily lives.

Transaction costs aside, the difference between current and future prices in these asset and commodity markets will essentially reflect the cost of borrowing funds to purchase and store what is available today with a view to selling it in future at a price that will be enough to repay the amount that was borrowed and to pay any costs of storage and insurance, along with the interest on the loan. If, at the current rate of interest, such a strategy would leave a profit after these payments have been made, it would make sense to buy more of the asset in question. If people did this on a big enough scale, they would bid up its current price to the point at which the profit surplus is eliminated beyond any amount that speculators require in compensation for the risk that the future price will be smaller than expected. So, in order to understand why the current prices of these kinds of assets and commodities are as they are, we need to understand how speculators form their expectations of future prices.

The traders in these markets have traditionally been viewed as specialists with expert knowledge of the underlying supply and demand conditions for the particular financial assets or commodities that they trade. Hence, they have a good sense of the long-term trends of prices in the market in which they trade. Their trading behavior is presumed to make prices much more stable than would otherwise be the case, since their willingness to hold stocks provides a buffer that absorbs disturbances on either side of the market.

We can get a sense of how this is supposed to work if we consider the market for a storable commodity whose entire annual output is harvested around the same time but whose consumption is spread evenly across the year. At harvest time, the price of such a commodity does not plunge because of the limited current demand for the commodity for consumption relative to the sudden increase in supply. Rather, traders will compete to buy it from the farmers who have harvested it, since the traders expect to be able to sell it later in the year and make a profit by selling it for a price that exceeds the price that they paid to get it by an amount larger than what it will cost to store in the meantime. The longer the product is held, the greater the storage costs will be, so the commodity's price will rise gradually after the harvest and peak just before the next harvest. However, the release of supplies from storage through the year will prevent a steeper price gradient during the year than is necessary to cover storage costs and leave traders with normal profits. The traders will not know who will be trying to unload their stocks on any day through the year, but if they see that the today's price is being pushed down due to many of their fellow traders trying to unload their holdings, they can defer doing likewise in order to try to get a better price tomorrow or further into the future. They thereby help to limit both the downward pressure on prices today and the upward pressure there will be in days to come. In other situations, where the underlying forces of supply and demand would generate a cyclical movement of prices, a similar process would cause the peaks and troughs to be smaller if speculative traders are present.

This classical view of speculation implies that speculative traders play a useful social function by smoothing out price fluctuations and limiting the need for users of commodities to incur the costs of holding stocks themselves. But a very different perspective on how speculation works and of its social desirability is to be found in the work of Keynes (1936) and Irwin (1937), both of whom had considerable experience and expertise in this area. Keynes was an active stock and futures trader, both on his own account (from which he amassed a considerable personal fortune) and as bursar of his Cambridge college, while Irwin was an economist at the US Department of Agriculture in Chicago, the main US hub for trade in wheat futures and other agricultural commodities. Both saw speculators as tending to act in ways that increase the volatility of asset and commodity prices, while Irwin also emphasized how prices could be manipulated profitably by groups of devious traders.

Before we consider the volatility issue, it should be noted that, since Irwin's time, manipulation of these types of markets has sometimes been very disruptive, as with the dramatic oil price hikes engineered by the Organization of Petroleum Exporting Countries (OPEC) in the 1970s, and the UK's so-called Black Wednesday (September 16, 1992) when currency trader George Soros earned himself $1 billion via a speculative move that forced the UK government to leave the European Currency Mechanism and float the pound, which fell sharply against major currencies the following day. Interestingly, in the OPEC case, it appears that the cartel did not push up the price of oil as far as it might readily have done, for negative marginal revenues appear to have been implied at the prices the cartel's actions generated, in contrast to what we might expect from the theory of monopoly. In seeking to draw attention to this, Wilson (1979) pointed out that, as with manufacturing firms in Andrews's (1949) "normal cost" theory of pricing, owners of oil resources need to be mindful of the risk that what they do today could spoil their future markets. In OPEC's case, there was not merely the risk that the reduction in real incomes that higher oil prices would cause would trigger a global downturn if the oil producers did not immediately spend their increased revenues; there was also the risk that the higher price would encourage more exploration for oil and more research into ways of reducing oil consumption.

Irwin and Keynes both present a view of speculator as being primarily focused on the likely behavior of other speculators, since this will affect price movements. This focus opens scope for asset and commodity prices to become detached from where they ought to be heading in terms of the underlying fundamentals and hence for speculation to distort the market signals observed by would-be investors. Keynes (1936, ch. 12) likens the speculators' situation to that of those who entered newspaper competitions in the 1930s where the task was to look at a set of photographs of beautiful women and pick which photograph would be viewed by the most entrants to the competition as being the one depicting the most beautiful woman, rather than to pick which of the photographs showed the woman who was the most beautiful. Irwin's view similarly highlights crowd behavior, but in a more dynamic way that emphasizes bandwagon effects. Instead of Keynes's "beauty contest" analogy, Irwin drew parallels between commodity markets and the tale of a US troopship that was returning to New York on a foggy day in 1919, fully laden with soldiers: it was said that the ship very nearly capsized when, as the fog started to clear and the lookout shouted that he could see the city, those on board rushed to one side of the ship to look in the direction to which the lookout was pointing.

Irwin used the phrase "movement traders" to characterize the speculators who concentrated on trying to predict the behavior of the other speculators rather than operating with a focus on underlying fundamentals. His concern was that if young traders who lacked expertise in relation to the underlying fundamentals were able to make good incomes from movement trading, they might not take the trouble to engage in the "arduous study of the numerous conditions which affect demand and supply" (Irwin, 1937, p. 277). If speculative markets increasingly become populated by movement traders, the extent to which they overshoot will increase, due to the trading by those who have knowledge of underlying fundamentals and trade on that basis being increasingly outweighed by the actions of movement traders.

When it comes to their trading behavior, we might be wise to see movement traders as highly promiscuous agents who lack the old-fashioned professionals' commitment to trading in a particular market. In its most determined form, movement trading entails always trying to be holding the asset whose price is going to rise relative to all other assets and always trying to predict, and be willing to shift one's portfolio into, whatever is going to be the "next big thing," regardless of what it might be. Since bounded rationality stands in the way of comprehensive knowledge across a wide range of assets and commodities, most movement traders will take their cues from relative price movements that are already happening because others are somewhat ahead of them in spotting the right capital gains to chase.

12.3   Herding, Information Cascades and Decision Rule Cascades

If all market participants were equally alert to the implications of unexpected new information for the yield of a particular asset, there would be no place for movement traders: the asset's price would immediately jump to the appropriate level and stay there until further unexpected information became available. In the real world, however, the implications of new information are construed differently and at different speeds by different speculators. Moreover, as Shiller (2020) emphasizes, economic narratives, like contagious diseases, take time to spread. Initially, the information may not even be noticed immediately by everyone, and subsequently, as some people belatedly discover and act upon it, others may change their views of its significance, especially after seeing its initial impact in the market. The initial impact may surprise some speculators and be viewed as potentially implying there will be further changes in the same direction. This may result in bandwagon effects whereby those who had not initially decided to buy an asset whose price has risen may now do so, with consequent price changes again not necessarily being seen as the end of the price adjustment process. It is via this mechanism that bubbles can be initiated in asset markets. The steepness of the price rise in the upswing is commonly the result of the assets in question being intrinsically nonreproducible (as with credentialed old masters in the art world) or whose supplies are inherently hard to expand (as with gold) or having significant initial lags in the scaling up of their production when prices of the existing stock have started to rise (as with real estate).

Although bubbles can be modeled using multiagent computer simulations as if they result from people choosing via simple decision rules, I concur with Michelle Baddeley's (2010) view that behavioral economists would be wise also to consider the psychological and sociological drivers of bubbles. When a bubble is in process, it often appears as though some kind of population-wide psychological mania has taken hold, with the population obsessively watching for news on the latest price movements (unless they are living wildly as they celebrate their increased wealth, as in the United States in the "Roaring Twenties" prior to the 1929 Wall Street Crash, or in the "Greed is good" yuppie era of the mid-1980s that followed the deregulation of financial markets prior to the stock market crash of October 19, 1987). Many people who would not normally take speculative risks seem to be sucked into such behavior, perhaps for fear of missing out and/ or fear of being viewed as boringly overcautious. For those at the bottom of the social ladder (such as the Wall Street shoeshine men in the 1920s, who might have hoped to pick up investment tips from their clients), the steepness of the increase in asset prices seems to offer the prospect of rapid elevation in their fortunes if they can somehow scrape together enough to get a foothold in the market: they have little to lose and everything to gain. Charles Kindleberger (1978) captured in his book *Manias, Panics and Crashes* how history has tended to repeat itself in this kind of way across the centuries, and it has continued to do so since then, as documented in that book's successive editions.

A variety of forms of crowd behavior can contribute to an economic bubble. One of these is "herding," which Baddeley (2010, p. 282) defines as "the phenomenon of individuals deciding to follow others and imitating group behavior rather than deciding independently and atomistically on the basis of their own, private information." In this sense, a herd of speculators may function rather like a herd of wild buffalo that starts to stampede; it is not like a herd of domesticated farm animals that are being guided by shepherds and their dogs, though we might see central bank governors as attempting at times to operate like shepherds, with the regulatory rules of financial systems there to limit wanton behavior by participants.

As we saw in Section 5.5, Keynes (1937) viewed such imitative behavior as a means of coping with extreme uncertainty when people have very little private information on which to base their decisions. It can entail copying the population at large, or groups within it, or merely copying particular individuals, possibly even by delegating one's choices in the area in question to a particular individual or entity (such as by buying a share in Warren Buffet's Berkshire Hathaway holding company). Imitation in principle could be a one-step process, whereby the actions of leaders are copied directly by their followers, but it typically works more gradually, spreading through social networks via a sequence of replicating choices: for example, Dave copies Alicia and is in turn copied by Edward, and so on. Such a process is known as an "information cascade" (Bikhchandani et al., 1992).

Related to the information cascade idea is the idea of a "decision rule cascade" that Jason Potts and I developed, as an extension to our earlier "market for preferences" notion, with our graduate student Ti-Ching Peng (Earl et al., 2007). How the two cascade notions differ will be more easily appreciated if I explain the origins of our paper. Ti-Ching was studying the dynamics of Brisbane's real estate prices and had written a paper in which she tried to predict median house prices for each suburb purely on the basis of each suburb's locational attributes, such as distance from the CBD, whether the suburb had a railway station, a school, and so on. Despite deliberately ignoring the quality of the housing stock in each suburb, her simple hedonic model supported quite well the maxim that what matters when choosing a place to own is "location, location, location." As we considered her results, our discussion turned to the boom in demand for investment properties and whether her analysis might have any lessons about which suburbs would be best if one were looking to buy a property to rent to others. To us, an obvious issue was the fact that Ti-Ching's model was a compensatory one, whereas, given the number of variables and suburbs, it seemed likely that investors might use non-compensatory checklist-style decision rules. What might these rules be, and how would investors arrive at them?

I then recalled a suggestion about the social side of investment property demand that Daly (1982) made in his book *Sydney Boom, Sydney Bust* about that city's housing market in the 1970s. To show how property investment habits could start, he had given an example that began with a wealthy real estate professional talking to his dentist about how things have been going and what his investment strategy has been. The dentist thereby picks up information about his patient's method of choosing investment properties and decides to try to apply these rules himself. He, too, starts doing well and talks to his friends and dental practice colleagues about his success with rental properties, throwing in some examples of his recipe for choosing them. Before long, the dentist's assistant and her partner have set out to do likewise.

We realized that this process was more subtle than an information cascade, for rather than copying the behavior of others and giving up trying to make a particular choice via what they knew, the players in the story did not know *precisely what the expert had done* but they were inferring and then applying decision rules from the tale of *how* the choices were made. The idea of a decision rule cascade was thus born, and it seemed to have potential to be employed in analyzing how the demand for a wide variety of investment assets could mushroom through social networks.

Given the process entailed in the story of the Sydney dentist, there is obvious potential for a variant of the tacit knowledge problem to apply with increasing significance as a decision rule cascade takes place. Because details of decision rules are revealed during short social interactions, there is scope for the quality of the decision rule that is inferred to be degraded repeatedly as it passes along the chain, away from the expert source. Rather as in a game of "Chinese whispers," elements may be lost or scrambled as the knowledge spreads from person to person. Those at the end of a decision rule cascade will fare relatively poorly not merely because they end up with a simpler and/or garbled decision rule but also because they act later, after the best opportunities have been seized. Indeed, what they end up buying might be properties that experts are selling with a view to moving their funds to different suburbs that they now see as relatively undervalued and likely soon to enjoy far better rates of capital appreciation.

12.4   Animal Spirits, Investment and Discretionary Consumption

When people stake their wealth, time and reputations on risky ventures in bold departures from conventions or merely seek to profit by trying to copy others, they will need an emotional impetus to go ahead rather than play safe and venture nothing. As we saw in Section 5.5, Keynes (1936, p. 161) encapsulated this via the notion of "animal spirits," which he defined as "a spontaneous urge to action rather than inaction." Keynes's use of the term is much narrower than its use in Akerlof and Shiller's (2009) book (as they acknowledge) but the role that he assigns to animal spirits still represents a major departure from how economists usually close their answer to the question of how people ultimately decide whether to venture into the unknown. Economists have usually avoided referring to the role of emotions when theorizing in this area. It is as if they subsume emotions within the assumption that individuals have "risk preferences," with some people being more willing than others to take on risks. There are well-established techniques for uncovering people's risk preferences, which are very widely employed in experimental economics. However, while such techniques may capture the risk preferences of research subjects at the time of such experiments, the risk preferences concept seems altogether too static. It sits uneasily with the volatility that is commonly observed in asset and commodity markets or the way that people can seem sometimes to flip from hesitancy into action, or suddenly lose their nerve, without acquiring any additional information of relevance to the risk they are contemplating.

The questions of what Keynes meant, or should have meant, by the term "animal spirits" and what it implies in relation to the concept of rationality have been addressed in a variety of ways, as Alexander Dow and Sheila Dow (2011) have demonstrated. Sheila Dow (2014) has subsequently characterized animal spirits in terms of optimism that has not been substantiated but results from having low uncertainty aversion and low awareness of uncertainty. The Dows prefer to avoid the "rational versus emotional" dichotomy when thinking about animal spirits, for animal spirits play a vital role in keeping capitalism moving in the face of fundamental uncertainty that makes it impossible to specify what constitutes "rational" behavior from the standpoint of rational choice theory. Here, I commend the Dows' survey to readers rather than attempting to summarize it. This leaves me with space to add a further contender on the wellsprings of animal spirits, a perspective framed in relation to ideas covered earlier in this book.

Keynes clearly was thinking along similar lines to Festinger's (1957) cognitive dissonance theory when he wrote (1936, pp. 161–162), "Enterprise only pretends to itself to be mainly activated by the statements in its own prospectus, however candid and sincere." However, in saying that entrepreneurs deal with their lack of knowledge of how their schemes might turn out by acting on the basis of their animal spirits, he seems to be appealing to something more basic than what we had said earlier in this book in relation to the nature of "gut feelings" and intuition as drivers of behavior in the face of fundamental uncertainty where choices may involve crucial experiments.

The "urge to action" to which Keynes refers can, I think, be usefully analyzed in relation to the identity of the decision-maker, a self-construct that stands to be reinforced or called into question by taking a particular kind of risk. As far as entrepreneurs are concerned, a study by Woods (2002) using Kelly's (1955) repertory grid technique revealed that "making things happen" is central to how they see themselves. The entrepreneurs in Woods's study would thus have experienced cognitive dissonance if they were not "making things happen" due to holding back from making investment commitments or from undertaking other business experiments. Likewise, people will experience cognitive dissonance if they see themselves as "ambitious" but fail to do the kinds of things that they, and their social referents, view as "what an ambitious person would do." Clearly, in such situations, these "entrepreneurs" or "ambitious" folk could seek to remove cognitive dissonance by rethinking their self-constructs. However, doing this would open a major can of worms in the absence of an acceptable, preexisting alternative vision of whom they might construe themselves to be and what kind of future that construct implies.

If one has a self-construct centered on being open to risk-taking, taking a risk is an act of self-actualization in Maslow's (1970) sense, and it may also be a means to meeting more basic needs. However, this does not mean that those who regard themselves as entrepreneurs or as ambitious will always be willing to take risks, for their rules for forming constructs will probably also include rules for what constitutes being "reckless" and/or "a fool" in relation to business, career choices, and so forth. Hence, if what Shackle (1974) calls "the state of the news" has taken a kaleidic turn from rosy to troubling, a self-styled "entrepreneur" or "ambitious person" may switch to being more cautious, for now there are clouds evident where previously they had not been imagined (cf. Sheila Dow's idea that someone with strong animal spirits tends to have low uncertainty awareness). Of course, this will generate cognitive dissonance, but switching into a more cautious mode avoids seeming to be a reckless fool. Such a person will then construct a narrative that removes the cognitive dissonance between their self-construct and their behavior, such as a story centered on the possibility of better opportunities being just around the corner. Such stories may be particularly easy to construct in a Schumpeterian world of innovation: loss of nerve today may, for example, preclude being the originator of a new meso rule, but one might tell oneself about the possibility of being able to make a bigger fortune by building on lessons learned from mistakes by those who, in one's absence, become the originators. Clearly, if the state of the news is such that everyone starts thinking like this, innovative investments will suddenly dry up and be replaced by a preference for liquidity.

12.4.1　Animal Spirits and Consumption

Keynes was only writing about business investment when he wrote about the impact of shifts in animal spirits and confidence on aggregate investment in a world of long-term expectations that have flimsy foundations. However, a contemporary advertisement of the UK carmaker Austin soon triggered in the mind of Townshend (1937, p. 160, n. 1) the idea that what Keynes was saying might apply to any durable or financial asset. The Austin advertisement was trying to signal the long-term value of the brand's cars by emphasizing, "You *buy* a car. You *invest* in an Austin." Like highly specific industrial equipment, a car usually cannot readily be sold at a price whose discount on what had been paid for it merely reflect how much physical depreciation its current owner has inflicted upon it. Hence, anyone who buys a car or, by extension, a durable asset of any kind (such as a booking for a vacation or a ticket to a live event, flight or rail journey) needs to be confident of not wanting or needing to reverse their decision at an unexpectedly early date, before it has served its purpose.

Townshend's insight implies that consumer expenditure may be driven by animal spirits, too. This implication seems especially significant once we recognize that people often dispose of their durable assets long before these assets cease to be worth maintaining and repairing. This means that consumers can readily decide to put on hold thoughts about upgrading their durable assets without losing the services that these assets yield. Something akin to this was pointed out very soon after Townshend's paper appeared: Reddaway (1937, p. 300) noted that, as economies became more affluent, the increased capacity for discretionary consumption expenditure could make it more difficult to sustain full employment. Reddaway argued, first, that demand for luxury and semi-luxury products is, at the best of times, less firmly grounded between such products than between necessities, which can make demand for discretionary purchases subject to fads, fashions and happenstance. Secondly, he argued that demand for luxury and semi-luxury products would be the first thing to be cut back in times of adversity. This, in turn, makes investment in producing items of discretionary consumption especially susceptible to shifts in confidence: returns could be poor both due to consumers opting to buy other products or simply to exercise a preference for liquidity.

These insights were not picked by other economists at that time. However, after World War II, the significance of discretionary consumption and of consumer sentiment as a driver of aggregate demand was the preoccupation of George Katona, a Hungarian psychologist who pioneered the study of consumer confidence with his colleagues at the University of Michigan's Center for Survey Research. (For useful commentaries on Katona's life and work, and how Katona's thinking intersects with that of Keynes, see, respectively, Wärneryd, 1982, and King, 2016.) As far as Katona was concerned, economists are mistaken if they attempt to model discretionary spending as a function of the ability to spend and ignore the significance of the *willingness* of consumers to spend. Affluent consumers in modern economies can suddenly increase their spending by running down their savings balances or by taking out secured or unsecured loans, but they do not have to do so. Likewise, they do not have to spend increased disposable income that they receive when governments cut income taxes. If they are to spend – and in the process use up future spending potential that they might need to call upon if they lose their jobs, face major medical bills, and so on – they need to be in the mood to spend.

Consider, by way of illustration, the first significant downturn in the United States in the 1950s. There was no obvious "economic" reason for consumers to have cut back on demand for new cars in the way that they did in 1957–1958, for their indebtedness had not become unsustainable and the average age of cars in the United States had not become unusually low (see the Katona-influenced study by Smith, 1975). However, this was a time when there was a sudden shift in consumer confidence: when the USSR beat the US into space by launching the first Sputnik satellite in 1957, this technological feat raised questions about the scale of the threat that the USSR posed to the US, rekindling Cold War concerns. Ironically, it was at this time that Packard (1957) and Galbraith (1958) offered their famous critiques of the notion of consumer sovereignty and portrayed consumer demand as being driven by the power of advertising. Katona (1960) challenged their claims in his book *The Powerful Consumer*. He also argued that sudden swings in consumer sentiment could derail the predictions of macroeconomic models and make it difficult for governments to make reliable estimates of the impact of their attempts to use fiscal and monetary measures to manage aggregate demand in the finely tuned way that Keynesian economists aspired to achieve with the aid of their econometric models. Later, Katona and Strumpel (1976) argued that consumer perceptions regarding the ability of the government to manage the economy have a major role in shaping consumer sentiment. They also demonstrate that the 1973–1975 US economic downturn was driven by a fall in "consumer investment" that preceded the fall in business investment and was associated with a sharp fall in consumer sentiment.

Katona's (1960) book is listed as in the references section in Akerlof and Shiller's *Animal Spirits* and certainly seems to be very much present in the latter in spirit despite Katona never otherwise being mentioned. This sense is confirmed by the fact that, in his autobiographical notes at the Nobel website, Shiller (2013) explains that it was the sole lecture of Katona that he attended while he was an undergraduate at the University of Michigan that alerted him to the importance of psychology for understanding the economy. Shiller goes on to say that for years Katona's ideas had been at the back of his mind. Katona is further lauded in Shiller's (2020) *Narrative Economics*. Shiller's endorsement of Katona matters, for as King (2016, pp. 71–72) points out, despite Katona's concerns being taken seriously by some of the pioneers of macroeconomic modeling, such as Lawrence Klein and James Tobin, both of whom went on to become Nobel Laureates, the issues that Katona raised were largely ignored in textbook on macroeconomics (the notable exception is the text written by Katona's Michigan colleague, Gardner Ackley, 1961). Despite this, and despite the associated neglect of Katona's thinking in the teaching of macroeconomics, the University of Michigan's Consumer Sentiment Index that Katona developed in the late 1940s is still being compiled over forty years after his death. Indeed, many consumer confidence indices are constructed nowadays, with some countries, such as the United States and Australia, having multiple indices of this kind, constructed by different bodies and with different methodologies. Since the levels of such indices are sometimes reported not merely in the business press but also in finance segments on primetime TV news programs, there is potential for them to have feedback impacts on the state of consumer confidence.

12.5   Saving Behavior in a World of Weak-Willed Homeowners

An economy populated by "econs" would not be characterized by excitable, jittery responses to changes in the state of the news, of the kind that Katona's work invites us to take seriously. Economic agents who knew the probability distributions of all kinds of events and were not constrained in their computational capacities would be able to construct plans for how they would spread their consumption over their entire lives. If they went through periods of unemployment or underemployment, this would not result in them reducing their consumption: they would simply draw on savings they had accumulated partly with such eventualities in mind, and when they enjoyed periods of overtime working, they would not celebrate their temporarily higher incomes with a temporary hike in their consumption. Similarly, when they retired, they would not make a step-reduction in their spending; indeed, they might bring into play plans to increase it to make the most of their extra leisure time, for which they would pay with savings accumulated carefully with such plans in mind and on the basis of competent applications of the arithmetic of compound interest. They would not know for sure how long they would live, but they would purchase annuities to ensure that they did not run out of money before they died. Moreover, they would make their consumption plans mindful of the probabilities of having their capacities to enjoy particular activities affected by particular health issues as they got older.

There is clearly more than a grain of truth in the conventional "as if" optimizing models of saving and consumption that predict the kinds of behavior outlined in the previous paragraph. But behavioral economics leads us to a different vision of this area of behavior. Given the potential to have a miserable retirement due to failing to accumulate enough savings, people would be procedurally rational if they were to research carefully what their options are in relation to savings opportunities and associated tax breaks. They would also be wise to be assiduous users of the calculating engines that providers of such services often offer on their websites, and to invest in some advice from a professional financial planner. Yet few of us do this to the degree that we might. Moreover, as the success of Thaler and Benartzi's (2004) Save More Tomorrow initiative shows, whether or not people will bother to take up their employers' savings programs can depend upon whether these programs are offered as defaults, even though it might only take a few minutes to sign up for them if they were presented on an opt-in basis. How much we amass for retirement can thus be significantly affected by factors such as:

- how uncomfortable we feel when confronting our mortality,
- whether we have simple heuristics – such as "a sum invested at a 3 percent return doubles in nominal value in about twenty-five years" – that help us keep in mind, when young, the power of compound interest,
- our self-control in the face of tempting opportunities to spend now, regardless of whether we simply allow the amount that we save to accumulate as a residual or whether we have bothered to formulate and set out to achieve any targets for our savings,
- whether we have so much happening in other areas of our lives that we repeatedly fail to ensure we invest a few minutes switching funds into higher-earning accounts or an evening on consolidating superannuation balances from various past employment saving schemes to find out where we stand, or on refreshing our minds on what the current tax rules are regarding concessions for retirement savings; and so on.

The materialistic temptations that are ever-present in modern affluent economies are to some extent countered by policies that require people to contribute to savings plans that lock up the funds until retirement or that succeed in nudging people to enter such plans voluntarily. However, since the early 1990s, these efforts by policymakers to contain the future budgetary burden of supporting those who do not accumulate adequate retirement funds have increasingly had to contend with the home equity mortgage meso, a financial innovation that leaves weak-willed homebuyers at risk of still having mortgage payments when they reach retirement age. In discussing this issue, Thaler (2015, ch. 9) emphasizes the role that unscrupulous mortgage brokers played in the run-up to the GFC in selling such mortgages to customers who had poor financial literacy. Having signed up for such mortgages in an environment of rising property prices, many people felt entitled to use their mortgage credit lines as means of turning the capital gains on their homes into consumer durables or memories from expensive vacations.

As we try to understand the growing phenomenon of retirees with mortgages, we should expect that the processes of cognitive dissonance reduction will conjure up reasons to spend in the minds of those who have the urge to draw on their lines of credit even if they have previously set themselves goals for when they will be mortgage-free. For example, we should expect them to construct narratives that emphasize the prospect of their incomes growing due to promotion, or that mortgage interest rates have a good chance of falling (pre-GFC) or staying very low (post-GFC). They might apply the heuristic that "the bank wouldn't have given us this spending capacity if they thought we wouldn't be able to make use of it and still be able to retire debt-free."

Insofar as consumers acknowledge the risk of still being in debt by the time they cease receiving income from employment, the dissonance reduction processes can get to work on their capacity to deal with the debt by drawing on their retirement savings and downplaying their likely expenditure needs in retirement, even though potentially they could remain active to a ripe old age or end up having to pay considerable sums due to succumbing to chronic health problems. The scope for taking an overoptimistic view is enhanced to the extent that consumers are on retirement saving schemes that do not offer a "defined benefit" based on a formula that takes account of their years of service and salary and which instead simply entail having the retirement fund invest their contributions on the stock market, which they might view as having great potential to rise before they retire. Of course, if all this proves to be a dream, the banks can come to their rescue by providing them with access to a "reverse mortgage" – a logical extension of the home equity loan concept that enables them to live by running down the remaining equity in their homes.

Serious attention needs to be given to the macroeconomic implications of the growing population of retirees with mortgages, and of those who pay off their homes before they retire but who retire with far smaller retirement balances than they might have accumulated if they had lived less materialistically. Ultimately, consumers who delay paying off their home loans will, other things equal, be able to consume less than they might have done over their lives because they spend more on interest payments. However, the "other things equal" condition may not apply to consumers as a group, since the bringing forward of consumption spending will have complex feedback effects on the macroeconomy further down the track.

If consumers do not make their saving decisions in ways that are procedurally rational, what kinds of heuristics should we expect them to be using to judge how much they can afford to spend or how much they ought to save? Part of the answer may lie in mental accounting procedures (Thaler, 1985). For example, if we receive a legacy, we are likely to put it in a mental account of its own instead of treating it as a fungible addition to our lifetime wealth to be used, as an "econ" would use it, as the basis for an incremental increase in our consumption for the rest of our life. Using the legacy to treat ourselves to something by which we can remember the donor will, as a rule, seem more appropriate than the "econ's" way of operating. For our general consumption, we may use the behavior of "people like us" as role models.

These social referents may not even be actual people we know. In his TV documentary series on the GFC, the Irish economic journalist David McWilliams (2009, episode 1) suggests that consumer reference standards could rise via the subconscious impact of changes in how sets are dressed in TV soap operas as time passes. He illustrates how these standards have changed with material from the long running, widely syndicated Australian show *Neighbors*. With its focus on the outsourcing of aspirations, McWilliams's suggestion is not altogether different from the role that Akerlof and Shiller (2009, pt. 2, ch. 10) assign to international differences in national narratives as means of understanding why, for example, the near-zero average savings rate of the US's materialistic population contrasts so sharply with the rates in some Asian nations, most notably that of China's nationalistic, future-oriented population. International differences in the guiding narratives that drive saving and spending behavior can have major macroeconomic effects: Ferguson and Schularick (2007) argue that the reluctance of the US's population to save has produced a trade deficit, fed in no small part by imports from China and supported by capital inflows from China. The latter are made possible by the Chinese population's willingness to "save their way out of poverty" (Akerlof and Shiller, 2009, p. 125). (For further behavioral analysis of saving behavior, see the excellent survey volume, *The Psychology of Saving*, by Wärneryd, 1999.)

12.6 Financial Institutions' Rules and Housing Affordability

Financial institutions have much in common with the vision of manufacturing and retailing firms presented earlier in this book:

- Their pricing involves the use of markup rules (though they often use the term "spread" when referring to the markup on deposit rate that they use to arrive at the interest rate they charge their borrowers).
- They are often skilled at finding ways to profit from customer inertia and ignorance, though they ought to be concerned about preserving customer goodwill (though

in recent decades those with ethically challenged cultures have sometimes failed to do so), since they have potential to retain their customers for many decades if they do not alienate them.

- They use points-based or box-ticking procedures as means for coping with uncertainty and complexity when they are, so to speak, producing new loans, whether for individuals, firms or sovereign states.
- They typically must deal with time-wasting would-be customers who turn out not to be creditworthy.

Their lending rules evolve as they try to deal with competitive pressure, take up opportunities that have been opened up by changes to regulations or respond to increased rates of defaulting on loans. This entails processes that have much in common with those outlined in Section 11.12 as drivers of the investment strategies of firms in manufacturing and creative industries. If a lender experiments successfully with less demanding loan rules in a bid to increase its market share, it puts pressure on its rivals and signals what they, too, might try to do. This results in further pressure to experiment by "pushing the envelope" even further by introducing less demanding rules for making loans. If this process eventually leads to a financial crisis, the lending rules will be dramatically tightened until the fallout from previous excesses becomes clear, whereupon the rule relaxation process begins again. This process is central to the financial instability hypothesis of Hyman Minsky that is discussed in Section 12.7 with an emphasis on changes in the types of risks that get taken. But before we move on to Minsky, it is instructive to consider how the relaxation of home lending rules can dramatically affect housing affordability.

Consider first a case where the lending rule is that a couple can borrow two and a half times the biggest earner's annual pretax income if they can offer a 20 percent deposit. (This was the kind of rule followed in the UK in the late 1970s.) If Billy earns $80,000 per year and his partner Meg earns $60,000, and if they can meet the deposit requirement, they can borrow $200,000 and buy a property that costs $250,000. However, if they only have a deposit of $30,000, the most expensive property they will be able to purchase will be one that costs $150,000. Being able to find an extra $20,000 will make a huge difference to the kind of property they can buy, and the manager of their bank might take the risk of nudging them into trying to find out if they can borrow this amount from the credit union at Billy's workplace and thereby put together a $50,000 deposit. It is a bit sneaky to do this (and thereby create what was called a "loan cocktail" by the bank manager who pointed me in that direction, despite barely knowing me, shortly after I arrived in Australia), but getting round the rule imposed by the bank's head office might help the branch manager meet her branch's lending targets. Billy and Meg are pleased to hear that, unlike when their parents were young, the bank does not require them to be married, for the expense of a wedding would chew up a sizable chunk of their deposit.

But now suppose that the lending rule allows lending three times the joint annual pretax income of the would-be buyers (who might even be allowed merely to be a group of friends rather than a couple), so long as they can come up with a 10 percent deposit. (This is what seemed to have become the rule in the UK by the late 1980s.) If this is the rule, Billy and Meg will be able to borrow $420,000 and buy a property whose price is $466,666 if they can offer a $46,666 deposit. If their deposit is only $30,000, the maximum they can spend on a property will be $300,000. We could extend our scenarios to include, say, rules that allowed mortgages of up to four times the combined incomes of the buyers, and with a zero deposit, subject to the mortgage being no more than 10 percent more than the value of the property. Such mortgages, with negative initial equity, appeared in the run-up to the GFC, and they enabled homebuyers to spend on furnishing their homes and/or to own newer, cheaper-to-maintain cars without having to incur the much higher interest rates that finance companies would charge. If property prices rose rapidly, the negative equity period would not last long, and the bank would hope to go on to achieve a bigger return from the clients in question than would have been possible via a more cautious strategy. Note how the negative equity mortgage might even make default less likely if the client's monthly repayment costs are less than the costs of having a smaller mortgage but paying for consumer durables through a finance company on a loan of shorter duration and/or having to incur the costs of keeping an old car going. Offering loans with a lower "teaser" rate of interest for the first few years also helps to ensure that defaults do not occur while such loans entail negative equity. But the creation of such lax lending rules also fuels the increases in real estate prices that is necessary to eliminate the initial negative equity.

In periods when real estate prices have been skyrocketing, the banking sector has tried to give the impression that it has been doing as much as it can to help its customers address the housing affordability problem: smaller deposit ratios make it easier to get on to or move up the "property ladder," and longer repayment periods make it easier for borrowers to service loans based on larger mortgage to income ratios. However, if we reflect on the figures in the aforementioned scenarios, we might be rightly suspicious that housing affordability crises are in no small part the result of banks having relaxed their lending rules and created the money that they let their clients borrow, from which the banks have profited considerably.

While this has been going on, banks have often given the impression that how much they can lend is limited by their abilities to attract deposits. However, when a bank (as distinct from a nonbank financial intermediary) expands its lending, it is able to do this simply by an electronic ledger entry so long as it has enough reserve assets to avoid breaching its minimum reserve asset rules or can obtain these assets from the central bank (by borrowing from the central bank to purchase eligible short-term government bonds from the central bank) or the nonbank private sector (purchasing private sector holdings of eligible short-term government bonds, for which it pays by creating matching deposits). The mortgage is a new asset and the money created to pay for it is a new deposit that is passed to the vendor of the property. Hence, the challenge for the banks is not to attract deposits that they then can lend; rather, it is to stop deposits from leaking out *after* they have been created. If there is a tendency for bank deposits to drain from the economy via a trade deficit, the banks will need to replenish them by attracting deposits from overseas, with the arrival of these deposits helping to stop the country's exchange rate from depreciating. In economies whose populations are on average very bad at saving but are keen to borrow to buy real estate, the banks may thus be significant drivers of rising foreign indebtedness as well as fueling booming real estate prices.

12.7   Minsky's Financial Instability Hypothesis

The material from the previous sections of this chapter complements the intensely financial approach to macroeconomics offered over several decades by Hyman Minsky (1919–1996) (see, particularly, Minsky, 1975, 1982a, 1982b, 1986; Papadimitriou and Wray, 2019; Wray, 2016; Neilson, 2019). If Minsky had lived to see that 2008 GFC, he would have been able to say, "I told you so," for his core contention was that capitalism is inherently prone to generate financial crises. He arrived at this view via what is implicitly a complex adaptive systems way of thinking that focuses on feedback loops and changes in the connective architecture of the financial system, i.e., the multilayered nexus of financial balance sheets. From this perspective, the demand for, and supply of, financial and real assets evolve in ways that gradually produces increasingly interconnected and fragile financial structures that can collapse like a house of cards if the monetary authorities do not intervene rapidly when insolvent financial institutions start to appear. Bounded rationality is an implicit feature of Minsky's vision, too, for it is only when a financial crisis breaks out that players in the financial system discover how terribly interconnected balance sheet have become and how inadequate were the financial reserves that many players had come to view as sufficient for buffering against nasty surprises.

Minsky's analysis is set in the context of a much richer view of the financial system than that on which Keynes (1936) built his *General Theory*. Minsky's view of the financial sector is very Schumpeterian, as might be expected given that he had studied under Schumpeter when doing his doctorate at Harvard in the 1940s. Hence, although Minsky accepts Keynes's concerns regarding the instability and weak foundations of long-term expectations, he also recognizes the potentially disruptive impacts of the experiments that financial institutions conduct in pursuit of greater profits, whose creativity often comes as a surprise to market regulators. These experiments have included the kinds of innovative mortgage contracts and changes to lending rules that were mentioned in Sections 12.5 and 12.6, along with financial innovations such as securitization and sophisticated financial derivatives that were viewed and marketed as means of passing risks to other players. Such experimentation can be triggered by changes that the authorities make to the rules of the game under which the financial system operates. These changes can include deregulatory initiatives such as those undertaken in many countries in the 1980s that triggered diversification experiments by financial institutions into territories where they had previously not been major players and where inexperience could result in costly mistakes. But whatever form they take, competitive ploys that seem to be working generate pressures for other players to follow suit or to try something even bolder.

In Minsky's analysis, the creation of a fragile financial system is a driven by changes in the kind of financing that is offered to borrowers and taken up by them. Minsky calls the safest form "hedge finance." This term denotes a loan on an asset (for example, an investment property) whose income yield (the property's net income after paying maintenance costs, property taxes and management fees) is expected to be adequate to cover both the interest on the loan and the repayment schedule for the loan principal. The question of whether the asset will rise in value is not at issue with this sort of finance; what matters is whether the income stream will be viewed as adequate by both the lender and the borrower. Neither side wants to see the loan fail and the asset in question then having to be subject to a forced sale. However, the lender's risk will be limited by how much equity the borrower offers as a deposit, for this provides a buffer if a forced sale has to be instigated and the realized price of the asset proves to be less than the amount of the loan.

A step up from this in terms of risk is what Minsky labels "speculative finance," where the expected net income flow from the asset whose purchase is to be financed covers the interest charges on the loan but not repayment of (all) the principal. This situation could apply if the borrower is allowed to operate with a higher debt to equity ratio and buys, on the basis of a given deposit, more units of the asset in question than would be possible under hedge finance. Here, if things go well, the lender may profit from making a bigger, interest-only loan. The higher debt to equity ratio may not seem to be a problem if the value of the asset is expected to rise rapidly, as this would reduce the debt to equity ratio and thereby reduce the risk associated with a forced sale if the borrower fails to keep up the interest payments. From the borrower's standpoint, there is the risk of ending up no better off if the asset's price does not rise, even if, as expected, the net income from the asset covers the interest charges. However, the attraction of such a deal to the borrower is that leveraging the deposit in this way, compared with a hedge finance deal, will result in greater net wealth if the asset's price rises so much that it will be possible to make a bigger profit on owning it than would have been possible if the deposit had been used to obtain a smaller, hedge finance investment loan. This will be the case if it becomes possible to sell the asset and realize a greater net amount, after paying back the loan principal, than the amount that it would have been possible to get in the same period by only taking on a smaller, hedge finance loan (which would include a smaller capital gain but also some repayment of the principal). Someone who might in a static market have, say, bought a single investment property via hedge finance might thus opt in a rising market to buy a couple of investment properties via speculative finance.

Clearly, if the latter deal can be done without crowding out other borrowers on a dollar-per-dollar basis, switching to speculative finance increases demand for the asset type in question, helping to confirm the expectation that its price was going to rise. If the general mood favors engaging in more speculative finance, those who end up borrowing more may indeed be able to do so without crowding out occurring. This is because banks may be in a mood to create more credit and, even if they are not, their depositors may become more willing to shift their funds to nonbank financial intermediaries or take the risk of engaging in direct lending. If bank deposit owners behave in this way, the ownership of the bank deposits changes but there will then be additional lending based on them, beyond that in the banks' balance sheets. Moreover, as Wray (2008) reminds us, Minsky repeatedly emphasized that, from the 1950s onward, banks that are in a mood to increase their lending have been able repeatedly to come up with innovative strategies to get around attempts of the monetary authorities to restrain them. As Minsky (1957, p. 186) pointed out early in his career, these kinds of innovations also mean that "the next financial crisis will never be just like the last one." This will make it more challenging for the monetary authorities to anticipate when the next financial crisis is going to take place and to know how to act when it happens: to a degree, it will be unprecedented and thus inherently hard to construe.

The riskiest form of lending and borrowing is what Minsky calls "Ponzi finance" (after the early twentieth-century Boston financial swindler, Charles Ponzi). This is where the debt to equity ratio at the time the deal commences is so high that the net income stream from the asset that is being financed is not big enough even to service the interest on the loan. Because of this, the investor must pay the rest of the interest by running down his or her financial reserves or by borrowing more and more. Clearly, for the investor not to make a loss relative to what might have been achieved by borrowing on a smaller scale on a speculative finance basis, this will require that the assets that are being financed rise in value at a far faster rate than that required for the speculative finance strategy to dominate over an even smaller hedge finance loan. However, if the class of asset in question does rise spectacularly in value, those who are prepared to risk losing all their equity by spreading it very thinly with very high gearing rations and then borrowing even more may be able to make their fortunes.

But if one is to make a fortune via a Ponzi finance investment strategy, it will be necessary to find a supplier of finance who has a similarly rosy view of the price trajectory for the asset that is being financed: given the very high gearing ratio, even a small fall in the asset's value could result in a loss if the borrower becomes unable to keep borrowing more to maintain interest payments on loans already taken out and the lender then has to foreclose and engage in a forced sale of the asset. If the lender is a financial intermediary that is likewise borrowing in an increasingly highly geared manner, the failure of the loans that it makes on a Ponzi finance basis may result in its own insolvency due to it not having enough reserves to write off against what it loses on these loans. This, in turn, will impose losses on those from whom it has borrowed, who may in turn be unable to honor their own financial obligations. Unfortunately, lenders' fears that many players in the financial system are heading toward such solvency crises may be self-fulfilling if they decide to hold back from further lending until it becomes clear who is in trouble. Those who have borrowed on a Ponzi finance basis may then suddenly discover that they cannot continue to extend their borrowing. Forced sales of their assets may then trigger a fall in asset values that also dashes the hopes of more cautious investor. Eventually, this could even impact upon those who had borrowed on a hedge finance basis: for example, if the economy moves into a recession, rental yields on real estate investments might tumble due to those who lose their jobs being unable to afford to pay as much as they have been paying to meet their housing needs.

Minsky sees transitions from hedge finance to speculative finance and, in some cases, ultimately to Ponzi finance as commencing due to people starting to notice unexpectedly rapid increase in the prices of particular types of assets, such as shares and/or real estate. We should recognize further, the potential for decision rule cascades to set in and, following Shiller (2020), the related role of viral narratives that people share about how others are prospering from particular kinds of investments. If they add their own funds, and what they can currently borrow, to the pool that is competing for the assets in question, they guard against the possibility of ending up regretting their failure to jump on the bandwagon (or, worse still, in the case of property investment, of being unable to join the ranks of homeowners at a later stage). If the supply of new assets runs behind the growth of demand for this class of assets, their behavior will help to fuel the increase in the prices of these assets. The capital gains that they make "on paper" can then be used as collateral for further borrowing to build larger but more highly geared portfolios, further fueling the process. At some point, Minsky contends, a euphoric mood will take hold: it will seem that, right now, as far as capital gains are concern, "The sky's the limit!"

In situations of financial euphoria, either within a particular sector or across markets much more widely, people can be observed to enter risk habitats that they would not frequent in normal times – as with the "mom and pop" small investors who start taking out margin loans to buy equities, or retail bankers that start engaging in markets that would normally be the preserve of investment banks. Such behavior should not necessarily be seen as indicating that they have changed their risk preferences, for they could simply be viewing the risk that they could do poorly in these unfamiliar territories as now being much smaller than in the past. With asset price increases increasingly seeming to be a sure thing, their lack of expertise in these markets may not seem to constitute a barrier to doing better there than in their familiar habitats, even if their achievements fall short of the seasoned players. Indeed, the success stories that they hear may include tales of people prospering despite having no idea, or the wrong idea, about the nature of the companies whose shares they purchased.

Unfortunately, these inexperienced investors are likely to be failing to notice several things that should have been of concern to them:

- Assets will not keep rising in value simply because people believe they are going to keep rising in value. Ultimately, assets will need to have an income stream-based reason for their values relative to other assets: if their income yield is less than the cost of financing their purchase, investors will sooner or later start to question the long-run sustainability of their current values, let alone their potential to enjoy further capital gains. Ultimately, the capacity of people to borrow to buy real estate will be constrained by their incomes, and lenders ultimately will become reluctant to extend even further loans that entail Ponzi finance.
- They may have a mistaken view of what is going on if they hear respected financial journalists speaking of prices as rising due to investors "getting into" housing, shares, etc., for the assets that these people are buying are being sold by those who

have decided to move their wealth elsewhere. The sellers may have more expertise than the naive buyers and have good reasons for suspecting that the asset price rises will slow or be reversed.

- If they purchase new assets (e.g., new equity issues or new real estate) rather than existing ones being sold by those who exit the market in question, they may not have done enough research about the extent of further supplies of these assets that are in the pipeline and could have negative impacts on the yields and prices of the assets they buy.

- They may not realize that similar speculative frenzies in the past have normally ended with disastrous capital losses; very few will have read books such as Kindleberger's (1978) classic, *Manias, Panics and Crashes* (available in its seventh edition as Aliber and Kindleberger, 2015).

- Insofar as they make their investments with the aid of complex contracts and under pressure to conclude their deals soon to avoid missing out on imminent gains, they would be wise to consider whether they really understand what they are getting into and who really stands to benefit from the deal. The problem of inadequate financial literacy afflicts not merely the inexperienced subprime mortgage customer; it can also apply to financial market participants who trade derivatives that are so complex as to obscure who ultimately is carrying the risk and hence what one's own risk position actually is (as is well captured in the movie *The Big Short* in relation to the run-up to the GFC). But unfamiliar and fast-changing environments make the risks of financial illiteracy and of not applying the "If it looks too good to be true, it's probably a scam" heuristic especially acute, as such environments make it easier for devious players to fleece those who feel an urgent need to place their financial bets. Moreover, if those who sign up borrowers are rewarded based on how many borrowers they sign up, rather than how many of those whom they sign up go on to establish themselves as reliable borrowers, it is dangerous for financially illiterate borrowers to apply the heuristic "If they didn't think I would be able to service this loan, they wouldn't be giving it to me."

In such environments, financial regulators will have a hard time keeping up with what is going on if they lack the entrepreneurial creativity of those whom they are there to police. Meanwhile, there is the risk that those who argue too soon that a bubble has emerged, and that it will surely burst, will lose their credibility, with financial fragility increasing until one significant financial failure brings on a crash due to its cascading effects across the nexus of balance sheets. Once such defaults start to occur, attempts to switch into "safe haven" assets will make matters worse. The private sector holders of "safe haven" assets will be those who have previously been playing safe – a group that will be especially unlikely to be interested in taking on assets that have suddenly begun to seem too dangerous even for the erstwhile risk-lovers to hold. Hence, if the monetary authorities do not step in as buyers of assets that private sector holders now view as unduly risky to hold, the end of euphoria will be followed by a precipitous fall in the prices of such asset relative to those of "safe haven" assets. Investors will only part with their safe assets in exchange for risky ones when they perceive the latter have fallen so far that it is unlikely they can fall any further.

If such a fall in asset prices takes place due to the authorities being unwilling to pump liquidity into the system and take over failing financial institutions, it will have depressive consequence for output and employment. Those who have lost financial wealth will become less willing to spend, and the inducement to invest in newly produced assets (e.g., brand-new factories) will be inhibited by the cheapness with which existing assets can now be purchased (e.g., by taking over companies whose market valuations have plunged). In the absence of fiscal stimulus, an economic recovery may not materialize until people have to increase their spending due to their durable assets wearing out or until there is an improvement in "animal spirits," with people becoming confident enough to start engaging in hedge finance deals because it appears that contractionary multiplier processes have gone as far as they are going to go. A key factor in the return of confidence to borrow and spend may be a sense on the part of individuals and financial institutions that their financial reserves have been replenished to more prudent ratios by, respectively, increased rates of personal saving and profits on the loans that remain after bad debts have been written off. However, in the interim, these attempts to rebuild reserves would only aggravate the downturn by holding down demand, directly in the former case and, in the latter case, insofar as spending power was held back due to banks increasing their retained profits by reducing their dividend payments to shareholders or raising the spread between what they pay to depositors and what they charge for borrowing.

Sadly, Minsky was not honored with a Nobel Memorial Prize in Economic Sciences despite the significance of his work. His ideas have figured at length in my own writing over many years, most notably in Dow and Earl (1982, chs. 11 and 12) and Earl (1990, ch. 12), both of which include case material. Many members of the Post Keynesian school of economics have likewise long been trying to draw attention to Minsky's work, and his research program has remained prominently the focus of the Levy Institute of Bard College, where he had the role of Distinguished Scholar. It is disappointing, then, to see how, in setting out "their" theory in *Animal Spirits*, Akerlof and Shiller fail to highlight the extent to which Minsky's work is a precursor to their own. Yet it is clear – to scholars who read prefaces and endnotes – that this is not because they are unfamiliar with Minsky's work. In their preface, Akerlof and Shiller (2009, p. xxiv) make a passing reference to Minsky having commented on the "banality" of versions of Keynesian economics that omit animal spirits, but otherwise they only refer to him briefly in four endnotes, two of which are especially worthy of attention. The first of these is an endnote to their preface (p. 177, n. 2). Here, they refer to Minsky as someone who had asked whether something like the Great Depression could happen again, after which they say that "our line of thinking . . . parallels that of Minsky." A later endnote to their preface (p. 177, n. 7) then refers to Minsky, along with Galbraith and Kindleberger, as having given "seminal historical accounts of bubbles and panics" – thereby promoting the impression that Minsky was an economic historian, not a theorist.

12.8   Wage Stickiness and Unemployment

When episodes of financial instability result in major recessions, or when there are less dramatic recessions due to other factors, the microeconomic fallout typically includes cases of people experiencing financial and psychological distress who claim that they are simply unable to find work despite applying for dozens of jobs. In such situations, where there are far fewer job vacancies than the number of people who are unemployed and actively seeking employment, it may seem entirely reasonable to a layperson to infer that involuntary unemployment exists and that the government should be trying to engineer an increase in aggregate demand to eliminate it. However, to many economists, such imbalances between the aggregate supply of labor and the aggregate demand for labor are due to money wage rates that result in real wages being at levels such that more workers want to work, and employers find it profitable to offer fewer jobs, than would be the case if the money wage rates, and hence real wages, were lower. To these economists, such a situation begs the question of why money wages have failed to fall swiftly so that more jobs will be available.

As Trevithick (1976) has emphasized, Keynes's (1936, pp. 13–15) answer was that although workers may be prepared to accept lower real wages than are currently being enjoyed by those who have jobs, they are also concerned about maintaining their wages relative to those received by other groups of workers. If any group of workers leads the way in trying to reduce (or, in an inflationary environment, limit increases in) money wages, there is no guarantee that other groups of workers will follow suit. In the absence of any system to ensure that others will follow, the members of any group of workers will fear that they will suffer a reduction in relative pay on top of the intended reduction in real pay, which they may view as unfair given the nature of their jobs relative to the jobs of members of other groups. Keynes's thinking thus foreshadows Wood's (1978) relativities-based view of pay, clashing with the orthodox theory of labor supply choices in which economic agents are only concerned about the net benefits that they will personally receive if they accept a job offer. From the orthodox standpoint, labor supply decisions are affected by occupational relativities only insofar as these affect the opportunity costs of working in one kind of job rather than another. To an "econ," distributive justice is an irrelevant factor when making labor supply choices.

An alternative way of looking at wage stickiness is to see it as arising from the demand side of the labor market. It was such a view that Keith Glaister and I proposed (Earl and Glaister, [1979] 1980) with the aid of ideas from the behavioral theory of the firm. We set out to show that, regardless of whether managers set their prices by applying a markup to "normal costs" or by equating marginal costs and revenues, they might fear that, if their sales fell, it could be counterproductive to try to drive wages down as a means of permitting price reductions aimed at making it viable to maintain output and employment. The problem, as we saw it, was that wage cuts could result in reductions in worker productivity, reducing profits even further. At the heart of our analysis were the following four considerations:

(a) Employment contracts are incompletely specified (Coase, 1937).

(b) Relationships between workers and other stakeholders in a firm take the form of an incompletely specified coalition in which bargaining over returns is conducted with uncertainty about its impact on the productivity of workers and their willingness to move elsewhere (Cyert and March, 1963).

(c) Wage rates are often attached to job slots (for example, "an electrician" or "a level-three administrative officer") rather than to individual workers, due to the unpredictable idiosyncrasies of what workers end up having to do while employed in a particular job (Williamson et al., 1975).

(d) Workers compete internally for promotion (Andrews, [1958] 1993, ch. 9).

Under these conditions, workers with the same class of role in a firm could be receiving similar wages but offering different levels of productivity, with the more productive ones hoping eventually to be rewarded by promotion. The problem for firms is that if they cut wages when sales fall, they risk losing their more productive workers, whereas if they keep wages unchanged and make some of their employees redundant, they can pick and choose which ones to let go based on what they have come to know about relative performance. Furthermore, employers might fear that if wages were cut when there was a major downturn in demand, workers might retaliate by being less cooperative within their vague employment contracts, whereas if some workers were instead retrenched and the rest continued to receive the same rates of pay, those who remained might offer consummate cooperation, grateful to be maintaining their living standards but fearing that they might suffer a similar fate if sales continue to decline and further job cuts are made.

That paper remains unpublished (though a scanned version is available at my personal website), as journal referees at the time were bemused by its behavioral foundations and pluralistic approach. With hindsight, we should have persisted with it, for others had similar ideas in that time of mounting unemployment amid the neoconservatism of the Thatcher government in the UK and the Reagan administration in the US. The others positioned their approach to wage stickiness as emerging from research on "efficiency wages" in the labor economics literature that had previously been focused not on microeconomic foundations of macroeconomics but on, for example, how remuneration systems should be designed to deter shirking. By 1986, in the introduction to their edited volume on efficiency wage models, Akerlof and Yellen (1986, pp. 1–2) were unequivocal in their claim that these kinds of models provide the best basis for understanding wage stickiness.

Behavioral economists who take this demand-side view of wage stickiness typically maintain, like Akerlof and Shiller (2009), that workers are concerned about fairness and relativities when bargaining for pay (in line with Keynes's view). They also argue that workers suffer from "money illusion" in the sense that, unlike "econs," workers are prone to fail to anticipate, or be unable to compute with any accuracy, the relationship between changes in money wages and changes in real wages. Given such a view of the supply side of the labor market, it makes all the more sense for their bosses to adjust the quantity of labor that they demand and reduce output, rather than to attempt to cut wages and try to sell their output more cheaply, when their sales fall below levels that make labor hoarding a prudent strategy.

However, although behavioral economics has plenty to say about why wages do not fall to clear the labor market when effective aggregate demand is insufficient to support full employment, many contributors to the theory of wage stickiness seem to have failed to appreciate that, as far as Keynes himself was concerned, it seemed most unlikely that fully flexible money wages would eliminate involuntary unemployment. Indeed, he viewed highly flexible money wages as a potential source of macroeconomic instability, not as a prerequisite for attaining a full employment equilibrium (see Keynes, 1936, chs. 17 and 19). His view is underpinned by two issues that are easily overlooked if one makes the "fallacy of composition" error of presuming that if an individual firm will find it profitable to expand production and employment if it can reduce its wage costs, then the same will be true if firms in general do this.

The first problem is that cutting money wages does not merely reduce production costs; it also reduces the purchasing power of workers. This means that if wages in general were cut by a particular percentage and prices were marked down by a similar percentage, firms would see no sign of demand for extra output if they did *not* hire more workers. The real economy would be unchanged, but all nominal values would have been reduced by the same percentage. (We may view the reverse of this process as what happens in an inflationary spiral at any level of unemployment, without that level having necessarily to tend to change.) Given this, the key question is what would happen if wages and prices were reduced in this way and firms *did* expand production in the belief that, with a lower price level, there will be more demand.

To see the answer, let us begin by supposing that, in response to a reduction in aggregate demand, firms have initially retrenched some workers and reduced production. Those who lose their jobs set out to find work elsewhere. Now suppose that money wages do indeed fall after newly unemployed workers discover they cannot find jobs. Firms then hire more workers and increase output. Reduced wages do not pose a problem for selling the aggregate volume of output that would have been produced without the wage cut, for prices can be marked down in line the reduced costs of production. But what about the extra output? The firms that produce the extra output will be hoping for an increase in revenue in real terms that covers the costs of producing it and leaves an increase in profits. This will happen if all the extra wage payments and expected extra profits are spent. However, this brings us to the second issue that has been overlooked in modern mainstream macroeconomics, namely Keynes's assumption that the marginal propensity to consume has a value less than one. This implies that, unless investment increases by an amount equal to what is saved from the marginal income, firms will indeed be disappointed if they hire more workers in response to offers to work for lower wages. If firms cannot sell the expected extra output at the prices they expected to get, they can either dispose of it, for a loss, at knockdown prices or increase their inventories. The latter strategy will make them even less willing to hire workers in the following period. The money wage cuts thus fail to solve the problem of inadequate effective aggregate demand, but if money wages are cut further, the process will merely repeat itself.

In the days when orthodox economists were aware of these issues, textbooks on macroeconomics acknowledged that, if money wages were flexible, there could be a downward spiral of money wages and prices in a situation of deficient aggregate demand. However, the textbook wisdom was that the deflationary gap would eventually be offset by the so-called real balance effect. At this point, prices and wages would cease to fall and macroeconomic equilibrium would be attained with zero involuntary unemployment. The idea here was that, as the price level fell, holdings of money would rise in value, thereby leading people to feel wealthier and therefore to increase their spending. However, as we move increasingly to a cashless economy, the potential for a positive real balance effect has withered toward zero. Instead, we need to acknowledge that a free fall in wages could instead lead to *rising* unemployment because of the havoc it would cause in personal balance sheets and in the financial sector: with mortgages and other debts not indexed to the price level, they would be impossible to service by those whose money wages collapsed. The defaults on these debts would then lead to bank failures that wiped out the gains in wealth that holders of bank deposits would initially experience as tumbling wages led to falling prices. This would be exacerbated not merely by collapsing confidence but also by discretionary spending being reined in simply because of expectations that products would be available more cheaply in future. In other words, given the problems that Keynes identified in moving up from microeconomic analysis to macroeconomics, we should be grateful that wage stickiness exists and should not view it as a labor market "imperfection."

12.9   Inflation

It is presumed in conventional macroeconomics that firms face rising marginal costs as they expand output, with the equilibrium level of output being the level at which marginal costs and marginal revenues are equal. Given their rising marginal costs, an expansion of output will only occur if there is an increase in expected demand that makes it possible to sell more at higher prices than the prices that they are currently charging and which entail increases in marginal revenue. From this standpoint, an increase in the number of workers employed thus seems inevitably to entail a rise in the price level and a fall in real wages.

If involuntary unemployment is present, such a rise in prices should not trigger a wage–price spiral, for although some workers might decide that they are not prepared to keep working for a reduced amount of purchasing power, firms will be able to replace them and maintain the increased volume of output by hiring from the ranks of those who had previously been unable to find jobs and are still willing to work despite the reduced return from doing so. By contrast, if the observed unemployment were due to people voluntarily opting to search for better jobs than they had so far been able to find, the rise in the price level that firms are presumed to require in order to expand output would be problematic. At first, the firms might be able to hire more workers because those who had been searching received offers of better paying jobs than they had previously been able to get. However, these workers and those who already had jobs would subsequently observe the rise in the price level and realize that the returns to working were not as good as expected. To continue working, they would require jobs with higher money wages, which firms would only be offering if they expected to be able to get higher prices for their output as a result of more demand being pumped into the system. Soon, so the orthodox story goes, workers would lose any money illusion that had blighted their previous decisions and would start to anticipate price increase and be unwilling to work unless money wages were increased to compensate both for the price increases that had occurred and for the increases that were expected. Attempts by the authorities to run the economy with a higher real level of demand than was consistent with underlying real supply conditions would therefore result in accelerating inflation.

This analysis is called into question by the "normal cost" view of pricing (outlined in Section 11.2) proposed by Andrews (1949), and by empirical work that is consistent with the normal cost view, most notably the research reported in Coutts et al. (1978) as well as Means (1972) and many other studies surveyed in Lee (1999). It should be recalled that Andrews's analysis is not an equilibrium-focused, market-clearing view of pricing: firms offer their products at take-it-or-leave-it prices that are based on their average variable costs plus a markup that they judge will deter existing and potential competitors from trying to steal market share from them via more aggressive pricing or building more features into their products without raising the products' prices. They use a target rate of sales as the output reference point when predicting their costs, but if sales exceed the target, they will be able to deliver more output due to having opted to have spare capacity for such an eventuality: they simply produce more without changing their prices. Similarly, if sales fall short of their targets, they reduce output and consider whether their marketing strategies could be improved, but they do not normally engage in a price war with their rivals. They only change their prices if they revise their long-term views of what their costs will average out to be across cycles of business activity.

From this perspective, changes in the level of demand will result in changes in the volume of output and employment without changes to prices and the real wages of employed workers. (The number of workers hired will not necessarily match the volume of output particularly closely, as some positions are nondivisible, and firms may also engage in labor hoarding to maintain the goodwill of their workforces and reduce hiring and firing costs across the business cycle.) Hence, if governments feel that recorded levels of unemployment are too high, they should not be fearful that an injection of purchasing power will *necessarily* lead to a rise in the price level that might then turn into an inflationary spiral. Yet, of course, such spirals are sometimes evident and can be difficult to bring under control, as in the period from the late 1960s to the early 1990s. To understand them, our behavioral toolkit offers insights when we consider the significances of productivity differences among suppliers, natural resource limitations and the competing aspirations of different economic stakeholder.

In some industries, an expansion of demand will entail a hike in prices because the industry has a rising supply curve even though, at the level of the production unit, marginal costs are nonincreasing. The "Salter diagram" framework employed in Section 11.3 can be adapted to capture the essence of such a situation, where the rising industry supply curve results from efficiency differences between production units. In Section 11.3 we used the Salter framework to consider industries that were not in a "normal" situation, either because of a long-term decline in demand or because of a disruptive new production technology. However, the stepped-block approach to industry supply curves that Salter devised for understanding structural change can also be applied to sectors such as electricity production, agriculture and mining in which prices emerge from a market-clearing process rather than by suppliers setting take-it-or-leave-it prices based on their assessments of competitive conditions. If major economies have entered a recession, prices for energy, agricultural and mining products may decline, with the highest-cost producers ceasing production until there is a recovery in demand. This will have some impact on real wages due to workers facing changes in food and energy prices across the business cycle. Workers might also experience cyclical movements in housing rental charges and mortgage interest rates.

However, from the standpoint of normal cost theory, the pricing of manufactured products may be unaffected by changes in the prices of raw material inputs if the economy is viewed as going through a "normal" kind of business cycle. Thus, if raw material prices follow the business cycle, they essentially play an offsetting role to profit reductions that manufacturers experience due to being able to sell less during the downturn. However, if falling raw material costs in a downturn are, contrary to normal cost theory, passed through to customers in lower prices for manufactured goods than would otherwise have been set, the impact on prices would be proportionately much smaller due to the extent of value-adding that manufacturing entails. By extension, when the economy recovered, the recovery of raw materials prices would push up manufactured goods prices by a far smaller proportion. As behavioral economists, we would also note that an economic downturn could, on the one hand, reduce learning curve effects on normal costs but, on the other hand, there could be reductions in normal costs as a result of failures to meet aspirations leading to successful searches for ways of reducing X-inefficiency.

Any downward impacts of an overall economic downturn on prices via the impact of reduced demand on the primary goods sectors would mean that, when the economy returns to full employment, those who kept their jobs during the downturn will have to give up the gains in their living standards that they had enjoyed. If workers demand increased pay to offset this recovery in the cost of living, we have a kind of ratchet effect in operation in the labor market: they act as if they have forgotten that the cost of living had been reduced by the onset of the downturn, either by prices falling or by them not rising as fast as they would have done if the downturn had not occurred. In other words, the problem is that consumers may not apply normal-cost thinking when looking at the cost of living except, perhaps, insofar as they judge their living costs with reference to official "seasonally adjusted" consumer price indices. This forgetting- and/or ratcheting-based view of what some might call a form of "money illusion" is a different story from that offered in orthodox macroeconomics.

But there is a complication that we need to consider in relation to the potential inflationary impact of a recovery from a sustained downturn. If sales in an industry fall so far in a downturn that some of the highest-cost production systems are taken out of operation, we need to consider whether they will be brought back into operation when demand recovers, with any reduction in prices also being reversed. (This would be akin to the scenario considered in relation to Figure 11.2 in Section 11.3 being reversed in the recovery.) If demand recovered to such an extent that it could not be satisfied by taking up spare capacity within production units that had remained in use, then the owners of the most productive of the less efficient capacity that had been left idle might indeed discover that they can now win sales when quoting prices that would cover the per-unit paying-out costs that they would need to incur to put their plant back into operation. However, as Hicks (1974) emphasizes, a long recession may result in idle capacity being scrapped or sold and shipped off to firm newly industrializing economies before the recovery happens. If so, inadequate domestic output during the recovery may result in increases in imports, with a depreciation of the currency of the country in question, thereby leading to higher import prices. Note, too, that the extent to which primary sector prices rise when a particular economy enters an upswing will depend on the extent to which other economies are also expanding.

Clearly, if a macroeconomic recovery does entail higher primary product prices, workers may start getting more aggressive in their wage bargaining to try to restore their real incomes to the levels that those who remained employed had enjoyed in the downturn. If so, there is potential for a wage–price spiral to emerge if employers are unable to absorb worker demands by cutting managerial and shareholder returns or via increased productivity. If such a spiral does take off, normal-cost pricing will result in wage increases being passed forward into prices, triggering wage demands elsewhere in the system to protect relative wages and real incomes. Hence, what started out merely as a step up in prices in some sectors as aggregate demand recovered may turn into an ongoing, economy-wide inflation problem. Matters may not be helped if competitive discipline breaks down due to firms starting to observe that customers simply acquiesce to price increases because their buying behavior is based on routines. With prices generally on the move but with different firms changing their wages and prices at different times, it is challenging for buyers to keep track of trends in relative prices. This makes it easier for firms to raise their prices without losing market share (see Leibenstein, 1981).

The risk that an upswing will generate a long-term problem of inflation will depend on the underlying rate of, and sectoral differences in, productivity growth in the economy and on how readily those involved in wage bargaining adjust their aspirations. If productivity growth is generally rapid, prices may fall, either due to the productivity increases being seen as implying reductions in "normal costs" and/or the costs of potential competitors or because upward-sloping supply curves will shift downward in sectors characterized by market-clearing pricing. This might enable workers to meet their aspirations for growth in real wages during an upturn, with no inflationary process kicking off. By contrast, matters could be very problematic in an economy with poor productivity growth that is recovering from a long recession that has resulted in aspirations for wage growth not being met and still not capable of being met even if aggregate demand increases. In the latter kind of economy – say, the UK in the 1970s and 1980s, unlike Germany or Japan around that time – inflation becomes the means by which the economic system deals with incompatible aspirations of workers and managers rather than something that can be eliminated by the uptake of organizational slack. As explained in Section 10.10, such slack is a product of aspirations not growing as fast as attainments in good times, but it will tend to get absorbed during periods of lackluster performance where productivity growth in overseas rivals is more rapid. In a flexible exchange rate system, slow-growth economies whose workers and employers have incompatible aspirations can be expected to have falling currencies as firms pass into higher prices the wage increases that they grant to their workers.

The sectoral distribution of productivity growth could affect inflationary pressures if collective bargaining is done with a keen eye on maintaining intersectoral wage differentials. Although we might expect that, under competitive pressure, improvements in labor productivity would reduce normal costs and be passed on to customers via lower price, such price reductions may be attenuated if employers concede to worker demands for pay increases that seem fair and reasonable given the growth in productivity. (For a detailed behavioral analysis of concession costs and negotiation costs of employers and workers during wage negotiations, see Tylecote, 1981.) However, as Jackson et al. (1972) emphasize, the trouble is that if workers in a sector where productivity is growing well above the norm succeed in getting pay increases at rates that are well above average rate of productivity growth, their rate of increase could become the rate to which other groups aspire. Wage increase will count as increases in normal costs and be passed forward into higher prices if the latter's employers concede such demands but are unwilling or unable to absorb the higher wage bill by reducing managerial and shareholder returns and reducing the size of their markup. So prices in the leading sector fail to fall due to workers capturing the benefits of productivity growth and preventing normal costs from falling, whereas in other sectors, the "follow the leader" approach to wage bargaining result in price increases whose scale is inversely related to sectoral rates of productivity growth.

Where incompatibility between the aspirations of workers and employers leads to a wage–price spiral, a solution needs to entail a lowering of workers' wage-growth aspirations and/or managers and shareholders taking less. It should not entail a squeeze on retained profits, for it is these that provide the means for investing in raising productivity and delivering the rising living standards to which the workers aspire. The obvious question here is how managers can get the workers to lower their aspirations. Achieving this will require the workers to accept a loss of some kind, which will in turn require their loss aversion to be overcome. Managers might seek to do this by showing the workers that they face bigger losses if they do not back down and thereby accept slower growth in wages.

If workers are more concerned about the growth in their wages not falling behind relative to what other groups of workers are achieving than with preventing small reductions in their absolute standards of living, then the key to eliminating inflation is to have the kind of system suggested by Wood (1978). This would entail sectoral or occupational wage bargaining being focused on what multiple or fraction of the sector- or occupation-weighted economy-wide average wage a particular type of worker will be paid. The rate of growth of this economy-wide average wage would be determined separately by bargaining between national bodies that represent employers and labor unions. If any reduction in real average purchasing power is needed, such a system should enhance cooperation between different interest groups by bringing questions of fairness and justice to the fore: it supplies everyone with a reference point from which to assess their prospects, thereby preventing bargaining from being shaped by loss aversion associated with more ambitious reference points. (Something akin to this seems to have been achieved during the operation of the so-called Prices and Incomes Accord in Australia in the mid-1980s, a time when that economy was wrestling with both high inflation and sharply falling terms of trade – see McDonald, 2017 for further details.) This is a much more humane way of addressing inflation than the neoconservative approach that ignores the relativities issue and combines restrictive monetary policy with attempts to crush the bargaining power of labor unions and prune back the value of unemployment benefits. The latter policy combination eliminates the incompatibility between worker and employer or shareholder aspirations by forcing down the former. In the neoconservative approach, worker docility is achieved by supplying workers with the prospect that they could end up unemployed, and with a major loss in their living standards relative to their current situation, if they do not accept that their real wages are not going to grow as rapidly as they had hoped.

12.10   Exchange Rates and International Trade

Conventional accounts of the relationship between exchange rates and international trade typically begins with something akin to the following simple and seemingly intuitive analysis. If a country is trying to import more than it is exporting, attempts to purchase foreign currency to pay for the excess of imports will tend to drive down the value of its currency. This will make imports more expensive, so domestic residents and firms will start buying more from domestic suppliers and reduce their demand for imports, while domestic producers will be able to price their products more cheaply in export markets. Hence, if exchange rates are allowed to float freely, trade deficits will tend rapidly to be eliminated and economies whose products have become unattractive and/or overpriced compared with those of their foreign rivals will not tend to suffer from rising unemployment and deindustrialization. However, the per-capita incomes of their populations may languish relative to those of residents in more dynamic and productive rival economies that grow more rapidly.

This account is then extended by recognizing that imports and exports can differ due to flows of financial capital between countries. A country can import a bigger value of goods and services than it exports if it can borrow from overseas or attract flows of investment funds. These capital flows may enable the government of an internationally uncompetitive country to prop up aggregate demand and maintain full employment despite there being a trade deficit. This may help ensure that firms can earn profits to fund improvements in their products and production methods to help them recover their shares of international markets. Indeed, some of the trade deficit could be due to imports of state-of-the-art equipment and paying for capability-enhancing educational services supplied by overseas universities. Inflows of foreign investment, such as from overseas multinational companies, may also help turn the country's balance of trade into surplus in the long run, which then makes it possible to repay overseas debts and provide profit and dividend payments to offshore suppliers of financial capital. Indeed, foreign lenders and other suppliers of long-term international capital would not lend or invest funds in a country that had a significant trade deficit unless they were confident that it would eventually turn its position around: if it failed to do so and continued to try to "live beyond its means" by borrowing increasingly large amounts to fund both the trade deficit and interest, profits and dividend payments to overseas claimants, it would be heading for a Ponzi-style disaster.

This view has two major shortcomings on which behavioral economics can shed some light. The first is that it is based on a very optimistic view of the rationality of international capital markets that also neglects the significance of speculative short-term capital flows as drivers of exchange rates. By value, these capital flows completely overwhelm foreign currency transactions concerning trade and long-term capital movements.

Harvey (2006, 2009a, 2009b) has attempted to synthesize a realistic account of how exchange rates between currencies are determined amid these flows. His work blends institutional and psychological elements with ideas from Keynes and emphasizes that the world of foreign currency dealers is one in which exchange rate volatility and the high stakes that it brings are viewed as entirely normal and an exciting part of the job of being a currency dealer or trader. These traders learn their business largely via experience on the job, as it has tacit knowledge aspects that cannot be taught. In order to avoid being left behind as markets move, the dealers are always on the lookout for information that may provide clues about what may trigger changes in currency values. They get it via routinely scanning favored sources and via trusted contacts. Harvey (2006) assigns three heuristics key roles in causing those involved in foreign currency markets to reach biased assessments that drive volatility. One is representativeness: in other words, the more aspects that a country has of things (for example, ever-growing foreign indebtedness and dependence on earnings from a narrow range of primary products) that are viewed features or drivers of a particular condition (for example, becoming a "banana republic"), then the more that country will be viewed as being or likely to become a country that has that condition, even if it might be viewed very differently in terms of other factors that are not being considered. (For example, a claim that a particular country is heading down the road of become a "banana republic" might look far less credible if one noted that its institutions and educational system were of high quality, that it was not displaying increasing incidence of corruption and political scandals involving nepotism, that its foreign debt was not largely owed by the public sector, etc.) The extent to which representativeness results in overreactions will depend on how the information has been framed and whether the anchoring heuristic leads to attention being captured by first impressions (for example, a news report by a credible authority suggesting that a particular country is heading down the "banana republic" track). We should also note that whether currency traders in major financial centers pick up a particular, potentially significant piece of information in relation to a small economy's international economic situation may depend on whether that economy happens to be in the news for other reasons that are receiving international coverage; if not, it might not be "on their radar" at all.

Harvey (2009b) contends that currency dealers use rather simple mental models to assess which new information is significant and what it implies for exchange rate movements. These mental models permit rapid responses following the discovery of surprising new information. From the "indicators" that the dealers routinely monitor, they seek to infer what is going to happen to what Harvey calls "base factors", namely differences in rates of interest, inflation and economic growth between the country in question and its trading partners, plus the perceived liquidity of the currency (i.e., how readily it can be exchanged for other assets or used in purchasing goods and services). These "base factors" feed into the dealer's view of what will happen to the "processes" that determine the direction of movement of the currency in question, namely net exports, net direct foreign investment in the country in question and net portfolio investment. Harvey suggests that these very simply causal mental links for predicting currency movements are supplemented by "technical analysis" conducted by the organization for whom the dealer works. Such analysis typically attempts to predict trend values based on time-series data on the currency's past trajectory. If such predictions are built into portfolio strategies, they can result in positive feedback effects (for example, if the rule is "Make US portfolio investments if the US dollar's trend is upward," this will tend to push up the value of the US dollar, other things equal). Finally, Harvey argues that the currency traders' short-term positions will also be colored by their medium-term views of economic prospects (bullish, bearish or neutral) and by how confident they are about their predictions of which way the currency in question will move.

Because so much of the volume of international currency trading is associated with short-term capital flows, changes in exchange rates do not accurately reflect long-term changes in the underlying fundamentals that determine international trade in goods and services. Rather, short-term currency movements reflect swings in the bets that bodies such as hedge funds opt to place when acting as movement traders or market manipulators. Given the resulting exchange rate volatility, exporters will be concerned that they could end up confusing their rivals and prospective customers if they frequently adjusted the prices they charged in their overseas markets. Hence, they only change their export prices in order to reflect longer-term trends, i.e., changes in what they view as "normal" exchange rates and in their "normal" costs. Until they are confident that they can see that such changes have occurred, they will let their profit margins for overseas sales rise (fall) as their domestic currency falls (rises) against foreign currencies (cf. the interview-based study conducted by Holmes, 1978). Firms in other countries will do likewise in respect of their export markets and when assessing the wisdom of setting up offshore operations.

The second major shortcoming of conventional wisdom on the relationship between exchange rates and international trade is that it overemphasizes the role of changes in relative prices as drivers of changes in the volumes of exports and imports between counties. Behavioral analysis of firms and consumer calls into question orthodox tendencies to view international trade with a focus on factor endowments and a static view of comparative advantage that leads to exchange rate adjustments being assigned a key role in allowing adjustments in international relative prices to ensure that factors of production remain fully employed. Foreign trade performance will evolve through time in ways that depend on the motivation and capacity of firms to develop new products, capabilities and markets, and their capacities to transfer their capabilities and sources of competitive advantage to other economies by operating as multinational enterprises or engaging in franchising and licensing arrangements.

Other things equal, institutional and cultural differences between domestic and foreign markets will favor a focus by firms on selling in their home territory if they are able to meet their aspirations by doing so. Given this, an obvious question is how changes in domestic demand pressure will affect export sales. The analysis in Chapters 10 and 11 implies an asymmetric relationship between domestic demand and exports, and this has been observed in empirical studies of exporters' behavior in the UK during the 1960s (Cooper et al., 1970) and for Portugal more recently (Esteves and Rua, 2015). On the one hand, we would expect disappointing domestic sales to trigger a search that might result in firms experimenting with foreign markets in ways that they might have done earlier had their aspirations been higher. (Likewise, if firms lose a particular foreign market due to the imposition of a restrictive trade policy, they may engage in search and discover other export markets that they could have been serving – as was the case with some Australian suppliers in sectors hit by punitive Chinese tariffs in 2020–2021: see Daly et al., 2021.) However, having been driven to go beyond a local search for customers, firms will normally proceed with a view to creating foreign bridgeheads for generating goodwill relationships and growing their business in the long run; as Cooper et al. (1970) emphasize, in line with the views of Marshall and Andrews, managers will not normally view such ventures as temporary ways of keeping their factories busy while planning to abandon the foreign markets when domestic demand recovers.

It would be unwise for firms to use foreign markets as temporary dumping grounds for their products each time there was domestic downturn: they would run into reputational problems of significance where after-sales support was a concern for customers. Taking a long-term view will make it easier to justify the sunk costs that will be necessary to get established in foreign markets. Moreover, having made such investments, sunk cost bias will reinforce the motivation of managers to maintain their foreign market presence. Similar considerations imply that, if the domestic currency falls in value and makes export markets potentially more profitable, firms normally will only respond by trying to sell overseas if they believe they will be able to do so in a viable manner in the long run in the face of future currency volatility. We would not normally expect foreign markets to be supplied in a "fly-by-night" or "hit-and-run" manner, and any attempt to cultivate them would be done mindful of the need to ensure that foreign sales growth does not jeopardize their capacity to maintain local customer goodwill.

On the demand side, the uptake of foreign products will be affected by the problems that buyers are trying to solve, how they construe foreign products, their openness to behaving in a non-patriotic manner by not buying local products and the extent of their resistance to buying from particular countries on the basis of a particular principle. Unless it had implications in relation to quality, the origin of an item of consumption would be a supposedly irrelevant factor in the decision-making of an "econ." However, it may have significance in real-world markets where consumers are affluent enough to be able to rule out products from particular countries (for example, via a "Nothing from China" kind of rule based on abhorrence of China's political system) despite then having to pay more to purchase from somewhere else. International trade may also be driven by some consumers seeking to differentiate themselves from their peers, which they may be able to do by choosing imported products that are otherwise functionally like those that are made domestically. An "econ" would not be expected to choose on such a basis, but it may help explain the extent to which international trade in consumer products between developed countries is of trade in similar products, a phenomenon not predicted by the theory of comparative advantage.

Insofar as buyers make their choices by applying non-compensatory decision rules, the impact of changes in exchange rates on patterns of international trade will be muted and will arise mainly via their impacts on real incomes and how products fare if a "choose the cheapest" rule is used as a tiebreaker. As a case study, it is useful to consider the UK car market in the 1970s, which inspired much of my early thinking about non-compensatory decision rules and their significance.

At that time, British carmakers were losing market share as their products came to be seen as having quality control and reliability problems compared with those from, particularly, German and Japan, and their supplies were often disrupted by poor industrial relations. If overseas carmakers raised the UK prices of their cars when the value of the British pound fell, this might take their vehicles beyond the maximum that some buyers of new cars were prepared to pay. But this would not necessarily drive those buyers to switch to British-made cars. Instead, they might switch to lower-tier models within the same overseas firms' product ranges, or switch to a cheaper imported brand that "ticked the boxes" in high-priority areas where the British products seemed deficient. At that time, Japanese cars were typically not a match for British ones in terms of their on-road dynamic capabilities (steering, ride, cornering, etc.) but they were viewed by a growing part of the market as adequate in this area and as not having the problems that the British cars were prone to have. The Japanese brands were thereby able to get established in the UK.

A fall in the value of the pound would also have had little impact on the UK's vehicle exports if their sales were being hampered due to overseas buyers choosing via non-compensatory decision rules that classified British cars as "not good enough" in key areas. Although such a fall in the UK's currency would have made it possible for the British firms to offer their products more cheaply in overseas markets, the non-price reasons for which they were being rejected would still apply. Thus, if European CEOs shunned Jaguar cars because of their woeful reliability, lower prices that brought Jaguars within the budgets of senior managers would not win sales if these managers had a similar view of them.

To prevent their market shares from declining, the British manufacturers needed to fix things that potential customers viewed as deal breakers rather than offering their cars more cheaply relative to foreign rivals. Jaguar thus needed to fix its reliability problems by buying better electrical components, even though this would increase production costs and be carried into higher prices. In export markets, a falling pound might have enabled such improvements to be made without raising prices, but there would then be the challenge of convincing customers that reliability had been improved. Otherwise, currency depreciations would only have helped the British firms to the extent that customers used compensatory decision rules and by enabling these firms to turn their remaining overseas currency earnings into more domestic currency from which to fund investment in better products and production processes.

If a country has run into balance of trade and unemployment problems due to non-price problems with its products, policymakers may be wise to consider a strategy that combines an expansionary fiscal policy (to reduce unemployment) and a finite period (say, five years) of import controls to prevent the fiscal stimulation from leaking out as an increase in demand for imports (cf. the prescription for the UK offered by Cripps and Godley, 1978). If, say, quotas were used to prevent more cars being imported when demand expanded, some domestic consumers who wanted to buy imported new cars would instead have to sacrifice some of their non-price aspirations and buy local output. This would help local producers to keep production going and earn profits to plough back into developing new and better products that were more congruent with common non-compensatory decision rules.

12.11   The Making of Macroeconomic Policy

Before concluding, we should consider the plight of those involved in designing and implementing macroeconomic policy in the real world of complex economic inter-actions and loosely grounded, shifting expectations. This is fertile territory for behavioral economics, as is evident from the theoretical and empirical work of Paul Mosley (1976, 1981, 1984). In principle, we might imagine that politicians would have in mind the social welfare function that they were seeking to optimize in order to maximize their chances of staying in power. Their bounded rationality and, in many cases, limited economic training would not necessarily prevent them from discovering the optimal policy means for achieving this goal, for they could call upon the expertise of many well-trained advisors, who would be able to run simulation models on high-powered computers: this is their equivalent of the consumer's market for preferences. But in practice, according to Mosley, policymaking is a satisficing activity in which many policy options fail to get modeled even in situations where a crisis triggers a search for something that will make the problem go away.

Mosley's analysis of macroeconomic policymaking in the UK and US between 1945 and 1973 presents a picture that has much in common with Cyert and March's (1963) idea that mangers of firms give "sequential attention to goals" rather than trading off multiple decision criteria in relation to a single overall objective such as long-term profit maximization. In the UK, the attention of politicians oscillated between the level of unemployment and the size of the foreign trade deficit, whereas in the US it swung between unemployment and inflation. The policymakers did not seem to find optimal trade-offs between these variables. Moreover, there seemed to be a tendency to overstimulate demand to get unemployment down to acceptable levels if an election was approaching. From a "heuristics and biases" standpoint, one might consider the latter behavior in terms of electoral loss aversion and present bias.

With the emergence of "stagflation" from the late 1960s, life became far simpler for the policymakers who accepted the argument that there was no trade-off between unemployment and inflation in the long run. When major economies adopted freely floating exchange rates during the 1970s, the cognitive challenge of policymakers became simpler still, with foreign trade deficits supposedly becoming self-correcting. Neoconservative economists offered a very simple "monetarist" approach to macroeconomic management: simply limit the growth of the monetary base to a rate close to the rate of real output growth and wait for inflationary expectations to adjust to a near-zero rate, whereupon the economy would settle at around the "natural rate" of unemployment, with minimal, non-accelerating inflation and no balance of payments problems. All that the politicians had to do was weather the discontent that came from their electorates as the sluggish adjustment of expectations took their economies past successive politically sensitive thresholds regarding the unemployment rate or total number of workers who were unemployed. As Mosley (1981) shows via testimony of government ministers and senior officials to the UK parliament's Treasury Committee, this simple view of how to manage the economy by making the elimination of inflation the overriding goal, and monetary targeting the means to achieving it, was so alluring that there was a general failure to consider the costs and benefits that the policy entailed relative to other approaches. Margaret Thatcher's government continued to run the UK's macroeconomic policy on this "TINA" (There Is No Alternative) basis long after Mosley's (1981) paper was published. Thatcher's approach was certainly simple in cognitive terms, especially after the 1982 cessation of funding for the key team of dissenting macroeconomic modelers, the Cambridge Economic Policy Group (CEPG). But it was hardly procedurally rational to ignore what was being tried elsewhere (such as the "Prices and Incomes Accord" that the Hawke Labor government introduced in Australia in April 1984, a couple of months before I emigrated there to escape the economic gloom of the UK). It is noteworthy that, after the CEPG was disbanded, its erstwhile leader Wynne Godley went on to develop, with Marc Lavoie, a "stock–flow consistent" approach to macroeconomic modeling that keeps track of the relationship between financial balances and real activity. This approach was well suited to spot, via computer simulations, increasing financial fragility, the impossibility of sustaining growth by increasing the level of indebtedness and hence potential for a Minsky-style meltdown. Set out in Godley and Lavoie (2007), the technique predicted the GFC (see Bezemer, 2009).

Bounded rationality is an inherent issue when policymakers are forced to contend with a macroeconomic crisis, even if those who ultimately have to decide what to do are being supported by large teams of advisors. The inherent problem is the perceived urgency of the need to act to prevent matters from getting worse. This may require decisions to be reached in a matter of hours and possibly without being able to call upon some of those whose expertise is required. On top of the difficulties of devising alternative scenarios and modeling their implications, the decisions may have to be made without accurate knowledge of which other entities may soon emerge seeking support (which matters if seats in a financial lifeboat are limited and/or not all applicants for assistance will be supported, in order to signal that reckless behavior can have consequences for those who fund it) or without time to discover the full scale of the immediate problem and the details of which parties it affects.

It is instructive to close this section with a short case study that embodies many of these issues, namely the Irish banking crisis that was part of the GFC. The Irish crisis arose as a result of local banks fueling a property bubble on the back of liabilities that involved largely offshore obligations. When the bubble burst, there was widespread defaulting on housing-related loans, including those to property developers. The latter left the country blighted by estates of partly built houses. One of the main financial institutions exposed to this was the Anglo Irish Bank (AIB), one of the three Irish banks that were nationalized in early 2009 for recapitalization. At the time, the Irish government was led to believe that the AIB's debt overhang was less than a third of what it turned out to be. The fact that those at AIB who provided the misleading information knew what they were doing did not come to light until over four year later when recordings of telephone conversations between some of the perpetrators came to light (see Williams, 2013).

But the eventual scale of the Irish bank bailouts – widely reported as being around €64 billion, for a nation with a 2008 population of less than 4.5 million – was a consequence of a decision that the Irish government had taken in the early hours of September 30, 2008 to guarantee pretty much the entire liabilities of the six largest Irish banks for the next two years, a measure that went way beyond the existing deposit insurance for retail customers. At the time, the decision horrified Victor Duggan, an economic advisor of the opposition's finance spokesperson. Ten years later, Duggan (2018) recalled what had happened and characterized the decision in psychological terms as a case of succumbing to the "do something" fallacy. With bank shares collapsing and people trying to turn their deposits into cash, it was clear that something had to be done, and what was chosen had been advocated earlier that month by David McWilliams (2008a, 2008b), a high-profile economics journalist whose credibility was strong since he had been one of very few commentators who had long predicted the property bubble and that it would cause a banking crisis.

McWilliams's op-ed articles in Ireland's *Business Times* succinctly pointed to the dangers of applying, in the Irish context, the three main kinds of responses that had been applied elsewhere (allowing a bank to collapse, nationalization by the state or engineering the takeover of a failed bank by a larger, more solvent one). That left his proposed fourth strategy – the guarantee strategy that the Irish government adopted – as the most attractive "something" that could be done, even though he acknowledged it would be a "leap of faith" for the authorities, as it had not been tried elsewhere. McWilliams referred to episodes of financial history as demonstrating that banks had found many ways of dealing with loans that were never going to be repaid in full. We might note, for example, that if a bank has insufficient reserves to write off against its nonperforming loans, it may be able to avoid declaring itself insolvent by not declaring the loans to be nonperforming and instead reschedule payments and/or give the borrower a payment "holiday." If this cognitive dissonance-removing fiction about the state of the loans can be sustained, profits from loans that are performing properly may enable it to build up its reserves to such a point where they are big enough to absorb writing off the loss on the loans that arises when, at that stage, the bank is able to sell the loans at a discount. (This is the essence of how, for example, the Latin American sovereign debt crisis was contained by the international banking system during the 1980s until the banks offloaded these debts via the "Brady bonds" scheme.)

In other words, what McWilliams envisaged was that the authorities would be able to restore depositor and bondholder confidence and thereby end the liquidity crisis, with the banks then gradually trading their way out of their solvency crises. But Duggan (2018) portrays the government as having a much more simplistic view: the policy involved no immediate outlay, as it was merely a guarantee, and they failed to appreciate the probability that a major bailout would soon be necessary because some of the banks' balance sheets were so toxic that it would prove impossible for them to devise ways of trading out of their difficulties. The banks' difficulties were exacerbated by their need to roll over significant liabilities to bondholders in a market that knew the expiry of the guarantee was (originally) scheduled to occur after only two years. What soon followed was a decade of austerity for the Irish population, whereas the offshore holders of claims on Irish banks were not subject to a "haircut."

12.12   Conclusion

The behavioral perspective that this chapter has offered on macroeconomic issues contrasts sharply with the dominant view of macroeconomics derived by aggregating up from optimizing micro-foundations. But it also sits rather uneasily with the "Keynesian" view of macroeconomic policymaking from the 1950s and 1960s that construed economic aggregates as ripe for continual fine-tuning by pulling on the levers of monetary and fiscal policy. This view was aptly characterized by Coddington (1976) as "hydraulic Keynesianism." (He probably had in mind the literally "hydraulic" Monetary National Income Analog Computer [MONIAC] models built by Bill Phillips early in that era.) However, as Hutchison (1977a) has argued, Keynes himself did not advocate that kind of policy and instead saw his *General Theory* as instructive in relation to macroeconomic interventions that would be needed from time to time when major problems emerged. From the perspective of this chapter, macroeconomic fine-tuning is problematic due to the dependence of aggregate demand on shifting investor and consumer confidence, which are in turn shaped by crowd behavior. Moreover, the challenge of making accurate predictions is compounded by the structural complexity and always evolving nature of both the "real" economy and the financial sector. Some economists might hope that the impacts of shifts in confidence on aggregate demand are susceptible to being modeled insofar as the psychological drivers of aggregate demand are affected by news about the state of the economy, since stock market indices change with changes in the state of the news. On this view, confidence is merely what statisticians call an "intervening variable" in the chain of causation between "economic" variables. However, macroeconomic fine-tuning seems doomed to be reactive and unreliable due to variability in the feedback relationships between stock prices and confidence and the chronic failure of attempts to forecast stock prices.

This does not mean that we should agree with Coddington's (1982) later view that accepting the effects of deficient foresight on economic actors and forecasters takes us down a nihilistic road as far as economic policy is concerned, though we might agree with the "fire the forecaster" suggestion of Akerlof and Shiller (2009, pp. 146–148). As behavioral economists, we would expect economic actors to try to cope with the complexity of their economic environments by using simple rules that, subject to one proviso, most of the time would keep them from switching into moods of euphoria or panic and would instead make them operate in a "business as usual" manner. The key proviso is that policymakers set up the rules of the game for decision-makers to preclude the kinds of events in the economic environment that are likely to trigger feelings of euphoria or panic.

In other words, and in line with the conclusions of Akerlof and Shiller, the macroeconomic policy focus should be on regulating how capitalism is allowed to work. So, for example, if we want to prevent dangerous inflation of property prices, we should impose rules that limit the size of mortgages relative to the homeowner's equity and income, while if we are concerned about avoiding bank failures, we should set (and monitor adherence to) rules about the composition of the balance sheets of financial intermediaries, and so on. This should be accompanied by the kind of modeling proposed by Godley and Lavoie (2007) that integrates the financial sector and the structure of indebtedness with what can happen in the "real" sector, in contrast to traditional approaches to modeling in which the monetary side of the economy is grossly simplified.

What we should not do is try to make the economy resemble as closely as possible the idealized "free market" system of orthodox economic theorists and neoconservative politicians. Furthermore, we should also be mindful of scope for using nudges and boosts, as discussed in Chapter 9 in relation to retirement savings and financial literacy. We should also take seriously the potential roles of political leaders and state propaganda as means for calming incipient euphoria or – as former US president Franklin D. Roosevelt recognized when he said in 1933 in his inaugural address, "We have nothing to fear but fear itself" – for trying to maintain or restore confidence.

13 Can We Be Happy without Destroying the Environment?

13.1 Introduction

As foreshadowed at the end of Chapter 1, this final chapter takes us into the territories of ecological economics and happiness economics. The works that kick-started these two fields appeared within a few years of each other in the early 1970s.

In the case of ecological economics, the seminal economic contribution was *The Entropy Law and the Economic Process*, by the Romanian evolutionary economist Nicholas Georgescu-Roegen (1971). In essence, he married Schumpeter's evolutionary view of economic growth as powered by advances in technology, and ideas from thermodynamics that focus on what happens when sources of energy are applied to other resources. The economic process neither creates nor destroys matter; rather, it aggregates scattered resources by mining, harvesting and refining them and then turns them into new combinations to serve economic ends. Inevitably, processes of production and consumption result in by-products, scrap and waste. The waste products end up in sinks in the natural environment in forms that, if concentrated, are often toxic or, if dispersed and/or mixed with other compounds, are difficult to recycle for further use.

From this standpoint, it appears that compounding economic growth is not sustainable in the long run. Even an economic steady state seems unlikely to be feasible without harnessing renewable energy sources and taking steps to ensure that key nonrenewable production inputs do not end up irretrievably in entropy sinks and that the natural ecosystems that yield food, fiber and pharmaceutical inputs are not wiped out by habitat destruction or collapse due to being poisoned and losing species diversity. In some cases, the destruction of ecosystems and/or species that inhabit them would also mean that humans would lose the experiential consumption benefits of being able to marvel at them for their intrinsic value. Global warming and its effects on climate illustrate this lesson from Georgescu-Roegen's analysis: allowing the atmosphere to be used as a sink for the by-products of burning fossil fuels has consequences that could prove catastrophic even before the supply of fossil fuels runs out.

Happiness economics began when Richard Easterlin (1974) sparked controversy by suggesting that the international data on happiness seemed to be contradictory: at any point in time, people with higher incomes seemed to be happier than those with lower incomes, whereas happiness did not seem to rise for everyone if they all experienced rising incomes as time passed. Two decades later, a growing body of happiness data yielded a similar picture: see Easterlin (1995). An obvious way of making sense of this is to view happiness as if it depends on how people see their incomes relative to others, rather than on its absolute level.

Taken together, the contributions of Easterlin and Georgescu-Roegen point to a fundamental question: if making everyone richer does not make everyone happier but wrecks the environment and cannot continue indefinitely, how can we enable people to be happy in a sustainable way? This chapter examines what lessons can be gleaned from analysis earlier in this book to help address this vital question; it does not offer surveys of the two fields that the question brings together. Such surveys can readily be found elsewhere: in the case of happiness economics, see Easterlin (2002) for a collection of key early papers, along with Layard (2011) and Bruni (2021); for a handbook on ecological economics, see Spash (2017); and for a one-stop handbook covering happiness, well-being and the environment, see Maddison et al. (2020).

In contrast to the kinds of lighthearted puzzles that Richard Thaler used so effectively to engage his readers and popularize his approach to behavioral economics, this chapter focuses on what is arguably the most serious issue that humans must get to grips with soon. It is quite likely that many readers will feel uncomfortable on seeing what I suggest people are going to need to do or stop doing if the economy is not to wreck the biosphere that is a prerequisite for the happiness of future generations. However, I hope readers will get a sense that the time they have invested in the earlier chapters leaves them with a way of thinking that is useful for analyzing some deadly serious issues that humans ignore at their peril.

Although the focus of this chapter is on changing consumer behavior in ways that enable people to be happier and yet have smaller environmental footprints, much of what follows could readily be adapted to the task of analyzing how to affect the meso trajectories of more environmentally sustainable practices in firms. Policies aimed at prodding firms to search for ways of limiting their energy consumption or use of other resource inputs are likely initially to be viewed as inconvenient impositions. However, they may sometimes turn out to be ways of reducing X-inefficiency that could have been implemented long before by using technologies that already existed. In other cases, policy-induced problem-solving activities may have unexpected benefits via the new knowledge that they push firms to create. For example, if carmakers are required to bear the costs of recycling the vehicles that they sell, the process of trying to figure out how to make them easier to take to pieces may have an unexpectedly beneficial by-product, namely that they discover how to design their vehicles to be cheaply assembled in the first place.

13.2   The Materialists versus the Greens

In the half-century that has passed since the seminal works of Georgescu-Roegen and Easterlin were published, our planet has been able to yield enough resources to accommodate many more people, with higher per-capita incomes, than many doomsayers of the early 1970s may have been able to envisage. It has therefore been easy for most people to operate as if there is no problem of environmental sustainability. This frame of mind has also been fostered by success in cleaning up some of the environmental impacts of economic growth in richer nations. But this does not mean that Georgescu-Roegen's analysis and other claims about the limits to growth have been refuted. Certainly, the growth experience of recent decades reflects a combination of the discovery of previously unknown supplies of natural resources, new technologies that made it possible to use resources that previously could not be extracted or recycled, and improvements in agricultural yields achieved via better plant breeding, genetic engineering, and so on. But the growth came at the price of habitat loss, many extinctions of species and the faster filling of entropy sinks, leaving greater environmental challenges than there would otherwise have been.

To give a sense of the difference between where consumption has been heading and where it may need to go in order to be sustainable, this section presents a pair of contrasting vignettes of lifestyles in an affluent economy that is a world leader in per-capita greenhouse gas emissions. These vignettes have been designed to show how people with similar educational backgrounds – probably rather like those of many readers of this book – can end up pursuing lifestyles that entail very different environmental impacts and sources of mental stress.

13.2.1   The Materialists

First, meet William, a very successful corporate lawyer. He grew up in Australia, where he still lives, and is a partner in a law firm whose clients include top-tier mining and energy companies. His parents were both lawyers, and it was clear at an early stage that they expected him not merely to be a lawyer, too, but to do even better than they had done rather than enter their suburban solicitors' practice. He graduated in the early 2000s with a dual degree in law and economics. William worked hard in both areas, but topping off his economics with the grades to which he felt he was entitled sometimes necessitated applying his stronger litigious capabilities when requesting his work to be remarked. He is married to Melissa, now a senior executive in a shipping company, whom he met at university. They have three young children, known by some of their friends and relatives as "the designer babies" because all there were conceived by IVF methods – not because of any fertility issues but to control their dates of birth to ensure their birthday celebrations would all happen around the same time, with Melissa not having to be pregnant during the humidity and blazing heat of summer. This extreme family planning was so precise, aided by Caesarian sections, that the three birthdays were on adjacent days, spread across five years. However, they had originally planned only to have two children to limit the impact of maternity leave on Melissa's career progress. They ended up deciding to have a third child after their second turned out, like the first, to be a boy. Since the Australian system did not allow gender selection in IVF processes, they flew to the US to have their daughter conceived, leaving the two young boys to be looked after by their live-in nanny.

Because William and Melissa are often extremely tied up with their work, the nanny's role includes looking after the other family members, namely their cat and two large pedigree dogs. At the time they acquired their pets, they did not investigate the carbon emissions or wider ecological impacts that could be attributed to these kinds of pets. It did not even occur to them that such issues were being studied and debated. They were simply following social norms: almost every house in their suburb seemed to have such pets. Like the rest of the city, their suburb is rather bereft of small birds these days, largely due to them being preyed upon by pet cats, but William has not made this connection.

When he drives off to work, William often observes his less leisure-poor neighbors out power walking their respective dogs, just as he imagined he would do when he and Melissa chose their pooches. This is not the only area where he gets less exercise than he had hoped. The swimming pool at home has proved mainly to be the domain of the children, under the watch of the nanny. So far, though, William's health has been good. Melissa had a big health scare with her digestive system around the time she hit forty. It took a long while before a diagnosis came and they were very fearful in the meantime. This was quite a jolt to them, as they had been used to being able swiftly to buy solutions to problems that they were unable to use their own skills to solve. Eventually, after switching to another doctor, Melissa was diagnosed to be both gluten and fructose intolerant. Consequently, they had to start thinking about food carefully, rather than just choosing what to eat based on whether they liked the taste. William enjoys not having to take such care when having business lunches, of which there are many, whereas Melissa always feels embarrassed at having to be very fussy when dining socially. She regards it as fortunate that normally she can still order a steak so long as she checks that the sauce will be OK.

Although William always has to keep in mind the need to maintain the lucrative relationships between his firm and its clients, it is the transactional side of his work that gives him the biggest buzz. Not every deal can be completed, or every case won, but the prospect of success with whatever he is working on fires him up and his success rate had been consistently good enough to have earned him a partnership at an early age. He sees each big career step, or major deal that comes to fruition, as something to mark with a trophy of some kind. However, he has to be careful not to allow thoughts about getting the next trophy to divert his attention from the job at hand. The trouble is, there is so little time to relax and enjoy the trophies, given his willingness to "do what it takes" to achieve the next success. He had hoped that after making it to the partnership, the pressure would lessen but, if anything, the stakes seem to have got higher. He and Melissa are both concerned that they are not getting enough "quality time" with their children.

William and Melissa live in a mature, leafy suburb of "executive homes" that were built in the period 1985–2005. It is easy to guess the ages of the houses in their suburb, as the sizes of the houses grew relative to the block sizes during the development process, and the later houses have much more elaborate exterior designs that feature complex roof layouts (that can make it very difficult to install solar photovoltaic electricity systems) and facades with columns and balconies. The later designs were clearly intended to be impressive: they give these homes looks that are on the way to emulating those of the homes of the elites from centuries past. These designs are poorly suited to the subtropical local climate and require powerful air-conditioning systems to keep them cool during the summer due to not having wide eaves and verandahs. They are the kinds of homes that urban sociologists often class as "McMansions" and, as they age, they become expensive to maintain. This is not simply due to them being old enough for the Diderot effect to kick in via kitchen and bathroom upgrades but also because of the complex roof designs and the plumbing systems entailed due to having multiple bathrooms. Leaks from the roof and plumbing would have been difficult to get fixed were it not for the live-in nanny being able to liaise with and monitor contractors while William and Melissa are at work.

Although their suburb is full of McMansions, it is William and Melissa's house that the locals refer to as "The Mansion," as it is conspicuously bigger than all the others – bigger even than the huge house next door (that is known locally as "The Little Mansion" and only occupies a single block, unlike "The Mansion"). It has, according to the realtor ad that attracted them to it, "commanding" views from its hilltop location. Their gardening contractor keeps the grounds looking beautifully manicured, and it never occurs to the couple that there are environmental costs to the irrigation system that go beyond the cost of the dam and pipelines that feed the water to it – such as the emissions associated with powering all the pumps that get the water to them. They have not yet got around to installing a rainwater tank to reduce these impacts, and their water bills, as the latter, paid by direct debit, are something they can readily afford and barely notice among their many other outgoings.

They bought the house when its original owner decided to have a "sea change" retirement. Melissa was smitten with the scale of the master bedroom's walk-in robe facilities, for they included a huge alcove that she now describes as her "shoe room." It is where she keeps, in their original boxes, her huge and still expanding collection of designer-brand shoes, which currently consists of about 150 pairs. Melissa does not think her shoe collection is a sign that she has more money than sense: if you were to challenge her about it, her reply would allude to the infamous first lady of the Philippines and point out that, when it comes to shoes, she is "only a half Imelda."

Even so, Melissa's shoe fetish has so far involved a similar outlay to William's purchase of the thirty-foot cabin cruiser that is usually to be seen on its trailer in their driveway. Like many trophy boats around their suburb, it is rarely used: William and Melissa tend to fly overseas for their vacations, and the hoped-for long weekends of relaxation and fishing from the boat frequently fail to come to fruition due to them being called on to attend to urgent business tasks. Despite the boat's presence, their double-entry driveway will be easily big enough to accommodate the cars that their children will no doubt get when they turn seventeen, with space still left for visitors' cars. Presently, aside from the boat, the driveway is home to William's twin-turbo, V8-engined Mercedes-Benz AMG E63 sedan and Melissa's BMW X5 SUV.

William's friends sometimes try to "wind him up" by pointing out that he rarely gets to enjoy his Merc on the open road and that he could have bought even better performance more cheaply by buying a top-line Tesla Model S instead. This fact came as a surprise to him when he first faced this jibe, for the Tesla was available when he bought the Merc that he had so long aspired to get and which was not a more basic E-series of the kind that seemed to be the default career success trophy in their suburb. But he rapidly concluded that he had made the right choice after all: a Tesla would lack the instant brand recognition of the Merc's three-pointed star radiator logo and it could be an embarrassing car to be seen in by, or to have to explain to, senior clients from the kinds of companies with whom he works.

At the time William and Melissa first purchased their house, one of their key criteria that it met was the fact that it was within a half-hour drive of both the airport (which William uses particularly frequently) and their respective workplaces. However, in just a few years, these travel times have increased significantly due to traffic congestion, with rising variance in journey times making much earlier departures necessary in order to be sure to arrive in time for flights or meetings. Sometimes, when stuck in traffic on the freeway, William notices that the users of the adjacent cycleway are moving faster than he is. However, he views them as poor, or keep-fit fanatics, or simply "weirdos" (cf. Pooley et al., 2011), and he notes to himself that they do not have the luxury of his air-conditioned, leather-upholstered cocoon. (He did not even check to see whether this model might be available with the MB-Tex artificial leather that is standard fare on more lowly models; this would have been a waste of his time, as the choice is not offered at this level.) Parking in the city is always easy and secure for him, as it is for Melissa at the city's port, as they both have personal parking bays at their workplaces.

When interest rates came down after the Global Financial Crisis, William and Melissa did not see the change as an opportunity to reduce their debts much more rapidly. Rather, in the years since the GFC, they used cheap money both to move up to owning The Mansion and to leverage capital gains by borrowing against the equity in their home to raise deposits on a couple of investment properties closer to the city center. These properties have, in effect, 100 percent loan finance, but this does not worry William and Melissa, as they have never seen the local property market take a serious dive. So long as they have no further health scares, William and Melissa believe that their careers have put them in a position where they will be able to pay off all their debt by the time they retire, despite the looming costs of putting their three children through the best private schools in the city.

The tenants of their investment properties are young professional couples that William imagines to be the sort of people who fritter their money away by dining out far too often (for example, having smashed avocado toast for breakfast) while bemoaning their inability to save enough for a deposit to get a foot on the property ownership ladder. (For a perspective from the millennials' side, see Sternberg, 2019.) As far as William is concerned, the problem with such people is that they feel entitled to start their adult lives with all the benefits that two decades of economic growth have brought since he and Melissa started out in the early 2000s.

13.2.2   Two Shades of Green

Back in Section 8.7, we considered the dilemma faced by Emma, a green Australian consumer, as she tried to find a suitable electric car for her needs. Now let me introduce Jude, her former partner. Jude is an ecological economist, who works as an analyst and advisor in a government agency concerned with energy and environmental policy. His thinking has been greatly influenced by the work of Clive Spash, an eminent ecological economist who is editor-in-chief of the journal *Environmental Values*. Whenever he makes a choice, Jude tries to limit his own environmental impact as much as he can.

After completing his PhD in the early 2000s, Jude chose to pursue a public-service career rather than becoming an academic, as he considered that being directly involved in policymaking gave him his best chance of contributing to a sustainable future. His career provides him with a very comfortable living despite his pay being far less than it would have been if he had not had the epiphany that led him down that road instead of sticking to his original plan of using his skills to make his fortune by working for an investment bank. His epiphany came as a result of seeing the movie *Erin Brockovich* in 2000 while he was an undergraduate and enrolled in the same law and economics dual degree program as William the materialist. As a result of seeing the film, he started thinking seriously about the relationship between capitalism and the environment and went on to take courses in environmental economics. Looking back, he finds it depressing that so little progress has been made since then despite books such as Spash's (2002) *Greenhouse Economics* having already been around when he was doing his PhD. Spash is not the only Clive whose work Jude admires. His favorite quotation – "People buy things they don't need, with money they don't have, to impress people they don't like" – is from Clive Hamilton's book *Growth Fetish* (2003), though it appears from Quote Investigator (2016) to be a variation on a saying that originated seventy years earlier to characterize the lifestyle of Broadway stars.

Jude's green principles have frequently made him a controversial figure where he works, though, unlike Spash, he has not yet been put in a position where the alternative to acceding to a demand from his boss was to resign on principle. (Spash hit the headlines in 2009 when he resigned from a research leadership role at Australia's CSIRO rather than withdraw from publication a paper exposing limitations of climate change policies, which had been accepted in a peer-reviewed journal: see Earl, 2009, and Pincock, 2009; for the article in question, see Spash, 2010.) It is not simply a result of him questioning the value-integrating methodologies of techniques such as contingent valuation and social cost–benefit analysis that his agency often uses (cf. O'Connor and Spash, 1999; Spash, 1999); Jude also has a reputation among his colleagues due to his stances over more mundane matters.

One such area has been office equipment. His agency has a policy of providing staff with all-in-one desktop computers that it normally replaces soon after their extended warranties expire. Jude has refused to accept this for reasons that go beyond the policy error of buying extended warranties. He has been concerned with the computers being replaced long before they are obsolete, the failure to purchase modular systems (which would have made it possible merely to replace only the components that failed or became obsolete), and the failure to take account of energy consumption when choosing computers, given that his colleagues merely put their computers into "sleep" mode when they head for home. All he thinks he needs his employer to provide him with is a monitor into which he can plug the laptop that he brings from home in a backpack when he cycles to work. Jude rarely writes on paper, and when he does, it is with a wooden pencil, not a plastic ballpoint pen, on the reverse of a printed page from his stash of paper for recycling. He is aware that e-books do not have zero marginal environmental costs but long ago vowed, on environmental grounds, to avoid buying hardcopy books anymore. He reads books and papers on his laptop wherever possible and sees no need to buy an e-reader.

Because Jude always has his laptop at hand, he had found no need for a smartphone or tablet until the introduction of QR check-in codes during the Covid-19 pandemic forced him to get a smartphone so that he could scan these codes. Up to that point, he had simply used a traditional no-frills mobile phone for calls and SMS messages, and a broadband USB dongle for mobile Internet access on his laptop. However, he regards smartphones and tablet computers much more favorably than we might first expect. These devices may seem to be designed to be disposable status symbols, given their short product life cycles and the absence of user-replaceable batteries. But Jude has checked the facts on whether, say, iPhones and iPads can be kept going if key parts fail (just as he checks for anything that he might need to buy one day or that the general public tends to buy) and he knows that screens, batteries and home buttons can be replaced. He accepts that there are significant costs to the environment in mining the rare minerals required for some of the components but notes that the well-developed systems for recycling mobile phones greatly reduce the chances of these materials ending up being lost in landfills. What he admires about these devices is the fact that, as complex systems with multiple capabilities, they enable their users to do things that used to require multiple devices that collectively used far more energy and materials but embodied far less knowledge. For many people, these devices even remove the need for a laptop or desktop computer.

Jude likes the way that, as well as eliminating many more resource-hungry devices from many consumer lifestyles, smartphones and tablets also reduce the living space that consumers require and the need to travel to enjoy entertainment. (In terms of the micro–meso–macro framework, the "macro" impacts of these products thus include their impacts on the home audio and video electronics sector, such as limiting the uptake of home theater systems and the residual market for hi-fi audio systems, impacting on the meso trajectory of the cinema market, changing the economics of the book market, news media, and so on.) Thus, although Jude suspects that there may be negative social and developmental impacts on those whose lives become overly concentrated on the small screens of these devices (see Wigley, 2021), and although the infrastructure of servers and digital delivery networks consume energy and materials on a large scale, he thinks that they may have a significant role to play in limiting per-capita environmental footprints.

His colleagues have long known him for his determination to apply Herbert Simon's (1991, p. 307) travel theorem at every opportunity. The theorem claims that if the point of travelling somewhere is merely to gather information, then the journey should not be made unless the information is of a site-specific kind that is being generated over a period of at least six months; in any other situation, it should be possible, and less costly, to obtain the information remotely. Jude can see the point of ethnographic researchers visiting sites and embedding themselves for long periods, but otherwise, like Simon, he is opposed to travelling anywhere to attend meetings or conferences. He also regards the management consultants that his agency sometimes hires as wasting time and needlessly imposing environmental costs when they insist on coming in for face-to-face meetings. Jude's colleagues mostly seem to relish being sent off to represent the agency at conferences and workshops, whereas Jude views such events as often being little more than taxpayer-funded junkets. He wishes that his colleagues would gather and share information and knowledge by using online resources, phone calls and webinars. He was an early adopter of Skype and a strong advocate of Zoom, but it was only in the Covid-19 pandemic that his colleagues started to see what he had been getting at. They also began to be less skeptical about his long-made suggestion that he should be allowed to work from home since there was generally no reason why he had to be at the office in order to do his job now that reliable broadband Internet was available. His colleagues still seem to be skeptical when he suggests that their college-age children should never be required or need to attend a campus for study purposes and that online dating services logically should provide a far more efficient way than chance campus encounters for finding a life partner.

Back in 2005, as singles with unusual preferences, Jude and Emma had certainly found the large pool of an online dating site to be an excellent way of overcoming the thin-market problem they each had been experiencing. They were both passionate about recycling and reusing (which included getting many of their clothes on op-shopping expeditions), were strongly opposed to pet ownership due to concerns about environmental paw-prints and had agreed to give up jetting off on long-distance overseas trips. They did not end up feeling they had lost much – aside from bragging rights and being able to "dine out" on their travelers' tales – as a result of abandoned international tourism. Instead, they became avid viewers of travel documentaries and readers of travel books, learning more than they would have done by "being there." This was another application of Simon's travel theorem and it also meant that they could learn about distant lands without having to worry about issues such as food safety. Unfortunately, their relationship gradually started to become stressful, as Jude developed a clearer picture of the implications of trying to be as green as possible (which he calls "lexicographic green'). To put it simply: he began to view Emma as not green enough for him.

Tensions between Jude and Emma arose across a wide range of areas. For example:

- Jude had insisted they should try to confine their diets as far as possible to locally sourced fruit and vegetables and adapt what they ate according to seasonal availability. This would reduce the environmental costs of their food in terms of "food miles" measures. However, discussions about what they should eat became even more problematic after he read Saunders and Barber (2008) and discovered that the emissions associated with food depended greatly on production technologies, too, and to such an extent that lamb and dairy products shipped from New Zealand to the UK could have a smaller environmental footprint than similar products consumed in the UK that had been produced there. The food sourcing issue even cast a cloud over dining out at local restaurants rather than eating at home. Previously, given their dietary preferences, they had viewed eating out as an eco-friendly way of using their discretionary income, for they walked to local eateries and would need to eat at home if they did not eat out. But Jude had begun to be concerned about whether food at local ethnic restaurants had a bigger eco-footprint than a home-cooked meal of vegetables from the local growers' market.

- Emma had chosen to be a vegan for ethical reasons but also argued that it was an environmentally better diet, since it avoided the conversion losses of turning plant matter into meat and dairy products, along with the greenhouse gas emissions from livestock and land clearing. However, after reading Fairlie (2010), Jude came to take the view that if one ranked overall environmental sustainability ahead of animal ethics, it might be better to be open to eating meat from cattle raised on rangelands that were not suited to arable crops, and from pigs that were being fed waste products rather than being reared in feedlots. Jude also came to view leather shoes as possibly better in environmental terms than the vegan shoes that Emma insisted on wearing, for the latter seemed less biodegradable.

- Jude would have preferred Emma not to own a car at all, rather than to try to have a vehicle chosen for its low emissions. He felt that, were it not for the frequent weekend visits Emma made to her mother, they could readily have got by using bicycles, taxis/Uber and public transport. Indeed, he could not see why her mother resisted the idea of moving close to them, given that she was no longer working. Otherwise, it seemed to Jude that all they would have needed to do would have been to rent a car for vacations – though only because living in Australia meant that the very limited passenger rail network and climate, in conjunction with great distances, ruled out the idea of rail- and cycling-based vacations. But Emma was reluctant to brave the city streets on a bicycle, found local bus timetables inconvenient and thought that the costs of using taxis or Uber and renting cars for vacations would add up to more than the annual cost of owning and running a small car – though neither of them could say what these costs typically were.

- Difficulties arose for the couple when Emma agreed to accompany her mother on a cruise that took them along the coast of Canada and Alaska after they had made a long flight across the Pacific Ocean to Vancouver. Jude views the emissions of cruise ships with alarm and, mindful of Simon's travel theorem, he was unimpressed by Emma's comment that, after seeing many icebergs, she now had an even stronger sense of what is at stake if global greenhouse gas emissions are not eliminated.

Emma came to think that she was doing enough – way more than most people she knew – to limit her environmental footprint and that Jude seemed to be operating as if he was bearing the whole weight of humanity's environmental problems on his shoulders. She sensed that he was viewing every choice as an ethical dilemma, with many decisions leaving him feeling guilty that, despite all his careful consideration, his choice would still have a negative environmental impact. He seemed unable to accept that generating entropic by-products was an inevitable consequence of being alive.

They finally decided to split up due to irreconcilable differences over the issue of having children. By this point, Emma was already in her late thirties and felt she was approaching a "now or never" reproductive point in her life. Her mother frequently reminded her of this, too, and of how much she was looking forward to becoming a grandmother. Jude had been stalling for years over this issue but ultimately decided that fathering children was one of the worst things he could do for ecological sustainability. He suggested that an intercountry adoption might be a compromise solution for them, since it would not entail an addition to the overall population. It might also result in the adopted children having fewer children than they might have done if they stayed in the country of their birth, though he was concerned that this might be more than offset by them growing up to enjoy much more affluent lifestyles than they otherwise would have done. This suggestion was not well received, despite also enabling her to avoid the downsides of pregnancy and childbirth: Emma wanted the full experience of being a woman and was wary of taking on a child that was likely to be damaged by a sense of having been rejected as well as due to poor nurturing prior to the adoption.

Jude's green principles result in him spending little of his discretionary income, so he gives significant amounts to charities whose missions focus on sustainability. He is debt-free, having paid off the mortgage on his apartment, so he could readily afford to switch to part-time work. However, it seems unlikely that he will do this. He finds his work fulfilling and worries that if he does less for the agency, projects that he might have handled will be undertaken by colleagues who are less fastidious in their focus on ethical and environmental aspects. He has no plans to use his surplus spending capacity to fund a bigger home, but he wishes that he had been able to find a Danish-style cohousing scheme with shared facilities and constructed from more eco-friendly materials than the apartment he ended up having to choose. The dominance of concrete in the construction of apartments and townhouse complexes in Australian cities remains disappointing to him, and he feels unable to move to a lifestyle block on the city's fringe due to the commuting challenges this would present to him on days when he is not able to work from home (given the sheer sprawl of the city, along with the limited public transport and cycle lanes) and the very real threat of bushfires that climate change has greatly exacerbated.

13.2.3   Discussion

Although the two vignettes were designed to contrast sharply, they are not wildly extreme or detached from reality. The materialists live in the expensive end of a suburb modeled on the one in which I live, rather than in the manner of the superrich. Even the "designer babies" and "half Imelda" elements are based on lives of actual consumers from the same socioeconomic group as William and Melissa. Similarly, the way in which I have depicted green living is a composite of the lifestyles of urban green professionals with which I am familiar, rather than representations of those who try to live self-sufficient, off-grid lifestyles in rural areas. The materialists' lifestyle would have an ecological footprint many times greater than that of even Emma's version of green living, while Jude's version probably keeps his impact to a level more like that of someone living comfortably in a country well down the league table of per-capita incomes.

Given the question that this chapter addresses, it is hard not to reflect upon how happy William, Melissa, Jude and Emma would be if they were real people. From Maslow's (1971) standpoint, it appears that how happy people will be with how their lives are going will depend on how far along their need hierarchy they can get beyond their most basic needs, without preventing themselves from meeting any of their other basic needs. On this basis, the happiest person in the vignettes is Jude, despite what may appear to be his rather grim determination to be part of the solution to the sustainability problem. He can concentrate on this without it interfering with his self-actualization goals, since his job is consistent with doing the right thing for the environment and he seems not to have a burning desire to pursue hobbies that would keep presenting him with dilemmas related to sustainability. He also seems not to care about what other people think of him and to have no urge to have children, which makes it easier to meet his middle-ranking needs. Clearly, he was not so besotted with Emma that he was willing to forgo his higher-level needs to help her fulfill her greater need to have children. In meeting his basic needs, he may feel he has some environmental impacts that are inherent to living in a modern society, but he can resolve the cognitive dissonance that this entails by telling himself that if he dropped out to pursue a "back to nature" kind of lifestyle (for which he may be woefully short of the necessary skills), it would mean giving up the chance to make a difference to the impact that others have on the environment. His life is very fulfilling, though he often feels frustrated by the failure of others to take up more sustainable ways of living. By contrast, his former partner Emma may now be preoccupied with the more basic frustration of trying to become a mother as her biological clock ticks increasingly loudly. She resolves the cognitive dissonance of her more compromised adherence to green principles by applying a distributive justice principle: why should she be expected to make an even bigger contribution to sustainability when others are doing much less?

The organizing principles that William and Melissa use to run their lives keep them from engaging in self-transcending behavior: they seem to be too busy even to contribute to community projects such as those undertaken by Rotary or Lions groups. They may feel that they dominate on the status ladder in their suburb, given the consumption trophies that their careers enable them to buy. It is difficult to separate their status attainments from what seems to be their approach to self-actualization: they operate as if, in the words of Helga Dittmar (1992), "To have is to be." But this leaves them frustrated, as they end up with a puritan work ethic that results in them being unable to relax and take the time necessary to enjoy the non-status benefits of the trophies they accumulate – benefits that would help them toward feeling that they are succeeding in what they really would like to be doing in a broader sense. Their way of "being" is akin to that of the hypothetical entrepreneur, challenged by Scitovsky (1943), who pursues profit "for its own sake," regardless of the effects that this has on the time available for doing anything else, including enjoying benefits that profit-financed consumption would make possible. From the standpoint of Maslow's analysis, William and Melissa would find their lives less stressful and more fulfilling if they could moderate their status aspirations and negotiate to start working part-time without being perpetually on call for work tasks. They could still get the buzz they get from using their professional skills in problem solving and stitching up deals, but less often. If such negotiations were ruled out as being at odds with the nature of their jobs, they might be wise to move to less demanding jobs that enabled them to use their skills in a different context (as with the big-city corporate lawyer who learns to enjoy life as a magistrate in a laid-back surfing community in the 1998–2000 Australian television drama series, *SeaChange*, more recently available on Netflix and Stan).

Maslow's analysis can also help us make sense of real-world examples of lifestyles that seem to entail strange hybrids of both materialistic and green lifestyles. An example of this would be the lifestyle of a couple in their fifties who live in a standalone five-bedroom property that is a long way from their different workplaces, to which they commute separately by bus and a hybrid car, and who make a determined effort to do the right thing in terms of the environment everywhere else in their lives. On the surface, such a lifestyle might seem internally contradictory (cf. the fragmentation corollary in Kelly's psychology of personal constructs), but it could have a backstory that is perfectly coherent. For example, it would be consistent with them being "empty-nesters" who had several grown-up children and only adopted green principles quite recently. Supply-side constraints and social embeddedness may explain why they have not opted to downsize after the children have "left the nest": it may be impossible to find suitable small properties in the same neighborhood and the location may matter not merely because their workplaces are in opposite directions from where they live, making it the least bad location for them despite the long commutes, but also because they have elderly parents in retirement homes nearby, or some of their children and grandchildren live nearby, and they are heavily involved in the local community. They may also be reluctant to move to somewhere smaller, since they have a passion for gardening and the large house enables them to have space also to pursue their indoor hobbies via a dedicated craft room and a music room, while also maintaining a guest room that is used quite often. Such a couple might seem to have surprisingly little concern about achieving status by collecting conspicuous consumption trophies, but they certainly live more comfortably than most people. However, the scale of their aspirations in respect of their social and self-actualization needs limits their ability to pursue their lately recognized need for self-transcendence in relation to the environment.

Even though the vignettes focus on in-country rather than between-country lifestyle differences and only refer to people in one age group, they give us a taste of the distributional challenges of transitioning to a more sustainable future. Jude seems to have few opportunities to reduce further his environmental footprint, but it seems unjust to Emma that she should go further in the same direction when others are making little or no attempt to start on that road. If those who are already more attuned to the kinds of changes that are necessary take such a view, policies that focus successfully on changing the behavior of those with the biggest per-capita environmental footprints will have secondary payoffs due to making the "already-attuned" group fell happier and more willing try even harder at living in a sustainable manner.

However, we must recognize that in some areas there are limits on what people like William and Melissa could do even if they suddenly decided to try to operate in a less resource-hungry manner. It is too late for them to decide to have fewer children than they already have and if they sell The Mansion, William's boat and their cars, they will be making it easier for others to acquire such assets – and the new owners might even make more use of them. Here, we have another manifestation of the slow replacement of assets discussed in Chapter 11 via the Salter diagram. If Melissa starts to feel uncomfortable about continuing to drive her BMW SUV and many other consumers start to feel likewise, the secondhand prices of such vehicles will plunge to the level necessary to attract buyers who have no such qualms about owning them and are willing to incur the costs of running and maintaining them. Such buyers may include status-hungry motorists in poorer countries where environmental attitudes are less progressive and there is a thriving market for imported used vehicles. By contrast, if consumers in high-income countries opt to replace their clothes less frequently, the trickle-down effects of donating clothing to charities will be reduced. This will not only raise the cost of living for their poorer compatriots or those like Jude and Emma who love to "op-shop"; it may also limit the flow of used clothing to, say, poor consumers in Africa whose ability to obtain cheap used clothing has already been reduced by the popularity of cheaper but less durable "fast fashion" clothes in high-income economies. (For analysis of the global trade in secondhand consumer goods, see Minter, 2019.)

13.3   The Need to Rein in Consumption Aspirations

The super-busy lifestyle of William and Melissa contrast sharply with what may be called the "overdose of leisure" scenario that Keynes (1930) outlined in his famous essay in which he considered the implications of compound rates of productivity growth for the "economic possibilities for our grandchildren." Like many people in affluent societies, William and Melissa have not viewed rising real hourly rates of pay as providing opportunities to work fewer hours per week or days per year. Instead, those with materialistic mindsets have kept expanding the range and complexity of the products that they consume. In many cases, as Frank (2007) has emphasized, there has been a tendency for consumption to resemble an arms race between status-hungry consumers that manifests itself in a preference for larger and larger products. Inequality has risen sharply since the early 1980s as a result of moves toward the globalization of markets and implementation of neoconservative policies of cutting marginal rates of income tax and "reforming" labor markets to limit the bargaining power of labor unions. Those whose wages have failed to rise and/or whose job prospects have shrunk have been courted by, and have often voted for, politicians who promise "jobs and growth" rather than redistributive policies and better social welfare safety nets. Almost everyone seems to want to consume more.

If viewed from the behavioral standpoint, this situation is not the result of people having insatiable hardwired wants of the kind that an "econ" is assumed to have. Rather, it can readily be understood in terms of how human cognitive processes have evolved to work in ways that ratchets up aspiration levels as higher levels of attainments become possible. As was emphasized earlier in this book, choices based on whether or not an option will enable pertinent aspiration levels to be met help to ensure that humans are able to avoid decision paralysis when faced with open-ended problems. But this evolutionary benefit of being genetically programmed to use aspiration levels in choice would have limited human progress if it meant that humans would stop striving to find ways of doing better in areas where they met their aspirations. If aspiration levels were static, humans would never have got to where they are today. However, evolutionary processes have selected two cognitive mechanisms that drive us to keep setting more demanding aspirations.

The first of these mechanisms is the tendency to habituate to new levels of attainment. Instead of remaining content with our success, the novelty wears off, our joy evaporates, and we become bored (see Scitovsky, 1976). We then raise our aspirations and start searching once again. This helps drive technological progress but makes us inherently restless as consumers. For example, we are initially excited by a fifty-inch television that seems like a cinema screen compared with its thirty-two-inch predecessor, but we soon get used to it and, after visiting an appliance store on some other missions, we see that seventy-inch televisions are now available at a price we can afford, so we start hankering after one of these. (Jude, of course, would point out that we might merely need to get some reading glasses to get a more cinematic experience, for viewing video content on an iPad held close to our faces can provide a more immersive field of view than that offered by a very large television at distance in a large lounge.) Unfortunately, the tendency to habituate also makes us prone to allow slowly worsening conditions in our external environments to go unnoticed: like a frog in water that is gradually taken to boiling point, we may fail to realize that our reference points are changing and hence that we may simply get used to changes that we would have objected to had they taken place in one hit. Because of this, we may not realize the gravity of where we have got to until it is too late to reverse the situation.

In order to prevent us from giving up trying to do better when success does not come immediately, we need to operate in a way that ensures we feel confident that we have a good chance of succeeding. Hence, the second cognitive process that drives the ratcheting up of aspiration levels entails our use of social comparisons when deciding what might be a reasonable level to try to attain. When those that we use as external reference standards are doing better, we take it as a sign that we can follow suit; indeed, we will need to do so if we are not to suffer reduced relative social standing. Inequality thus fuels rising aspirations, which in turn fuels the economic growth that results in consumer restlessness (see further Genicot and Ray, 2017). However, if others, for whatever reasons, seem to be lowering their sights, we will not automatically follow them, since we may enjoy higher social standing if we demonstrate we do not have to lower our sights. If our incomes fall, we may keep up appearances by continuing to spend, if we are able to do so, by reducing our rates of saving (Duesenberry, 1949).

Previously, it was not a problem for humanity that evolutionary processes selected these cognitive mechanisms, for humans were able to keep increasing in number despite periodic Malthusian episodes, by increasing their geographical reach and by innovations that raised productivity. But now, despite the increasing awareness of the threat posed by global warming and climate change as global per-capita level of consumption increase, there appears to be no growing sense among the world's biggest per-capita consumers that they need to rein in their aspiration levels as per-capita incomes rise in newly industrializing economies. Rather, climate change seems to be viewed by most adults as the only environmental challenge and as a problem that can be brought under control if the politics of setting appropriate emissions reduction targets can be resolved. In some countries, as renewable energy technologies become cheaper than those based on fossil fuels, people are even getting excited about the positive impact that, say, a transition to a hydrogen economy will have on per-capita incomes. The view seems to be that there may be some adjustment problems but, hey, the winners will be readily able to compensate the losers and, from then on, the sky's the limit!

As behavioral economists, we should not be surprised by either the emergence of such a simplified view of the relationship between economic activity and the environment or the associated tendency to keep voting for more economic growth. We probably slip quite often into taking such a view ourselves, due to our limited attentive capacity, rather than always looking for environmental issues associated with our choices in the manner of Jude, the obsessively green consumer. If so, we badly need, like the mass of the population, to get out of such a System 1 way of thinking about the environment, remind ourselves about present bias and adopt a good measure of Jude's grimly analytical way of operating.

William and Melissa's McMansion should be viewed as a pointer to the fundamental contradiction between long-run rising per-capita incomes with increasing populations versus environmental sustainability. Mansion-like living becomes increasingly ordinary as mass production methods are applied to the housing industry and as per-capita incomes rise, though middle-class households finance their lifestyles by long hours of paid work rather than from the incomes generated by inherited assets in the manner of Veblen's leisure class. They end up too time-poor to make the most of what they can afford to buy. This happens even where their possessions are expensive, lumpy items (such as William's boat and high-performance luxury car) rather than members of a large collection of items that cannot be consumed at the same time (as with Melissa's many pairs of designer shoes). But they nonetheless buy their trophies for their symbolic value as possessions, rather than merely renting such products for occasions when they have time to use them to their full potential. (See also Linder's 1970 book, *The Harried Leisure Class*.)

If there were no environmental constraints, economic growth would, in the long run, enable anyone to live the McMansion lifestyle or inner-city variants of it that entail living in very spacious luxury apartments. Indeed, if productivity growth enabled per-capita real incomes to compound without limit, techniques of mass production might then be applied to the construction of what would inevitable be tagged as "McPalaces," to enable upper middle-class families to differentiate themselves from the lower middle-class and working-class consumers who had become able to afford McMansions. Robots would solve the "positional good" problem of finding servants (raised by Hirsch, 1976), so everyone could live like royalty without anyone having to work as a servant. Despite this, the superrich could still differentiate themselves by living in even more lavish palaces in superior locations and by taking vacations at exclusive resorts.

Likewise, cars as good as William's Mercedes-Benz would become mass consumption products, while the Bentleys, Rolls-Royces and suchlike cars that are nowadays the preserve of the superrich would become affordable to people in the equivalent of William's position on the socioeconomic status ladder. And, of course, this process would not be confined to today's advanced industrial economies: given enough time, such profligate lifestyles would spread globally. The global spread of McDonald's hamburger restaurants that has symbolized the start of a country's transition into economic development (as emphasized in Friedman, 1999) is, from this unconstrained growth perspective, just the tip of the McDonaldization iceberg that the growth of knowledge and systems of mass production would make possible in evolving economies (cf. Ritzer, 2004).

Sooner or later, however, all this will run into the constraints that Georgescu-Roegen identified. The "positional good" issue that Hirsch (1976) raised is beginning to bite in the tourism sector, now that so many people can afford to travel to the world's best beaches, scenic locations and cultural heritage sites (e.g., Venice), wrecking the tranquility and causing problems of crowding, waste management, and so on. Already, as Beiser (2018) emphasizes, there are growing problems in sourcing supplies of the type of sand that is a prerequisite for building a vast array of things that we take for granted or to which we aspire (including, of course, McMansions), as well as concrete sea walls for holding back rising sea levels that result from global warming. However, even before key resource supplies are exhausted without substitutes being found, there is the risk that the environmental impact of economic growth may result in a catastrophic inability to enable the human population to meet basic survival needs: consider, for example, the prerequisite role that particular insects, such as bees, play in pollinating food crops, and hence what would happen if the populations of such insects collapsed as a result of the increased use of highly intensive forms of agriculture, pollution in their environments, pesticides, and so on.

The fact that most adults go about their lives as if these physical limits to sustainable economic growth do not exist is neither surprising nor due to these limits being too hard for ordinary people to understand. People are busy trying to cope with everyday life and messages about sustainability are allowed by their leaders and legislators to be crowded out by stimuli aimed at promoting consumption.

The implication of these limits is simple: sustainability requires the reining in of per-capita consumption and halting (and then reversing) human population growth. This needs to be done without denying the world's poor the opportunity to get their living standards up to a level at which they are no longer preoccupied with meeting their basic needs, so it requires a very major change in the global and within-country distribution of income and wealth. How is such change from materialistic to sustainable lifestyles to be achieved, and can it be done without making those who need to make substantial reductions in their environmental impacts feel unhappy about making these sacrifices?

13.4   The Macroeconomics of Downsizing an Economy

Before considering the lessons that behavioral economics offers at the microeconomic level about the transition to environmentally sustainable lifestyles, let us consider the macroeconomics of achieving a world in which people in advanced industrial economies on average spend less of their lives in paid work, earn less and hence consume fewer resources. Macroeconomic downsizing will be a politically challenging task in materialistic societies, so it is vital that it does not result in mass unemployment and/or a growing part of the population struggling to find the wherewithal to meet their basic needs. The latter apply even in the absence of any attempt at overall economic downsizing, as technological unemployment looms due to advances in, and associated falling costs of, automation and artificial intelligence that enable more and more activities to be undertaken more cheaply by machines than humans. Robots can work a three-shift, seven-day week for many years without wearing out or getting tired and letting quality slip. Hence, they may be cheaper than human labor for some tasks even if they cost, say, fifteen times the annual wages a worker would require for his or her basic needs. With some industrial robots costing as little as $20,000, the problem looms even in newly industrializing economies where it had been hoped that the combination of far lower wages than advanced economies and productivity-raising technologies from the latter would provide a path the elimination of poverty.

Jobs will then remain only for workers who have any of the following capabilities:

(a) Expertise for addressing infrequently asked questions that the fixed costs of programming make it uneconomic to have addressed by machines.
(b) Valuable know-how that cannot be programmed into machines because it takes the form of tacit knowledge that is beyond the capacity of artificially intelligent machines to "learn by doing."
(c) Valuable critical and creative thinking skills that are superior to those available via artificial intelligence.
(d) Skills as personal service providers that have human qualities (for example, genuine empathy and sympathy) that affect the quality of the service outcome, and which cannot be programmed into machines.

For everyone else, job prospects are grim even before we bring macroeconomic downsizing into the picture. But if economic downsizing takes place, even those with the capabilities listed above could find it challenging to find jobs: for example, if fewer goods are being shipped internationally, the problem-solving expertise in the shipping industry may not be enough to ensure that Melissa can continue to work in that sector.

Except for one key difference, the macroeconomics of achieving environmental sustainability and limiting fallout from technological unemployment are, ultimately, rather like the macroeconomics of dealing with the Covid-19 pandemic. The key difference is that, in the pandemic, output per head only had to be restrained for a relatively short period, whereas environmental sustainability will, ideally sooner rather than later, require the long-term suppression of production. This difference has implications for the design of policies for addressing the reduction in employment opportunities that the downsizing of output entails.

The macroeconomic challenge in the pandemic was to ensure that curtailing output based on face-to-face interactions was done without causing multiplier effects that made the reduction of economic activity bigger than it needed to be to have the desired impact on the spread of the virus. During pandemic lockdowns, those with essential service jobs and those who could work from home could continue to receive their income, but they could not spend it on some of the product they normally would have bought. To some degree, this group substituted in favor of other products that were produced by members of the group, but otherwise they increased their saving rates, pending recovery from the pandemic. Workers in sectors such as hospitality, aviation and tourism were laid off, but if their incomes collapsed, their abilities to spend in sectors that were still operating would have fallen, too. If a levy had been imposed on the extra saving by those who were still working and the proceeds had been transferred to those who had been laid off, the latter would have been able to fill in the gap in demand that their loss of income would otherwise cause in the sectors that were able to continue producing. With such a redistribution, an economy could run steadily with a smaller volume of activity, rather than imploding (see further Earl 2020a). However, this was not how governments supported the incomes of those who were laid off. Instead, income support was funded by selling bonds and/or engaging in "quantitative easing." The policies that were chosen enabled those who kept working as normal to avoid losing any spending power during the pandemic. However, there would eventually be a need to impose tax increases or monetary restraints to prevent an inflationary gap when the pandemic-period savings ultimately came to be spent (see further Earl 2020b). These policies were thus less equitable than the saving levy approach would have been.

One way to scale back production to improve the environmental sustainability of economic activity would be to engineer a supply-side shock. It could entail decreeing that a list of products and services whose production and/or consumption were particularly environment-damaging could no longer be offered or could only be offered in specified quantities, with suppliers of the latter having to purchase supply permits for the period in question. As in a pandemic lockdown, the loss of income in the restricted sectors could result in reduced demand elsewhere. Macroeconomic balance could be achieved by taxing away the amount that those the unrestricted sector would otherwise have spent on the now-restricted products, with the revenue being transferring to those who have lost their jobs in the restricted sector. Note here that, unlike in a pandemic, the long-term nature of the restrictions could mean that the workers in the unrestricted sector would not save income they could no longer spend on the restricted products; they might instead spend more in their own sectors. If so, employment in the unrestricted sectors could be maintained with much smaller (possibly even zero) income support transfers to those who lost their jobs in the restricted sectors. This begs the question of what then would happen to the latter group.

Similar intersectoral issues arise in relation to technological unemployment. In principle, we can envisage an economy in which no one works and everything that is consumed is produced by machines. In such an economy, income would be received by the owners of shares in firms that own the machines that are used in producing marketed output. Those who do not own physical capital or shares would live on transfer payments paid by the government and funded by taxes on the incomes and/or wealth of the owners of capital, with further taxes (or borrowing by the government) being used to fund public sector spending and ensure macroeconomic balance. In such an economy, the usual macroeconomic coordination problems could arise due to policymakers being surprised by the aggregate willingness to spend on consumption and investment.

Clearly, as with the need to redistribute from those who own capital to those who become permanently unemployed as a result of investment in automation, there are significant distributional issues with engineering supply-side shocks to bring about economic downsizing in a way that aims to get the biggest benefit in terms of environmental sustainability. If the workers laid off from the restricted sector are to work again, it will have to be in the unrestricted sector, either via that sector being allowed to grow (thereby limiting the overall environmental benefits of the policy measures) or by some of its existing workers retiring or working fewer hours. If those who lost their jobs in the restricted sector could not obtain jobs elsewhere, those in the unrestricted sector would then end up support them via transfers in the long run.

Alternatively, the government could engineer a less finely targeted reduction in economic activities on the demand side via tax and/or interest rate increases and cuts in government expenditure, with transfer payments being made to those who lose their jobs. Either way, since the policy would be deliberately taking employment to a lower long-term level than the level that had prevailed, the policy might be augmented by measures to promote earlier retirements, job sharing or reduced working hours.

An important consideration with policies aimed at achieving macroeconomic downsizing is whether they can be implemented without causing financial and real estate markets to collapse. If, say, international air travel is one of the sectors that is forced to contract, this will hit not merely those who work in that sector and its supply chains but also the shareholders in these businesses. However, wealth effects associated with such losses on shares in the restricted sector could be contained by aggregate demand management to ensure that businesses in the rest of the economy did not suffer from reduced revenues, with transfer payments to those who lose their jobs in the restricted sector flowing back to the unrestricted sector as demand for its output. If so, there would not be a basis for a fall in shares of firms in the unrestricted sectors despite the fall in per-capita spending and the reduced wealth of those who owned shares of firms in the restricted sector. Similarly, it may appear that, so long as the taxes and transfers are in place, the capacity of the laid-off workers to service their debts would, as a group, be unchanged. Even so, we should be mindful that cascading effects may be triggered during a macroeconomic downsizing, due to individuals differing in their financial commitments. For example, a worker who lost his or her job in a sector on which environmentally based restrictions were imposed might be under mortgage stress and not have been spending a significant proportion of his or her income in the sectors on which the restrictions are imposed. Such a worker might end up becoming a mortgage defaulter due to the income support transfer payment not being big enough to cover monthly mortgage payments as well as other nondiscretionary spending.

It might be easier to make macroeconomic downsizing to achieve environmental goals politically acceptable if it is preceded by the introduction of a "universal basic income" (UBI) system in which the UBI payments were paid to everyone as a basic human right and were big enough to enable anyone to pay for the necessities of life. UBI would remove much of the anxiety about coping with losing one's job. UBI would also make it easier for those who lost their jobs to find employment, since it would facilitate voluntary switches by other workers to part-time work or voluntary breaks from working.

Ideally, the introduction of UBI would entail also the removal not merely of unemployment and means-tested social welfare benefits but also of child-support welfare payments. In place of the latter, there could be per-child UBI payments to custodial parents. These payments would be age-related due to the different costs of bringing up children at different stages but, in order help rein in population growth, UBI payments might only be made for two surviving children per mother, and women would be provided with ready access to means of limiting the number of children to which they gave birth. (Thus, a single mother might be more mindful about allowing herself to get pregnant with a second child via a casual liaison, since this would potentially limit her chances of ending up with a long-term partner who wanted to become a parent. By contrast, a widower with two children who goes on to marry a woman with one child would be able to father one UBI-eligible child with her.) With the UBI payments for children going to the bank accounts of custodial parents, victims of domestic violence would find it financially much easier to exit abusive relationships if the granting of a domestic violence order against their partner automatically ensured the children's UBI payments came to them rather than the partner. This kind of system would also be a means of ensuring that custodial parents were not impoverished after a relationship breakdown if their former partner failed to contribute to supporting their children.

From a behavioral standpoint, it would appear desirable to accompany the UBI program by an expenditure tax of the kind proposed by Kaldor (1955), in place of income tax. A steeply progressive expenditure tax seems likely to be more acceptable than income tax as a means of financing UBI and reining in consumption, since it is not framed in terms of taking income from those who work to support those who do not. It thus counters the loss aversion and fairness concerns that voters would have if UBI were accompanied by much higher income tax rates. Voters would be able legally to avoid paying penal expenditure tax rates by deferring expenditure that they might have financed from current income. A highly progressive expenditure tax could thereby deter status-seeking consumption and get closer to hitting directly the environmental costs of consumption while making it more likely that those with well-paid but high-stress jobs would end up opting for a "sea-change" or "tree-change" whereby they scaled back their work commitments after years of stashing away their income and limiting their consumption to limit their tax liabilities.

13.5   Happiness as a Frame of Mind

It is clear what policymakers in affluent economies should try to engineer at the micro level if they are concerned about the environmental sustainability of economic activity and take Maslow's analysis of human needs seriously but can see little hope of being able to change the hierarchical ranking of the needs that Maslow identified. Their task is rather like that of managers of a firm who hope they can find enough organizational slack that can be taken up and thereby allow the firm to survive. To create happier populations that live in more sustainable ways, they need to figure out how to get people to do two things. One is to lower their aspirations in relation to needs more basic than self-actualization and which are not physiologically determined. The other is to reduce consumption in excess of what is required to meet the basic needs that are physiologically determined. There is also a need for policies that foster forms of self-actualization that have minimal environmental impacts. The goal would be to arrive at a situation in which people operate with what we might call "mindful restraint" and end up being happier while reducing their environmental impacts because they are:

- well nourished without being obese,
- not allowing the sizes of their living space to exceed what is necessary for each household member to have adequate personal space and privacy while also allowing adequate space for intra-household interactions,
- tolerating temperatures in their homes than are in line with human physiological needs rather than operating with needlessly cool summer and needlessly hot winter temperatures simply because they can afford to do so,
- satisfied with fewer children and
- focusing their concerns about their social standing not on where they rank in terms of their income and wealth, but on whether others respect and admire them because they see them as living to high ethical and environmental standards and because they contribute selflessly and creatively to the well-being of their communities.

Such outcomes would also be consistent with what other views of basic needs (such as those explored in Fellner and Goehmann, 2020) imply for improving social and environmental well-being.

In attempting to steer economies to such outcomes, it is vital that policymakers shake off established tendencies to equate well-being and happiness with levels of employment and per-capita Gross Domestic Product. The total amount that people spend on consumption each year may be a poor proxy for their happiness. It tells us nothing about the following:

- the quality of their consumption experiences,
- the extent to which what they consume in the year in question is possible because of what they spent in previous years on durable goods or the time they invested in previous years in developing skills that they now use as consumers,
- the sacrifices they made to be able to finance their consumption,
- how their personal lives are going and
- how their hopes and fears are being affected by how they feel about the state of the world in general.

Indeed, consumption patterns may not be independent of how happy people are feeling due to how their lives are going in particular areas. As the phrase "retail therapy" acknowledges, consumption spending may in some cases be undertaken as an antidote to feeling that life is not working out well in other areas. The same may be said of spending on drinking, drugs and gambling that is undertaken as a means of diverting one's attention from difficulties and disappointments.

Orthodox economic theory invites us to view happiness in terms of the total net utility that people obtain from the desired and undesired experiences they have within the period being studied. What's done is done, so, if things went awry, an "econ" would not get despondent and would only look back with a view to learning how similar kinds of disappointments could be avoided in future or to judge whether there is a need to reassess the probabilities of such disappointments. Orthodox utility theory does not portray an "econ" as experiencing dread or enjoyment by anticipation, yet it does presume an "econ" is able to compute the present value of expected future experiences.

This view of happiness presumes that we can, in principle, be compensated for experiencing things that we did not want to experience. In such situations, the compensation needs to be big enough to provide us with the ability to experience things that will give us enough utility to offset the disutility from the experiences that we did not want to have. From this standpoint, we should view the unhappiness of a woman after hearing of the death of her partner in an accident as being due to the couple having failed to purchase a life insurance policy with a payout large enough to enable her to purchase goods and services that would have given her enough utility to offset the loss of utility that she would have got from the things she would have experienced had her partner not died. If there is enough life insurance, she should, on this analysis, be able to ensure her children remain happy, too, as in, "Don't feel sad that Daddy's dead; it means we can all go to Disneyland as soon as the life insurance payout is in the bank, which is something we wouldn't have been able to afford if he'd not had the accident!"

From a behavioral perspective, such a view seems questionable from several angles:

- Long-held expectations that have been frequently activated will not be instantly deleted from the mind of a person as soon as the events to which they pertain are rendered impossible. Rather, they will have high probabilities of coming to mind when forming expectation in that context despite no longer having the same relevance. Until new templates come to have higher probabilities of being firmed up in this area due to the repeated previous activation of their neural connections, the person in question will experience grief via this process.
- Some people appear to think in a way that denies that gains in other areas can ever compensate for losses in other areas. They see their lives as being ruined if they suffer the loss of something or someone whose presence in their lives they have assumed when building many of their expectations. They also seem to underestimate their capacity to rebuild their lives on alternative assumptive foundations.
- People may be unable to see today's losses and gains as merely temporary upsets or windfalls, owing to their finite information processing capacity in the heat of the moment and/or their habitual failure to think reflectively, along with limited personal experience and limited knowledge of the experience of others. As a result, disappointments make them unhappy to an unwarranted degree, whereas success makes them feel euphoric (cf. Minsky's "financial instability hypothesis," discussed in Section 12.7). In effect, they operate as if they live purely in the present moment, for they seem oblivious to lessons from the past that might be taken to imply that the change in their fortune will probably only be temporary.

Implied here is a more basic point about happiness that is at the heart of Kelly's (1955) psychology of personal constructs: things and events do not "make" us happy or unhappy; rather, how we feel about something depends on how we construe it, and the notion of "happiness" is itself a personal construct. However, this is not to say that how happy we feel is independent of the stimuli we receive from our environment. Insofar as we view our happiness in terms of the extent to which we are able to predict and control events, we may feel needlessly unhappy because we allow ourselves to be exposed to stimuli from media companies (and from some of the firms who use them as advertising platforms) that seek to grab attention by presenting information that could be construed as implying that we have a smaller capacity to predict and control events than we need to have. We may also feel happier than perhaps we should feel about the world around us due to the ways in which others seek to frame things for us. For example, the switch in messaging from "global warming" to "climate change" during the presidency of George W. Bush seems to have been designed to limit the alarm that voters might be feeling (see Shepherd, 2018): "global warming" was thought to sound more troubling (e.g., like something from an apocalyptic science-fiction story) than "climate change" sounds. Reducing voters' concerns would reduce the likelihood that they might start adopting more sustainable ways of living that threatened the fossil fuel industry.

If people view being in control as a key aspect of being happy, they appear to have potential to become happier if they can increase their spending on means to achieving control. They will also become happier if they can switch to jobs that offer better opportunities for being in control and/or for buying means to making events easier to predict and control. But they might be able to become happier if they could negotiate to work fewer hours in their present jobs and cut their spending in line with their reduced income. They may be able to become happier while reducing their expenditure on goods and services, and their environmental impacts, if they can change how they live by following strategies such as the following:

(a) *Change the sources of stimuli in their lives.*

For example, switch to using public broadcasters' television and radio channels that do not have a commercial interest in making viewers anxious as a means to keep them tuning in to discover areas to avoid and ways of keeping in control.

(b) *Routinely look with more determination for reasons to be cheerful and hopeful.*

If events confound their hopes and expectations, they should: attempt to identify lessons from what happened, to enhance their capacities for predicting and controlling events; look for upsides to what has happened; and consider why the disappointment in question might "not matter anyway." (From this positive psychology perspective, the tendency to resolve the cognitive dissonance associated with disappointment by employ a "sour grapes" way of downplaying the significance of what one has failed to attain might be viewed as a resilience-enhancing habit of thought that has become part of human nature via evolutionary selection processes.)

(c) *Change the ways that they view social status.*

It is common for people to assign superior status to those who have more senior, better-paying jobs and higher consumption levels than themselves. They look up to these people and assume they would be happier if they had higher social status. Hence, they set about achieving status via job promotions, career moves and conspicuous consumption, and they feel unhappy if they fail to ascend the status ladder. Social well-being would be much better if such people recognized that – just as in Barnard's (1938) analysis of the firm, where executive authority is granted by lower-level operatives rather than coming automatically via the position that the executive holds – *they* are the ones who are granting superior social status to those they seek to emulate. Given this, they should be able to make themselves happier by taking a different view of who deserves to be viewed as of higher status than themselves: this could be an effective means to reduce cognitive dissonance arising from the gap between where they see themselves in society and where they would prefer to be.

Such a view could be based on whether a person appears to deserve respect because of the things they do and how they go about doing them, on the obstacles they had to overcome to get where they are, on the things that they have to tolerate or contend with as a result of the position they occupy, and so on. On this basis, a corporate lawyer such as William may not seem to be the kind of person one should or would want to be, and his house and other trophies from his legal and transaction-making capabilities may seem to symbolize moral shortcomings. We might also view him as very dull and as a rather poor parent due to his "all work, no play" puritan way of operating. However, at least he does not court the pity that some might accord to those who try to draw attention to their earning power or wealth by driving around noisily in a Ferrari, Porsche or suchlike vehicles, unaware that some of their audiences are construing these cars as phallic symbols that are intended to compensate for their owners' shortcomings in that area. (As my partner observed, a man driving a Tesla Model 3 that has a Sakura pink wrap would surely have a bigger chance that onlookers would have no doubts about his manhood. Moreover, they would not be likely to view him with the disdain they might have felt if he were driving a similarly priced BMW that they viewed as the sort of car that a drug dealer or obnoxiously pushy young professional might drive.)

Those who adopt a virtue-based view of status and operate in a congruent manner should be able, without reducing their happiness, to rein in their pursuit of higher-tier jobs and items of conspicuous consumption that have normally been viewed as signifiers of one's social status and importance for how the economic and social system functions. They will also find it easier to avoid getting depressed if it starts appearing that they now "have a bright future behind them." (For further analysis of the long-term dynamics of personal happiness, see Rauch, 2018.) If a virtue-based view of status became widespread, the rich would be more likely to feel uncomfortable about how they were seen if they engaged in conspicuous consumption rather than philanthropy. Meanwhile, the less well off would be more likely to vote for redistributive policies: those who are keen to avoid damaging the world that their children will inherit and who feel contempt for the superrich and harbor no hope of getting as far as possible down the track to joining them, should have no reason to support neoconservative policies.

(d) *Choose products and activities that have potential to provide "flow" experiences with minimal environmental consequences.*

Time spent having "flow" experiences can be, and often is, time that is free of worries about where we stand in terms of social status or how others see us, for we are too engrossed in processing a flood of exciting stimuli. For example, we may be caught up in the "thrill of the chase," discovering fascinating new things by using our problem-solving skills to reveal our family history or may be "in the zone" performing a challenging task that we are confident we can complete successfully (such as playing music, cooking an unfamiliar recipe or riding on a mountain bike track). Ideally, people should engage in "flow"-rich activities that have minimal per-minute environmental impacts and help them toward self-actualization and develop their capacities to predict and control events. Something as mundane as, say, time spent catching up with a friend over coffee, without having to keep watching the time, could come into this category so long as its impact on well-being is not compromised due to the conversation turning into a "gripe-fest" and/or toward status-related issues.

Clearly, it is possible to choose to do things both for their prospective "flow" experiences while doing them and for the bragging rights and status that comes from having dared to do them and having survived the experience. High-excitement tourism experiences epitomize the "flow-with-status" phenomenon but often are of very short duration and in some cases entail very high rates of energy consumption (as with, say, jet-boat rides), as well as potentially inciting others to take retaliatory measures in the war for status. Much more desirable, in terms of personal, social and environmental well-being are flow-generating activities such as gardening, reading a book that one "can't put down" or getting sucked into following a succession of links on Wikipedia or suggestions on YouTube from which one emerges with extra knowledge but wondering where the last few hours had gone.

(e) *Choose products that have potential to be reused in a creative manner.*

Leisure activities can be chosen mindful of whether they involve purchasing products that only have a one-time or fixed-function role. For the price of a ticket to a live show that will leave me with bragging rights but only incomplete memories of the performance, I might instead purchase a music notation app such as Guitar Pro that will enable me to spend as many hours as I can muster, year after year, writing music scores (and probably enjoying "flow" as I do so) and hearing digital renditions of how they sound.

These creative, open-ended types of consumption may not only offer us better value than single-use products and be more fulfilling than those that we consume passively; they may also get in the way of shopping and spending on other things that have bigger environmental impacts. But because they entail active involvement without instructions to take us to a particular result, their uptake may be impeded by anxiety about whether we will have what it takes to end up with outcomes that will bolster out self-esteem. If we can get over fears that we will end up merely confirming our limitations, sunk cost bias may help to keep us engaged. The challenge for producers of these kinds of products is to design them so that they enable us to develop our creative skills via a learning-by-doing process that initially entails producing a defined result by following a set of instructions.

Lego provides an interesting case here, having morphed from offering packs of building blocks for design-it-yourself use by children to offering increasingly complex and expensive kits designed to appeal even to adults. Such kits could appeal to, say, affluent retirees who have time on their hands (as was the case with an old friend of mine whose extensive international tourism plans were wrecked in 2020 by pandemic-related travel restrictions). Working up the Lego range to more and more elaborate projects offers potential to develop the confidence required to graduate to the stage of conceiving one's own major Lego projects using building blocks obtained by demolishing the models that were built from the kits. There are also lessons here for parents considering presents for their children. If a toy cannot be used creatively, it is unlikely to engage the child repeatedly; indeed, parents who ignore this proposition risk suffering the disappointment of seeing that the child finds it more attractive to play creatively with the packaging than the toy it contained.

The notion that the scale and form of non-physiological needs, aspirations and means of satisfying them are not "given" applies also to the need for self-actualization. Rather than being "born" to have a particular self to actualize, a person's ideal-self is a personal construct, as are the means for actualizing it. The ideal-self constructs that people form seem likely to depend on the role models to which people are exposed and the experiences they have had, rather than being created out of nowhere. If so, there is potential for educational and cultural policies to provide ideas about what one might strive to be and to provide settings in which it is possible to acquire the capabilities necessary for making it a reality – or, at least, for having fulfilling experiences in going some way in the idealized direction and being able to arrive at a revised ideal-self that seems more realistic rather than suffering endless frustration.

The ability to construct a feasible vision of one's target self is clearly an area where many people lack the necessary capabilities, as is evidenced by how lost people can become when they retire after decades of having much more limited control over how they spend their days. This capability problem is going to become more widespread as the application of robotics and artificial intelligence technologies puts more and people in situations where they cannot absorb themselves so much in paid work due either to fewer hours or days being worked each week or to technological unemployment. The scale of the problem will be bigger the more that output growth is reined in to make economic activity more environmentally sustainable. Policymakers would be wise to try to ensure people develop the capacity to come up with workable and eco-friendly answers to the question, "What do I *really* want to do?" Failure to foster such capabilities will lead to widespread boredom and discontent and increased risks that, as Keynes (1930) foresaw, the dysfunctional aspects of the elite leisure class will befall the wider population. There needs to be more to life than killing time indoors by passively watching Netflix, fueled by alcohol and drugs, or engaging in active outdoor pursuits at the expense of other species.

In short, this section's view of happiness bodes well for the possibility that people could learn to be happier while simultaneously having smaller environmental impacts. Aside from the issue of how to prevent vested interests from using spin and shock tactics to distort how people see the world, the main policy challenge is to overcome the impermeability of the personal construct systems of those whose lifestyles are far from eco-friendly. The difficulties that some people have in coming up with their own positive perspectives should be less of a concern, for external suppliers of ideas (such as those who work as "motivational speakers" and writers of "self-improvement" books) might be used to boost such capacities. Those with construct systems in which even small changes carry major implications about the entire system's functionality are not going to be willing to engage with a presentation that seeks to supply them with an entire new system that offers them, and the planet, a better future. Opening their minds without causing them anxiety requires a foot-in the-door or step-by-step process that begins with something that will engage their attention with positive prospects that are available from a single change that happens to have environmental benefits and nothing to which they can object.

If there are some downsides to adopting a more sustainable lifestyle, the key to people being able to look happily toward the future is that they keep thinking about the upsides and are diverted from dwelling on what they have to give up. From the standpoint of Hayek's *Sensory Order*, nostalgic thinking needs to be seen as an inhibitor of brain plasticity, thereby inhibiting the firming up of new habits of thought and habituating to areas in which it is necessary but not difficult to make sacrifices to achieve sustainability.

13.6   Alternative Ways of Influencing Lifestyle Meso Trajectories

The micro–meso–macro framework provides a clear way of appreciating the process of transitioning to a sustainable economic future. It invites us to view materialistic lifestyles and green lifestyles as meso rules whose trajectories policymakers can attempt to influence by designing systems of rules, incentives, nudges and boosts. It remains to be seen whether they will be able to exercise enough influence in time to prevent human activities from degrading Earth's ecosystems so much that they become cumulatively and irreversibly unable to serve even the basic needs of humanity, let alone bring a halt to human-induced extinctions of other species. The policy challenge is not merely to induce existing adherents to the materialistic meso to adopt the green meso; it also entails finding ways of diverting consumers in newly industrializing economics (NICs) into green lifestyles instead of using the fruits of their rising productivity as means of adopting materialistic lifestyles that their counterparts in advanced industrial economies have long enjoyed.

To a conventional economist, the path to changing consumer lifestyles in more sustainable directions entails using taxes to adjust the relative prices of different types of products so that they properly reflect differences in environmental costs. For example, if taxes on vehicle fuels are increased, thirsty vehicles will arrive more rapidly at the point where no one aside from a scrap dealer is prepared to purchase them, due to their annual operating costs exceeding the total annual amount that anyone is prepared to pay for the combined capital and operating costs of motoring in a vehicle of the quality in question. Likewise, property taxes can be used to limit urban sprawl and reduce per-capita emissions from heating and air-conditioning by making large single-household residences more expensive to live in, leading them to be converted into apartments or demolished and replaced by higher-density property complexes.

Clearly, there can be merit in such tax- or price-based policies. However, given the urgency of the need to rein in adverse human impacts on the environment, we need to be mindful of their limitations. One issue is that if redistributive income tax changes are not implemented, too, it may be politically difficult to maintain support for policies that increase sharply the prices of things that are commonly viewed as essentials. If compensating income tax cuts and increases in social welfare payments are not offered to poorer consumers, sharp increases in unit costs of, say, residential water and vehicle fuels might have their impacts on usage mainly via poor consumers being unable to expand their spending in these areas, while the rich mainly continued watering their lawns, topping up their swimming pools and driving their gas-guzzling status symbol vehicles as if nothing had happened. The rich might simply maintain their consumption in the face of reductions in their real incomes by reducing their rates of saving (cf. the "relative income hypothesis" analysis of the consumption function proposed by Duesenberry, 1949). For equity reasons, and to sidestep the risk that tax- or price-based policies may have disappointingly meager impacts on demand, it may be wiser to use quantity-based policies – such as consumption limits for water that are based on household size, and vehicle emissions standards – heretical though this may seem to orthodox economists and libertarians.

From the standpoint of behavioral economics, policies that impose new constraints have benefits that go beyond their ability to ensure equity (much as with rationing of basic items during wartime, as discussed in Keynes, 1940) and in better guaranteeing that targets will be met: if it is impossible to get around such policies by trading consumption rights with others, there is an incentive to engage in creative problem-solving to find innovative ways of reducing consumption. This is essentially how vehicle emission standards and product recycling standards work: instead of merely offering a fallible incentive for manufacturers to raise their game, the policy forces them to innovate. However, the "ways" by which problem-generating policies are addressed may not necessarily entail investing in new technologies; in some cases, all that may be necessary is a change in one's consumption routines, such as saving water by showering rather than taking a bath.

We also need to be mindful that orthodox economic thinking arrives at tax- or price-based environmental policies via theories that presume consumers engage in constrained optimization in terms of fixed preferences whose form ensures they always "have their price" if presented with policies aimed at inducing substitution. From such a perspective, we would view William and Melissa, and Jude and Emma, as behaving differently due to having different preference orderings. We would accept that "they are as they are" but nonetheless presume that by engineering appropriate changes to relative prices (and possibly also by increasing income taxes), we can induce William and Melissa to behave like Jude or Emma except insofar as the former couple are constrained because they have children and pets. (Of course, if they thought like an "econ," they could happily sell their pets or terminate their pets' lives if they faced a set of relative prices that made such actions optimal.)

However, from our behavioral standpoint, the lifestyles in the two vignettes should not be viewed "as if" they are based on immutable preferences. Rather, these lifestyles are driven by the goals and operating principles that these consumers use to make sense of the world and cope with life. These goals and principles preclude some forms of substitution. If all options clash with some of the principles, the preferred option will be one that allows the consumer to avoid violating their principles in order of priority. Thus, if a woman like our imaginary Emma ultimately decides, with her reproductive clock close to the point of no return, that the principle of trying to be as green as possible is less important than the goal to have a family, then she will push ahead with trying to have the desired family and only be as green as is possible given the primacy of having the family.

As well as differing in their choices in relation to environmental sustainability because they rank goals and principles differently, consumers may also behave differently because they differ in their aspiration levels for particular goals and in the sets of goals they pursue. Materialistic consumers like William and Melissa may thus not even have a goal "to do the right thing for the environment so long as it does not preclude meeting higher-level goals," and a real-world Jude may simply have had no desire to have children rather than feeling that he had to abandon that desire in order to conform to his lexicographic green principle. It could even be possible that when Jude used his green principle as the basis for ending his relationship with Emma, his "real reason" was that he had a very strong desire *not* to become a father, that had other foundations (such as the expected loss of control it would entail), with this aversion to parenthood merely being amplified by concerns about adding to population pressures.

If lifestyle differences are seen as reflecting differences in principles, goals, priorities and aspirations, rather than differences in immutable preferences, the challenge for policymakers is – in line with the analysis in Section 13.5 – to devise ways to promote changes in these areas conducive to more environmentally sustainable behavior. In other words, the task is to ensure that consumers reprogram their minds in ways that result in them being (more) environmentally mindful, changing their priorities about what matters for a fulfilling life, and moderating their resource-hungry aspirations.

It is going to be difficult to do this if attention from the desired audience is in short supply and if it cannot be quickly argued, in ways admissible to the audience's existing rule systems, that nothing of significance has to be given up or that the benefits to them of pro-environment changes are so great as to overcome tendencies toward loss aversion. If we accept Hayek's *Sensory Order* analysis of cognition, it is evident that more environmentally sustainable mindsets will be easier to achieve in totalitarian countries where media are under state control and can be used as means for brainwashing the population by bombarding them with stimuli designed to crowd out materialistic ways of thinking. I am not advocating that democracies should go down that kind of road, but it is not hard to envisage them ending up there if individuals are too slow to change themselves and if gentler nudges and boosts fail to generate enough of a speeding up of the adoption of the green meso to prevent ecological disaster.

Even if one has time to discuss issues carefully (for example, if people with different operating systems are talking at a dinner party or other kind of social function), it may prove difficult to win over, or even merely to plant the seeds for later reflection and change in the minds of smart, well-educated materialists like William and Melissa if the changes in question clash with core constructs. In such situations, we may find that, rather than viewing the discussion as an opportunity for getting a clearer picture of why others behave differently and possibly discovering important implications for themselves, they treat it as an occasion for demonstrating their skills in arguing that there is nothing particularly wrong with how they live and that others should aspire to live as they do. In other words, because their general operating mode is essentially transactional, their attention becomes focused not on what they might learn for longer-term benefit but on winning the current joust by doing whatever it takes rhetorically for the other side to back away. These kinds of people may thus be no easier to enlighten than those who lack their brains and education and who deal with challenges simply by refusing to engage with opponents and/or by taking a libertarian stance and saying that they should be free to spend their money as they wish.

Such considerations may initially seem merely to reinforce the orthodox economist's perspective by implying that it may be impossible to use complex, evidence-based reasoning to induce people to change their minds in significant ways. Certainly, the chances of "boost"-style policies succeeding in promoting more sustainable behavior seem to be far greater within school- and college-age segments of the population who are keen to enhance their cognitive operating systems, than with mature adults who have long since created systems that they view as generally serving them well. However, other ideas from our behavioral toolbox imply that policymakers should neither simply accept that "people are what they are" nor only focus, as orthodox economists would do, on trying to use changes in relative prices to drive behavior in environmentally sustainable directions.

Consider again the relevance of Hayek's (1952) *Sensory Order* in this context. Despite my comments about its implications in relation to brainwashing, Hayek's view of the mind does provide a basis for expecting that more and more people in democratic societies will switch to more sustainable lifestyles in the long run, even in the absence of drastic taxes on environmentally harmful products and even if people commonly choose largely by following what they view to be the norms and rules of their social reference groups. As we have seen, Hayek's analysis predicts that what will come to mind as the normal thing that "someone like me" should do in a particular situation is a probabilistic function of both the cumulative and recent recall rates of stored memories about behavior in that context. Hence, if people increasingly have to process stimuli associated with "people like me" who engage in more sustainable forms of consumption, the chances of such behavior coming to mind as normal for "people like me" will increase, too. This will be the case regardless of whether "people like me" have been trying to "do the right thing" or have simply been doing, for other reasons, things that reduce environmental impacts.

If virtually no one on my reference group behaves in a green manner, the chances that I will think of doing so will be near to zero, but the probability of me thinking in this way will rise as others whom I view as "like me" adopt the green meso, so long as the rules of my personal construct system do not require me to reconstrue the adopters as "no longer like me." If the adopters continue to seem "like me" in other respects, any thoughts that perhaps they are no longer "like me" will tend to get crowded out by all the other instances of them behaving "like me" that will tend to come to mind. Thereby, I may evolve through time from seeing materialistic choices as the sole norm for people like me, to a pluralistic view whereby people like me can display aspects of being both materialistic and applying green principles, through to viewing green principles as the only acceptable basis for my behavior.

Via this sort of process, those who never view themselves as anything but normal for their social group may come to be horrified if they reflect on the ways in which they and their peers used to behave, despite having seen nothing wrong with it "back then." So, just as society has been able to evolve toward being free of norms such as smoking, racism, sexism and homophobia, so we may expect that people will become increasingly open to following those who in most respects seem normal but who are prepared to experiment by pioneering or becoming early adopters of green alternatives to driving SUVs, 4WDs and light trucks, having pets and (more than two) children, flying overseas for their vacations and aspiring to live in entry-level McMansions, and so on. The prerequisites for this to happen will be the availability of affordable green options and that green alternatives are not tainted by being associated purely with those who are seen as weird, fanatical or of low social standing.

The transition toward more sustainable lifestyles may thus be speeded up where the following conditions apply:

(a) *Where pioneering eco-friendly products can readily be justified on other, perfectly "normal" grounds and do not seem to involve any "abnormal" sacrifices.*

The electric cars offered by Tesla are exemplars of this, for they can appeal to those who want an attention-grabbing luxury product that delivers in terms of performance, styling and self-drive capabilities, without suffering from an unacceptably small range. By contrast, the original Toyota Prius and Honda Impact hybrid petrol-electric cars were doomed to be little more than "proof of concept" products and real-world reliability test beds for their respective manufacturers. Unlike the hybrid versions of "normal" models that Toyota and Honda later came to offer, these vehicles had many limitations relative to "normal" cars, so buying one signaled determination to be green, regardless of the downsides. Indeed, the first hybrid petrol-electric cars needed to be offered as unique models in order to make it harder to compare them with "normal" cars due to the cost penalties of early hybrid power systems and their smaller fuel savings compared with those achieved by later generations of the technology.

(b) *Where products that are both appropriate in environmental terms and feasible for mass-market adoption are adopted by those that are viewed as fashion leaders and are supported, where necessary, via the emergence of institutions that facilitate and promote adoption and use (i.e., the emergence of a market for preferences and a user commons).*

For example, switching to "trashion" and "op-shopping" and away from "fast fashion" clothing and other goods that are produced cheaply by being designed to last for only one season would be both appropriate and feasible for mass-market consumers, even if the switch were led by celebrities. The creative repurposing of pre-owned products obtained cheaply via op-shopping or as giveaway items via community social networking sites may then be facilitated via exemplars posted on interest-group websites, as with the Facebook page "I Love to Op-Shop." By contrast, consider what we should expect to result from celebrities receiving publicity for adopting luxury electric vehicles and from the showcasing, via television programs, of "grand designs" of one-off eco-homes commissioned by rich consumers with seemingly unlimited capacities to succumb to pressures for cost escalation. Even if such cases of conspicuous consumption point the way to a greener future, they will do little to foster more eco-friendly consumption in these areas unless down-market equivalents or, at least, affordable "halfway-house" products are available. In the absence of such products, the supply of information about the high-end versions is more akin to a form of consumption pornography than a market institution, though perhaps it may prompt entrepreneurs to consider trying to supply products that make the technologies affordable by the masses.

(c) *Where events take place that truncate materialistic meso trajectories by serving as "wake-up calls" that lead people to question behavioral norms.*

When considered together, Hayek's (1952) *Sensory Order* and Kelly's (1955) *Psychology of Personal Constructs* are useful tools for understanding how an event can trigger an enduring rethink of our way of life. For an event to have such an impact, it must be seen, *from the standpoint of our existing system of constructs* to have such a dramatic set of implications for our ability to predict and control events that we cannot stop thinking about the need to find a new operating system for coping with life until we find one that looks like it could be good enough. Events that we find distressing but whose flows of distressing stimuli soon dry up will be less likely to have such an impact: the return to normality will enable us to return to making sense of the world using memories stored prior to them. Hence, despite the flurry of concern when they happened, they will gradually get crowded out by the cumulative impact of other memories on what comes to mind when we think about how we should behave and view the world.

So what kinds of events will be dramatic enough to arrest the attentive capacity of the population at large and serve as wake-up calls in relation to the environment? At the very least, they need to be events whose *possible* connections with human behavior cannot be denied outright by the rules that the bulk of the population use for making sense of the world. If events threaten erstwhile outright climate-change deniers *to the core of their construct systems*, we might see them shift from a position of outright denial to skepticism, which then opens them up to acting via the precautionary principle that it is worth trying to limit greenhouse gas emissions in case they are indeed responsible for the type of event that has been experienced. Concern about long-term personal physical survival may trump, say, fears about one's ability to cope with the implications of pro-environment policy changes or having to lose face due to shifting one's political stance (for example, away from having been a devotee of former US president Donald Trump).

Events that have this capacity probably need to entail types of misfortunes that both befall and can, to some degree, potentially be attributed to the behavior of "people like me." This should ensure that they generate sympathy toward the victims as well as feeling of guilt about possibly contributing to such events and anxiety that one might someday suffer in a similar manner. Such events also need to be problematic to explain away without recourse to arguments that seem ad hoc, implausibly tortuous and/or purely self-serving. This does not necessarily require that ordinary people in general need habitually to operate in a deeply analytical manner. Rather, it merely requires the presence of some respected critical thinkers within groups of ordinary people or among those, such as journalists, to whom ordinary people outsource ways of interpreting events and who are capable of understanding flaws in arguments put forward by those who deny the significance of the event in question.

For example, suppose the dramatic events are bushfires that are encroaching on urban areas and which are being argued to result from drier climates that are being generated by global warming. Resistance to making costly changes toward lifestyles with lower emissions might seem reasonable to ordinary people in Australia if journalists allow politicians to get away with arguing (as members of the Liberal–National Coalition government argued repeatedly during the writing of this book) that "Our greenhouse gas emissions account for a tiny fraction of world emissions, so any reduction in our emissions is not going to make a significant difference to climate change." Such an argument works via the attention-diverting methods that we considered in Section 9.6. Ordinary consumers generally see journalists reporting this view without seeing them having made any attempt to ask these politicians to comment on the suggestion, "On a per-capita basis, we are among the worst contributors to global warming despite also being among the best endowed for achieving reductions in our emissions, so isn't it the case that a failure to 'do our bit' is self-serving and morally reprehensible? This country did not opt out of standing up to fascism in World War II because of our small population relative to the nations that Hitler sought to invade, or because of our distance from them; we did the right thing then, so should we not do the right thing now in relation to climate change?" A critical mode of reporting such as this may be difficult for journalists to practice without breaking conventions about the duration of sound bites in news reports. However, we may wonder whether some of them do not even go so far as trying to think critically about what they are being told, let alone reflect on their moral duties as journalists to prevent the medium from dictating the message they send out to their audiences.

To the extent that mindlessness is impeding switches to more environmentally sustainable products and lifestyles, policymakers who wish to promote such changes may seem best advised to focus on two kinds of measures. One is to accept that decisions may be driven by what Kahneman (2011) calls System 1 thinking and then to try to work out how to require choice architectures to be designed to nudge people in the desired direction. For example, electricity utility companies might be required to make their "green power" options (i.e., those with carbon offsets) to be presented as the default setting for prospective customers so that an opt-out would be necessary to take the nongreen offers. (However, the offsets in question will also need to be credible: see Spash, 2010, for a critique of reliance on carbon offsets.) The other approach is to try to drive consumers into more reflective and analytical System 2 styles of thinking and present greener options for them to consider. Nudges may be tools here, too, not merely to steer consumers to question whether they could be doing better but also to provide targets at which they might aim. Regulations that require white goods, electronics products and motor vehicles to be displayed with official energy consumption figures and star ratings are designed both to prod prospective buyers to include the energy-consumption dimension in their decision rules and to remove the need to search for the relevant information.

Water and electricity utilities frequently employ mindfulness-inducing strategies rather than simply trying to use higher prices to rein in consumption and reduce their need to create additional capacity. They do this by including in their billing documents information about how the recent period's consumption compares with previous periods and with local norms for various household sizes. This information may then be viewed by some customers as a signal that they need to be more careful about their usage, if previously they were doing better or if others with similar-size households are doing better than they are. But utility companies have generally failed to try to reduce usage rates by the kind of application of "foot-in-the-door" (minimal justification) psychology used in experiments by Katzev and Johnson (1983, 1984) in which energy conservation outcomes were compared for treatment groups that differed in whether they had initially only been asked to complete an energy conservation questionnaire, whether they were asked to reduce their energy use by a target amount and whether they were given a financial incentive to reduce their energy consumption by the target amount. Katzev and Johnson found that while the groups given the conservation target did on average reduce their consumption relative to the control group, the group with the biggest proportion of energy conservers was the one that was initially only asked to complete the questionnaire, and that the incentivized group did not perform better. Energy companies thus might be able to reduce demand on their systems, without having to offer any incentives to their customers, if they first run a similar kind of survey or ask customers to keep energy-use diaries to learn their energy-use patterns through time and then invite them to try to meet energy conservation targets that are gradually ramped up. Clearly, such a strategy might include "boost" aspects in the form of newsletters about the energy savings available from the latest generation of household appliances.

Strategies aimed at promoting more environmentally responsible behavior by making people mindful of their own behavior in relation to environmental issues need to be designed mindful of the likelihood of backsliding. The problem here is that System 1 thinking happens not just as a result of System 2 being lazy but as a result of cognitive overload and exhaustion. Being green requires discipline, which is unlikely unless green operating principles are part of System 1 as well as System 2. Thus, although Katzev and Johnson (1983, p. 282) report that a follow-up study showed that energy conservation continued among their subjects after their twelve-week experiment ended, we should not be surprised to observe backsliding where new policies are not implemented for long enough for new habits of action and thinking to be developed to the point where myelination takes place along the relevant neural pathways. If backsliding from eco-friendly behavior is to be avoided, consumers need to be as alert to the possibility of such behavior as, say, a person with coeliac disease needs to be to food that may contain gluten. This is a tall order, given the finite attentive capacity of real-world decision-makers, especially in social environments in which the norm is not to concentrate on pro-environment behavior. If, unlike Jude, we have not established firm green principles, it is easy to lapse from what we have been trying to do and end up on a slippery slope under pressure from peers or when short of attentive capacity and the time needed to explore the implications of what we do.

An important role for policymakers may therefore be that of supplying specific new routines (such as those for "How to make the most of rooftop solar photovoltaic power systems") that are easily adopted by the target audience, rather than just concentrating on advocating a particular generic kind of behavior (such as "Buy a rooftop solar photovoltaic system month-by-month on your power bill") and dispelling myths and popular misconceptions about its costs and benefits. Such routines might, of course, be supplied in conjunction with simple messages aimed at promoting the uptake of domestic renewable energy technologies (such as "Rooftop solar systems have fallen in price so much that usually they now pay for themselves in only X years").

13.7   Systems That Make It Easier to Reduce Environmental Impacts

Before concluding this chapter (and the book as a whole), it is important to note that the complex systems view that we have frequently employed in earlier chapters can be very helpful for understanding what may need to be done in order for human impacts on the natural environment to be reduced. For example, if people really do need to travel, their choices of travel mode may be shaped by systems issues rather than being simply a function of relative prices. Those who are using non-compensatory decision rules may view systems that have lower environmental impacts as having "fatal flaws," as in the following cases:

- A "soccer mom" may find it logistically impossible to get her children to their various after-school activities on time by public transport, due to the timetabling of the bus routes. (Due to overweighting low-probability events, she may also be unduly anxious about letting her children walk to school and/or the activities on their own.)
- A manager who likes the idea of cycling from home in suburbia to work in the city on both environmental and health grounds may nonetheless continue to commute by car because of fears about safety associated with the aggressive behavior of cyclists that he views as "Lycra louts" or "Tour de France wannabes" and having to contend with some difficult intersections in heavy traffic on the parts of the journey that are not on cycleways. He also does not want to feel that he is terrorizing his wife with the prospect that he could have a serious accident. Cycling to work is also problematic in terms of being professionally presented and groomed after arriving, since there are no shower facilities at his workplace and compulsory helmets generate "hat hair" issues. Moreover, unlike his academic friends who keep their bicycles in their offices, there is no secure place for him to keep his bicycle during office hours. His alternatives to commuting by car are problematic, too: his suburb is poorly served by buses, and the railway station is a half-hour walk from home.

If he drives to the station to get a train that would get him the rest of the way to work at the right time, the parking spaces are invariably already taken, whereas he can park readily in his firm's car park if he drives all the way to work.

In these kinds of situations, it may take a change of system design for people to change their transport mode choices. In other words, policy measures may need to include changes in road design and lighting, to improve perceived safety, installing workplace showers and secure bicycle storage, addressing "missing link" problems with cycleways, and so on. Change may be hard to engineer where resistance results from a cultural issue that produces antipathy between different users of the system. However, problematic cultural norms may evolve in ways that cumulatively promote the desired change in transport choices as other issues are addressed: for example, the more that cycling becomes widespread as a means of getting around (as in, say, Denmark) rather than mainly undertaken as a fitness activity by those whose risk tolerance also results in them paying little attention to road rules, the more that mutual respect will develop between cyclists and other road users and the safer and more attractive cycling will become.

Of course, to a conventional economist, the way to tip such choices in more environmentally friendly directions would be to change relative prices, such as by taxing parking spaces and introducing bigger fines for the drivers of vehicles who drive too close to cyclists. But if systems-related issues affect choices (that are made via compensatory decision rules) or are decisive (when non-compensatory decision rules are being used), policymakers may be wise to consider using rules to interfere with the functionality of systems that are relatively costly in environmental terms. For example, consider a policy of trying to reduce motor vehicle use in city centers by regulations that reduce the number of public and privately provided parking spaces. This will impose greater search costs for finding parking spaces, but if prices of public parking are not increased, the outcome may be more equitable than what might be achieved via a policy of taxing private parking and raising public parking fees without restricting the number of spaces. A quantity-restricting policy can limit the extent to which the well paid can simply carry on doing what they do so long as they pay for the privilege. If such a policy makes parking "too unpredictable" for senior staff, it may serve as a prompt to introduce or lobby for measures that will enhance the functionality of more environmentally friendly systems. The bosses may not actually switch to such systems, but to the extent that the improvements encourage their subordinates to do so, the former's parking difficulties may diminish.

13.8   Conclusion

This final chapter could have been a short wrap-up summary of the ground covered in earlier chapters rather than a lengthy attempt to apply ideas from earlier chapters to the economics of environmental or ecological sustainability. The decision to offer the latter was partly a consequence of reflecting on *After the Warming*, an apocalyptic futuristic climate-change documentary, made by the broadcaster and science historian James Burke in 1989. The date is not a mistake: it really was aired that long ago, and that is what makes it so disturbing to watch. I had been unaware of it until the mid-2010s when I came across it on YouTube when looking for some of Burke's other films. It presents his distillation of the history and science of climate change and explores, from the standpoint of his vision of 2050, solutions that he imagined might be adopted in the battle to halt global warming. Much of his scenario was remarkably prescient, but Burke inevitably misjudged the trajectories of many of the technological and political changes that he canvassed, and he completely overlooked some that we might now view as "on the horizon."

One of the things that Burke got wrong makes his film especially chilling to watch in the 2020s but is easy to understand from the perspective of this book. This error was his estimate of how long it would take before politicians accepted warnings from the scientific community and put in place a set of institutions to rein in climate change. (He envisaged a global body to manage a system of tradeable greenhouse gas emission permits, allocated to nations according to their populations, not their per-capita incomes.) Burke called the period 1980–2000 "the two lost decades," but he envisaged world leaders coming to their senses by 2000, the year by which he also imagined people would have given up eating meat. In his view, 2000 was tragically late for dealing with the environmental consequences of economic growth. Clearly, despite his prodigious historical knowledge of the evolution of science and technology, Burke was an optimistic pessimist when it came to anticipating how rapidly people would accept the need to change to avert a looming disaster – in contrast to their adaptability when faced with a here-and-now crisis (as evidenced during the Covid-19 pandemic).

The answer that this chapter has offered to the question that its title posed is that we can, *in principle*, be happy without destroying the environment that supports us, but that ensuring that this happens could be a tall order for policymakers in democratic societies, since it necessitates major changes in how most people look at the world. Policies that entail "nudging" people to behave differently will have a role to play, but they will need to be accompanied by a much more dramatic set of paternalistic interventions, educational "boosts" and redistributive policies than libertarian conservative politicians are likely to find palatable. There is a very real risk that people will fail to vote for politicians who have enough vision of what needs to be done. Hence, there is the risk that, like firms that have gone out of business due to the inability of their managers to see that they needed to change their business models (as with the cases in Schoenberger, 1997), humanity will inflict an irreversible environmental disaster on itself as a result of too few people adopting the green meso soon enough. The plasticity of the human brain gives us the potential to change voluntarily to – and to enjoy – sustainable lifestyles, but it does not guarantee that we will do so before it is too late. Looking back, I can see myself as adapting far more slowly than I should have done. Despite floating some of the ideas from this chapter in earlier work (Earl and Wakeley, 2009; Earl, 2017a), it was only after the first couple of chapters of this book had been written that the computer used for writing it came to be powered via rooftop solar panels, with a further two years elapsing before the household car became even a petrol-electric hybrid. Most of us can readily do better at being green, without making ourselves miserable.

This chapter has been much closer in its style to the work of Veblen than to that of modern behavioral economists such as Thaler. But we owe much to Thaler for the way he used trivial examples from everyday life to win support for a behavioral approach to economics. He would have been ignored if he had tried to question the assumed rationality of decision-makers by offering a critique of materialistic lifestyles and proposing that there should be paternalistic efforts to make consumers more mindful of the consequences of, and alternatives to, following social norms. But with Thaler and others having got a "foot in the door" for behavioral economics via a modest approach that was politically acceptable, the path may be more open to the uptake of a wider-ranging and more radical behavioral economics meso of the kind proposed in this book. At the very least, I hope this book provides a thought-provoking answer to those who have looked at modern work built around prospect theory and decision-making seen as compromised by "heuristics and biases" and have asked themselves, "Is that all there is to behavioral economics?"

References

Abolafia, M. Y. (1996). *Making Markets: Opportunism and Restraint on Wall Street.* Cambridge, MA: Harvard University Press.

Abolafia, M. Y. (1998). Markets as cultures: An ethnographic approach. *Sociological Review*, *46*(May), 69–85.

Ackley, G. (1961). *Macroeconomics Theory*. New York: Collier Macmillan.

Adams, T. F. N., & Kobayashi, N. (1969). *The World of Japanese Business*. London: Ward Lock.

Ainslie, G. (1992). *Picoeconomics: The Strategic Interaction of Successive Motivational States within the Person*. Cambridge: Cambridge University Press.

Aitken, S. (Writer/Director). (2010). *Seduction in the City: The Birth of Shopping*. Sydney: Essential Media & Entertainment Pty. Ltd., Screen Australia, ARTE, Screen NSW, and Tel France Ltd.

Akerlof, G. A. (1970). The market for "lemons": Quality uncertainty and the market mechanism. *Quarterly Journal of Economics*, *84*(3), 486–500.

Akerlof, G. A., & Dickens, W. T. (1982). The economic consequences of cognitive dissonance. *American Economic Review*, *72*(3), 307–319.

Akerlof, G. A., & Kranton, R. E. (2000). Economics and identity. *Quarterly Journal of Economics*, *115*(3, August), 715–753.

Akerlof, G. A., & Kranton, R. E. (2010). *Identity Economics: How Our Identities Shape Our Work, Wages, and Well-Being*. Princeton, NJ: Princeton University Press.

Akerlof, G. A., & Shiller, R. J (2009). *Animal Spirits: How Human Psychology Drives the Economy, and Why It Matters for Global Capitalism*. Princeton, NJ: Princeton University Press.

Akerlof, G. A., & Shiller, R. J. (2015). *Phishing for Phools: The Economics of Manipulation and Deception*. Princeton, NJ, and Oxford: Princeton University Press.

Akerlof, G. A., & Yellen, J. L. (Eds.). (1986). *Efficiency Wage Models of the Labor Market*. Cambridge: Cambridge University Press.

Alchian, A. (1950). Uncertainty, evolution, and economic theory. *Journal of Political Economy*, *58*(3, June), 211–221.

Alchian, A. (1969). Information costs, pricing, and resource unemployment. *Western Economic Journal (Economic Inquiry)*, *7*(2), 109–128.

Aldred, J. (2012). Climate change uncertainty, irreversibility and the precautionary principle. *Cambridge Journal of Economics*, *36*(5), 1051–1072.

Aliber, R. Z., & Kindleberger, C. P. (2015). *Manias, Panics and Crashes: A History of Financial Crises* (7th ed.). Basingstoke: Palgrave.

American Psychiatric Association. (1980). *Diagnostic and Statistical Manual of Mental Disorders (DSM–III)* (3rd ed.). Washington, DC: American Psychiatric Association.

Ames, A. (1952). *The Ames Demonstrations in Perception*. New York: Hafner Publishing.

Anand, P. (1982). How to be right without being rational (the von Neumann & Morgenstern way). *Oxford Agrarian Studies*, *11*(1), 158–172.

Anderton, P. (2020). The Captain Meets His Dad – The History of Andertons Music Co (L. Anderton, Interviewer). Video interview, March 29, 2020, YouTube. www.youtube.com/watch?v=MjT1XD0tKW0

Andreozzi, L., & Bianchi, M. (2007). Fashion: Why people like it and theorists do not. In M. Bianchi (Ed.), *The Evolution of Consumption: Theories and Practices*. Advances in Austrian Economics, Volume 10 (pp. 209–229). Oxford: Elsevier.

Andrews, P. W. S. (1949). *Manufacturing Business*. London: Macmillan.

Andrews, P. W. S. (1964). *On Competition in Economic Theory*. London: Macmillan.

Andrews, P. W. S. (1993). *The Economics of Competitive Enterprise: Selected Essays of P. W. S. Andrews* (F. S. Lee and P. E. Earl, Eds.). Aldershot: Edward Elgar.

Andrews, P. W. S., & Brunner, E (1975). *Studies in Pricing*. London: Macmillan.

Ansoff, H. I. (1965). *Corporate Strategy: An Analytic Approach to Business Policy for Growth and Expansion*. New York: McGraw-Hill.

Aoki, M., Gustafson, B., & Williamson, O. E. (Eds.). (1990). *The Firm as a Nexus of Treaties*. London: Sage.

Ariely, D. (2008). *Predictably Irrational: The Hidden Forces That Shape Our Decisions*. New York: HarperCollins.

Arnould, E. J., & Price, L. L. (1993). River magic: Extraordinary experiences and the extended service encounter. *Journal of Consumer Research*, *20*(1, June), 24–45.

Arrow, K. J. (1962). Economic welfare and the allocation of resources for invention. In Universities-National Bureau Committee for Economic Research and Committee on Economic Growth of the Social Science Research Council (Eds.), *The Rate and Direction of Inventive Activity: Economic and Social Factors* (pp. 609–626). Princeton, NJ: National Bureau of Economic Research.

Augier, M., & March, J. G. (2008). Realism and comprehension in economics: A footnote to an exchange between Oliver E. Williamson and Herbert A. Simon. *Journal of Economic Behavior & Organization*, *66*(1), 95–105.

Baddeley, M. (2010). Herding, social influence and economic decision-making: Socio-psychological and neuroscientific analyses. *Philosophical Transactions: Biological Sciences*, *365* (1538, January 27), 281–290.

Baddeley, M. (2013). *Behavioural Economics and Finance*. London and New York: Routledge.

Bain, A. D. (1964). *The Growth of Television Ownership in the United Kingdom since the War: A Lognormal Model*. University of Cambridge, Department of Applied Economics Monographs, No. 12. Cambridge: Cambridge University Press.

Bannister, D., & Fransella, F. (1971). *Inquiring Man: The Theory of Personal Constructs*. Harmondsworth: Penguin Books.

Barberis, N. C. (2013). Thirty years of prospect theory in economics: A review and assessment. *Journal of Economic Perspectives*, *27*(1, Winter), 173–196.

Barley, S. R. (2015). Why the Internet makes buying a car less loathsome: How technology changes role relations. *Academy of Management Discoveries*, *1*(1), 31–60.

Barnard, C. I. (1938). *The Functions of the Executive*. Cambridge, MA: Harvard University Press.

Baumeister, R. F. (2014). Self-regulation, ego-depletion, and inhibition. *Neuropsychologia*, *65* (December), 313–319.

Baumeister, R. F., Bratslavsky, E., Muraven, M., & Tice, D. M. (1998). Ego depletion: Is the active self a limited resource? *Journal of Personality and Social Psychology*, *74*(5), 1252–1265.

Baumeister, R. F., Sparks, E. A., & Stillman, T. F. (2008). Free will in consumer behavior: Self-control, ego depletion, and choice. *Journal of Consumer Psychology*, *18*(1), 4–13.

Baumol, W. J. (1959). *Business Behavior, Value and Growth*. New York: Macmillan.

Baumol, W. J., Panzar, J., & Willig, R. (1982). *Contestable Markets and the Theory of Industrial Structure*. New York: Harcourt Brace Jovanovich.

Baumol, W. J., & Quandt, R. E. (1964). Rules of thumb and optimally imperfect decisions. *American Economic Review*, *54*(2, March), 23–46.

Bausor, R. (1982). Time and the structure of economic analysis. *Journal of Post Keynesian Economics*, *5*(Winter), 163–179.

Bausor, R. (1984). Towards a historically dynamic economics: Examples and illustrations. *Journal of Post Keynesian Economics*, *6*(Spring), 360–376.

Becker, G. S., & Murphy, K. (1988). A theory of rational addiction. *Journal of Political Economy*, *96*(4), 675–700.

Beckert, J. (2020). Markets from meaning: Quality uncertainty and the intersubjective construction of value. *Cambridge Journal of Economics*, *44*(2, March), 285–301.

Beiser, V. (2018). *The World in a Grain: The Story of Sand and How It Transformed Civilization*. New York: Riverhead Books/Penguin Random House.

Belsky, G., & Gilovich, T. (1999). *Why Smart People Make Big Money Mistakes and How to Avoid Them*. New York: Simon & Schuster.

Benartzi, S., & Thaler, R. H. (2007). Heuristics and biases in retirement planning. *Journal of Economic Perspectives*, *21*(3, Summer), 81–104.

Berg, N., & Gigerenzer, G. (2010). As-if behavioral economics: Neoclassical economics in disguise? *History of Economic Ideas*, *18*(1), 133–166.

Berger, L. A. (1989). Economics and hermeneutics. *Economics and Philosophy*, *5*(2, October), 209–234.

Berle, A. A., & Means, G. C. (1932). *The Modern Corporation and Private Property*. New York: Macmillan.

Berne, E. (1964). *Games People Play: The Psychology of Human Relationships*. Harmondsworth: Penguin Books.

Bernstein, C., & Woodward, B. (1974). *All the President's Men*. New York: Simon & Schuster.

Bertrand, M., Mullanathan, S., & Shafir, E. (2004). A behavioral-economics view of poverty. *American Economic Review*, *94*(2, May), 419–423.

Bettman, J. R. (1979). *An Information-Processing Theory of Consumer Choice*. Reading, MA: Addison-Wesley.

Bezemer, D. J. (2009). "No one saw this coming": Understanding financial crisis through accounting models. MPRA Paper No. 15892. Available online at https://mpra.ub.uni-muenchen.de/15892/

Bianchi, M. (Ed.) (1998). *The Active Consumer: Novelty and Surprise in Consumer Choice*. London and New York: Routledge.

Bianchi, M., & Patalano, R. (2017). *Storytelling and Choice*. Rounded Globe eBook. Retrieved from https://roundedglobe.com/books/ad46e83f-b971–4a96–8efc-662855976998/Storytelling%20and%20Choice/

Bikhchandani, S., Hirshleifer, D., & Welch, I. (1992). A theory of fads, fashion, custom and cultural change. *Journal of Political Economy*, *100*(5), 992–1026.

Blatt, J. M. (1979). The utility of being hanged on the gallows. *Journal of Post Keynesian Economics*, 2(2), 231–239.

Block, L. G. (1999). Fear appeal and persuasion. In P. E. Earl & S. Kemp (Eds.), *The Elgar Companion to Consumer Research and Economic Psychology* (pp. 239–246). Cheltenham: Edward Elgar.

Blois, K. J. (1972). Vertical quasi-integration. *Journal of Industrial Economics*, 20(3, July), 253–272.

Boland, L. A. (1986). *Methodology for a New Microeconomics: The Critical Foundations*. Boston, MA: Allen & Unwin.

Borg, L. (2001). Jeans leap ahead as the "Jeremy Clarkson effect" fades. *The Daily Telegraph*, 12 April. Available online at www.telegraph.co.uk/news/uknews/1315886/Jeans-leap-ahead-as-Jeremy-Clarkson-effect-fades.html

Bradbury, R. ([1953] 1977). A sound of thunder. In R. Bradbury, *Golden Apples of the Sun* (pp. 88–99). St Albans: Granada (originally published 1953, London: Rupert Hart-Davis).

Brooks, R. (2011). *Sex, Genes and Rock 'n' Roll: How Evolution Has Shaped the Modern World*. Sydney: University of New South Wales Press.

Bruni, L. (Ed.) (2021). *A Modern Guide to the Economics of Happiness*. Cheltenham: Edward Elgar.

Burke, J. (Writer). (1989). After the Warming. Maryland Public Television/Film Australia/ Wisemans/Electric Image/Principal Film Company.

Burnham, T. C., & Phelps, J. (2019). Ordinaries: Thomas Kuhn, Adam Smith, and Charles Darwin. *Journal of Bioeconomics*, 21(3, October), 145–155.

Burns, T., & Stalker, G. M. (1961). *The Management of Innovation*. London: Tavistock Publications.

Butos, W. N. (Ed.) (2010). *The Social Sciences of Hayek's 'The Sensory Order.'* Advances in Austrian Economics, Volume 13. Bingley: Emerald.

Cairncross, A. K. (1958). Economic schizophrenia. *Scottish Journal of Political Economy*, 5(1, February), 15–21.

Camerer, C., Babcock, L., Lowenstein, G., & Thaler, R. H. (1997). Labor supply of New York cabdrivers: One day at a time. *Quarterly Journal of Economics*, 112(2, May), 407–440.

Camerer, C., Issacharoff, S., Lowenstein, G., O'Donoghue, T., & Rabin, M. (2003). Regulation for conservatives: Behavioral economics and the case for "asymmetric paternalism." *University of Pennsylvania Law Review*, 151(3), 1211–1254.

Camerer, C., & Vepsalainen, A. (1988). The economic efficiency of corporate culture. *Strategic Management Journal*, 9(Summer), 115–126.

Cameron, S., & Golby, D. (1990). An economic analysis of personal debt. *Bulletin of Economic Research*, 42(3, July), 241–247.

Carlson, S. (1951). *Executive Behaviour*. Stockholm: Stromberg.

Carter, C. F. (1953). A revised theory of expectations. *Economic Journal*, 63(252, December), 811–820.

Cartwright, E. (2014). *Behavioral Economics* (2nd ed.). Abingdon and New York: Routledge.

Catmull, E. (2014). *Creativity, Inc*. New York: Random House.

Celsi, R. L., Rose, R. L., & Leigh, T. W. (1993). An exploration of high-risk leisure consumption through skydiving. *Journal of Consumer Research*, 20(1, June), 1–23.

Chabris, C., & Simons, D. (2010). *The Invisible Gorilla: How Our Intuitions Deceive Us*. New York: Crown Publishers/Random House.

Chai, A., Earl, P. E., & Potts, J. (2007). Fashion, growth and welfare: An evolutionary approach. In M. Bianchi (Ed.), *The Evolution of Consumption: Theories and Practices*. Advances in Austrian Economics, Volume 10 (pp. 187–207). Oxford: Elsevier.

Chandler, A. D. (1962). *Strategy and Structure: Chapters in the History of the American Industrial Enterprise*. Cambridge, MA: MIT Press.

Chandler, A. D. (1977). *The Visible Hand: The Managerial Revolution in American Business*. Cambridge, MA: Belknap Press/Harvard University Press.

Chandler, A. D. (1990). *Scale and Scope: The Dynamics of Industrial Capitalism*. Cambridge, MA: Belknap Press/Harvard University Press.

Chang, H.-J. (2010). *23 Things They Don't Tell You About Capitalism*. London: Penguin Books.

Chase, W. G., & Simon, H. A. (1973). Perception in chess. *Cognitive Psychology, 4*(1, January), 55–81.

Choi, Y. B. (1993). *Paradigms and Conventions: Uncertainty, Decision Making and Entrepreneurship*. Ann Arbor: University of Michigan Press.

Christandl, F., & Fetchenhauer, D. (2009). How laypeople and experts misperceive the effect of economic growth. *Journal of Economic Psychology, 30*(3), 381–392.

Christensen, C. (1997). *The Innovator's Dilemma: When New Technologies Cause Great Firms to Fail*. Boston, MA: Harvard Business Review Press.

Cialdini, R. B. (1984). *Influence: The Psychology of Persuasion*. New York: William Morrow & Company.

Cialdini, R. B. (2009). *Influence: Science and Practice* (5th ed.). Boston, MA: Pearson Education.

Cialdini, R. B. (Writer). (2014). *The Power of Persuasion (Stanfor Business Breakfast Presentation)*. San Francisco, CA: Kanopy Streaming.

Clydesdale, G. (2021). *Reducing Inter-generational Ethnic Poverty: Economics, Psychology and Culture*. Abingdon and New York: Routledge.

Coase, R. H. (1937). The nature of the firm. *Economica (New Series), 4*(16, November), 386–405.

Coddington, A. (1976). Keynesian economics: The search for first principles. *Journal of Economics Literature, 14*(4, December), 1258–1273.

Coddington, A. (1982). Deficient foresight: A troublesome theme in Keynesian economics. *American Economics Review, 72*(3, June), 480–487.

Coelli, T., Rao, D. S. P., O'Donnell, C. J., & Battese, G. E. (2005). *An Introduction to Efficiency and Productivity Analysis* (2nd ed.). New York: Springer.

Cohen, J. L., & Dickens, W. T. (2002). A foundation for behavioral economics. *American Economic Review, 92*(2), 335–338.

Cohen, M. D., March, J. G., & Olsen, J. P. (1972). A garbage can model of organizational choice. *Administrative Sciences Quarterly, 17*(1, March), 1–25.

Cooper, R. A., Hartley, K., & Harvey, C. R. M. (1970). *Export Performance and the Pressure of Demand: A Study of Firms*. London: Allen & Unwin (Reprinted 2018 London: Routledge).

Cosmides, L., & Tooby, J. (1994). Better than rational: Evolutionary psychology and the invisible hand. *American Economic Review Papers and Proceedings, 84*(2), 327–332.

Coutts, K., Godley, W., & Nordhaus, W. (1978). *Industrial Pricing in the United Kingdom*. University of Cambridge, Department of Applied Economics, Monograph 26. Cambridge: Cambridge University Press.

Cripps, F., & Godley, W. (1978). Control over imports as a means to full employment and the expansion of world trade: The UK's case. *Cambridge Journal of Economics, 2*(3, September), 327–334.

Csibra, G., & Gergely, G. (2011). Natural pedagogy as an evolutionary adaptation. *Philosophical Transactions of the Royal Society (B)*, *366*, 1149–1157.

Csikszentmihalyi, M. (1990). *Flow: The Psychology of Optimal Experience*. New York: Harper & Row.

Cunningham, M. T., & White, J. G. (1974). The behaviour of industrial buyers in their search for supplier of machine tools. *Journal of Management Studies*, *11*(May), 115–128.

Cyert, R. M., Feigenbaum, E. A., & March, J. G. (1959). Models in a behavioral theory of the firm. *Behavioral Science*, *4*(2, April), 81–96.

Cyert, R. M., & March, J. G. (1955). Organizational structure and pricing behavior in an oligopoly. *American Economic Review*, *45*(1, March), 129–139.

Cyert, R. M., & March, J. G. (1956). Organizational factors in the theory of oligopoly. *Quarterly Journal of Economics*, *70*(1, February), 44–64.

Cyert, R. M., & March, J. G. (1963). *A Behavioral Theory of the Firm*. Englewood Cliffs, NJ: Prentice-Hall (2nd ed. 1992, Malden, MA and Oxford: Blackwell).

Daly, J., Mercer, D., & Kuang, W. (2021). Is the dream over? Amid China's trade war, producers grapple with new world order. *ABC Rural News*, 16 May. Australian Broadcasting Corporation. Available online at www.abc.net.au/news/rural/2021-05-17/after-12-months-of-the-trade-war-is-the-china-dream-over/100127874

Daly, M. T. (1982). *Sydney Boom, Sydney Bust: The City and Its Property Market, 1854–1981*. Sydney: Allen & Unwin.

Damasio, A. (1994). *Descartes' Error: Emotion, Reason, and the Human Brain*. New York: Putnam.

Darby, M. R., & Karni, E. (1973). Free competition and the optimal amount of fraud. *Journal of Law & Economics*, *16*(1, April), 67–88.

Davies. J. E., & Lee, F. S. (1988). A post Keynesian appraisal of the contestability criterion. *Journal of Post Keynesian Economics*, *11*(1, Autumn), 3–25.

Day, R. H. (1967). Profits, learning and the convergence of satisficing to marginalism. *Quarterly Journal of Economics*, *81*(2), 302–311.

de Montaigne, M. ([1533–1592] 1963). *Essays and Selected Writings* (bilingual edition, translated and edited by D. M. Frame). New York: St Martin's.

De Vany, A. (2004). *Hollywood Economics: How Extreme Uncertainty Shapes the Film Industry*. London and New York: Routledge.

DellaVigna, S., & Malmedier, U. (2004). Contract design and self-control: Theory and evidence. *Quarterly Journal of Economics*, *119*(2, May), 353–402.

DellaVigna, S., & Malmedier, U. (2006). Paying not to go to the gym. *American Economic Review*, *96*(3), 694–719.

DeRiviere, L. (2008). Do economists need to rethink their approaches to modeling intimate partner violence? *Journal of Economic Issues*, *42*(3, September), 583–606.

DeVoe, C. (2019). Dentists with Alembics. *Steve Hoffman's Music Forums*, https://forums.stevehoffman.tv/threads/dentists-with-alembics.887394/

Dewey, J. (1910). *How We Think*. New York: D. C. Heath.

Dhami, S. (2016). *The Foundations of Behavioral Economics*. Oxford: Oxford University Press.

Diderot, D. (1775–1777). Regrets sur ma vieille robe de chambre [Regrets on my old dressing gown]. In J. Assézat & M. Tourneux (Eds.), *Miscellanea Philosophiques* (pp. 5–12). Paris: Garnier (via Wikisource).

Dittmar, H. (1992). *The Social Psychology of Material Possessions: To Have is to Be*. Hemel Hempstead: Harvester Wheatsheaf.

Doidge, N. (2007). *The Brain that Changes Itself: Stories of Personal Triumph from the Frontiers of Brain Science*. New York: Viking Penguin.

Dopfer, K. (2012). The origins of meso economics. *Journal of Evolutionary Economics*, 22(1), 133–160.

Dopfer, K., Foster, J., & Potts, J. (2004). Micro-meso-macro. *Journal of Evolutionary Economics*, 14(3), 263–279.

Dore, R. P. (1973). *British Factory, Japanese Factory: The Origins of National Diversity in Industrial Relations*. Berkeley and Los Angeles: University of California Press.

Dore, R. P. (2012). *Flexible Rigidities: Industrial Policy and Structural Adjustment in the Japanese Economy, 1970–1980*. London: Bloomsbury.

Dow, A., & Dow, S. C. (2011). Animal spirits revisited. *Capitalism and Society*, 6(2), Article 1, 25. Available online at https://papers.ssrn.com/sol23/papers.cfm?abstract_id=2208040

Dow, S. C. (2013). Formalism, rationality, and evidence: The case of behavioural economics. *Erasmus Journal for Philosophy and Economics*, 6(3, Special Issue), 26–43.

Dow, S. C. (2014). Animal spirits and organization. *Journal of Post Keynesian Economics*, 37(2), 211–231.

Dow, S. C., & Earl, P. E. (1982). *Money Matters: A Keynesian Approach to Monetary Economics*. Oxford: Martin Robertson.

Downie, J. (1958). *The Competitive Process*. London: Duckworth.

Drakopoulos, S. A. (1994). Hierarchical choice in economics. *Journal of Economic Surveys*, 8(2), 133–153.

Drakopoulos, S. A., & Karayiannis, A. D. (2004). The historical development of hierarchical behavior in economic thought. *Journal of the History of Economic Thought*, 26(3), 363–378.

Duesenberry, J. S. (1949). *Income, Saving and the Theory of Consumer Behavior*. Cambridge, MA: Harvard University Press.

Duggan, V. (2018). "That's insane... did they guarantee everything?": Reliving the night of the bank bailout. *The Journal*, 30 September. Available online at www.thejournal.ie/readme/night-of-the-bank-guarantee-4258897-Sep2018/

Duhen, P. M. M. (1906). *The Aim and Structure of Physical Theory*. (Translated by P. Weiner.) Princeton, NJ: Princeton University Press.

Dunn, S. P. (2000). Fundamental uncertainty and the firm in the long run. *Review of Political Economy*, 12(4), 419–433

Dutton, D. (2003). Aesthetics and evolution. In J. Levinson (Ed.), *The Oxford Handbook of Aesthetics* (pp. 693–705). New York: Oxford University Press.

Eagleman, D., & Brandt, A. (2017). *The Runaway Species: How Human Creativity Remakes the World*. Edinburgh: Canongate.

Earl, P. E. (1983a). A behavioral theory of economists' behavior. In A. S. Eichner (Ed.), *Why Economics is Not Yet a Science* (pp. 90–125). Armonk, NY: M. E. Sharpe (London: Macmillan).

Earl, P. E. (1983b). The consumer in his/her social setting: A subjectivist view. In J. Wiseman (Ed.), *Beyond Positive Economics?* (pp. 176–191). London: Macmillan.

Earl, P. E. (1983c). *The Economic Imagination: Towards a Behavioral Analysis of Choice*. Brighton: Wheatsheaf.

Earl, P. E. (1984). *The Corporate Imagination: How Big Companies Make Mistakes*. Brighton: Wheatsheaf.

Earl, P. E. (1986a). A behavioural analysis of demand elasticities. *Journal of Economic Studies*, *13*(3), 20–37.

Earl, P. E. (1986b). *Lifestyle Economics: Consumer Behaviour in a Turbulent World*. Brighton: Wheatsheaf.

Earl, P. E. (Ed.) (1988). *Behavioural Economics*. Aldershot: Edward Elgar.

Earl, P. E. (1990). *Monetary Scenarios: A Modern Approach to Financial System*. Aldershot: Edward Elgar.

Earl, P. E. (1992). On the complementarity of economic applications of cognitive dissonance theory and personal construct psychology. In S. E. G. Lea, P. Webley, & B. Young (Eds.), *New Directions in Economic Psychology* (pp. 49–65). Aldershot: Edward Elgar.

Earl, P. E. (1995). *Microeconomics for Business and Marketing: Lectures, Cases and Worked Essays*. Aldershot: Edward Elgar.

Earl, P. E. (1996). Contracts, coordination, and the construction industry. In P. E. Earl (Ed.), *Management, Marketing, and the Competitive Process* (pp. 149–171). Cheltenham: Edward Elgart.

Earl, P. E. (2001). Simon's Travel Theorem and the demand for live music. *Journal of Economic Psychology*, *22*(3, June), 335–358.

Earl, P. E. (2002). *Information, Opportunism and Economic Coordination*. Cheltenham: Edward Elgar.

Earl, P. E. (2003). The entrepreneur as a constructor of connections. In R. Koppl (Ed.), *Austrian Economics and Entrepreneurial Studies*. Advances in Austrian Economics, Volume 6 (pp. 113–130). Oxford: Elsevier.

Earl, P. E. (2009). Update on censorship of critique of emissions trading schemes. *Eclectic Real-World Economics*. Posted 6 December, at https://shredecon.wordpress.com/2009/12/06/update-on-censorship-of-critique-of-emssions-trading-schemes/

Earl, P. E. (2011). From anecdotes to novels: Reflective inputs for behavioural economic. *New Zealand Economic Papers*, *45*(1/2), 5–22.

Earl, P. E. (2012). Experiential analysis of automotive consumption. *Journal of Business Research*, *65*(7, July), 1067–1072.

Earl, P. E. (2013). The robot, the party animal and the philosopher: An evolutionary perspective on deliberation and preference. *Cambridge Journal of Economics*, *37*(6, November), 1263–1282.

Earl, P. E. (2017a). Lifestyle changes and the lifestyle selection process. *Journal of Bioeconomics*, *19*(1, April), 97–114.

Earl, P. E. (2017b). The evolution of behavioural economics. In R. Frantz, S.-H. Chen, K. Dopfer, F. Heukelom, & S. Mousavi (Eds.), *Routledge Handbook of Behavioral Economics* (pp. 5–17). London and New York: Routledge.

Earl, P. E. (2018). Richard H. Thaler: A Nobel prize for behavioural economics. *Review of Political Economy*, *30*(2), 107–125.

Earl, P. E. (2020a). COVID-19 macroeconomics from the standpoint of Keynes's "How to Pay for the War." *Eclectic Real-World Economics*. Posted 21 March, at https://shredecon.wordpress.com/2020/03/21/covid-19-macroeconomics-from-the-standpoint-of-keyness-how-to-pay-for-the-war/

Earl, P. E. (2020b). Is it inevitable that macroeconomic stimulus packages "ultimately have to be paid for" after the COVID-19 recession is over? *Eclectic Real-World Economics*. Posted 6 August, at https://shredecon.wordpress.com/2020/08/06/is-it-inevitable-that-macroeconomic-stimulus-packages-ultimately-have-to-be-paid-for-after-the-covid-19-recession-is-over/

Earl, P. E., Friesen, L., & Shadforth, C. (2017). The efficiency of market-assisted choices: An experimental analysis of mobile phone connection service recommendations. *Journal of Institutional Economics*, *13*(4), 849–873.

Earl, P. E., Friesen, L., & Shadforth, C. (2019). Elusive optima: A process-tracing analysis of procedural rationality in mobile phone connection plan choices. *Journal of Economic Behavior & Organization*, *161*, 303–322.

Earl, P. E., & Glaister, K. W. ([1979] 1980). Wage stickiness from the demand side. University of Stirling Discussion Papers in Economics, Finance, and Investment, No. 78 [December 1979]. Slightly revised (1980) journal submission version available online at https://shredecon.files.wordpress.com/2021/01/earl-and-glaister-1980wage-stickiness.pdf

Earl, P. E., & Littleboy, B. (2014). *G. L. S. Shackle*. Basingstoke: Palgrave Macmillan.

Earl, P. E., & Peng, T.-C. (2012). Brands of economics and the Trojan horse of pluralism. *Review of Political Economy*, *24*(3, July), 451–467.

Earl, P. E., Peng, T.-C., & Potts, J. (2007). Decision rule cascades and the dynamics of speculative bubbles. *Journal of Economic Psychology*, *18*(3, June), 351–364.

Earl, P. E., & Potts, J. (2000). Latent demand and the browsing shopper. *Managerial and Decision Economics*, *21*(3–4), 11–22.

Earl, P. E., & Potts, J. (2004). The market for preferences. *Cambridge Journal of Economics*, *28*(4), 619–633.

Earl, P. E., & Potts, J. (2013). The creative instability hypothesis. *Journal of Cultural Economics*, *37*(2), 153–173.

Earl, P. E., & Potts, J. (2016). The management of creative vision and the economics of creative cycles. *Managerial and Decision Economics*, *37*(7, October), 474–484.

Earl, P. E., & Wakeley, T. (2005). *Business Economics: A Contemporary Approach*. Maidenhead: McGraw-Hill.

Earl, P. E., & Wakeley, T. (2009). Price-based versus standards-based approaches to reducing car addiction and other environmentally destructive activities. In R. P. F. Holt, S. Pressman, & C. L. Spash (Eds.), *Post Keynesian and Ecological Economics* (pp. 221–236). Cheltenham: Edward Elgar.

Earl, P. E., & Wakeley, T. (2010). Economic perspectives on the development of complex products for increasingly demanding customers. *Research Policy*, *39*(8, October), 1122–1132.

Earl, P. E., & Wicklund, R. A. (1999). Cognitive dissonance. In P. E. Earl & S. Kemp (Eds.), *The Elgar Companion to Consumer Research and Economic Psychology* (pp. 81–88). Cheltenham: Edward Elgar.

Easterlin, R. A. (1974). Does economic growth improve the human lot? Some empirical evidence. In P. A. David & M. W. Reder (Eds.), *Nations and Households in Economic Growth: Essays in Honor of Moses Abramovitz* (pp. 89–125). New York: Academic Press.

Easterlin, R. A. (1995). Will raising the incomes of all increase the happiness of all? *Journal of Economic Behavioor and Organization*, *27*(1), 35–47.

Easterlin, R. A. (Ed.) (2002). *Happiness in Economics*. Cheltenham: Edward Elgar.

Economist (2011). Burberry and globalization: A checkered story: Burberry's revival reflects the power of globalisation, and its limits', *The Economist*, 20 January. Available online at www.economist.com/node/17963363?story_id=17963363

Edwardes, M. (1983). *Back from the Brink*. London: Collins.

Ehrenberg, A., & Scriven, J. (1999). Brand loyalty. In P. E. Earl & S. Kemp (Eds.), *The Elgar Companion to Consumer Research and Economic Psychology* (pp. 52–63). Cheltenham: Edward Elgar.

Elster, J. (1983). *Sour Grapes: Studies in the Subversion of Rationality*. New York: Paris Cambridge University Press and Editions de la Maison des Sciences de l'Homme.

Elster, J. (1984). *Ulysses and the Sirens: Studies in Rationality and Irrationality* (rev. ed.). New York: Cambridge University Press; Paris: Editions de la Maison des Sciences de l'Homme.

Elster, J., & Lowenstein, G. (1992). Utility from memory and anticipation. In G. Lowenstein & J. Elster (Eds.), *Choice Over Time* (pp. 213–234). New York: Russell Sage Foundation.

Endres, A. M. (1991). Marshall's analysis of economising behaviour with particular reference to consumption. *European Economic Review*, *35*(2, April), 333–341.

Endres, A. M., & Harper, D. A. (2012). The kinetics of capital formation and economic organisation. *Cambridge Journal of Economics*, *36*(4), 963–980.

Endres, A. M., & Harper, D. A. (2020). Economic development and complexity: The role of recombinant capital. *Cambridge Journal of Economics*, *44*(1, January), 157–180.

Engel, J. F., Kollat, D. T., & Blackwell, R. D. (1968). *Consumer Behavior*. Hinsdale, IL: Dryden Press.

Ericsson, K. A., & Simon, H. A. (1993). *Protocol Analysis: Verbal Reports as Data* (rev. ed.). Cambridge, MA: MIT Press.

Esteves, P. S., & Rua, A. (2015). Is there a role for domestic demand pressure on export performance? *Empirical Economics*, *49*(4), 1173–1189.

Etzioni, A. (1988). *The Moral Dimension: Toward a New Economics*. New York: Free Press.

Fairlie, S. (2010). *Meat: A Benign Extravagance*. East Meon: Permanent Publications.

Fasolo, B., McClelland, G. H., & Todd, P. M. (2007). Escaping the tyranny of choice: When fewer attributes make choice easier. *Marketing Theory*, *7*(1), 13–26.

Fellner, W., , & Goehmann, B. (2020). Human needs, consumerism and welfare. *Cambridge Journal of Economics*, *44*(2), 303–318.

Ferguson, N., & Schularick, M. (2007). Chimerica and the global asset market boom. *International Finance*, *10*(3), 215–239.

Fernandez, K. V., & Lastovicka, J. L. (2011). Making magic: Fetishes in contemporary consumption. *Journal of Consumer Research*, *38*(2, August), 278–299.

Festinger, L. (1957). *A Theory of Cognitive Dissonance*. New York: Harper & Row.

Fishbein, M., & Ajzen, I. (1975). *Belief, Attitude, Intention, and Behavior*. Reading, MA: Addison-Wesley.

Foley, C. A. (1893). Fashion. *Economic Journal*, *3*(11, September), 458–474.

Foss, N. J. (Ed.) (1997). *Resources, Firms and Strategies: A Reader in the Resource-Based Perspective*. Oxford: Oxford University Press.

Foss, N. J., & Knudsen, C. (Eds.) (1996). *Towards a Competence theory of the Firm*. London: Routledge.

Foxall, G. (1990). *Consumer Psychology in Behavioural Perspective*. London: Routledge.

Frank, E. (Director). (2016). *Victorian Slum [DVD]*. UK: Dazzler Media (DVD)/Amazon Instant View.

Frank, R. H. (2007). Does context matter more for some goods than others? In M. Bianchi (Ed.), *The Evolution of Consumption: Theories and Practices*. Advances in Austrian Economics, Volume 10 (pp. 231–248). Amsterdam: Elsevier.

Frankel, M. (1955). Obsolescence and technical change in maturing economies. *American Economic Review*, *45*(June), 296–319.

Frantz, R., & Leeson, R. (Eds.) (2013). *Hayek and Behavioral Economics*. Basingstoke: Palgrave Macmillan.

Friedman, M. (1953). The methodology of positive economics. In M. Friedman (Ed.), *Essays in Positive Economics* (pp. 3–43). Chicago, IL: University of Chicago Press.

Friedman, T. L. (1999). *The Lexus and the Olive Tree: Understanding Globalization*. London: HarperCollins.

Friesen, L., & Earl, P. E. (2015). Multipart tariffs and bounded rationality: An experimental analysis of mobile phone plan choices. *Journal of Economic Behavior & Organization, 116* (August), 239–253.

Friesen, L., & Earl, P. E. (2020). An experimental analysis of regulatory interventions for complex pricing. *Southern Economic Journal, 86*(3), 1241–1266.

Friston, K. (2010). The free-energy principle: A unified brain theory? *Nature Reviews Neuroscience, 11*(2), 127–138.

Frost, R. O., & Stekatee, G. (2010). *Stuff: Compulsive Hoarding and the Meaning of Things*. Boston, MA and New York: Houghton Mifflin Harcourt.

Fry, A., & Silver, S. (2010). First person: We invented the post-it note. *FT Magazine*, 3 December. Available at www.ft.com/cms/s/2/f08e8a9a-fcd7-11df-ae2d-00144feab49a .html#axzz18hyDnyKX

Fullbrook, E. (1998). Caroline Foley and the theory of intersubjective demand. *Journal of Economic Issues, 32*(3), 709–731.

Gabaix, X., & Laibson, D. (2006). Shrouded attributes: Consumer myopia, and information suppression in competitive markets. *Quarterly Journal of Economics, 121*(2, May), 505–540.

Gabor, A., & Granger, C. W. J. (1966). Price as an indicator of quality: Report on an enquiry. *Economica, 33*(129, February), 43–70.

Galbraith, J. K. (1958). *The Affluent Society*. London: Hamish Hamilton.

Garfinkel, H. (1967). *Studies in Ethnomethodology*. Engleood Cliffs, NJ: Prentice-Hall.

Genicot, A., & Ray, A. (2017). Aspirations and inequality. *Econometrica, 85*(2, March), 489–519.

Georgescu-Roegen, N. (1971). *The Entropy Law and the Economic Process*. Cambridge, MA: Harvard University Press.

Gigerenzer, G. (2015). On the supposed evidence for libertarian paternalism. *Review of Philosophy and Psychology, 6*(3, September), 361–383.

Gigerenzer, G., & Brighton, H. (2009). Homo Heuristicus: Why biased minds make better inferences. *Topics in Cognitive Sciences, I*(1), 107–143.

Gigerenzer, G., & Goldstein, D. G. (1996). Reasoning the fast and frugal way: Models of bounded rationality. *Psychological Review, 103*(4), 650–669.

Gigerenzer, G., Todd, P. M., & the ABC Research Group (1999). *Simple Heuristics that Make Us Smart*. New York: Oxford University Press.

Gilleard, C. (1999). McClelland hypothesis. In P. E. Earl & S. Kemp (Eds.), *The Elgar Companion to Consumer Research and Economic Psychology* (pp. 380–382). Cheltenham: Edward Elgar.

Gimpl, M. L., & Dakin, S. R. (1984). Management and magic. *California Management Review, 27*(1, October), 125–136.

Godley, W., & Lavoie, M. (2007). *Monetary Economics: An Integrated Approach to Credit, Money, Income, Production and Wealth*. Basingstoke: Palgrave.

Goldratt, E. (2004). *The Goal: A Process of Ongoing Improvment (Third Revised Edition)*. Great Barrington, MA: North Rivers Press.

Gomes-Casseres, B. (2009). NUMMI: What Toyota learned and GM didn't. *Harvard Business Review Blog*. Posted September 1 at https://hbr.org/2009/09/nummi-what-toyota-learne

Goodhart, C. A. E. (2008). Risk, uncertainty and financial stability (2nd G. L. S. Shackle biennial memorial lecture, St Edmund's College, Cambridge, 6 March. LSE Financial Markets Group Paper Series. London School of Economics. London. Available online at www.lse.ac.uk/fmg/assets/documents/papers/special-papers/SP178.pdf

Gould, S. J. (1991). The self-manipulation of my pervasive, perceived vital energy through product use: An introspective-praxis perspective. *Journal of Consumer Research, 18* (September), 194–207.

Gould, S. J. (1993). The circle of projection and introjection: An introspective investigation of a proposed paradigm involving the mind as a "consuming organ". In K. A. Costa & R. W. Belk (Eds.), *Research in Consumer Behavior* (pp. 185–230). Greenwich, CT: Association for Consumer Research.

Gould, S. J. (1995). Researcher introspection as a method in consumer research: Applications, issues and implications. *Journal of Consumer Research, 21*(Mach), 719–722.

Gouldner, A. W. (1954). *Patterns of Industrial Bureaucracy*. Glencoe, IL: Free Press.

Granovetter, M. (1985). Economic action and social structure: The problem of embeddedness. *American Journal of Sociology, 91*(3, November), 481–510.

Grant, A. T. K. (1977). *Economic Uncertainty and Financial Structure*. London: Macmillan.

Green, S. (1988). Understanding corporate culture and its relation to strategy. *International Studies of Managment & Organization, 18*(2, Summer), 6–28.

Griliches, Z. (1957). Hybrid corn: An exploration in the economics of technological change. *Econmetrica, 25*(4, October), 501–522.

Grimsdale, P. (Writer). (1990). *Nippon: Japan since 1945 (Part 5: Taking on Detroit)*. London: BBC.

Grove, A. S. (1996). *Only the Paranoid Survive*. New York: Doubleday Business.

Grüne-Yanoff, T., & Hertwig, R. (2016). Nudge versus Boost: How coherence are policy and theory? *Minds and Machines, 26*(1–2), 149–183.

Grubb, M. D. (2015). Failing to choose the best price: Theory, evidence and policy. *Review of Industrial Organization, 47*(3), 303–340.

Grupp, H., & Maital, S. (2001). *Managing New Product Development and Innovation: A Microeconomic Toolbox*. Cheltenham: Edward Elgar.

Güth, W., & Weiland, T. (2011). Aspiration formation and satisficing in search with(out) competition. *New Zealand Economic Papers, 45*(1–2, April–August), 23–45.

Gutman, J. (1982). A means–end chain model based on consumer categorization processes. *Journal of Marketing, 46*(2, Spring), 60–72.

Gutman, J., & Alden, S. D. (1985). Adolescents' cognitive structures of retail stores and fashion consumption: A means–end chain analysis of quality. In J. Jacoby & Olson, J. C. (Eds.), *Perceived Quality* (pp. 99–114). Lexington, MA: D. C. Heath (for New York University Institute of Retail Management)

Hall, R. L., & Hitch, C. J. (1939). Price theory and business behaviour. *Oxford Economic Papers, Old Series 2*(1), 12–45.

Hamilton, C. (2003). *Growth Fetish*. Crows Nest: Allen & Unwin.

Hanson, J. D., & Kysar, D. A. (1999a). Taking behavioralism seriously: The problem of market manipulation. *New York University Law Review, 74*(3), 630–749.

Hanson, J. D., & Kysar, D. A. (1999b). Taking behavioralism seriously: Some evidence of market manipulation. *Harvard Law Review, 112*(7, May), 1420–1572.

Hanson, P. G. (2013). *The Joy of Stress*. Atascadero, CA: Sressworks

Hare, P. (2010). *Vodka and Pickled Cabbage: Eastern European Travels of a Professional Economist*. London: Athena Press

Harper, D. A. (1996). *Entrepreneurship and the Market Process*. London and New York: Routledge.

Harper, D. A., & Earl, P. E. (1996). Growth of knowledge perspectives on business behaviour. In P. E. Earl (Ed.), *Management, Marketing and the Competitive Process* (pp. 306–328). Cheltenham: Edward Elgar.

Harper, D. A., & Endres, A. M. (2010). Capital as a layer cake: A systems approach to capital and its multi-level structure. *Journal of Economic Behavior & Organization, 74*(1), 30–41.

Harper, D. A., & Endres, A. M. (2012). The anatomy of emergence, with a focus upon capital formation. *Journal of Economic Behavior & Organization, 82*(2), 352–367.

Harper, D. A., & Endres, A. M. (2017). From Quaker Oats to Virgin Bridge: Brand capital as a complex adaptive system. *Journal of Institutional Economics, 14*(6, December), 1071–1096.

Harrigan, K. R. (1980). *Strategies for Declining Businesses*. Lexington, MA: Lexington Boos/ D.C. Heath.

Hart, N. (2013). *Alfred Marshall and Modern Economics*. Basingstoke: Palgrave Macmillan.

Harvey, J. T. (2006). Psychological and institutional forces and the determination of exchange rates. *Journal of Economics Issues, 40*(1), 153–170.

Harvey, J. T. (2009a). *Currencies, Capital Flows and Crises: A Post Keynesian Analysis of Exchange Rate Determination*. London and New York: Routledge.

Harvey, J. T. (2009b). Currency market participants' mental models and the collapse of the dollar 2001–2008. *Journal of Economic Issues, 43*(4), 931–949.

Hawtrey, R. G. (1926). *The Economic Problem*. London: Longmans, Green & Co.

Hayek, F. A. (1952). *The Sensory Order: An Inquiry into the Foundations of Theoretical Psychology*. Chicago, IL: University of Chicago Press.

Heath, C., & Heath, D. (2010). *Switch: How to Change Things When Change is Hard*. New York: Random House.

Heiner, R. A. (1983). The origin of predictable behavior. *American Economic Review, 73* (September), 560–595.

Heiner, R. A. (1986). The economics of information when decisions are imperfect. In A. J. MacFadyen & H. W. MacFadyen (Eds.), *Economic Psychology: Intersection in Theory and Application* (pp. 293–350). Amsterdam: North-Holland.

Hertwig, R. (2017). When to consider boosting: Some rules for policy-makers. *Behavioral Public Policy, 1*(3), 143–162.

Heukelom, F. (2014). *Behavioral Economics: A History*. Cambridge: Cambridge University Press.

Hey, J. D. (1982). Search for rules for search. *Journal of Economic Behavior & Organization, 3* (1), 65–81.

Hicks, J. R.(1935). Annual survey of economic theory: The theory of monopoly. *Econometrica, 2*(1, January).

Hicks, J. R. (1939). *Value and Capital*. Oxford: Clarendon Press.

Hicks, J. R. (1974). *The Crisis in Keynesian Economics*. Oxford: Basil Blackwell.

Hicks, J. R., & Allen, R. G. D. (1934a). A reconsideration of the theory of value (Part I). *Economica (New Series), 1*(1, February), 52–76.

Hicks, J. R., & Allen, R. G. D. (1934b). A reconsieration of the theory of value (Part II). *Economica (New Series), 1*(2, May), 196–219.

Hinkle, D. N. (2010 [1965]). The change of personal constructs from the viewpoint of a theory of construct implications. (PhD dissertation, Ohio State University, 1965). *Personal Construct Theory and Practice, 7*(Supp. No. 1), 1–61.

Hirsch, F. (1976). *Social Limits to Growth*. Cambridge, MA: Harvard University Press.

Hirschman, A. O. (1970). *Exit, Voice and Loyalty*. Cambridge, MA: Harvard University Press.

Hodgson, G. M. (1988). *Economics and Institutions: A Manifesto for a Modern Institutional Economics*. Cambridge: Polity Press.

Hodgson, G. M. (1994). Optimisation and evolution: Winter's critique of Friedman revisited. *Cambridge Journal of Economics, 18*(4, August), 413–439.

Hodgson, G. M. (1997). The ubiquity of habits and rules. *Cambridge Journal of Economics, 21* (6), 663–684.

Hodgson, G. M. (2003). The hidden persuaders: Institutions and individuals in economic theory. *Cambridge Journal of Economics, 27*(2), 159–175.

Hodgson, G. M. (2004). Opportunism is not the only reason why firms exist: Why an explanatory emphasis on opportunism may mislead management strategy. *Industrial and Corporate Change, 13*(2), 401–418.

Hodgson, G. M. (2010). Choice, habit and evolution. *Journal of Evolutionary Economics, 20* (1), 1–18.

Hofstadter, D. R. (1979). *Godel, Escher, Bach: An Eternll Golden Braid*. Hassocks, Sussex: Harvester Press.

Holbrook, M. B. (1995). *Consumer Research: Introspective Essays on the Study of Consumption*. Thousand Oaks, CA: Sage.

Holmes, P. M. (1978). *Industrial Pricing Behaviour and Devaluation*. London: Macmillan.

Horne, D. (1964). *The Lucky Country: Australia in the Sixties*. Ringwood, VIC: Penguin Books.

Hsiao, Y. C. (2018). An Experimental Investigation of the Secretary Problem: Factors Affecting Sequential Search. PhD dissertation, University of Canterbury.

Huising, R., & Silbey, S. (2018). From nudge to culture and back again: Coalface governance in the regulated organization. *Annual Review of Law and Social Sciences, 14*, 91–114.

Hutchison, T. W. (1938). *The Significance and Basic Postulates of Economics*. London: Macmillan (reprinted in 1965, New York: Augustus M. Kelley).

Hutchison, T. W. (1977a). *Keynes Versus the Keynesians …?: An Essay in the Thinking of J. M. Keynes and the Accuracy of its Interpretation by his Followers*. London: Institute of Economic Affairs.

Hutchison, T. W. (1977b). *Knowledge and Ignorance in Economics*. Oxford: Blackwell.

Ironmonger, D. S. (1972). *New Commodities and Consumer Behaviour*. Cambridge: Cambridge University Press.

Irving, J. (1978). P. W. S. Andrews and the Unsuccessful Revolution. Ph.D. dissertation, University of Wollongong, NSW.

Irving, J. L., & Feschback, S. (1954). Personality differences associated with responsiveness to fear-arousing communications. *Journal of Personality, 23*(2), 178–188.

Irwin, H. S. (1937). The nature of risk assumption in the trading on organized exchanges. *American Economic Review, 27*(2, June), 267–278.

Iyengar, S. S., & Lepper, M. R. (2000). When choice is demotivating: Can one desire too much of a good thing? *Journal of Personality and Social Psychology, 79*(6), 995–1006.

Jackson, D., Turner, H. A., & Wilkinson, F. (1972). *Do Trade Unions Cause Inflation?* University of Cambridge Department of Applied Economics Occasional Paper 36. Cambridge: Cambridge University Press.

Jacobsen, L. (2017). P. W. S. Andrews' Manufacturing Business reconsidered. *Review of Political Economy, 29*(2), 190–208.

Jefferson, M. (1983). Economic uncertainty and business decision-making. In J. Wiseman (Ed.), *Beyond Positive Economics? Proceedings of Section F (Economics) of the British Association for the Advancement of Science, York 1981* (pp. 132–159). London: Macmillan.

Jefferson, M. (2012). Shell scenarios: What really happened in the 1970s and what may be learned for current world prospects. *Technological Forecasting and Social Change, 79*, 186–197.

Jefferson, M. (2014). The passage of time: Shackle, Shell and scenarios. In P. E. Earl & B. Littleboy (Eds.), *G. L. S. Shackle (Great Thinkers in Economics)* (pp. 190–214). Basingstoke: Palagrave Macmillan.

Jevons, W. S. (1905). *Essays on Economics*. London: Macmillan.

Jolls, C., Sunstein, C. R., & Thaler, R. H. (1998). A behavioral approach to law and economics. *Stanford Law Review, 50*, 1471–1550.

Jones, J. M., & Jetten, J. (2011). Recovering from strain and enduring pain: Multiple group memberships promote resilience in the face of physical challenges. *Social Psychology and Personality Science, 2*(3), 239–244.

Kahneman, D. (2011). *Thinking, Fast and Slow*. New York: Farrar, Strauss & Giroux.

Kahneman, D., Knetsch, J. L., & Thaler, R. H. (1986). Fairness as a constraint on profit seeking entitlements in the market. *American Economic Review, 76*(4, September), 728–741.

Kahneman, D., Knetsch, J. L., & Thaler, R. H. (1990). Experimental tests of the endowment effect and the Coase theorem. *Journal of Political Economy, 98*(6), 1325–1348.

Kahneman, D., Knetsch, J. L & Thaler, R. H. (1991). Anomalies: The endowment effect, loss aversion and status quo bias. *Journal of Economic Perspectives, 5*(1m Winter), 193–206.

Kahneman, D., & Tversky, A. (1972). Subjective probability: A judgment of representativeness. *Cognitive Psychology, 3*(3), 430–454.

Kahneman, D., & Tversky, A. (1979). Prospect theory: An analysis of decision under risk. *Econometrica, 47*(2), 263–291.

Kaldor, N. (1955). *An Expenditure Tax*. London: George Allen & Unwin.

Kamstra, M., Kramer, L., & Levi, M. (2002). Winter Blues: A SAD Stock Market Cycle. Working Paper. Federal Reserve Bank of Atlanta. Atlanta, GA.

Kaptein, M. (2017). The battle for business ethics: A struggle theory. *Journal of Business Ethics, 144*(2, August), 343–361.

Katona, G. (1951). *Psychological Analysis of Economic Behavior*. New York: McGraw-Hill.

Katona, G. A. (1960). *The Powerful Consumer: Psychological Studies of the American Economy*. New York: McGraw-Hill.

Katona, G., & Strumpel, B. (1976). Consumer investment versus business investment. *Challenge, 18*(6, January), 12–16.

Katzev, R. D., & Johnson, T. R. (1983). A social-psychological analysis of residential electricity consumption: The impact of minimal justification techniques. *Journal of Economic Psychology, 3*(3–4), 267–284.

Katzev, R. D., & Johnson, T. R. (1984). Comparing the effects of monetary incentives and foot-in-the-door strategies in promoting residential electricity conservation. *Journal of Applied Social Psychology, 14*(1), 12–27.

Kay, N. M. (1979 *The Innovating Firm: A Behavioural Theory of Corporate R&D*. London: Macmillan

Kay, N. M. (1982). *The Evolving Firm: Strategy and Structure in Industrial Organization*. London: Macmillan.

Kay, N. M. (1984). *The Emergent Firm: Knowledge, Ignorance and Surprise in Economic Organization*. London: Macmillan.

Kay, N. M. (1997). *Pattern in Corporate Evolution*. Oxford: Oxford University Press.

Kelly, G. A. (1955). *The Psychology of Personal Constructs*. New York: W. W. Norton.

Kelly, G. A. (1963). *A Theory of Personality*. New York: W. W. Norton.

Kelly, G. A. (1969). The autobiography of a theory. In B. Maher (Ed.), *Clinical Psychology and Personality Theory: The Collected Papers of G. A. Kelly*. New York: Wiley.

Kets de Vries, M. F. R., & Miller, D. (1984). *The Neurotic Organization: Diagnosing and Changing Counterproductive Styles of Management*. San Francisco, CA: Jossey-Bass.

Kets de Vries, M. F. R., & Miller, D. (1988). Personality, culture and organization. In P. J. Albanese (Ed.), *Psychological Foundations of Economic Behavior* (pp. 82–99). New York: Praeger.

Keynes, J. M. (1921). *A Treatise on Probability*. London: Macmillan.

Keynes, J. M. (1930). Economic possibilities for our grandchildren (parts I and II). *The Nation and Athenaeum, 48*(2, October 11 [part I]; 3, October 18 [part II]), 36–37; 96–98.

Keynes, J. M. (1936). *The General Theory of Employment, Interest and Money*. London: Macmillan

Keynes, J. M. (1937). The general theory of employment. *Quarterly Journal of Economics, 51* (2, February), 209–223.

Keynes, J. M. (1940). *How to Pay for the War: A Radical Plan for the Chancellor of the Exchequer*. London: Macmillan.

Kilmann, R., Saxton, M. J., & Serpa, R. (Eds.). (1985). *Gaining Control of the Corporate Culture*. San Francisco, CA: Jossey-Bass.

Kindleberger, C. P. (1978). *Manias, Panics and Crashes*. London: Macmillan.

King, J. E. (2016). Katona and Keynes. *History of Economics Review, 64*(1), 64–75.

Klein, B., & Leffler, K. B. (1981). The role of market forces in assuring contractual performance. *Journal of Political Economy, 89*(4, August), 615–641.

Klein, B. H. (1977). *Dynamic Economics*. Cambridge, MA: Harvard University Press.

Koestler, A. (1975). *The Act of Creation*. London: Picador.

Koestler, A. (1979). *Janus: A Summing Up*. London: Picador.

Koppl, R., & Whitman, D. G. (2004). Rational choice hermeneutics. *Journal of Economic Behavior & Organization, 55*(3, November), 295–317.

Kotler, P., & Levy, S. (1971). Demarketing, yes, demarketing. *Harvard Business Review, 49*(6), 74–80.

Koutsobinas, T. (2014). Keynes as the first behavioral economist: The case of the attribution substitution heuristic. *Journal of Post Keynesian Economics, 37*(2), 337–355.

Koutsobinas, T. (2021). Attribute substitution, earlier-generation economic approaches and behavioural economics. *Review of Social Economy*, Published online 23 January, DOI: 10.1080/00346764.2021.1874498.

Kreps, D. M. (1990). Corporate culture and economic theory. In J. E. Alt & A. Shepsle (Eds.), *Perspective on Positive Political Economy* (pp. 90–143). Cambridge: Cambridge University Press.

Laaksonen, P. (1994). *Consumer Involvement: Concepts and Research*. London: Routledge.

Lakatos, I. (1970). Falsificaton and the methodology of scientific research programmes. In I. Lakatos & A. Musgrave (Eds.), *Criticism and the Growth of Knowledge* (pp. 91–196). London: Cambridge University Press.

Lamfalussy, A. (1961). *Investment and Growth in Mature Economies: The Case of Belgium.* London: Macmillan.

Lancaster, K. J. (1966a). A new approach to consumer theory. *Journal of Political Economy, 75* (2, April), 132–157.

Lancaster, K. J. (1966b). Change and innovation in the technology of consumption. *American Economic Review, 56*(1, March), 14–23.

Langer, E. J. (1991). *Mindfulness: Choice and Control of Everyday Life.* London: HarperCollinns.

Langlois, R. N. (2003). The vanishing hand: The changing dynamics of industrial capitalism. *Industrial and Corporate Change, 12*(2), 351–385.

Langlois, R. N., & Robertson, P. L. (1995). *Firms, Markets and Economic Change: A Dynamic Theory of Business Institutions.* London and New York: Routledge.

Latsis, S. J. (1972). Situational determinism in economics. *British Joural for the Philosophy of Science, 23*(3, August), 207–245.

Lavoie, D. (1990). Hermeneutics, subjectivity and the Lester/Machlup debate: Towards a more anthropological approach to empirical economics. In W. J. Samuels (Ed.), *Economics as Discourse: An Analysis of the Language of Economics* (pp. 167–184). New York: Springer.

Layard, R. (2011). *Happiness: Lessons from a New Science* (2nd ed.). London: Penguin.

Lazonick, W. (1990) *Competitive Advantage on the Shopfloor.* Cambridge, MA: Harvard University Press.

Lazonick, W. (1991) *Business Organization and the Myth of the Market Economy.* Cambridge: Cambridge University Press.

Lea, S. E. G., Mewse, A. J., & Wrapson, W. (2012). The psychology of debt in poor households in Britain. In R. Brubaker, R. M. Lawless, & C. J. Tabb (Eds.), *A Debtor World: Interdisciplinary Perspective on Debt* (pp. 151–166). Oxford: Oxford University Press.

Lea, S. E. G., Webley, P., & Levine, R. M. (1993). The economic psychology of consumer debt. *Journal of Economic Psychology, 14*(1, March), 85–119.

Lee, F. S. (1984). Full cost pricing: A new wine in a new bottle. *Australian Economic Papers, 23*(42), 155–166.

Lee, F. S. (1999). *Post Keynesian Price Theory.* Cambridge: Cambridge University Press.

Leff, N. H. (1985). Optimal investment choice for developing countries: Rational theory and rational decision-making. *Journal of Development Economics, 18*(2–3, August), 335–360.

Leibenstein, H. (1950). Bandwagon, snob, and Veblen effects in the theory of consumers' demand. *Quarterly Journal of Economics, 64*(2, May), 183–207.

Leibenstein, H. (1966). Allocative efficiency vs. "X-efficiency." *American Economic Review, 56*(3, June), 392–414.

Leibenstein, H. (1976). *Beyond Economic Man: A New Foundation for Economics.* Cambridge, MA: Harvard University Press.

Leibenstein, H. (1978). *General X-Efficiency Theory and Economic Development.* New York: Oxford University Press.

Leibenstein, H. (1981). The inflation process: A micro-behavioral analysis. *American Economic Review, 71*(2), 368–373.

Leibenstein, H. (1989). *The Collected Essays of Harvey Leibenstein, Volume 2: X-Efficiency and Microeconomic Theory* (edited by K. Button). Aldershot: Edward Elgar.

Lenton, A. P., & Stewart, A. (2008). Changing her ways: The number of options and mate-standard strength impact mate choice strategy and satisfaction. *Judgment and Decision Making, 3*(7, October), 501–511.

Lester, R. A. (1946). Shortcomings of marginal analysis for wage–empmloyment problems. *American Economic Review, 36,* 63–82.

Linder, S. B. (1970). *The Harried Leisure Class.* New York: Columbia University Press.

Loasby, B. J. (1967). Making location policy work. *Lloyds Bank Review, 83*(January), 34–47.

Loasby, B. J. (1973). *The Swindon Project.* London: Pitman.

Loasby, B. J. (1976). *Choice, Complexity and Ignorance.* Cambridge: Cambridge University Press.

Loasby, B. J. (1978). Whatever happened to Marshall's theory of value? *Scottish Journal of Political Economy, 25*(1, February), 1–12.

Loasby, B. J. (1982). The entrepreneur in economic theory. *Scottish Journal of Political Economy, 29*(3, November), 235–245.

Loasby, B. J. (1983). Knowledge, learning and enterprise. In J. Wiseman (Ed.), *Beyond Positive Economics?* (pp. 104–121). London: Macmillan.

Loasby, B. J. (1989). *The Mind and Method of the Economist.* Aldershot: Edward Elgar.

Loasby, B. J. (1990). Problem-solving institutions. *Scottish Journal of Political Economy, 37* (2), 197–201.

Loasby, B. J. (1998). The organisation of capabilities. *Journal of Economic Behavior & Organization, 35*(2), 136–160.

Loasby, B. J. (2000). How do we know? In P. E. Earl & S. F. Frowen (Eds.), *Economics as an Art of Thought: Essays in Memory of G.L.S. Shackle* (pp. 1–24). London and New York: Routledge.

Loasby, B. J. (2004). Hayek's theory of the mind. In R. Koppl (Ed.), *Evolutionary Psychology and Economic Theory.* Advances in Austrian Econoomics, Volume 7 (pp. 101–134). Oxford: Elsevier.

Lodge, D. (1975). *Changing Places.* London: Martin Secker & Warburg.

Loomes, G., & Sugden, R. (1982). Regret theory: An alternative theory of rational choice under uncertainty. *Economic Journal, 92*(368), 805–824.

Lorsch, J. W. (1986). Managing culture: The invisible barrier to strategic change. *California Management Review, 28*(2, Winter), 95–109.

Lowenstein, G. (1987). Anticipation and the valuation of delayed consumption. *Economic Journal, 97*(387, September), 666–684.

Lowenstein, G., & Thaler, R. H. (1989). Anomalies: Intertemporal choice. *Journal of Economic Perspectives, 3*(4, Fall), 181–193.

Luce, M. F., Bettman, J. R., & Payne, J. W. (2001). *Emotional Decisions: Tradeoff Difficulty and Coping in Consumer Choice.* Chicago, IL: University of Chicago Press.

Lutz, M. A., & Lux, K. (1979). *The Challenge of Humanistic Economics.* Menlo Park, CA: Benjamin–Cummings Publishing.

Lutz, M. A., & Lux, K. (1988). *Humanistic Economic: The New Challenge.* New York: Bootstrap Press.

Lydall, H. F. (1959). The distribution of employment income. *Econometrica, 27*(1, January), 110–115.

Macaulay, S. C., Steen, J., & Kastelle, T. (2017). The search environment is not (always) benign: Reassessing the risks of organizational search. *Industrial and Corporate Change,* published online 27 November. doi:10.1093/icc/dtx045

Machlup, F. (1946). Marginal analysis and empirical research. *American Economic Review, 36* (4, September), 519–534.

Mack, A., & Rock, I. (1998). *Inattention Blindness.* Cambridge, MA: MIT Press.

Macmillan, P. J. (2015). Thinking Like an Expert Lawyer: Measuring Specialist Legal Expertise Through Think-Aloud Problem Solving and Verbal Protocol Analysis. PhD dissertation, Bond University, QLD.

Maddison, D., Rehdanz, K., & Welsch, H. (Eds.). (2020). *Handbook on Wellbeing, Happiness and the Environment*. Cheltenham: Edward Elgar.

Maital, S. (1982). *Mind, Markets and Money: Psychological Foundations of Economic Behavior*. New York: Basic Books.

March, J. G. (1988). *Decisions and Organizations*. Oxford: Basil Blackwell.

March, J. G., & Simon, H. A. (1958). *Organizations*. New York: Wiley.

Markey-Towler, B. (2018). *An Architecture of the Mind*. London: Routledge.

Marris, R. L. (1964). *The Economic Theory of "Managerial" Capitalism*. London: Macmillan.

Marschak, J. (1968). Economics of inquiring, communicating, decidin. *American Economic Review*, *58*(2, May), 1–18.

Marshall, A. (1890). *Principles of Economics* (1st ed.). London: Macmillan.

Marshall, A. (1923). *Industry and Trade* (4th ed.). London: Macmillan.

Martin, J. P. (1978). X-inefficiency, managerial effort and protection. *Economica*, *45*(179, August), 273–286.

Maslow, A. H. (1943). A theory of human motivation. *Psychological Review*, *50*(4), 370–396.

Maslow, A. H. ([1954] 1970). *Motivation and Personality* (2nd ed.). New York: Harper & Row.

Maslow, A. H. (1971). *The Farther Reaches of Human Nature*. New York: Viking.

Mason, R. S. (1981). *Conspicuous Consumption: A Study of Exceptional Consumer Behaviour*. Farnborough: Gower (New York: St Martin's Press.

Mason, R. S. (1998). *The Economic of Conspicuous Consumption: Theory and Thought Since 1799*. Cheltenham: Edward Elgar.

McClelland, D. C. (1961). *The Achieving Society*. Princeton, NJ: Van Nostrand.

McCracken, G. (1988). *Culture and Consumption: New Approaches to the Symbolic Character of Consumer Goodes and Activities*. Bloomington and Indianapolis: Indiana University Press.

McDermott, S., Linahan, K., & Squires, B. (2009). Older people living in squalor. *Australian Social Work*, *62*(2), 245–257.

McDonald, I. M. (2017). "We will end up being a third-rate economy … a banana republic:" How behavioural economics can improve macroeconomic outcomes. *Australian Economic Review*, *50*(2), 137–151.

McWilliams, D. (2008a). State must act as a safeguard. *Business Post*, 20 September. Available online at www.davidmcwilliams.ie/state-must-act-as-a-safeguard/

McWilliams, D. (2008b). State guarantees can avert depression. *Business Post*, 27 September. Available online at www.davidmcwilliams.ie/state-guarantees-can-avert-depression/

McWilliams, D. (Writer). (2009). Addicted to Money. Sydney and Dublin: Electric Pictures, Screen Australia, Screen West, Radio Telefis Eireann, ABC and S4C.

Means, G. C. (1935). Industrial prices and their relative inflexibility. *Journal of the American Statistical Association*, *30*(190, June), 401–413.

Means, G. C. (1972). The administered-price theory reconfirmed. *American Economic Review*, *62*(3, June), 292–306.

Meeks, G. (1977). *Disappointing Marriage: A Study of the Gains from Merger*. Cambridge: Cambridge University Press.

Mehta, J. (2013). The discourse of bounded rationality in academic and policy arenas: Pathologising the errant consumer. *Cambridge Journal of Economics*, *37*(6, November), 1243–1261.

Menger, C. ([1871] 1950). *Principles of Economics*. Glencoe, IL: Free Press (English translation by J. Dingwall and B. F. Hoselitz).

Miller, D., & Friesen, P. H. (1984). *Organizations: A Quantum View*. Englewood Cliffs, NJ: Prentice-Hall.

Miller, G. A. (1956). The magical number seven, plus or minus two: Some limits on our capacity for processing information. *Psychological Review, 101*(2), 343–352.

Miller, R., Williams, P., & O'Neill, M. (2018). *The Healthy Workplace Nudge: How Healthy People, Culture and Buildings Lead to Higher Performance*. Hoboken, NJ: Wiley.

Minsky, H. P. (1957). Central banking and money market changes. *Quarterly Journal of Economics, 71*(2, May), 171–187.

Minsky, H. P. (1975). *John Maynard Keynes*. New York: Columbia University Press.

Minsky, H. P. (1982a). *Can "It" Happen Again? Essays on Instability and Finance*. Armonk, NY: M. E. Sharpe (Published in the UK as *Inflation, Recession and Economic Recovery*. Brighton, Wheatsheaf, 1982).

Minsky, H. P. (1982b). The financial instability hypothesis: A restatement. In P. Arestis & T. Skouras (Eds.), *Post Keynesian Economic Theory* (pp. 24–55). Brighton: Wheatsheaf/ Armonk, NY: M.E. Sharpe.

Minsky, H. P. (1986). *Stabilizing an Unstable Economy*. New Haven, CT: Yale University Press.

Minter, A. (2019). *Secondhand: Travels in the New Global Garage Sale*. London: Bloomsbury.

Mosley, P. (1976). Towards a "satisficing" theory of economic policy. *Economic Journal, 86* (341, March), 59–72.

Mosley, P. (1981). The Treasury Committee and the making of economic policy. *Political Quarterly, 52*(3), 348–355.

Mosley, P. (1984). *The Making of Economic Policy: Theory and Evidence from Britain and the United States since 1945*. Brighton: Wheatsheaf.

Moss, S. J. (1981). *The Economic Theory of Business Strategy: An Essay in Dynamics Without Equilibrium*. Oxford: Martin Robertson.

Motz, B., Mallon, M., & Quick, J. (2021). Automated educative nudges to reduce missed assignments in college. *IEEE Transactions on Learning Technologies*. doi:10.1109/ TLT.2021.3064613

Munkirs, J. R. (1985). *The Transformation of American Capitalism: From Competitive Market Structures to Centralized Private Sector Planning*. Armonk, NY: M, E. Sharpe, Inc.

Murray, H. A. (1938). *Explorations in Personality*. New York: Oxford University Press.

Muth, J. F. (1959). Rational expectations and the theory of price movements. *Econometrica, 29* (3, July), 315°333.

Neild, R. (2002). *Public Corruption: The Dark Side of Social Evolution*. London: Anthem Press.

Neilson, D. H. (2019). *Minsky*. Cambridge: Polity Press.

Nelson, P. (1970). Information and consumer behavior. *Journal of Political Economy, 78*(2, March–April), 311–329.

Nelson, R. R., & Winter, S. G. (1982). *An Evolutionary Theory of Economic Change*. Cambridge, MA: Belknap Press of Harvard University Press.

Nicosia, F. M. (1966). *Consumer Decision Processes: Marketing and Advertising Implications*. Englewood Cliffs, NJ: Prentice–Hall.

Nightingale, J. (1997). Anticipating Nelson and Winter: Jack Downie's theory of evolutionary economic change. *Journal of Evolutionary Economics, 7*(1), 147–167.

Nightingale, J. (1998). Jack Downie's Competitive Process: The first articulated population ecological model in economics. *History of Political Economy, 30*(3), 369–412.

Nisbett, R. E., & Ross, L. (1980). *Human Inference: Strategies and Shortcomings of Social Judgment*. Englewood Cliffs, NJ: Prentice Hall.

Norman, A., *et al.* (2004). On the computational complexity of consumer decision rules. *Computational Economics, 23*(2), 173-192.

O'Connor, M. P., & Spash, C. L. (Eds.). (1999). *Valuation and the Environment: Theory, Method and Practice*. Cheltenham: Edward Elgar.

O'Donnell, C. J. (2018). *Productivity and Efficiency Analysis: An Economic Approach to Measuring and Explaining Managerial Performance*. Singapore: Springer Singapore.

O'Donoghue, T., & Rabin, M. (1999). Doing it now or doing it later. *American Economics Review, 89*(1, March), 103–124.

OECD. (2017). *Behavioural Insights and Public Policy: Lessons from Around the World*. Paris: OECD.

Olshavsky, R. W., & Granbois, D. H. (1979). Consumer decision-making – Fact or fiction? *Journal of Consumer Research, 6*(2, September), 93–100.

Olson, J. C., & Reynolds, T. J. (1983). Understanding consumers' cognitive structures: Implications for advertising strategy. In L. Percy & Woodside, A. (Eds.) *Advertising and Consumer Psychology* (pp. 77–90). Lexington, MA: Lexington Books, D. C. Heath.

Ormerod, P. (1998). *Butterfly Economics*. London: Faber & Faber.

OSC (Open Science Collaboration) (2015). Estimating the reproducibility of psychological science. *Science, 349*(6251 [28 August]), aac4716.

Packard, V. (1957). *The Hidden Persuaders*. London: Longmans Green.

Papadimitriou, D. B., & Wray, L. R. (Eds.) (2019). *The Elgar Companion to Hyman Minsky*. Cheltenham: Edward Elgar.

Paroush, J. (1965). The order of acquisition of consumer durables. *Econmetrica, 33*(1, January), 225–235.

Parsons, S. D. (2000). Shackle and the project of the enlightenment: Realism, time and imagination. In P. E. Earl & S. F. Frowen (Eds.), *Economics as an Art of Thought: Essays in Memory of G. L. S. Shackle* (pp. 124–148). London and New York: Routledge.

Payne, J. W. (1976). Task complexity and contingent processing in decision making: An information search and protocol analysis. *Organizational Behavior and Human Performance, 16*(2), 366–387.

Payne, J. W., Bettman, J. R., & Johnson, E. J. (1993). *The Adaptive Decision Maker*. Cambridge: Cambridge University Press.

Peneder, M., & Woerter, M. (2014). Competition, R&D and innovation: Testing the inverted-U in a simultaneous system. *Journal of Evolutionary Economics, 24*(3, July), 653–687.

Penrose, E. (1959). *The Theory of the Growth of the Firm*. Oxford: Basil Blackwell.

PEP (1965). *Thrusters and Sleepers: A Study of Attitudes in Industrial Management (A PEP Report)*. London: George Allen & Unwin.

Peters, G., Ruiter, R. A., & Kok, G. (2014). Threatening communication: A critical re-analysis and a revised meta-analytic test of fear appeal theory. *Health Psychology Review, 7*(S1), S8–31.

Piketty, T. (2014). *Capitalism in the Twenty-First Century* (translated by A. Goldhammer). Cambridge, MA: Belknap Press of Harvard University Press.

Pil, F. K., & Cohey, S. K. (2006). Modularity: Implications for imitation, innovation and sustained advantage. *Academy of Management Review, 31*(4, October), 995–1011.

Pincock, S. (2009). Researcher quits over science agency interference. *Nature News*, 4 December. Available online at www.nature.com/news/2009/091204/full/news.092009 .091126.html

Pitelis, C. N. (2007). A behavioral resource-based view of the firm: The synergy of Cyert and March (1963) and Penrose (1959). *Organization*, *18*(3, May/June), 478–490.

Polanyi, M. (1962). *Personal Knowledge*. New York: Harper Torchbooks.

Polanyi, M. (1967). *The Tacit Dimension*. Garden City, NY: Doubleday Anchor.

Pooley, C., *et al.* (2011). *Understanding Walking and Cycling: Summary of Key Findings and Recommendations*. Lancaster: Lancaster University.

Port, I. S. (2019). *The Birth of Loud: Leo Fender, Les Paul, and the Guitar-Pioneering Rivalry That Shaped Rock "n" Roll*. New York: Scribner.

Potts, J. (2000). *The New Evolutionary Microeconomics*. Cheltenham: Edward Elgar.

Potts, J. (2019). *Innovation Commons: The Origins of Economic Growth*. Oxford: Oxford University Press.

Pyatt, F. G. (1964). *Priority Patterns and the Demand for Household Durable Goods*. Cambridge: Cambridge University Press.

Quine, W., van O. (1951). Two dogmas of empiricism. *Philosophical Review*, *60*(1, January), 20–43.

Quote Investigator (2016). Using money you haven't earned to buy things you don't need to impress people you don't like. *QuoteInvestigator*, 21 April, https://quoteinvestigator.com/ 2016/04/21/impress/

Rabin, M., & Thaler, R. H. (2001). Anomalies: Risk aversion. *Journal of Economic Perspectives*, *15*(1), 219–232.

Rauch, J. (2018). *The Happiness Curve: Why Life Gets Better After Midlife*. London: Bloomsbury Publishing.

Raviv, S. (2018). The genius neuroscientist who might hold the key to true AI. Retrieved from www.wired.com/story/karl-friston-free-energy-principle-artificial-intelligence/

Rawson, R. A. (2006). Meth and the brain: The meth epidemic. *Frontline*, 14 February. Retrieved from www.pbs.org/wgbh/pages/frontline/meth/body/methbrainnoflash.html

Rayo, L., & Becker, G. S. (2007). Evolutionary efficiency and happiness. *Journal of Political Economy*, *115*(2), 302–337.

Reddaway, W. B. (1937). Special obstacles to full employment in a wealthy community. *Economic Journal*, *47*(186, June), 297–307.

Reynolds, T. J., & Gutman, J. (1983). Developing images for services through means–end chain analysis. In L. L. Berry, Shostack, G. L., & Upah, G. D. (Eds.) *Emerging Perspectives in Service Marketing* (pp. 40–44). Chicago, IL: American Marketing Association.

Reynolds, T. J., & Gutman, J. (1984). Laddering: Extending the repertory grid methodology to attribute–consequence–value hierarchies. In R. E. Pitts & Woodside, A. (Eds.) *Personal Values and Consumer Psychology* (pp. 155–167). Lexington, MA: D. C. Heath.

Reynolds, T. J., & Jamieson, L. F. (1985). Image representations: an analytic framework. In J. Jacoby & Olson, J. C. (Eds.) *Perceived Quality* (pp. 115–138). Lexington, MA: D. C. Heath (for New York University Institute of Retail Management).

Richardson, G. B. (1953). Imperfect knowledge and economic efficiency. *Oxford Economic Papers*, *5*(2, June), 136–156.

Richardson, G. B. (1959). Equilibrium, expectations and information. *Economic Journal*, *69* (274, June), 223–237.

Richardson, G. B. (1960). *Information and Investment*. Oxford: Oxford University Press.

Richardson, G. B. (1972). The organisation of industry. *Economic Journal, 82*(327, September), 883–896.

Ritzer, G. (2004). *The McDonaldization of Society.* Thousand Oaks, CA: Pine Forge Press.

Robertson, P. L., & Langlois, R. N. (1994). Institutions, inertia and changing industrial leadership. *Industrial and Corporate Change, 3*(2), 359–378.

Robinson, E. A. G. (1939). Review article on Oxford Economic Papers. *Economic Journal, 49* (September), 538–543.

Robinson, J. (1964). *Economic Philosophy.* Harmondsworth: Penguin Books.

Robson, A. J. (2001a). The biological basis of economic behavior. *Journal of Economic Literature, 39*(1, March), 11–33.

Robson, A. J. (2001b). Why would nature give individuals utility functions? *Journal of Political Economy, 109*(4), 900–914.

Robson, A. J. (2002). Evolution and human nature. *Journal of Economic Perspectives, 16*(2, Spring), 89–106.

Roe, A. R. (1973). The case for flow of funds and national balance sheet accounts. *Economic Journal, 83*(330), 399–420.

Rostow, W. W. (1960). *The Stages of Economic Growth: A Non-Communist Manifesto.* Cambridge: Cambridge University Press.

Ryle, G. (1949). *The Concept of Mind.* London: Hutchinson (republished 2009. London: Routledge).

Salter, W. E. G. (1960). *Productivity and Technical Change.* Cambridge: Cambridge University Press.

Samuelson, P. A. (1938). A note on the pure theory of consumer's behaviour. *Economica (New Series), 5*(17, February), 61–71.

Samuelson, P. A. (1948). Consumption theory in terms of revealed preference. *Economica, 15* (60, November), 243–253.

Saul, J. R. (1993). *Voltaire's Bastards: The Dictatorship of Reason in the West.* Toronto, Ontario: Penguin.

Saunders, C., & Barber, A. (2008). Carbon footprints, life cycle analysis, food miles: Global trade trends and market issues. *Political Science, 60*(1), 73–88.

Schein, E. H. (1984). Coming to a new awareness of organizational culture. *Sloan Management Review, 24*(2, Winter), 3–16.

Schimmack, U. (2018). Why the Journal of Personality and Social Psychology should retract article DOI: 10.1037/a0021524 "Feeling the future: Experimental evidence for anomalous retroactive influences on cognition and affect" by Daryl J. Bem." Retrieved from https://replicationindex.wordpress.com/2018/01/05/why-the-journal-of-personality-and-social-psychology-should-retract-article-doi-10-1037-a0021524-feeling-the-future-experimental-evidence-for-anomalous-retroactive-influences-on-cognition-a/

Schoenberger, E. (1997). *The Cultural Crisis of the Firm.* Oxford: Blackwell.

Schouten, J. W., & McAlexander, J. H. (1995). Subcultures of consumption: An ethnography of the new bikers. *Journal of Consumer Rsearch, 22*(1, June), 43–61.

Schulte-Mecklenbeck, M., Kuhberger, A., & Ranyard, R. (2011). *A Handbook of Process Tracing Methods for Decision Research.* Hove and New York: Psychology Press.

Schumacher, E. F. (1973). *Small is Beautiful: A Study of Economics as if People Mattered.* London: Blond and Briggs.

Schumpeter, J. A. (1943). *Capitalism, Socialism and Democracy.* London: George Allen & Unwin (new edition, 1992, London and New York, Routledge).

Schwartz, B. (2005). *The Paradox of Choice: Why More is Less*. New York: Harper Perennial.

Scitovsky, T. (1943). A note on profit maximisation and its implications. *Review of Economic Studies*, *11*(1, Winter), 57–60.

Scitovsky, T. (1944). Some consequences of the habit of judgin quality by price. *Review of Economic Studies*, *12*(2, May), 100–105.

Scitovsky, T. (1976). *The Joyless Economy: An Inquiry into Human Satisfaction and Consumer Dissatisfaction*. New York: Oxford University Press.

Scitovsky, T. (1981). The desire for excitement in modern society. *Kyklos*, *34*(1), 3–13.

Scitovsky, T. (1985). Pricetakers' plenty: A neglected benefit of capitalism. *Kyklos*, *38*(4, November), 517–536.

Selznick, P. (1957). *Leadership in Administration*. Evanston, IL: Harper & Row.

Sent, E.-M. (2004). Behavioral economics: How psychology made its (limited) way back into economics. *History of Political Economy*, *36*(4), 735–760.

Shackle, G. L. S. (1943). The expectational dynamics of the individual. *Economica*, *10*(38, May), 99–129.

Shackle, G. L. S. (1949). *Expectation in Economics*. Cambridge: Camrbidge University Press.

Shackle, G. L. S. (1955a). *Uncertainty in Economics and Other Reflections*. Cambridge: Cambridge University Press.

Shackle, G. L. S. (1961). *Decision, Order and Time in Human Affairs*. Cambridge: Cambridge University Press.

Shackle, G. L. S. (1972). *Epistemics and Economics: A Critique of Economic Doctrines*. Cambridge: Cambridge University Press.

Shackle, G. L. S. (1974). *Keynesian Kaleidics*. Edinburgh: Edinburgh University Press.

Shackle, G. L. S. (1979). *Imagination and the Nature of Choice*. Edinburgh: Edinburgh University Press.

Shackle, G. L. S. (1988). *Business, Time and Thought* (edited by S. F. Frowen). London and Basingstoke: Macmillan.

Shefrin, H. M., & Thaler, R. H. (1988). The behavioral life-cycle hypothesis. *Economic Inquiry*, *26*(4, October), 609–643.

Shepherd, M. (2018). Climate change or global warming? Three reasons not to be distracted by the name game. *Forbes Magazine*, 13 April. Available online at www.forbes.com/sites/marshallshepherd/2018/04/13/climate-change-or-global-warming-three-reasons-not-to-be-distracted-by-the-name-game/?sh=430d1c325088

Shiller, R. J. (2013). Robert J. Shiller facts: Biographical. *The Novel Prize*, www.nobelprize.org/prizes/economic-sciences/2013/shiller/facts/

Shiller, R. J. (2020). *Narrative Economics: How Stories Go Viral and Drive Major Economic Events*. Princcton, NJ: Princeton University Press.

Shiozawa, Y., Morioka, M., & Taniguchi, K. (2019). *Microfoundations of Evolutionary Economics*. Tokyo: Springer Japan.

Shove, E., Pantzar, M., & Watson, M. (2012). *The Dynamics of Practice: Everyday Life and How It Changes*. London: Sage.

Shrum, L. J., *et al.* (2013). Reconceptualizing materialism as identity goal pursuits: Functions, processes, and consequences. *Journal of Business Research*, *66*, 1179–1185.

Sickles, R. C., & Zelenyuk, V. (2019). *Measurement of Productivity and Efficiency: Theory and Practice*. Cambridge: Cambridge University Press.

Silver, M. (1984). *Enterprise and the Scope of the Firm*. Oxford: Martin Robertson.

Simon, H. A. (1947). *Administrative Behavior*. New York: Macmillan (3rd edition 1976. New York: Free Press).

Simon, H. A. (1951). A formal theory of the employment relationship. *Econometica, 19*(3, July), 293–305.

Simon, H. A. (1955). A behavioral model of rational choice. *Quarterly Journal of Economics, 69*(1, February), 99–118.

Simon, H. A. (1956). Rational choice and the structure of the environment. *Psychological Review, 63*(2), 129–138.

Simon, H. A. (1957a). *Models of Man*. New York: Wiley.

Simon, H. A. (1957b). The compensation of executives. *Sociometry, 20*(1, March), 32–35.

Simon, H. A. (1959). Theories of decision-making in economics and behavioral science. *American Economic Review, 49*(3, June), 253–283.

Simon, H. A. (1962). The architecture of complexity. *Proceedings of the American Philosophical Society, 106*(6, December), 467–482.

Simon, H. A. (1969). *The Sciences of the Artificial*. Cambridge, MA: MIT Press.

Simon, H. A. (1976). From substantive to procedural rationality. In S. J. Latsis (Ed.), *Method and Appraisal in Economics* (pp. 129–148). Cambridge: Cambridge University Press.

Simon, H. A. (1982a). *Models of Bounded Rationality, Volume 1: Economic Analysis and Public Policy*. Cambridge, MA: MIT Press.

Simon, H. A. (1982b). *Models of Bounded Rationality, Volume 2: Behavioral Economics and Business Organization*. Cambridge, MA: MIT Press.

Simon, H. A. (1991). *Models of My Life*. New York, NY: Basic Books.

Simon, H. A. (1992). Altruism and economics. *Eastern Economic Journal, 18*(1), 73–83.

Simon, H. A. (1993). Altruism and economics. *American Economic Review, 83*(2, May), 156–161.

Simon, H. A. (1997). *Models of Bounded Rationality, Volume 3: Empirically Grounded Economic Research*. Cambridge, MA: MIT Press.

Simon, H. A. (2005). Darwinian altruism and economics. In K. Dopfer (Ed.), *The Evolutionary Foundations of Economics* (pp. 80–88). Cambridge: Cambridge University Press.

Simon, H. A., & Chase, W. G. (1973). Skill in chess. *American Scientist, 61*(4, July–August), 394–403.

Sjåstad, H., & Baumeister, R. F. (2018). The future and the will: Planning requires self-control and ego-depleiton leads to planning aversion. *Journal of Experimental Social Psychology, 76*(May), 127–141.

Smircich, L. (1983). Concepts of culture and organizational analysis. *Administrative Sciences Quarterly, 28*(3, September), 339–358.

Smith, A. ([1759] 1976). *The Theory of Moral Sentiments* (edited by D. D. Raphael and A. L. MacFie). Oxford: Clarendon Press.

Smith, A. ([1795] 1980). The principles which lead and direct philosophical enquiries; illustrated by the history of astronomy. In W. P. D. Wightman (Ed.), *Essays on Philosophical Subjects* (pp. 33–105). Oxford: Oxford University Press.

Smith, R. A. (1963). *Corporations in Crisis*. Garden City, NY: Doubleday.

Smith, R. P. (1975). *Consumer Demand for Cars in the USA*. University of Cambridge Department of Appiled Economics Occasional Paper No. 44. Cambridge: Cambridge University Press.

Smith, V. L. (1991). *Papers in Experimental Economics*. Cambridge: Cambridge University Press.

Smith, V. L. (2008). *Rationality in Economics: Constructivist and Ecological Forms*. Cambridge: Cambridge University Press.

Smyth, R. L. (1967). A price-minus theory of costs? *Scottish Journal of Political Economy, 14* (2, June), 110–117.

Spash, C. L. (1999). Contingent valuation. In P. E. Earl & S. Kemp (Eds.), *The Elgar Companion to Consumer Research and Economic Psychology* (pp. 124–134). Cheltenham: Edward Elgar.

Spash, C. L. (2002). *Greenhouse Economics: Value and Ethics*. London: Routledge.

Spash, C. L. (2010). The brave new world of carbon trading. *New Political Economy, 15*(2), 169–195.

Spash, C. L. (Ed.) (2017). *Routledge Handbook of Ecological Economics*. Abingdon: Routledge.

Spellman, B. A. (2015). A short (personal) future history of revolution 2.0. *Perspectives on Psychology, 100*(6), 886–899.

Spread, P. (2011). Situation as determinant of selection and valuation. *Cambridge Journal of Economics, 35*(2), 335-356.

Spurling, G. (1985). Industry and human resources. In J. Scutt (Ed.), *Poor Nation of the Pacific? Australia's Future* (pp. 70–74). Sydney: George Allen & Unwin.

Staw, B. M. (1976). Knee-deep in the big muddy: A study of escalation of commitment to a chosen course of action. *Organizational Behavior and Human Performance, 16*(1), 27–44.

Steinbruner, J. D. (1974). *The Cybernetic Theory of Decision: New Dimensions of Political Analysis*. Princeton, NJ: Princeton University Press.

Sternberg, J. (2019). *The Theft of a Decade: How the Baby Boomers Stole the Millennials' Economic Future*. New York: PublicAffairs.

Stigler, G. J. (1961). The economics of information. *Journal of Political Economy, 69*(3, June), 213–225.

Stigler, G. J. (1976). The Xistence of X-efficiency. *American Economic Review, 66*(1, March), 213–216.

Stigler, G. J., & Becker, G. S. (1977). De gusitbus non est disputandum. *American Economic Review, 67*(2, March), 76–90.

Strotz, R. H. (1957). The empirical implications of a utility tree. *Econometrica, 25*(2, April), 269–280.

Sugden, R. (2009). On nudging: A review of Nudge: Improving Decisions About Health, Wealth and Happiness by Richard H. Thaler and Cass R. Sunstein. *International Journal of the Economics of Business, 16*(3, November), 365–373.

Sugden, R. (2018). "Better off," as judged by themselves: A reply to Cass Sunstein. *International Review of Economics, 65*(1), 9–13.

Sunstein, C. R., & Thaler, R. H. (2003). Libertarian paternalism is not an oxymoron. *University of Chicago Law Review, 70*(4, Fall), 1159–1201.

Szmigin, I., & Rutherford, R. P. (2013). Shared values and the impartial spectator. *Journal of Business Ethics, 114*(1), 171–182.

Tajfel, H., & Turner, J. C. (1979). An integrative theory of intergroup conflict. In W. G. Austin & S. Worchel (Eds.), *The Social Psychology of Intergroup Relations* (pp. 44–47). Monterey, CA: Brooks/Cole.

Thaler, R. H. (1980). Toward a positive theory of consumer choice. *Journal of Economic Behavior & Organization, 1*(1), 39–60.

Thaler, R. H. (1985). Mental accounting and consumer choice. *Marketing Science, 4*(3, Summer), 199–214.

Thaler, R. H. (1992). *The Winner's Curse: Paradoxes and Anolmalies in Economioc Life*. Princeton, NJ: Princeton University Press.

Thaler, R. H. (1999). Mental accounting matters. *Journal of Behavoral Decision Making, 12*(3, September), 183–206.

Thaler, R. H. (2015). *Misbehaving: The Making of Behavioral Economics*. New York: W. W. Norton.

Thaler, R. H., & Benartzi, S. (2004). Save more tomorrow: Using behavioral economics to increase employee saving. *Journal of Political Economy, 112*(1, pt. 2), S164–S187.

Thaler, R. H., & Shefrin, H. M. (1981). An economic theory of self-control. *Journal of Political Economy, 89*(2m April), 291–406.

Thaler, R. H., & Sunstein, C. R. (2008). *Nudge: Improving Decisions About Health, Wealth and Happiness*. New Haven, CT: Yale University Press.

Thompson, C. J. (1996). Caring consumers: Gendered consumption meanings and the juggling lifestyle. *Journal of Consumer Research, 22*(4, March), 388–407.

Thompson, M. (1979). *Rubbish Theory: The Creation and Destruction of Value*. Oxford: Oxford University Press.

Thomson, M., MacInnis, D., & Park, C. W. (2005). The ties that bind: Measuring the strength of consumers' emotional attachment to brands. *Journal of Consumer Psychology, 15*(1), 77–79.

Tinbergen, N. (1951). *The Study of Instinct*. Oxford: Clarendon Press.

Tomer, J. F. (2007). What is behavioral economics? *Journal of Socio-Economics, 36*(3), 463–479. doi:10.1016/j.socec.2006.12.007

Townshend, H. (1937). Liquidity premium and the theory of value. *Economic Journal 47*(185, March), 157–169.

Trevithick, J. A. (1976). Money wage inflexibility and the Keynesian labour supply function. *Economic Journal, 86*(342, June), 327–332.

Tuck, M. (1976). *How Do We Choose?: A Study in Consumer Behaviour*. London: Methuen.

Tversky, A. (1969). Intransitivity of preferences. *Psychological Review, 76*(1), 31–48.

Tversky, A. (1972). Elimination by aspects: A theory of choice. *Psychological Review, 79*(4, July), 281–299.

Tversky, A., & Kahneman, D. (1971). Belief in the law of small numbers. *Psychological Bulletin, 76*(2), 105–110.

Tylecote, A. (1981). *The Causes of the Present Inflation*. London: Macmillan.

Underhill, P. (2001). *Call of the Mall: How We Shop*. London: Profile.

Veblen, T. B. (1899). *The Theory of the Leisure Class: An Economic Study of Institutions*. New York: Macmillan.

Veblen, T. B. (1914). *The Instinct of Workmanship and the State of the Industrial Arts*. New York: Macmillan.

von Neumann, J., & Morgenstern, O. (1944). *Theory of Games and Economic Behavior*. Princeton, NJ: Princeton University Press.

Wallendorf, M., & Bruchs, M. (1993). Introspection in consumer research: Implementation and implications. *Journal of Consumer Research, 20*(September), 339–359.

Wallis, J., Dollery, B., & Crase, L. (2009). Political economy and organizational leadership: A hope-based theory. *Review of Political Economy, 21*(1), 123–143.

Wärneryd, K.-E. (1982). The life and work of George Katona. *Journal of Economic Psychology, 2*(1), 1–31.

Wärneryd, K.-E. (1999). *The Psychology of Saving: A Study on Economic Psychology*, Cheltenham: Edward Elgar.

Waterson, M. (2003). The role of consumers in competition and competition policy. *International Journal of Industrial Organization, 21*(2, February), 129–150.

Watzlawick, P., Weakland, J. H., & Fisch, R. (1974). *Change: Principles of Problem Formation and Problem Resolution*. New York: Norton.

Weber, E. J. (2009). *Wilfred Edward Graham Salter: The Merits of a Classical Economic Education*. University of Western Australia Economics Discussion/Working Papers. Nedlands, WA.

Wells, W. D. (1975). Psychographics: A critical review. *Journal of Marketing Research, 12*(2, May), 196–213.

Wigley, R. (2021). *Born Digital: The Story of a Distracted Generation*. London: Whitefox.

Wilkinson, N. (2012). *An Introduction to Behavioral Economics* (2nd ed.). Basingstoke: Palgrave.

Williams, P. (2013). Inside Anglo: The secret recordings. *The Irish Independent*, 24 June. Available online at www.independent.ie/business/irish/inside-anglo-the-secret-recordings-29366837.html

Williamson, O. E. (1964). *The Economics of Discretionary Behavior: Managerial Objectives in a Theory of the Firm*. Englewood Cliffs, NJ: Prentice-Hall.

Williamson, O. E. (1970). *Corporate Control and Business Behavior*. Englewood Cliffs, NJ: Prentice-Hall.

Williamson, O. E. (1975). *Markets and Hierarchies: Analysis and Anti-Trust Implications*. New York: Free Press.

Williamson, O. E. (1985). *The Economic Institutions of Capitalism: Firms, Markets and Relational Contracting*. New York: Free Press.

Williamson, O. E., Wachter, M. L., & Harris, J. E. (1975). Understanding the employment relation: The analysis of idiosyncratic exchange. *Bell Journal of Economics, 6*(1, Spring), 250–278.

Wilson, T. (1979). The price of oil: A case of negative marginal revenu. *Journal if Industrial Economics, 27*(4, June), 301–315.

Winter, S. G. (1964). Economic "natural selection" and the theory of the firm. *Yale Economic Essays, 4*, 225–272.

Winter, S. G. (1971). Satisficing, selection and the innovating remnant. *Quarterly Journal of Economics, 85*(2), 237–261.

Winter, S. G., Szulanski, G., Ringov, D., & Jensen, R. J. (2012). Reproducing knowledge: Inaccurate replication and failure in franchise organizations. *Organization Science, 23*(3, May–June), 672–685.

Witte, K., & Allen, M. (2000). A meta-analysis of fear appeals: Implications for effective public health campaigns. *Education and Behavior, 27*(5), 591–615.

Wolf, C., jr. (1970). The present value of the past. *Journal of Political Economy, 78*(4), 783–792.

Wolnizer, P. W. (2006). *Auditing as Independent Authentication*. Sydney, NSW: Sydney University Press.

Wood, A. (1978). *A Theory of Pay*. Cambridge: Cambridge University Press.

Woods, C. (2002). Entrepreneurial Action: Casting the Entrepreneur in the Market Process. PhD dissertation, University of Auckland.

Woodward, J. (1965). *Industrial Organization: Theory and Practice*. London: Oxford University Press.

Woollett, G. J. (2007). Structural Change in the Australian Economy: The S-Shaped Curve Applied to Consumer Demand. PhD dissertation, University of Queensland, QLD.

Wray, L. R. (2008). Lesson from the subprime meltdown. *Challenge, 51*(2, March–April), 40–68.

Wray, L. R. (2016). *Why Minsky Matters: An Introduction to the Work of a Maverick Economist*. Princeton, NJ: Princeton University Press.

Wright, T. P. (1936). Factors affecting the cost of airplanes. *Journal of Aeronautical Sciences, 3* (4), 122–128.

Ziman, J. (1978). *Reliable Knowledge: An Exploration of Grounds for Belief in Science*. Cambridge: Cambridge University Press.

Index

Printed in the United States
by Baker & Taylor Publisher Services